T0213548

Lecture Notes in Computer Science 10325

Commenced Publication in 1973
Founding and Former Series Editors:
Gerhard Goos, Juris Hartmanis, and Jan van Leeuwen

More information about this series at http://www.springer.com/series/7412

Lucio Tommaso De Paolis · Patrick Bourdot
Antonio Mongelli (Eds.)

Augmented Reality, Virtual Reality, and Computer Graphics

4th International Conference, AVR 2017
Ugento, Italy, June 12–15, 2017
Proceedings, Part II

 Springer

Editors
Lucio Tommaso De Paolis
University of Salento
Lecce
Italy

Patrick Bourdot
University of Paris-Sud
Orsay
France

Antonio Mongelli
University of Salento
Lecce
Italy

ISSN 0302-9743   ISSN 1611-3349   (electronic)
Lecture Notes in Computer Science
ISBN 978-3-319-60927-0   ISBN 978-3-319-60928-7   (eBook)
DOI 10.1007/978-3-319-60928-7

Library of Congress Control Number: 2017943083

LNCS Sublibrary: SL6 – Image Processing, Computer Vision, Pattern Recognition, and Graphics

Printed on acid-free paper

This Springer imprint is published by Springer Nature
The registered company is Springer International Publishing AG
The registered company address is: Gewerbestrasse 11, 6330 Cham, Switzerland

Preface

Virtual Reality (VR) is a simulation in which computer graphics is used to create a realistic-looking where the feeling of immersion and realistic presence is very high.

Augmented Reality (AR) technology allows for the real-time fusion of computer-generated digital contents with the real world with the aim of enhancing the users' perception and improve their interaction or assist them during the execution of specific tasks.

Human–Computer Interaction technology (HCI) is a research area concerned with the design, implementation, and evaluation of interactive systems that make more simple and intuitive the interaction between user and computer.

This book contains the contributions to the 4th International Conference on Augmented Reality, Virtual Reality and Computer Graphics (SALENTO AVR 2017) that has held in Ugento (Italy) during June 12–15, 2017. We cordially invite you to visit the SALENTO AVR website (http://www.salentoavr.it) where you can find all relevant information about this event.

SALENTO AVR 2017 intended to bring together researchers, scientists, and practitioners to discuss key issues, approaches, ideas, open problems, innovative applications, and trends on virtual and augmented reality, 3D visualization, and computer graphics in the areas of medicine, cultural heritage, arts, education, entertainment as well as industrial and military sectors.

We are very grateful to the Program Committee and local Organizing Committee members for their support and for the time spent to review and discuss the submitted papers and doing so in a timely and professional manner. We would like to sincerely thank the keynote and tutorial speakers who willingly accepted our invitation and shared their expertise through illuminating talks, helping us to fully meet the conference objectives.

In this edition of SALENTO AVR, we were honored to have the following keynote speakers:

- Mariano Alcañiz, Universitat Politècnica de València, Spain
- Vincenzo Ferrari, Università di Pisa, Italy
- Fabrizio Lamberti, Politecnico di Torino, Italy
- Roberto Scopigno, ISTI-CNR, Pisa, Italy
- Fabrizio Nunnari, German Research Center for Artificial Intelligence (DFKI), Germany

We extend our thanks to the University of Salento for the enthusiastic acceptance to sponsor the conference and to provide support in the organization of the event.

We would also like to thank the EuroVR Association, which has supported the conference since its first edition, by contributing each year to the design of the international Program Committee, proposing the invited keynote speakers, and spreading internationally the announcements of the event.

SALENTO AVR attracted high-quality paper submissions from many countries. We would like to thank the authors of all accepted papers for submitting and presenting their works at the conference and all the conference attendees for making SALENTO AVR an excellent forum on virtual and augmented reality, facilitating the exchange of ideas, fostering new collaborations, and shaping the future of this exciting research field.

For greater readability of the two volumes, the papers are classified into five main parts that include contributions on:

- Virtual Reality
- Augmented and Mixed Reality
- Computer Graphics
- Human–Computer Interaction
- Applications of VR/AR in Medicine
- Applications of VR/AR in Cultural Heritage

We hope the readers will find in these pages interesting material and fruitful ideas for their future work.

June 2017

Lucio Tommaso De Paolis
Patrick Bourdot
Antonio Mongelli

Organization

Conference Chair

Lucio Tommaso De Paolis   University of Salento, Italy

Conference Co-chairs

Patrick Bourdot   CNRS/LIMSI, University of Paris-Sud, France
Marco Sacco   ITIA-CNR, Italy
Paolo Proietti   MIMOS, Italy

Honorary Chair

Giovanni Aloisio   University of Salento, Italy

Scientific Program Committee

Andrea Abate	University of Salerno, Italy
Giuseppe Anastasi	University of Pisa, Italy
Selim Balcisoy	Sabancı University, Turkey
Vitoantonio Bevilacqua	Polytechnic of Bari, Italy
Monica Bordegoni	Politecnico di Milano, Italy
Pierre Boulanger	University of Alberta, Canada
Andres Bustillo	University of Burgos, Spain
Massimo Cafaro	University of Salento, Italy
Bruno Carpentieri	University of Salerno, Italy
Marcello Carrozzino	Scuola Superiore Sant'Anna, Italy
Pietro Cipresso	IRCCS Istituto Auxologico Italiano, Italy
Arnis Cirulis	Vidzeme University of Applied Sciences, Latvia
Lucio Colizzi	CETMA, Italy
Mario Covarrubias	Politecnico di Milano, Italy
Rita Cucchiara	University of Modena, Italy
Matteo Dellepiane	National Research Council (CNR), Italy
Giorgio De Nunzio	University of Salento, Italy
Francisco José Domínguez Mayo	University of Seville, Spain
Aldo Franco Dragoni	Università Politecnica delle Marche, Italy
Italo Epicoco	University of Salento, Italy
Vincenzo Ferrari	EndoCAS Center, Italy
Francesco Ferrise	Politecnico di Milano, Italy
Emanuele Frontoni	Università Politecnica delle Marche, Italy
Francesco Gabellone	IBAM ITLab, CNR, Italy

Damianos Gavalas	University of the Aegean, Greece
Osvaldo Gervasi	University of Perugia, Italy
Luigi Gallo	ICAR/CNR, Italy
Viktors Gopejenko	ISMA University, Latvia
Mirko Grimaldi	University of Salento, Italy
Sara Invitto	University of Salento, Italy
Fabrizio Lamberti	Politecnico di Torino, Italy
Leo Joskowicz	Hebrew University of Jerusalem, Israel
Tomas Krilavičius	Vytautas Magnus University, Kaunas, Lithuania
Salvatore Livatino	University of Hertfordshire, UK
Silvia Mabel Castro	Universidad Nacional del Sur, Argentina
Luca Mainetti	University of Salento, Italy
Andrea Martini	CETMA, Italy
Antonio Mongelli	University of Salento, Italy
Sven Nomm	Tallinn University of Technology, Estonia
Roberto Paiano	University of Salento, Italy
Andrea Pandurino	University of Salento, Italy
Giorgos Papadourakis	Technological Educational Institute (TEI) of Crete, Greece
Gianfranco Parlangeli	University of Salento, Italy
Gianluca Paravati	Politecnico di Torino, Italy
Nikolaos Pellas	University of the Aegean, Greece
Roberto Pierdicca	Università Politecnica delle Marche, Italy
Sofia Pescarin	CNR ITABC, Italy
James Ritchie	Heriot-Watt University, Edinburgh, UK
Jaume Segura Garcia	Universitat de València, Spain
Robert Stone	University of Birmingham, UK
João Manuel R.S. Tavares	Universidade do Porto, Portugal
Daniel Thalmann	Nanyang Technological University, Singapore
Nadia Magnenat-Thalmann	University of Geneva, Switzerland
Carlos M. Travieso-González	Universidad de Las Palmas de Gran Canaria, Spain
Antonio Emmanuele Uva	Polytechnic of Bari, Italy
Volker Paelke	Bremen University of Applied Sciences, Germany
Krzysztof Walczak	Poznań University of Economics and Business, Poland
Anthony Whitehead	Carleton University, Canada

Local Organizing Committee

Ilenia Paladini	University of Salento, Italy
Silke Miss	Virtech, Italy
Valerio De Luca	University of Salento, Italy
Pietro Vecchio	University of Salento, Italy

An Introduction to Unity3D, a Game Engine with AR and VR Capabilities (Tutorial)

Paolo Sernani

Università Politecnica delle Marche, Ancona, Italy

Games, Augmented Reality, and Virtual Reality are capturing the attention of the research community as well as the industry in many application domains with purposes such as education, training, rehabilitation, awareness, visualization, and pure entertainment.

From a technical perspective, scientists, researchers, and practitioners need tools and integrated frameworks that allow them running a fast prototyping as well as an accurate development and production of applications and gaming experiences.

The tutorial presents the Unity3D game engine, describing its main features (cross-platforms applications, cloud build, the asset store, and the wide community of users). Moreover, the tutorial introduces the integration of Unity3D with AR and VR tools.

Keynote Abstracts

The Future Fabrics of Reality: Socio-psychological Aspects of Human Interaction in Advanced Mixed Reality Environments

Mariano Alcañiz

Universitat Politècnica de València, Valencia, Spain

In the last two years, technological tools known as Mixed Reality Interfaces (MRIs) have appeared on the market, which not only allow user interaction with a virtual environment, but also allow the physical objects of the user's immediate real environment to serve as elements of interaction with the virtual environment. That is, MRIs are perfect tools to introduce into our reality new virtual elements (objects and virtual humans) that will generate a new reality in our brain. Today, MRIs are the most technologically advanced tools that human beings have used to date to improve their reality and generate artificial realities that improve the reality they live. In the last year, there is an unusual interest in MRI in the ICT industry. That means that MRI will be a revolution in human communication mediated by new technologies, as in the moment was the irruption of the mobile phone. Therefore, the central question that motivates the present talk is: what capacity will MRIs have to alter the reality that we are going to live in a few years and hence alter the social communication between humans? To date, only a very basic aspect of MRIs is being investigated, its ability to simulate our current reality. However, the above question calls for a paradigm shift in current MRI research. It is necessary to advance towards this new paradigm by proposing a basic research scheme that will allow to analyse the influence of individual personnel variables and MRI interaction aspects will have on basic aspects of human behaviour, like decision making. In this talk, we present several examples of how MRI can be used for human behaviour tracking and modification, we describe different research projects results and we conclude with a discussion of potential future implications.

Potentialities of AR in Medicine and Surgery

Vincenzo Ferrari

Università di Pisa, Pisa, Italy

Patient safety and the surgical accuracy can be nowadays significantly improved thanks to the availability of patient specific information contained in particular in medical images. AR is considered an ergonomic way to show the patient related information during the procedure, as demonstrated by the hundreds of works published in the last years. To develop useful AR systems for surgery there are many aspects to take into account from a technical, clinical and perceptual point of view. During the talk particular attention will be posed to the using of HMD for surgical navigation describing also current doubts related to the using of this kind of technologies to perform manual tasks under direct view.

AR offers also the possibility to improve surgical training outside the surgical room. Surgical simulation based on AR, mixing the benefits of physical and virtual simulation, represents a step forward in surgical training. In this talk the last advancements in visual and tactile AR for surgical simulation will be showed.

Phygital Play: Where Gaming Intersects Mixed Reality, Robotics and Human-Machine Interaction

Fabrizio Lamberti

Politecnico di Torino, Turin, Italy

Developments in Virtual Reality (VR) and Augmented Reality (AR) technologies are dramatically changing the way we perform many of our everyday activities. One of the fields that is expected to be more profoundly influenced by this technological revolution is entertainment and, especially, gaming. With VR and AR, players will be able to fully immerse in computer-generated environments and become part of them, while gaming elements will be allowed to enter the real word and interact with it in a playful way. The physicality ensured by the possibility to move in open spaces as well as to touch, move and, in a word, feel both real and virtual objects will make gaming more engaging, as it will bring players' experience to a more primordial level. The "physicalization" of gaming is a process that will encompass a number of other fields. For instance, ways to make players interaction with computers and computer-generated contents ever more concrete, e.g., by exploiting haptic, tangible or hand and body tracking-based interfaces will have to be experimented. Similarly, the contribution of non-technical research fields will have to be taken into account. As a matter of example, according to behavioural studies, robotic elements could be introduced in the playing area, e.g., as players' avatars, artificial companions, etc. to strengthen the relation between the digital and physical worlds. By leveraging the above considerations, the aim of this talk is to present the activities that are being carried out to create a cloud-based platform supporting a systematic use of VR/AR technologies, robotic components and human-machine interaction paradigms with the aim to further push the transformation of real-world settings in ever more amazing gaming environments.

VR/AR: Success Stories and Opportunities in Cultural Heritage and Digital Humanities

Roberto Scopigno

ISTI-CNR, Pisa, Italy

Virtual and Augmented Reality have already a quite long story and a consolidated status. There are a number of projects and installations specifically developed for presenting or navigating Cultural Heritage (CH) data. But CH or, more broadly, Digital Humanities are domains with specific needs and constraints. Previous projects have selected these domains either to assess new technologies or to provide new tools and navigation experiences. The users in this domain belong to two well differentiated classes: ordinary public (museum visitors, web surfers) or experts (scholars, archaeologists, restorers). The talk will present in a comparative manner some selected previous experiences, aiming at deriving a critical assessment and suggest issues and open questions.

Populating Virtual Worlds: Practical Solutions for the Generation of Interactive Virtual Characters

Fabrizio Nunnari

German Research Center for Artificial Intelligence (DFKI),
Saarbrücken, Germany

Creating a state-of-the-art virtual character is a job which requires the employment of many professionals–dedicated artists do modeling, texturing, and rigging. However, since few years it is possible to find some software tools allowing nonskilled users to generate fully functional virtual characters quickly. The characters, which feature a compromise between quality and creation speed, are ready to be employed for either movie production or in real-time applications. In this tutorial, I will give an overview of some modern virtual character generators, and I will show how to use them to populate with characters real-time interactive applications.

Contents – Part II

Contents – Part I

Augmented and Mixed Reality

Application of VR/AR in Medicine

Augmented Reality to Enhance the Clinician's Observation During Assessment of Daily Living Activities

M. De Cecco[1]([✉]), A. Fornaser[1]([✉]), P. Tomasin[1]([✉]), M. Zanetti[1]([✉]),
G. Guandalini[2], P.G. Ianes[2], F. Pilla[2], G. Nollo[1]([✉]), M. Valente[1]([✉]),
and T. Pisoni[1]([✉])

[1] University of Trento, Trento, Italy
{mariolino.dececco,alberto.fornaser,paolo.tomasin,
matteo.zanetti,giandomenico.nollo,martina.valente,
tommaso.pisoni}@unitn.it
[2] Apss (Apss.Tn.It), Trento, Italy
{giovannimariaachille.guandalini,
patriziagabriella.ianes,francesco.pilla}@apss.tn.it

Abstract. In rehabilitation medicine and in occupational therapy (OT) in particular the assessment tool is essentially the human eye observing the person performing activities of daily living to evaluate his/her level of independence, efficacy, effort, and safety, in order to design an individualized treatment program. On the contrary, in other clinical settings, diagnostics have very sophisticated technological tools such as the Computed Axial Tomography, 3D ultrasound, Functional Magnetic Resonance Imaging, Positron Emission Tomography and many others. Now it is possible to fill this gap in rehabilitation using various enabling technologies currently in a phase of real explosion, through which it will be possible to provide the rehabilitator, in addition to the evidence provided by the human eye, also a large amount of data describing the person's motion in 3D, the interaction with the environment (forces, contact pressure maps, motion parameters related to the manipulation of objects, etc.), and the 'internal' parameters (heart rate, blood pressure, respiratory rate, sweating, etc.). This amount of information can be fed back to the clinician in an animation that represents the reality augmented with all the above parameters using methodologies of Augmented Reality (AR). The main benefit of this new interaction methodology is twofold: the observed scenarios depicted in animations contain all the relevant parameters simultaneously and the related data are well defined and contextualized. This new methodology is a revolution in rehabilitative evaluation methods that allow on one hand to increase the objectivity and effectiveness of clinical observation, and on the other hand to re-define more reliable assessment scales and more effective rehabilitation programs, more user-centered.

© Springer International Publishing AG 2017
L.T. De Paolis et al. (Eds.): AVR 2017, Part II, LNCS 10325, pp. 3–21, 2017.
DOI: 10.1007/978-3-319-60928-7_1

1 Introduction

AR has many applications that span from gaming, military, space, marketing, jour-nalism, tourism, education and training, location-based services for mobile devices, to the service of industrial maintenance for parts analysis, simulation and/or staff support. AR and Virtual Reality (VR) are used in the field of mental health, rehabilitation medicine and OT. VR, which completely immerses the person in a simulated envi-ronment (Pratt et al. 1995), has a long standing use in field of mental health, psy-chotherapy (Glantz et al. 1997), to treat acrophobia (Hodges et al. 1995) and the fear of flying (Hodges et al. 1996, Rothbaum et al. 1996). In rehabilitation it has been applied during the assessment of upper extremities (Broeren et al. 2002) and cognitive deficits (Kim et al. 2004, Josman et al. 2014). In addition, VR has been used in cognitive and physical rehabilitation using video games (Halton 2008, William et al. 2009, Gustavo et al. 2010, Confalonieri et al. 2012, Confalonieri et al. 2013) and for gait training (Ichinose 2003, Andreas et al. 2007, Alexander et al. 2007), as well as during the retraining of activities of daily living (Lee et al. 2003). Furthermore, it has been used in combination with robotics (Sanchez 2005), treadmill training (Saiwei et al. 2011), during driving assessments for persons with head injuries (Liu et al. 1999), and to optimize driving interfaces and learning, for example with individuals who use wheelchairs (Maule et al. 2016).

However, in these situations, they are used by the patient, not the clinician. In rehabilitation the main assessment 'instruments' are the clinician's eyes, and the use of standardized clinical assessments. Their observational skills could be supplemented and enhanced with technology, facilitating a more comprehensive assessment. To our knowledge, this has not yet occurred. In order to cover this gap, the engineering team of the University of Trento in the context of the AUSILIA (Pisoni et al. 2016) project (http://ausilia.tn.it/) developed an augmented domotics environment which acquires individual's motion/actions, his/her interactions with the environment (forces, contact pressure maps, motion parameters related to the manipulation of objects, etc.), and internal status via physiological parameters (heart rate, blood pressure, respiratory rate, sweating, etc.) while performing self-chosen activities of daily living, and provides it via immersive AR to the clinician.

This system provides additional information and data to the clinicians, thus giving them not only a clearer picture regarding the performance of the individual under observation, but also an additional quantitative mean for assessment and classification. This innovation could positively affect not only rehabilitation outcomes, but also the assessment protocols and related clinical scales.

2 Target Observations

AUSILIA's main goal is to increase independence in activities of daily living, increase quality of life, decrease level of care and assistance, and postpone or prevent institu-tionalization, by identifying the most effective technological solutions and/or providing specifications regarding architectural redesign of an individual's living environment. AUSILIA consists of a Domotics Apartment and a Laboratory for Analysis and Design, both equipped with sensors for quantitative and qualitative evaluation, embedded systems for data acquisition and pre-processing, networks for data collection. Data are then fed to the AR-based Human Machine Interface (HMI) for clinical evaluation.

The protocol foresees that, after an initial physiatrist assessment, the individual is observed in the domotics apartment (see Fig. 1) performing the self-chosen activities of daily living important to him/her, identified with an occupational therapist using the Canadian Occupational Performance Measure (Law et al. 2014). The occupational therapist's observation assesses the individual's level of independence, efficacy, physical effort and safety, using the Assessment of Motor and Process Skills (AMPS; Fisher and Bray Jones 2012) and the Performance Quality Rating Scale (PQRS; Martini et al. 2014). Table 1 lists the main observation scenarios (bathroom, kitchen, bedroom, house management and safety) for the domotics apartment with the associated daily activities. After this preliminary clinical assessment, the second phase foresees that the interdisciplinary team of AUSILIA shares with the individual and his/her caregiver a preliminary personalized project, which can exploit innovative technological and/or personalized assistive solutions appropriate for them. This phase foresees the possibility that for the individual and his/her caregiver to try the identified solutions in the domotics apartment. This project may include spending up to 8 h a day for a maximum of five days in the domotics apartment that is able to collect the augmentative parameters/measurements and then feed them back in AR to the clinician, providing a the more complete/objective picture regarding the individual's day, his/her routine and performance, and his/her physiological state in relation to with the different technological solutions employed. At the end of the testing period, the clinician, enabled by the AR HMI, reassesses to determine if the identified technological solutions identified in the preliminary project improved the level of independence, efficacy, physical effort and safety during the performance of daily activities, or if other solutions shall be identified and tested.

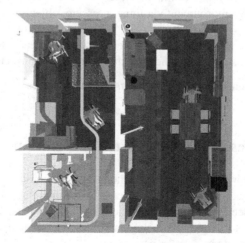

Fig. 1. Rendering of the domotics apartment.

Table 1. Overall clinical observation requirements.

Observation scenario	Relevant daily activity
1. Bathroom	1.1 I want to use the toilet for bodily needs 1.2 I want to wash my hands, face, teeth, head, upper arms/arts underarms, shave with a razor blade and foam 1.3 I want to wash up: shaving with an electric razor, comb my hair, wear put on makeup 1.4 I want to wash my whole body (bath, shower …)
2. Kitchen	2.1 I want to eat 2.2 I want to drink 2.3 I want to prepare a meal 2.4 I want to fix/tidy up the kitchen
3. Bedroom	3.1 I want to go to/get up from bed 3.2 I want to manage the activities in bed 3.3 I want to dress/undress 3.4 I want to make the bed
4. House management, safety	4.1 I want to do the laundry 4.2 I want to clean the rooms 4.3 Monitor the house environment 4.4 Security of the house environment 4.5 Patient Safety

In order to be compliant with the clinical observation requirements, we introduced a set of observation parameters that are common in the different scenario and that can be hereafter summarized in three main categories:

- users motion/actions via 3D Time of Flight (ToF) technology that allow to navigate in the video sequence both temporally and spatially, i.e. to freeze the subject posture and observe it from infinite points of view;
- interaction with the environment via force, pressure, objects handling accelerations, etc.;
- internal status via physiological parameters such as heart rate, blood pressure, breath frequency, skin conductance, electroencephalography etc.

To the above current domotics parameters, additional ones can be added for a more complete picture.

3 Possible Means to Provide AR to the Clinician

The main benefit of this new interaction methodology is twofold: the observed scenario contains all the relevant parameters simultaneously and the related data are well defined and contextualized (see Fig. 2) for a proper use by a clinician. On the other hand, the more traditional way to display data singularly has the advantage to allow a deeper analysis of each time series.

There are different possibilities to provide a proper feedback to the clinician in order to enhance his/her point of view while observing an individual that uses different

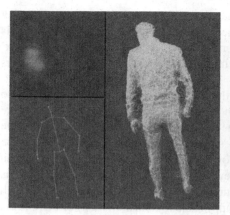
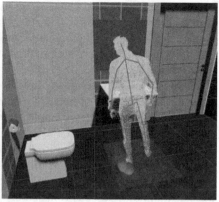

Fig. 2. Domotics scenario with the following relevant data acquired: patient shape, motion (estimated via skeletonization), pressure on the floor. Right picture shows a possible representation of AR in a domotics environment with all the relevant data reported in a virtual context (model) of the environment. Left picture represents the same data reported singularly and decontextualized.

technological solutions in a domotics scenario. In order to choose the best one we considered the main differences between the domain within which to present the data recorder and to perform the reality augmentation. We define as AR-on-2D the augmented reality achieved in a two-dimensional domain and AR-on-3D the one in a three-dimensional one. Further element to consider it is the choice on the most suitable hardware support for the data and AR: immersive interfaces and standard flat displays.

Considering AR-on-2D or AR-on-3D, it is possible to consider the following:

- In 3D domain, it is possible to link the information with the corresponding object. As an example it is possible to explore the mixed environment, find a specific object, select it and then display different kind on information directly linked to the specific object.
- In 2D it is possible to choose the time instant and in some sense navigate in 'time', in 3D it is possible both to navigate in time and in 'space' by choosing the best viewpoint (see Fig. 3).

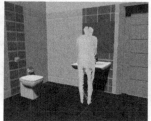

Fig. 3. (left) Traditional camera view; (middle) ToF 3D camera view; (right) the 'best' viewpoint in the same 3D context to observe the user's actions in a suitable way.

- In 2D domain traditional cameras are used, in the 3D one it is possible to employ both traditional and 3D ToF cameras. The main advantage of the 2D technology is its higher resolution and chromatic rendering. Main advantage of 3D is its 'direct' three-dimensional representation even though, currently, the technology suffers from a lower resolution.

- In 3D it is possible to estimate directly the 3D shape. In 2D it is also possible to estimate the shape of objects or human subjects at the expense of much more elaborated algorithms. For example Shape-From-Silhouette (SFS) methods are able to recover the Visual Hull (VH) from silhouette images and thus a 3D shape estimate. One of the limitations of SFS, however, is that the approximated shape can be very coarse when there are only a few cameras. To solve this limitation it is possible to fuse different silhouettes captured across time (Cheung et al. 2003) with the constraint of rigid body (thus barely applicable to human motion) or there is the need to fuse texture and silhouette information (Hernández and Schmitt 2004). Methods that rely on texture can be very effective in some cases but require a proper texture suitable to extract features and complex procedures not perfectly suited for real time applications. The same applies to the problem of object detection with the only current limit of ToF camera resolution that could make traditional 2D technologies more suitable for some applications.

- From the 3D shape it is possible to improve/enable the skeleton estimation via modelling and fitting a human mannequin on the 3D data (Zhang et al. 2012, Huang et al. 2013), or estimating skeleton accuracy by comparing the skeleton and the 3D data and then fusing the result (Pathirana et al. 2016, Moon et al. 2016).

- In 3D it is possible to exploit modern animation frameworks to animate virtual and real objects as a function of the distributed augmentative measurements. This enables to create proper links between cause and effect that best suits the human brain representation of the specific context (see Fig. 4), thus improving the feedback to the user in terms of intuitiveness and thus 'readability'.

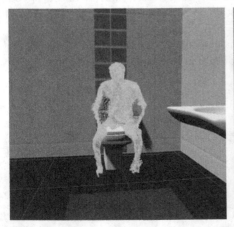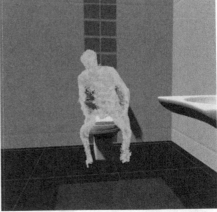

Fig. 4. Example of the use of UNITY™ to animate a toilet seat as a function of the actual user force exerted. The formulation applied in this case is the following, where the numeric values were chosen to optimize the visualization:

- In 3D dimensional perception and thus shape measurement display are much more effective.
- 3D ToF data are much more privacy friendly: it is indeed possible to blur, by smoothing, the 3D shape of the subject while keeping intact its overall physiognomy, still useful for motion and action analysis. The same kind of operation on standard 2D vision based technologies causes a higher loss of information.

$$Vertical_{Displacement} = \frac{1}{5000} \frac{\left(P_{left} + P_{right} - 280\right)}{2}$$

$$Angular_{Displacement} = \frac{\left(P_{left} - P_{right} - 280\right)}{30}$$

This enables to create a proper link between force and 3D motion that, magnified, best suits the human brain representation of the force that is currently perceived via its effect (motion in vertical direction as a function of the total weight and rotation as a function of its unbalance). The same could have been achieved also for a 2D representation but the elaboration chain would have been more cumbersome (requiring anyway the 3D context for simulation, fitting or shape reconstruction).

Difference between immersive interface and 2D display:

- With the 2D display based solution it is possible to use the traditional display technology that is certainly of lower cost both in terms of the display itself and the required computing/graphics resources. With this solution it is possible to display both the 2D and the 3D data.
- With the immersive solution it is possible to navigate within the environment with natural gestures (i.e. looking around, turning the head, etc.) so that observation through navigation results much more effective in terms of speed and truthfulness.
- With the immersive solution there is the possibility to use 3D joysticks over which it is possible to link several variables of interest (such as physiological wearable data as in our case). Those data can appear or disappear just raising or dropping the hand. Further possibilities are: a haptic feedback driven by the 3D interaction between the joysticks and the objects displayed in the 'virtual' environment and more friendly but also effective manipulation or selection of the data, such as a 3D lasso or a 3D laser pointer operating directly inside the scene.

Combining the capture with the display technology it is possible to foresee the following architectures:

1. by 2D camera only and traditional display;
2. AR over 2D camera and traditional display;
3. camera 3D only and traditional display;
4. AR over 3D camera and traditional display;
5. 3D camera and immersive AR

The user experience in an AR system is primarily affected by the display type that, in turn, is affected by the sensing technology employed (2D or 3D) and the means for interaction. The display and sensing techniques determine in fact the effectiveness and realism in the blending of the two realities.

Optical see-through devices that use an optical combiner, such as a half-silvered mirror or a holographic material, were not considered as far as our application does not requires a real time interaction between the clinician and the user, neither some sort of AR to gain user attention. The user is essentially immersed in activities of daily life within a domotics environment without the presence of any 'external' factors that could disturb or change his/her usual behaviour.

Considering the advantages provided by the 3D technology and by the immersive solution we combined those technologies to develop our Immersive 3D Augmented Domotics Environment. One further advantage of this combination is the depth perception that is straightforward also in 'difficult' cases such as the one reported in Fig. 5.

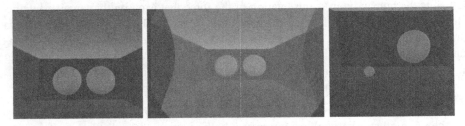

Fig. 5. (left) Bidimensional view of a three-dimensional environment with two spheres at different distances from the rear wall and different radii defined appear similar; (middle) immersive view: left and right eye superimposed; (right) bidimensional view, rotated, showing the difference in radius and distance from the wall.

In Fig. 5 it is reported a traditional LCD (bidimensional) view of a three-dimensional environment with two spheres at different distances from the rear wall and different radii defined in such a way to appear similar. In the middle picture it is shown the right and left eye view of the immersive view. It is evident the disparity difference that provides a clear sense of depth. In the last (right) picture the same bidimensional view rotated revealing the actual difference in radius and distance from the wall: with a 2D display it is needed to rotate the view to perceive the depth.

From the above we choose to adopt the 3D camera and immersive AR as an additional tool in the Ausilia interface. The more traditional 2D LCD based interface that allow a deeper analysis for each variable and the proposed one are not in antithesis as far as both are be proposed to the clinician in a proper interface that show the most suitable for the current analysis.

4   The Proposed Measurement Framework

The framework is realized as three independent elements able to share information. The first is the sensing infrastructure (Fig. 6), which is constituted by a set of sensors and technologies distributed inside the apartment. The measurement solutions are designed to collect and locally pre-process the signals in order to minimize the amount of data to send and store. The collectors of the information are a set of PC placed in proper locations in order to provide the better coverage and thus allow a proper connection with the sensors. These are connected by a local network to a router.

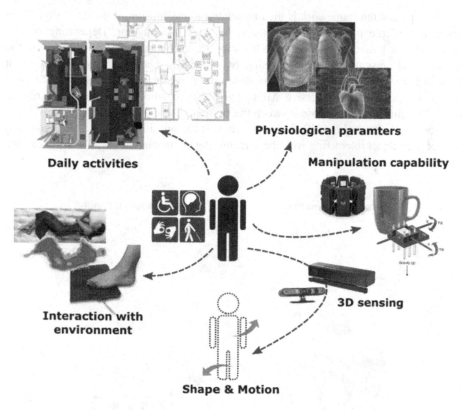

Fig. 6. Framework, sensing infrastructure of the apartment.

Second element of the framework is the main data collection unit (Fig. 7), represented by a displaced server and a database. This is connected as master to the local network of the apartment. It manages:

- the supervision on the state of the apartment;
- the activation of the area/zones with respect to the status/actions/motions of the user;
- the time synchronization between PCs, devices and data;
- the data collection and transit from the PC and sensors to the database (NTP based).

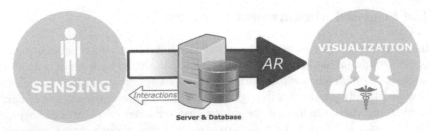

Fig. 7. Framework, interconnection and management structure.

Third part of the framework is the one related to the fruition of the data (Fig. 8). In this case multiple hardware supports can be used as collector. Depending on the characteristics, kind and potentiality of the support, the data are here retrieved from the database and presented to the user using two modalities: a web-based interface that allow to retrieve and analyse all the data stored in the database by means of a traditional LCD interface and the immersive AR in the 3D framework that is the focus of this paper. The clinician can choose between the two interfaces. If his/her aim is to focus in deep on single data he/she will choose the first. If his/her aim is to have an aggregated view of the subject interacting with the surrounding environment he/she will choose the second.

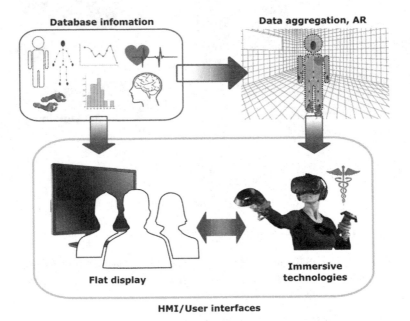

Fig. 8. Framework, data visualization.

About the AR interface, the Unity engine was chosen for the implementation. Further valid alternative is the Unreal Engine. Both software environment are indeed optimized for the development of 2D/3D virtual scene, provide more functionalities than more standard software solution, have plugins for an easy integration of VR headsets. Main drawback of the software solution is however a lack of libraries for a versatile matricial manipulation, advanced computation and management of devices. The issue was solved by developing ad-hoc DLLs from C++ solutions for C#.

From the above considerations we choose the following configuration for the AR feedback to the clinician:

- online registering sensors signals within the domotics environment;
- post processing for features extraction and data compression;
- offline presentation to the clinician via the HTC VIVE. These are not strictly AR devices as far as they were developed primarily for VR applications. Anyhow, in the VR provided by the device we mixed the model of the domotics house (thus virtual) with the 3D sensors data (thus real) and different kind of feedback from the various environmental and user linked sensors.

The sensors that were identified are several. To provide a meaningful example the sensors embedded in the bathroom are listed in Table 3 with the corresponding relevant activity (reported in Table 2) together with the corresponding measurement requirements.

Table 2. Sensors with main specifications and measurement requirements with the correspondence to the relevant daily activity to monitor in the domotics apartment.

Sensor	Relevant daily activity	Measurement requirements
Pressure matrix	1.1 I want to use the toilet for bodily needs 1.2 I want to wash my hands, face, teeth, head, upper arms/arts, shave with a razor blade and foam 1.3 I want to wash up: shaving with electric razor, comb my hair, wear makeup	• Thin device/instrument (not invasive) • Minimum size: 0,4 × 0,7 m (sink) • Sampling frequency: >30Hz • Pressure range: 0–100 N/cm^2 • Pressure resolution: 0.01 N/cm^2 • Spatial resolution: >2 dpi
Local pressure	1.1 I want to use the toilet for bodily needs 1.2 I want to wash my hands, face, teeth, head, upper arms/arts, shave with a razor blade and foam	• Thin device/instrument (not invasive) • Sampling frequency: >30Hz • Pressure range: 0–100 N/cm^2 • Pressure resolution: 0.01 N/cm^2

(continued)

Table 2. (*continued*)

Sensor	Relevant daily activity	Measurement requirements
RFID	1.2 I want to wash my hands, face, teeth, head, upper arms/arts, shave with a razor blade and foam 1.3 I want to wash up: shaving with electric razor, comb my hair, wear makeup	• Multiple synchronous tags identification • Thin tag, possibly adhesive • Maximum operative range: >20 cm
IMU	1.2 I want to shave with a razor blade and foam 1.3 I want to wash up: shaving with electric razor, comb my hair, wear makeup	• Triaxial accelerations • Triaxial rotation • Minimum sampling frequency: >20Hz (Parkinson detection) • maximum device size:5 × 5 × 2 cm
ToF 3D camera	1.1 I want to use the toilet for bodily needs 1.2 I want to wash my hands, face, teeth, head, upper arms/arts, shave with a razor blade and foam 1.3 I want to wash up: shaving with electric razor, comb my hair, wear makeup 1.4 I want to wash the whole body (bath, shower…)	• Sampling frequency: > 15Hz • 3D surfaces point density: >2 pt/cm^2 • Skeletonization accuracy: 5 cm • Joints angular accuracy • Measurement area/FOV: 16 m^2 (4 × 4 m)
Wearable sensors	1.1 I want to use the toilet for bodily needs 1.2 I want to wash my hands, face, teeth, head, upper arms/arts, shave with a razor blade and foam 1.3 I want to wash up: shaving with electric razor, comb my hair, wear makeup	• The device should be comfortable and minimally invasive • The device must not restrict the user movements • Wireless connectivity • Robustness to motion artefacts • ECG minimum sampling frequency ≥ 250 Hz • EDA minimum sapling frequency ≥ 4 Hz

5   Preliminary Exploitation in the Clinical Setting

The proposed system was implemented in a preliminary test field. The bathroom of the AUSILIA apartment in Villa Rosa Hospital was structured with some of the afore-mentioned technologies, with reference to the list of actions indicated for such environment, and organized for demo sessions. A test subject, with no previous instructions, was left alone in the room, free to achieve whatever action he prefers. During this time, the therapists did not observe him.

Table 3. Selected sensors and specifications.

Sensor	Identified hardware/device	Compliant level
Pressure matrix	*Sa.Ni. Corporate "Ultrasensor"* • Data transmission rate: 30–200 Hz • Size: 0,5 × 0,5 m • Spatial resolution: 42 dpi • Max pressure: 150 N/cm^2 • Pressure resolution: 0.02 N/cm^2 • Accuracy ±5%	Highly compliant
Local pressure	*Interlink "FSR 400 Series"* • Force sensitivity range: 0.2 N–20 N • Force resolution: 1024 point • Force repeatability • Single part: ±2% • Standing load durability 2.5 kg for 24 h: −5% average	Compliant
RFID	*CaenRFID, "Slate R1260l"* • RF power: 15 levels → 12 dBm–26 dBm • Size: 297 × 205 × 15 mm •Frequency band: 902–928 MHz • Maximum range: 40 cm • Provided with adhesive sample tags	Compliant
IMU	*lp-research "LPMS-B2"* • Data transmission rate: up to 400 Hz • Size: 39 × 39 × 8 mm • Accelerometer: 3 axes, ±2 / ±4 / ±8 / ±16 g, 16 bits • Gyroscope: 3 axes, ±125 / ±245 / ±500 / ±1000 / ±2000°/s, 16 bits • Magnetometer: 3 axes, ±4 / ±8 / ±12 / ±16 gauss, 16 bits • Resolution: <0.01° • Accuracy: <2° (dynamic) <0.5° (static)	Compliant
ToF 3D camera	*Microsoft "Kinect V2"* • Data transmission rate: 30 Hz • Depth resolution: 414 × 512 3d points → 3D surfaces density variable with depth, approximately 2–5 pt/cm^2 • Skeletonization accuracy < 5 cm • Maximum operative distance: 5 m	Highly compliant

(*continued*)

Table 3. (*continued*)

Sensor	Identified hardware/device	Compliant level
Wearable sensors	*Smartex WWS (ECG)* • ECG sampling frequency: 250 Hz • Derived parameters: heart rate, RR interval, heart rate variability *Smartex WWS (Piezo-resistive sensor)* • Sampling frequency: 25 Hz • Derived parameters: breathing rate, breathing amplitude *Empatica E4 (PPG Sensor)* • Sampling frequency: 64 Hz • Sensor output: blood volume pulse • Sensor output resolution: 0.9 nW/digit *Empatica E4 (EDA Sensor)* • Sampling frequency: 4 Hz • Resolution: 1 digit ∼900 pSiemens • Range: 0.01 µS–100 µS *Empatica E4 (Infrared thermopile)* • Sampling frequency: 4 Hz • Range: −40…115 °C for skin temperature • Resolution: 0.02 °C • Accuracy: ±0.2 °C within 36–39 °C Sensor output resolution: 0.9 nW/digit *Empatica E4 (EDA Sensor)* • Sampling frequency: 4 Hz • Resolution: 1 digit ∼900 pSiemens • Range: 0.01µS–100 µS *Empatica E4 (Infrared thermopile)* • Sampling frequency: 4 Hz • Range: −40…115 °C for skin temperature • Resolution: 0.02 °C • Accuracy: ±0.2 °C within 36–39 °C	Compliant

Fig. 9. Comparison of occupational therapy support/interaction: on the left, the standard approach based on the presence of the therapist side by side to the patient; on the right, the proposed AR structure in which the patient is independent and the therapist/s can assess his state from an augmented view.

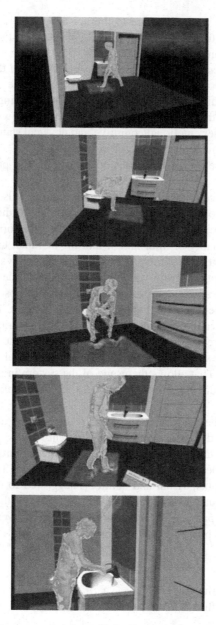

Fig. 10. Sequence of actions recorded form the bathroom and aggregated in the AR interface. From the top to the bottom, the sequence shows the walk of the subject over the pressure mat (blue surface), the interaction with the toilet (load transfer, stability), the actions related to the sink. Together with the 3D data, the therapist can monitor the physiological parameters from the joystick (held in the physical word, but also displayed in the 3D environment). (Color figure online)

Objective of the test was to provide to therapists a demo sample from the acquisition and AR infrastructure, Fig. 9 (right), comparable with the standard practice of 'side-by-side' observation, Fig. 9 (left).

In Fig. 10 are reported some of the most relevant frames of the acquired in a demo sequence, the same observed by therapists. The idea is that the AR environment (data acquisition, stream and display) must be self-sufficient, allowing the therapist both to understand and monitor the actions performed by the subject (without being to his/her side), both to assess his/her emotional/cognitive and physical status, this time supported by more objective information.

The avoidance of the therapist to be side by side to the patients potentially has various benefits.

First, the independence of the subject during the actions. It is indeed known that the presence of an external observer influences the behaviour of the observed subject. In order to avoid such distracting/influencing element the monitoring system must grant the same amount and quality of information that the therapist usually assess from the physical observation. In this preliminary exploitation, no relevant loss of information was reported by the therapists, who were able to properly understand and analyse the actions of the subject in a way comparable to the standard observation practice.

Important improvement regards the privacy of the subject. Despite the recording, necessary for the observation and analysis, the privacy is granted because the data collected is always filtered by an automatic process before the transfer to the server, blurring the shape of the subject while keeping intact the global volume (useful for the analysis of the actions). That allows the usage of the system in areas in which it is not possible to apply the direct observation unless in a 'simulated' form, as in the bathroom.

Further element is the augmentation of the reality, which allows the natural integration of parameters and measurements from different realms in a unique, contextual and meaningful representation. In our case one of the most significant example was the aggregation of the heartbeat (as a sound) synchronous with the 3D shape and motion of the subject. The two inputs, visual and auditory, suggested to the therapists a natural correlation of the two quantities with respect to the status of the subject, assessing in this way stress, fatigue, pain etc. In addition, other elements were recorded, integrated in the AR interface and presented to the therapists:

- Breath rate
- Sweat
- Pressure/stability of the gait
- Pressure/stability of the sit
- Tremor

In our preliminary test, all these parameters were reported by the therapists as meaningful and useful for a better comprehension of the actions of the patient. Among the various tested and observed actions, the most interesting ones were: transfer from wheelchair to toilet bowl, hand washing, teeth brushing. In all cases the therapists managed to analyse the parameters of interest and motions with no effort.

Unique criticism underlined was the density of the 3D point cloud: perceived as not sufficiently dense in some area of the environment, with a loss in details for the reconstruction of the hand and fingers. No other issues were highlighted.

All these elements proved therefore the effectiveness of the proposed structure in the application context.

6 Conclusions

The work describes a new framework able to empower what the rehabilitator can experiment of a phase of user experience inside a domotics setting while performing daily routine actions fundamental to restore his/her autonomy. The clinician will be able to evaluate in an aggregated view gestures, interactions with the environment and the person's physiological parameters via an immersive augmented reality framework. The main innovation lies is the fact that the system will go beyond the subjective view of the rehabilitator being able to collect a quantitative and objective view that embody not only the subject interactions with the environment but also the user internal status via physiological parameters thus allowing, for the first time in clinical rehabilitation protocols, an empathic observational experience.

The data provided by the system are innumerable. The actual use for clinical protocols has still to be explored in the clinic context through the use of ad hoc rehabilitative protocols able to exploit the full potential of the new paradigm.

Acknowledgement. This project was partially funded by the Provincia Autonoma di Trento in the framework of the AUSILIA project.

References

Pisoni, T., Conci, N., De Natale, F., De Cecco, M., Frattari, A., Guandalini, G.: AUSILIA: assisted unit for simulating independent living activities. In: IEEE International Smart Cities Conference (2016)

Confalonieri, M., Guandalini, G., Da Lio, M., De Cecco, M.: Force and touch make video games 'serious' for dexterity rehabilitation. Stud. Health Technol. Inform. **177**, 139–144 (2012). H Index: 31

Confalonieri, M., Tomasi, P., Depaul, M., Guandalini, G., Baldessari, M., Oss, D., Prada, F., Mazzalai, A., Da Lio, M., De Cecco, M.: Neuro-physical rehabilitation by means of novel touch technologies. Stud. Health Technol. Inform. **189**, 158–163 (2013). ISBN 978-1-61499-267-7

Maule, L., Fornaser, A., Leuci, M., Conci, N., Lio, M., Cecco, M.: Development of innovative HMI strategies for eye controlled wheelchairs in virtual reality. In: Paolis, L.T., Mongelli, A. (eds.) AVR 2016. LNCS, vol. 9769, pp. 358–377. Springer, Cham (2016). doi:10.1007/978-3-319-40651-0_29

Cheung, K.M.G., Baker, S., Kanade, T.: Shape-from-silhouette of articulated objects and its use for human body kinematics estimation and motion capture. In: Proceedings 2003 IEEE Computer Society Conference on Computer Vision and Pattern Recognition, vol. 1. IEEE (2003)

Hernández, E.C., Schmitt, F.: Silhouette and stereo fusion for 3D object modeling. Comput. Vis. Image Underst. **96**(3), 367–392 (2004)

Hodges, L.F., Kooper, R., Meyer, T.C., Rothbaum, B.O., Opdyke, D., de Graaff, J.J., Williford, J.S., North, M.M.: Virtual environments for treating the fear of heights. IEEE Comput. **28**(7), 27–34 (1995)

Hodges, L.F., Watson, B.A., Kessler, G.D., Rothbaum, B.O., Opdyke, D.: Virtually conquering fear of flying. IEEE Comput. Graph. Appl. **16**(6), 42–49 (1996)

Rothbaum, B.O., Hodges, L., Watson, B.A., Keller, G.D., Opdyke, D.: Virtual reality expo-sure therapy in the treatment of fear of flying: a case report. Behav. Res. Ther. **34**(5–6), 477–481 (1996)

Glantz, K., Durlach, N.I., Barnett, R.C., Aviles, W.A.: Virtual reality (VR) and psychotherapy: opportunities and challenges. Presence **6**(1), 87–105 (1997)

Liu, L., Miyazaki, M., Watson, B.: Norms and validity of the DriVR: a virtu-al reality driving assessment for persons with head injuries. Cyberpsychology Behav. **2**(1), 53–67 (1999)

Alexander, K., et al.: Virtual gait training for children with cerebral palsy using the Lokomat gait orthosis. Stud. Health Technol. Inform. **132**, 204–209 (2007)

Andreas, M., et al.: Prospective, blinded, randomized crossover study of gait rehabilitation in stroke patients using the Lokomat gait orthosis. Neurorehabil. Neural Repair **21**(4), 307–314 (2007)

Ichinose, W., Reinkensmeyer, D., Aoyagi, D., Lin, J., Ngai, K., Edgerton, V., Harkema, S., Bobrow, J.: A robotic device for measuring and controlling pelvic motion during locomotor rehabilitation. In: Proceedings of the 2003 IEEE Engineering in Medicine and Biology Society Meeting, pp. 1690–1693 (2003)

Saiwei, Y., et al.: Improving balance skills in patients who had stroke through virtual reality treadmill training. Am. J. Phys. Med. Rehabil. **90**(12), 969–978 (2011)

William, L., et al.: The development of a home-based virtual reality therapy system to promote upper extremity movement for children with hemiplegic cerebral palsy. Technol. Disabil. **21** (3), 107–113 (2009)

Sanchez, R.J., et al.: A pneumatic robot for re-training arm movement after stroke: Rationale and mechanical design. In: 9th International Conference on Rehabilitation Robotics, ICORR 2005. IEEE (2005)

Halton, J.: Virtual rehabilitation with video games: A new frontier for occupational therapy. Occup. Ther. Now **9**(6), 12–14 (2008)

Gustavo, S., et al.: Effectiveness of virtual reality using Wii gaming technology in stroke rehabilitation a pilot randomized clinical trial and proof of principle. Stroke **41**(7), 1477–1484 (2010)

Amy, H., Korner-Bitensky, N., Levin, M.: Virtual reality in stroke rehabilitation: a systematic review of its effectiveness for upper limb motor recovery. Top. Stroke Rehabil. (2014)

Martini, R., Rios, J., Polatajko, H., Wolf, T., McEwen, S.: The performance quality rating scale (PQRS): reliability, convergent validity, and internal responsiveness for two scoring systems. Disabil. Rehabil. early online, pp. 1–8 (2014)

Fisher, A.G., Jones, K.B.: Assessment of Motor and Process Skills: Volume II – User Manual, 7 Revised edn. Three Star Press Inc., Fort collins (2012)

Law, M., Baptiste, S., Carswell, A., McColl, M.A., Polatajko, H.J., Pollack, N.: Canadian Occupational Performance Measure, 5th edn. CAOT Publications ACE, Ottawa (2014)

Day, H., Jutay, J.: Measuring the psycosocial impact of assistive devices: the PIADS. Can. J. Rehabil. **9**(2), 159–168 (1996)

Demers, L., Weiss-Lambrou, R., Ska, B.: Item analysis of the quebec user evaluation of satisfaction with assistive technology (QUEST). Assistive Technol. **12**(2), 96–105 (2000)

Pratt, D.R., Zyda, M., Kelleher, K.: Virtual reality: in the mind of the beholder. IEEE Comput. **28**, 17–19 (1995)

Im, D.J., Ku, J., Kim, Y.J., Cho, S., Cho, Y.K., Lim, T., Lee, H.S., Kim, H.J., Kang, Y.J.: Utility of a three-dimensional interactive augmented reality program for balance and mobility rehabilitation in the elderly: a feasibility study. Annuals Rehabil. Med. **39**(3), 462–472 (2015)

Broeren, J., Björkdahl, A., Pascher, R., Rydmark, M.: Virtual reality and haptics as an assessment device in the postacute phase after stroke. CyberPsychology Behav. **5**(3), 207–211 (2002)

Kim, K., Kim, J., Ku, J., Kim, D.Y., Chang, W.H., Shin, D.I., Lee, J.H., Kim, I.Y., Kim, S.I.: A virtual reality assessment and training system for unilateral neglect. CyberPsychology Behav. **7**(6), 742–749 (2005)

Lee, J.H., Ku, J., Cho, W., Hahn, W.Y., Kim, I.Y., Lee, S.M., Kang, Y., Kim, D.Y., Yu, T., Wiederhold, B.K., Wiederhold, M.D., Kim, S.I.: A virtual reality system for the assessment and rehabilitation of the activities of daily living. CyberPsychology Behav. **6**(4), 383–388 (2004)

Josman, N., Kizony, R., Hof, E., Goldenberg, K., Weiss, P.L., Klinger, E.: Using the virtual action planning-supermarket for evaluating executive functions in people with stroke. J. Stroke Cerebrovasc. Dis. **23**(5), 879–887 (2014)

Zhang, L., Sturm, J., Cremers, D., Lee, D.: Real-time human motion tracking using multiple depth cameras. In: International Conference on Intelligent Robots and Systems (IROS), 2012 IEEE/RSJ, pp. 2389–2395. IEEE, October 2012

Pathirana, P.N., Li, S., Trinh, H.M., Seneviratne, A.: Robust real-time bio-kinematic movement tracking using multiple kinects for tele-rehabilitation. IEEE Trans. Ind. Electron. **63**(3), 1822–1833 (2016)

Moon, S., Park, Y., Ko, D.W., Suh, I.H.: Multiple kinect sensor fusion for human skeleton tracking using Kalman filtering. Int. J. Adv. Rob. Syst. **13**(2), 65 (2016)

Huang, H., Wu, S., Cohen-Or, D., Gong, M., Zhang, H., Li, G., Chen, B.: L1-medial skeleton of point cloud. ACM Trans. Graph. **32**(4), 65:1 (2013)

Augmented Robotics for Electronic Wheelchair to Enhance Mobility in Domestic Environment

Luca Maule[1]([✉]), Alberto Fornaser[1]([✉]), Paolo Tomasin[1]([✉]),
Mattia Tavernini[2]([✉]), Gabriele Minotto[1]([✉]), Mauro Da Lio[1]([✉]),
and Mariolino De Cecco[1]([✉])

[1] Department of Industrial Engineering,
University of Trento, Via Sommarive 9, Trento, Italy
{luca.maule,alberto.fornaser,paolo.tomasin,
gabriele.minotto,mauro.dalio,
mariolino.dececco}@unitn.it
[2] Robosense srl, Via G. Segantini 23, Trento, Italy
m.tavernini@robosense.it

Abstract. This paper focuses on the development of a novel Human Machine Interaction strategy based on Augmented Reality for the semi-autonomous navigation of a power wheelchair. The final goal is the development of a shared control, combining direct control by the user with the comfort of an autonomous navigation based on augmented reality markers. A first evaluation has been performed on the real test bed.

Keywords: Augmented Reality · Virtual reality · Eye tracking · Assistive technologies · Shared control · Autonomous navigation

1 Introduction

Mobile robotics is the discipline that studies the development of autonomous systems in order to provide support or help to human users. Applications of this kind range from industrial application to medicine. Power wheelchairs represent a good example of assistive tool that could benefit from the technological transfer from the mobile robotic field. Indeed the wheelchair has a strong impact on the quality of life of patients affected by mobility limitations, example are spinal cord injuries or degenerative diseases as Amyotrophic Lateral Sclerosis (ALS). The pathological state generates in these subjects many physical inabilities but also psychological distress. The capability of moving autonomously plays therefore an important role for their quality of daily life.

The necessity of a caregiver, common condition, does not improve the self-esteem of the disabled subjects. An assistive technology should be designed to be as much comfortable as possible and not invasive in order to improve the autonomy of the patients. For this reason, a robotic wheelchair can be of great benefits restoring the human mobility.

Common techniques to control a wheelchair are based on a physical interaction between the user and a device such as joysticks, keyboards or breath. Recently, eye tracker technologies have become a promising tool as control input for any kind of user

© Springer International Publishing AG 2017
L.T. De Paolis et al. (Eds.): AVR 2017, Part II, LNCS 10325, pp. 22–32, 2017.
DOI: 10.1007/978-3-319-60928-7_2

[3, 4, 7]. Indeed, eye movement is one of the fastest human movement, although are mainly conceived for exploration, less for control [2]. Gaze-based control devices represent very useful tools able to guarantee a good mobility also to the more critical patients. Pathologies like ALS affect the people starting from the peripheral organs, moving progressively to the rest of the body. The last part involved are the eye muscles. On top of this, the Human Machine Interface (HMI) based on eye tracking can play a fundamental role for actual usability and manoeuvrability of a wheelchair.

Many solutions for gaze-based control are quite invasive due to the necessity to wear external devices such as glasses [3] or electrodes for Electrooculography [4]. Other solutions are based on less invasive techniques like Video Oculography (VOG) [5, 6]. Due to the delicate health condition of the patients, it would be highly desirable to have interfaces the least tiring and invasive possible.

Regarding the interaction modalities, current interfaces require a continuous control by the user. This control modality results very tiring for the patients, especially for the gaze-based control technique where the user has to keep all the time the attention on the monitor. Moreover, houses are usually characterized by small spaces and narrow passages. Unfortunately, not all the disabled people have the possibility to adapt their house to the required particular necessities. For these reasons, the exploitation of a robotic path planning control of power wheelchair would be of great benefit to relief the patient. Indeed, in this manner, he/she does not have to keep attention on the HMI. An assisted guide could be very useful and comfortable especially for the movement in narrow spaces. The solution presented in this paper aims to create a novel technology to support the control of a power wheelchair during difficult manoeuvres. Furthermore, using an autonomous wheelchair the patient does not need to keep the attention on the monitor, resulting less tiring.

In our work, we propose an integration of our previous gaze-based HMI [1] with a robotic framework able to plan and control a part of the route according to a normal HMI based on AR. With this novel technology, we aimed to guarantee the freedom of movement and at the same time the comfort of the assisted guide. We use UNITY Game Engine for the development of the HMI. Moreover, we use ArUco[1] (a library for Augmented Reality AR applications based on OpenCV) to identify the possible targets and then OpenCV[2] for image processing. The proposed AR-based application is able to recognize points of interest (POIs) visible to the camera, to plan a path and to give to the patient the possibility to eventually perform the preferred path after proper checking. From an applicative point of view, when a POI enters in the field of view of the camera the user can select it, starting in this way the autonomous navigation.

The tests on the application developed were performed evaluating the repeatability of the manoeuvres starting from different positions. In this way, the impact of the uncertainty of the camera position was evaluated, with respect to the wheelchair, on the reached position.

---

[1] https://www.uco.es/investiga/grupos/ava/node/26.

[2] http://opencv.org/.

2   System Architecture

The project involves the integration of a hardware and software module on a commercial wheelchair. The system was designed in order to enhance the mobility of the user giving him/her the possibility to control the wheelchair through both manual and autonomous navigation via gaze-based technique.

With manual navigation, the user acts directly on the wheels by selecting the forward and the rotational speed. A continuous law, to determine the forward and the steering velocities, characterizes the control strategy as described in [1]. The velocities are calculated proportionally to the position of the gaze on the monitor.

With semi-autonomous navigation, the wheelchair is able to reach a selected target without any other input from the user. To achieve such task, it is necessary to assess the actual position of the wheelchair with respect to the surrounding environment. Given the start and the end positions and attitudes, the vehicle calculates the best path to reach the goal. Then another specific algorithm, that calculates the control parameters for the motors, realizes the tracking of the path (path-following task).

Figure 1 presents a schematic representation of the system. In the left part a commercial device (power wheelchair) where the proposed technology is integrated. In the central part, the module developed, and added on the wheelchair, represented by a Windows PC that reads the navigation camera, acquires the information about the gaze position and shows the HMI on the monitor. The surrounding environment is shown in the right part, where ArUco markers are used to define all the point of interest for the user.

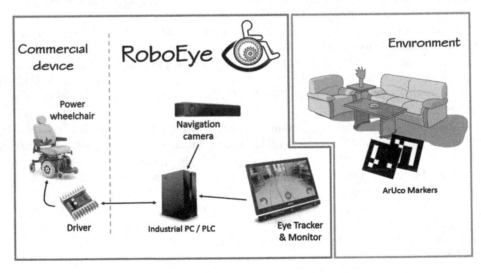

Fig. 1. Conceptual model of the project

In addition to the real wheelchair, the application was applied also on a simulator in order to perform some evaluation tests and theoretical analyses with control quantities.

2.1 Augmented Robotic Wheelchair

The system is made by a power wheelchair commercialized by Invacare[3] (model: Storm XR) integrated with some additional devices useful at including advanced robotic functionalities. From a kinematic point of view, the wheelchair corresponds to a differential drive vehicle with the traction wheels on the back part of the chassis. An industrial B&R PLC and a Windows PC perform all the logical computations. Two encoders were mounted on the wheels for the odometric localization. The motors used are the original ones of the wheelchair while a commercial driver was added for powering them.

The PLC calculates the control parameters (voltage related to forward and rotational speeds) and pilots the driver of the two motors. It also collects the data from the encoders about the rotations of the wheels, calculating in this way the position of the wheelchair. The odometric localization is performed by an incremental recursion, dead reckoning, technique that suffers of a drift in the estimation of the position and attitude. Because of that, it is necessary an absolute localization algorithm in order to compensate such effect, mainly due to the uncertainty of the vehicle parameters.

Common absolute localization systems, used in industrial application, are based on cameras or laser scanners, like NAV[4]. On the other hand, these systems are usually slower than the incremental ones and require a map of the surrounding environment. The combination (data fusion) of the two localization systems represents the optimal solution, with the update rate of the incremental and the accuracy of the absolute. In our case, the absolute localization is designed differently from the canonical ones to prevent the usage of a map of the environment. Each POI (for example doors or tables) represents a localization element, centred with respect to a couple of markers, coded and uniquely identifiable, and associated to the target position and attitude.

The identification of the markers and the localization of the wheelchair with respect to the POI is implemented with a Time Of Flight (TOF) camera, a Kinect V2.0, mounted on the frontal part of the wheelchair, few centimeters above the knees of the patient, as shown in Fig. 2. The position of the sensor was the result of the advices from a pool of tester: the presence of the knees in the field of view of the camera was defined as very useful in the depth perception of the surrounding environment and in particular for movements close to obstacles or narrow passages.

The images coming from the camera are displayed on a monitor mounted in front of the user. On that image are overlapped the HMI and the information about the POI detected in the field of view of the camera. The patient interacts with the system using an eye tracker (TOBII EyeX[5]) mounted below the monitor. A Windows PC manages the camera, the monitor and the eye tracker. It is connected to the PLC through a TCP/IP connection using PVI library from B&R[6].

---

[3] http://www.invacare.com.

[4] https://www.sick.com/de/en/product-portfolio/detection-and-ranging-solutions/2d-laser-scanners/nav3xx/c/g91916.

[5] http://tobiigaming.com/product/tobii-eyex/.

[6] https://www.br-automation.com/en/perfection-in-automation/.

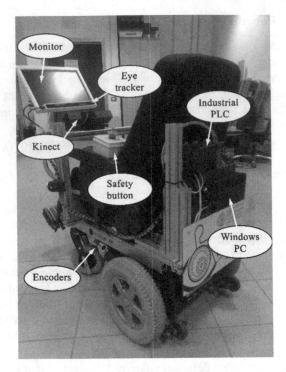

Fig. 2. Hardware architecture

A safety button, connected directly to the voltage supply of the motors, ensures the safety of the user during the learning and test phase.

2.2 Virtual Reality Architecture

The proposed HMI was developed using UNITY game engine. The aim was both to maximize the usability of the wheelchair, both to minimize the stress resulting from the intense use.

The user has in front of him/her a monitor where are shown all the commands for both the manual and autonomous navigation. On the background, the application shows the RGB frames captured by the Kinect. This video stream is useful to perceive the surrounding environment and to pilot the wheelchair but also to see the location of POIs in the Kinect field of view.

A C++ Dynamic-link library (DLL) simultaneously analyses the same images coming from Kinect to detect markers. If at least a couple of markers related to a POI are detected, the DLL performs also the relative localization with respect to the wheelchair, the planning of the path and the communication with the industrial PLC. At the end of the processing, the algorithm gives back to the UNITY application information about POI detected and associated paths planned. Such information are used by the main application to create an augmented image with a pin icon on the target point and lines that show in perspective the path planned. The described processing is performed on each new frame acquired, ensuring in this way an on-line update of the path planned.

The commands for the trig of the various actions are displayed on the foreground as the icons related to the POI detected. In order to start the semi-autonomous manoeuvre, the user must explicitly select the POI by gazing it for 3 s.

The DLL, operative core of the structure, can be conceptually divided in three levels with two parallel tasks, Fig. 3.

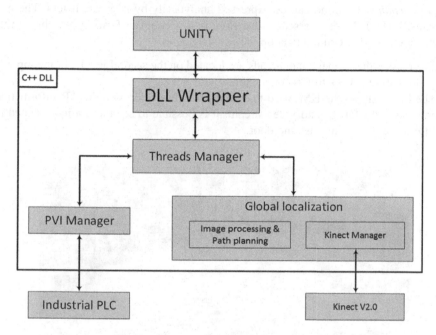

Fig. 3. Conceptual model of the C++ DLL

Starting from the lower level, two threads perform the localization and the communication with the industrial PLC. The localization includes the Kinect management, the image processing and the path planning modules.

Overall the following steps are performed at this level:

- *Data acquisition:* the algorithm acquires the information about colour and depth map from the Kinect;
- *Assessment of Kinect position:* the Kinect and the chassis are connected through a joint and so the position of the camera could be easily changed. Using RANSAC (RANdom SAmple Consensus) algorithm it is possible to calculate the height and the attitude of the Kinect with respect to the ground plane;
- *Roto-translation of the 3D points associated to the depth:* the Kinect provides the depth information in the camera reference frame. The data is then transformed to the reference system of the wheelchair;

- *Target detection:* the RGB frames retrieved from the Kinect are analysed using ArUco library to detect the markers in the field of view. The algorithm searches for couples of markers related to POIs, evaluates their 3D positions and then calculates the position and the attitude of the middle point, the POI;
- *Path calculation:* the path to reach the target is determined by using clothoids, a curve characterized by continuous third order curvature. The movement toward the target has to be as safe as possible. For this reason the paths are divided in two consecutive parts; a dynamic path that change according to the current position of the wheelchair and a fixed path for the final approach to the target;
- *Path sending:* a clothid can be expressed analytically by five parameters. The two paths, both clothoids, are sent to the PLC in this compact form by the thread that manages the PVI communication.

The classes that manage the threads are located on the second level. On the top, the wrapping class for C++ to C# conversion.

The Fig. 4 shows the HMI used to control the wheelchair with the AR information superposed to the foreground video stream. It is possible to see the pin icon related to the POI detected, in this case the door.

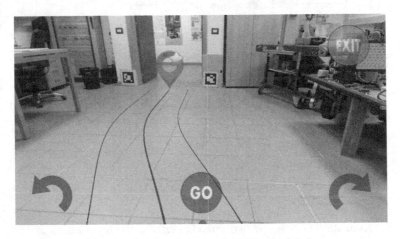

Fig. 4. HMI for the control of the wheelchair

3   Experimental Testing

The assessment of the performance of the semi-autonomous navigation was performed through a repeatability analysis on the final positions reached by the wheelchair.

Figure 5 shows the scheme considered during the test campaign. Two markers were attached on the jambs of a door, with a clearance of about 1.2 m.

Initial position and attitude of wheelchair (x', y', θ) are referred to the target reference frame (x, y), while (X_M, Y_M) define the wheelchair reference frame in (x, y). Initial conditions are the distance from target along x and y axis, respectively x' and y', and the initial wheelchair attitude θ.

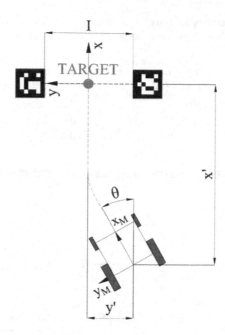

Fig. 5. Example of test scenario with the wheelchair arrangement with respect to the target position and attitude.

To evaluate the performance of the system the following tests were performed by analysing the final position and attitude repeatability. The tests are:

- The wheelchair always starts from a fixed position and attitude;
- The wheelchair initial position shifts only along the y' direction with respect to the target. The y' distance, related to each group of samples, was varied from -0.90 ± 0.01 m to $+0.90 \pm 0.01$ m with steps of 0.30 ± 0.01 m;
- The wheelchair starts from a randomly generated initial condition (x', y' and θ).

Table 1 shows the initial conditions related to the tests. The uncertainty on the initial attitude for all tests was calculated using the uncertainty propagation law combining the information about the initial conditions (x', y').

Table 1. Description of the three tests performed for the repeatability analysis.

Test number	x' distance	y' distance	θ vehicle attitude	Number of samples
1	(4.26 ± 0.01) m	(0.61 ± 0.01) m	(0.0 ± 0.1) rad	30
2	(4.26 ± 0.01) m	Variable	(0.0 ± 0.1) rad	30
3	Variable	Variable	Variable	30

In Table 2 is reported the offset between the target position and the mean final wheelchair position, which represents the systematic error and can be compensated with a calibration, and the standard deviation which is the index of data dispersion (Figs. 6, 7 and 8).

Table 2. Results of repeatability analysis for the three types of test explained above, in terms of offset between target position and mean acquired one and principal axis of acquired data covariance.

	Offset from target in X axis [m]	Offset from target in Y axis [m]	Maximum principal std [m]	Minimum principal std [m]
1	−0.045	−0.003	0.024	0.014
2	0.034	0.028	0.049	0.013
3	−0.014	−0.054	0.064	0.026

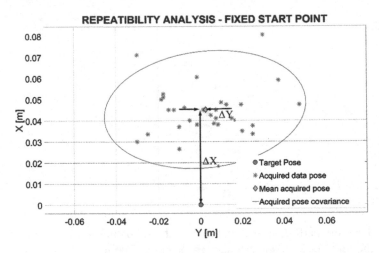

Fig. 6. Repeatability analysis results with the wheelchair starting from fixed position and attitude.

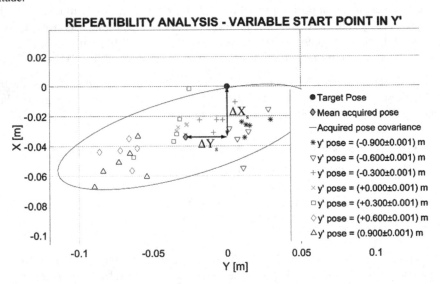

Fig. 7. Repeatability analysis results with the wheelchair starting from different y′ distances from the target position.

On the test characterized by a shift along the y' direction, Fig. 7, it is possible to notice a correlation between the initial position of the wheelchair and the final position reached. Indeed, it can be noticed that the samples related to the same initial position are grouped close to each others.

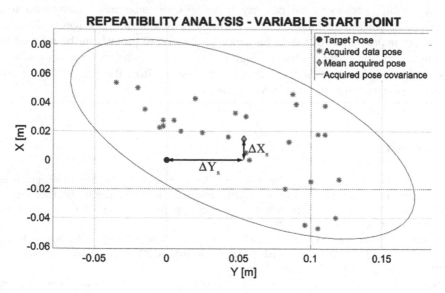

Fig. 8. Repeatability analysis results with the wheelchair starting from different positions and attitudes.

4 Conclusions

This paper focuses on the development of an Augmented Reality application based on a gaze interaction technology that is able to control semi-autonomously a wheelchair in a domestic environment. The performance of the system was evaluated by performing a repeatability analysis on the final positions reached, starting from different positions with respect to the target. In this way, it was possible to assess the influence of the starting position.

The repeatability analysis shows a maximum value (test with complete variable start point, Fig. 8) of deviation from the target position, transversal to the final desired direction of 0.18 m and 0.08 m longitudinally. From this information, we can conclude that considering a wheelchair width of 0.62 m, the minimum space actually that is required to reach autonomously a target is 0.98 m. Moreover, it is possible to notice a systematic deviation represented by the distances between the mean position of the sample and the target. This deviation can be related to the extrinsic parameters of the Kinect with respect to the vehicle that are not precisely known. As reported before, the Kinect is mounted on the chassis through a revolute joint characterized by backlashes in particular in the angle. This causes the systematic deviation highlighted in the final position reached by the wheelchair.

A future development is an on-line calibration of the Kinect extrinsic parameters by considering the changes in terms of position and attitude recorded by the odometric localization and by the Kinect absolute localization during the execution of the path. In this way, it is possible to compensate the systematic deviation and to prevent errors due to the possible variations of the position and attitude of the Kinect in the long periods.

As overall conclusion, we can say that the semi-autonomous navigation tool developed is suitable for indoor use in common houses having passages wider than 98 cm. An improvement of the performance of the overall project can be reached by the implementation of the on-line calibration tool together with an error budget analysis. Architectural house design criteria can take benefits from the error budget results in order to enhance the user mobility experience.

References

1. Maule, L., Fornaser, A., Leuci, M., Conci, N., Da Lio, M., De Cecco, M.: Development of innovative HMI strategies for eye controlled wheelchairs in virtual reality. In: Paolis, L.T., Mongelli, A. (eds.) AVR 2016. LNCS, vol. 9769, pp. 358–377. Springer, Cham (2016). doi:10.1007/978-3-319-40651-0_29
2. Fornaser, A., De Cecco, M., Leuci, M., Conci, N., Daldoss, M., Maule, L., De Natale, F., Da Lio, M.: Eye trackers uncertainty analysis and modelling. In: XXIII Convegno Nazionale A.I. VE.LA., Perugia, 12–13 Novembre 2015
3. Jain, M., Puri, S., Unishree, S.: Eyeball motion controlled wheelchair using IR sensors. Int. J. Comput. Electr. Autom. Control Inf. Eng. 9(4), 906–909 (2015). World Academy of Science, Engineering and Technology
4. Champaty, B., et al.: Development of EOG based human machine interface control system for motorized wheelchair. In: 2014 Annual International Conference on Emerging Research Areas: Magnetics, Machines and Drives (AICERA/iCMMD). IEEE (2014)
5. Ktena, S.I., Abbott, W., Aldo Faisal, A.: A virtual reality platform for safe evaluation and training of natural gaze-based wheelchair driving. In: 2015 7th International IEEE/EMBS Conference on Neural Engineering (NER). IEEE (2015)
6. Armanini, A., Conci, N.: Eye tracking as an accessible assistive tool. In: 2010 11th International Workshop on Image Analysis for Multimedia Interactive Services (WIAMIS), 12–14 April 2010, pp. 1–4 (2010)
7. Mahajan, H.P., et al.: Assessment of wheelchair driving performance in a virtual reality-based simulator. J. Spinal Cord Med. 36(4), 322–332 (2013)

Semi-automatic Initial Registration for the iRay System: A User Study

Tian Xie[1] , Mohammad M. Islam[1], Alan B. Lumsden[2],
and Ioannis A. Kakadiaris[1(✉)]

[1] Computational Biomedicine Lab, Department of Computer Science,
University of Houston, Houston, USA
ioannisk@uh.edu
[2] Methodist Research Institute, Houston, USA

Abstract. Simultaneous localization and mapping based augmented reality (AR) is trending in mobile AR applications. With the help of depth sensors, both accuracy and speed have improved. However, the method that performs the initial registration to align virtual objects with real scenery is not well developed, especially for some applications requiring very accurate registration (e.g., systems used in medical applications). For the iRay system, which is a mobile AR system using the Structure Sensor, we propose to use an iterative closest point algorithm to initially register the scanned mesh with the torso surface obtained pre-operatively, and then use SLAM to track pose. In this paper, a semi-automatic initial registration strategy is evaluated by a user study. This strategy is designed to help the user modify the selection of the 3D scanning area, so that the errors introduced by subjective differences can be reduced. The results indicate that the proposed strategy helps the users improve initial registration quality and reduces the average needed time.

Keywords: Medical AR · Mobile AR · 3D registration · User study

1 Introduction

Simultaneous localization and mapping (SLAM) based augmented reality (AR) systems are becoming more and more popular in recent years. SLAM differs from traditional marker-based registration strategies in its ability to track camera pose from the spatial environment, not just markers. This provides AR freedom to explore the space rather than just observing small markers. It also generates a new demand for placing virtual objects directly into the 3D reconstruction.

For most mobile AR applications, the traditional techniques are based primarily on 2D information, such as markers [1]. When SLAM is applied, additional 3D information is available [2, 3]. Virtual objects can be placed directly into 3D locations. The efficiency and accuracy of the placement are limited by the performance of the SLAM algorithm used for mobile platforms.

With the advent of depth sensors, SLAM has become much more accurate and faster in recent years. Some AR glasses (e.g., Hololens [4] and Meta 2 [5]) are using depth-enhanced tracking systems to achieve robust pose estimation in real time.

© Springer International Publishing AG 2017
L.T. De Paolis et al. (Eds.): AVR 2017, Part II, LNCS 10325, pp. 33–42, 2017.
DOI: 10.1007/978-3-319-60928-7_3

However, the registration methods have limited efficiency. In general, authoring requires an initial registration between virtual objects and a real 3D scene. It is application-specific, but always involves 3D shape/surface recognition. For instance, Hololens provides an interactive 3D authoring method based on surface recognition so that users can place models on the desk and walls with simple gestures. Although user-friendly, this kind of 3D authoring is not accurate and always depends on the user's perception.

When used in the medical domain, the initial registration accuracy for 3D authoring would be very restricted. It is necessary to develop accurate 3D registration methods for SLAM-based mobile AR applications.

In our previous work, we presented a mobile AR system named iRay [6]. It is implemented on the iPad and uses a Structure Sensor to obtain an accurate (1.5 mm) depth map. We have shown that the registration between 3D point clouds is useful for initial registration. However, the accuracy is highly dependent on the similarity of the two objects to be registered because we are using a simple iterative closest point (ICP) algorithm to ensure real time performance.

Currently, in iRay, we are using the MRI data of a male volunteer and his scanned torso surface mesh to perform our initial registration. Performance is not stable due to factors such as clothing, fullness of the stomach, and mostly the scanning area's size and location, which are selected by users with individual differences.

Focused on reducing these unstable inputs, a visual guidance strategy is proposed to help understand which area should be scanned for a better registration. The designed visual guidance includes an adjustable 3D box and semi-transparent overlay of the actual pre-operative torso surface model. Users can adjust the box's depth distance to fit the model onto the real torso. A user study was performed and indicated that this semi-automatic strategy can help the user to avoid most incorrect selections and improve their selection quality and speed.

The rest of the paper is organized as below. Section 2 illustrates the iRay system's constraints and major factors that make authoring unstable. Section 3 describes the user study with statistical results. Finally, Sect. 4 includes our discussion.

2   System Overview

2.1   The iRay System

The iRay system [6] uses mobile AR devices in a medical domain. Currently, the mobile platform is an Apple iPad and later will be extended to include AR glasses. A Structure Sensor [7] is used as the depth and SLAM information provider. Both 3D cloud points of the scanned area and active camera pose can be obtained by the Structure Sensor SDK.

Figure 1 depicts the framework of the iRay system noting the semi-automatic initial registration module. In Fig. 1, the blue arrows indicate offline related to patient data preparation. The green arrows indicate online processing running in every frame. The yellow arrows indicate the initial authoring functions performed only once just before the tracking loop starts. Note that the user selection of the scanning area is the only manual input in this system.

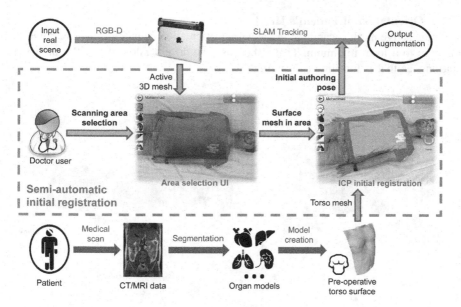

Fig. 1. Initial registration for iRay. (Color figure online)

2.2 Factors of Instability

Figure 1 depicts the area selection user interface (UI). A preview of the 3D scanning area is drawn in red-to-yellow. This preview is decided by the cube box, which is rendered as a white wireframe in the middle of the display screen. Users can control this box's size and depth (the physical focal distance relative to iPad camera). They can also change the iPad's pose to focus on the region of interest.

This step is manual because automatically searching for or recognizing a torso surface in an unknown 3D environment is challenging. Sometimes the user may not notice small details. The area they selected might be too large, too small, too slanted, or sometimes may not include the whole surface. These incorrect selections are under-estimated because they appear normal and tiny. Unfortunately, their influence is sometimes significant and cannot be corrected.

In our system, ICP is applied to register the 3D point clouds because ICP has been proven to be very efficient in depth-related work [8, 9]. In the iRay system, the reference point cloud is always set to the scanned torso mesh, and the comparison point cloud is the pre-operative model's vertices. When ICP registration is complete, the estimated 3D transformation can be directly applied to virtual organ models. The ICP fitting method is point-to-plane, and the iterations end when the transformation matrix is stable. Both point clouds are sampled to 500 points to balance accuracy and speed.

Under this specific setting, there are three factors that cause instability to the registration: (1) orientation of patient's head, (2) size of scanning area, and (3) horizontal and vertical displacement. The details are discussed in the following.

2.2.1   Orientation of Patient's Head

When the active mesh is captured in the wrong orientation (Fig. 2), iRay's ICP will just converge to a local minimum. That is because we do not allow the ICP search large rotations, as that is too time consuming.

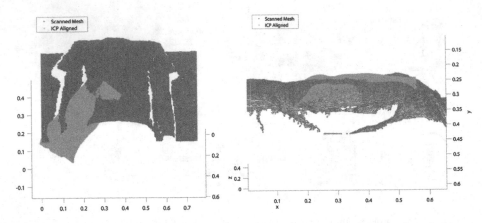

Fig. 2. Depicted are two examples of incorrect orientation registration. The red mesh denotes the pre-operative torso model that needs to register. The blue mesh denotes the reference mesh captured by the depth sensor. Both meshes are presented in full idensity without sampling. (Color figure online)

This incorrect orientation occurs consistently if there is only an empty wireframe rendered in the screen. The user always needs guidance to find the correct orientation. Thus, in the strategy we propose in this paper, the comparison torso mesh is overlaid in the middle of the cube box. The user can easily infer the orientation as they can quickly recognize the shoulder, chest or other anatomical features, so the two meshes will be in the same orientation.

2.2.2   Size of Scanning Area

Size of scanning area matters because it affects the quantity of information contained in the reference mesh. If the size is too large, too many points and noise are introduced. If the size is too small, there is not enough data to achieve good registration.

Figure 3 depicts examples of a small scanning size issue. The registration quality cannot be measured as the reference mesh is just a flat patch and we do not know which body part it is. Figure 4 depicts an example of large scanning size. The registration result is adequate but still has a small drift. That is because the reference (blue) point cloud is always sampled to 500 points as discussed earlier; therefore, larger size implies sparser mesh. Too sparse mesh leads to low registration quality.

In some cases, larger scanning size is preferred as it generally contains additional information. For these reasons, in the strategy presented in this paper, the size of the cube box is unchangeable to prevent the small scanning size issue. Specifically, the new size is a little larger than the actual size of the torso model, so that the reference

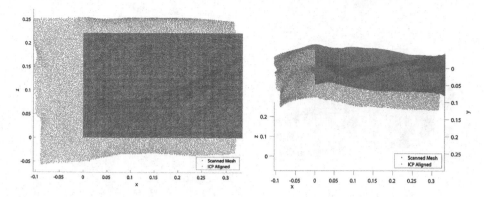

Fig. 3. Registration example when the reference (blue) mesh is too small. Depicted are two views of the same data. (Color figure online)

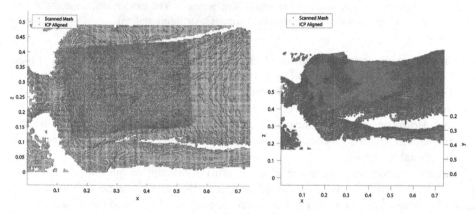

Fig. 4. Registration example when the reference (blue) mesh is too large. Depicted are two views of the same data. (Color figure online)

mesh has additional vertices and the system can be more tolerable to the user's subjective biases.

2.2.3 Horizontal and Vertical Displacement

The vertical displacement is caused by the incorrect depth of the scanning box relative to the iPad camera. The horizontal displacement occurs on the perpendicular plane of the camera focal line. Figure 5 depicts two examples of these two kinds of displacement.

Figure 5(L) depicts an example of vertical displacement where the top surface of torso is incomplete because the scanning box is set too low, which means the depth is too far from the camera. This occurs even when a red depth preview has been shown. Some users may not care about the preview due to their individual preferences. Figure 5(R) depicts an example where the left side of torso has not been scanned

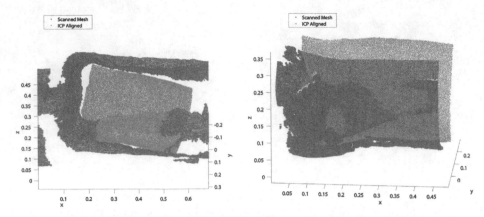

Fig. 5. Depiction of two registration examples with different displacement. (L) Depicted is an example of vertical displacement. The middle part of the torso has not been included in the box space. (R) Depicted is an example of horizontal displacement. The torso mesh is incomplete as one side has not been included in the scanning box. (Color figure online)

because the scanning box is displaced horizontally. This occurs when the user stands too far away from the patient, and s/he forgets to include the whole torso.

To overcome the vertical displacement, the depth sensor automatically finds a supporting surface so the box can always stand above the background and will not be too low. However, when the patient is lying on a narrow bed (or similar situation), the system fails to find a correct or valid surface, so the strategy has been changed to a depth-adjustable version.

Another option was to scan the whole depth information within the selected frustum, so the top surface would always be complete. However, in some scenarios, there could be some medical equipment placed on the patient's body, and those data should not be included in the scanning mesh. Due to these constraints, training of the user is the best solution.

3 User Study

3.1 Selection Quality

Due to the above factors of instability, we propose a semi-automatic initial registration strategy to help the user modify the selection of the 3D scanning area. The interface is shown in Fig. 6. The major change of the strategy over our prior work is to overlay the actual pre-operative torso surface model in the middle of the scanning box. When presented with this pre-rendered surface, the users can easily understand where to put the scanning box, so they can better avoid the factors of instability.

The box's size is automatically defined by the pre-operative model depicted in green color (Fig. 6). This surface model serves as the comparison mesh in the initial registration. The major target of authoring is to align this model onto the patient data so that when the user fits this green model onto the real torso, it is a good selection.

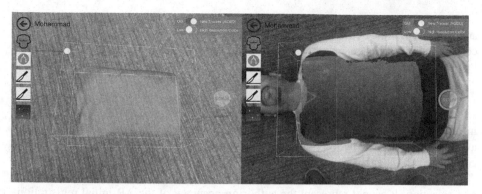

Fig. 6. Examples of new initial registration strategy. (L) Depicted is an example of the new User Interface. (R) Depicted is an example of good selection. (Color figure online)

Figure 6(R) depicts an example of good selection. The registration accuracy of this good selection can be inspected in Fig. 7.

The distances visualized in Fig. 7 are computed using a k-d tree-based nearest neighbor search. The search is performed among all the points without any sampling. The reference cloud contains 17,383 points. They are all generated from a 2D depth map with 1.5 mm precision. The comparison cloud has 14,726 points with a distribution density of about 2–3 mm.

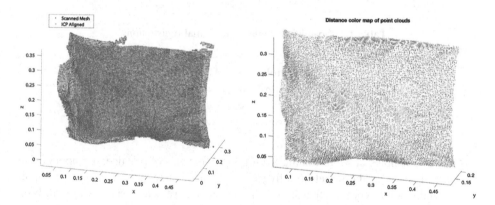

Fig. 7. Depiction of the registration result of the selection depicted in Fig. 6. (L) Depiction of the aligned meshes. (R) Color map of the distances (computed by nearest neighbor search) between the point clouds. Red color denotes large distances while blue color small distances. (Color figure online)

In this example, the smallest distance is 0.15 mm while the largest distance is 21.14 mm. The red color denotes the largest value, which is located in the top middle of Fig. 7(R). In that region, the reference mesh was not complete, so the nearest neighbor is still far away.

This phenomenon of incomplete mesh can be used to estimate the quality of box area selection. If the quality is very low, such as in Fig. 5, many points do not have any corresponding reference, and their nearest neighbor will be very far away. For example, in Fig. 5(L), the average distance of two point clouds is 42.86 mm, while in a good example such as Fig. 6, the average distance is only 3.72 mm.

Therefore, we apply this *average distance measure* to describe the quality of box selection in the user study. If the user's selection does not contain enough useful information, such as some important parts are cut out from the box (as in Fig. 5), the average distance will be very high. On the other hand, if the user has selected the correct area, this value will be small.

It should be mentioned that this average distance can only describe the quality of box selection. It cannot represent the authoring accuracy of the AR initial registration. The AR registration accuracy should be measured by FRE and TRE [10].

3.2   Experimental Design

We designed a user study to compare the proposed strategy with the strategy presented in our previous work [6]. This strategy (V2.0) is described above and depicted in Fig. 6, rendering the pre-operative model before registration starts. The old strategy (V1.0) can be used to change the box size but has no visual guidance. Table 1 summarizes the comparison of these two strategies. The new strategy does not use the size control and allows for model overlay.

Table 1. Capabilities available for initial registration.

Functions	V1.0	V2.0
Size control	✓	
Depth control	✓	✓
Depth preview	✓	✓
Model overlay		✓

After five minutes of short training and one to two times of practice, the operator is being asked to select the target area five times with the new strategy, and then five times with the old. Every selection starts with the same parameters, such as default box size and depth. The devices used are the same pair of iPad mini and Structure Sensor. The volunteer to be scanned is the same person wearing the same type T-shirt in the same pose (lying down on the same couch). The time that the user takes from the moment s/he starts controlling the iPad to when s/he presses the scan button is recorded. Every scan is recorded as 3D mesh, as is the ICP registration result. The average distance described in Sect. 3.1 is being computed after the experiments. Users do not receive any measurable feedback about the quality of their selection; they just try to select the whole torso area as they have been told in the training step.

3.3   Results

Eighty trials from eight different operators are evaluated in this study. The operators are between 24–31 years old, with at least a college education. None of them have any knowledge of iRay, nor do they have any medical experience. After the tests, there is a survey to rate themselves and provide feedback.

Time and Quality: Figure 8 depicts the average distance and average operation time of 80 tests (40 tests of each version). Note that comparing to the old strategy, new strategy has reduced the average distance by 11.3% and the average operation time by 28.1%. That means the users are achieving a better selection quality in less time, which indicates that our new strategy is very effective.

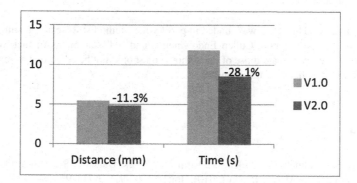

Fig. 8. Depicted are the average distance and operation time of all tests.

Reduction of Error: Although the average selection quality appears good (around 5 mm in Fig. 8), subjective error is inevitable. As described above, our new strategy is designed to reduce factors of instability. For each selection in the user study, if the final average distance is larger than 6 mm, it will be labeled as an error, and the reason will be analyzed.

The final result indicates that there are 17.5% subjective errors among all trials in the test of old version and only 7.5% in the new; all of these errors are caused by displacement, as the factors of orientation and size are all voided after the training. This result demonstrates that our new strategy can efficiently reduce the subjective errors by 57.1%, which also proves its effectivity.

Survey: Users indicated that they agree with the description "new version strategy is easier to use" with an average score of 8.1, and they agree that "New version strategy has better performance (UI design)" with an average score of 8.5.

4   Conclusion

In this paper, we propose a new initial registration strategy to be used with our iRay system. It overlays the actual pre-operative torso surface model in the middle of a scanning box to help the user avoid some factors of instability caused by the user's subjective decision.

A user study has been performed to evaluate the new strategy. The results show that the new strategy can help the users reduce subjective errors by 57%, improve the selection quality by 11.3% and increase the operation speed by 28.1%, which demonstrates the efficiency of the design.

Note that the testers in this study are young in age and have no medical knowledge. As our application is designed for physicians, we plan to conduct tests with physicians to receive their feedback.

Acknowledgements. This work was funded in part by the Methodist Research Institute and the UH Hugh Roy and Lillie Cranz Cullen Endowment Fund. All statements of fact, opinion or conclusions contained herein are those of the authors and should not be construed as representing the official views or policies of the sponsors.

References

1. Coquillart, S., Brunnett, G., Welch, G.: Virtual Realities: Dagstuhl Seminar 2008. Springer Science & Business Media, Berlin (2010). doi:10.1007/978-3-211-99178-7
2. van den Hengel, A., Hill, R., Ward, B., Dick, A.: In situ image-based modeling. In: Proceedings 8th IEEE International Symposium on Mixed and Augmented Reality, Orlando, FL, USA, pp. 107–110 (2009). doi:10.1109/ISMAR.2009.5336482
3. Langlotz, T., Mooslechner, S., Zollmann, S., Degendorfer, C., Reitmayr, G., Schmalstieg, D.: Sketching up the world: in situ authoring for mobile augmented reality. Pers. Ubiquit. Comput. **16**(6), 623–630 (2012). doi:10.1007/s00779-011-0430-0
4. Hololens. https://www.microsoft.com/microsoft-hololens/en-us
5. Meta 2. http://buy.metavision.com/products/meta2
6. Kakadiaris, I.A., Islam, M.M., Xie, T., Nikou, C., Lumsden, A.B.: iRay: mobile AR using structure sensor. In: Proceedings 15th IEEE International Symposium on Mixed and Augmented Reality, Merida, Mexico (2016)
7. Structure sensor. https://structure.io
8. Newcombe, R.A., Izadi, S., Hilliges, O., Molyneaux, D., Kim, D., Davison, A.J., Kohi, P., Shotton, J., Hodges, S., Fitzgibbon, A.: KinectFusion: real-time dense surface mapping and tracking. In: Proceedings 10th IEEE International Symposium on Mixed and Augmented Reality, Basel, Switzerland, pp. 127–136. (2011). doi:10.1109/ISMAR.2011.6092378
9. Newcombe, R.A., Fox, D., Seitz, S.M.: DynamicFusion: reconstruction and tracking of non-rigid scenes in real-time. In: Proceedings IEEE Conference on Computer Vision and Pattern Recognition, Boston, MA, USA, pp. 343–352 (2015)
10. Shamir, R.R., Joskowicz, L., Spektor, S., Shoshan, Y.: Localization and registration accuracy in image guided neurosurgery: a clinical study. Int. J. Comput. Assist. Radiol. Surg. **4**(1), 45–52 (2009). doi:10.1007/s11548-008-0268-8

Teaching Materials Using AR and VR for Learning the Usage of Oscilloscope

Takashi Miyazaki[1(✉)], Yusuke Ohira[1], Hiroaki Yamamoto[2], and Masaaki Nishi[3]

[1] National Institute of Technology, Nagano College,
716 Tokuma, Nagano 381-8550, Japan
{miya, ohira}@nagano-nct.ac.jp
[2] Faculty of Engineering, Shinshu University,
4-17-1 Wakasato, Nagano 380-8553, Japan
yamamoto@cs.shinshu-u.ac.jp
[3] Faculty of Education, Shinshu University,
6-Ro Nishinagano, Nagano 380-8544, Japan
nishi@shinshu-u.ac.jp

Abstract. In order to have students enjoy experimental practice and exercises, it is important to acquire information beforehand on how to use the measuring instruments used in experiments. In this research we developed educational teaching materials that let students learn the principle and usage of an oscilloscope in an enjoyable way using Augmented Reality (AR) technology and Virtual Reality (VR) technology with a tablet. The most important feature of the tools is that they use not only explanations by the text-based 2D world, but also effective explanations by 3D modeling using AR and VR technology. The results of a questionnaire by the students who used the teaching materials of the oscilloscopes for the first time show a very good response.

Keywords: Augmented Reality · Virtual Reality · Oscilloscope · Teaching material · Wearable device

1 Introduction

Recently, the interest of AR and VR technologies has significantly increased with the widespread adoption of smartphones and tablets. Many attempts to incorporate this technology into education and practice in various fields have been actively made [1–4]. Various measuring instruments are often used in the experimental practice of electric and electronic systems, and it is important to instruct students to operate measuring instruments efficiently. In particular, oscilloscopes among measuring instruments are very important instruments for students conducting experimental practice of electric and electronic systems, but it takes time to master the operation method due to the number of buttons and the number of operation procedures. Also, in addition to learning how to use an oscilloscope, knowing its operation principle is important because students can understand phenomena of electrons in the electric field. However, because students in lower grades have only learned about the basics of electricity it is

© Springer International Publishing AG 2017
L.T. De Paolis et al. (Eds.): AVR 2017, Part II, LNCS 10325, pp. 43–52, 2017.
DOI: 10.1007/978-3-319-60928-7_4

uncertain that they have sufficient knowledge to really understand the principle of oscilloscopes. In addition, the concept is difficult for lower grade students to grasp because it is a phenomenon in the three-dimensional world when trying to understand the movement of electrons. So far we have developed applications using AR technology that works on tablets [7, 8, 9]. In this application, when the tablet is turned to the oscilloscope, a virtual oscilloscope button appears on the tablet, and when touching the button to be operated next the explanation is displayed. When conducting an experimental practice using this teaching material, students are giving a favorable evaluation that it is much more interesting and easier to understand than the conventional paper-based text. However, since it is necessary to use both hands to manipulate the tablet both hands are restricted, causing the problem of making it impossible to see the explanation while operating the oscilloscope.

In this study we thought that the learning of operating principles could be presented in an easy-to-understand manner using the VR (Virtual Reality) technology. Wearing goggles for AR and a smartphone for VR on a headset, we developed a wearable teaching material that the user can understand while feeling the operation method and principle of operation of the oscilloscopes.

2   Teaching Materials to Learn the Principle of Oscilloscope

In this research we developed a teaching material that can be understood while wearing a device, so that students can experience the operating principle and operation method of the oscilloscope. At our school we explain the principle of a cathode-ray tube oscilloscope as shown in Fig. 1. The features of this educational material are the following four functions. (i) Since both hands are free, the user can see the explanation in real time while actually operating the oscilloscope. (ii) Stereoscopic viewing becomes possible by dividing the display for the right eye and the left eye by using the wearable device, and it is possible to experience a realistic three-dimensional feeling. (iii) When presenting the operating principle, the user can see how the traveling electron direction changes with the voltage applied to the electrode plate, almost as if the user is going inside the oscilloscope itself. (iv) When presenting the operation method, it is possible to intuitively understand by animating the concrete operation method in addition to the virtual button using AR technology. In the case of using the VR technology, it is desirable to make the user unable to see the outside world in order to raise immersion. Therefore, this teaching material uses smartphone and headset in combination. Because a smartphone is fixed into the headset, the user cannot operate a conventional touch screen, so the user can operate the buttons of the headset for operation. On the other hand, in order to use the AR technology, it is necessary not to see the outside world through the camera, but to be directly visible. When images are displayed through a camera set a smartphone, it takes time to process. Therefore the operation performed by the user is delayed as compared with the action actually performed by the user. Because of this time delay, the feeling of the user often becomes nauseous. Hence, it turned out that it is better to use a device capable of displaying AR objects on translucent glasses.

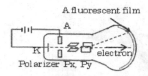

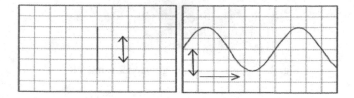

Fig. 1. Principle of the cathode ray tube (CRT) and electron shift by polarizers

2.1   Teaching Material Using VR to Learn the Principle of Oscilloscope

In our laboratory experiments, we taught how to use an oscilloscope through text, but it was not enough for students to understand the movement of three-dimensional electrons. Therefore, the movement of electrons inside the cathode ray tube of the oscilloscope was constructed in a three-dimensional virtual space by utilizing the VR technology and the teaching material for reproducing the movement of electrons. Thus the learning of the principle of oscilloscopes was created. This allows students to experience the feeling of entering into the oscilloscope and observe the movement of electrons in it. As the VR device, we use Gear VR by the SAMSUNG Company shown in Fig. 2. Its feature was that the buttons for operation are provided in the headset, and it is easy to understand the operation of the Galaxy smartphone used in combination with them. As the software development environment, we used Unity 5 of Unity Technologies. In addition, since realism can be enhanced by giving a stereoscopic effect, a virtual left eye camera and right eye camera are prepared for the development environment. The positions of these cameras are slightly shifted from each other, and the images seen from the respective cameras are displayed separately for the left eye and the right eye on the display of the smartphone VR as shown in Figs. 3 and 4. By performing this process, parallax can be expressed, and students can feel the depth of the object placed in the VR space as shown in Fig. 5. Furthermore, VR allows the user to naturally see the direction which the user wants to see by using the acceleration sensor built in the smartphone and matching the orientation of the user's head with the orientation of the camera in the VR. Also, the user can change the position of the viewpoint freely by using the operation buttons. In addition, since it was understood that the operation using the operation button was somewhat difficult through testing, we make it possible to operate even small controller using Bluetooth. Therefore, the user can experience the operation of the oscilloscope in the sense that the user are in the space inside the VR.

Fig. 2. Goggles of teaching material using VR

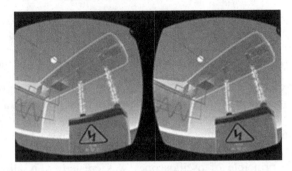

Fig. 3. Teaching material using VR

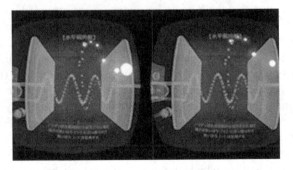

Fig. 4. Electron motion in the CRT

2.2 Teaching Material Using AR with a Tablet

The AR library includes a marker type for recognizing a specific fixed figure and a markerless type for recognizing an object existing in reality rather than a specific fixed figure. In the case of a marker type, as it is necessary to paste the marker at the same position of all the oscilloscopes, we choose the markerless type Vuforias. For the voice of character, we select AquesTalk which is used for movies such as live comment slowly being used in "Nico Nico Douga". As the 3D development environment, we

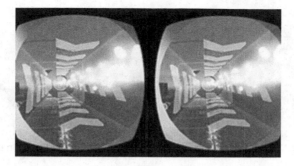

Fig. 5. Stereoscopic view with parallax

chose Unity because it is easy to write to iOS, use AR library in Vuforia, draw 3D objects, play audio and so on. Figure 6 shows the landscape using the tablet of this teaching material facing the operation surface of the oscilloscope. The teaching material has the following two modes when explaining the operation method of the oscilloscopes. One is the mode of operating procedure as shown in Fig. 7. It is presented when it is required a series of procedures such as initial setting and probe adjustment. For the operation the character on the upper side of the screen explains with letters and sounds, the buttons necessary for the operation blink, and the setting item is superimposed on the screen and displayed. The other is the mode of explaining button. When the button on the screen is touched, the character on the lower side explains what kind of function the button has by letter and voice.

Fig. 6. Scenery of using AR teaching material

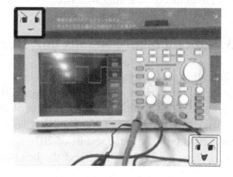

Fig. 7. Display of operation procedure

2.3   Teaching Material Using AR with Goggles

The MOVERIO BT-300 from EPSON can add information on semi-transparent goggles as a device for AR as shown in Fig. 8. In addition, Vuforias PTC was used as a library, and Unity 5, same as the working principle learning material using VR, was used for integrated development environment. As students do not have the AR teaching materials, they can use both hands freely during experiment classes. As shown in

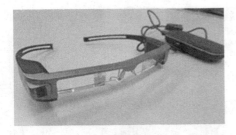

Fig. 8. Goggles of teaching material using AR   **Fig. 9.** Display the operation procedure

Fig. 9, the explanations of operating oscilloscope start to be presented when the cursor is superposed on the button of the oscilloscope. The descriptions of the operation method continue to be displayed even if the cursor is out of the position of the button so that the positioning of the cursor and the button can be easily performed. Two types of 2D and 3D are prepared as the screen display method to the BT - 300. In the case of 2D, the same screen is displayed in front of the left and right eyes, so a clear image is displayed. When operating the oscilloscope, the user needs to focus on the operation button of the oscilloscope, but the explanatory image displayed is displayed at the same position irrespective of the position of focus. On the other hand, in the case of 3D, the screen for the left eye is displayed on the left display and the screen for the right eye is displayed on the right display. As frequent changes in focus are reduced by adjusting both images at almost the same position as the oscilloscope button, eye fatigue is suppressed. For that reason, it seems that the explanatory texts and cursor images are sticking on the oscilloscope. Therefore, 3D display technology is chosen to enhance the effectiveness of teaching materials.

3   Questionnaire Results and Discussion

Since this work is being expanded year by year, we conduct questionnaire survey for students who used the materials from 2014 to 2016. Therefore we cannot easily compare, but we summarize the results of the survey as shown in Figs. 10, 11, 12, 13, 14 and 15. The results of 2014 and 2015 questionnaires indicate when the students used only iPad type. And the results of 2016 questionnaire show when the students used the iPad type, the goggles type and the headset type.

(a)   Fun of materials (see Fig. 10)

The percentage of students answered that the teaching materials are fun is almost 100%, and 70% of the students said that these tools are very fun in 2016. We believe it is because we adopted the goggles type the VR teaching materials from 2016.

(b)   Operability of teaching materials (see Fig. 11)

Since operability has been improved year by year, 100% of students said that it was easy to use in 2016. As for this, 60% of students said that it was particularly easy to use because we adopted the goggle type the VR teaching material from 2016.

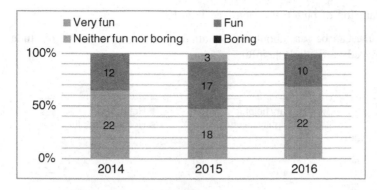

Fig. 10. Fun of teaching materials

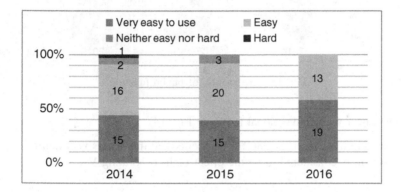

Fig. 11. Operability of teaching materials

(c) Explanation of operation procedure (see Fig. 12)

The answer that it was helpful was nearly 100% every year, and the ratio that said it was helpful this time was almost 60%.

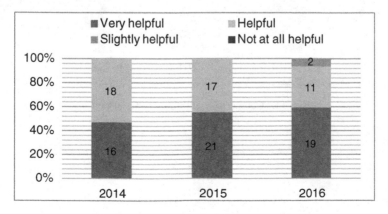

Fig. 12. Explanation of operation procedure

(d) Explanation of button function (see Fig. 13)

The same can be said about the explanation of the button; 60% of students from 2015 answered particularly helpful.

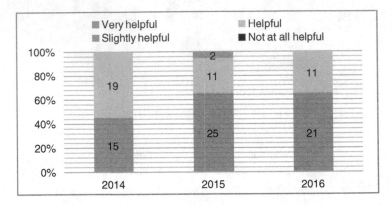

Fig. 13. Explanation of button function

(e) Comparison with conventional text (see Fig. 14)

Compared to traditional text, 80% of students said that it was very helpful in 2016. The best reason is considered to be the effect of incorporating VR.

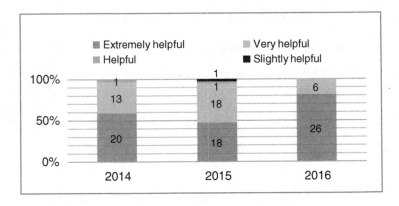

Fig. 14. Comparison with conventional text

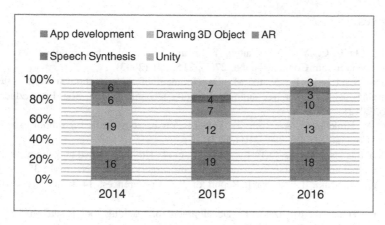

Fig. 15. Interested technology (Multiple answers allowed)

(f) Interested technology (see Fig. 15)

Figure 15 shows which technology the students had interested in. Especially, the interest in developing applications that run on tablets is high and it is near 70% to be combined with 3D technology, because the principle of the oscilloscope is explained by 3D animation. AR increases every year and it became about 20% in 2016.

4 Conclusion

In order to learn the operating principle of the oscilloscope, we developed the VR teaching material using a smartphone and a headset. We also developed the AR teaching material using translucent goggles to present the operation method of the oscilloscope. In addition, as a whole impression of this teaching material, "easy to understand", "touching on technologies such as AR", "similar teaching materials for other experimental equipment", "Using Unity which is a development environment" is mentioned. Therefore, in addition to fulfilling the purpose of "making experimental practice fun", this study material has made it possible for many students to be interested in various technologies used as their development environments. Finally, we plan to improve the ease of use of the teaching materials.

Acknowledgement. We would like to thank students of NIT Nagano College who answered to the questionnaire using the developed teaching materials. This study was supported by JSPS KAKENHI Grant Number 25910022 and JP16H00234.

References

1. Caia, Y., Chuib, C., Yec, X., Wangb, Y., et al.: VR simulated training for less invasive vascular intervention. Comput. Graph. **27**(2), 215–221 (2003)
2. Watanuki, K., Kaede, K., Muto, M.: Development of an education support system for mechatronics using marker free augmented reality technology. Jpn. Soc. Eng. Educ. **60**(6), 99–105 (2012)
3. Sigitov, A., Hinkenjann, A., Roth, T.: Towards VR-based systems for school experiments. Procedia Comput. Sci. **25**, 201–210 (2013)
4. Pelargosa, P.E., Nagasawaa, D.T., Lagmana, C., et al.: Utilizing virtual and augmented reality for educational and clinical enhancements in neurosurgery. J. Clin. Neurosci. **35**, 1–4 (2017)
5. Ohira, Y., Miyazaki, T.: Research Report of JET Conferences, 14 January, pp. 167 172 (2014)
6. Ohira, Y., Yodo, Y., Miyazaki, T.: Development of teaching tool based on AR for the experiments using oscilloscope. In: The 9th International Symposium on Advances in Technology Education, ISATE 2015, pp. 218–222 (2015)
7. Ohira, Y., Miyazaki, T.: Development of the oscilloscope teaching materials using AR and VR. In: Research Report of JET Conferences (2017, in press)

An Augmented Reality System for Maxillo-Facial Surgery

Francesco Ricciardi[1], Chiara Copelli[2], and Lucio T. De Paolis[3(✉)]

[1] Innovation and Research Division, Casa Sollievo della Sofferenza Hospital,
San Giovanni Rotondo, Italy
f.ricciardi@operapadrepio.it
[2] Operative Unit of Maxillo-Facial Surgery,
Casa Sollievo della Sofferenza Hospital, San Giovanni Rotondo, Italy
chiaracopelli@hotmail.it
[3] Department of Engineering for Innovation, University of Salento, Lecce, Italy
lucio.depaolis@unisalento.it

Abstract. Maxillo-facial surgery is a surgical field where surgical planning and navigation tools are commonly used but there is still a visualization gap among planned surgical activities and those in the operating room. We propose an Augmented Reality platform that includes a planning module and a drill guidance system. Some laboratory tests on 3D printed mandibles have been carried out in order to evaluate the system guidance uncertainty with different sets of fiducial points. The obtained mean value of guidance uncertainty has been of 1.37 mm when 2 anatomical points and 3 implanted screws were used and 1.43 mm when 5 anatomical points were used. The use of three fixed screws reduces the system mean guidance uncertainty and surgeons judged the augmented reality technology helpful in this kind of surgical procedures.

Keywords: Augmented reality · Computer-aided surgery · Maxillo-facial surgery

1 Introduction

In the context of the image-guided surgery, the development of platforms based on the augmented reality may represent a significant improvement and support that provide a surgeon an accurate knowledge of the patient's anatomy and pathologies inside the patient's body. The augmented reality technology makes it possible to overlay virtual models of the organs on the real patient; this allows the surgeon to have a sort of 'X-ray vision' of the patient's internal anatomy.

Several research groups presented the use of augmented reality technology in many surgical fields including spinal surgery [1], orthopaedics [2], neurosurgery [3], minimally invasive surgery [4, 5], hepatic surgery [6] and biopsy procedures [7] due to the possibility to face in a more easy and precise way the surgical procedures.

In maxillo-facial surgery ablative and reconstructive tumour surgery as well as the treatment of complex congenital and acquired deformities are often difficult due the anatomical complexity of the facial skeleton and the functional and aesthetic importance of the structures involved.

© Springer International Publishing AG 2017
L.T. De Paolis et al. (Eds.): AVR 2017, Part II, LNCS 10325, pp. 53–62, 2017.
DOI: 10.1007/978-3-319-60928-7_5

Surgical techniques of the craniofacial area have been refined and developed during the past 30 years, but despite these technological advances, there are still problems with regard to the correct definition of margins of complex oncological resections, the accuracy in repositioning skeletal components into optimal relationships and the restablishment of facial symmetry. Several factors contribute to poor outcomes. First of all there is the surgical reliance on 2-dimensional imaging for treatment planning on a 3-dimensional problem. There are also the difficulties in assessing the intraoperative position and the poor visualization of deep skeletal contours and the variations in head position and craniofacial development.

Recent technological improvements led to the availability of different aiding systems in the field of cranio-maxillo-facial surgery in preoperative planning and intra-operative navigation. Pre-surgical planning tools allow the surgeon to analyse CT or MRI data and to simulate and plan the surgical procedure [8]. The simulation is usually based upon patient's virtual reality 3D models reconstructed from these datasets. The virtual data produced with these planning tools can be imported into a virtual reality navigation system that can be used to provide guidance indications for the accurate and safe placement of the anatomical structures, the movement of bone segment, the resection of tumour and/or osteotomy design [9].

All these innovations are useful and important but sometimes the results have a lack of accuracy and it is difficult for the surgeon to adapt the virtual planning to the surgical field.

The augmented reality technology can bypass these problems merging the virtual preoperative planning within the real operative field. By means of this technology the surgeon has the capability to visualize in real time the operative scenario overlapped with virtual 3D models of organs such as a tumour or other anatomical structures of interest [10, 11].

2 Related Works

Several works about the use of augmented reality technology in maxillo-facial surgery can be found in literature.

Salb et al. [12] presented an augmented reality system for cranio-facial surgery. The system is based on the use of a Sony Glasstron HMD and two micro cameras placed on the visor in order to realize an optical see-through overlay. An NDI Polaris optical tracking system has been used for the camera and the surgical instruments tracking. Some tests were carried out and a very low guidance uncertainty value was obtained.

Kahrs et al. [13] experimented an augmented reality system for maxillo-facial surgery based on the use of two video-projectors that permit to give additional 3D information for patient localization and orientation in order to achieve a self alignment tool.

Mischkowski et al. [14] presented an augmented reality tool for computer assisted surgery named X-Scope. The system, used in the orthognathic surgery, is constituted of a portable display that can be used to show the virtual models superimposed on the patient's face; an optical tracker is used to track the display location.

Swiatek-Najwer et al. [15] presented a navigation system based on virtual reality to support oncologic surgery in the maxillo-facial area. The proposed system provides an interesting and advanced module for surgical planning.

Badiali et al. [16] presented an augmented reality system for maxillo-facial bone surgery; for registration and tracking modality they used the "wearable augmented reality for medicine (WARM)" that doesn't require external infrared cameras or electromagnetic field generator, but only the visible light. Alignment between the real and virtual world is achieved via processing of video frames grabbed by the cameras.

In this paper we describe the development of an augmented reality platform designed for maxillo-facial surgery in order to help surgeons in the tumour ablations and resections to define more precise resection margins and to reduce the risk of recurrence. The system permits a useful healthy tissue removal. The platform includes a virtual reality-based surgical navigation module and an augmented reality guidance system and permits surgeon to speed-up time between the surgical planning and the surgery and also to make adjustments to the planned surgery flow during the live surgery.

3 Technological Platform

The developed maxillo-facial surgery platform consists of a software platform provided with an optical tracking system and a webcam.

From the medical image of a patient (MRI or CT), an efficient 3D reconstruction of his anatomy can be provided in order to improve the standard slice view by the visualization of the 3D models of the organs; colors associated to the different organs replace the grey levels in the medical images. In order to build 3D models of the organs from the patient's CT scans we used 3D Slicer [17].

The surgeon, after building the 3D models of the organs, has the possibility to customize the appearance of each organ by modifying color and opacity.

The surgical guidance module comprises a virtual reality surgical navigator and an augmented reality guidance system. In order to use these modules the surgeon has to perform the registration procedure that permits to align the patient reference system with the virtual world reference system. The tools have been designed in order to reduce the complexity of the surgical procedure and to maximize the positive outcomes of the surgery. A drill guidance tool based on a crosshair paradigm helps the surgeons during the screw-positioning task.

The application development is based on the use of the IGSTK framework [18] and of the C++ language. IGSTK, Image-Guided Surgery Toolkit, is an open-source framework developed for image-guided surgery applications. The most important feature of this cross-platform framework is the robustness. The use of a state machine ensures a formal validation of the software and an error free behaviour.

VTK framework [19] is used for the development of the mesh editor, the reconstruction planning tools and the drill guidance tool. VTK is an open-source visualization framework written in C++ for 3D computer graphics, scientific visualization, image processing and much more.

Qt framework [20] was used to develop the application interface. It provides a multi-platform support that permits to have a highly portable application. Qt is also compatible with IGSTK framework.

To perform the measurements of the position of fiducial points on the patient body and track position and orientation of surgical tools we used a NDI Polaris Vicra optical tracker [21]. The tracker uses two IR cameras to detect the infrared-emitting or retro-reflective markers. Real-time measurements could be achieved in a specific interaction volume that is defined by the tracker itself and cannot be changed. The tracking system accuracy is of 0.2 mm and 0.1 tenth of a degree.

Philips SPC1330NC webcam has been used for images capturing; it offers good image quality with 2.0 Mpixel sensor, a maximum frame rate of 90 fps and 16 bit color depth. Camera position is tracked using an NDI tracker tool fastened to the camera.

4   Surgical Planning Module

A surgical planning module could be used in order to plan the surgical procedure; it consists of three sub-modules that are: anatomy inspector, mesh editor and reconstruction planner [22].

The anatomy inspector tool, shown in Fig. 1, permits to have a better view of the patient's anatomy and pathology. Using CT images together with anatomy models it offers to surgeons many visualization modalities that can be used in order to have a more detailed view of the area of interest.

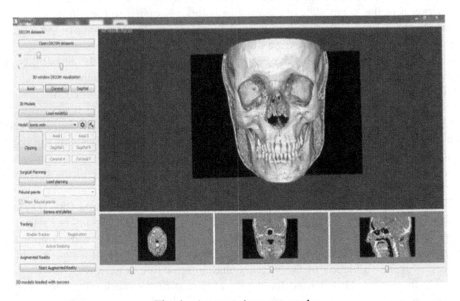

Fig. 1. Anatomy inspector tool

The anatomy inspector tool offers many visualization modalities that can be used on 3D virtual models. A 3D view window can combine the visualization of 3D models with the patient's CT scans along the three traditional medical projections.

For each model surgeons can customize color and opacity of the mesh using the user interface. In this way visualization effects can be used to watch inside closed volumes without loosing the perception and the extension of the container body.

This user interface can also be used in order to obtain some advanced visualization effects, as shown in Fig. 2, where the skin is rendered with a lower opacity to permit to see inside and the tumour mass colored in green. This kind of visualization permits to identify in a clear manner the tumour extension and its positioning as well as the relationship with the other structures.

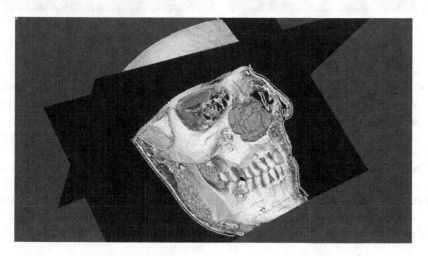

Fig. 2. Mesh advanced visualization (Color figure online)

A selective mesh clipping tool permits to cut the virtual models and watch inside; it permits to obtain an alternative view of the tumour. Clipping planes coincide with CT slices and the user can adjust the corresponding cursor in order to move the cutting plane and re-compute the clipping in real-time. Mesh clipping can also be used in the operating room during surgery; in this case the tip of a surgical pointing tool can be linked to the CT slices cursors in order to obtain a dynamic and real-time mesh clipping. The mesh editor tool provides users with some basic mesh editing commands that are useful for the reconstruction planning. The integration of a mesh editing tool in the application permits to avoid the use of external software and tools to edit the meshes.

In order to avoid an unwanted translation or rotation of these models could result in a harmful guidance indication. For this reason we decided to add an alert message when the user starts a command that could translate or rotate a mesh.

The mesh editor tool allows the mesh reflection with respect to a reflection plane that is aligned with the traditional medical projections planes. By means of this tool the user can adjust the position of the reflection plane along its normal axis.

In Fig. 3 the results of the reflection of a clipped mandible, maxilla and part of cheekbone are shown. In this case the reflection could be combined with transparency effects to make a comparison between the two sides of the face.

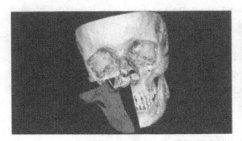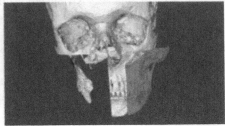

Fig. 3. Mesh editor tool

Maxillo-facial surgeons often use screws and plates to keep together bones, to define a reconstruction shape and favourite the process of osteosynthesis. Most effective reconstruction results come from a careful planning of the positioning of these support tools. For this reason a reconstruction planning module permits the surgeon to plan the reconstruction phase; actually this module supports only the screws positioning.

The application permits, using small red spheres, to compute the intersection points between the screw trajectory and a given mesh. These data can be used for the screw positioning not only in the pre-operative phase, but also to guide the surgeon by means of an augmented view during the real surgical procedure. It permits to increase the screw positioning accuracy.

5   Surgical Navigation and Augmented Reality Modules

The planning obtained through the surgical planning module can be used in the operating room in the Surgical Navigation Module or by means of Augmented Reality Module.

In order to use the Augmented Reality Module which permits a correct alignment among real objects and virtual ones, it is necessary to compute the mathematical transformation that permits to align the virtual world coordinate system with the real world coordinate system. Several methods are available in order to compute the image registration in surgical guidance systems. We have chosen a point-based registration method that is based on some fiducial points defined both on the patient body and in the CT scans.

The registration procedure asks the user to measure the position of the fiducial points showed in the application interface in the tracker reference system; this measurement is made by means of an optical tracker. The surgeon has to touch the fiducial points with the tracker probe and the tracker acquires the positions in the tracker coordinate system. During the registration procedure the patient must not be moved.

Once the positions of all fiducial points are acquired the application computes the registration transformation using the Horn algorithm [23].

During and after the registration phase, the relative position between the patient and the tracker must not change, otherwise the registration will not be valid and the virtual model not correctly aligned. A sterilized tracker tool can be rigidly fixed on the patient skull by means of a surgical screw to solve this problem. In this way the tracker measurements will be referred to the reference system associated to this tool and both the patient and the tracker can be freely moved.

Once the registration phase is completed, the surgeon can navigate in the patient's virtual models. This visualization modality can also be used during the surgery as a surgical navigator. In this case the surgeon watches the models presented on the screen and uses a tracker probe to measure their anatomical positions on the real patient.

The augmented reality visualization (Fig. 4) can be optionally activated and the camera starts to acquire a real-time video of the patient body. The surgeon can move the camera and visualize the virtual models superimposed to the patient body; the constraint that the camera must remain in the tracker measurement volume.

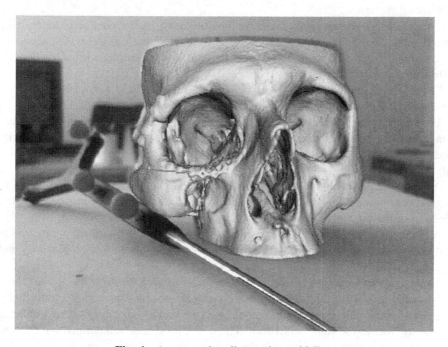

Fig. 4. Augmented reality cutting guidelines

A drill guidance module is provided in virtual reality and augmented reality modalities. A tracked tool must be fixed on the drill and the drill bit calibrated by means of a pivot calibration. The module uses the screw intersection points computed by the reconstruction planning module to automatically detect when the drill tip is next to one of these points.

When the distance between the tip and the intersection point falls below 15 mm, a crosshair tool is shown in the upper left part of the screen and the point is evidenced by a red transparent sphere. The opacity of the tool and sphere visualization is inversely proportional to the distance. Once the tip reaches the screw intersection point, the angle between the screw trajectory and the drill bit is shown on the sphere pointer of the crosshair.

6   System Tests

Some laboratory tests were conducted in order to evaluate the application guidance uncertainty in a well controlled environment. These tests are important and must be done in order to put in evidence the system guidance uncertainty without the typical influence factors present in the operating room.

During the tests four 3D-printed models of human mandible and a model of the frontal half part of the human skull were used. All these models were reconstructed and printed from real patient's CT scans. The cut outliner tool produces the information used during the test.

Three surgical screws were placed on the surface of each model in order to have some fixed fiducial points. Once all the screws were fixed, each model was scanned by a CT scanner and these scans were used in order to reconstruct virtual reality 3D models of the 3D printed models.

During the planning phase of the experiment each virtual model was loaded into the application as well as its CT scan and six cutting planes were defined.

The fiducial points were placed on the models surface. Three fiducial points were defined on the center of the screws head screwed on the samples. Other two fiducial points were defined in two easily recognizable anatomical points characterized by a high convexity.

A first set of measuring was done in order to investigate the registration accuracy in a mixed environment and study if the use of fixed fiducial points contributes to the reduction of the guidance uncertainty.

A second set of measures was carried out using five anatomical points easily recognizable anatomical points characterized by a high convexity, low co-planarity and easy accessibility.

The maximum value of system uncertainty is less then 2.5 mm when at least three rigid fiducial points (in this case screws) contributes to the registration phase. Only using anatomical points as registration points, the same value of system guidance uncertainty reaches the value of 3.1 mm. The use of rigid and well defined registration points contributes to the system guidance uncertainty reduction in terms of mean value and variance. In the opinion of the surgeons the mean values of guidance uncertainty are acceptable in both cases.

Although it needs to be improved, surgeons judged the developed system to be useful in reduction of the gap between the existing surgical planned visualization approach and the treatment in the operating theatre. The possibility to have the custom guidance information directly on the patient anatomy reduces effectively the surgeon distraction if compared with the actual guidance systems.

7 Conclusions

In this paper is presented an augmented reality guidance system for the maxillo-facial surgery. Although the technological improvements of the last years, there is a gap between the virtual reality-based surgical planning tools and the surgical theatre.

The presented system consists of a software platform with an optical tracking system and a webcam. The developed software consists of two modules: a surgical planning module and a surgical guidance module. The application permits a complete surgical workflow from the planning phase to the surgical phase since it includes an advanced surgical planning module, a virtual reality based navigation module and an augmented reality guidance system.

Two experimental tests were made in order to compare the guidance uncertainty in two different experimental settings.

References

1. Bastien, S., Peuchot, B., Tanguy, A.: Augmented reality in spine surgery: critical appraisal and status of development. Stud. Health Technol. Inf. **88**, 153–156 (2002)
2. Blackwell, M., Morgan, F., Di Gioia, A.M.: Augmented reality and its future in orthopaedics. Clin. Orthop. Relat. Res. **354**, 111–122 (1998)
3. Meola, A., Cutolo, F., Carbone, M., Cagnazzo, F., Ferrari, M., Ferrari, V.: Augmented reality in neurosurgery: a systematic review. Neurosurg. Rev., 1–12 (2016). Springer, Heidelberg
4. De Paolis, L.T., Pulimeno, M., Aloisio, G.: An augmented reality application for minimally invasive surgery. In: Katashev, A., Dekhtyar, Y., Spigulis, J. (eds.) 4th Nordic-Baltic Conference on Biomedical Engineering and Medical Physics (NBC 2008). IFMBE, vol. 20, pp. 489–492. Springer, Heidelberg (2008)
5. Marescaux, J., Diana, M., Soler, L.: Augmented reality and minimally invasive surgery. J. Gastroenterol. Hepatol. Res. **2**(5), 555–560 (2013)
6. Paolis, L.T., Ricciardi, F., Dragoni, A.F., Aloisio, G.: An augmented reality application for the radio frequency ablation of the liver tumors. In: Murgante, B., Gervasi, O., Iglesias, A., Taniar, D., Apduhan, B.O. (eds.) ICCSA 2011. LNCS, vol. 6785, pp. 572–581. Springer, Heidelberg (2011). doi:10.1007/978-3-642-21898-9_47
7. Khamene, A., Wacker, F., Vogt, S., Azar, F., Wendt, M., Sauer, F., Lewin, J.: An Augmented Reality system for MRI-guided needle biopsies. Stud. Health Technol. Inf. **94**, 151–157 (2003)
8. Bell, R.B.: Computer planning and intraoperative navigation in cranio-maxillofacial surgery. Oral Maxillo-Facial Surg. Clin. North Am. **22**(1), 135–156 (2010)
9. Pham, A.M., Rafii, A.A., Metzger, M.C., Jamali, A., Strong, B.E.: Computer modeling and intraoperative navigation in maxillo-facial surgery. Otolaryngol. Head Neck Surg. **137**(4), 624–631 (2007)
10. De Paolis, L.T., Aloisio, G.: Augmented Reality in Minimally Invasive Surgery. In: Mukhopadhyay, S.C., Lay-Ekuakille, A. (eds.) Advances in Biomedical Sensing, Measurements, Instrumentation and Systems. LNEE, vol. 55, pp. 305–320. Springer, Heidelberg (2010)

11. Wagner, A., Rasse, M., Millesi, W., Ewers, R.: Virtual reality for orthognathic surgery: The augmented reality environment concept. J. Oral Maxillo-Fac. Surg. **55**(5), 456–462 (1997)

12. Salb, T., Brief, J., Welzel, T., Giesler, B., Hassfeld, S., Muehling, J., Dillmann, R.: Inpres (intraoperative presentation of surgical planning and simulation results) – augmented reality for craniofacial surgery. In: SPIE 5006, Stereoscopic Displays and Virtual Reality Systems (2003)

13. Kahrs, L.A., Hoppe, H., Eggers, G., Raczkowsky, J., Marmulla, R., Wörn, H.: Visualization of surgical 3D information with projector-based augmented reality. Stud. Health Technol. Inf. **111**, 243–246 (2005)

14. Mischkowski, R.A., Zinser, M.J., Kübler, A.C., Krug, B., Seifert, U., Zöller, J.E.: Application of an augmented reality tool for maxillary positioning in orthognathic surgery – a feasibility study. J. Cranio-Maxillofac. Surg. **34**(8), 478–483 (2006)

15. Swiatek-Najwer, E., Majak, M., Popek, M., Pietruski, P., Szram, D., Jaworowski, J.: The maxillo-facial surgery system for guided cancer resection and bone reconstruction. In: 36th International Conference on Telecommunications and Signal Processing, pp. 843–847. IEEE (2013)

16. Badiali, G., Ferrari, V., Cutolo, F., Freschi, C., Caramella, D., Bianchi, A., Marchetti, C.: augmented reality as an aid in maxillo-facial surgery: validation of a wearable system allowing maxillary repositioning. J. Cranio-Maxillofac. Surg. **42**(8), 1970–1976 (2014)

17. Pieper, S., Halle, M., Kikinis, R.: 3D slicer. In: 1st IEEE International Symposium on Biomedical Imaging: From Nano to Macro, pp. 632–635 (2004)

18. Enquobahrie, A., Cheng, P., Gary, K., Ibanez, L., Gobbi, D., Lindseth, F., Yaniv, Z., Aylward, S., Jomier, J., Cleary, K.: The image-guided surgery toolkit igstk: An open source C++ software toolkit. J. Digit. Imaging **20**(Suppl. 1), 21–33 (2007)

19. Schroeder, W.J., Martin, K., Lorensen, W.: The visualization toolkit: an object-oriented approach to 3D graphics, 3rd edn. Kitware, Inc. (formerly Prentice-Hall), New York (2003)

20. Qt - cross-platform application & UI development framework. http://www.qt.io

21. Ndi Polaris Vicra. http://www.ndidigital.com

22. Ricciardi, F., Copelli, C., Paolis, L.T.: A pre-operative planning module for an augmented reality application in maxillo-facial surgery. In: Paolis, L.T., Mongelli, A. (eds.) AVR 2015. LNCS, vol. 9254, pp. 244–254. Springer, Cham (2015). doi:10.1007/978-3-319-22888-4_18

23. Horn, B.K.: Closed-form solution of absolute orientation using unit quaternions. J. Opt. Soc. Am. **4**, 629–642 (1987)

Augmented Reality and MYO
for a Touchless Interaction with Virtual Organs

Chiara Indraccolo$^{(\boxtimes)}$ and Lucio T. De Paolis

Department of Innovation for Engineering, University of Salento, Lecce, Italy
{chiara.indraccolo,lucio.depaolis}@unisalento.it

Abstract. Recent years have seen revolutionary changes in CAS field thanks to the introduction of advanced Augmented Reality technologies. In this brief will be presented the overall study carried out in order to develop an AR application to support the doctor during the surgery. It will be described the way the surgeon can perform a more accurate diagnosis by using not just the traditional bidimensional grey-scale CT/MRI images, but also a more realistic three-dimensional marker-based visualization of the patient's organs. Specific focus will be given to the extremely beneficial way the surgeon can interact with this kind of digital information in the operating room. It will be presented a highly innovative *gesture-control* device which allows the doctor to interact with IT equipment in a touchless and as natural as possible way, without coming into contact with it or interrupting the surgery, thus preserving the surgical environment from the danger of contamination.

Keywords: Augmented reality · Computer aided surgery · 3D Modeling · Myo Armband · Touchless interaction

1 Introduction

Nowadays speaking about technological development is no more surprising. Anyone know what technology is and constantly has to do with some kind of tech. Now we can speak about technological evolution and about a man who wants to try make possible the impossible. In this framework fit innovative technologies like Virtual Reality (VR) and Augmented Reality (AR).

Founded as a branch of VR, Augmented Reality has gradually claimed its spaces and its role, becoming a technology that evolves in a parallel but independent way. VR models a fictitious world entirely computer constructed, which excludes the real world. It gives the user the *immersive effect*, namely the feeling of being within a virtual and otherwise nonexistent world, where he can also do things that in real life would be impossible because they defy the laws of physics and human limits. The AR, instead, maintains a strong contact with the real world, familiar to the user, and with its own rules. This technology enriches the reality with additional virtual information of various nature, seamlessly integrated in the real physical space and optimally processed, thus giving the user

L.T. De Paolis et al. (Eds.): AVR 2017, Part II, LNCS 10325, pp. 63–73, 2017.
DOI: 10.1007/978-3-319-60928-7_6

the perception of a single scene in which real and virtual are two indistinguishable entities. The main purpose of the AR applications development is to convey information that otherwise the user could not perceive only through his senses. Even if the first applications were pure exercises in style, acting mainly to elicit the "wow effect", nowadays the AR proved itself to provide support, valuable opportunities, and concrete benefits in many areas.

Computer Aided Surgery. Medicine and Engineering have always been two antithetical disciplines. Medicine has very ancient origins; it is strongly attached to its rules, to a knowing and a "know-how" that has been passed down over the centuries and which is based on inviolable principles. However Engineering science has been able to provide Medicine in general, and Surgery in particular, with new tools for the diagnosis and definition of the therapy, clinical support and advantages in every aspect of the health care system [1]. This collaboration gives rise to the expression of *Computer Aided Surgery* (CAS) which refers to an innovative computer-assisted surgical approach and that represented an extraordinary renewal of the operating way in the surgical rooms.

The introduction of emerging AR technology, moreover, make the surgeons free from the technical limitations of the imaging and visualization equipment, thus improving their surgical experience with the use of 3D information gathered from patient medical images. An advantage of using AR in minimally invasive surgery could be found in a better spatial perception and in the duration of the surgical procedure that could be shorter than in conventional way [2]. At the current state of research, the most benefits coming from an augmented visualization are in oncology; De Paolis et al. [3] present a guidance system for needle placement in the treatment of the liver tumours with the radiofrequency ablation. The software offers to surgeon also a set of tool to study the patients pathology during preoperative planning task.

One of the most amazing use of Augmented Reality in surgery was carried out by the IRCAD (*Istitute de Recherche Contre le Cancers de l'Appareil Digestif*) [4], leading center in minimally invasive surgery, in Strasbourg, France. In 2001, Professor Jacques Marescaux amazed the world of surgery by performing what became known as "Operation Lindbergh" [5]: from New York, he was able to skillfully remove the diseased gallbladder of a patient hospitalized physically in Strasbourg, just driving a robotic console.

Luc Solér, head of the Research & Development Department at IRCAD, award-winning by the international community for his research and his projects in the field of digital applications for medicine [1], he enthusiastically endorsed the use of AR applications in abdominal surgery: *"The 3D models - says - allow a better definition of the tumor area as far as to take action on tumors that were previously not considered operable"*.

A few years ago, in Monaco, Germany, was founded the CAMP, a laboratory specialized in *Computer Aided Medical Procedures* [6] with the aim to develop next-generation solutions for computer-assisted interventions.

Gestural Technologies. Gestures are new forms of communication based on the association of particular messages and meaningful commands with well-defined positions or movements of some parts of the human body. They typically deal with finger and hand movements. Gestures represent a more natural form of human-computer interaction than traditional devices such as mouse and keyboard. Moreover, gestures are a more practical alternative to voice-recognition systems, which require a long and complex training phase to adjust to the voice tone and the users diction. In the last years a lot of devices and systems have been designed for gesture detection by engineers and software developers. However, hints provided by human-interaction experts should be taken into account in the design process to make gestural technologies more usable and consistent with natural interaction forms. Furthermore, the distinction between real control gestures and accidental movements is still an open problem.

Wearable devices are often cumbersome and may limit hand movements due to the presence of sensors and wires. The consequent constraints on the degree of freedom of movements partially reduce the range of users' gestures. Moreover, the general user experience may be negatively affected. Users often do not perceive this form of interaction as being as natural as that offered by vision-based systems. Nevertheless, nowadays the most common gestural technologies, introduced by videogame and entertainment companies (e.g., Microsoft, Nintendo, and Sony), rely either on handheld devices or on cameras performing motion tracking [7].

The Leap Motion controller [8] is a small, easy to-use, and low-cost device designed to capture the movements of human hands and fingers. Figure 1 shows the use of the Leap Motion during the experiments.

The Sony PlayStation Move controller [9] detects movements in the 3D space thanks to a multi-colored light source and a webcam.

The Nintendo Wii remote controller (Wiimote) [10] is equipped with accelerometers, infrared detectors, and a LED sensor bar. The MotionPlus add-on can detect change in orientation along the three axes thanks to some inertial gyroscopes.

Unlike Sony and Nintendo, Microsoft introduced Kinect [11], a markerless webcam-based system that does not need any handheld device.

Myo Armband is a wearable gesture-control and motion-control device, developed by Thalmic Labs [12]. What most surprising is that Myo it's the first input device in the world that employs the extraordinary capability of eight separate electromyography (EMG) metal sensors which, in contact with the skin, are able to literally read the electrical activity of forearm muscles and to translate them into digital commands. From here its name "Myo", the scientific prefix for muscles.

1.1 Motivation

In surgical field some data related to the patient's medical records are digitalized in order to be displayed on a monitor placed in the operating room and, generally, the surgeon needs to consult these information during surgery.

The main limitation, in such a situation, is that he handles surgical instruments and, above all, that he wears sterile gloves and coat and he cannot in any way come into contact with IT equipment that are potentially vehicle of bacteria. Thus, as often happens, in this case the surgeon has to interrupt the surgery or to avail the help of medical staff at the expense of precision and time optimization.

In this perspective, the goal of the developed system would be to enhance the practice of the surgeon who, by using an innovative wearable device that allows touchless gesture-control, can both interact with 3D models of the patient's organs and consult medical information of the traditional slices in an absolutely autonomous way, simply by performing natural arm and hand movements.

2   Developed Application

2.1   Preliminary Work

Realization of 3D Models. In a preliminary diagnostic phase, the patient is subjected to the X-rays practice that produces stack of images taken from different angles. Subsequently these CT and MRI scans are processed by sophisticated *segmentation* softwares [13], as *3DSlicer* [14] and *ITKSnap* [15], and the 3D volume of the specific anatomical structure is derived (in the specific of this work heart and liver shown in Fig. 1).

The next step is the *classification* process based on the evaluation of the radiodensity value which depends on the different consistence of the various human tissues and that influences the shade of gray with which they appear in the slices [16]. Radiodensity value is classified by the so called *Hounsfield Scale*, the standard quantitative measure commonly used in computed tomography scanning [17]. So, given that in the Hounsfield Scale the air is characterized by the value of -1000 HU, the water by 0 HU and dense cortical bone has the value of $+1000$ HU, the slices are evaluated with the help of a physician and each region is labeled as corresponding to a specific anatomical component of the human body.

Finally, an advanced 3D modeling software is used in order to shape the final three-dimensional virtual model. The information about the tissue consistence is used to graphically model the organ deformations [18] and to simulate their response to external stimuli.

Fig. 1. Three-dimensional heart and liver virtual models

Camera Calibration. This is a crucial step that aims to align the virtual camera with the real one and to ensure a consequent accurate and reliable tracking by reducing the jitter. In technical terms, it consists in the identification of the camera's intrinsic parameters that system needs in order to derive the undistortion function.

This AR system camera has been calibrated by using a specific utility provided by ARToolKit SDK. Knowing that when viewed through the camera, lens distortion causes the straight lines to appear curved [19], a default number of 10 images of the pattern *"Calibration chessboard (A4).pdf"* have been captured at a variety of angles to the camera lens. So the *calib_camera* program used the OpenCV library to process all the images, locate the corners of the squares (whose real size was known), measure the spacing between the corners, and to finally calculate the distortion factor associated to the camera device.

Marker Registration. A marker-based tracking approach has been used and, although there exist different types of marker, black and white square ones have been used. It's because they can be customized with an explanatory pattern, the computational burden of the tracking process is not cumbersome and they are robust with respect to the the lighting changes.

The output of the *marker registration* phase, performed by running the *mk_patt.exe* file provided by ARtoolKit SDK, is a pattern recognition data file associated to each marker, that enables ARToolKit algorithms to detect, recognize, identify and track them in a captured video stream.

3 Design and Implementation

The application has been developed by using Unity3D, a powerful 3D graphics engine [20], combined with the ARToolKit plugin [19] in order to manage all basic aspects of the augmentation of the scene. It consists of a framework scene composed by some Unity elements hierarchically organized that are:

- CONTROL COMPONENT, that manages the core of augmentation system
- SCENE ROOT COMPONENT, that is the origin element and keeps track, if any, of the base marker, that is the currently marker in view
- 2 MARKER COMPONENTS, that handles everything related to the process of marker tracking
- CAMERA COMPONENT, that is a very important element responsible for the correct tracking of the marker and, consequently, for the correct visualization of the augmented scene
- LIGHT COMPONENT, that is an optional element added in order to just illuminate the virtual objects and allow the physician a more accurate analysis
- 3D OBJECT COMPONENTS, that allow the rendering of 3D virtual models

3.1   3D Models Rendering

The basic idea of an AR application is that the virtual scene is projected on an image plane using a virtual camera and this process is called "rendering".

The video camera continuously captures individual frames of the real world and an ARToolKit utility makes the virtual objects be merged into the frame. This final merged image is what users finally see on a standard monitor [21]. Naturally, there is a previous processing step in which the ARToolKit system calculates camera transformation matrix to render the virtual object in the right scale and perspective, in the same orientation as the coordinate axes, and in different poses. This way the Unity virtual camera is moved to the same pose as the real camera to avoid an unrealistic result.

When the developed application runs and the liver marker is detected, the 3D virtual model *LiverTumor.fbx* is rendered showing a human liver affected by tumor. A little more complex, instead, is the rendering of virtual heart. When a surgeon is faced heart surgery, the preliminary diagnostic phase can not ignore important information such as the heartbeat and the pulse beat since the presence of any anomalies in cardiac rythm can greatly influences the planning of surgery. For this reason, when heart marker is detected by the camera and identified by computer vision algorithms, the rendering of the 3D virtual model *Heart.obj* has been associated with the rendering of a mp3 audio track reproducing a real beating heart sound, and with the rendering of a dynamic behaviour simulating the pulse beat.

The simulation of heartbeat movements have been implemented via scripting by acting on the scale property of the heart model. Furthermore, to give the surgeon a more realistic perception of beating effect, the code has been written in shuch a way that the heart's contractions were synchronized with the heartbeat reproduced by audio file. So, the effective heart rate and time interval (in microseconds) that elapse between a beat and another one have been calculated and, in the *Pulse()* function shown the following, it has been implemented a repetitive and alternating scaling of the heart, based on those exact time intervals. Specifically in the code *t1* is the time interval between two beats, *t2* is the heart rate, and *t3* is a starting delay in order to synchronize the animation with the audio track.

```
public IEnumerator Pulse(float t1, float t2, float t3){
    yield return new WaitForSeconds(t3);

    while (true) {
        rb.transform.localScale = new Vector3(0.003f, 0.003f,
        0.003f);

        yield return new WaitForSeconds(t1);

        rb.transform.localScale = new Vector3(0.0028f, 0.0028f,
        0.0028f);

        yield return new WaitForSeconds(t2);
    }}
```

3.2   Touchless Interaction

From a technical point of view, when we speak about any form of interaction with organs' 3D models, we can't ignore that we are facing with objects that are virtual and not real. Hence, ideally, it is necessary to simulate the application of specific forces on these objects, and so, to translate physics and real forces to virtual and inexistent ones. To this end a "Rigidbody" Unity component has been attached to the heart and liver virtual models, thus ensuring them to behave as physical objects. The rigid body property helps to represent the objects' solid volume in terms of physics and so enables them to receive forces and torque in order to get a move or interact each other in a realistic way [20].

Applying and controlling these essential physics forces have been implemented via scripting. A C# file named *OrganControl.cs* has been created in order to convert a key directional arrow pression into motion impulse impressed to the virtual object. Some methods derived from *MonoBehaviour* Unity's library class have been leveraged. In particular, by using the *GetKey()* function it has been accomplished the goal to catch a keyboard user input event and to associate it a transformation in either *rotate* or *scale* property of the rigidbody.

In the following excerpt of the code is shown the *FixedUpdate()* function which Unity reserves to the implementation of anything is related with a rigid body [20]. It is shown as a left/right arrow key pression will be detected by the AR application and will be converted in a virtual model leftward/rightward rotation of five degrees around the y-axis. In the same way, a detected up/down arrow key pression, will be transformed to a scaling up/scaling down of the virtual model. It is important to note that, in the case of scaling down of the virtual organ it is set an additional constraint in order to avoid an excessive zoom out and the consequent reversal of the model (caused by the negative values of the scale property).

```
void FixedUpdate(){
    if (Input.GetKey(KeyCode.LeftArrow))
    {
        // leftward rotation of the model
        rb.transform.Rotate(0, 5, 0, Space.Self);
    }
    else if (Input.GetKey(KeyCode.RightArrow)){
        // rightward rotation of the model
        rb.transform.Rotate(0, -5, 0, Space.Self);
    }
    else if (Input.GetKey(KeyCode.UpArrow)) {
        // zoom in of the model
        rb.transform.localScale += new Vector3(0.0001f, 0.0001f,
        0.0001f);
    }
    else if (Input.GetKey(KeyCode.DownArrow)) {
        if (rb.transform.localScale.x > 0.0007) {
```

```
      // zoom out of the model
      rb.transform.localScale += new Vector3(-0.0001f,
      -0.0001f, -0.0001f);
} } }
```

Myo Armband. The actually innovative aspect of this work has been the realization of an AR system which allows the user to interact with the augmented scene in a really natural way by using Myo Armband.

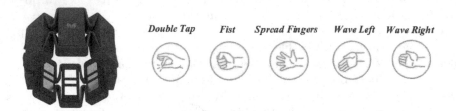

Fig. 2. Myo Armband and the five preconfigured gestures

The preconfigured gestures are 5 (Fig. 2): *double tap, fist, fingers spread, wave left* and *wave right*, to be combined with forearm movement and twist.

Interaction with AR Elements. With the aim to design the touchless control of the application and implement its interactive behaviour, the "Keyboard Mapper" utility provided with the *Myo Connect* has been used. Each of the 5 gestures that Myo recognizes has been associated with one of the specific keyboard commands previously implemented in the "OrganControl.cs" Unity script and with an additional very important task. The association between gestures the surgeon performs and commands executed on the virtual models has not been made in a random manner but in such a way to provide the surgeon an experience of interaction as natural as possible. So, assuming the Myo worn on the right arm, the resulting mapping has been the following:

- **Wave Left - left arrow key**: by moving the hand towards the inside, surgeon can intuitively rotate the virtual object leftwards
- **Wave Right - right arrow key**: similarly, by moving the hand towards the outside, surgeon can easily rotate the virtual object rightwards
- **Fist - down arrow key**: surgeon can zooming in the augmented element by closing the hand in a fist, as if he wanted grab it
- **Spread Fingers - up arrow key**: surgeon can zooming out the augmented element by spreading his fingers, as if he wanted move it away
- **Double Tap - toogle lock**: to turn on and off the motion control system

The last mapping provides surgeon with a very important fifth additional gesture. It deals with the lock of the device which allow the surgeon, in any time, to interrupt the touchless interaction and carry out the surgery by prevent the interpretation of accidental gestures (Fig. 3).

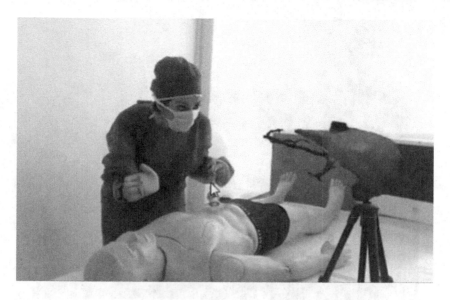

Fig. 3. Testing phase of the interaction between Myo and AR elements

Interaction with Slices. In order to make surgeon able to hands-free consult also the slices displayed on a monitor, the default "Presentation Mode" built in the *Myo Connect* utility has been used. It can be activated through the "Myo Application Manager" window just flipping the switch on and allows surgeon to interact with the slices by performing just four simple gestures:

- **Double Tap**: move forward in the presentation
- **Wave Left and Hold**: holding the wave left gesture until Myo stops vibrating to move backward in the presentation
- **Make a Fist and Rotate** it's a combination of gestures that activates:
  - a **Pointer**: if the fist is rotated counter-clockwise. Double Tap to turn the pointer off
  - the **Zoom-in**: if the fist is rotated clockwise. Double Tap to zoom out

Finally, thanks to the Bluetooth technology used for the connection with the computer system, this device is really useful in this specific use case. In fact, as long as it is in contact with the skin, the surgeon could wear it under the white coat without compromising the communication signal and thus preserving the surgical environment from a possible external contamination. In addition, his arm doesn't have to be pointed in any direction so he feels free to assume the more confortable position.

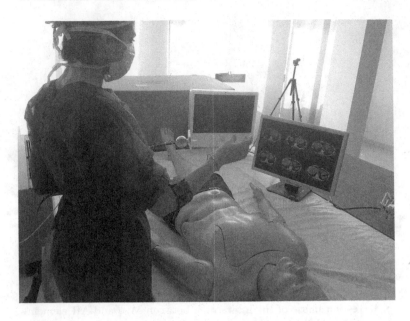

Fig. 4. Testing phase of the interaction between Myo and slices

4   Conclusion and Future Work

The results of this work have been extremely interesting. They led to the development of a first prototype of an application very useful, easy to use and that does not completely upset the "modus operandi" already consolidated in the surgeon's experience. The AR system too has a minimal structure composed by just a computer, a camera, a marker for each organ to be displayed, and obviously the Myo, and doesn't interfere with the work of the medical staff (Fig. 4).

With a view to the future development of this work, the objective is to make the rendering of both graphic aspect and real natural movements of the organs (such as respiratory movement or heartbeat) to be synergically integrated in real time and not virtually reconstructed.

Then, it will be the possibility to intervene in greater detail on the libraries that implement the functioning of the Myo device in order to implement the recognition of additional gestures. This would provide the surgeon the ability to interact with the virtual models of the patient's organs by exploiting a wider range of operations.

Finally, it will certainly be subject of future study also the possibility to realize the rendering of the virtual organs with advanced AR techniques which aim to display them in the form of holograms. In this way, the surgeon would have the ability to interact with them using an extra degree of freedom.

References

1. Solér, L.: Realtá Aumentata e Realtá Virtuale applicata alla chirurgia. In: 12th International Computer Graphics Conference, Torino, Piemonte, 27 Ottobre 2011
2. De Paolis, L.T., Pulimeno, M., Aloisio, G.: An augmented reality application for minimally invasive surgery. In: Katashev, A., Dekhtyar, Y., Spigulis, J. (eds.) 14th Nordic-Baltic Conference on Biomedical Engineering and Medical Physics. IFMBE Proceedings, vol. 20, pp. 489–492. Springer, Heidelberg (2008)
3. De Paolis, L.T., Ricciardi, F., Dragoni, A.F., Aloisio, G.: An augmented reality application for the radio frequency ablation of the liver tumors. In: Murgante, B., Gervasi, O., Iglesias, A., Taniar, D., Apduhan, B.O. (eds.) ICCSA 2011. LNCS, vol. 6785, pp. 572–581. Springer, Heidelberg (2011). doi:10.1007/978-3-642-21898-9_47
4. IRCAD. Institute de Rechérche Contre le Cancers de l'Appareil Digestif, Strasburgo, Francia. http://www.ircad.fr/research/computer/
5. "Operation Lindbergh". A World First in TeleSurgery: The Surgical Act Crosses the Atlantic! Press Conference, 75007, Paris, 19 September 2001
6. CAMP. Computer Aided Medical Procedures, Monaco, Germania. http://camp.lcsr.jhu.edu/ar/
7. Invitto, S., Faggiano, C., Sammarco, S., De Luca, V., De Paolis, L.T.: Haptic, virtual interaction and motor imagery: entertainment tools and psychophysiological testing. Sensors 2016 **16**, 394 (2016)
8. The Leap Motion Controller. http://www.leapmotion.com
9. Sony PlayStation. http://www.playstation.com
10. Nintendo Wii System. http://wii.com
11. Microsoft Kinect. http://support.xbox.com/en-US/browse/xbox-one/kinect
12. MYO Armband. http://www.myo.com
13. Tran, D.T., Sakurai, R., Yamazoe, H., Lee, J.H.: Phase segmentation methods for an automatic surgical workflow analysis. Int. J. Biomed. Imaging **2017** (2017). Article ID 1985796
14. 3DSlicer. 3DSlicer Documentation. http://www.slicer.org/
15. ITKSnap. ITKSnap Documentation. http://www.itksnap.org/pmwiki/pmwiki.php
16. AMIC. Advanced Medical Imaging Center. http://www.amic-chicago.com/
17. Radiopaedia. The dictionary of radiology. http://radiopaedia.org
18. De Paolis, L.T., De Mauro, A., Raczkowsky, J., Aloisio, G.: Virtual model of the human brain for neurosurgical simulation. Stud. Health Technol. Inf. **150**, 811–815 (2009)
19. ARToolKit. ARToolKit Documentation. http://artoolkit.org/documentation
20. Unity3D. Unity3D User Manual. http://docs.unity3d.com/Manual/UnityManual.html
21. Malik, S.: Master of Computer Science. Robust Registration of Virtual Objects for Real-Time Augmented Reality. Carleton University, Ottawa, Ontario, Canada, 8 May 2002

Architecture of a Virtual Reality and Semantics-Based Framework for the Return to Work of Wheelchair Users

Sara Arlati[1], Daniele Spoladore[2], Stefano Mottura[2(✉)],
Andrea Zangiacomi[2], Giancarlo Ferrigno[1], Rinaldo Sacchetti[3],
and Marco Sacco[2]

[1] Politecnico di Milano, Milan, Italy
{sara.arlati, giancarlo.ferrigno}@polimi.it
[2] Istituto di Tecnologie Industriali e Automazione – Consiglio
Nazionale delle Ricerche, ITIA-CNR, Milan, Italy
{stefano.mottura, daniele.spoladore, andrea.zangiacomi,
marco.sacco}@itia.cnr.it
[3] Istituto Nazionale Assicurazione Infortuni sul Lavoro, INAIL, Budrio, Italy
r.sacchetti@inail.it

Abstract. Being reintegrated at work after an accident constitutes an important milestone to recover a good quality of life, especially for severely injured people forced on a wheelchair after a trauma. The presented framework exploits virtual reality technologies with the aim of supporting these people in gaining awareness of their new conditions, providing them training in simulated and riskless environments. During the training, that addresses key aspects related to mobility, upper body preservations and return to work, the behaviors of the users are tracked to assess their functional level. The evaluation of these data, in addition to the expertise of the clinical personnel, is used to determine the wheelchairs user's health condition, which is properly formalized in a semantic data model. This model then allows inferring the jobs that are still suitable for each specific user and the most appropriate level of difficulty of the tasks proposed in the virtual environments.

Keywords: Virtual reality · Ontology · Semantic data model · User-centered design · Return to work · Wheelchair users · Vocational rehabilitation

1 Introduction

Accidents that leads the involved person to the complete or partial lower limbs loss are adverse events, which deeply affect the injured subject's physical, social, and psychological well-being and constitute a significant burden on the health care system and on the families of the injured person. People who underwent these traumatic events often can only rely on a wheelchair to complete daily mobility-related tasks after the trauma. A recent statistic has highlighted that each year, in the US, there are 2 million new wheelchair users and there that this numbers are due to increase during the next years [1]. Though this increase is surely related to the population aging [2], studies

© Springer International Publishing AG 2017
L.T. De Paolis et al. (Eds.): AVR 2017, Part II, LNCS 10325, pp. 74–85, 2017.
DOI: 10.1007/978-3-319-60928-7_7

have shown that nearly 25% of mobility-device users in working age has actually a job, whereas the remaining fraction is unemployed [3]. These pieces of evidence call for the definition of proper measures and instruments to support a successful reintegration of injured people in working age [4, 5], especially considering that pathologies leading to wheelchair forced use are various: spinal cord injury, head injuries, amputations, stroke, poliomyelitis and are only a few examples. Promoting the successful return to work of wheelchair users is thus a fundamental concern that should be addressed by all countries, since it not only reduces the social burden and the economic and time-costing support required from the family members, but also increases the quality of life of the disabled person him/herself. Different studies have in fact highlighted the positive correlation between employment and quality of life and, on the contrary, have shown that long term unemployment has a negative impact on mental and physical health [6, 7].

In this context, the work presented in this paper aims at designing a framework that takes advantage of Virtual Reality (VR) and semantic models to support the return to work and, more in general, to achieve a satisfactory daily life of people forced to use a wheelchair because of a traumatic event. Occupational reintegration of injured people must take into account different critical aspects due to the different kind of psychological and motor challenges experimented with the new physical condition, which deeply affect activities of daily life (ADL). For this reasons, it is necessary that wheelchair users (WUs) are supported and properly trained during their rehabilitation path, starting from the acute phase, till the reacquisition of their autonomy both in working and daily living activities, in order to improve as much as possible their quality of life [5].

2 Aims of the Framework

The development of the proposed integrated framework addresses two key aspects of vocational rehabilitation; on one hand, it provides the WU with a new awareness, making him/her able to deal with the challenges related to the return to work. On the other hand, it supports the vocational personnel with a technological means able to discriminate the still suitable jobs for that specific user.

To achieve the former goal, VR represents a promising tool since it allows the user to train in safe environment, where repeatability is guaranteed, and where she/he can experiment the consequences of specific behaviors without the risk of harming him/herself or other people [8]. Because of this *safety*, the level of anxiety of users training in VEs is often very low: this also contributes to a better performance and to an improved decision-making process [9]. Moreover, VEs are able to increase the user's motivation providing engaging and less-boring experience and may implement monitoring systems to provide different types of feedbacks, with the aim of keeping a high attentional level and increasing the performance [10]. Thus, the use of VR can bring different advantages in the rehabilitation field, where the injured people act as unexperienced users because of their (partial) unawareness of their new sensory-motor physical condition. The motivational aspect, in this case, gains even more value, especially if we consider that rehabilitation treatments are often composed of series of repetitive and effortful tasks [11].

The virtual training foreseen in this framework is structured in three different phases, designed to respond to the major needs of a novice WU: locomotion, preservation of upper limbs functionalities and retention of a good quality of life, through participation in the social and work life [12, 13, 15]. Therefore, in the first virtual environment (VE) for training, the user learns how to drive a wheelchair; in the second, he/she learns optimal techniques to perform common ADL (as transfers, weight-lifting, etc.) and proper physical exercises to prevent injuries and pain in the upper body [14, 15]. Finally, in the third VE, the user is trained to perform job-contextualized tasks, with the aim of facilitating and speeding up the work reintegration, after the de-hospitalization and the return to home.

Thus the designed system trains the user on these three critical aspects to make him/her regain autonomy in daily life, and, also allows him/her to make an auto-evaluation of his/her new capabilities, while trying to perform physical exercises and tasks of increasing difficulty.

Moreover, the system offers the possibility to collect objective data on the user performance, acquiring biomedical signals and tracking body movements, thanks to specific sensors and systems. These data constitute a valuable help for the clinician who has to formalize the health condition of the novice WU using the International Classification of Functioning (ICF), an internationally recognized standard for the description of health and disability [16]. The ICF-based evaluation of the subject, inserted in a proper ontological model [17], is in fact the entry point of two other models capable of discriminating which jobs are still suitable for that specific WU, considering his/her residual capabilities, and suggesting to the rehabilitation personnel the most proper difficulty level for the tasks proposed in the VE.

3   The Integrated Framework Architecture

The achievement of the research aims is pursued thanks to the development virtual environments for training and semantic models, which are the two key modules constituting the framework (as shown in Fig. 1).

Beyond these two modules, the framework foresees the development of a mechatronic platform, on which the wheelchair is anchored, able to collect the data needed to navigate the virtual environments and to return to the user the proper vestibular and force feedback, according to what happens in the VEs (e.g. brakes, obstacles hit, slopes, etc.) [8] and the use of different types of sensors with the aim of monitoring the WU performance in real time.

3.1   The Virtual Environments for Training

The three virtual environments described hereinafter have been designed to support the novice WU while regaining autonomy in daily life, by learning how to move around, how to prevent health-related secondary issues and how to perform specific job-tasks.

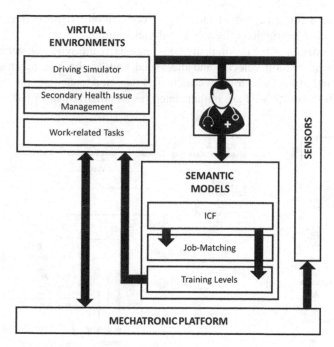

Fig. 1. The two key elements composing the framework and their relationships with other blocks.

It has to be highlighted that, in this context, VR not only provides the user with a realistic (but safe) context in which he/she can experience different behaviors, but also allows giving the users feedback on their performance in real time. In the three VEs presented hereinafter, feedbacks are generated considering both the activities and the interaction of the WU in the VEs, (i.e. the number of hit obstacles), and the information gathered by different sensors (described in Sect. 5), properly combined in an "evaluation algorithm", implemented *ad hoc*. Data are also stored to evaluate the progress of the WU from session to session.

The driving simulator. The main issue to be addressed when dealing with novice WU is indeed locomotion [12]. Thus, this first VE is dedicated to the simulation of the wheelchair driving and presents various scenarios, both outdoor and indoor. In the former case, different types of soil – such as tarmac, cobbles, grass, sand, etc. – can be experienced by the user, with the aim of making him/her gaining awareness of the potential risks of each of them. In the latter case, the proposed scenarios represent living environments, as the house and the workplace, with particular focus on places where maneuvering a wheelchair can be potentially more difficult, as the kitchen, the office and the shop floor. The user is encouraged to perform in the proposed situations specific maneuvers included in the Wheelchair Skills Training Program (WSTP) [18], a means designed to formalize WUs training and tested in different RCTs with positive outcomes [19, 20]. Other indications, reported in the WSTP manual, are also taken in consideration and implemented in the VE: demonstration of the correct maneuver, provision of verbal instructions, feedback and their timing.

The functionalities of the driving simulator, especially the synchronization between the wheelchair propulsion velocity and the visual flow in the VE, together with the mechatronic platform on which the wheelchair is mounted, constitute the fundamental layer on which the other VEs are implemented, as summarized in Fig. 2.

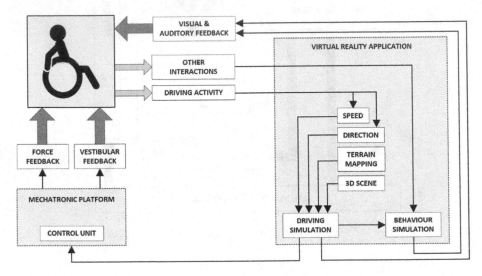

Fig. 2. The pipeline showing the main actors, data-flow, devices and processes involved in the core functionalities of the training environments.

Upper body preservation training. Wheelchair-bound people often have to face secondary health conditions that are either a consequence of the primary condition (i.e. spinal cord injury, traumatic brain injury, amputation, back and musculoskeletal disorders, etc.) or the result of atypical behaviour, such as the prolonged stay in the sit position or the overuse of the upper limbs [14, 15]. Since these secondary issues can seriously affect the quality of life and the participation in this type of population [12], the strengthening of upper body muscles and the prevention of wrong behaviours represent key aspects for the maintenance of autonomy in ADL and the capability of work. With this aim, the second VE assists the WU while performing: (1) specific physical exercises and (2) daily wheelchair user's actions. In the former case, the exercises are mostly aimed at stretching the anterior shoulder muscles and strengthening the back and the shoulder posterior muscles, as indicated in different studies dealing with the management of musculoskeletal pain in WUs [14, 21]. In the latter case, instead, the tasks are presented by the system with precise indications on how to optimize them, in order to reduce the exerted forces and optimize the muscles' performance, while maintaining the functional ability of the individual. Particular attention is paid on the manual propulsion technique, since different parameters have been proven to affect in a significant way the efficacy of the stroke and the energy consumption required to the users. Different studies have compared the biomechanics of different propulsion pattern varying with the speed and the axle position [15, 22]. The outcome of this trials resulted in the identification of the semicircular pattern as the most effective and the less risky in terms of acquired upper-body pathologies, since it is characterized by highest ratio of push time with respect to cadence and reduced abrupt change in direction. It is therefore suggested to teach novice wheelchair users to apply this type of pattern, letting the hand travelling below the pushrim during the recovery phase (Fig. 3).

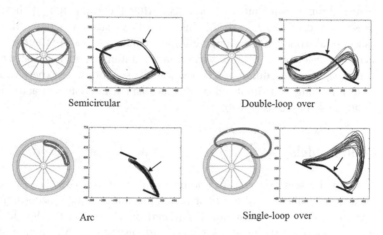

Semicircular   Double-loop over

Arc   Single-loop over

Fig. 3. The four manual wheelchair propulsion patterns, identified among expert WU. (Figure adapted from [22]).

Beyond the propulsion patterns, other tasks commonly performed in daily-life and potentially harmful for upper limbs are, among others, transfers and push-ups for pressure relief. Indications on the correct position of all the body segments while performing these tasks, provided by both the WSTP and the guidelines developed by the Consortium for Spinal Cord Medicine are implemented in the VE [15]. The same indications provided by the WSTP about tasks demonstration, feedback and provision of the instructions are also integrated in this scenario.

Work training environments. The work-related VE is a digital scenario aimed at reproducing real life's situations and the interactions that normally occur in work-places. The acting of the WU, in this case, is contextualized in a digital environment representing the specific working scenario, where the WU is likely to return to, as for example an office or a shop floor. In these scenarios, the WU has to perform a set of specific exercises aimed at training not merely physical capabilities, but also job-related tasks that necessarily have to be performed in different way for a user forced to remain in the sit position. General examples that are valid for different kind of professionals are: picking an object from the floor, lifting a weight and getting through an hinged door. To develop more specific activities, a finite number of case studies are considered at first stage. Activities and environments are created and differentiated, according to the job place and tasks of a specific WU. Each of these situations includes also the reaching of specific locations with the wheelchair, as the office or a workstation, and the interaction with specific designated objects in the scene. For some particular objects, as the furniture, the WU has the opportunity, during the VEs experience, of digitally annotating comments to advise the technical personnel about wrong placements or objects obstructing the pathway. This constitutes an important outcome, not only for the WU, who became aware of the distances and the space required to maneuver the wheelchair, but also for occupational therapists who can test the effects of the implementation of different assistive and accessibility measures in the work environment, before turning them into real practice. After the validation of these environments based on case studies, if the instrument reveals an actual efficacy in promoting successful work reintegration, the implementation of a sort of authoring tool will be taken in consideration. In this way, non-programmers, such as occupational therapists, can design and test different VEs without the support of an expert, providing each WU with a training in a simulated work-place and with simulated activities that will be as much customized as possible.

4 Semantic Models

The main goal of the semantic web technologies in this framework is to assess the WUs' residual functional capacity and their general health condition, according to the ICF classification, that is an international standard developed by the World Health Organization to describe and measure health and disability [16]. Basing on this assessment, a second goal is to provide a list of jobs eligible for the patients' health condition, according to their residual capabilities. Finally, thanks to specific data set collected from the sensors and properly elaborated, in conjunction with the health condition assessed by medical personnel, it is possible to set the difficulty of the training exercise in the VEs.

The whole semantic data model is composed of three domain sub-modules, and includes two sets of rules (Fig. 4). The first ontology collects the ICF subdomains, called Core Sets, that are relevant for the WU population and their work reintegration: Spinal Cord Injury Core Set [23], Traumatic Brain Injury Core Set [24], Stroke Core Set [25], and Vocational Rehabilitation Core Set [26]. This semantic model allows the formalization of a standard and sharable model of the patient's current health condition, useful to facilitate communication between different stakeholders (physicians, physiotherapists, vocational counsellors). The result is, from one hand, a classification of the patient's health condition according to the cause that brought him/her on a wheelchair – using the suitable ICF Core Sets – and, on the other, an instrument able to assess his/her residual functional capability – using the Vocational Rehabilitation ICF Core Set and the raw data coming from the VE and sensors. Clinical personnel, as well as vocational therapists, are requested to identify the proper qualifiers for each relevant ICF code, but the consultation of the objective data coming from the VEs can constitute a valuable help in identifying residual capabilities and progress through time.

The aim of the second model is to provide a semantic description of jobs (and of the related tasks composing them) to assess the maximum impairment grade acceptable for

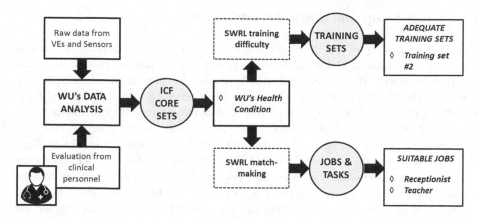

Fig. 4. The flow along the three semantic models. For a WU having that specific Health Condition, the ontology infers the proper training sets (#2 in this case) and a list of suitable jobs (receptionist, teacher, etc.).

a user to perform a certain job. This purpose is achieved analyzing the jobs available in a specific work-related context and assigning them ICF-based employment factors, with the aim of identifying the acceptable functional conditions that a worker must have to perform a job and its constituting tasks. In contrast with the research area that explores the semantic matchmaking between candidates' resumes and skills and available job offers [27, 28], in this framework, the semantic model is used to describe on ICF basis all jobs available in a specific work environment, so that WU workers can be re-employed into new working roles, possibly in the same company. The model takes into account the new health condition of workers in wheelchair and finds new suitable roles according to it.

The evaluation of the patient's health condition is also necessary to set the training difficulty in the VR environment. For this purpose, a third semantic model, containing different training sets, is developed. The training sets include a different range of physical capabilities and takes into account some physiological measurements, essential to determine the training difficulty level (e.g. range of motion, postural control, velocity of propulsion, EMG signals, number of obstacles hit, etc.). The higher the capabilities values are, the more difficult the training set for the exercise will be. Using a set of rules it is possible to provide to each single patient an appropriate training difficulty. It is indeed fundamental to provide the patients with challenging tasks, which are neither too difficult nor too easy [9].

Thanks to a periodical assessment of the patient's health condition, it is possible to update the data regarding the user's functional capabilities, thus obtaining new entailments about the list of suitable tasks and jobs and new training sets or difficulty levels. The semantic approach described above allows to implement new ICF Core Sets about different pathologies which may be the cause of the wheelchair-bounding of a patient. For instance, the semantic model can be enriched by the modeling and insertion of the ICF Core Set for persons following an amputation [29], which is currently being developed.

5 System Setup and Software Technologies

The implementation of the proposed framework requires the adoption of various technological solutions. The wheelchair is mounted on a mechatronic platform actuated in order to provide the proper vestibular feedback according to the simulated environment. The visualization of the VE scenes either relies on a semi-cylindrical powerwall (as the one in [30]) or on head mounted displays, since they seems to be the devices which elicit the highest users' sense of presence without affecting their performance [31, 32]. A marker-based stereo motion capture system is used for tracking the movements and the posture of the WU during the simulated experience, giving the clinical personnel the possibility to evaluate not only the WU performance, but also the change in performances according to the wheelchair setup. Dynamometers – integrated in the platform - are used for measuring the force exerted by the WU, whereas the use of electromyography can be evaluated to study muscles' activations and synergies in the WU upper limbs in case of upper body pathologies and (even suspected) not-full functioning of the arms (Fig. 5).

Fig. 5. A simplified representation of the system setup. The user is sit on the wheelchair, anchored on the mechatronic platform, facing the powerwall. Different sensors (the motion tracking system, EMG and dynamometers) monitor the WU performance in real-time.

Different devices are taken in consideration to permit the interaction of the WU with the user interface of the VE: the motion tracking system itself, data-gloves, the Leap Motion [33] and the special pads of the HTC-Vive head mounted display [34]. According to the tasks that the WU has to perform in a certain VR-based scenario, the choice of the interaction device is evaluated based on the easiness of use, the comfort and the affinity of the virtual gesture with the one performed in the real life. The software engine of the VE is developed and programmed with Unity3D [35].

The semantic models can be developed in RDF/OWL [36], supported by inference rules written in SWRL [37]. An RDF-store and SPARQL endpoint allow a high level of expressivity to represent inference rules and a large amount of semantic data. The most likely editor yet for the development of the ontologies is Protégé, that also allows reasoning with Pellet [38] and the use of SWRL. Anyway, during the course of the project possible alternative solutions will be evaluated.

6 Conclusions

This work presents the design of a VR-based framework aimed at supporting people who lost their legs' functionality in regaining autonomy during daily life and at work. The training activities enabled by the proposed solution are focused on different aspects influenced by the new condition: maneuvering the wheelchair, even in challenging environments, optimizing the upper body movements, to decrease the possibility of developing secondary pathologies, and performing specific job-related tasks. The approach here described represents an opportunity to fill the gap between de-hospitalization and return to work for the injured person, reducing the time spent in rehabilitation/training centers and risks of accidents after the de-hospitalization, which is high during the first years of wheelchair usage.

In addition, the data collected during the training sessions, properly formalized thanks to the semantic model, could provide important information on the WU's possible re-employment to the physicians, the occupational therapists and all the technical personnel involved in the work-reintegration process, facilitating their collaboration (even from different sites) through the use of a standard language, such as ICF.

This framework will be implemented within a project financed by the National Institute for Insurance against Accidents at Work (INAIL). This will assure that in all project development phases, users' requirements and indications provided by experts will be always taken into account. The results of the implementation of the first VEs – which will be developed according to specific use-case and necessities – and feedbacks provided by vocational rehabilitators will constitute the first step for including the system among the standard services available at the INAIL Prostheses Center in Budrio (Bologna, Italy) to enable the successful reintegration of the WUs in the job market.

References

1. Brault, M.W., et al.: Americans with disabilities: 2010. Current population reports, vol. 7, pp. 0–131. US Census Bureau Washington, DC (2012)
2. Smith, E.M., Sakakibara, B.M., Miller, W.C.: A review of factors influencing participation in social and community activities for wheelchair users. Disab. Rehabil. Assistive Technol. 11(5), 361–374 (2016). Taylor & Francis
3. Gray, D.B., Morgan, K.A., Gottlieb, M., Hollingsworth, H.H.: Person factors and work environments of workers who use mobility devices. Work 48(3), 349–359 (2014). IOS Press

4. Valtonen, K., Karlsson, A.-K., Alaranta, H., Viikari-Juntura, E.: Work participation among persons with traumatic spinal cord injury and meningomyelocele1. J. Rehabil. Med. **38**(3), 192–200 (2006). Medical Journals Limited
5. Leduc, B.E., Lepage, Y.: Health-related quality of life after spinal cord injury. Disab. Rehabil. **24**(4), 196–202 (2002). Taylor & Francis
6. Melin, R., Fugl-Meyer, K.S., Fugl-Meyer, A.R.: Life satisfaction in 18-to 64-year-old Swedes: in relation to education, employment situation, health and physical activity. J. Rehabil. Med. **35**(2), 84–90 (2003). Taylor & Francis, Stockholm, Sweden (2001)
7. Huppert, F.A., Whittington, J.E.: Evidence for the independence of positive and negative well-being: Implications for quality of life assessment. British J. Health Psychol. **8**(1), 107–122 (2003). Wiley Online Library
8. Pithon, T., Weiss, T., Richir, S., Klinger, E.: Wheelchair simulators: a review. Technol. Disab. **21**(1, 2), 1–10
9. Maclean, N., Pound, P.: A critical review of the concept of patient motivation in the literature on physical rehabilitation. Soc. Sci. Med. **50**(4), 495–506 (2000). Elsevier
10. Bayón-Calatayud, M., Peri, E., Nistal, F.F., Duff, M., Nieto-Escámez, F., Lange, B., et al.: Virtual Rehabilitation. In: Pons, L.J., Raya, R., González, J. (eds.) Emerging Therapies in Neurorehabilitation II, pp. 303–318. Springer International Publishing, Cham (2016)
11. Flores, E., Tobon, G., Cavallaro, E., Cavallaro, F.I., Perry, J.C., Keller, T.: Improving patient motivation in game development for motor deficit rehabilitation. In: Proceedings of the 2008 International Conference on Advances in Computer Entertainment Technology, pp. 381–384. ACM (2008)
12. Trotter, J.: Wheelchair users' problems with community living. Can. Fam. Physician **31**, 1493 (1985). College of Family Physicians of Canada
13. Adriaansen, J.J., Post, M.W., de Groot, S., van Asbeck, F.W., Stolwijk-Swüste, J.M., Tepper, M., et al.: Secondary health conditions in persons with spinal cord injury: a longitudinal study from one to five years post-discharge. J. Rehabil. Med. **45**(10), 1016–1022 (2013). Medical Journals Limited
14. Mulroy, S.J., Thompson, L., Kemp, B., Hatchett, P.P., Newsam, C.J., Lupold, D.G., et al.: Strengthening and optimal movements for painful shoulders (STOMPS) in chronic spinal cord injury: a randomized controlled trial. Phys. Therapy **91**(3), 305–324 (2011). American Physical Therapy Association
15. PV of America Consortium for Spinal Cord Medicine, et al.: Preservation of upper limb function following spinal cord injury: a clinical practice guideline for health-care professionals. J. Spinal Cord Med. **28**(5), 434 (2005). Maney Publishing
16. International Classification of Functioning, Disability and Health (ICF). http://www.who.int/classifications/icf/en/
17. Gruber, T.R., et al.: A translation approach to portable ontology specifications. Knowl. Acquisition **5**(2), 199–220 (1993)
18. Kirby, R.L.: Wheelchair Skills Program (WSP), Version 4.1. Wheelchair Skills Test (WST) Manual (2008)
19. Best, K.L., Routhier, F., Miller, W.C.: A description of manual wheelchair skills training: current practices in Canadian rehabilitation centers. Disab. Rehabil. Assistive Technol. **10**(5), 393–400 (2015). Taylor & Francis
20. MacPhee, A.H., Kirby, R.L., Coolen, A.L., Smith, C., MacLeod, D.A., Dupuis, D.J.: Wheelchair skills training program: A randomized clinical trial of wheelchair users undergoing initial rehabilitation. Arch. Phys. Med. Rehabil. **85**(1), 41–50 (2004). Elsevier

21. Hicks, A., Martin, K., Ditor, D., Latimer, A., Craven, C., Bugaresti, J., et al.: Long-term exercise training in persons with spinal cord injury: effects on strength, arm ergometry performance and psychological well-being. Spinal Cord **41**(1), 34–43 (2003). Nature Publishing Group

22. Boninger, M.L., Koontz, A.M., Sisto, S.A., Dyson-Hudson, T.A., et al.: Pushrim biomechanics and injury prevention in spinal cord injury: recommendations based on CULP-SCI investigations. J. Rehabil. Res. Dev. **42**(3), 9 (2005). Superintendent of Documents

23. ICF Core Set for Spinal Cord Injury. https://www.icf-research-branch.org/icf-core-sets-projects2/neurological-conditions/development-of-icf-core-sets-for-spinal-cord-injury-sci

24. ICF Core Set for Traumatic Brain Injury. https://www.icf-research-branch.org/icf-core-sets-projects2/neurological-conditions/development-of-icf-core-sets-for-traumatic-brain-injury-tbi

25. ICF Core Set for Stroke. https://www.icf-research-branch.org/icf-core-sets-projects2/cardiovascular-and-respiratory-conditions/icf-core-set-for-stroke

26. ICF Core Sets for Vocational Rehabilitation. https://www.icf-research-branch.org/icf-core-sets-projects2/diverse-situations/icf-core-sets-for-vocational-rehabilitation

27. Francescutti, C., Frattura, L., Troiano, R., Gongolo, F., Martinuzzi, A., Sala, M., et al.: Towards a common disability assessment framework: theoretical and methodological issues for providing public services and benefits using ICF. Disabil. Rehabil. **31**(Suppl. 1), S8–S15 (2009). Taylor & Francis

28. Colucci, S., Di Noia, T., Di Sciascio, E., Donini, F.M., Mongiello, M., Mottola, M.: A formal approach to ontology-based semantic match of skills descriptions. J. UCS **9**(12), 1437–1454 (2003)

29. ICF Core Set for persons following an amputation. https://www.icf-research-branch.org/icf-core-sets-projects2/other-health-conditions/icf-core-set-for-persons-following-an-amputation

30. Gait Real Time Analysis Interactive Lab (GRAIL). https://www.motekforcelink.com/product/grail/

31. Alshaer, A., Hoermann, S., Regenbrecht, H.: Influence of peripheral and stereoscopic vision on driving performance in a power wheelchair simulator system. In: 2013 International Conference on Virtual Rehabilitation (ICVR), pp. 164–152. IEEE (2013)

32. Alshaer, A., Regenbrecht, H., O'Hare, D.: Immersion factors affecting perception and behaviour in a virtual reality power wheelchair simulator. Appl. Ergon. **58**, 1–12 (2017). Elsevier

33. Leap Motion. https://www.leapmotion.com/

34. HTC Vive. https://www.htcvive.com/eu/

35. Unity3D Game Engine. https://unity3d.com/

36. Web Ontology Language (OWL). https://www.w3.org/OWL/

37. SWRL: A Semantic Web Rule Language Combining OWL and RuleML. https://www.w3.org/Submission/SWRL

38. Sirin, E., Parsia, B., Grau, B.C., Kalyanpur, A., Katz, Y.: Pellet: a practical owl-dl reasoner. Web Semant. Sci. Serv. Agents World Wide Web **5**(2), 51–53 (2007). Elsevier

Virtual Environments for Cognitive and Physical Training in Elderly with Mild Cognitive Impairment: A Pilot Study

Sara Arlati[1,2(✉)], Andrea Zangiacomi[2], Luca Greci[2],
Simona Gabriella di Santo[3], Flaminia Franchini[3], and Marco Sacco[2]

[1] Dipartimento di Elettronica, Informazione e Bioingegneria,
Politecnico di Milano, Milan, Italy
sara.arlati@polimi.it
[2] Institute of Industrial Technologies and Automation,
National Research Council, Milan, Italy
{andrea.zangiacomi,luca.greci,
marco.sacco}@itia.cnr.it
[3] IRCCS Fondazione Santa Lucia, Rome, Italy
{s.disanto,f.franchini}@hsantalucia.it

Abstract. This work aims at providing an evaluation of the acceptability and the usability of a virtual reality-based intervention developed for the physical and cognitive training of mild cognitive impaired elderlies. To perform this evaluation, participants enrolled in the intervention group (n = 4) of a randomized controlled trial to test the system were interviewed, and their adherence and their performances in the virtual environments for cognitive training were evaluated. In spite of the small sample, the active participation and the unanimous positive judgement of all the participants led to the conclusion that the training program was well accepted and enjoyable. Participants also claimed reduced level of anxiety in their ADL. On the basis of these encouraging results, a second trial, with enlarged sample and with a system implementing the improvements required to overcome the limitations and the problems highlighted with this pilot study, will be performed in the next future.

Keywords: Virtual reality · Dementia · Aging · Mild Cognitive Impairment

1 Introduction

Alzheimer's Disease (AD) is a neurodegenerative progressive disorder causing in advanced stages cognitive impairment and dementia. It is the most common cause of dementia among the elderly population, and accounts for 50-60% of dementia cases observed among the over-65. Its prevalence increases almost exponentially (less than 1% < 65 years and more than 20% between 80 and 84 years). The World Health Organization (WHO) estimated that about 7 million people were having dementia in Western Europe in 2011, and they are expected to continue to rapidly increase [1]. Such circumstances entail severe social, economic and healthcare consequences, such

L.T. De Paolis et al. (Eds.): AVR 2017, Part II, LNCS 10325, pp. 86–106, 2017.
DOI: 10.1007/978-3-319-60928-7_8

as lesser quality of life (QoL), increasing health care demand and family burden, longer utilization of care facilities, higher expenses for families and health systems.

The impairment of memory has long been considered the main symptom of AD; however, recent evidence indicates the existence of forms of AD involving mainly or exclusively other cognitive domains, which have been included in the new diagnostic criteria. A variant form of AD may affect initially brain's posterior regions [2, 3], and manifest with primary deficits in visual-perceptual processing and visual-spatial elaboration [4, 5]. Visual-spatial deficits directly correlate with functional impairment [6] in early stages of AD [7] and they are the strong predictors of augmented probability of traffic accidents in people with AD [8, 9].

Before converting to dementia, persons with AD may initially manifest the so-called Mild Cognitive Impairment (MCI), characterized by the impairment in at least one cognitive domain, but without a significant deterioration of autonomy in activity of daily living [10]. People with MCI (pMCI) have increased risk to develop dementia, even if a consistent percentage of them remain stable or return normal during the years [11]. Thus, they represent the target population for interventions aimed at halting/reducing AD progression, in particular for strategies centered on modifiable risk factors for dementia [12]. Accordingly, a growing amount of clinical trials has been initiated to inquire the separate and combined effect of cognitive stimulation (CS), physical exercise (PE), or other non-pharmacological strategies [13]. In spite of these trials, the efficacy of CS in pMCI is still unclear: an issue of CS-based programs is the transferability of benefits in real life. Meta-analyses suggest little benefit on the trained tasks [14–16] and data from observational studies showed the presence of plasticity even in the elderly population [17] and pMCI [18], giving a possible explanation of why cognitive stimulation could delay cognitive decline. A recently published study reported that combining physical activity and cognitive stimulation may delay cognitive decline in older persons with dementia [19].

Virtual Reality (VR) is a computerized approach used in neuroscience to provide interventions in a controlled environment with a high degree of ecological validity, where movement, cognitive and other variables can be monitored [20]. There is evidence [20] that patients may feel a sense of control and enjoyment while interacting with the VR during CS [21]. Furthermore, VR training may address various diverse treatments for pMCI, such as navigation and orientation, face recognition, cognitive functioning, as well as on instrumental activities of daily living. A systematic review of studies evaluating computerized cognitive training (CCT) and virtual reality cognitive training (VRCT) interventions for individuals at high risk of cognitive decline [22] documented consistent improvement in the domains of attention, executive function, visual and verbal memory, and also on the psychological symptoms (depression, anxiety, apathy) of participants. Instead, further studies are needed to verify their efficacy on ADLs [22].

Starting from these considerations, the Goji project [23] proposes a preventive program for elderly people with minor cognitive disorders, based on the use of VR, with the purpose of providing an effective and easily accessible technological tool for physical, cognitive and functional stimulation, in order to improve the quality of life of MCI and AD patients and their families.

2 Aim of the Study

The main aim of this work is to assess during the pilot trial the usability and accept-ability of the designed physical and cognitive training system and to determinate the real difficulty of the proposed tasks in a reduced sample of elderlies experiencing the first symptoms of AD. The acceptability of a new technology is a field of study extensively analyzed in the last two decades [24] and the acceptability of users is defined as the demonstrable availability to use technology and the way people perceive, accept, and adopt it [25]. The user's acceptance represents a critical success factor for the adoption of innovative technologies and this aspect is particularly relevant when dealing with older population, as in this case. In fact, while this kind of applications is in general well-accepted by children and young people, older adults are usually not very familiar with technology and have greater difficulty to use and accept them. This makes essential to overcome these barriers for the adoption of new technology-based treatments/services [26].

For what concerns acceptability assessment, in this work, the opinions of the patients undergoing the training were collected to determine how they feel about the program, what they would change or improve, and their satisfaction after its conclusion.

3 The Training System

Three different scenarios have been designed and implemented to support users while performing the physical activity and to train their cognitive capabilities. In particular, they are dealing with tasks that are common in daily life: riding a bike in a park (Sect. 3.1) and crossing roads - avoiding cars - (Sect. 3.2) to reach a supermarket and, when arrived, buy certain products indicated in the shopping list (Sect. 3.3). The former scenario is dedicated to the performance of the physical activity, whereas the latter two imply the use of cognitive functions.

The hardware devices composing the training system (shown in Fig. 1, on the left) are a cycle-ergometer (EuroBike 320, Lumed, Opera, MI, Italy), a smart garment, aimed at measuring the hearth rate in real time (Wearable Wellness System, Smartex, Navacchio, PI, Italy), a finger touch projector (EB-1430WI, Epson, Long Beach, CA, USA) and a Playstation controller anchored on the cycle-ergometer handlebars (Sony, Minato, Tokyo, Japan). The Virtual Environments (VEs) described hereinafter have been developed using Unity 3D.

3.1 The Park Scenario

While performing the physical task, the user rides the cycle-ergometer, facing the projected screen and wearing the smart garment. In this case, the virtual environment has the aim of increasing the user's engagement and of providing him/her with information on the exercise, like speed, covered distance, round per minute, time elapsed and heart rate; it represents a trail in the park (see Fig. 1) that the user travels in

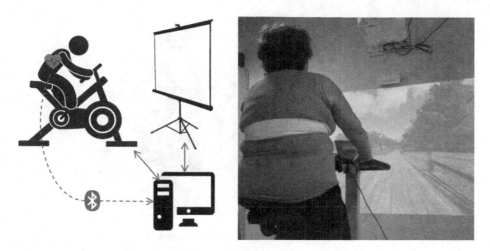

Fig. 1. An exemplificative scheme of the setup designed for the physical task (on the left) and a patient biking in the park scenario (on the right).

first person and that flows according to the pedals velocity. In this first prototype of the VE, the user can only follow the predefined path, which foresees turns and slopes, but cannot interact to choose a different itinerary. To increase the realism of the projected scene and thus the user's presence in the VE, trees' leaves and grass move as the wind is blowing and, sometimes, wild animal appear in the sky or on the trail sides. Moreover, realistic 3D sounds have been added to the scene.

The cycle-ergometer workload is adjusted according to the heart rate of the user, measured through the garment, with the aim of maintaining a constant level of fatigue during the exercise. For further details about the rationale and the implementation of such cycle-ergometer control algorithm, see [27].

Before the training session starts, the operator, who is thought to assist the patient during the entire session, has the chance to set the duration of the physical training, choosing between 15 or 20 min.

3.2   The Road Crossing Scenario

After the completion of the physical training, the park displayed on the projected screen turns into an urban route. In this second scenario, the user has still to ride the cycle-ergometer, but the task is not more physical (the workload is set to 0), but cognitive; he/she, in fact, has to face the crossing of five traffic-congested and non-regulated crosswalks (see Fig. 2).

In details, the tasks that the user has to perform in this scenario are: (1) pedaling to reach the border of the sidewalk, (2) brake when being near it, (3) check on both sides if there are cars moving closer and, if not, (4) restart pedaling to reach the following cross. To reach the crosswalk and proceed forward the user has to pedal on the cycle-ergometer, while to brake he/she must stop pedaling and press the X button on the PlayStation controller. Because of the structure of the ergometer, in fact, it was

Fig. 2. A user performing the road-crossing scenario.

impossible to access the wheel compartment and create a physical brake, able to stop the wheel rotation due to the inertia. The joystick placed on the controller is used to turn the point of view when the sidewalk border is reached to check if cars are moving closer and, thus, if it is possible to cross the road safely.

Cars are generated by the application at fixed interval time, but their velocities are randomly set. If a car hits the user while crossing, 3D sounds simulating an accident are reproduced and, after a few seconds, he/she is brought in a safe-position and can restart to pedal as the cars disappears from that cross. The number of total accidents and the total time needed to reach the supermarket are saved on a XML file, containing also the patient data and the data coming from the shopping scenario, that is described in Sect. 3.3.

3.3   The Shopping Scenario

The shopping takes place in a virtual supermarket, in which the user has to buy five grocery items indicated on the shopping list that is displayed on the left side of the projected screen. To perform the tasks proposed in this last scenario, the user gets down from the cycle-ergometer, stands in front of the projected screen and touches it to select either the aisle or the product on the shelves. To buy a product, in fact, the user has to accomplish two subsequent tasks: find and tap on the aisle whose sign is containing the name of product (*aisle task*) and touch the right product, placed on the shelves in a random position, among other distractors (*shelf task*).

Five levels of difficulty have been implemented for both tasks. They are independent so the operator can set, at the beginning of each virtual shopping session, the level he/she prefers for the aisle and for the shelves tasks. The target product and the "distractors" provided in the task, with the aim of increasing the difficulty, are always selected randomly, allowing the generation of a potentially unlimited number of different combinations for each tasks [28]. For the aisle scenario, the parameters used to implement the increasing difficulty are shown in Table 1.

Table 1. Parameters to set the difficulty of the aisle task for each level.

Level no.	No. aisles	No. elements per aisle	Misleading word
1	2	1	No
2	2	3	No
3	2	3	Yes
4	3	4	Yes
5	4	4	Yes

Beyond the increasing number of aisles and elements on displayed on the signs, starting from the third level, a word that semantically or orthographically "looks similar" to the name of the target object is placed in one of the non-target aisles, with the aim of misleading the patient if he/she does not pay enough attention to the task. An example of orthographical similarity is the misleading word "melagrana" [pommegranade] used instead of the target object "melanzana" [eggplant]; an example of semantically similar word is "braciola" [pork chop] used instead of "bistecca" [steak].

Dealing with the development of the five levels of difficulty for the choice of the correct product on the shelves, the algorithm implemented foresees the setting of different parameters:

- Distractors number: defines how many distractors are placed on the shelving unit.
- Discount products: determines if discounted products are allowed on the shelves or not. Each product has a correspondent discounted product.
- Small products: determines if small products are allowed on the shelves or not. Some of the products in our database are classified by dimension (i.e. bottles and jars), while other not (fruits, clothes, etc.).
- Variability: determines the percentage of the products on the shelves that are placed picking random object from the whole database of products.
- Similarity: determines how similar the products not randomly placed are. It is computed attributing each object the belonging (value 1) to a certain category or not (value 0) and then comparing the binary numbers hence created using an algorithm based on the Hamming distance [29]. Examples of the categories used to classify the products in the database are round fruits, refrigerated section, boxes, jars, bottles, etc. In practice, having a similarity value equal to 1 means to have on the shelves non-random products that – at least – have one category in common, whereas 2 means having two categories in common.
- Shelf area: determines the area of the shelving unit in which the target object can be found; in the first levels, only central positions are allowed, whereas in the second, only the border of the shelf can be occupied with products.

The detailed parameters used to implement the five levels for the shelf task are shown in Table 2. An example of two possible shelves is reported in Fig. 3.

For both the described tasks, if the user commits an error or does not interact with the VE for more than 20 seconds, the system intervenes giving him/her a hint to help him/her proceed to the next task. More in details, for the aisle scenario the first hint is given by a guiding voice remembering the user the name of the product to look for and the wrong aisle sign – that was touched by the user – is blurred out. This type of hint is

Table 2. Parameters to set the difficulty of the shelf task for each level.

Level no.	Distractors no.	Discounted products	Small products	Variability	Similarity	Shelf area
1	9	No	No	0.6	1	Center
2	9	No	No	0.6	1	Border
3	9	No	No	0.5	1	All
4	15	No	Yes	0.3	1	All
5	25	Yes	Yes	0.2	2	All

Fig. 3. An example of the shelves proposed to the user in Level 1 (on the left) and in Level 5 (on the right). In the latter case, the target is a package of pasta, thus due to the similarity implementation, the shelf is filled with many box food products. (Color figure online)

repeated for each error (or hesitation), until just one aisle remains active; in this case, the last remained aisle sign is also highlighted in yellow. For the shelf task, after an error or 20 seconds of hesitation, hints are given as follow: the voice repeats the name of item to collect; the target item on the shelf blinks 3 times; the target item is highlighted in yellow.

For each session of the virtual shopping, the current level of difficulty, the total time used to complete the task, the target object and eventual errors or hesitations were stored on a XML file, containing also the patient ID and the date of the session.

4 Participants and Methods

4.1 Participants

A cohort of 202 patients with subjective disturbances in one or more cognition areas was evaluated for the enrollment in the study. Each subject underwent a clinical assessment to identify risk factors (comorbidities, life style, familiarity, cardiovascular issues) and a neuropsychological and functional assessment, through the submission of standardized tests. Inclusion criteria were age $\geq$ 65 years, one or more test scores indicating compromised visuospatial abilities, one or more test scores indicating cognitive decline. Exclusion criteria were: functional impairment; cardiovascular issues preventing the capabilities of undergoing a physical training; cognitive impairment that would influence the ability to participate in the study; inability to provide informed consent.

Ten subjects were enrolled in the study that was organized as a randomized controlled trial. Intervention and control groups' characteristics are reported in Table 3.

Table 3. Baseline characteristics of the study patients according to the treatment group.

	Intervention group (n = 5)	Control group (n = 5)
Age	71.6 ± 4.8	74.4 ± 6.0
Years of schooling	8.4 ± 6.3	6.8 ± 1.6
Mini-Mental State Examination (MMSE)	23.1 ± 3.6	23.0 ± 3.5
Rey–Osterrieth Complex Figure (ROCF)	23.5 ± 12.0	21.2 ± 10.3
Clock Drawing Test (CDT)	1.5 ± 0.7	1.5 ± 1.2

The study protocol was approved by the Ethics Committee of IRCCS Fondazione Santa Lucia and each subject enrolled in the study signed an informed consent form.

4.2   Intervention

Patients belonging to the intervention group were asked to perform three training session per week for six consecutive weeks. Each training session was composed of a three phases, each one respectively foreseeing the setup and the VEs described in Sect. 3 subparagraphs. During the first phase participants had to perform physical activity on the cycle-ergometer for 15 (during the first 3 weeks) or 20 minutes; in the second phase, they had to cross the road five times, regardless of time; finally, during the third phase, they were asked to perform 20 minutes of cognitive training in the shopping VE. Since each shopping list was composed of five items to buy, time was prolonged when there was the need of concluding the started grocery shopping. All the participants started the training at level 1 for both the aisle and the shelf tasks; both levels were decided to be always increased accordingly. To move on to the next level, participants had to perform each level (aisle + shelf) for three times, without committing any kind of error. An operator explained the protocol to each patient and gave him/her the chance to get familiar with the system, in a brief tutorial session preceding the first week of intervention. The operator was also in charge of setting the right levels of difficulty before each training session, checking the correctness of the previous repetitions, and assisting the patients if unexpected events occurred (i.e. participant forgot how to proceed, the system got stuck, etc.). Subjects enrolled in the control group did not undergo any kind of treatment.

4.3 Outcomes

Both at the beginning and at the end of the six weeks, participants enrolled in the intervention group were interviewed using specific questionnaires to gather qualitative information assessing the acceptability and usability of the training system. This qualitative component represented an important opportunity to understand participants' experiences in the intervention and allowed assessing outcomes – such as patients' feelings – that were difficult to measure quantitatively. Finally, these data enabled to examine participants' perspectives on the effects of the intervention.

The two versions of the questionnaire – administered by a psychologist due to the impaired conditions of participants – consisted of three parts and differed only in the first one. The first part of the initial questionnaire, besides collecting personal information as past or present job, aimed at investigating the patients' level of confidence in their own use of different devices (TV, mobile phones, tablet or PC), which may affect the patient performance when dealing with new technologies as in this intervention and patients' motivations and expectations towards the training. On the other hand, the objective of the first part of the questionnaire administered at the end of the training period was to investigate if users were satisfied with the training and if their expectations had been met. Moreover, participants were also asked if they wish to continue such training, also at their homes, if possible.

The two other sections of both questionnaires aimed at assessing users' opinions about different aspects related to the three scenarios, divided into the first two (park and road crossing), involving the use of the cycle-ergometer, and the last one, the supermarket, which foresees the use of the projected touch screen. In details, the items investigated for the two cases are reported in Fig. 4 (Sect. 5.1). The first five aspects (satisfaction, desire to continue, enjoy, comfort) were taken from questionnaires used to evaluate the acceptability of the robotic therapy [26, 30]; in addition, aspects related to the VEs, negative states of feeling and general suggestion were investigated.

Each patient was asked to assign a score (0-4) to each of the questions defined (with the exception of the open ones), according to the following classification: not at all (0), not really (1), neutral (2), somewhat (3) and very much (4).

To assess the difficulty of the proposed tasks, data coming from the VR-based software were recorded and analyzed with the aim of determining the parameters that affected more the patients' performances. In particular, the collected data were:

- Errors committed in the aisle task;
- Hesitations (more than 20 s) in the aisle task;
- Errors committed in the shelf task;
- Hesitations (for more than 20 s) in the shelf task;
- Number of accidents.

The last parameter is related to the road-crossing scenario, whereas all the others come from the purely cognitive training environment (the supermarket). Since each error/hesitation was stored in the XML file associated with the current difficulty level and the target product, further analysis on the difficulty proposed by the graphical representation of a specific grocery item, the presence on the shelf of the same item with multiple dimension and the presence of the discount label were made.

Patients in both groups also underwent full neuropsychological and physiological assessments; for details, see [27].

5   Results

5.1   Acceptability and Usability

Of the five participants randomized in the intervention group, one withdrew from the study after the second session for reasons that were independent from the present study. One dropout for reasons not related to the study was registered also in the control group. No adverse event was reported among other participants.

Of the four patients in the intervention group, adherence was judged good (more than 75%) for three of them, and partial (more than 50% and less than 75%) for one patient (67%).

Dealing with the intervention provided, all the patients reached and performed the Level 5 of both tasks before the end of the 6th week of intervention. Because of this reason, the operator assisting the sessions made a change in the protocol with the aim of not boring the patients, and made them do the shopping just showing the shopping list once – at the beginning – and making the patient buy the products by heart. Since a precise analysis of these sessions' data was not possible because the operator intervention is no longer quantifiable – especially in terms of execution time –, the following paragraph is considering for the cognitive tasks (aisle and shelf tasks) only the data acquired during the first sessions in which the intervention protocol was followed.

Concerning acceptability assessment, results from the final questionnaires are summarized in Fig. 4. No particular negative effects arose during all the three steps of the intervention and the interaction with technology revealed to be quite easy. Some suggestions for improving the environments were focused on the recognition of specific products: "I suggest clearer labels on the items; I could not distinguish some of them". P4 requested to introduce more difficulties, more unpredictable scenarios and other environments and tasks to perform. All patients wish to continue the training: "If I were sure to get better and better, I would do it to prevent new symptoms" and, except one ("No, I don't. I prefer to come to the hospital because at home I have other duties distracting me."), they would continue it at home.

Expectations were met for all of participants and, in particular, concerning the self-perceived improvements, they reported better performance in real life: "I noticed that I do not forget some things anymore", regardless of real improvements revealed from results of cognitive tests.

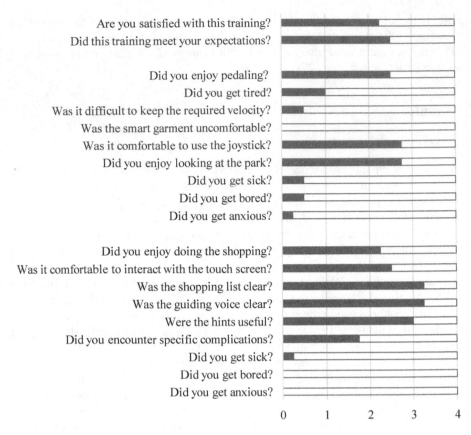

Fig. 4. The results of the questionnaire at the end of the trial. The rating corresponds to: not at all (0), slightly (1) average (2), quite a lot (3) and very much (4).

5.2   Evaluation of the Difficulty

The four patients recruited in the intervention groups underwent at least 3 trial for each level of difficulty, as shown in Fig. 5. Before changing the protocol, each patient performed at least 20 trials with the difficulty level set on 5.

In two cases, a slip of the operator was identified by the analysis of the data: P2 performed Level 2 three times, but she committed an error in the aisle task while performing the last trial, so she should have repeated Level 2 at least three times more. The same happened for P3 who committed two errors while performing the aisle task in Level 3 that were not taken into account by the operator.

The supermarket - Aisle Task. The number of errors committed by each patients, the hesitations of at least 20 s - weighted on the numbers of the total products bought - and the time needed to complete the aisle task were considered to evaluate the patients' performance with respect to the level of difficulty. For the first two variables, no clear tendency among data can be identified: in general, errors and hesitations ratio are pretty low (always ≤ 0.4) for all the patients and for all the levels. Considering both, there

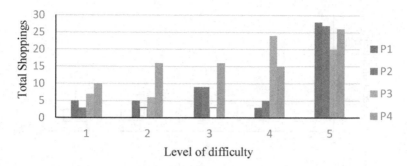

Fig. 5. The number of trials of shelf task performed for each level of difficulty by each patient. Blank columns represent the cases in which the operator made a mistake in making the participant proceed to the next level.

seems to be a slight increase in difficulty in Level 4 and 5, where the number of aisles is increased to 3 and 4, respectively. No increase in errors/hesitations can to be attributed to the insertion of a misleading word on the aisle sign, which starts from Level 3.

Instead, analyzing the execution time median values, it can be noticed that the more the level difficulty increased, the more time the patients required to complete the task (Fig. 6).

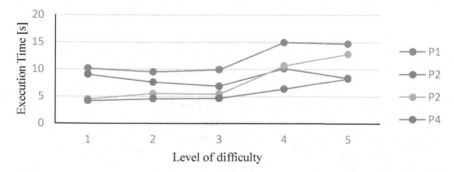

Fig. 6. The time required to complete each aisle task according to the level of difficulty.

The increase in time appears even clearer looking at the boxplots representing the distribution of execution times over the five levels of difficulty. One exemplificative boxplot, relative to P2, is reported in Fig. 7. Though not shown, other patients' distributions follow the same tendency: while the median value slightly increases, the upper quartile becomes larger and larger when increasing the level of difficulty, meaning that in some configurations of aisles and aisle signs, the target was very hard for the participant.

Looking more precisely at the cases in which the participants committed errors or waited longer than 20 s while choosing the right aisle, some of the products' names were highlighted since they induced more hesitations than others. In particular, the trickiest words – especially when associated with the misleading word – are reported in Table 4.

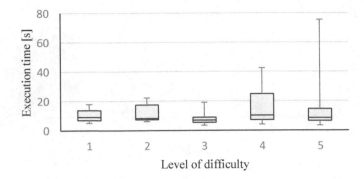

Fig. 7. Boxplot representing the aisle execution time for P2. The median is the horizontal dark line; the interquartile range is the gray box.

Table 4. The product's names which induced more than 4 errors (E) and/or hesitations (H).

Product name	Misleading word	E	H	E + H
Vino rosso (red wine)	Viso rosso	5	6	11
Spugnette (sponges)	Spaghetti	8	0	8
Dash liquido (liquid soap)	Rash liquido	3	5	8
Bottiglia olio (bottled oil)	Battigia olio	7	1	8
Uva rossa (red grapes)	Usa rossa	5	2	7
Caffettiera (coffee maker)	Canottiera	3	4	7
Acqua gasata (sparkling water)	Acuta gasata	3	3	6
Vino bianco (white wine)	Viso bianco	3	3	6
Dash Ecodosi	Rash ecodosi	3	3	6
Carta igienica (toilet paper)	Sarta igienica	5	1	6
Acqua naturale (still water)	Acuta naturale	4	1	5
Martello (hammer)	Cartello	3	2	5
Tortiglioni	Maccheroni	1	4	5
Dixan liquido	Doxa liquido	3	2	5
Fagioli (beans)	Fagiani	3	2	5

The supermarket - Shelf Task. In the shelf task, in contrast with what happened for the aisle task and even not considering the two cases in which the operator made mistakes (blank dots), a general tendency to increase the errors and the hesitations was highlighted by the analysis of the saved data (Figs. 8 and 9).

The two ratio values are higher with respect to the aisle task for all the patients. Looking at the graphs, it can be seen that P1 reached almost 1 (0.96) in error ratio and almost 0.6 in the hesitations ratio, indicating that he had at least one issue for each one of the products he had to buy in Level 5.

Dealing with execution time, the median values, reported in Fig. 10, show a general tendency to the increase moving toward Level 5, as it happened for the aisle task.

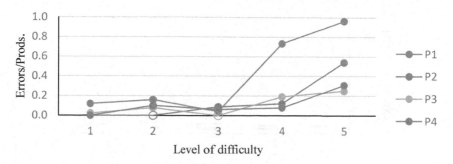

Fig. 8. The number of errors, weighted on the total products picked from the shelf, for all the participants at each level of difficulty. Blank dots indicates the cases in which the operator made a mistake in making the participant proceed to the next level.

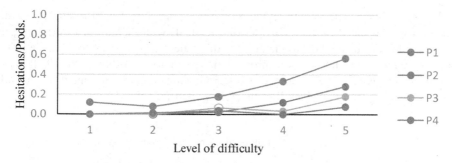

Fig. 9. The hesitations, weighted on the total products picked from the shelf, for all the participants at each level of difficulty. Blank dots indicates the cases in which the operator made a mistake in making the participant proceed to the next level.

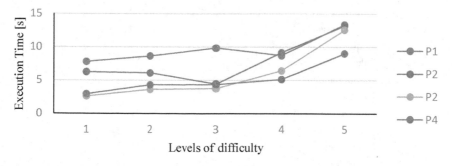

Fig. 10. The time required to complete each shelf task according to the level of difficulty.

The distribution of the tasks time in the boxplot preserves as in the aisle task: less wide intervals for the first levels and upper quartiles growing with the increase of difficulty. This is valid for all the patients; the exemplificative case of P2's execution time is reported in Fig. 11.

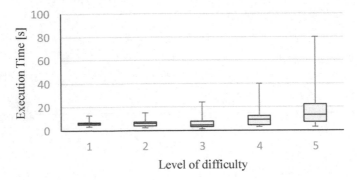

Fig. 11. Boxplot representing the shelf execution time for P2. The median is the horizontal dark line; the interquartile range is the gray box.

The same analysis performed on the products' names that caused more errors and hesitation was repeated for the items put on the shelf, with the aim of determining if some were trickier than others to identify for the patients. In addition to the aisle task, which required only choosing the product name without attributes, the shelf task required the patients to perform also a discrimination among discounted and small products (starting from Level 3). Results are reported in Table 5.

Table 5. The list of products that induced more than 10 errors and/or hesitations.

Product	Small	Discount	H	E	E + H
Tortiglioni piccoli sconto	✓	✓	9	17	26
Acqua naturale sconto		✓	1	17	18
Tortiglioni			4	14	18
Tortiglioni piccoli	✓		3	15	18
Spugnette			5	9	14
Acqua gasata			4	9	13
Acqua naturale piccola	✓		4	9	13
Sale grosso			6	7	13
Acqua naturale			3	9	12
Biscotti			4	8	12
Deodorante sconto		✓	5	7	12
Guanti sconto		✓	5	7	12
Riso venere			7	5	12
Clementina			4	7	11
Collutorio			5	6	11
Dash liquido piccolo	✓		3	7	10
Dentifricio			3	7	10
Latte bottiglia piccolo	✓		2	8	10
Latte cartone piccolo	✓		1	9	10

Number of accidents. The data saved by the system relative to the number of accidents occurred during the second part of the training were analyzed (Table 6). With the exception of P1, who reached the 16%, all the other participants had an accident in less than 10% of the road crossings.

Table 6. Accidents registered during the 18 sessions for all the participants. The dash indicates the patient did not attend that session.

# Ses.	1	2	3	4	5	6	7	8	9	10	11	12	13	14	15	16	17	18	TOT	Accs/Trials
P1	–	1	0	0	2	2	1	1	0	1	0	0	2	2	0	–	2	0	14	0.16
P2	0	1	0	–	–	0	1	–	0	–	0	0	–	0	0	–	0	0	2	0.03
P3	0	0	1	0	–	0	0	–	0	0	–	2	–	1	0	–	0	1	5	0.07
P4	3	0	0	1	0	0	0	0	0	0	1	0	0	0	–	1	–	0	0	6	0.07

6 Discussion

All the four patients who concluded the training program for six consecutive weeks attended the training session with good adherence. The administration of the questionnaire revealed that the only patient (P2) whose adherence was less than 75% was the only one without a driving license, so she needed to be driven by her daughter who not always was available.

All the patients were able and willing to conclude all the sessions without the need of taking breaks; they were all able to understand the tasks and to reach Level 5 within the 13th session. Qualitative data retrieved from the questionnaire revealed high levels of engagement and motivation, enabled mainly by the use of the virtual reality technologies that were "new" to them. Feedbacks on the VEs design revealed appreciation, leading to the conclusion that the training was well accepted by all the patients, who would continue with the program also at home. Moreover, what is important to notice is that self-perceived improvements helped the patient to decrease the anxiety levels in their activities of daily living, thus enabling an improvement of their quality of life (QoL). This trend of improvement is also in line with the results of psychometric tests performed pre/post the trial [27]; even if these outcomes were not statistically significant, this effect was probably due to the reduced size of the sample.

Dealing with the evaluation of the difficulty of the proposed tasks, different considerations can be made looking at the analyzed data. As expected, the general tendency is that the increasing level of difficulty led to an increased number of trials to move on with the next level. Some exceptions may be attributed to either a learning effect or an intrinsically higher or lower difficulty associated to a specific product to select. For the aisle task, a slight increase in difficulty (more errors/hesitations and longer execution time) can be attributed to the appearance of new aisles, as it happens in Level 4 and Level 5. No increase, instead, seems to be related to the increase of the product names appearing on the aisle signs (Level 1 and Level 2). This might be attributed to a the increased visuospatial demand and to the increased mean distance of the target with respect to patient initial position [31]. Instead, no significant increase in difficulty seemed to be attributable to the insertion of the misleading word, though it has to be highlighted that most common errors were related either to slight ortho-graphical changes in the original product name (i.e. only one letter substituted: "vino rosso" − "viso rosso") or to substitutions with words semantically different, but meaningful (i.e. "spugnette" − "spaghetti"). Other studies have actually identified issues in reading, spelling and recognizing the semantic meanings of words in patients with dementia [32].

With respect to the aisle task, the shelf task led to a higher number of errors and hesitations and increased execution time. This was expected due to the higher number of elements among which the user had to choose and the additional difficulty due to items of different dimension and discounted items and in agreement with evidences from previous studies, which reported higher reaction times in association with increased visuospatial demand [33, 34].

Looking more in detail at the most problematic products, the item that induced the worst performance - in all its formats (small and discounted) - was a kind of pasta, "tortiglioni". Investigating the reason of this issue with the operator who attended all the sessions, it was discovered that, though the brand and the package were quite common in all the Italian supermarkets, participants found it very difficult to be identified and claimed to call that type of pasta "rigatoni" and not "tortiglioni". "Tortiglioni" and "Rigatoni" are actually very similar and difficult to discriminate, mainly because the resolution of the projector, 1280×1020, on a large screen (3×2 meters) makes reading the labels difficult. Moreover, the items distribution over the Italian supermarkets is probably different across the Country: preliminary tests on healthy individuals performed in Lombardy - where the application was developed - did not highlighted any issues with this product, as it happened in Lazio where the trial took place. The same happened for water bottles, since the colors of the packages, which represented the most important cue to discriminate between still and sparkling water, are actually different depending on the geographical area. Another issue that was hypothesized looking at the most problematic items is the lack of familiarity of the participants with some specific products. In fact, some of them are probably not common as other items in the grocery shopping of an elderly, as socks − that were represented as sporty socks −, wool gloves and black rice, and some are probably bought in different packages or from a different brand, or as in the case of biscuits, sponges, deodorant and toothpaste.

A last consideration on the supermarket scenario should be made taking into account what participants reported at the end of the trial. They explained that they felt uncomfortable in picking a non-discounted product (as written in the shopping list) when, on the shelf, there is the discounted version of the same item, because this goes against common sense.

Dealing with the road-crossing scenario, neither clear tendency, nor a sort of learning effect can be identified looking at the data. Accidents are a few and distributed randomly all over the sessions and further studies are required to identify which are the main causes of accidents: attentional deficits, cognitive impairments or the techno-logical setup. Dealing with the last point, a previous study has shown a high correlation between crossing decisions and perceptions of safety by younger and older adults in real world and filmed versions of traffic scenes, indicating that the difference between 2D or 3D scenarios is not likely to affect the crossing decision of participants [35].

Different hypotheses are found in literature to try to explain the increased number of risky crossing decisions in old-old population (>75 years old): general cognitive decline that leads to wrong evaluations [8], the underestimation of age-related losses on performance [36], the increased latency when initiating the crossing [37] and the lack of compensations for the slower pace [38]. Another possible explanation could be related to the appearance of visuospatial deficits as first symptoms of still undiagnosed AD [6]. In this context, the presented system that is able to provide a training in a safe environment, where the user has the chance to become aware of his/her limitations with no or very limited anxiety (as reported in the questionnaires answers) constitutes for sure an instrument that is worth for further investigations.

7   Limitations and Future Work

This work aims at studying the acceptability of a treatment to train patients with MCI trying to delay as much as possible the appearance of (new) symptoms, and the usability of the VR-based system developed to accomplish this goal. Though it has to be acknowledged that the sample was small, the active participation in the training sessions and the unanimous positive judgement of the participants had led to the conclusion that the training program was well accepted and enjoyable for the patients. Data about the psychometric tests conducted pre-post the intervention showed promising results, though not significant [27]. However, these results induced the psychologists of the Santa Lucia hospital to conduct a second trial, for longer periods of time and with an enlarged sample of participants – with an application that will be free of any potential bias.

In fact, this pilot trial gave the possibility not only to test the system with AD patients, but also to highlight what are the critical aspects not emerged in the preliminary test phase performed with healthy subjects. Starting from the analysis of these issues, different improvement to the system have being identified, from both the technological and the intervention protocol point of view. First, the software will be made able to handle automatically the level selection, excluding the intervention and the potential errors committed by the operator. Dealing with the supermarket scenario, all the users will perform exactly the same tasks: all the aisles and shelf tasks proposed to the users will be computed previously, saved and loaded when it is the time. In this way, not only the target object will be saved, but also all the distractors and their position will be available for further analysis. Therefore, it will be possible to examine in a more precise way the nature of the difficulties encountered by the patients, such as the position of the target, the similarity of the distractors, the image of the product itself, etc. Moreover, the levels of difficulty will be increased (from 5 to 50) with the aim of introducing a memory task in the protocol (the shopping list can either be shown or hidden) and to create different scenarios with respect to the few levels developed for this trial. For instance, there will be easier levels – so that the intervention can be extended to patients with more severe symptoms –, levels "in the middle", with a small number of products but very similar to each other, and levels more complicated, with the entire shelf filled with products (40 items). All the objects that resulted problematic in this pilot trial will be substituted: the water bottles will be characterized more clearly, adding a label indicating "sparkling" or "still", the "tortiglioni" package will be replaced with another pasta package (i.e. "farfalle", which are uniquely recognized); other cited product will be replaced with ones more familiar for elderlies.

For the park scenario, the smart garments used in this trial will be substituted with a more practical heart rate monitor, which will allow to more participants to use the same equipment. This was not possible in the trial described in this work, due to size and hygienic reasons. A finger pulse oximeter and a chest band are now under evaluation. Finally, even if there were not particular criticism from the participants of this trial, a 3D printed brake integrating a potentiometer will be attached to the cycle-ergometer to make the stopping at the road crossing more natural. Instead, no interventions allowing a more natural the rotation of the point of view at the road crossing will be performed, since the setup comprising the projected screen does not allow so. A possibility of improvement, in this case, may be achieved using a head mounted displays (HMD), but due to balance and motion sickness issues, different preliminary tests must be conducted on healthy and pathological subjects, with the aim of assessing the effective usability of this technology in this type of task.

References

1. World Health Organization, Dementia: a public health priority. World Health Organization (2012)
2. Haxby, J.V., Rapoport, S.I.: Abnormalities of regional brain metabolism in Alzheimer's disease and their relation to functional impairment. Progress Neuro-Psychopharmacol. Biol. Psychiatry **10**(3), 427–438 (1986). Elsevier
3. Prvulovic, D., Hubl, D., Sack, A., Melillo, L., Maurer, K., Frölich, L., et al.: Functional imaging of visuospatial processing in Alzheimer's disease. Neuroimage **17**(3), 1403–1414 (2002). Elsevier
4. Crutch, S.J., Lehmann, M., Schott, J.M., Rabinovici, G.D., Rossor, M.N., Fox, N.C.: Posterior cortical atrophy. Lancet Neurol. **11**(2), 170–178 (2012). Elsevier
5. Mendez, M.: Posterior cortical atrophy: a visual variant of Alzheimer's disease. In: Vision in Alzheimer's Disease, pp. 112–125. Karger Publishers (2004)
6. Fukui, T., Lee, E.: Visuospatial function is a significant contributor to functional status in patients with Alzheimer's disease. American Journal of Alzheimer's Disease & Other Dementias® **24**(4), 313–321 (2009). SAGE Publications Sage CA, Los Angeles, CA
7. Johnson, D.K., Storandt, M., Morris, J.C., Galvin, J.E.: Longitudinal study of the transition from healthy aging to Alzheimer disease. Arch. Neurol. **66**(10), 1254–1259 (2009). American Medical Association
8. Rizzo, M., Reinach, S., McGehee, D., Dawson, J.: Simulated car crashes and crash predictors in drivers with Alzheimer disease. Arch. Neurol. **54**(5), 545–551 (1997). American Medical Association
9. Ball, K., Owsley, C.: Driving competence: It's not a matter of age. J. Am. Geriatrics Soc. **51**(10), 1499–1501 (2003). Wiley Online Library
10. Petersen, R.C., Smith, G.E., Waring, S.C., Ivnik, R.J., Tangalos, E.G., Kokmen, E.: Mild cognitive impairment: clinical characterization and outcome. Arch. Neurol. **56**(3), 303–308 (1999). American Medical Association

11. Mariani, E., Monastero, R., Mecocci, P.: Mild cognitive impairment: a systematic review. J. Alzheimer's Dis. **12**(1), 23–35 (2007). IOS Press
12. Beydoun, M.A., Beydoun, H.A., Gamaldo, A.A., Teel, A., Zonderman, A.B., Wang, Y.: Epidemiologic studies of modifiable factors associated with cognition and dementia: systematic review and meta-analysis. BMC Public Health **14**(1), 643 (2014). BioMed Central
13. Andrieu, S., Coley, N., Lovestone, S., Aisen, P.S., Vellas, B.: Prevention of sporadic Alzheimer's disease: lessons learned from clinical trials and future directions. Lancet Neurol. **14**(9), 926–944 (2015). Elsevier
14. Willis, S.L., Tennstedt, S.L., Marsiske, M., Ball, K., Elias, J., Koepke, K.M., et al.: Long-term effects of cognitive training on everyday functional outcomes in older adults. JAMA **296**(23), 2805–2814 (2006). American Medical Association
15. Reijnders, J., van Heugten, C., van Boxtel, M.: Cognitive interventions in healthy older adults and people with mild cognitive impairment: a systematic review. Ageing Res. Rev. **12**(1), 263–275 (2013). Elsevier
16. Wolinsky, F.D., Unverzagt, F.W., Smith, D.M., Jones, R., Wright, E., Tennstedt, S.L.: The effects of the ACTIVE cognitive training trial on clinically relevant declines in health-related quality of life. J. Gerontol. **61**(5), S281–S287 (2006). Oxford University Press
17. Calero-Garcia, M.D., Navarro-González, E., Muñoz-Manzano, L.: Influence of level of activity on cognitive performance and cognitive plasticity in elderly persons. Arch. Gerontol. Geriatr. **45**(3), 307–318 (2007)
18. Calero, M.D., Dolores, M., Navarro, E.: Cognitive plasticity as modulating variable on the effects of memory training in elderly persons. Arch. Clin. Neuropsychol. **22**(1), 63–72 (2007)
19. Bamidis, P.D., Fissler, P., Papageorgiou, S.G., Zilidou, V., Konstantinidis, E.I., Billis, A.S., Tsilikopoulou, G.: Gains in cognition through combined cognitive and physical training: the role of training dosage and severity of neurocognitive disorder. Frontiers Aging Neurosci. **7**, 152 (2015)
20. García-Betances, R.I., Jiménez-Mixco, V., Arredondo, M.T., Cabrera-Umpiérrez, M.F.: Using virtual reality for cognitive training of the elderly. Am. J. Alzheimer's Dis. Other Dementias **30**(1), 49–54 (2015). SAGE Publications
21. Flynn, D., Van, S.P., Blackman, T., Femcott, C., Hobbs, B., Calderon, C.: Developing a virtual reality–based methodology for people with dementia: a feasibility study. CyberPsychol. Behav. **6**(6), 591–611 (2003). Mary Ann Liebert, Inc.
22. Coyle, H., Traynor, V., Solowij, N.: Computerized and virtual reality cognitive training for individuals at high risk of cognitive decline: systematic review of the literature. Am. J. Geriatric Psychiatry **23**(4), 335–359 (2015). Elsevier
23. Sacco, M., Redaelli, C., Zangiacomi, A., Greci, L., Di Santo, S., Leone, A., Vezzoli, A.: GOJI an advanced virtual environment supporting training of physical and cognitive activities to prevent dementia occurrence in elderly with minor cognitive disorders. In: Andò, B., Siciliano, P., Marletta, V., Monteriù, A. (eds.) Ambient Assisted Living. Biosystems & Biorobotics, vol. 11, pp. 429–437. Springer International Publishing, Switzerland (2015)
24. Venkatesh, V.: Determinants of perceived ease of use: Integrating control, intrinsic motivation, and emotion into the technology acceptance model. Inf. Syst. Res. **11**(4), 342–365 (2000). Informs
25. Dillon, A., Morris, M.G.: User acceptance of new information technology: theories and models. In: Annual Review of Information Science and Technology. Information Today, Medford (1996)

26. Mazzoleni, S., Turchetti, G., Palla, I., Posteraro, F., Dario, P.: Acceptability of robotic technology in neuro-rehabilitation: Preliminary results on chronic stroke patients. Comput. Methods Programs Biomed. **116**(2), 116–122 (2014). Elsevier

27. Marzorati, M., Di Santo, S.G., Mrakic-Sposta, S., Moretti, S., Jesuthasan, N., Caroppo, A., et al.: Supporting physical and cognitive training for preventing the occurrence of dementia using an integrated system: a pilot study. In: 6th EAI International Conference on Wireless Mobile Communication and Healthcare - Transforming Healthcare Through Innovations in Mobile and Wireless Technologies, Milan, Italy, 14–16 November 2016. Springer (2016) (In press)

28. Alloni, A., Sinforiani, E., Zucchella, C., Sandrini, G., Bernini, S., Cattani, B., et al.: Computer-based cognitive rehabilitation: the CoRe system. Disab. Rehabil., 1–11 (2015). Taylor & Francis

29. Hamming, R.W.: Error detecting and error correcting codes. Bell Syst. Techn. J. **29**(2), 147–160 (1950). Wiley Online Library

30. Krebs, H.I., Hogan, N., Aisen, M.L., Volpe, B.T.: Robot-aided neurorehabilitation. IEEE Trans. Rehabil. Eng. **6**(1), 75–87 (1998). IEEE

31. García-Vergara, S., Howard, A.M.: Three-dimensional fitt's law model used to predict movement time in serious games for rehabilitation. In: Shumaker, R., Lackey, S. (eds.) VAMR 2014. LNCS, vol. 8526, pp. 287–297. Springer, Cham (2014). doi:10.1007/978-3-319-07464-1_27

32. Ferris, S.H., Farlow, M.: Language impairment in Alzheimer's disease and benefits of acetylcholinesterase inhibitors. Clin. Interv. Aging **8**, 1007–1014 (2013)

33. Daum, I., Quinn, N.: Reaction times and visuospatial processing in Parkinson's disease. J. Clin. Exp. Neuropsychol. **13**(6), 972–982 (1991). Taylor & Francis

34. Carpenter, P.A., Just, M.A., Keller, T.A., Eddy, W., Thulborn, K.: Graded functional activation in the visuospatial system with the amount of task demand. J. Cogn. Neurosci. **11**(1), 9–24 (1999). MIT Press

35. Oxley, J.A., Fildes, B., Ihsen, E., Charlton, J.L., Day, R.H.: Simulation of the road crossing task for older and younger adult pedestrians: a validation study. In: Road Safety Research and Enforcement Conference, 1997, Hobart, Tasmania, Australia (1997)

36. Holland, C.A., Rabbitt, P.: People's awareness of their age-related sensory and cognitive deficits and the implications for road safety. Appl. Cogn. Psychol. **6**(3), 217–231 (1992)

37. Daigneault, G., Joly, P., Frigon, J.Y.: Executive functions in the evaluation of accident risk of older drivers. J. Clin. Exp. Neuropsychol. **24**(2), 221–238 (2002)

38. Oxley, J.A., Ihsen, E., Fildes, B.N., Charlton, J.L., Day, R.H.: Crossing roads safely: an experimental study of age differences in gap selection by pedestrians. Accid. Anal. Prev. **37**(5), 962–971 (2005)

Virtual System for Upper Limbs Rehabilitation in Children

Edwin Pruna$^{(\boxtimes)}$, Andrés Acurio, Jenny Tigse, Ivón Escobar,
Marco Pilatásig, and Pablo Pilatásig

Universidad de las Fuerzas Armadas ESPE, Sangolqui, Ecuador
eppruna@espe.edu.ec

Abstract. A virtual system is presented for upper limbs rehabilitation in children using a haptic device and oculus rift. Two interactive games were created in Unity 3D with daily tasks and easy execution. In addition, the virtual system was used by two groups of children (CP and Down Syndrome) with mild spasticity, the same ones who performed the exercise. The movements allowed by the system help in the rehabilitation of the hands and in hand-eye coordination. The participants completed a SEQ usability test with results (52 ± 0.43) by group 1 and ($53,5 \pm 0,72$) by group 2. The outcomes allow determining that the system has a good acceptance to be used in rehabilitation. Children in group 2 (Down Syndrome) achieved to manage the system successfully despite intellectual and ocular difficulties.

Keywords: Haptic device · Oculus Rift · Unity 3D · SEQ · Rehabilitation

1 Introduction

Childhood cerebral palsy (CP) has been considered one of the most common causes of motor disability in children. CP refers to a group of non-progressive movement and posture alterations due to a brain injury that occurred during fetal brain development, childbirth or in the first years of child life. [1]. Studies have shown that the prevalence of CP worldwide is 2.11 per 1000 live births [2]. Approximately half of children with CP may suffer from dysfunctions in upper limb activities such as extending, grasping and manipulation [3]. On the other hand, Down syndrome is a genetic disorder that hinders the general development of children. It mainly affecting muscle tone, posture, movement coordination and the development of fine motor skills or manual ability. This sensory stimulation has been an important factor for children to improve their motor skill [4].

Physical therapy in children with mild motor impairment of hemiplegic type is one of the elements in a childhood development program where therapists have to incorporate authentic efforts to achieve stimulating, varied and quality environment, so a child with cerebral palsy, like any child, needs new experiences and interaction with the outside world in order to learn new things [5, 6]. Searching in literature for children with CP, emphasizing the importance of repetitive practice of functional activities in various contexts focused on feedback and performance [7–14]. However participating

L.T. De Paolis et al. (Eds.): AVR 2017, Part II, LNCS 10325, pp. 107–118, 2017.
DOI: 10.1007/978-3-319-60928-7_9

in practices or repetitive movements can cause boredom in children because of limitations in the performed exercises [15].

Therapy based in virtual reality is an increasingly recognized tool that is used for immersion and motivation of the patient in a virtual environment [16–18]. Studies have shown an improvement in manual function and cortical organization in children with CP after therapies based on Virtual Reality (VR) [19, 20]. The use of VR games in the upper limb motor rehabilitation process has been increasing [20–23]. Environments created with VR present places very close to reality that provide visual and audition feedback, factors that can be manipulated in a precise and systematic way and allow an individualized training in motor learning [25, 26]. A virtual game can also presents tactile feedback through the interaction of haptic devices with virtual environments, factors that get more immersion from patient in the task performed [27–29].

As mentioned in this work is presented a 3D virtual reality application. The system is constituted by a haptic device that acquires the movement generated by the user and an oculus rift device that provides immersion in the use of the system. Two interactive virtual environments were designed. The first application presents the interface of a virtual garden where an activity of daily life is developed, which is watering plants. The second application presents a task to order objects according to a targets system organized by color. These games allow performing rehabilitation exercises such as extension and flexion of wrist and finger pinch. Finally, this system presents a menu of choice, where the user can choose the number of objectives. In Fig. 1 the implemented system is presented.

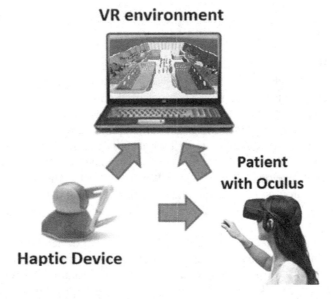

Fig. 1. 3D virtual system for rehabilitation in children (Color figure online)

The present work is divided into five sections including the introduction, Sect. 2 presents the methodology used for system development, Sect. 3 explains the use of the system, Sect. 4 shows the tests and results and finally Sect. 5 presents the conclusions.

2 Methodology for System Development

This section explains the stages of virtual system; Fig. 2 shows the system block diagram.

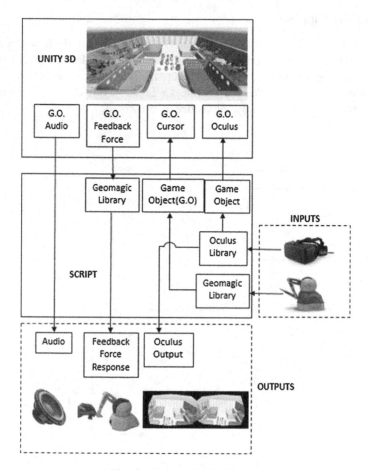

Fig. 2. System block diagram

Next, the stages are presented:

2.1 Signals Acquisition from Input Peripherals

Oculus Rift and Haptic Device (Geomagic Touch) are the input peripherals in this system.

Through the haptic device manipulator the movements that the user makes in the real space are collected, this process is carried out with the digital encoders that are inside the haptic device. With the HMD (Head-Mounted Display) (Oculus Rift) catches the movement that the user makes with the head, after placing the device, this movements are transferred to camera control that sees the virtual reality environment. The movements capture is done through an infrared camera placed on the computer top and in front of the device mounted on user's head.

2.2   Script Development

In this stage, data is collected and interpreted from the input devices through the libraries programmed in C to communicate with each of these devices. Using the code developed in Visual Studio organizes and directs the information received to each one of the activities proposed in the application. In Fig. 3 a flowchart of the input and output information management by the device is presented.

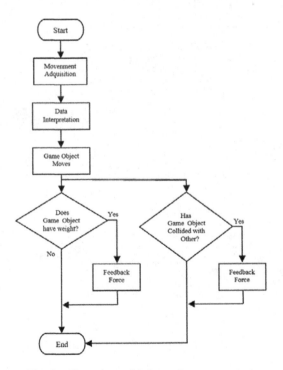

Fig. 3. Flow chart of information management

In the interaction between the virtual objects, a script is used that is responsible for counting of objects and includes an error detection system that indicates if a target was placed in wrong position, which is presented, in the next diagram (Fig. 4).

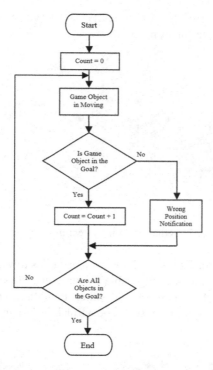

Fig. 4. Flow chart of object count and error detection.

2.3   Unity3D Environment Design

To create and design virtual objects, specific programs are used like Blender and 3ds Max, in these programs are designed figures with great visual appeal for children. Then these virtual objects are imported with a compatible format to the project in Unity3D so that they can be used in the application visual interface. For a correct and real execution of the game dynamic is necessary to add to the virtual objects some components of Unity3D like Rigid body, Mesh Collider, Audio source, Animation and Script. In the case of scripts included to objects, which were previously encoded in Visual Studio, their programming goes according to the task that each object must perform based on the total application dynamics.

Virtual environments were designed considering rehabilitation movements like flexion and extension wrist and pinch.

3   Description of 3D System Use

This section shows how to use the system:

The user is placed in a seated position in front of Oculus Rift camera obtaining the better position to execute the movements. Then the patient must take the Geomagic Touch manipulator like a pencil.

In the main screen, one of the virtual reality games (garden or basket) is selected. Figure 5 presents the system main menu.

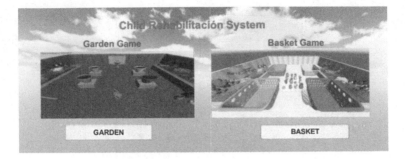

Fig. 5. Rehabilitation System main menu

The first game is a virtual garden where the patient has to water plants in pots until they grow (plant growth time is configurable by the user), the system provides a force feedback when a virtual object collides with other. In addition, an audio indicates that the task was completed. Figure 6 presents the virtual environments.

Fig. 6. Garden virtual environment

The second game is about organizing the objects that are located in the center, according to the basket color. The game has four levels of difficulty (Each level increases the number of objects) (Fig. 7).

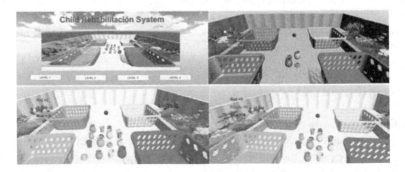

Fig. 7. Basket game virtual environment (Color figure online)

4   Tests and Results

4.1   Test

Experimental tests are performed to evaluate the response of the haptic device in rehabilitation therapies. A trajectory was created to be compared with the patient movements (with feedback of the haptic device) to save data of the positions in x, y and z axis.

Furthermore, system usability tests are carried out on two group of children. The first group integrated by five children (3 girls and 2 boys) with mild spasticity in the upper limbs in order to ASWRTH 1 + scale. They were between 7 and 12 years old. The second group integrated by four children (2 girls and 2 boys) with Down syndrome and moderate difficulty of movement in upper limbs. They were between 9 and 12 years old. The procedure detailed in Sect. 3 are explained before the tasks execution. Figure 8 presents the users performing the rehabilitation tasks.

Fig. 8. Virtual system used by children.

4.2   Results

The next outcomes are presented: rehabilitation movements performed, haptic device response signals and usability test (SEQ).

Rehabilitation Movements Performed. Supported by the rehabilitation professional, three types of useful movements are identified that allow the system to be used for fine motor rehabilitation of upper limbs. The first movement is pinch that is developed when the patient holds the haptic device manipulator, the second and third movements are flexion and rotation of wrist developed when the patient is performing the tasks proposed in the applications. In Fig. 9 the movements performed by users of the rehabilitation system implemented are presented.

It is verified that the applications were developed with the appropriate approach for fine motor rehabilitation in upper limbs, which allows the patients perform similar exercises to the physical therapies rehabilitation with more motivation.

Haptic Device Response Signals. The virtual system defines a trajectory, which will be compared with the patient movements in a rehabilitation therapy. Figure 10 shows data of the positions in the x, y, and z axis that the patient performed during the game

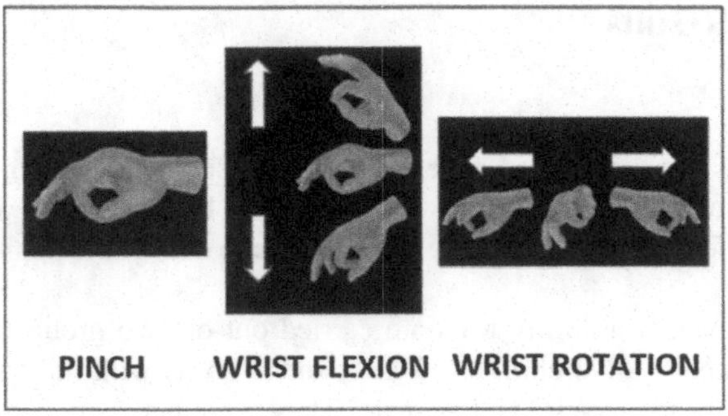

PINCH   WRIST FLEXION   WRIST ROTATION

Fig. 9. Movements that the rehabilitation system allows to be performed.

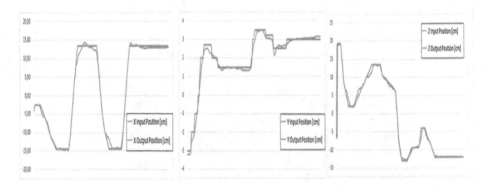

Fig. 10. Defined trajectory (red line) vs patient movement (blue line). (Color figure online)

execution time compared with a set reference value of the route to be followed. It can be noticed that these movements follow according to reference value. That allows patient has an appropriate rehabilitation.

Suitability Evaluation Questionnaire (SEQ). Finally, it presents the results of virtual 3D system usability. In several scientific works authors validate the virtual tools for rehabilitation through usability tests [30–33]. The studies allow to determine the patient acceptance, this information is of great importance to determine the security, sensation, discomfort when a virtual system is used. The test for usability evaluation is SEQ developed by Gil-Gómez [30]. Has 14 questions, where 13 questions have a score of 1 to 5 points according to the following scheme. The first seven questions (Q1–Q7) are related to acceptance and immersion level that caused the experience after the patient having used the application. The next four questions (Q8–Q11) are connected to the effects and discomfort that this type of system could cause like nausea, disorientation or eyes discomfort. The next two questions are related to the difficulty at the time of performing the task and use the equipment for the execution and the last question is an open question where patient indicates if he was uncomfortable with the virtual reality system and the reasons. Questions Q1, Q2, Q3, Q4, Q5, Q6 and Q11 are normally scored from 1 to 5. Questions Q7, Q8, Q9, Q10, Q12, and Q13 have a negative form, so at the time of score it should be noted that the score of 2 will change in 4 and the score of 1 will have a value of 5.

If the result obtained is in the range of 40–65 the application is considered as acceptable for rehabilitation (Table 1).

Table 1. Presents the questions asked to users of the system as well as the results.

Questions	Group 1		Group 2	
	Result (N = 5)		Result (N = 4)	
	Mean	SD	Mean	SD
Q1. How much did you enjoy your experience with the system?	4,6	0,49	4,75	0,43
Q2. How much did you sense to be in the environment of the system?	4,6	0,49	4,75	0,43
Q3. How successful were you in the system?	4,6	0,8	4,5	0,5
Q4. To what extent were you able to control the system?	3,2	0,75	4	1
Q5. How real is the virtual environment of the system?	4,2	0,75	4,5	0,86
Q6. Is the information provided by the system clear?	4,4	0,8	5	0
Q7. Did you feel discomfort during your experience with the system?	1,4	0,8	1,25	0,43
Q8. Did you experience dizziness or nausea during your practice with the system?	1,4	0,8	1,75	1.29
Q9. Did you experience eye discomfort during your practice with the system?	1,2	0,4	1	0
Q10. Did you feel confused or disoriented during your experience with the system?	1,8	0,75	1,75	1,29
Q11. Do you think that this system will be helpful for your rehabilitation?	4	0,63	5	0
Q12. Did you find the task difficult?	1,6	0,8	3	2
Q13. Did you find the devices of the system difficult to use?	2,2	0,75	1,25	0,43
GLOBAL SCORE (total)	52	0,43	53,5	0,72

The outcomes in the test are: group 1 (52 ± 0.43) and group 2 (53,5 ± 0,72).

5 Conclusions and Future Work

A virtual 3D system was created using a haptic device and oculus rift as input peripherals. The virtual environment is designed in Unity 3D and is conformed of two interactive games that allow the generation of rehabilitation movements like flexion and extension of wrist and bidigital clamp. The system presents a high level of immersion having an Oculus Rift and speakers as output devices. Also the system has force feedback when there is collision between virtual objects. This in an innovating system and causes a great interest in children.

The virtual system allows to perform movements that help fine motor rehabilitation and improve hand-eye coordination in children. The results obtained in the usability test are group 1: (52 ± 0.43) and group 2 (53.5 ± 0.72) and indicate that the system has an acceptance to be used in rehabilitation, so users feel Immersion and enjoy the game. Patients don't have discomfort and have little difficulty in using it. Considering that children with Down Syndrome have a certain level of intellectual disability and visual impairments, however this hasn't been a problem to use the system successfully.

As future work is intended to create games using two haptic devices that increase motivation and interest in participation.

Acknowledgements. We thank the "Universidad de las Fuerzas Armadas ESPE" for financing the investigation project number 2016-PIC-0017.

References

1. Li, D., Tan, Z., Kang, P., Shen, B., Pei, F.: Effects of multi-site infiltration analgesia on pain management and early rehabilitation compared with femoral nerve or adductor canal block for patients undergoing total knee arthroplasty: a prospective randomized controlled trial. Int. Orthop. **41**(1), 75–83 (2017)
2. Bax, M., Goldstein, M., Rosenbaum, P., et al.: Proposed definition and classification of cerebral palsy. Dev. Med. Child Neurol. **47**, 571–576 (2005)
3. Oskoui, M., Coutinho, F., Dykeman, J., et al.: An update on the prevalence of cerebral palsy: a systematic review and meta-analysis. Dev. Med. Child Neurol. **55**, 509–519 (2013)
4. Aicardi, J.: Disease of the Nervous System in Childhood. MacKeith Press, London (1992)
5. Candel, I.: Programa de atención temprana. Intervención en niños con síndrome de Down y otros problemas de desarrollo, CEPE, Madrid (2005)
6. De Campos, A.C., da Costa, C.S., Rocha, N.A.: Measuring changes in functional mobility in children with mild cerebral palsy. Dev. Neurorehabil. **14**, 140–144 (2011)
7. Prosser, L.A., Lee, S.C., Barbe, M.F., VanSant, A.F., Lauer, R.T.: Trunk and hip muscle activity in early walkers with and without cerebral palsy – a frequency analysis. J. Electromyogr. Kinesiol. **20**, 851–859 (2010)
8. Boyd, R.N., Morris, M.E., Graham, H.K.: Management of upper limb dysfunction in children with cerebral palsy: a systematic review. Eur. J. Neurol. **8**(Suppl. 5), 150–166 (2001)
9. Fetters, L.: Measurement and treatment in cerebral palsy: an argument for a new approach. Phys. Ther. **71**(3), 244–247 (1991)
10. Ketelaar, M., Vermeer, A., Hart, H., Van Petegem-van Beek, E., Helders, P.J.M.: Effects of a functional therapy program on motor abilities of children with cerebral palsy. Phys. Ther. **81** (9), 1534–1545 (2001)
11. Sakzewski, L., Ziviani, J., Boyd, R.: Systematic review and meta-analysis of therapeutic management of upper-limb dysfunction in children with congenital hemiplegia. Pediatrics **123**(6), e1111–e1122 (2009)
12. Sakzewski, L., Ziviani, J., Boyd, R.N.: Efficacy of upper limb therapies for unilateral cerebral palsy: a meta-analysis. Pediatrics **133**(1), e175–e204 (2014)
13. Novak, I., Mcintyre, S., Morgan, C., et al.: A systematic review of interventions for children with cerebral palsy: state of the evidence. Dev. Med. Child Neurol. **55**(10), 885–910 (2013)

14. Löwing, K., Bexelius, A., Carlberg, E.B.: Activity focused and goal directed therapy for children with cerebral palsy: do goals make a difference? Disabil. Rehabil. **31**(22), 1808–1816 (2009)
15. Fetters, L.: Perspective on variability in the development of human action. Phys. Ther. **90**(12), 1860–1867 (2010)
16. Galil, A., Carmel, S., Lubetzky, H., Heiman, N.: Compliance with home rehabilitation therapy by parents of children with disabilities in Jews and Bedouin in Israel. Dev. Med. Child Neurol. **43**(4), 261–268 (2001)
17. Mitchell, L., Ziviani, J., Oftedal, S., Boyd, R.: The effect of virtual reality interventions on physical activity in children and adolescents with early brain injuries including cerebral palsy. Dev. Med. Child Neurol. **54**, 667–671 (2012)
18. Snider, L., Majnemer, A., Darsaklis, V.: Virtual reality as a therapeutic modality for children with cerebral palsy. Dev. Neurorehabil. **13**, 120–128 (2010)
19. Levac, D.E., Galvin, J.: When is virtual reality "therapy"? Arch. Phys. Med. Rehabil. **94**(795), 8 (2013)
20. Golomb, M.R., McDonald, B.C., Warden, S.J., Yonkman, J., Saykin, A.J., Shirley, B., et al.: In-home virtual reality videogame telerehabilitation in adolescents with hemiplegic cerebral palsy. Arch. Phys. Med. Rehabil. **91**, 1–8 (2010)
21. Shin, J., Song, G., Hwangbo, G.: Effects of conventional neurological treatment and a virtual reality training program on eye-hand coordination in children with cerebral palsy. J. Phys. Ther. Sci. **27**(7), 2151–2154 (2015) http://doi.org/10.1589/jpts.27.2151
22. Sucar, L.E., et al.: Gesture therapy: an upper limb virtual reality - based motor rehabilitation platform. Trans. Neural Syst. Rehabil. Eng. **22**, 634–643 (2014)
23. Laver, K.E., George, S., Thomas, S., Deutsch, J.E., Crotty, M.: Virtual reality for stroke rehabilitation. Cochrane Database Syst. Rev. (2015). doi:10.1002/14651858
24. Tatla, S.K., Shirzad, N., Lohse, K.R., Virji-Babul, N., Hoens, A.M., Holsti, L., et al.: Therapists' perceptions of social media and video game technologies in upper limb rehabilitation. JMIR Serious Games. **3**(1), e2 (2015). doi:10.2196/games.3401
25. Colomer, C., Llorens, R., Noé, E., Alcañiz, M.: Effect of a mixed reality-based intervention on arm, hand, and finger function on chronic stroke. J. Neuro Eng. Rehabil. **13**, 45 (2016). http://doi.org/10.1186/s12984-016-0153-6
26. Sveistrup, H., Thornton, M., Brvanton, C., et al.: Outcomes of intervention programs using flatscreen virtual reality. In: Conference Proceedings IEEE Eng Medicine and Biology Society vol. 7, 4856–4858 (2004)
27. Chen, Y.-P., Kang, L.-J., Chuang, T.-Y., Doong, J.-L., Lee, S.-J., Tsai, M.-W., Jeng, S.-F., Sung, W.-H.: Use of virtual reality to improve upper-extremity control in children with cerebral palsy: a single-subject design. Phys. Ther. **87**(11), 1441–1457 (2007). doi:10.2522/ptj.20060062
28. Dhiman, A., Solanki, D., Bhasin, A., Bhise, A., Das, A., Lahiri, U.: Design of adaptive haptic-enabled virtual reality based system for upper limb movement disorders: a usability study. In: 2016 6th IEEE International Conference on Biomedical Robotics and Biomechatronics (BioRob), Singapore, pp. 1254–1259 (2016)
29. Li, S., Zhang, X.: Eye-movement-based objective real-time quantification of patient's mental engagement in rehabilitation: a preliminary study. In: 2014 IEEE International Conference on Mechatronics and Automation, Tianjin, pp. 180–185 (2014)
30. Shah, N., Basteris, A., Amirabdollahian, F.: Design parameters in multimodal games for rehabilitation. Games Health Res. Dev. Clin. Appl. **3**(1), 13–20 (2014)

31. Gil-Gómez, J.A., Gil-Gómez, H., Lozano-Quilis, J.A., Manzano-Hernández, P., Albiol-Pérez, S., Aula-Valero, C.: SEQ: suitability evaluation questionnaire for virtual rehabilitation systems. application in a virtual rehabilitation system for balance rehabilitation. In: 2013 7th International Conference on Pervasive Computing Technologies for Healthcare and Workshops, Venice, pp. 335–338 (2013)
32. Fitzgerald, D., Kelly, D., Ward, T., Markham, C., Caulfield, B.: Usability evaluation of e-motion: a virtual rehabilitation system designed to demonstrate, instruct and monitor a therapeutic exercise programme. In: Proceedings Virtual Rehabilitation, pp. 144–149 (2008)
33. Kalawsky, R.S.: VRUSE–a computerised diagnostic tool: for usability evaluation of virtual/synthetic environment systems. Appl. Ergon. **30**, 11–25 (1999)
34. Cameirao, M.S., Badia, S.B., Oller, E.D., Verschure, P.F.: Neurorehabilitation using the virtual reality based rehabilitation gaming system: methodology, design, psychometrics, usability and validation. J. Neuroeng. Rehabil. **7**, 48 (2010)

3D Virtual System Trough 3 Space Mocap Sensors for Lower Limb Rehabilitation

Edwin Pruna[✉], Marco Pilatásig, Hamilton Angueta,
Christian Hernandez, Ivón Escobar, Eddie D. Galarza,
and Nancy Jacho

Universidad de las Fuerzas Armadas ESPE, Sangolqui, Ecuador
eppruna@espe.edu.ec

Abstract. A 3D virtual system is presented for rehabilitation of lower limbs trough 3 Space Mocap Sensors and the Unity 3D environment, also, two games are designed to allow the flexion, extension and strengthening movements. The games have some difficulty levels thought for every rehabilitation stage. The system was used by 4 people with knee problems, which completed the whole exercise. In addition the participants performed a SEQ usability test with results of ($53 \pm 0{,}56$), this shows that the systems has a good acceptation to be used for rehabilitation.

Keywords: 3 Space Mocap · Unity 3D · Rehabilitation · SEQ

1 Introduction

Nowadays, there are people who suffer from illness affecting their lower limbs, this is the case of the knee Osteoarthritis, this causes pain and joint dysfunction. Osteoarthritis is present in people with medium and advanced ages, being women the most prone to have this illness [1]. The treatment to this pathology involves physical rehabilitation with the help of a physiotherapist in which the patient seats over the border of a table and performs the flexion and extension movements. Every movement must be done 10 times with speed established by the physiotherapist [2, 9]; the same movements could be done home with the disadvantage that they could not be done correctly, this would cause the rehabilitation process to last longer [3].

Virtual reality has great importance in rehabilitation of lower limbs, consequently implementing videogames based applications allow patients to perform exercises in an interactive and personalized way [4]. The virtual environment provides the patient's immersion and in the same time it allows feedback, for example, visuals, sound, strength, etc. [5, 6], this causes the patient to be motivated to keep performing the exercises to finally rehabilitate the affected lower limb. The therapies using VR are based on tracking the movements in real time. This movements could be from upper limbs, lower limbs or the whole body and the information is shown in a graphic interface provided by a computer [7]. VR is considered like a complement to traditional rehabilitation, to improve movements through computational tools that simulate the environments and objects which the patient can interact with.

© Springer International Publishing AG 2017
L.T. De Paolis et al. (Eds.): AVR 2017, Part II, LNCS 10325, pp. 119–128, 2017.
DOI: 10.1007/978-3-319-60928-7_10

In this context, there are many investigation work which allows to perform the rehabilitation of upper limbs through virtual reality by using Inertial Measuring Units (IMU) to acquire data, in [9] it is presented the monitoring of knee and hip angles using IMU during the rehabilitation of lower limbs, the results are the 3D cinematic estimation of the lower limbs joints, in [10] it is shown the detection of lower limbs movements based on Life Performance Research Motion Sensor (LPMS), as result it was obtained a method to detect the movement of lower limbs in hemiplegic patients based on sensors with inertial technology; the development of a rehabilitation robot for lower limbs based on free walking and virtual reality is described in [11], the obtained result was that the motor disability patients could walk with free running in a virtual environment and also they could choose the passive and active training modes. In [11] it was developed an evaluation system for lower limbs rehabilitation based on virtual reality technology, it shows as result an interface for human – computer interaction and it can be seen the movements of the affected limb. A training system for lower limbs rehabilitation with active and passive co stimulation is presented in [12], as result it gets the improvement of the nerve center based in the neuronal mirror theory.

Therefore, in this work it is presented a 3D virtual system for knee rehabilitation with the use of 3 Space Mocap Sensors, it is also designed an interaction interface between the patient and the computer in which there is the immersion so the knee rehabilitation exercises can work through video games, in addition, there is visual and audible feedback that guarantees the exercises be finished and performed correctly. In Fig. 1 the implemented system is shown.

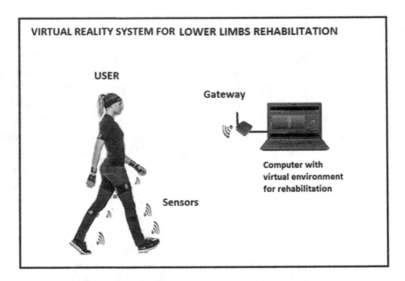

Fig. 1. 3D virtual system for lower limbs rehabilitation

The present work is organized in five sections including the introduction, in Sect. 2 it is presented the used methodology for the system development, in Sect. 3 the system utilization is explained, in Sect. 4 the tests and results are shown, finally in Sect. 5 the conclusions are presented.

2   Methodology for System Development

This chapter describes the stages that make up the virtual system, the following figure shows the block diagram (Fig. 2).

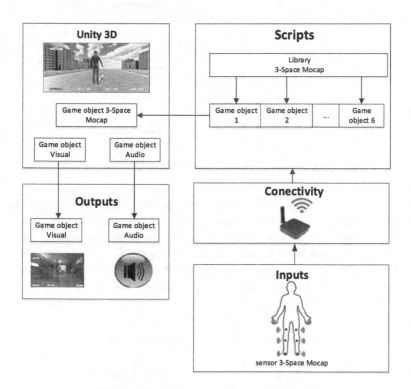

Fig. 2. Block diagram of the system virtual

2.1   Signal Acquisition from the Input Peripheral

As input peripheral it was used the YEI 3-Space Mocap movement capture devices, for the extents of this work it was used 6 sensors (3 for the left leg and 3 for the right leg); the used communication is Wireless under the 802.11 standard, the communication mode between the devices is question – answer, the Gateway sends a frame with question commands and the sensors answer the request via an answering frame.

Figure 3 shows the format of the question frame which is used for communications; this allows the gateway to request information about the axis x, y and z from the sensor in real time; in the frame the first byte is to control and allows the beginning of communication, the second byte shows the address of the device to communicate, the third byte provides information about the task to be done by every sensor, the fourth, fifth and the other bytes send information about the required data, finally the last byte has the detection method and errors correction.

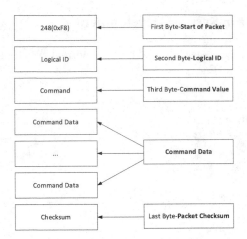

Fig. 3. Format of the binary packet "Question"

Figure 4 shows the answer frame from the sensors to the gateway, this answer frame provides the Gateway with the information about the status of each one of the 6 sensor, the first byte shows if the command was received and processed, the second byte allows the Wireless logic identification of the answering sensor, the third byte shows the length of the following answer (it is not shown in case of failure), the fourth, fifth and other bytes send information about the sensor status.

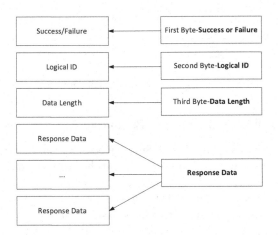

Fig. 4. Format of the binary packet "Answer"

2.2   Script Development

Scripts were developed to the system design, these are explained below:

Transformation from Quaternion Data to Euler. The 3 space mocap sensors provide data in Quaternion Format (q) which show a real dimension and three imaginary, (w, x, y, z) respectively, as shown in the following formula:

$$|q|^2 = q_w^2 + q_{x1}^2 + q_y^2 + q_z^2 = 1 \tag{1}$$

To visualize the data in the Unity Software, it must be done the transformation from Quaternion Format to Euler through the next matrix.

$$\begin{bmatrix} \Phi \\ \theta \\ \psi \end{bmatrix} = \begin{bmatrix} atan2(2(q_0q_1 + q_2q_3), & 1 - 2(q_1^2 + q_2^2)) \\ asin(2(q_0q_2 - q_3q_1)) \\ atan2(2(q_0q_3 + q_1q_2), & 1 - 2(q_2^2 + q_3^2)) \end{bmatrix} \tag{2}$$

Where:
Φ (Roll) Represents the x axis rotation.
Θ (Pitch) Represents the y axis rotation.
Ψ (Yaw) Represents the z axis rotation.

Scene Activation and Deactivation Script. Ascript was created which is in charge of the activation and deactivation of the scenes, its name is "Función_botones" which shows or remove objects in each scene through the command Set.Active, where the true or false command show or not those objects, also it can remove the operation of some scripts that are not necessary in all the games.

Sensor Calibration Script. The option to calibrate the sensor is "tare", which allows the interaction with any button of the device, it allows to give a predetermined position to the sensor, in the frame, the "tare" function is activated with 0×60 shown in the third byte. Below it is shown the instructions to calibrate the sensors.

2.3   Design of Virtual Environment

In the virtual objects design it was used two dedicated programs, they are Blender and 3ds Max, in this programs, shapes of the environment are designed, then the objects are imported to the Unity3D environment and then they are used in the virtual environment design. For the application implementation it is included the virtual objects as Unity 3d components like: Rigid Body, Mesh Collider, Audio Source, Animation and Script. Additionally, it was designed interactive games: (a) Obstacles Skipping games with the left or right leg in an alternated way (this is thought so the user can perform the flexion and extension exercises). (b) A game based on avoiding objects thrown by a monkey in a random way (focus to strengthen the knees). In Figs. 5 and 6 it is shown the designed virtual environments.

Each environment is composed of 4 scenes which are described below:

Start Menu. Is the main window and is composed of 3 buttons from which it can be accessed the following options: calibrate, play and exit.

Fig. 5. Virtual environment designed to perform flexion and extension exercises.

Fig. 6. Virtual environment designed to perform strengthening exercises.

Calibration Window. Allows to calibrate the sensors prior to be used.
Play Window. Allows to select the available exercises and shows a small tab to go back to main menu.
Exit Window. Allows to end the application.

3 Utilization Mode of the Virtual Reality System

In this chapter it is described how to use the virtual system in rehabilitation, the following figure shows the flow diagram of the way of use (Fig. 7).

4 Test and Results

4.1 Test

It was performed system usability tests by 4 people (3 men and 1 woman), with ages between 61 and 78 years old (69.5 ± 8.5), it was uses the following inclusion criteria: age >20 years and <80 years, have knee osteoarthritis. The exclusion criteria was: have visual deficiency and/or several audible deficiency. Before the task execution there were and explanation of how to use the virtual games. Figure 8 shows the users performing the rehabilitation tasks.

4.2 Results

Below is shown the results of the system usability, in many scientific articles the authors validate the virtual tools for rehabilitation through usability tests [13, 14], they

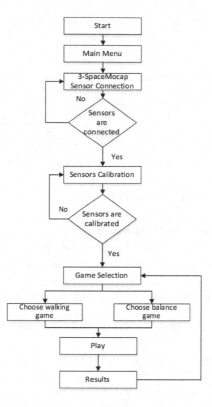

Fig. 7. Flow diagram of the system's way of use.

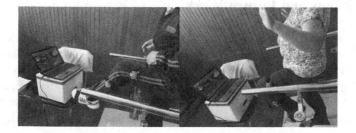

Fig. 8. 3D virtual system used by the patients

allow to determine the acceptation or not of the patients; the performed test for the usability evaluation is SEQ developed by Gil-Gomez et al. [15], it allows to obtain patient's information related to the virtual reality system usability, for example: easiness, secureness, sensation, inconveniences, etc. SEQ has 14 clear questions, which 13 has a value of 1 to 5 points and the last is an open question so the patient indicates if he felt uncomfortable with the virtual reality system and what were the reasons. If the obtained results are between the ranges of 40–65 points it is considered that the application is acceptable for rehabilitation.

In Table 1 it is presented the questions performed to the system's users as well as the obtained results.

Table 1. Average SEQ and standard deviation

Question	Result (N = 4)	
	Mean	SD
Q1. How much did you enjoy your experience with the system?	4	0,71
Q2. How much did you sense to be in the environment of the system?	3,5	1,11
Q3. How successful were you in the system?	4,75	0,43
Q4. To what extent were you able to control the system?	3,5	0,5
Q5. How real is the virtual environment of the system?	4,75	0,43
Q6. Is the information provided by the system clear?	5	0
Q7. Did you feel discomfort during your experience with the system?	1,25	0,43
Q8. Did you experience dizziness or nausea during your practice with the system?	1	0
Q9. Did you experience eye discomfort during your practice with the system?	1,25	0,43
Q10. Did you feel confused or disoriented during your experience with the system?	1,75	1,29
Q11. Do you think that this system will be helpful for your rehabilitation?	5	0
Q12. Did you find the task difficult?	2,25	1,08
Q13. Did you find the devices of the system difficult to use?	1	0
GLOBAL SCORE (total)	53	0,56

5   Conclusions and Future Work

It was implemented the 3D virtual system using the 3 Space Mocap sensors for movement acquisition, the design of the virtual environment was developed in the Unity 3d Software based on two interactive games that allow the execution of flexion and extension movements as well as knee strengthening; the created virtual environments provide visual and audible feedback to the users so it generates entertainment and immersion, the systems has many difficulty levels that are essential in the stages of rehabilitation.

The virtual reality system was used by 4 people which have knee osteoarthritis problems, it was evaluated the usability with the SEQ test with results of (53 ± 0,56), this result shows that the virtual reality system presents enough acceptation to be used in rehabilitation, since the users feel the immersion and enjoy the game, they don't have inconveniences and have low difficulty when using it.

As future work the implemented system will be used in rehabilitation therapies for patients with knee problems; the patients that used the system show great interest in using the system as an alternative of rehabilitation. Finally, by using the 17 3 Space Mocap sensors it will be developed a virtual environment to strengthen the upper and lower limbs.

Acknowledgements. We thank the "Universidad de las Fuerzas Armadas ESPE" for financing the investigation project number 2015-PIC-006.

References

1. Li, D., Tan, Z., Kang, P., Shen, B., Pei, F.: Effects of multi-site infiltration analgesia on pain management and early rehabilitation compared with femoral nerve or adductor canal block for patients undergoing total knee arthroplasty: a prospective randomized controlled trial Int. Orthop. **41**(1), 75–83 (2017)
2. Van Baar, M.E., Dekker, J., Oostendorp, R., Bijl, D., Voorn, T.B., Bijlsma, J.W.J.: Effectiveness of exercise in patients with osteoarthritis of hip or knee: nine months' follow up. Ann. Rheum. Dis. **60**(12), 1123–1130 (2001)
3. Gonzalez, A., Fraisse, P., Hayashibe, M.: Adaptive interface for personalized center of mass self-identification in home rehabilitation. IEEE Sensors J. **15**(5), 2814–2823 (2015)
4. Ferreira dos Santos, L., Christ, O., Mate, K., Schmidt, H., Krüger, J., Dohle, C.: Movement visualisation in virtual reality rehabilitation of the lower limb: a systematic review. Biomed. Eng. **15** (2016). Art. no. 144
5. Valvoda, J.T.: Virtual humanoids and presence in virtual environments. Ph.D. thesis. Rheinisch-Westfälische Technische Hochschule Aachen, Fakultät für Mathematik, Informatik und Naturwissenschaften (2007)
6. Schüler, T., Ferreira dos Santos, L., Hoermann, S.: Harnessing the experience of presence for virtual motor rehabilitation: towards a guideline for the development of virtual reality environments. In: Sharkey, P.M., Pareto, L., Broeren, J., Rydmark, M. (eds.) Proceedings of the 10th International Conference on Disability, Virtual Reality and Associated Technologies (ICDVRAT), Gothenburg, 2–4 September 2014, pp. 373–376. The University of Reading, Reading (2014)
7. Holden, M.K.: Virtual environments for motor rehabilitation: review. Cyberpsychol. Behav. **8**, 187–211 (2005)
8. Cho, K.H., Lee, K.J., Song, C.H.: Virtual-reality balance training with a video-game system improves dynamic balance in chronic stroke patients. Tohoku J. Exp. Med. **228**, 69–74 (2012)
9. Bonnet, V., Joukov, V., Kulić, D., Fraisse, P., Ramdani, N., Venture, G.: Monitoring of hip and knee joint angles using a single inertial measurement unit during lower limb rehabilitation. IEEE Sensors J. **16**(6), 1557–1564 (2016). Art. no. 7352303
10. Sun, T., Wang, C., Liu, Q., Lu, Z., Duan, L., Chen, P., Shen, Y., Li, M., Li, W., Liu, Q., Shi, Q., Wang, Y., Qin, J., Wei, J., Wu, Z.: Development of lower limb motion detection based on LPMS. In: 2016 IEEE International Conference on Real-Time Computing and Robotics, RCAR 2016, pp. 243–248 (2016). Art. no. 7784033
11. Zhang, J., Li, M., Song, R., Zhang, X.: Development of a lower limb rehabilitation robot based on free gait and virtual reality. In: 2014 IEEE International Conference on Robotics and Biomimetics, IEEE ROBIO 2014, pp. 808–813 (2014). Art. no. 7090431
12. Zhang, X., Xu, G., Xie, J., Li, M., Pei, W., Zhang, J.: An EEG-driven lower limb rehabilitation training system for active and passive co-stimulation. In: Proceedings of the Annual International Conference of the IEEE Engineering in Medicine and Biology Society, EMBS 2015, November, pp. 4582–4585 (2015). Art. no. 7319414
13. Fitzgerald, D., Kelly, D., Ward, T., Markham, C., Caulfield, B.: Usability evaluation of e-motion: a virtual rehabilitation system designed to demonstrate, instruct and monitor a therapeutic exercise programme. In: Virtual Rehabilitation, pp. 144–149 (2008)

14. Kalawsky, R.S.: VRUSE–a computerised diagnostic tool: for usability evaluation of virtual/synthetic environment systems. Appl. Ergon. **30**, 11–25 (1999)
15. Gil-Gómez, J.A., Manzano, P.H., Albiol, S.P., Aula, C.V., Gil-Gómez H., Lozano, J.A.Q.: SEQ: suitability evaluation questionnaire for virtual rehabilitation systems. In: Proceedings Application in a Virtual Rehabilitation System for Balance Rehabilitation (2012)

Robust Laparoscopic Instruments Tracking Using Colored Strips

Virginia Mamone[1(✉)], Rosanna Maria Viglialoro[1,2],
Fabrizio Cutolo[1], Filippo Cavallo[3], Simone Guadagni[4],
and Vincenzo Ferrari[1,5]

[1] EndoCAS, Department of Translational Research and of New Surgical
and Medical Technologies, University of Pisa, Pisa, Italy
virginiam989@gmail.com, {rosanna.viglialoro,
fabrizio.cutolo,vincenzo.ferrari}@endocas.org
[2] Vascular Surgery Unit, Cisanello University Hospital AOUP, Pisa, Italy
[3] Sant'Anna School of Advanced Studies, Pisa, Italy
filippo.cavallo@santannapisa.it
[4] General Surgery Unit, Department of Oncology Transplantation
and New Technologies, University of Pisa, Pisa, Italy
simone5c@virgilio.it
[5] Department of Information Engineering, University of Pisa, Pisa, Italy

Abstract. To assist surgeons in the acquisition of the required skills for the proper execution of the laparoscopic procedure, surgical simulators are used. During training with simulators it is useful to provide a surgical performance quantitative evaluation. Recent research works showed that such evaluation can be obtained by tracking the laparoscopic instruments, using only the images provided by the laparoscope and without hindering the surgical scene. In this work the state of the art method is improved so that a robust tracking can run even with the noisy background provided by realistic simulators. The method was validated by comparison with the tracking of a "chess-board" pattern and following tests were performed to check the robustness of the developed algorithm. Despite the noisy environment, the implemented method was found to be able to track the tip of the surgical instrument with a good accuracy compared to the other studies in the literature.

Keywords: Optical tracking · Single camera · Laparoscopic training · Surgical simulation · Surgical performance evaluation

1 Introduction

In recent decades, laparoscopic surgery proved to be an effective alternative to open surgery techniques for the treatment of various abdominal diseases. However, the laparoscopic technique introduces new issues for surgeons, due the using of the laparoscope and elongated instruments passing through the access ports, as the availability of the sole endoscopic camera mediated view, the lack of tactile feedback and the limited force feedback, and the fulcrum effect on the instruments that imposes restrictions on the movements [1]. These technique-related issues impose on novices a

© Springer International Publishing AG 2017
L.T. De Paolis et al. (Eds.): AVR 2017, Part II, LNCS 10325, pp. 129–143, 2017.
DOI: 10.1007/978-3-319-60928-7_11

complex and long learning curve. Surgical simulators can shorten the training period and reduce patient's risks in the early stages of the learning curve [2, 3]. Surgical simulators allow novices to improve their technical abilities as manual dexterity and the hand-eye coordination, and, for some simulators, learn the main difficult steps up to a complete operation. Through the analysis of certain parameters, it is possible to obtain a surgical performance quantitative evaluation, which constitutes a feedback of the progress and can be used to determine the achieving of an appropriate level of competence (proficiency level). Novices who have reached the proficiency level are ready, while other ones can need additional training. A literature search showed that significant parameters for this purpose, as path length and jerk [4], can be extracted from the movements of the laparoscopic instruments. In case of virtual reality simulators [5–7] the kinematics of the instruments is offered by the simulator itself, while in case of physical simulators (for example box trainer or mannequins) or hybrid AR simulators [5, 8] laparoscopic instruments tracking is required.

Since the laparoscopic images are available both in physical and hybrid AR simulators, machine vision based techniques are a suitable choice.

In [9] the authors combine machine learning methods with optical flow information to track the 3-D pose of the end-effector of a surgical robot for laparoscopy. Through a completely marker-less tracking, they are able to determine the 6° of freedom (DoF) of the instrument in respect to the camera but the achievable tracking accuracy of 4.09 [mm] might be not enough for our purposes. In [10], laparoscopic surgical instruments are equipped with a non-bulky marker consisting in a colored strip attached to the instrument shaft. Machine vision methods allow the estimation of the projected diameter of the surgical instrument onto the camera images; taking into account the cylindrical shape of the surgical instrument shaft, this information is then used to determine the position of the instrument and its rotation along pitch and yaw angles. Mean tracking accuracy in [10] is 2.5 mm "for working distances commonly found in laparoscopic training".

Our new approach improves the technique described in [10] to work with a more realistic and complex environment as the one provided by the cholecystectomy simulator being developed by the EndoCAS center for computer assisted surgery [11–14].

This paper describes the state of the art algorithm [10] and our improvements, the trial setup and the results. Finally the method and its application are discussed.

2 Materials and Methods

2.1 Experimental Set-up and Camera Calibration

The tests were carried out using the laparoscopic simulator being developed by the EndoCAS center for computer-assisted surgery [11–14]. It is an augmented reality simulator for the training of the critical phases in the cholecystectomy procedure. The simulator is composed of an external frame that replicates an insufflated abdomen while inside it faithfully reproduces the internal organs involved in the intervention. To get a more realistic render, liver and gallbladder are manufactured starting from computed tomography images [11, 15]. A laparoscope is reproduced through mounting on the distal part of a cylindrical tube, a consumer camera with a 4–6 cm focal length and a 56° viewing angle (REF-37131-919 by SOMIKON). The images are acquired at a 1280 × 720 resolution.

Colored Strip Implementation. Marker detection is based on a simple color segmentation by thresholding performed in the HSV (hue, saturation, value) color space because HSV allows robust segmentation of objects that undergo non-uniform levels of illumination intensity, shadows and shading [10, 16]. In particular, segmentation based on saturation and hue allows wider color range to be covered and therefore it is less dependent on the lighting conditions within the scene (mainly affecting the V channel). Furthermore, highly saturated colors are not present in our simulated surgical scene (Fig. 1). For these reasons, and as suggested in [17, 18], we adopted fluorescent dyes for the colored markers (strips) so as to peak the saturation channel in their own region of interest: the S values of the colored strips show a higher dynamic with respect to the neighboring pixels than their corresponding H values. In this way, the segmentation based on thresholding becomes more selective: it can be performed with a high cutoff value in the S-channel and it yields good results also at low lighting conditions like ours.

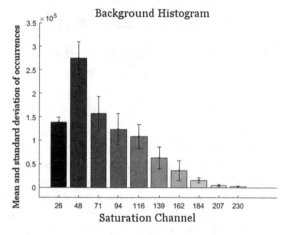

Fig. 1. Histogram of the Saturation channel (HSV-scale) of the images of the simulated surgical field: high saturated colors are infrequent.

Two laparoscopic grasping forceps, typically used during a cholecystectomy procedure, were modified by attaching to the distal part of each shaft a fluorescent colored strip. The colors were selected by analyzing the histogram of the hue channel of the operative field shown in Fig. 2. Red and, to a lesser extent, cyan prevail in the images of the operative field. Although the predominant color varies when different portions of the operative field are focused, the variance of the lower peaks is minimal. On the basis of these observations, a green marker and a blue marker were depicted with fluorescent dye respectively to the two shafts.

Camera Calibration. The camera is calibrated using the OpenCV libraries. The projective parameters of the camera and the distortion components due to lens non-linearity are estimated using the Zhang calibration procedure [19] and a "chessboard" pattern as calibration target.

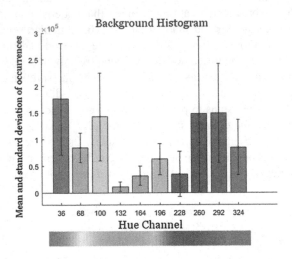

Fig. 2. Histogram of the Hue channel (HSV-scale) of the images of the simulated surgical field (background) (Color figure online)

2.2 Image Processing

The non-linear distortions onto the camera frames are compensated by applying an un-distortion function on the base of the calibration parameters.

The undistorted image is then processed by the two threshold-based segmentation procedures to detect the blue and green marker regions respectively. Segmentation returns a binary image but does not yield any topological information. Thereafter, a labeling technique is used to uniquely label the subsets of connected components. Among the identified regions, the one with the greatest area is associated to the marker mask, while the others are discarded. This will eliminate segmented areas not belonging to the marker. These areas may arise from the reflections of the marker on the metal surface of surgical instruments or on the silicon surface that makes up the internal organs (Fig. 3).

At this stage in [10], the authors apply the Hough transform to detect the straight lines associated to the profiles of the entire instrument. In the first video frame, they apply the Hough transform to the whole image and then in a sub-window taking into account the output of a Kalman filter to speed up the process. This step is not optimal for our set-up due to the inhomogeneous background. As showed in Fig. 4 (up) false straight lines not belonging to the instrument profile may be wrongly recognized by the Hough algorithm.

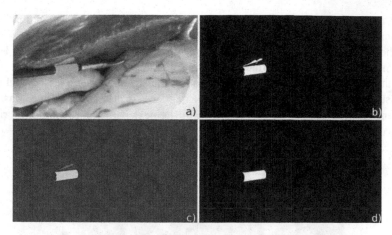

Fig. 3. (a) An image captured by the simulator laparoscope. (b) Image segmentation is altered by the reflection. (c) Labeling algorithm discerns the topologically separate areas. (d) Marker mask not affected by reflections in the starting image. (Color figure online)

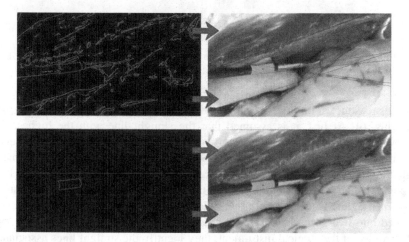

Fig. 4. (Up) application of the Canny detector to the whole image and corresponding identification of straight lines through Hough transform. (Down) application of the Canny detector to the segmented marker region and the corresponding identification of straight lines through Hough transform

In laparoscopic operations, the field of view (FOV) is usually very strict in order to magnify the view itself (Fig. 5). Therefore, the estimation of the lines passing through the profiles of markers is a good approximation of the profiles of the entire laparoscopic instrument. For this reason, we determine the straight lines applying the Hough transform only to the segmented regions corresponding to the markers. In this way, we drastically reduce the computational cost and, at the same time, we find only straight lines corresponding to the laparoscopic instrument (and not corresponding to the background as in the original version).

In the original version, the two straight lines with higher value in the Hough transform accumulator are identified as the two marker profiles. Nevertheless, it may happen that the two lines with the highest Hough transform are being associated to the same instrument profile (Fig. 5). When this happens, instrument tracking, based on instrument profiles knowledge (as described in the next paragraph), cannot be rightly performed.

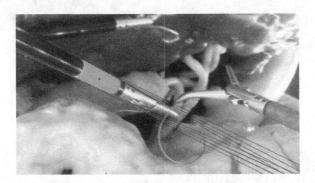

Fig. 5. Wrong identification of the instrument profiles selecting the 2 lines with higher Hough transform value: both red lines correspond to a single profile. (Color figure online)

For this reason, we improved the method to prevent wrong labeling of the marker profiles (Fig. 6). At first, it is assumed that the straight line with the highest accumulator value corresponds to one of the two instrument profiles (*profile 1*). Then, the algorithm determines the *perpendicular line* to the identified *profile 1* and passing through the *barycenter* of the region corresponding to the marker (detected after segmentation). The *points of intersection* of the *perpendicular line* with all the straight lines returned by the Hough transform are identified. Finally, the *points of intersection* are divided into two groups via K-mean clustering. The two clusters of points appear on both profiles of the surgical instrument: they identify the straight lines associated to the opposite profiles 1 and 2. In this way, it is possible to identify the straight lines associated to *profile 2* as those contained in the second cluster of points (which does not contain *profile 1*). The straight line relative to *profile 2* is then chosen from this second cluster selecting the straight line with the highest value of the Hough transform.

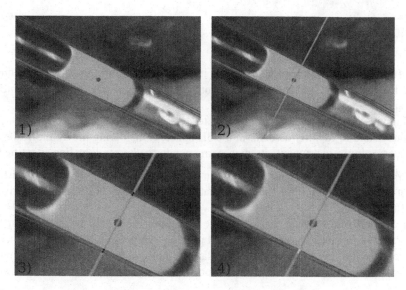

Fig. 6. Opposite profiles identification improvement: (1) Identification of the *profile 1*; (2) detection of the *perpendicular line* passing through the *barycenter* of the segmented region; (3) Intersection of the *perpendicular line* with all the straight lines returned by the Hough transform; (4) Profile 2 is identified via K-mean clustering.

2.3   Tracking of the Tip of the Surgical Instrument

The apparent diameters of the surgical instrument are used to estimate the marker depth. The *main axis* of the instrument on the image is calculated as the median line between *profile 1* and *profile 2*. The points of intersection of the *main axis* with the segmented region of the marker determine points A and B (Fig. 7). Then it is possible to determine the lines perpendiculars to the main axis and passing through A and B. These lines intersect the instrument profiles respectively in A_1, A_2 and B_1, B_2. Segments $\overline{A_1A_2}$ and $\overline{B_1B_2}$ approximatively correspond to the projection of the marker diameter in correspondence of A and B, and can be used to estimate the depth of their corresponding position in the 3-D space, as expressed in [10]:

$$Z_{A'} \approx d \frac{f_x f_y}{\sqrt{\left[(u_{A_1} - u_{A_2})f_y\right]^2 + \left[(v_{A_1} - v_{A_2})f_x\right]^2}}, \qquad (1)$$

where d is the actual diameter of the laparoscopic instrument, f_x and f_y, are the horizontal and vertical focal lengths respectively, while u_{A1}, v_{A1}, u_{A2} and v_{A2} are the coordinates on the image corresponding to A_1 and A_2: $A_1 = (u_{A_1}, v_{A_1})$, $A_2 = (u_{A_2}, v_{A_2})$. After the estimation of $Z_{A'}$ it is possible to determine:

$$X_{A'} = (u_A - c_x)\frac{Z_{A'}}{f_x}, \qquad (2)$$

$$Y_{A'} = (v_A - c_y)\frac{Z_{A'}}{f_y}, \tag{3}$$

where u_A, and v_A are the coordinates on the image corresponding to A, while c_x and c_y are the horizontal and vertical displacements of the optical axis from the center of coordinates.

Using the same equations it is possible to determine $X_{B'}$, $Y_{B'}$, and $Z_{B'}$.

Points A' and B' identify a vector in the 3D space. Considering the cylindrical shape of the laparoscopic instrument, its axis corresponds to the straight line identified by vector $\overrightarrow{A'B'}$ and the instrument tip lies on this line. Knowing the actual distance between the instrument tip P' and the marker, its spatial coordinates are trivially derived (Fig. 7).

We can perform a sanity check after the estimation of the tip position P' on each image frame taking into account current and previous tip positions. The sanity check is performed discharging tip positions estimations not compatible with the physical dimensions of the simulator or in case of too fast movements.

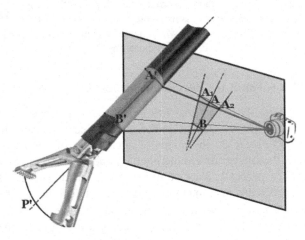

Fig. 7. Perspective projection of the points identified for estimating the position of the instrument tip (point P') and corresponding points in 3-D space

Tracking Correction at the Image Edges. In general, the whole marker should be visible to performs surgical instrument tracking. However, the implemented method works as long as the Hough transform is able to identify the profiles of the instrument. Applying some precautions, the tracking of the marker can proceed even when the latter is at the borders of the camera FOV, and it is only partially visible in the scene. In these conditions, the straight line at the image border may be wrongly identified as *profile 1* of the instrument (Fig. 8a). The lines whose Hough parameters fall within the ranges of the image edges are therefore excluded in advance. In this way the colored marker can be localized even if it is only partially displayed in the scene (Fig. 8b).

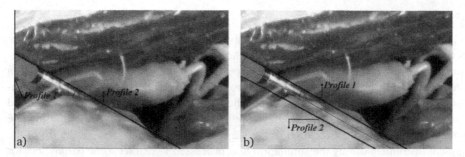

Fig. 8. Particular case with the marker partially contained in camera FOV. (a) Wrong detection of the profiles of the laparoscopic instrument on the image edge. (b) Proper identification of the profiles as a result of the exclusion of straight lines generated by the image edges (Color figure online)

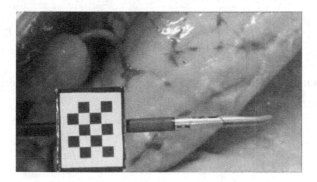

Fig. 9. Pattern used for obtaining the reference estimates

2.4 Accuracy Evaluation

The following section describes the validation tests performed in the realistic environment provided by the cholecystectomy simulator. Our solution has been validated through using a "chessboard" pattern, commonly used in AR applications, as gold standard. As shown in Fig. 9, the pattern was secured on a rigid support and attached to the laparoscopic instrument. Before proceeding with the test, the position of the laparoscopic instrument tip was mechanically calibrated (with a caliper) to both the marker and the grid reference. This configuration allows a direct comparison between the results obtained from the two tracking methods. The validation experiment was performed by randomly moving inside the cholecystectomy simulator and by simultaneously tracking the colored marker and the "chessboard" pattern. A total of 100 images were acquired and processed by the algorithm.

2.5   Robustness Evaluation

Experimental tests were conducted to analyze the robustness and suitability of the method for the evaluation of surgeons in the laparoscopic cholecystectomy intervention. The test involved two surgeons while performing the ligature of the cystic duct, a fundamental step of this surgical procedure. The test required the use of two laparoscopic grasping forceps, which were modified through the application of the colored markers. Figure 10 shows few frames captured during the test and highlighting the fundamental steps in the execution of the surgical knot. The trajectory of the tip of the surgical instrument during the simulation was processed to extract some parameters for the surgical performance evaluation. Path length D, normalized Jerk J, as well as task execution time T and time spent outside the camera FOV are calculated. The Path length D is the total length of the path taken by the tip of the surgical instrument. Chmarra et al. [20] have shown that this value is able to discern surgeons groups with different experience and is calculated as:

$$D = \int_0^T \sqrt{\left[\left(\frac{dX}{dt}\right)^2 + \left(\frac{dY}{dt}\right)^2 + \left(\frac{dZ}{dt}\right)^2 \right]} \, dt. \tag{4}$$

The Jerk J characterizes the smoothness of the movement and its normalized form [4] is obtained as:

$$J = \sqrt{\frac{T^5}{2D^2} \int_0^T \left[\left(\frac{d^3X}{d^3t}\right)^2 + \left(\frac{d^3Y}{d^3t}\right)^2 + \left(\frac{d^3Z}{d^3t}\right)^2 \right] dt}. \tag{5}$$

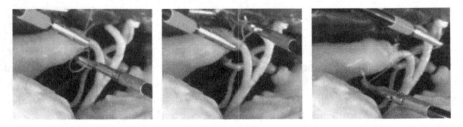

Fig. 10. Pictures taken during the experimental tests: the three sequential images illustrate the basic steps in the surgical knot execution.

3   Results

3.1   Accuracy

The accuracy of the tracking method was evaluated by analyzing the deviation of the tip coordinates obtained through our tracking method from the coordinates obtained through the gold standard method. Figure 11 shows points corresponding to the laparoscopic instrument tip. Pink points result from the "chessboard" pattern tracking whereas blue points result from the colored marker tracking method. Table 1 lists the average error and the standard deviation obtained via the new tracking method. Much of the data variability can be attributed to the Z coordinate error. Although the average error along the three directions is comparable, the standard deviation along Z is greater. This is due to the different way by which the depth is estimated: Z coordinate is estimated from the apparent diameter at the ends of the marker, the others are directly derived by the position of the 3D point in the image. Depth resolve through projective images is always an issue.

Table 1. The mean error and the standard deviation of each translational degree of freedom

	X	Y	Z
Mean	0.55 [mm]	0.24 [mm]	1.77 [mm]
Standard deviation	4.07 [mm]	1.82 [mm]	16.93 [mm]

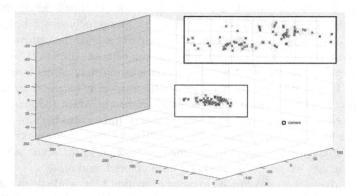

Fig. 11. Method quantitative validation results: Pink dots correspond to the instrument tip position obtained through the "chessboard" pattern. Blue points show the instrument tip position obtained through the colored marker. (Color figure online)

3.2   Robustness

Figure 12 shows an image processed by the algorithm. The arrows on the image plane correspond to vectors $\overrightarrow{AB}$ of each laparoscopic instrument as a result of the image processing. The figure highlights the projective geometry related to the 3-D localization of points A' and B'. The black straight lines represent the projection rays of points A and B. The Z coordinate estimate allows the localization of A' and B' in 3-D space therefore identifying $\overrightarrow{A'B'}$ vectors. The vectors are shown by the green and the blue arrows according to the color of the corresponding marker. The laparoscopic instruments tips, represented by points P_L and P_R in Fig. 12, are located along the direction of these vectors.

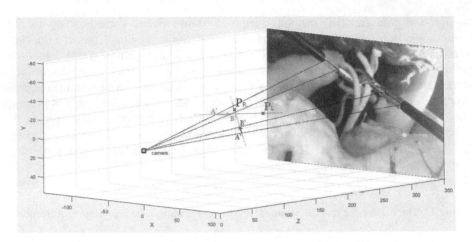

Fig. 12. Reconstruction process of the 3-D position starting from the identification of the colored markers in the image (Color figure online)

To verify the reliability of the algorithm, the frames captured during the experimental tests were divided into three groups. The first group includes the images where the marker is completely in the scene without any parts outside the camera FOV. The frames where the marker is not properly localized can be considered as *false negatives*. In the second group, the images where the marker is completely absent from the scene are collected. In this case, the frames in which the marker is localized correspond to *false positives*. Finally, the third group contains frames in which the marker is only partially displayed (because a part of it falls outside of the camera FOV or it is hidden by the other instrument or by an anatomical part). In this group, the images in which the marker was correctly located or was identified as external to the scene are assessed. Table 2 summarizes the results obtained for each colored marker.

False negatives are mostly limited to cases of motion blur, while thanks to the use of fluorescent paint for the colored markers, *false positives* has not occurred. Regarding the last group of frames, the visible part of the marker is not always enough to provide the data needed to a proper localization and so the performance is very bad in respect to the previous two groups, but, in any case, marker visibility should be a must in case of marker based tracking.

The tracking method has proven robust and through the processing of the tip trajectory it was possible to obtain the parameters characterizing the surgical performance. The extracted parameters are shown in Table 3.

Table 2. Error statistics: *False negatives* correspond to cases in which the marker is wrongly localized although it is completely displayed in the image. *False positives* correspond to cases where the marker 3D position is located within the simulator though it does not appear within the image. *Wrong partial detection* refers to frames in which the marker, partially displayed in the image, has not been correctly located.

Experiment run	Surgeon 1		Surgeon 2	
Error statistics	Green marker	Blue marker	Green marker	Blue marker
False negative	0 %	0.18 %	0.96 %	0 %
False positive	0 %	0 %	0 %	0 %
Wrong partial detection	31.67 %	23.83 %	13.8 %	12.66 %

Table 3. Parameters for the evaluation of the surgical performance

Experiment run	Surgeon 1		Surgeon 2	
Parameters	Green marker	Blue marker	Green marker	Blue marker
Path length [mm]	3530	3790	1580	1360
Time outside FOV [s]	0.5	8.5	0.5	1
Normalized Jerk	$9.36 \ 10^5$	$1.19 \ 10^6$	$8.56 \ 10^6$	$6.50 \ 10^5$
Time [s]	106		78	

4   Conclusions

In this work some fundamental improvements in respect to a previous work for the tracking of laparoscopic surgical tools using colored strips are described. The implemented method is consistent with the results obtained from [10] although the latter uses a simulator that provides a background less noisy that simplifies the tracking. Our improvements can be summarized in: (1) identification of the straight lines in the segmented region of the marker and not on the entire image; (2) use of the K-mean clustering to rightly identify the two profiles; (3) Tracking correction at the image edges.

Thanks to our improvements, the method allows performing the tracking of surgical instruments even in noisy and realistic environments such like the one provided by the cholecystectomy simulator developed at the EndoCAS center.

Acknowledgement. This research work was supported by VALVETECH project, FAS fund – Tuscany Region (Realization of a newly developed polymeric aortic valve, implantable through robotic platform with minimally invasive surgical techniques) and SThARS project, grant "Ricerca finalizzata e Giovani ricercatori 2011–2012" Young Researchers - Italian Ministry of Health (Surgical Training in identification and isolation of deformable tubular structures with hybrid Augmented Reality Simulation).

References

1. Freschi, C., et al.: Technical review of the da Vinci surgical telemanipulator. Int. J. Med. Robot. Comput. Assist. Surg. **9**(4), 396–406 (2013)
2. Champion, H.R., Gallagher, A.G.: Surgical simulation—a 'good idea whose time has come'. Br. J. Surg. **90**(7), 767–768 (2003)
3. Kneebone, R.: Simulation in surgical training: educational issues and practical implications. Med. Educ. **37**(3), 267–277 (2003)
4. Cavallo, F., et al.: Biomechanics-machine learning system for surgical gesture analysis and development of technologies for minimal access surgery. Surg. Innov. **21**(5), 504–512 (2014)
5. Lahanas, V., Georgiou, E., Loukas, C.: Surgical simulation training systems: box trainers, virtual reality and augmented reality simulators. Int. J. Adv. Robot. Automn. **1**, 1–9 (2016)
6. Moglia, A., et al.: Patient specific surgical simulator for the evaluation of the movability of bimanual robotic arms. Stud. Health Technol. Inform. **163**, 379–385 (2011)
7. Turini, G., et al.: Patient-specific surgical simulator for the pre-operative planning of single-incision laparoscopic surgery with bimanual robots. Comput. Aided Surg. **17**(3), 103–112 (2012)
8. Ferrari, V., et al.: Augmented reality visualization of deformable tubular structures for surgical simulation. Int. J. Med. Robot. Comput. Assist. Surg. **12**, 231–240 (2015)
9. Allan, M., Chang, P.-L., Ourselin, S., Hawkes, D.J., Sridhar, A., Kelly, J., Stoyanov, D.: Image based surgical instrument pose estimation with multi-class labelling and optical flow. In: Navab, N., Hornegger, J., Wells, W.M., Frangi, A.F. (eds.) MICCAI 2015. LNCS, vol. 9349, pp. 331–338. Springer, Cham (2015). doi:10.1007/978-3-319-24553-9_41
10. Loukas, C., Lahanas, V., Georgiou, E.: An integrated approach to endoscopic instrument tracking for augmented reality applications in surgical simulation training. Int. J. Med. Robot. **9**(4), e34–e51 (2013)
11. Viglialoro, R.M., Condino, S., Gesi, M., Ferrari, M., Ferrari, V.: Augmented reality simulator for laparoscopic cholecystectomy training. In: De Paolis, L.T., Mongelli, A. (eds.) AVR 2014. LNCS, vol. 8853, pp. 428–433. Springer, Cham (2014). doi:10.1007/978-3-319-13969-2_33
12. Viglialoro, R.M., et al.: AR visualization of "Synthetic Calot's Triangle" for training in cholecystectomy. In: 12th IASTED International Conference on Biomedical Engineering. BioMed, Austria (2016)
13. Viglialoro, R.M., et al.: A physical patient specific simulator for cholecystectomy training. In: Computer Assisted Radiology and Surgery (CARS) (2012)
14. Condino, S., Viglialoro, R.M., Fani, S., Bianchi, M., Morelli, L., Ferrari, M., Bicchi, A., Ferrari, V.: Tactile augmented reality for arteries palpation in open surgery training. In: Zheng, G., Liao, H., Jannin, P., Cattin, P., Lee, S.-L. (eds.) MIAR 2016. LNCS, vol. 9805, pp. 186–197. Springer, Cham (2016). doi:10.1007/978-3-319-43775-0_17
15. Condino, S., et al.: How to build patient-specific synthetic abdominal anatomies. An innovative approach from physical toward hybrid surgical simulators. Int. J. Med. Robot. **7**(2), 202–213 (2011)
16. Kyriakoulis, N., Gasteratos, A.: Light-invariant 3D object's pose estimation using color distance transform. In: IEEE International Conference Imaging Systems and Techniques (IST) (2010)
17. Diotte, B., et al.: Multi-modal intra-operative navigation during distal locking of intramedullary nails. IEEE Trans. Med. Imaging **34**(2), 487–495 (2015)

18. Cutolo, F., et al.: Robust and accurate algorithm for wearable stereoscopic augmented reality with three indistinguishable markers. Electronics **5**(3) (2016). Article number 59
19. Zhang, Z.: A flexible new technique for camera calibration. IEEE Trans. Pattern Anal. Mach. Intell. **22**(11), 1330–1334 (2000)
20. Chmarra, M.K., et al.: Retracting and seeking movements during laparoscopic goal-oriented movements. Is the shortest path length optimal? Surg. Endosc. **22**(4), 943–949 (2008)

Natural User Interface to Assess Social Skills in Autistic Population

Claudia Faita[(⊠)], Raffaello Brondi, Camilla Tanca, Marcello Carrozzino, and Massimo Bergamasco

Institute of Communication, Information and Perception Technologies, Scuola Superiore Sant'Anna, Perceptual Robotics Laboratory, Pisa, Italy {c.faita,r.brondi,c.tanca,m.carrozzino,m.bergamasco}@santannapisa.it

Abstract. The children suffering of autism spectrum disorder (ASD) present several limitations in social communication and interactive skills. State of the art showed that Virtual Reality (VR) represents a valid alternative to learn social skills in ASD. In particular VR offers the advantage to simulate daily life interaction in a replicable and controlled environment. In this paper, we present a novel methodology to evaluate social competence in ASD based on the immersive VR system, featuring natural interaction. The VR system is based on the theoretical model which aims to evaluate the intersubjective interchange in everyday relationship between autistic population and the surrounding environment. We suggest that this technological setup can be a useful tool to increase social competence in ASD and it can become a sophisticated outcome measurement tool for studying the improvement of social competence.

Keywords: Virtual reality · Immersive virtual environment · Natural interaction · Autism spectrum disorder · Social skills training

1 Introduction

Autism Spectrum Disorder (ASD) is a developmental disorder diagnosed on the basis of early-emerging social and communication impairments and rigid and repetitive patterns of behaviour and interests [1]. The first manifestation of ASD appears when the infant starts to interact with the surrounding world. ASD children show a low level of interest toward the environment, the caregivers and the other persons, and they have reduced abilities in social communication and interaction [2]. Because of the great difference in the level of impairments severity, the early diagnosis is very difficult. In particular social communication deficits have been related to limitation in interactive activities involving social attention and responsiveness to social reward [3]. Prelinguistic pattern of communication and the coordination of joint attention are severely compromised. People suffering of autism spectrum disorder are not able to interact with others because they do not understand the implicit processes of interpersonal coordination that occur during social interaction with others [4,5].

© Springer International Publishing AG 2017
L.T. De Paolis et al. (Eds.): AVR 2017, Part II, LNCS 10325, pp. 144–154, 2017.
DOI: 10.1007/978-3-319-60928-7_12

Because of the safe environment and nature of simulation experience, Virtual Reality (VR) provides a helpful tool for the autistic population. In particular, the Virtual Environment (VE) acts on two fronts: on one side it replicates the relationships occurring in the "real world", secondly it reduces the source of anxiety provided by the real practice [6]. Moreover, some people with ASD, especially the young children appear to prefer multimedia environments where they can actively participate as protagonists [7]. Also, thanks to the strong sense of presence, VE is accepted as a copy of reality [8]. Due to the spread of virtual reality on a commercial level and the consequent reduction of costs, VR is starting to be used in the field of autism research. More recently the spreading of devices interfacing VR user's (especially in VR game industry) using the innate human means of communication (e.g. voice and gestures), has empowered paradigms of natural interaction, namely Natural User Interfaces (NUIs), which relevantly impact both on communication and immersion [9]. The combination of highly immersive technology with NUI metaphor can substantially enhance social presence and empathy during social interaction in VR-game experience [10]. For this reason, we suppose that it might be an useful device to train social skills in ASD population. However, in the field of VR applications for ASD there is the emergence of a common methodology in order to improve the effectiveness of the studies.

In this paper an immersive VR system, featuring natural interaction aimed at evaluating and training social skills in ASD is presented. Moreover, a methodological approach for the use of VR for the investigation of social impairments in autism is provided.

In the following: first the state of the art in the VR application for autism then the technological setup fostering natural interaction in immersive VE together with the designed methodology are presented. Finally, the guideline for a user study and a general discussion for future applications are provided.

1.1   State of the Art

VR applications have demonstrated to be useful tools to investigate the social impairments in autism spectrum disorders. A lot of researches showed that VR can be used as enhanced learning environments, mainly for training social skills [11]. The first relevant pilot research making use of virtual reality system for ASD goes back to 1996. [12] investigated the level of acceptance and the ability to identify cars and colors in a three different virtual scenes. He found that children put on the helmets without any problem and completed the tasks properly (they identified car colors correctly even when they were presented different street scenes). Based on this preliminary good result, the following researches concentrated more on the investigation of the social patterns in ASD by using VR applications. [13] used a collaborative VE to evaluate the ability of autistic children to recognize emotions presented by the avatars (e.g. facial expressions) and to operate in the virtual context. Participants were successful at both operating the avatars, recognizing the emotions expressed by them, and identifying the appropriate context for those emotions. [14] used another collaborative VE, where autistic children participated in a virtual classroom with their avatar, and the avatar of a teacher. Social competence learning was evaluated, with encouraging results, in terms of the ability to listen to others, eye-contact, and understanding of others expressions and behaviors. Also the capability of joint attention with a virtual character has been studied in children with the autistic spectrum [15], showing that a virtual character in a VE may be perceived by young children with ASD as an intentional being. These children can learn to follow an avatar gaze and gesture cues, and can respond to them by means of a touch screen interface. [16] showed that autistic people were capable of recognizing avatars mental and emotional states by means of their facial expressions. Moreover, some researches demonstrated that VEs can represent powerful learning tools for children with ASD because the interaction, for example in terms of collaboration affordances, offered by VEs is highly accepted by autistic patients. VR applications, while offering a protected and safe setting, are capable of providing an ecological and controlled scenario for practicing tasks connected to the skills to be learned [17,18].

We believe that the effectiveness of VEs in ASD treatment can be utterly enhanced by the use of immersive virtual technologies such as CAVE-like systems or Head Mounted Displays (HMD). Recent studies have shown indeed that the immersion in VE enhances the social understanding and improve the social competences in individuals with ASDs [19,20].

All the presented works highlight several benefit of the use of VR technology in order to enhance and train social communication skills in the autistic population. The spreading of depth cameras and sensorized controllers is providing more natural form of communication with VE. Being able to naturally interact with the virtual objects is extremely important for person with social impairments because it permits to simulate the every day interaction with the surrounding world. Even more importantly, a natural interface with the virtual environment can create deeply benefits the social interaction. Because of the new richer interaction capabilities, NUI are becoming popular in the field of game industries. When coupled with immersive visualization system like HMD, the overall effect on the user experience in terms of immersion, social presence, flow and engagement is greatly improved [21]. For this reasons, new technologies offer powerful alternatives to enable new ways of communication. We suppose that the new NUIs combined with immersive IVEs can be a powerful alternatives to enhance social skills in ASD.

However, some issues such as the identification of the ASD sample and the creation of an organic methodology for assessing the effect of VR technology on ASD patients remain to be clarified. In fact, ASD is characterized by a wide range of impairments both in terms of typology and severity. Differences in the results obtained by [22,23] comparing user experiences for study conversation skills, revealed the importance of screening participants in order to sufficient ability to perform the tasks administered in the VE [24]. At the same time, the technological setup must be calibrated based on the social impairments and level of disability of the ASD patients. [24] provided the emergence of both a common terminology and a theoretical-based research questions to investigate the use of technologies for the treatment of autism research.

Starting from the above experimental framework and theoretical background this paper analyzed the possibility of adopting NUI-metaphor + IVE-technology in a wider research framework to assess social skills in the domain of autism spectrum disorder. Within this general goal the study also proposes a methodology for the evaluation of the novel technology and the creation of an experimental setup for the study of social impairments in autistic population. More in detail, the main hypotheses explored by this research are:

- **natural user interaction**: new interaction metaphor in Immersive VEs may be developed to elicit social communication skills in ASD;
- **interaction with virtual agent**: responsive virtual agent verbally communicate with the user depending on the performance;
- **methodological approach**: based on theoretical assumption the experimental protocol is designed to evaluate new technology in the field of ASD

In order to answer the above questions a technological setup has been designed in order to train social skills in the autistic population. In this paper we proposed an example of a protocol in which a user, helped by a virtual agent, must complete a puzzle game by using his own hand.

2 The Project

The goal of the project is to design a experimental setup based on NUI metaphor in order to enrich the IVE-based training program and transfer social skills to ASD. The procedure we adopted is summarize in the Fig. 1

In this section, the theoretical approached with related research questions are shown. Then the appropriate sample of users are described followed by the technological setup explanation. At the end the protocol experimental that we will adopt is illustrated.

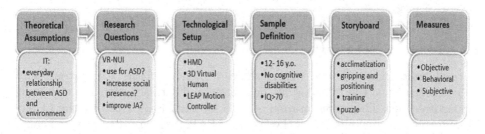

Fig. 1. Workflow of the methodological approach we adopted to design the experiment.

2.1 Theoretical Assumption and Experimental Questions

To date, the main theoretical approach to investigate cognitive and behavioral patterns of ASD is based on Theory Theory (TT) account, supporting the idea that the autistic population is not able to indirectly infer other persons' mental states by observing their external behavior [25, 26]. This approach does not explain the pre-theoretical/sensory-motor capabilities for understanding others and it left important questions unanswered [27]. By moving the problem from the mentalization to the perception, Interaction Theory (IT) explains the ASD pathology as a lack of pre-reflective embodied relationship of self and other that emerge in bi-personal interaction [28]. Based on the idea that we have a direct access to the other minds, IT claims that social impairments in ASD consist of the inability to understand the inner state of the other person through its overt behaviors. According to IT approach, we argue that the assessment of the cognitive patterns of social interaction and the rehabilitation process should be conducted taking into account the everyday relationship between autistic population and the surrounding environment. In particular, the inability in joint attention, imitation, attention to the peers, and the tendency to the isolation must be comprehended in the field of intersubjective interchange with the other during everyday-life. Because of the safety environment and replicability of social activities, VR can promote learning of social skills. Moreover, we believe that the use of a NUI metaphor, by facilitating the interaction with virtual objects and social agents, can improve the ecological validity of the virtual experience and produce improvement in social competences. For this purposes we have implemented a setup based on NUI and IVE paradigm for the ASD population. The user helped by a virtual-peer should complete a virtual puzzle game. In order to understand the game mechanism and to complete the puzzle, the participants must tackle joint attention tasks. Th research questions underline the entire experiments are the following:

– VR-NUI paradigm can be easily used from ASD children?
– VR-NUI paradigm can increase the level of social presence?
– VR-NUI paradigm can improve the joint attention abilities in habitual cooperative tasks?

2.2 Technological Set-Up

Natural Interaction was used during the development of the VR system. The user can grasp the tile by using his own hand and interact with the object in the environment. The representation of the user hand is provided by the LEAP Motion controller mounted on a HMD. The LEAP, making use of infrared camera, tracks the movement of hands and fingers with very low latency, converting them into 3D input[1]. The virtual scenario made of a room with a big windows and a desk located at the north side. Behind the desktop is present a virtual

---

[1] https://www.leapmotion.com/product/vr/.

agent which explains and helps the user to complete the task. The VE was created by using the Unity game engine, a cross-platform game engine developed by Unity Technologies[2]. The $3D$ virtual human model from Rocketbox library (Rocketbox Studios GmbH, Hannover) was animated through motion capture data from The Carnegie Mellon University Motion Capture (CMU) Database. CMU is a collection of a multimodal samples of everyday human actions and behaviors created with a Vicon Motion Capture System with 12 infrared mix-40 cameras, each one recording 4 mp images at 120 Hz [29]. The animations were retargeted, mounted and looped in order to create the body movements (pointing, gazing and natural idle position). For the facial animation Faceshift studio[3] a tool for high quality markerless motion capture and Microsoft Kinect sensor has been used [30]. The software also provides a plugin to bind the animations recorded to a custom model, both using morphtarget or facial bones. The body and facial animation has been made for mimicking the natural human movement.

2.3 Selection of ASD Sample

In the field of autism spectrum disorder, the HMD setup presents several limitation in particular in (i)- the heaviness on the user head and (ii)- the total occlusion of sight. Moreover the NUI metaphor foresee typical hands skills. In general the VR-NUI device can be used with patients with high cognitive functions. In the last version of Diagnostic and Statistical Manual of Mental Disorders $(DSM-5)$ the category "high-functioning" was abolished [31]. Conversely, $DSM-5$ identifies three different levels of severity based on social communication skills and restricted, repetitive behaviors. The individuals who are diagnosed with a level 3 have difficulties initiating social interactions, and clear examples of atypical or unsuccessful response to social overtures of others. They may appear to have decreased interest in social interactions. Moreover, they present significant difficulties in switching between activities and problems of organization and planning hamper independence.

In the previous researches in which VR-HMD devices were used, all the participants were target in general terms as as autistic subjects with high cognitive functions. We consider adapt to the study the individuals without cognitive disability with a level of diagnose of 3. Because of the helmet's size the technological set-up can not be worn by very young children. For this reason, the appropriate sample for these kind of research is composed by adolescents aged between $12-16$ with IQ more than 70, without cognitive disabilities.

2.4 Storyboard

The experimental task consist of the composition of a virtual jigsaw puzzle. The participant is located in a virtual room and a Virtual Character (VC) is located in front of him (as shown in Fig. 4). The procedure is divided in four phases, as followed:

---

[2] https://www.unity3d.com/.
[3] https://www.faceshift.com.

1. acclimatization
2. gripping and positioning
3. training
4. jigsaw puzzle game

In the first phase (a) the virtual character, called "Gino", introduce both himself and the system. Gino invites the participant to look and navigate all around. The goal of this phase is training the user comfortable with the VE and increase the sense of immersion and adaptation. In (b), the virtual agent explains the gripping mechanism and points at the tile that the user must grasp and position. During this phase there are two first Joint Attention (JA) task: (1)- virtual agent points at the tile to grip; (2)- virtual agent points the place holders where positioning the tiles. During the phase (c) there is the third JA task: VA points and gazes at the right tile to grip and indicate the right box to position the tile. The game starts when the Training session is ended (d). In this phase the user had to complete the jigsaw puzzle. The solution is placed in the right part of the desk, the tiles in the middle and the place holders are on the left. During the game the virtual agent does not help the user and remains behind the desk without speaking. The game finished when the entire puzzle is completed (Figs. 2 and 3).

Fig. 2. The user are pinching the tile during the completion of the jigsaw puzzle game

2.5   Evaluation Method

In order to evaluate the social interaction of ASD users with both the environment and the virtual agent, the following data will be collected:

- Objective Measures: task performances like tiles right placed; number of error; completion time; time tiles location;
- Behavioral Measures: joint attention abilities and attention to VC suggestion, and body movement;
- Subjective Measures: pre and post experience questionnaires and after experience interview to evaluate the interaction with environment and virtual agent.

Fig. 3. Testing session: joint attention task during the training phase

Fig. 4. Screenshot of the virtual environment. The position of the user is indicated with the symbol of the camera

The objective measures are collected automatically by the system during the game experience. Joint attention and attention to VC are evaluated by measuring head orientation during specific tasks. Moreover, the body movements are recorded using Kinect motion sensing device. The psychologist participated to the entire experimental procedure and he observes and collects information about the participants' behavior. After experience, a questionnaire to evaluate social presence, level of immersion and enjoyment during the game must be complete. Also, the user answers to an informal interview carried out by the experimenters. The interview topics are: the use of NUI technology; the sense of presence; the difficulty to perform the task; the interaction with the $3D$ characters.

3   Discussion and Future Works

In this paper was presented a VR system, featuring natural interaction aimed at evaluating and training social skills in children affected by autism. The lack of ecological validity in clinical investigation has stressed the exigence of a new methodology to assess social impairments in ASD. Because of simulation feature, VE revealed a enhanced tool to overcome this limitation. In fact, previous researches showed that VR can be used to study the behavior of autistic people by replicating context of everyday social interaction and the relationship with the surrounding environment [22].

The novelty introduced in our study is the introduction of a NUI metaphor in VR application for the investigation of social impairments in ASD. Based on the IT theoretical model we have adopted three main principles for the development of VR application:

- the metaphor of interaction with the environment must respect the rules of naturalness;
- interacting with the avatar should be based on the principles of joint attention;
- the evaluation method should be based on a phenomenological model (Interactive Theory Approach).

In order to fulfill these principles we have created an application in which ASD users complete a jigsaw puzzle game with own hands completely immersed in a virtual environments. Moreover, during the experience a virtual character helps participant to grasp and put the tile in the correct position.

We believe that this methodology may improve social skills of users for the following reason: (i)- the completion of the task requires a social communication between the participant and the virtual character; (ii)- the increasing of both the enjoyment and the sense of co-presence as a natural interaction effect [21] may stimulate the development of social skills; (iii)- the realism and the naturalness of VE create the conditions for a transfer of the acquire skills in the real world. A future study aims at demonstrating the ability of our system to elicit social skills will be carried out on a sample of ASD children that satisfied the cognitive characteristic described.

The application can also be used as outcome tool in ASD children by collecting and decoding a stream of data during controlled lifelike social interaction activities and it can become a sophisticated and personal measurement tool for studying the improvement of social competence.

References

1. Frith, U., Happé, F.: Autism spectrum disorder. Curr. Biol. **15**(19), R786–R790 (2005)
2. Wing, L.: The autistic spectrum. Lancet **350**(9093), 1761 (1997)
3. Chevallier, C., Parish-Morris, J., McVey, A., Rump, K.M., Sasson, N.J., Herrington, J.D., Schultz, R.T.: Measuring social attention and motivation in autism spectrum disorder using eye-tracking: stimulus type matters. Autism Res. **8**(5), 620–628 (2015)
4. Schilbach, L., Timmermans, B., Reddy, V., Costall, A., Bente, G., Schlicht, T., Vogeley, K.: Toward a second-person neuroscience. Behav. Brain Sci. **36**(04), 393–414 (2013)
5. Sebanz, N., Bekkering, H., Knoblich, G.: Joint action: bodies and minds moving together. Trends Cogn. Sci. **10**(2), 70–76 (2006)
6. Strickland, D.: Virtual reality for the treatment of autism. Stud. Health Technol. Inform. **44**, 81–86 (1997)
7. Mineo, B.A., Ziegler, W., Gill, S., Salkin, D.: Engagement with electronic screen media among students with autism spectrum disorders. J. Autism Dev. Disord. **39**(1), 172–187 (2009)
8. Bölte, S., Golan, O., Goodwin, M.S., Zwaigenbaum, L.: What can innovative technologies do for autism spectrum disorders? Autism **14**(3), 155–159 (2010)
9. Brondi, R., Avveduto, G., Carrozzino, M., Tecchia, F., Alem, L., Bergamasco, M.: Immersive technologies and natural interaction to improve serious games engagement. In: De Gloria, A., Veltkamp, R. (eds.) GALA 2015. LNCS, vol. 9599, pp. 121–130. Springer, Cham (2016). doi:10.1007/978-3-319-40216-1_13
10. Brondi, R., Alem, L., Avveduto, G., Faita, C., Carrozzino, M., Tecchia, F., Bergamasco, M.: Evaluating the impact of highly immersive technologies and natural interaction on player engagement and flow experience in games. In: Chorianopoulos, K., Divitini, M., Hauge, J.B., Jaccheri, L., Malaka, R. (eds.) ICEC 2015. LNCS, vol. 9353, pp. 169–181. Springer, Cham (2015). doi:10.1007/978-3-319-24589-8_13
11. Bellani, M., Fornasari, L., Chittaro, L., Brambilla, P.: Virtual reality in autism: state of the art. Epidemiol. Psychiatr. Sci. **20**(3), 235–238 (2011)
12. Strickland, D., Marcus, L.M., Mesibov, G.B., Hogan, K.: Brief report: two case studies using virtual reality as a learning tool for autistic children. J. Autism Dev. Disord. **26**(6), 651–659 (1996)
13. Moore, D., Cheng, Y., McGrath, P., Powell, N.J.: Collaborative virtual environment technology for people with autism. Focus Autism Dev. Disabil. **20**(4), 231–243 (2005)
14. Cheng, Y., Ye, J.: Exploring the social competence of students with autism spectrum conditions in a collaborative virtual learning environment-the pilot study. Comput. Educ. **54**(4), 1068–1077 (2010)
15. Adolphs, R.: Recognizing emotion from facial expressions: psychological and neurological mechanisms. Behav. Cogn. Neurosci. Reviews **1**(1), 21–62 (2002)
16. Tartaro, A., Cassell, J.: Playing with virtual peers: bootstrapping contingent discourse in children with autism. In: Proceedings of the 8th International Conference on International Conference for the Learning Sciences, International Society of the Learning Sciences, vol. 2, pp. 382–389 (2008)
17. Wallace, S., Parsons, S., Westbury, A., White, K., White, K., Bailey, A.: Sense of presence and atypical social judgments in immersive virtual environments responses of adolescents with autism spectrum disorders. Autism **14**(3), 199–213 (2010)

18. Fornasari, L., Chittaro, L., Ieronutti, L., Cottini, L., Dassi, S., Cremaschi, S., Molteni, M., Fabbro, F., Brambilla, P.: Navigation and exploration of an urban virtual environment by children with autism spectrum disorder compared to children with typical development. Res. Autism Spect. Disord. **7**(8), 956–965 (2013)

19. Lorenzo, G., Pomares, J., Lledó, A.: Inclusion of immersive virtual learning environments and visual control systems to support the learning of students with asperger syndrome. Comput. Educ. **62**, 88–101 (2013)

20. Cheng, Y., Huang, C.-L., Yang, C.-S.: Using a 3D immersive virtual environment system to enhance social understanding and social skills for children with autism spectrum disorders. Focus Autism Dev. Disabil. **30**(4), 222–236 (2015)

21. Brondi, R., Avveduto, G., Alem, L., Faita, C., Carrozzino, M., Tecchia, F., Pisan, Y., Bergamasco, M.: Evaluating the effects of competition vs collaboration on user engagement in an immersive game using natural interaction. In: Proceedings of the 21st ACM Symposium on Virtual Reality Software and Technology, p. 191. ACM (2015)

22. Trepagnier, C., Sebrechts, M., Finkelmeyer, A., Coleman, M., Stewart, W., Werner-Adler, M.: Virtual environments to address autistic social deficits. Annu. Rev. CyberTherapy Telemedicine Decade VR **3**, 101–108 (2005)

23. Cheng, Y., Chiang, H.-C., Ye, J., Cheng, L.-H.: Enhancing empathy instruction using a collaborative virtual learning environment for children with autistic spectrum conditions. Comput. Educ. **55**(4), 1449–1458 (2010)

24. Miller, H.L., Bugnariu, N.L.: Level of immersion in virtual environments impacts the ability to assess and teach social skills in autism spectrum disorder. Cyberpsychology Behav. Soc. Networking **19**(4), 246–256 (2016)

25. Baron-Cohen, S., Leslie, A.M., Frith, U.: Does the autistic child have a "theory of mind"? Cognition **21**(1), 37–46 (1985)

26. Goldman, A.I., et al.: Theory of mind. In: Margolis, E., Samuels, R., Stich, S.P. (eds.) Oxford Handbook of Philosophy. Oxford University Press, UK (2012)

27. Gallagher, S.: Understanding interpersonal problems in autism: Interaction theory as an alternative to theory of mind. Philos. Psychiatry Psychol. **11**(3), 199–217 (2004)

28. Fuchs, T.: Pathologies of intersubjectivity in autism and schizophrenia. J. Conscious. Stud. **22**(1–2), 191–214 (2015)

29. De la Torre, F., Hodgins, J., Bargteil, A., Martin, X., Macey, J., Collado, A., Beltran, P.: Guide to the Carnegie Mellon University multimodal activity (CMU-MMAC) database. Robotics Institute, p. 135 (2008)

30. Bouaziz, S., Wang, Y., Pauly, M.: Online modeling for realtime facial animation. ACM Trans. Graph. (TOG) **32**(4), 40 (2013)

31. Association, A.P., et al.: Diagnostic and Statistical Manual of Mental Disorders (DSM-5®). American Psychiatric Pub, Virginia (2013)

RRT-Based Path Planning for Virtual Bronchoscopy Simulator

Wilbert G. Aguilar[1,2,3(✉)], Vanessa Abad[4], Hugo Ruiz[1,5],
Jenner Aguilar[6], and Fabián Aguilar-Castillo[7]

[1] Departamento de Seguridad y Defensa,
Universidad de las Fuerzas Armadas, ESPE, Sangolquí, Ecuador
wgaguilar@espe.edu.ec
[2] Centro de Investigación, CICTE,
Universidad de las Fuerzas Armadas, ESPE, Sangolquí, Ecuador
[3] Research Group GREC, Universitat Politècnica de Catalunya,
Barcelona, Spain
[4] Departament de Genètica, Universitat de Barcelona, Barcelona, Spain
[5] Purdue University, West Lafayette, IN, USA
[6] Hospital Vicente Corral Moscoso, Cuenca, Ecuador
[7] IESS Hospital General, Machala, Ecuador

Abstract. In this paper, we offer a virtual bronchoscopy simulator as an assistance exploration tool and diagnosis of peripheral lung nodule lesions. We present a proposal for motion planning to a interest region in the lung nodule based on RRT. Navigation will be guided by this path in a 3d virtual lung reconstructed from CT images. We compare several RRT-algorithm looking for the optimal option for the virtual bronchoscopy problem.

Keywords: Path planning · RRT · Computational geometric · Kinematics · Virtual reality · Bronchoscopy

1 Introduction

In recent years, motion planning methods have been applied in several medical fields. This work introduces these methods into bronchoscopy [1, 2]. Bronchoscopy is a diagnostic test that allows lung exploration searching anomalies. The process introduces a flexible device called bronchoscope through the larynx, in order to transport a micro camera for the exploration into the bronchia. Medical doctors need a high training level to perform this process. An alternative proposal is the bronchoscope motion planning during the exploration. In this way, doctors can be guided by a virtual line that shows them the path.

There are multiple approach for solving path planning issues. These methods are classified in two groups: Classic methods [3], and sampling-based methods [4]. For high dimension configurations spaces [5], sampling methods are widely used. Sampling-based methods use representative point sets from the configuration space, and do not require an exact space representation. They are based on free collision sample generation, with a representative configuration from the work space as a

© Springer International Publishing AG 2017
L.T. De Paolis et al. (Eds.): AVR 2017, Part II, LNCS 10325, pp. 155–165, 2017.
DOI: 10.1007/978-3-319-60928-7_13

sample. The Collision detection algorithm [6] is a useful process that guarantees a collision free sample.

Some optimal algorithms are: The Rapidly Exploring Random Trees or communally known as RRTs [7, 8] and the Probabilistic Roadmap Planner or PRMs [9, 10].

We propose to use RRT as path planner because of the internal structure of the lung. In order to determine the solution path, the motion planner has 3 inputs: The reconstructed 3D model from a patient CT images (Computed Tomography), the bronchoscope structure, and the interest region location (target point) in the lung nodule. The system generates a 3D model with the bronchoscope kinematics. The path solution obtained from the RRT will be tracked by the simulated bronchoscope from the start position to the target point. Standard RRT and extended version will be tested.

This article is organized as: In the Sect. 2, we explains virtual model of the bronchoscope as a robot and its kinematics and constrains. Section 3 refers to the RRT planning algorithm and two extended versions, RRT-Connect and RRT of Dynamic Domain. Finally, in the last two Sections, we presents the results, conclusions and future lines of work.

2 Kinematic Modeling

There is necessary to define two main elements: Working Space and Robot.

One of the path planner inputs is a 3D virtual model of the lungs, reconstructed from CT images. Figure 1 shows a virtual model of the work space.

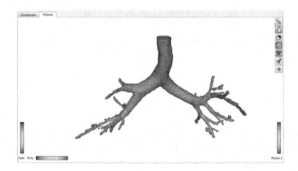

Fig. 1. Bronchia virtual model

For the planning problem, we require the a robot that, in this particular case, is defined by a virtual bronchoscope. The subsection bellow describes the virtual model of the bronchoscope.

2.1 Bronchoscope Model

A bronchoscope is a tubular device with a micro camera. During the bronchoscopy process, the device is inserted by the nose or mouth with the objective of exploring the interior of the respiratory tract looking for anomalies. Once the interest region is located, lung secretions or tissue can be collected for posterior tests.

There are two types of bronchoscopes: rigid and flexible. This work is focused on motion planning for a flexible bronchoscope. The flexible Bronchoscope is formed by optical fiber that transport the light along the bronchoscope.

Fig. 2. Bronchoscope movements

The bronchoscope is modelled as a kinematic chain of three links, where each link is a 2 mm diameter cylinder. The flexible segment of the bronchoscope has the dimensions of the Fig. 2. For the navigation through the irregular structure of the bronchia, the kinematic chain (tip of the bronchoscope) moves by three motion controls:

- *Forward*: The bronchoscope motion is defined by the translation Z in the orientation of the flexible bronchoscope head.
- *Rotation*: This is the rotation of the bronchoscope base around the forward motion Z. In Fig. 2 the rotation motion is α. This movement have not limits but can be defined between $-\pi$ and π.
- *Flexion*: This movement controls the robot joints, between $-\pi/2$ and $\pi/2$. The angle is the sum of θ angles of Fig. 2.

The bronchoscope model has 6° of freedom for the base and 2° for the joints, controlled by to three movements. Two controls affect 6° of freedom of the bronchoscope base, Forward and Rotation. The degree of freedom for the joints is the Flexion. A complex bronchoscope model can be structured by increasing the number of kinematic chain links. A bronchoscope model with 10 links and a 90° Flexion angle is shown on Fig. 3.

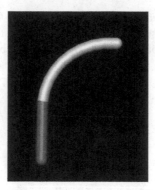

Fig. 3. 10 links Bronchoscope with a 90° Flexion angle.

2.2   Constrained Kinematic Model

The constrains from de model condition the movements of the bronchoscope. The forward motion is a circular movement is a plane defined by α which radius depends on θ. To explain the constrained kinematics, Fig. 4 shows the circular movement generated by these constrains, where:

- ΔZ is the Forward motion.
- α is the Rotation motion.
- θ is the Flexion motion.

The figure shows the controls and the follow parameters and reference frame:

- L is the length of each segment from the kinematic chain.
- R is the external circumference radius that is drawn by the kinematics chain motion.
- Rc is the internal circumference radius that is drawn by the kinematics chain motion.
- β is the traveled angle by the kinematic chain regarding the center C of the circumference.

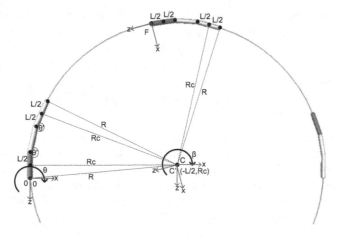

Fig. 4. Constrained kinematics.

- W is the world reference frame.
- O is the initial reference frame.
- O' is the rotated reference frame.
- C is the reference frame in the center of the circumference.
- C' is the rotated reference frame in the center of the circumference.
- F is the final reference frame.

For defining the β angle and the R and Rc radius, based on the motion ΔZ, α and θ:

$$R = \frac{L}{2\cos\left(\frac{\theta}{2}\right)} \tag{1}$$

$$\beta = \frac{\Delta Z}{R} = \frac{2\Delta Z \cos\left(\frac{\theta}{2}\right)}{L} \tag{2}$$

$$Rc = \frac{L}{2}\tan\left(\frac{\pi - \theta}{2}\right) \tag{3}$$

To obtain the constrained kinematic transformation from the world reference frame W, to the final reference frame F, the corresponding transformations between the reference frames are multiplied:

$$T_O^F = T_O^{O'} * T_{O'}^C * T_C^{C'} * T_{C'}^F \tag{4}$$

Where:

$$T_O^{O'} = \begin{bmatrix} \cos(\alpha) & -\sin(\alpha) & 0 & 0 \\ \sin(\alpha) & \cos(\alpha) & 0 & 0 \\ 0 & 0 & 1 & 0 \\ 0 & 0 & 0 & 1 \end{bmatrix} \tag{5}$$

$$T_{O'}^C = \begin{bmatrix} 1 & 0 & 0 & Rc \\ 0 & 1 & 0 & 0 \\ 0 & 0 & 1 & -\frac{L}{2} \\ 0 & 0 & 0 & 1 \end{bmatrix} \tag{6}$$

$$T_C^{C'} = \begin{bmatrix} \cos(\beta) & 0 & \sin(\beta) & 0 \\ 0 & 1 & 0 & 0 \\ -\sin(\beta) & 0 & \cos(\beta) & 0 \\ 0 & 0 & 0 & 1 \end{bmatrix} \tag{7}$$

$$T_{C'}^F = \begin{bmatrix} 1 & 0 & 0 & -Rc \\ 0 & 1 & 0 & 0 \\ 0 & 0 & 1 & L/2 \\ 0 & 0 & 0 & 1 \end{bmatrix}. \tag{8}$$

We obtain:

$$
\begin{bmatrix}
\cos\alpha\cos\beta & -\sin\alpha & \cos\alpha\sin\beta & \cos\alpha(1-\cos\beta)\,Rc + \cos\alpha\sin\beta\,L/2 \\
\sin\alpha\cos\beta & \cos\alpha & \sin\alpha\sin\beta & \sin\alpha(1-\cos\beta)\,Rc + \sin\alpha\sin\beta\,L/2 \\
-\sin\beta & 0 & \cos\beta & \cos\beta\,L/2 + \sin\beta\,Rc - L/2 \\
0 & 0 & 0 & 1
\end{bmatrix}
\tag{9}
$$

The effects of forward motion, using the constrained kinematics with flexion angles of 0 and 30°, are shown in Fig. 5.

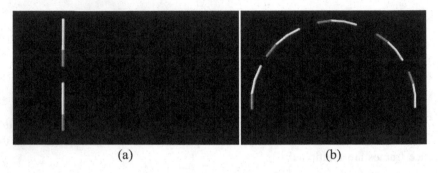

(a)   (b)

Fig. 5. Forward bronchoscope motion with (a) $\theta = 0°$. (b) $\theta = 30°$.

The bronchoscope is located in the bronchia virtual model and the initial and final configurations is defined. We can design the motion planner based on different approach.

3   Path Planning

RRT algorithm has been selected as path planning method because of its performance as kinematic chain motion planners in tubular environments.

3.1   Proposed RRT for Bronchoscopy Exploration

The RRT algorithm is able to find a solution path by defining an initial configuration in the trachea and a final configuration in the interest lung region. This solution method could be slow and expensive. The number of samples decreases when the RRT is developed from the interest lung region to the trachea. As shown in Fig. 6, a random sample Xrand is chosen in each algorithm iteration. This sample is obtained by giving random values to the 6° of freedom from bronchoscope base and to the 1° of freedom from flexion. T is the searching tree, we look for the nearest neighbor vertex Xnear to T [11]. Configurations are obtained from a PREDICTOR function based on the current configuration and controls. The PREDICTOR function is an incremental simulator.

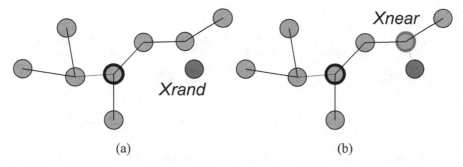

Fig. 6. Standard RRT. (a) Random sample. (b) Closer neighbor.

Other variations of the algorithm that decrease the searching time are RRT-Connect and Dynamic-Domain RRT.

3.2 RRT-Connect

Instead of a PREDICTOR function with Gaussian combinations of the Rotation, Flexion and Forward with a Δt interval, The PREDICTOR function in the RRT-Connect [12] performs several Gaussian combinations of Rotation, Flexion and forward until the Xnew collides with an obstacle of the work space, as shown in Fig. 7. Then, the controls combination gets the Xnew closer to the Xrand.

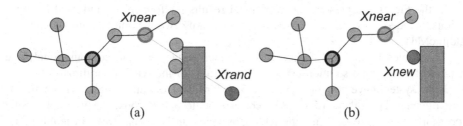

Fig. 7. RRT-Connect. (a) The closer sample gets random samples until to collide with an obstacle. (b) Selection of a control combination that gets the new sample closer to the random sample.

3.3 Dynamic-Domain RRT

In the Dynamic-Domain RRT [13], the domain is consider as a sphere which center is located in the closer Xnear sample to the obtained Xrand random sample. If the Xrand random sample is not inside this sphere, in other words, is located in a distance superior to a specified limit, the Xrand random sample is dismissed (Fig. 8). For the bron-choscope's motion planning, the limit taken in consideration is 0.1 of the total length of the work space.

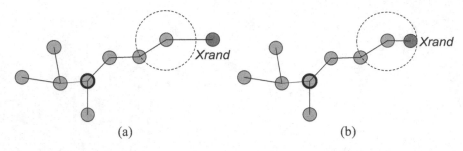

Fig. 8. Dynamic-Domain RRT. (a) The random sample is dismissed if it is located outside the domain. (b) The random samples are taken in consideration only if they are part of the domain.

4   Results and Discussion

We use as reference the path planner [14] based on RRT-Connect, in order to comparing the results for the dynamic domain RRT and RRT-Connect. For four different initial and final configurations we perform five variations of the RRT, five times each one:

- Standard RRT without kinematic constrains
- Standard RRT with kinematic constrains
- RRT-Connect
- Dynamic-Domain RRT
- RRT-Connect with Dynamic-Domain.

In the Fig. 9, we present the overlapped results for four initial and final configurations. Video results are provided on https://www.youtube.com/watch?v=4-ZldjmcMd4.

The Tables 1, 2, 3 and 4 shows the number of samples and computational time required for finding a solution using five variations of the RRT algorithms.

If the system have not constrains, the Standard RRT obtains a high performance as path planner. The others four RRTs correspond to a bronchoscope with kinematic constrains. Results reveals that the RRT-Connect with Dynamic Domain is the variation that requires minimum number of samples and computational time for finding the solution path.

Computational time depends on the processor used for executing the planning software. Algorithm were processed by an ACER 5630 laptop with the following characteristics: Intel Pentium Dual-Core T3400, 2.16 Hz, 2.17 Hz, 3 GB RAM.

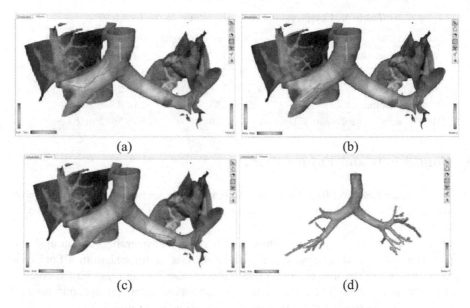

(a) (b)

(c) (d)

Fig. 9. Overlapped solution: (a) First test. (b) Second test. (c) Third test. (d) Four test.

Table 1. Comparison of RRT algorithms in the first test

RRT	Number of samples	Computational time
Without kinematic constrains	28–32	19 s–21 s
Standard RRT	60–66	40 s–44 s
RRT-Connect	34–39	25 s–28 s
Dynamic-Domain RRT	52–57	35 s–38 s
RRT-Connect with Dynamic Domain	33–37	24 s–27 s

Table 2. Comparison of RRT algorithms in the second test

RRT	Number of samples	Computational time
Without kinematic constrains	38–43	25 s–29 s
Standard RRT	77–86	51 s–57 s
RRT-Connect	46–52	33 s–37 s
Dynamic-Domain RRT	75–80	50 s–53 s
RRT-Connect with Dynamic Domain	41–47	29 s–33 s

Table 3. Comparison of RRT algorithms in the third test

RRT	Number of samples	Computational time
Without kinematic constrains	46–54	31 s–36 s
Standard RRT	93–105	62 s–70 s
RRT-Connect	59–67	42 s–47 s
Dynamic-Domain RRT	91–99	61 s–67 s
RRT-Connect with Dynamic Domain	52–61	37 s–43 s

Table 4. Comparison of RRT algorithms in the four test

RRT	Number of samples	Computational time
Without kinematic constrains	167–177	1 m 51 s–1 m 58 s
Standard RRT	284–298	3 m 9 s–3 m 19 s
RRT-Connect	179–191	2 m 2–2 m 10 s
Dynamic-Domain RRT	276–283	3 m 4 s–3 m 9 s
RRT-Connect with Dynamic Domain	171–179	1 m 56–2 m 2 s

5 Conclusions and Future Work

The path planner based on Rapidly Exploring Random Trees allows to determine with relative rapidness the solution path between an initial and final configuration of a virtual bronchoscope.

The bronchoscope kinematic constrains increase considerably the number of samples required to find a solution path. If the RRT is performed from a final configuration located in the interest lung region, the number of samples and the computational time is reduced. The RRT-Connect combination with the dynamic domain RRT, is the best approach for the bronchoscope motion planning.

As a future work, the virtual bronchoscopy simulation will be improved using a bronchoscope dynamic model. The motion planning for this dynamic system must consider the dynamic issues.

Acknowledgement. This work is part of the project Perception and localization system for autonomous navigation of rotor micro aerial vehicle in gps-denied environments, VisualNav-Drone, 2016-PIC-024, from the Universidad de las Fuerzas Armadas ESPE, directed by Dr. Wilbert G. Aguilar.

References

1. Cabras, P., Rosell, J., Aguilar, W.G., Pérez, A., Rosell, A.: Haptic-based navigation for the virtual bronchoscopy. In: Proceedings of the 18th IFAC World Congress, vol. 18, no. 1, pp. 9638–9643 (2011)
2. Vining, D., Liu, K., Choplin, R., Haponik, E.: Virtual bronchoscopy. Relationships of virtual reality endobronchial simulations to actual bronchoscopic findings. Chest **109**, 549–553 (1996)
3. LaValle, S.M.: Planning Algorithms. Illinois, Cambridge (2006)
4. Latombe, J.C.: Robot Motion Planning. Kluwer Academics, Massachussetts (1991)
5. Hsu, D., Latombe, J.C., Motwani, R.: Path planning in expansive configuration spaces. Int. J. Comput. Geom. Appl. **9**, 2719–2726 (1997)
6. Mirtich, B.: V-clip: fast and robust polyhedral collision detection. Technical Report TR97-05, Mitsubishi Electronics Research Laboratory (1997)
7. LaValle, S.M.: Rapidly-exploring random trees: a new toll for path planning. TR 98-11, Computer Science Department, Iowa State University (1998)

8. LaValle, S.M., Kuffner, J.J.: Rapidly-exploring random trees: progress and prospects. In: Algorithmic and Computational Robotics: New Directions, pp. 293–308 (2000)
9. Kavraki, L.E., Svestka, P., Lydia, E., Latombe, J.C., Overmars, M.H.: Probabilistic roadmaps for path planning in high-dimensional configuration spaces. IEEE Trans. Robot. Autom. **12**(4), 576–580 (1996)
10. Saha, M., Latombe, J.C.: On finding narrow passages with probabilistic roadmap planners. In: Workshop on the Algorithmic Foundations of Robotics (1998)
11. Atramentov, A., LaValle, S.M.: Efficient nearest neighbor searching for motion planning. In: Proceedings IEEE International Conference on Robotics and Automation, pp. 632–637
12. Kuffner, J.J., LaValle, S.M.: RRT-connect: an efficient approach to single-query path planning. In: Proceedings IEEE International Conference on Robotics and Automation, pp. 995–1001 (2000)
13. Yershova, A., Jaillet, L., Simeon, T., LaValle, S.M.: Dynamic-domain RRTs: efficient exploration by controlling the sampling domain. In: Proceedings IEEE International Conference on Robotics and Automation (2005)
14. Aguilar, W.G., Morales, S.: 3D environment mapping using the Kinect V2 and path planning based on RRT algorithms. Electronics **5**(4), 70 (2016)

Assistance System for Rehabilitation and Valuation of Motor Skills

Washington X. Quevedo, Jessica S. Ortiz, Paola M. Velasco,
Jorge S. Sánchez, Marcelo Álvarez V., David Rivas,
and Víctor H. Andaluz[✉]

Universidad de las Fuerzas Armadas, ESPE, Sangolquí, Ecuador
{wjquevedo,jsortiz4,pmvelascol,jssanchez,rmalvarez,
drrivas,vhandaluz1}@espe.edu.ec

Abstract. This article proposes a non-invasive system to stimulate the rehabilitation of motor skills, both of the upper limbs and lower limbs. The system
contemplates two ambiances for human-computer interaction, depending on the
type of motor deficiency that the patient possesses, *i.e.*, for patients with chronic
injuries, an augmented reality environment is considered, while virtual reality
environments are used in people with minor injuries. In the cases mentioned, the
interface allows visualizing both the routine of movements performed by the
patient and the actual movement executed by him. This information is relevant
for the purpose of *(i) stimulating* the patient during the execution of rehabilitation, and *(ii) evaluation of the movements* made so that the therapist can
diagnose the progress of the patient's rehabilitation process. The visual environment developed for this type of rehabilitation provides a systematic application in which the user first analyzes and generates the necessary movements in
order to complete the defined task. The results show the efficiency of the system
generated by the human-computer interaction oriented to the development of
motor skills.

Keywords: Rehabilitación · Realidad virtual · Kinect · Motricidad motora ·
Unity3d

1 Introduction

Disability worldwide is on the increase due to factors such as aging, injuries and
chronic diseases *e.g.,* diabetes, arthritis, muscle atrophy, mental health disorders,
among others which generate as main problem that people fail to achieve or maintain
an optimal functioning of autonomy in the performance of motor, sensory and intellectual activities [1, 2]; through the years rehabilitation has been used to counteract
these deficits, which provides mechanisms of strengthening, learning, and recovery of
mobility [3]. The daily activities, being repetitive or poorly performed, can generate
side effects that lead to different degrees of injuries that occur in the distinct types of
tissues, bones, tendons, ligaments and muscles [4–8].

To obtain an optimal physical recovery, techniques and tools are used to diagnose,
prevent, evaluate and treat the disease; by means of multiple procedures according to

© Springer International Publishing AG 2017
L.T. De Paolis et al. (Eds.): AVR 2017, Part II, LNCS 10325, pp. 166–174, 2017.
DOI: 10.1007/978-3-319-60928-7_14

the patient's pathology using physical or mechanical agents, that generate an increase in force, flexibility, and resistance, in addition, the learning about proper biomechanics [9]. Types of treatments may be classified according to their nature into *(i) passive treatments* that are unconsciously performed by the patient *i.e.,* the patient does not perform any movement voluntarily, thus generating a dependence on teams or third parties [10]; and *(ii) active treatments* are exercises performed voluntarily by the patient for which it is necessary to have motor awareness, it is considered necessary that the movement is desired by the patient, in addition to knowing the usefulness of the exercise, wich allows the construction a mental state that entails a correct execution of the treatment [9, 10].

Currently, there are different technological proposals that contribute to the implementation of passive and active rehabilitation treatments, research has been done and several studies mention electronic devices that stimulate the patient to perform movements [11–13]. The implementation of Virtual Reality, VR, is broad since it host applications from *(i)* industrial areas, in the development of virtual environments of training and control of a processes [14]; *(ii)* education, generating working environments that allow the integration of children with a certain level of disability in the teaching - learning process [15]; *(iii)* social, implemented to promote tourism and culture allowing the socio-economic development of each country [16]; *(iv)* military training, by means of simulators for the driving of vehicles airs, terrestrial and maritime, in addition to training in combat, planning, and preparation of special missions [17]; and *(v)* health, in development of mechanisms to improve the quality of life of people, through different applications *e.g.,* service robots capable of assisting in rehabilitation treatments, VR-based simulators for physicians, training them and perfecting robot-assisted procedures [2, 18–20].

Studies performed in people who suffered different injuries indicate that the use of virtual reality techniques improved the mobility and balance of patients [21]. The application of haptic devices allows interaction in the virtual environment, to perform exercise routines in patients requiring physical and motor rehabilitation, providing the person a different activity during treatment [22]. The multiple advancements generated in the field of rehabilitation, by the patients and specialists, through diverse ways of applying virtual reality in therapies, has generated a favorable impact on society. Among the VR applications in rehabilitation, various technologies have been developed presenting benefits in injuries and pathologies *e.g.,* in [23] it is proposing the design of immersive video games in a VR environment, which integrates motion capture sensors and electromyography sensors, EMG, to measure the effort of muscles according to the activity. In works like [24], immersive haptic devices are used to detect the movement in the execution of daily tasks, so that it is possible to analyze the kinematics in the reach and hooking of the objects. While in [25], the acquisition of spatial and gestural data is performed by means of the bracelet Myo in the healthy limb and through the VR which emulates an activity that is replicated by a robotic glove in the affected limb.

Hence, this article proposes a non-invasive rehabilitation system for both upper limb and lower limb motor. The proposed system allows sensing through the device Kinect v2 [26] the motions of the user. In addition, an application developed in virtual reality is presented using Unity 3D graphics engine [27]; the interface allows the user to visualize predetermined movements focused on the affected area of the lesion. This parameter is considered in the execution time of the routine of movements to be developed by the user. Finally, we present the experimental results in which a session of movements associated with daily tasks for the patient is considered; so one of the advantages of the proposed system is that in addition to being comfortable and affordable for the patient, it helps in its therapeutic process of rehabilitation while immersing it in a virtual world that stimulates and motivates during its recovery.

This article is divided into 4 sections including the Introduction. Section 2 presents the valuation of movements performed by the user and the graphical virtual reality environment are presented. Section 3 shows experimental results that validate the proposal, and finally, the conclusions are detailed in Sect. 4.

2   System Rehabilitation

This section describes the development of the augmented reality and virtual reality environment using Unity 3D graphics engine; environments in which several scenarios are considered to stimulate the user's neuronal system when executing the desired movements. It proposes the valorization of the movements made by users with the purpose of validating and diagnosing the progress of rehabilitation.

The programming for the operation of the scene in virtual reality and in augmented reality graphically shown in Fig. 1, links the components with the mechanics of movements performed by a person in front of a body tracking device.

In section (i) the scenes in Virtual and Augmented Reality are developed which are chosen in the user interface at the moment of starting the application. There are also objects that show the data captured by the Kinect device, as well as cameras and auxiliary objects.

In section (ii) corresponding to SCRIPTS, you have the main application controller which operate all interactions and displays information in virtual reality and augmented reality environments by management the inputs: Kinect, Oculus SDK, and Input/Output plugin It uses an algorithm that reads the positions of joints in space and overlays them to the color image that the Kinect device captures. By means of position comparators, it is determined whether the user's movements are correct. It also has a controller to export the data acquired from the user to databases so that external analysis can perform analyses that require dedicated calculation potential.

In section (iii) of Outputs the resulting responses of inputs and interaction with the user interface are received in audio, video and tracking outputs.

2.1   Virtual Environment

The initial process requires the proper positioning of a person in front of the Kinect device, for its corresponding detection, which based on a peripheral camera that acts as a sonar that manages to capture gestures and movements within a visual field in real time, this allows to structure an arrangement of points of the body, since it detects the main joints of the body within a cloud of points, in the following layer treatment is

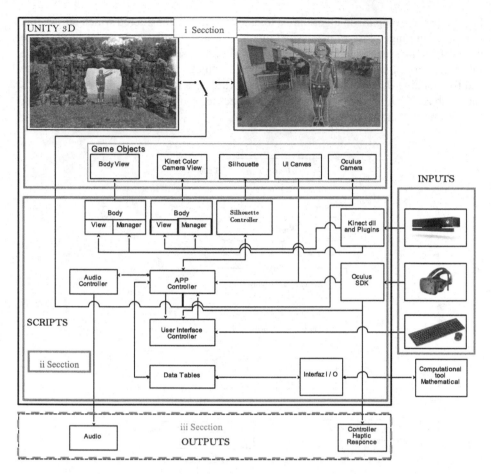

Fig. 1. Rehabilitation system scheme

given to these points within Unity, where an array of body points corresponding to A user, the system can simultaneously track 6 bodies with skeleton overlapping features within Unity.

The graph of joints is made using a representative GameObject that inherits the coordinates and the name of the joint, all joints will be child objects of a parent object with name body + id, where id is the identification number of the body detected. Accordingly, it is realized that lines are created that join the joints using LineRenderer with desired initial and final position. for the next layer of treatment of the data of the tracked body, a library of bodies is obtained in advance in the desired position for each exercise, strategic measures are taken, for example the measurement of the angle that forms the arm with respect to the body, the opening of the legs, etc. In the comparison block, the user is asked to place himself in a certain position so that the system evaluates the user's position to perform the exercise, then the strategic measures are compared between the user's tracked body in real time and the saved model in the library. In this comparison algorithm, a tolerance factor is considered which allows that in a position range close to the desired one is considered correct. In order to visualize this process, messages and stimuli are expressed in the user interface that informs of the fulfillment or not of the exercise performed. In addition, the data of the reference body and the tracking data can be transferred in real time to a database so that external tools can analyze the information and give more specific results of the exercise performed, the structure is shown in Fig. 2.

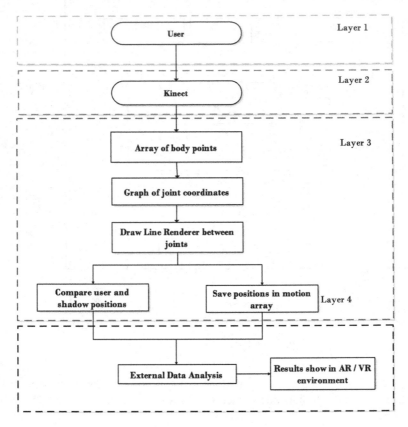

Fig. 2. Rehabilitation system process

3   Results

For the validation of the application, two types of exercises aimed at the rehabilitation of the shoulder and hip, the experimental tests were performed with 15 people, 11 men, and 4 women, ranging from 20 to 28 years of age.

For the first case, the shoulder joint is analyzed, which is composed of three bones: clavicle, shoulder blade, and humorous. The shoulder is the most mobile joints in the body. To remain in a normal position, the shoulder must be anchored by muscles, tendons, and ligaments. The most frequent lesions in this joint are: strains, dislocations, separations, tendinitis, bursitis, rupture of the rotator cuff, frozen shoulder, fractures and arthritis; The majority of these injuries are treated through physical therapy.

The application shows a scenario inspired by an environment that inspires calmness, as shown in Fig. 3(a). In the first stage of rehabilitation, the abduction movements are performed without loads, that is, it will only move the weight of its bone structure and muscle mass; For this test the application will explain the movement to be performed, which consists of moving the arm laterally, in the xz plane, for which it is necessary that the person is placed in front of the device, which traces the silhouette that serves the user. The realization of movements; Fig. 3(b) shows the beginning of the exercise, placing the silhouette in red color until the exercise is performed correctly; While in Fig. 3(c), it is shown when the exercise has been completed correctly, by painting the green silhouette; All the information will be stored in the corresponding database.

Fig. 3. Sequence of abduction motions (Color figure online)

The data obtained from the performance of the exercises are analyzed by statistical methods, In this case, the box diagram is used which visually represents the dispersion and symmetry of the data, this graph represents the quartiles and the minimum and maximum values of the data, on a rectangle aligned horizontally or vertically. In Fig. 4(a), the results obtained from this test are shown, it is observed that the samples are concentrated at 90° because it is the point that is recorded the most, obtaining the maximum values at 180° and the minimum values at 0°. Demonstrating in this way the consistency of the data acquired by the system.

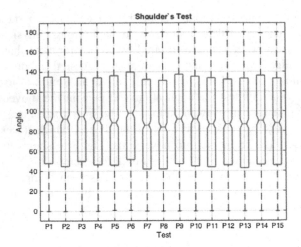

Fig. 4. Results of exercises.

The following study analyzes the articulation of the hip or coxofemoral, which relates the coxal bone to the femur, thus joining the trunk with the lower limb, together with the surrounding musculature, supports the weight of the body in both static postures and dynamics; the lesions that present in this joint are: Distensions, Bursitis, Dislocations, Fractures.

For the assessment, the flexion movement will be performed, which will allow the joint to be moved in a range of 90°; the data are monitored in a range from an initial angle of 180° to a final angle of 90°. Figure 5 shows the results obtained from this test, where it can be determined that the movement of the hip is maintained within the range, in addition, that means are maintained close to 135°.

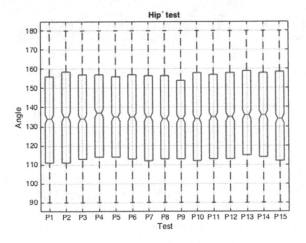

Fig. 5. Results flexion movements.

4 Conclusions

The results demonstrated by the development of virtual environments for motor skills rehabilitation demonstrate the efficiency of the proposed system, which allows the patient to substantially improve their motor skills, since the system stimulates the patient to perform an assisted rehabilitation, based on exercises Therapeutic, developed in different environments and classified according to their motor deficiency. In addition, the proposed system allows the therapist to have the assessment of the movements performed by the patient, in order to make a reliable diagnosis of patient recovery.

References

1. Organización Mundial de la Salud: Informe Mundial sobre la Discapacidad (2011)
2. Silver, B.: Virtual reality versus reality in post-stroke rehabilitation. Lancet Neurol. **15**(10), 996 (2016)
3. O'Sullivan, S., Schmitz, T., Fulj, G.: Physical Rehabilitation, USA, pp. 333, 443 (2014)
4. Chambers, A., Smith, P., Sim, M., LaMontagne, A.: Comparison of Two Measures of Work Functioning in a Population of Claimants with Physical and Pshychological Injuries. Springer Science+Business Media, Dordrecht (2016)
5. Chang, Y.-J., Chen, S.-F., Huang, J.-D.: A kinect-based system for physical rehabilitation: a pilot study for young adults with motor disabilities. Res. Dev. Disabil. **32**(6), 2566–2570 (2011). Cited 332 times
6. Lange, B., Chang, C.Y., Suma, E., Newman, B., Rizzo, A.S., Bolas, M.: Development and evaluation of low cost game based balance rehabilitation tool using the microsoft kinect sensor. In: 2011 Annual International Conference of the IEEE Engineering in Medicine and Biolog Society, Boston, MA, pp. 1831–1834 (2011)
7. Vela Nuñez, M., Avizzano, C.A., Carrozzino, M., Frisoli, A., Bergamasco, M.: Multi-modal virtual reality system for accessible in-home post-stroke arm rehabilitation. In: 2013 IEEE ROMAN, Gyeongju, pp. 780–785 (2013)
8. Hoei, T., Kawahira, K., Fukuda, H., Sihgenobu, K., Shimodozono, M., Ogura, T.: Use of an arm weight-bearing combined with upper-limb reaching apparatus to facilitate motor paralysis recovery in an incomplete spinal cord injury patient: a single case report. J. Phys. Therary Sci. **29**, 176–180 (2017)
9. Bejarano, N., Maggioni, S., Rijcke, L., Cifuentes, C., Reinkensmeyer, D.: Robot-Assisted Rehabilitation Therapy Recovery Mechanisms and Their Implications for Machine Design, Emerging Therapies in Neurorehabilitation II, pp. 197–223 (2015)
10. Vos-Vromans, D., Smeets, R., Hujinen, I., Koke, A., Hitters, W., et al.: Multidisciplinary rehabilitation treatment versus cognitive behavioural therapy for patients with chronic fatigue syndrome: a randomized controlled trial. J. Intern. Med. **279**, 268–282 (2016)
11. Tao, G., Archambault, P.S., Levin, M.F.: Evaluation of kinect skeletal tracking in a virtual reality rehabilitation system for upper limb hemiparesis. In: International Conference on Virtual Rehabilitation (ICVR), pp. 164–165 (2013)
12. Andaluz, V., Salazar, P., Silva, S., Escudero, V., Bustamante, D.: Rehabilitation of upper limb with force feedback. In: 2016 IEEE International Conference on Automatica (ICA-ACCA) (2016)

13. Andaluz, V.H., et al.: Virtual reality integration with force feedback in upper limb rehabilitation. In: Bebis, G., et al. (eds.) ISVC 2016. LNCS, vol. 10073, pp. 259–268. Springer, Cham (2016). doi:10.1007/978-3-319-50832-0_25

14. Andaluz, V.H., Chicaiza, F.A., Gallardo, C., Quevedo, W.X., Varela, J., Sánchez, J.S., Arteaga, O.: Unity3D-MatLab simulator in real time for robotics applications. In: De Paolis, L., Mongelli, A. (eds) Augmented Reality, Virtual Reality, and Computer Graphics. AVR 2016. LNCS, vol. 9768, pp. 246–263. Springer, Cham (2016). doi:10.1007/978-3-319-40621-3_19

15. Davis, M., Can, D., Pindrink, J., et al: Virtual Interactive Presence in Global Surgical Education: International Collaboration Through Augmented Reality, pp. 103–111. Science Direct (2016)

16. Huang, Y., Backman, K., Backman, S., Chang, L.: Exploring the implications of virtual reality technology in tourism marketing: an integrated research framework. Int. J. Tour. Res. **18**, 116–128 (2016)

17. Pallavicini, F., Argenton, L., Toniazzi, N., Aceti, L., Mantovani, F.: Virtual reality applications for stress management training in the militry. Aerosp. Med. Hum. Perform. **87**, 1021–1030 (2016)

18. Rothbaum, B.O., Price, M., Jovanovic, T., Norrholm, S.D., Gerardi, M., Dunlop, B., Ressler, K.J.: A randomized, double-blind evaluation of D-cycloserine or alprazolam combined with virtual reality exposure therapy for posttraumatic stress disorder in Iraq and Afghanistan War veterans. Am. J. Psychiatry **171**, 640–648 (2014)

19. Schreuder, H.W., Persson, J.E., Wolswijk, R.G., Ihse, I., Schijven, M.P., Verheijen, R.H.: Validation of a novel virtual reality simulator for robotic surgery. Sci. World J. **2014**, 1–10 (2014). ID:507076

20. Padilla-Castaneda, M.A., Sotgiu, E., Frisoli, A., Bergamasco, M., Orsini, P., Martiradonna, A., Laddaga, C.: A virtual reality system for robotic-assisted orthopedic rehabilitation of forearm and elbow fractures. In: International Conference on Intelligent Robots and Systems, pp. 1506–1511 (2013)

21. Menezes, R.C., Batista, P.K.A., Ramos, A.Q., Medeiros, A.F.C.: Development of a complete game based system for physical therapy with kinect. In: Serious Games and Applications for Health (SeGAH), pp. 1–6 (2014)

22. Faroque, S., Horan, B., Adam, H., Pangestu, M., Thomas, S.: Haptic virtual reality training environment for micro-robotic cell injection. In: Kajimoto, H., Ando, H., Kyung, K.-U. (eds.) Haptic Interaction, pp. 245–249. Springer, Japan (2015)

23. Rincon, A., Yamasaki, H., Shimoda, S.: Design of a video game for rehabilitation using motion capture, EMG analysis and virtual reality. In: International Conference on Electronic, Communications and Computers, pp. 198–204 (2016)

24. Levin, M.F., Magdalon, E.C., Michaelsen, S.M., Quevedo, A.A.: Quality of grasping and the role of haptics in a 3-D immersive virtual reality environment in individuals with stroke. IEEE Trans. Neural Syst. Rehabil. Eng. **23**, 1047–1055 (2015)

25. Lipovsky, R., Ferreira, H.: Hand therapist: a rehabilitation approach based on wearable technology and video gaming. In: 4th Portuguese Meeing on Bioengineering, Portugal (2015)

26. Yoshida, H., Honda, T., Lee, J., Yano, S., Kakei, S., Kondo, T.: Development of a system for quantitative evaluation of motor function using Kinect v2 sensor. In: Micro-NanoMechatronics and Human Science (MHS), pp. 1–6 (2016)

27. Harshfield, N., Chang, D., Rammohan: A Unity 3D framework for algorithm animation. In: Computer Games: AI, Animation, Mobile, Multimedia, Education and Serious Games (CGAMES), USA (2015)

Robotic Applications in Virtual Environments for Children with Autism

Christian P. Carvajal, Luis Proaño, José A. Pérez, Santiago Pérez, Jessica S. Ortiz, and Víctor H. Andaluz$^{(\boxtimes)}$

Universidad de las Fuerzas Armadas, ESPE, Sangolquí, Ecuador
{jsortiz4, vhandaluz1}@espe.edu.ec,
chriss2592@hotmail.com, joansll@hotmail.com,
luis.e.proa@gmail.com, ddsanty1992@gmail.com,
chriss2592@hotmail.com, joansll@hotmail.com

Abstract. In this paper, it proposes the development of a virtual reality system that works simultaneously with the physical environment, by creating an atmosphere that stimulates the abilities of children with autism spectrum disorder. This system is implemented through a human - machine interface, which has the possibility to simulate and work with functions focused on rehabilitation, so the patient will be involved in assisted therapies based on DSM - 5 protocols. Therefore, multiple environments and applications are presented for the interaction with the physical media to increase the stimulus of the affected one. The results of the application are presented to validate the project using the information collected through the interaction between the developer, therapist and patient.

Palabras Claves: Visión artificial · Entorno virtual · Simulación · Autismo · Humanoide · Avatar

1 Introduction

Children with autistic neurological disorder - ASD - simply interpret social cues as communication and relationships with others, so they are subject to activities whose patterns are repetitive in behavior and behavior [1], such as following routines Specific, lack of imaginative ability, impulsive and non-functional movements [2], among others. According to the World Health Organization (WHO), 1 in 160 children suffer from autism disorders worldwide according to the 2016 report [4]; With 1 in 38 children with autism in South Korea, while in the United States - The National Health Interview Survey suggests that 1 in 45 have ASD. However, at the Latin American level only three studies are known about the prevalence of this syndrome, which shows a very low average and not all are based on the population. In the Venezuelan clinic, a prevalence of 17/10,000 was found among children aged 3 to 9 years; In Argentina, among 839 children younger than 5 years. Finally, a study conducted in a city located at the southeastern of Brazil, we found that the prevalence of ASD is 27/10,000 [5].

Currently, the implementation of the technology and the use of conventional methods for the treatment of such disorder has shown that it can positively impact current therapeutic practices, providing highly significant results in terms of advances

© Springer International Publishing AG 2017
L.T. De Paolis et al. (Eds.): AVR 2017, Part II, LNCS 10325, pp. 175–187, 2017.
DOI: 10.1007/978-3-319-60928-7_15

and improvements of the affected. However, the deployment of intelligent spaces in these challenging environments is not an easy task, as most individuals living in these spaces face numerous cognitive behavioral challenges, which limit the ability to deploy new technologies [6].

Within the literature, there are several areas that focus on neurodevelopment, among which we have: (i) Intelligent devices are all those objects capable of identifying, locating, detecting, connecting and leading to new forms of communication between people. Today, children with autism are a subject of research because, as there is not current cure for autism, the goal of primary care is to create a supportive environment in which several intelligent devices interact with each other and allow users Control and monitor events that occur in therapies [7]; (ii) Video anecdotal and clinical reports indicate that for many young people with ASD, the use of television and video games may be clinically significant insofar as these behaviors interfere with adaptive functioning and social commitment [8]; (iii) Information and Communication Technologies in the field of medicine has allowed the development of different tools that have contributed to improve teaching methodologies. As for autism, the main objective of the study is to promote interaction and communication with children with ASD through the use of robots, which can be used as didactic tools for teaching and developing skills improving their social relationship with others in their Environment [7]; (iv) Virtual environments with the progressive advancement of Virtual Reality (VR), it is possible to create three-dimensional worlds directed towards the disorder in the neurodevelopment within which the patient can experience real-life sensations generated by computer, these environments have manual tasks, exercises, therapeutic routines, among others. Helping the child in a very satisfactory way with socialization, learning and communication [9].

A wide variety of treatments have been designed whose applicability has been directed to studies of a medical-psychological nature, especially within the field of study in therapies against autism. One of the platforms that offers practical opportunities with dynamic and real-life social interactions is Virtual Reality (VR), which consists of the simulation of reality in which visual representations are based on everyday life and are presented in a screen. VR has been used previously and has been shown to be an effective intervention tool in the treatment of various conditions, such as anxiety, phobias, fear of flight, stroke in treatments and studies of the autistic spectrum in several Levels, since it naturally facilitates specific responses based on actions or events that occur within virtual environments that the patient requires with a previous diagnosis of the therapist [10, 11]. VR has been found as a viable pathway for the treatment of ASD, in which it is described below: The project developed by Marcus et al. [12] presented a brief report on two cases analyzed using virtual reality as a learning tool for autistic children. Strickland et al. [13] implemented a virtual reality system for the treatment of autism by a flat-screen system with virtual scenes. Lahiri et al. (2014) [14] developed a system of social communication based on physiologically informed virtual reality for individuals with autism.

This article focuses on the implementation of a system in which robotics and virtual reality are adapted to the treatment of children with autism. The proposal of the work is based on the development of several virtual environments where the patient will be able to choose between characters such as robots, people, comics, animes, among others, which it will stimulate and immerse the child in virtual environments according to the chosen character. The system has several levels of interaction depending on the degree of affection of the child, the same as previously defined by the therapist. Additional, real-time through artificial vision is detected the emotions of the child with the purpose of assessing the degree of satisfaction in performing the task proposed by the therapist. The scenarios in the environment can be chosen depending on the age, gender and treatment to be followed, i.e., if a character is selected as "Goku", the virtual environment will take place in the clouds or in a city that allows more stimulation. Finally, the system is characterized by being intuitive and easy to use to improve the immersion between the therapist and the patient.

The paper is organized as follows. Section 2 presents the structure of the system; While Sect. 3 shows the virtualization process. The design of the interface and system options is presented in Sect. 4. In Sect. 5 the experimental results are indicated and the system performance is evaluated. Finally, the conclusions are presented in Sect. 6.

2 System Structure

The system developed is based on the interaction architecture between the patient and the Virtual Reality environments through a physical element that acts as an intermediary (Robot), with therapies and activities that are based on the behavioral treatment DMS-5 [11]. This rehabilitation system follows protocols which are performed after an analysis of the patient's state and with options depending on the level that affects the disorder, although there is the therapist's contribution, the system helps to stimulate the children with characters of their interest in selectable virtual environments in which they can have their virtual assistant to perform different activities and directly perform recovery therapy of psychological deficiency. Additionally, virtual reality, artificial vision and robotics technologies are adopted, which make the system capable of performing a repetitive feedback in the robot and within the virtual environment, maintaining consistency in the process.

Figure 1 shows the structure of the system developed where the robot is programmed to perform tasks autonomously and the results are presented in the virtual environment in an avatar way previously selected by the therapist with the aim of stimulating the senses and the attention of the patient. The system receives this information through non-verbal channels, allowing better validation of behavior based on treatment protocols.

In the virtual environment, the child is located with the avatar in a game environment, with the objective of fulfilling activities proposed by the therapist depending on their level of autism, by complying with the program, the system delivers important data to the doctor which can evaluate the progress of treatment. In the artificial vision part, the system focuses on capturing and discriminating the infant's emotions through facial recognition, to obtain an estimation of the child's behavior in response to environmental stimuli and the virtual assistant of work, in this case the system distinguishes happiness, sadness, anger and depending on this, the environment and the avatar will react if it must.

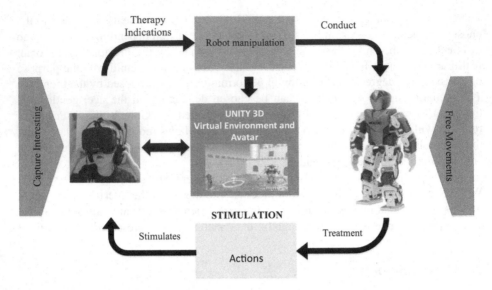

Fig. 1. Behavioral intervention assisted by the virtual reality system for the treatment of ASD.

3 Operating Scheme

The interaction between the patient and the virtual environment is done through a humanoid robot that allows to be manipulated - controlled - with ease, in order to provide the inputs to the virtual environment. The development of the virtual environment should allow the interaction between the robot and an avatar; the avatar can be selected according to the interest of the patient to be treated. In the virtual environment the movements of the avatar are executed according to the emotions of the patient which are captured by means of a vision sensor. The proposed block diagram is divided into five parts, see Fig. 2.

System Inputs, the inputs of the system are devices that capture signals to be interpreted and perform an action, *e.g.,* movements, emotions, sound, among others. The virtual devices used as inputs are: *(i)* virtual reality helmet allows the user to immerse in a virtual environment in order to stimulate the patient to perform the therapy proposed by the specialist; *(ii)* gesture control sensor, this electronic device allows interaction with the virtual interface by tracking gestures performed by the user's hand; *(iii)* vision sensor, allows to acquire the images of facial gestures performed by patients with the objective of obtaining numerical information to be processed and generate an output according to the algorithms used in artificial vision.

Controller Design, this section presents the control system for children with autistic disorder with the inclusion of vision and control technologies for the treatment of this condition, which consists of artificial vision, controller and actuators (Fig. 3).

Artificial vision, has as input to the vision sensor responsible for capturing the physical environment and the child's profile, the system is able to differentiate the patient's mood through child - robot interaction and then generate output data

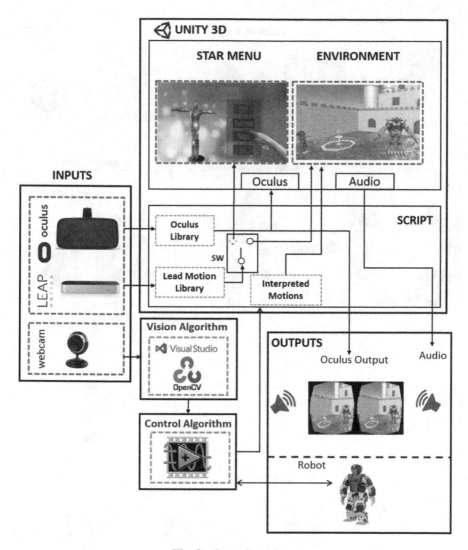

Fig. 2. Operating scheme

depending on the case. The process begins with the detection and capture of the face, so that the program can standardize the image and thus perform the detection of smile, eyes and other particularities necessary for optimal functioning (Fig. 4).

The communication, the protocol used to communicate with the artificial vision algorithm is RS-232, a serial communication in which virtual ports are created in the computer, i.e. The patient's status detection algorithm sends a character that represents the current state of the patient, through this character the Humanoid performs a specific movement, the control algorithm tabien obtains the position reading of the robot's extremities to be copied in the avatar Of 3D simulation.

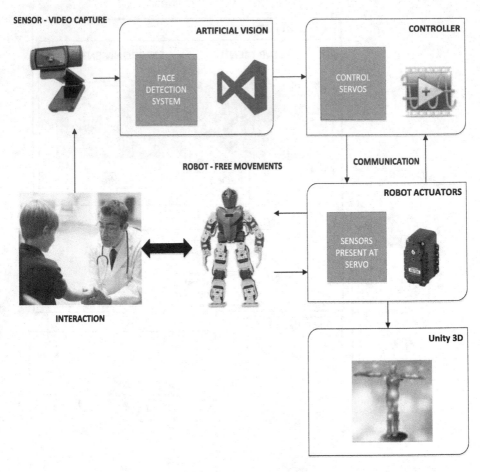

Fig. 3. Controller system

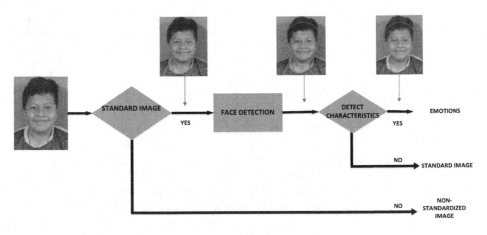

Fig. 4. Facial recognition algorithm

Control algorithm, receives the treatment's data emitted by the software of artificial vision, this one is in charge to relate to the computer with the assistant (robot). The information received is from the monitoring process in patients, as well as analyze their progress with each therapy, robot movements will be loaded and stored in vectors by each actuator present in the humanoid that can be accessed from the user interface or from the virtual environment.

Robot, has intelligent actuators which is able to be handled through libraries and commands, can also deliver and send data such as speed, position, voltage and torque.

Virtual Environment: The VR environment is developed in order to capture the attention of the patient, the interface simulates the motion of humanoid robot real in the selected avatar virtual, this environment was created in the platform of Unity 3D done, where it has the respective programming scripts that allow Interact with the system inputs and outputs (Fig. 2).

Outputs: The outputs of the system are electronic devices that emulate movements, environments, sounds, among others; these outputs devices of the system are: virtual reality helmet, audio speakers and the humanoid robot BIOLOID that executes the movements according to the state of the child and at the same time copies these to interpret them in the avatar virtually (Fig. 2).

4 Virtualization

The design of avatars, environments, 3D objects, among others, is done on specific platforms for this type of drawings, using software with parametric tools, in which specific properties can be assigned to 3D figures such as mobility points, textures, color and even in some cases animations are created which can be exported to be used in the Unity 3D environment, between others.

In the process to virtualize the system for Unity 3D, the following steps are taken into account (Fig. 5): *(i)* import parts of the 3D model or simply as an interface for children only exist on the internet some avatars to facilitate the developers creating these designs, these can be TV characters, cartoons, animes, among others; *(ii)* establish unique properties for 3D designs such as animations, colors, textures, among others; and *(iii)* structure and control, where the system inputs are programmed and configured.

To set properties and convert our design that is compatible with Unity 3D, AutoDesk-3DS MAX software is used because Unity 3D recognizes only specific files on its platform, this file format maintains its characteristics and designed properties and properties set. Figure 6 shows an avatar downloaded from the web, where property is established to be able to move its limbs, give it an orientation, and size; at the end of this process the file is exported in * .fbx format, compatible with Unity, i.e. In this type of format its hierarchies when using the 3D design remain according to the programmed.

Interface Unity 3D, the VR interface is developed with an interactive menu Fig. 7 with which the therapist or patient can operate without any difficulty, it has sub menus like; *(i) Star* serves to begin the interaction of the virtual environment according to the movements that the robot executes with the control algorithm; *(ii) Environment* executes

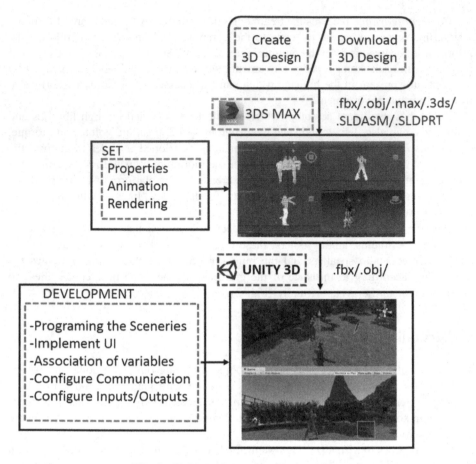

Fig. 5. Unity environment transformation.

a sub-menu of the scenarios available for the virtual simulation of the avatar, *(iii)* *Avatars*; you have available characters created or downloaded from the web with their respective hierarchies of movements and finally *(iv) Exit* ends the simulation in the VR.

5 Experimental Results

This procedure aims to develop social skills in children through robotics and virtual reality, whose program is based on the method of Treatment and Education of Autistic Children with Communication Problems. Applicable for children between 6 and 12 years old. Table 1.

The patient is placed in front of the computer, placing it in a comfortable position so that the artificial vision sensor fully captures his face in conjunction with the Oculus Rift virtual reality helmet used as shown in the Fig. 8.

Subsequently the artificial vision software proceeds to capture the image and discriminates the patient's mood with the objective of generating the reference signal for

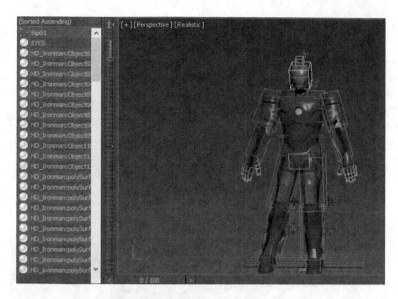

Fig. 6. Create objet to animation.

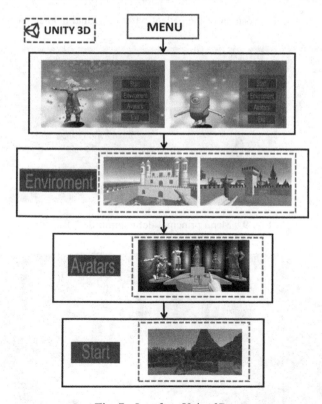

Fig. 7. Interface Unity 3D.

Table 1. Procedure for autistic children

Phase	Activities
Motivation	Play activities (Songs, Games)
Recognition of the environment	Recognize people and objects in the classroom
Explanation of rules for therapies	Pictogram use
Introduction of the robot within the environment	Pictogram use
Development of the therapy	Interaction with the robot
Evaluation	Patient evaluation
Closing	Pictogram use for indicating that the therapy session is over

Fig. 8. Position of the patient with the virtual helmet.

Fig. 9. Menú principal del entorno de VR.

Fig. 10. Avatar selection.

the controller, in the VR interface the initial menu is displayed Fig. 9, the Avatar can be selected according to the patient's preferences through gesture movements captured by the leap motion Fig. 10, then the patient or therapist chooses the simulation scenario, for this case was used with three examples (Figs. 11, 12 and 13).

Fig. 11. Open environment of a forest.

Fig. 12. Environment of an opened castle.

Fig. 13. Environment of a closed castle.

Running together the scenario of VR and the controller of the Robot BIOLOID in which if the patient moves the robot in a certain position it simulates it virtually the same, in the same way if the robot executes an action according to the patient's mood, this movement is replicated into the avatar (Fig. 14(a), (b), (c)).

(a) Position one

(b) Position two

(c) Position three

(d) Position four

Fig. 14. Motions of the humanoid robot and avatar virtual.

6 Conclusions

The results obtained in the virtual environment for autistic spectrum disorder demonstrate the efficiency of the system under the supervision of a therapist, allowing the patient to increase their stimulation. The routine has been developed by the patient and is established by the treatment according to a previously obtained diagnosis. The system contemplates two modes of operation, one in which it conforms to the mood of the patient selected to perform a specific movement, thus improving the patient's social relationship with other people in a controlled environment; The other is fed back to perform readings of the position of the BIOLOID Humanoid robot parts, in which the therapist asks the patient to perform a repetitive action, the same was visualized in the virtual environment in order to reflect the evolution of the patient's disorder.

References

1. Yun, S.-S., Kim, H., Choi, J., Park, S.-K.: A robot-assisted behavioral intervention system for children with autism spectrum disorders. Rob. Auton. Syst. **76**, 58–67 (2016)
2. Robinson, P.: A Review of Autism Spectrum Disorder, March 2012
3. Ennis-Cole, D.L.: Technology for Learners with Autism Spectrum Disorders. Springer, Berlin (2014)
4. Pauta-Pintado, J., Lima-Juma, D., Gal, J.: An intelligent system based on ontologies and ICT tools to support the diagnosis and intervention of children with autism, p. 5 (2016)
5. Dekkers, L.M.S., Groot, N.A., Delfos, M.F.: Prevalence of autism spectrum disorders in ccuador: a pilot study in quito. J. Autism Dev. Disord. **45**(12), 4165–4173 (2015)
6. Tentori, M., Escobedo, L., Balderas, G.: A smart environment for children with autism. IEEE Pervasive Comput. **14**(2), 42–50 (2015)
7. Sula, A.: Using Assistive Technologies in Autism Care Centers to Support Children Develop Communication and Language Skills. A Case Study: Albania, vol. 3, no. 1, pp. 203–212 (2014)
8. Mazurek, M.O., Shattuck, P.T., Wagner, M., Cooper, B.P.: Prevalence and correlates of screen-based media use among youths with autism spectrum disorders. J. Autism Dev. Disord. **42**(8), 1757–1767 (2012)
9. Rothbaum, B.O., Hodges, L.F., Kooper, R., Opdyke, D., Williford, J.S., North, N.: Effectiveness of computer generated (virtual reality) graded exposure in the treatment of acrophobia. Am. J. Psychiatry **152**(4), 626–628 (1995)
10. Kandalaft, M.R., Didehbani, N., Krawczyk, D.C., Allen, T.T., Chapman, S.B.: Virtual reality social cognition training for young adults with high-functioning autism. J. Autism Dev. Disord. **43**(1), 34–44 (2013)
11. Wang, M., Reid, D.: Virtual reality in pediatric neurorehabilitation: attention deficit hyperactivity disorder, autism and cerebral palsy. Neuroepidemiology **36**(1), 2–18 (2011)
12. Marcus, L., Mesibov, G., Hogan, K.: Brief report: two case studies using virtual reality as a learning tool for autistic children. J. Autism Dev. Disord. **26**, 9 (1996)
13. Strickland, D.: Virtual reality for the treatment of autism. Stud. Health Technol. Inform. **44**, 81–86 (1997)
14. Lahiri, U., Bekele, E., Dohrmann, E., Warren, Z., Sarkar, N.: A physiologically informed virtual reality based social communication system for individuals with autism. J. Autism Dev. Disord. **45**(4), 919–931 (2015)

Realism in Audiovisual Stimuli for Phobias Treatments Through Virtual Environments

Jessica S. Ortiz, Paola M. Velasco, Washington X. Quevedo,
Marcelo Álvarez V., Jorge S. Sánchez, Christian P. Carvajal,
Luis F. Cepeda, and Víctor H. Andaluz(✉)

Universidad de Las Fuerzas Armadas, ESPE, Sangolquí, Ecuador
{jsortiz4,pmvelascol,wjquevedo,rmalvarez,jssanchez,
lfcepedal,vhandaluz1}@espe.edu.ec,
chriss2592@hotmail.com

Abstract. This article proposes a system of perception of the real world through audiovisual stimulation for the treatment of different types of phobias. The proposed system is made up of various virtual environments which will be selected according to the phobia to be treated, *i.e.,* the user-environment integration depends on the type and degree of the phobia. The interface allows visualize the environment where the patient must comply with a predetermined therapy by the psychotherapist, in which the biometric signals of the patient are feed back in real time through wearables devices. This information is processed in order to ingest directly in the algorithm of the user's behavior; algorithm that controls the audiovisual stimuli related to the phobia during the interaction of the virtual environment with the user. In addition, the parameters of the biometric signals are displayed graphically/numerically in the virtual environment in order for the patient to control their behavior and face their irrational fear-phobia. The results are validated based on the realism of the virtual environments developed, and the audio-visual stimuli applied to the patient based on the change of the parameters of the biometric signals acquired through wearable devices.

Keywords: Phobias · Audiovisual stimulation · Wearable devices · Virtual reality · Unity3D

1 Introduction

The nature of the human being generates behaviors of survival that make them move away from situations considered as dangerous, according to the perspective of the person against circumstances of lived or acquired experiences, the different fears according [1, 2] generates physiological indicators, facials expressions, corporal reaction, behavior traits, among others; becoming from a simple fear to an exaggerated awe of certain situations taking the name of phobia. The phobias affect the everyday environment, of who suffer from it, to the point of generating conflict in affective, labor, social relationships surrounding the patient, in this sense several studies have been generated in recent years, these have made use of technology to try eradicate or

© Springer International Publishing AG 2017
L.T. De Paolis et al. (Eds.): AVR 2017, Part II, LNCS 10325, pp. 188–201, 2017.
DOI: 10.1007/978-3-319-60928-7_16

helping the patient to live with their condition, as the complexity of the disease in-creases, solutions are sought that encompass the complete analysis of the disease [3].

The phobia according to clinical psychology is an anxiety disorder, generated by irrational fear of situations or objects that do not represent any danger, these conditions are not considered new although in the last decade's new types of phobias have been generated, which may to generate impediments in performing daily activities in patients [4, 5]. People suffering from phobias undergo various changes as *(i) psychic symptoms*, that generate discomfort and suffering in the face of the patient's mistaken perception of himself, causing intense attacks, *e.g.,* anxiety, loss of control, depression, among others [6]; *(ii) vegetative symptoms*, also known as psychological symptoms are manifested by the anxiety that the patient shows in the face of the presence of objects or situations considered risky, *e.g.,* tachycardia, fainting, sweating, redness, pallor, among others [7]; and finally *(iii) symptoms of motor affections*, they generate disturbances in the patient's motor skill upon exposure of a dreaded situation, *i.e.,* the patient reacts with affections such as trembling voice, facial grimacing, muscle stiff-ness or the presence of involuntary movements [8]. Among treated patients, psychological symptoms are more common and more difficult to diagnose because of the similarity between natural human fear and phobia; usually this situation leads to being ignored by people. However, when the condition reaches severity indexes, the patient searches for means of defense, making integration difficult in the social environment [6].

According to [8–11] three main groups of phobias are recognized: *(i) Agoraphobia*, the name given to the dread of being in situations where there is no escape, *i.e.,* the patient is afraid of being trapped and unaided in desperate situations as overpopulated places or closed, this being a factor for which the person is isolated from the outside world; *(ii) Social phobias*, is the difficulty of relating in social situations, the person affected experiences embarrassment, lack of self-confidence, fear of being a cause of criticism or mockery, avoiding participation in social and public events; *(iii) Isolated or specific phobias*, is intense fear and persistent due to the presence or anticipation of specific environments, situations or objects [5], the following subtypes are distinguished: animal (spiders, rodents, snakes), environmental (heights, storms, darkness) blood-injections-damage (receive injections, blood from wounds, hospitals), situational (transports, tunnels, bridges), other types caused by other stimuli such as: fear of contracting disease or, to the persons in disguise [12]. In specific phobias, the reduction of the phobic response is achieved with the treatment of patient exposure, guided by a psychotherapist.

The treatment of phobias should be analyzed by a specialist to determine the type and degree of affection of the patient, knowing the factors that triggers the phobia establish the type of psychotherapy to be used, in addition allows him to know the antecedents causing his fear [13, 14]. In this context, the following techniques are determined to confront and control the triggering reaction to the phobia:

- *Exposure psychotherapy*, is the confrontation of the patient with the dreaded situation, to control their fears through gradual and progressive stimulation, for which it is necessary to work in real *"in live"* sites.

- *Systematic desensitization psychotherapy,* consists of projecting the object or situation of phobia, *"in live"*, to control the anxiety generated per the stimulus, through the repetition of ideas.
- *Cognitive psychotherapy,* is to generate confidence before the agents that cause fear in the patient, through the acquisition of information, details, characteristics, among other data of the situation to which he fears.
- *Psychotherapy of shock,* opts for forced exposure to the stimulus until the patient controls their fear, are used as a last resort to verify that the patient has not had a favorable response to previous treatments.

Technological advances have allowed to innovate the psychological treatments through tools and effective applications, where the psychotherapist can apply procedures for the treatment of phobias [13–15]. The Virtual Reality, VR, is being applied in the therapeutic treatment, due to the immersion of people in an environment where the senses of sight and hearing confuse the real with the virtual [14], giving the ease of to recreate environments like those used for this type of treatment in clinics, reducing costs and facilitating the changes required by the psychotherapist according to the needs of the patient [16]. Due the treatment depends of the type and degree of phobia, e.g., fear of height (acrophobia), fear of spiders (arachnophobia), fear of blood (hemophobia), among other types of fears; it is important that the virtual environment contain the necessary elements according to the case, that is why the use of VR tools, facility the development of appropriate environments for the patient immersion in real time [15, 16]. The applications focused on the treatment of phobias are of easy access and manipulation for the psychotherapist, so they can be applied in the initial stages of the treatment, where the patient will not be exposed to the phobia in real form [8].

Several VR applications have been developed in the treatment of phobias, allowing the patient the immersion in sessions controlled by the psychotherapist, *e.g.,* [17] details the efficiency of the use of VR for the creation of structured virtual environments, the same which are applied in treatments for patients with psychological dis-orders. This work contemplates the application of VR as an alternative of the conventional treatments used in phobias therapies. In studies, such as [10] the patient was immersed in claustrophobic virtual environments that allow to identify if the VR can lead to anxiety in the patient, for which various virtual environments are presented where characteristics such as color, textures, spatial opening, among others. The VR is indicated as a viable method to treat this type of disorders, but it is necessary the evaluation of this method to know its effectiveness. While [18] presents a system based on virtual reality for the treatment of acrophobia that allows the patient to move freely in the virtual environment, to provide greater presence and immersion; the patient has sequential and increasing access as he/she advances successfully, *i.e.,* that as the patient controls the anxiety generated by the fear increases the visual stimuli.

This research proposes a system implemented with technological innovation that allows to help the treatment of psychological disorders, allowing the use of the main techniques of treatment of therapies that simulate a real environment where the patient is gradually exposed to the object of fear that causes panic or facing the highest level of fear possible according to different types of phobias. The system comprises directly of a virtual environment developed with a graphic engine the same one that to give greater realism uses devices like OculusRift.

This article is divided into 6 sections including the Introduction. Section 2 presents the structure of the proposed phobia treatment system; while the valorization of the physiological responses emitted by the user in the estimation of the virtual environment are presented in Sect. 3. The description of the multilayer scheme of the application of development of virtual environments is contemplated in Sect. 4. Section 5 Shows experimental results that validate the proposal; and finally the conclusions are detailed in Sect. 6.

2 System Structure

This paper present the development of an application in a 3D virtual environment for phobia treatments by means of audiovisual stimulation in the real world perception; the user will find different working environments according to the type and degree of phobia that affects him. In addition, the proposed application allows psychotherapists to evaluate reactions to receptive stimuli during immersion in the virtual environment, for which wearable devices will be used; this in-formation will allow the psychotherapist to analyze the recovery progress of each user in the treatment process. The phobias treatment system allows feedback of the responses to stimuli received through wearable devices, see Fig. 1.

Fig. 1. Wearables devices

This phobia treatment system is safe and allows the user to determine the working environment according to the type and degree of phobia [14]. Figure 2 describes the user's interaction with the proposed system, establishing as comunication element the

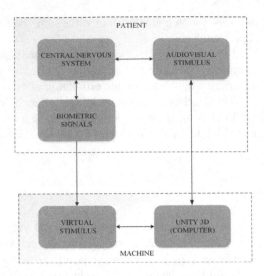

Fig. 2. Phobia treatment system block diagram

feedback, the response of the nervous system of the user through biometric signals, *e.g.*, heart rate, oxygen level in the blood, blood pressure, tremor Physiological, among others.

The patient's interaction with the system is established through bilateral communication, *i.e.*, first through a graphical interface the user selects the working environment in which he/she interacts; second to the user will be exposed to audiovisual stimuli while immersed in the preestablished environment. Due to the type and degree of phobia that the user presents, the responses to the stimuli are controlled in real time, allowing the monitoring of the biomechanical signals through wearable devices; the user's behavior data are acquired in order to determine if the stimulation is adequate and can be increased according to the perspective of the psychotherapist.

In addition, in the virtual environment where the user executes the therapy is implemented response indicators based on the biometric signals acquired through the wearable devices; these virtual indicators will allow the user to control their reaction in order to successfully accomplish the defined therapy, *i.e.*, the user's central nervous system becomes the controller of a closed loop control system. The visual environment developed for this type of treatment provides a systematic application which the user interacts with the environment controlled their reactions in order to complete the defined work.

3   Graphic Environment

The system is developed as a virtual 3D application, contains control scripts, the same ones that act according to the behavior of the devices applied in the Unity environment, view Fig. 3. In the simulation stage of the scene it's found the virtual reality programming, here different 3D environments are developed, the same ones that are focused on causing a patient immersion where the brain does not distinguish between

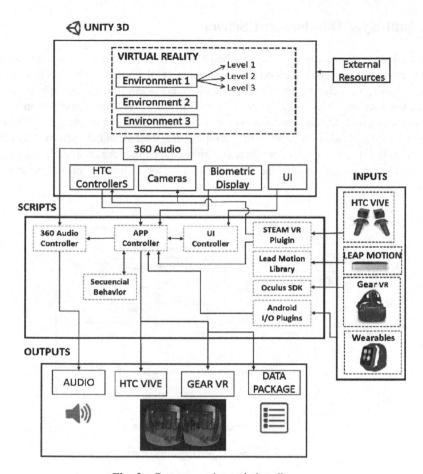

Fig. 3. Component interrelation diagram

the real and the virtual, besides Are designed according to the type of phobia to be addressed, as well as the level of stimulus that the subject is facing.

In the input and output stage different devices may be applied for the interaction between the user and the virtual environment, *e.g.* VR helmets (Oculus Rift, HTC VIVE and GearVR) and haptic controls, *e.g.* Tracking hands devices, (Leap Motion, Manus VR Myo Armband, Wearables devices). Depending on the diversity of devices that can be used, it is important that the code structure is general, so that automatic detection of a device, as well as cross-platform compatibility.

In the SCRIPTS stage the communication with the input and output devices is managed, so that the virtual environment has the required functionality, through the APP controller the movement and interaction with the application is managed, depending on different stimuli, the Level of the stimulus is administered according to the recording of the input signal using the technique of hierarchies. Finally, the output stage has 360 surround audio, haptic response to the inputs, visual response to the tracking of movements and visualization of recorded data during therapy.

4 Multi-layer Development Scheme

This section describes the multilayer schema for the development of applications in virtual environments, as a method for the treatment of phobias. This scheme works independently, i.e., can be replaced by other layers according to the application in which the user interacts, finding: *(i) Layer 1* in this layer the construction of the environment where the test environment is shown; *(ii) Layer 2* in charge of the execution of the task and configuration of the inputs that interact in the system; *(iii) Layer 3* develops the stimulus controller where the biometric signals are analyzed; and finally; *(iv) Layer 4* the visualization of the acquired data for the evaluation of the therapy, see Fig. 4.

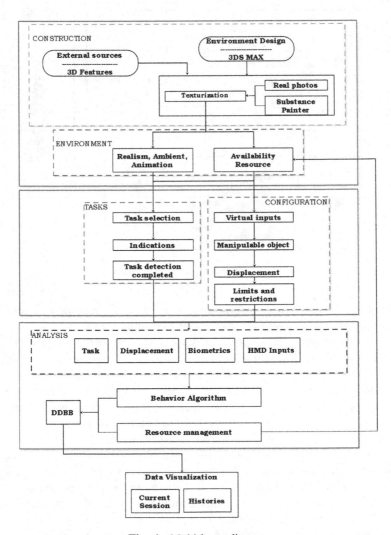

Fig. 4. Multi-layer diagram

Construction Environments

This layer allows to develop the virtual environment in function of the phobia that is wanted to treat, the virtual environment can be designed in a graphic animation engine or can be imported from CAD software, in the case of being exported must be considered the software 3ds Max or Blender, So that the motion hierarchies can be established and the resulting files are compatible with the Unity 3D graphics engine software. For the customization of the virtual environments can be considered external 3D sources of certain objects or elements that are not available in the software that is developing the application, e.g., rabbits, snakes and others. Once the designs and objects that are to belong to the virtual environment are obtained, these are the texturing, see Fig. 5, color-texture-rigorousness of the object through Albedo, Metallic, Normal y Heigh Map, obtained from an original image or using the tool Substance Painter, in such a way that they have the most real and convincing environments possible.

Fig. 5. Final textured environment

The sublayer environment is dynamic, here is the environment animation, inside this sublayer are considered two sections: *(i) Realism:* in which the setting of the whole virtual environment is done, the lighting and animation are added in the way that one has a greater immersion in the environment; *(ii) Availability of Resources:* this section is directly related to the controllers, here are all the resources available to interact in the virtual environment.

Settings and Tasks

In layer 2 two sublayers are considered: (i) Input configuration: for user interaction and elements that compose the virtual environment using the HTC VIVE and Gear VR devices. The configuration of input devices is done by using functions of OnTriggerEnter (), OnTriggerStay (), OnTriggerExit (). For manipulation of objects and elements of the virtual environment, the GRIP or TRIGGER button is considered. While for the displacement of the user in the virtual environment the user's own movement is considered and the "teleportation" is implemented, which consists in indicating a reference point on the surface for the purpose of moving the user to a desired location within the limits of the application, see Fig. 6. Here also the limits and restrictions of the virtual environment are fixed. Y (ii) Task: this section selects the type of task according to the phobia to be treated, e.g. for phobia to heights that crosses a rope between buildings; general guidelines of the task are given and the signage is presented within the virtual environment so that the user has a guide and does not lose interest in the development of the test. The completed task detection is implemented in order to know the exact moment the user finished the test.

Fig. 6. General indications

Analysis and Control
In layer three a block of analysis is established, the HMD Inputs are analyzed in order to know the state in which are the inputs or controls that the user manipulates, can be done an analysis of vital signs such as: heartbeat, sweating, trembling, pulsations, among others to determine the degree of relaxation or excitement of the user, in function on the data obtained, the degree of excitation can be determined, at higher excitation the intensity of the phobia level. It examines the movement and movement of the user, in order to know the exact place in which it is, determines where to go and control programmed limits and restrictions. It also analyzes the fulfillment of the task in order to: measure the compliance time of the task and increase or decrease the level of intensity of the test if necessary.

Within layer three the behavioral algorithms are implemented, i.e. the sequence of occurrence of events on how, when and where the stimuli that cause phobias are present, in a similar way, the administration of resources is done the same that are related to the section of availability of resources. The above will be stored in a database which will be available for manipulation and analysis by the therapist.

Data Visualization
In the last layer is considered the visualization of the data, the historicals that will help to see the evolution of the subject with respect to the phobias, and shows the current therapy session with the objective of planning a new session or to modify it according to the data analysis, this section is oriented to the analysis of the therapist.

5 Results

In this section presents the results of the application for the treatment of phobias according to the type and grade that the patient presents. The application displays a virtual menu for the purpose that the user selects the environment according to the type of phobia it has and the level of irrational fear (phobia), see Fig. 7.

(a) Type of phobia

(b) Phobia level

Fig. 7. Virtual environment selection

Figure 8 shows the virtual environments developed, in the same application is consider four of the most common phobias possessed by people (i) *claustrophobia* that is the fear of closed places see Fig. 8(a); (ii) *zoophobia* the medical name given to the fear of all kinds of animals see Fig. 8(b); (iii) *ophidiophobia* the irrational fear towards the serpents see Fig. 8(c), and finally (iv) *acrophobia* known as fear of height see Fig. 8(d). In each virtual environment, it is considered a behavioral algorithm that

(a) Claustrophobia

(b) Zoophobia

(c) Ophidiophobia

(d) Acrophobia

Fig. 8. Virtual environments for 4 types of phobias

considers the stimuli emitted to the patient based on the biometric data that are recorded, i.e. the patient will be gradually exposed to events that provoke a response related to the phobia, to verify the intensity in the response, so that a sudden change in the physiological activity of the user, causes a change in the environment that allows to keep the user within the normal parameters.

In Fig. 9, the interaction of the patient with the virtual environment for the treatment of acrophobia is shown. Working environments stimulate the patient visual and audibly, allowing the interaction with the environment to be as real as possible, *i.e.,* that the user will be exposed to sounds and animations according to the selected environment, for which use is made of Virtual devices such as HTC VIVE and GearVR, hearing aids and wearables devices for measuring biometric signals.

(a) Acrophobia   (b) Zoophobia

Fig. 9. User interaction in treatment phobias

In this therapy was considered the virtualization of a city with high-rise buildings, in which the user has as a mission to move from one building to another by means of a beam joining the two skyscrapers as shown in Fig. 10. The stimulation to which the patient is exposed allows an immersion with the virtual environment in such a way to sense in real time the parameter changes of the biometric signals obtained with the wearable device, *i.e.,* that as it advances in the path the device registers the vital signs, in order to compare them with the normal values, so that actions are taken regarding the increase of the stimulus that the user is facing, or the change of the environment so that the user can stabilize.

Fig. 10. Acrophobia therapy section.

6 Conclusions

In this article an application of virtual environments was presented in order to stimulate the audiovisual senses for medical treatment of phobias. The developed application considers a behavioral algorithm that controls the virtual environment according to the type and degree of phobia and the biological signals of the patients acquired in real time through wearable devices. The results are validated based on the realism of the virtual environments developed, and the audio-visual stimuli applied to the patient based on the change of the parameters of the biometric signals acquired through wearable devices.

References

1. Shunnaq, S., Raeder, M.: Virtual phobia a model for virtual therapy of phobias. In: XVIII Symposium on Virtual and Augmented Reality, pp. 59–63 (2016)
2. Monge, J.P., López, G., Guerrero, Luis A.: Supporting phobia treatment with virtual reality: systematic desensitization using oculus rift. In: Duffy, V.G., Lightner, N. (eds.) Advances in Human Factors and Ergonomics in Healthcare. AISC, vol. 482, pp. 391–401. Springer, Cham (2017). doi:10.1007/978-3-319-41652-6_36
3. Rosa, P., Esteves, F., Arriaga, P.: Beyond traditional clinical measurements for screening fears and phobias. IEEE Instrum. Measur. Soc. **64**, 3396–3404 (2015)
4. Horváthová, D., Siládi, V., Lacková, E.: Phobia treatment with the help of virtual reality. In: Scientific Conference on Informatics, pp. 114–119 (2015)
5. Tabbakh, S.K., Habibi, R., Vafadar, S.: Design and implementation of a framework based on augmented reality for phobia treatment applications. In: International Congress on Technology, Communication and Knowledge (ICTCK), pp. 366–370 (2015)
6. Takacs, B., Simon, L.: A clinical virtual reality rehabilitation system for phobia treatment. In: Information Visualization, pp. 798–806 (2007)

7. Depasquale, C., Pistorio, M.L., Corona, D., Mistretta, A., Zerbo, D., Sinagra, N., Giaquinta, A., et al.: Correlational study between psychic symptoms and quality of life among hemodialysis patients older than 55 years of age. Transplant. Proc. **48**(8), 2850 (2016)
8. Reger, G.M., Koenen-Woods, P., Zetocha, K., Smolenski, D.J., Holloway, K.M., Rothbaum, B.O., Mishkind, M.: Randomized controlled trial of prolonged exposure using imaginal exposure vs. virtual reality exposure in active duty soldiers with deployment-related posttraumatic stress disorder (PTSD) (2016)
9. Alcaniz, M., Monserrat, C., Botella, C., Banos, R.M., Guerrero, B.: Using augmented reality to terat phobias. IEEE Comput. Graph. Appl. **25**, 31–37 (2005)
10. Christofi, M., Michael-Grigoriou, D.: Virtual environments design assessment for the treatment of claustrophobia. In: Virtual System & Multimedia (VSMM), pp. 1–8 (2016)
11. Grillon, H., Riquier, F., Thalmann, D.: Eye-tracking as diagnosis and assessment tool for social phobias, pp. 138–145 (2007)
12. Singh, J., Singh, J.: Treatment options for the specific phobias. Int. J. Basic Clin. Pharmacol. **5**(3), 593–598 (2016)
13. Villani, D., Rotasperti, C., Cipresso, P., Triberti, S., Carissoli, C., Riva, G.: Assessing the emotional state of job applicants through a virtual reality simulation: a psycho-physiological study. In: Giokas, K., Bokor, L., Hopfgartner, F. (eds.) eHealth 360°. LNICSSITE, vol. 181, pp. 119–126. Springer, Cham (2017). doi:10.1007/978-3-319-49655-9_16
14. Miloff, A., Lindner, P., Hamilton, W.H., Reuterskiöld, L., Andersson, G., Carlbring, P.: Single-session gamified virtual reality exposure therapy for spider phobia vs. traditional exposure therapy: a randomized-controlled trial. In: Society for Research on Internet Interventions, Seattle (2016)
15. North, M.M., North, S.M.: Virtual reality therapy for treatment of psychological disorders. In: Maheu, M.M., Drude, K.P., Wright, S.D. (eds.) Career Paths in Telemental Health, pp. 263–268. Springer International Publishing, Switzerland (2017)
16. Gonzalez, D.S., Moro, A.D., Quintero, C., Sarmiento, W.J.: Fear levels in virtual environments, an approach to detection and experimental user stimuli sensation. In: Images and Artificial Vision (STSIVA), pp. 1–6 (2016)
17. Gebara, C.M., Barros-Neto, T.P.D., Gertsenchtein, L., Lotufo-Neto, F.: Virtual reality exposure using three-dimensional images for the treatment of social phobia. Revista Brasileira de Psiquiatria **38**(1), 24–29 (2016)
18. Costa, J., Robb, J., Nacke, L.: Physiological acrophobia evaluation through in vivo exposure in a VR CAVE, pp. 1–4 (2014)

Virtual Out-of-Body Experience as a Potential Therapeutic Tool After Kidney Transplantation

Péter Csibri[1]($\boxtimes$), Róbert Pantea[2], Attila Tanács[2], Alexandra Kiss[1], and Gyula Sáry[1]

[1] Department of Physiology, University of Szeged, Dóm tér 10, Szeged 6720, Hungary
{csibri.peter,sary.gyula}@med.u-szeged.hu
[2] Institute of Informatics, University of Szeged, Árpád tér 2, Szeged 6720, Hungary
tanacs@inf.u-szeged.hu

Abstract. The last wave of commercially available virtual reality (VR) devices opened ways to more immersive medical applications. We present a virtual reality system that exploits the virtual out-of-body experience to assist the acknowledgment of the transplanted body organ. We give an overview of the physiological background and set goals towards the VR system. An implementation using Oculus Rift hardware is presented. We describe the applied physiological evaluation process for kidney transplantation. The studies are currently still ongoing.

Keywords: Medical VR · Virtual out-of-body experience · Transplant adoption

1 Introduction

The technique behind virtual reality has been known for many decades including stereo photo displays around the end of the 19th century, early virtual reality (VR) approaches in the 1960's, and GPU–3D active glass based ones in the 2000's. Starting from the 1990's, an explosion of VR laboratories around the world can be witnessed.

Todays technological advances made it possible to create commercially available glass devices that can implement a new level of fully immersive experiences. A cheap solution is smartphone based like Google Cardboard costing few dollars to more expensive glasses containing extra motion sensors like the Samsung Gear VR. Although these can be treated as easy and cheap entry to VR, full fledged graphics with high enough and continuous frame rate can only be achieved utilizing massive computations produced by strong computers and graphics hardware nowadays. The necessary bandwidth still requires wired connection between the glass and the computer. It is also critical to immediately respond to patient movement using sensitive motion sensors (accelerometers, gyroscopes). Such commercially available devices are the Oculus Rift and HTC Vive.

L.T. De Paolis et al. (Eds.): AVR 2017, Part II, LNCS 10325, pp. 202–210, 2017.
DOI: 10.1007/978-3-319-60928-7_17

Besides gaming, telepresence and various industrial applications, VR usage in assisting medical tasks is more and more frequent. So called "serious games" are games with education, skill development or rehabilitation in mind instead of entertainment. These are used for either physician training as in case of laparoscopic intervention [1], or aimed towards the patients to help recovery in rehabilitation of stroke [2] or the legs [3]. For physician training the advantages of VR is clear, studies have demonstrated that these can significantly reduce intra-operative errors compared against traditional methods, e.g., [4]. As for the evidence in patient recovery, the papers show encouraging preliminary results albeit stating that the findings are usually limited [2,5]. A recent review paper on treatment of phantom limb pain [6] summarizes that papers published in this particular topic mainly show case studies and albeit the positive findings, studies of higher evidence are still yet to be conducted. The most similar work to ours is using the virtual out-of-body experience to reduce to fear of death [7].

We target our focus towards commercially available VR glass devices that provide sufficient frame rates and make deployment of such clinical systems cheaper and easier. As these type of devices are relatively new in the market, papers dealing with their applications are now starting to appear. E.g., in [8], the Oculus Rift was found applicable for standardized and reliable assessment and diagnosis of elementary cognitive functions in laboratory and clinical settings.

In this paper we describe a virtual reality system that exploits the virtual out-of-body experience to assist the acknowledgment of the transplanted body organ. First we introduce the physiological background and set the goals against the system. Then we introduce our implemented system. This project is a work in progress. Medical evaluation has started but we only have some preliminary feedback from physicians.

2   Physiological Background

There is an increasing number of evidence in transplantology proving that experiencing disease, own body sensation, and awareness of the transplanted organ may have an influence on the physical recovery [9,10,16,20]. The anxiety after the surgery can even increase [28] which is a strong negative impact on the life quality after the implantation of organs [11,17]. In addition in the case of kidney transplantation, a strong correlation was observed between the impaired renal functions (serum creatinine) and biological degradation associated with complications arising in the future [24].

In order to reduce anxiety following transplantation surgery, we developed an autogenous imaginaton anti-stress therapy. In order to improve the method we developed a virtual world to offer a new tool for the therapist. The essence of the method is to create a virtual body which will be used to make the illusory self-identification sensation on which the therapy will be carried out. In the classic form of therapy, the subject has to imagine a certain situation. The therapist can achieve the therapeutic effect with the continuous changing of this fictional world. In a stressful situation that arises after transplantation, this method is difficult to apply in practice as the test person's thoughts are difficult to control, so he/she might be unable to focus on the fictional world. With virtual reality, the therapist can present the imaginary world more easily and change it when he/she wants this. This simplifies the immersion to the test person and this way the control of the therapy is much easier for the therapist.

The virtual body sensation or out-of-body experience is very similar to the phenomenon known as heautoscopy, in which a person feels that there is a second body which is his/her own [12,15]. This phenomenon is very close to the rubber hand illusion when we can create an illusory hand ownership. In the case of healthy humans, we can create the feeling that the rubber hand lying in front of them is their own limb [14,18,29,30]. To induce the illusion, we place a rubber hand in front of the subject while we cover the real hand. After that we start stroking the real hand with a brush and simultaneously we stroke the rubber hand as well at the same place. After a while the illusory hand ownership and the proprioceptive drift will develop [30,31]. The illusion is created by means of parallel processing of the visuo-tactile stimuli in multisensory neurones of the premotor cortex (PMC) and intraparietal sulcus (IPS) [26]. The neurons are located here are able to respond to stimuli that come from the contralateral limb skin and for visual stimuli which approach these limb [23]. The receptive field of these neurons may change for example by moving the arm [23,27]. The illusory feeling is also due to the change of these receptive fields [26].

As the *self* is normally an autonomous and uniform experience rather than a collection that of various body parts, one could assume that the whole body illusion is of a different case. The experimental results confirm its contrary, however. In the case of full body, the origin of the illusion was testified with similar studies in primates [19,21]. In addition, the illusory self-identification is stably maintained even if the virtual body only partially reflects the current appearance of the subjects [15]. Based on all of these, it has been suggested that the heautoscopy as a disorder should be treated as it comes from multisensory processing – in this case visual tactile and proprioceptive [13], which can be induced in a similar way as the rubber hand illusion [22,25].

3   System Design Goals and Implementation

When designing the system the following goals were set by the physicians.

(i) It is crucial to precisely and effectively handle quick head motions of the patient keeping continuously high frame rate to avoid cybersickness [32].

(ii) It is desirable to make an avatar that resembles the body parameters (height, BMI, etc.) of the patient.

(iii) To be able to adopt the avatar as a living creature it should follow a biologically valid motion pattern and be placed inside a scene natural to the patient.

(iv) To reach the virtual out-of-body experience, it is expected to be able to make tactile and visual excitation in a synchronized manner [33].

(v) The size of the visual representation of the kidney should be easily modifiable.

(vi) The camera should be freely detachable from the avatar, so the avatar can move around in the room without a change of first person perspective of the observer, thus strengthening the feeling of being just a passive observer of his/her own body.

(vii) The distance set between the camera and the avatar should be saved for later reference.

We chose Oculus Rift as VR glass and a high end PC for the graphical computations. Development started with Oculus Rift DK2, that was later upgraded to its final commercial version. According to our preliminary tests, this configuration satisfied Goal (i).

Goals (ii) and (iii) relate to modeling of the avatar and the environment. We chose Unity 3D game engine[1] since it is easy to adopt and provides direct programming connection to Oculus Rift.

Creating a realistic model of a human character is of widespread interest in gaming and simulation. MakeHuman[2] is an open source tool for making such 3D models. We can choose from many predetermined shapes and can easily tailor the model to our needs adjusting self explanatory parameters. Our goal is to define a set of man and woman models the physician can chose from when the therapy of a new patient is started. If no satisfyingly similar model is available, it is possible to prepare a new one and import into the program. The generated models are of high resolution, containing more than 220 thousands of vertices.

MakeHuman also generates a skeleton to our model that can be used for character animation. The output of MakeHuman can be directly imported into Unity. Unity's default humanoid animation system can make use of the skeleton if the model is in an appropriate initial position: when arms are stretched in horizontal position (Fig. 1). The animation was based on using the `ThirdPersonController` script of Unity Standard Assets, overriding the idle animation script to follow the head movement of the patient. The script implements the biological movement patterns of walking and running making it more natural to accept by the patient as virtual body sensation.

Besides, the open source animation software Blender[3] is also compatible with MakeHuman skeletons. Thus, missing animations from Unity (e.g., a sitting character) can be produced here and forwarded to Unity.

The environment consist of a textured room with some furniture and two windows to a natural outside scene. We used a model from Blend Swap website[4] that we heavily modified in Blender. More walls and the ceiling was added, surface normal vectors were fixed and materials were affixed to surfaces to be able to add textures to them in Unity (Fig. 2). The outside garden was produced using tree and flower models from `NatureStarterKit2` and `Ornamental Flower`

---

[1] Official homepage: https://unity3d.com/.

[2] Official homepage: http://www.makehuman.org/.

[3] Official homepage: http://www.blender.org.

[4] http://www.blendswap.com/blends/view/59196.

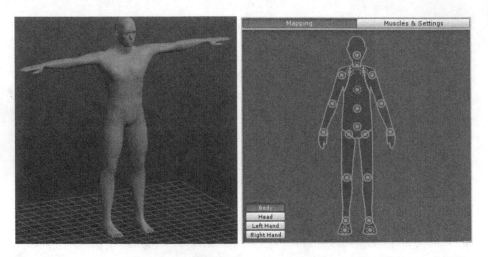

Fig. 1. Man avatar designed in Makehuman (left) and its skeleton joint points in Unity (right)

Fig. 2. Room scene prepared in Blender and further processed in Unity

Set packages available from Unity Asset Store. Lighting was switched to dynamic instead of the default Global Illumination model and Ambient Occlusion was applied to improve display speed.

A crucial point of the application is to statisfy Goal (iv). To reach to virtual out-of-body experience, the patient should be tactily and visually excited synchronously. The tactile excitation in the real world is performed by the physicist using a pen-like object. The visual one in the virtual world is represented by a spotlight animation effect. Four regions of the body is determined and excitation of these is repeated for 2–3 min maintaining 4–8 s for one stimulus (Fig. 3).

Fig. 3. Man avatar with spotlight positions representing visual touch regions

The size of the kidney is also represented by a spotlight attached to the virtual body. Its size can be changed interactively by the mouse wheel. As the therapy progresses, the size of the organ can be matched to the anxiety level of the patient thus satisfying Goal (v).

Goals (vi) and (vii) are purely technical that were successfully implemented.

4   Evaluation Method

According to Latos et al. [24] there is a strong correlation between the patient's belief about his/her own health status and the secreted creatinine and urea. If the mental state of the patient deteriorates, the deterioration of the renal function will follow, thus, the success of transplantation decreases.

After being instructed about the treatment process and signing the consent form, participants are asked to take up the Oculus Rift. The study is divided into two phases.

- **Reaching the virtual out-of-body experience.** It takes 3–4 min meanwhile we use tactile stimuli in the subjects back and simultaneously those appear as visual effects in the back of the VR body.
- **Treatment phase.** It lasts 25–30 minutes. The treatment is repeated 10 times after the operation in two-day intervals.

The test persons on the occasion of the control examinations participate in a psychotherapy session. In order to study the psychological state of the subjects, first we use psychological tests and questionnaires.

- To assess the severity of depressive symptoms we use the Beck's Depression Inventory (BDI) [34]. It is a 21-question multiple-choice self report inventory psychometric test.

- The Spielberger State and Trait Anxiety Inventory (STAIS and STAIT) measures the level of anxiety after transplantation [35], which is an emotional state test that included feelings of apprehension, tension, nervousness, and worry accompanied by physiological arousal. Anxiety can be adaptive in motivating behavior that helps the individual to cope with threatening situations but it can also be maladaptive when it is too high and paralyzes the patient.
- We apply the Posttraumatic Growth Inventory (PTGI) to quantify the coping with traumatic events [35]. This 21-item scale includes factors of new possibilities, relating to others, personal strength, spiritual change, and appreciation of life.
- An other questionnaire serves measuring the representations relating to the transplanted organ Transplanted Organ Questionnaire to check the feasibility of everyday life [17].
- For the monitoring of biological changes, at every treatment occassions we determine the serum creatinine level of the patient using a blood tests to examine renal function. We analyze the results with multifractal ANOVA and correlation tests. In a control condition we use the results from the classic therapy.

The results of the tests will not be shared with the test person, in this way these do not affect the outcome of the investigation.

5   Conclusions

Preliminary tests show that the application works properly for healthy subjects. People with less knowledge of IT can quickly learn to operate it. Following the positive feedback from professionals, the studies are currently going on at this very moment with kidney transplanted patients. Once the evaluation forms will be received, statistical analysis of the results can be conducted.

The aim of our work was to create an easy to use tool for therapists to facilitate their work thus saving their time and energy. We also aim to improve patients' quality of life and improve the success of transplantation ratio with reducing anxiety. And last but not least we want to show that virtual reality has a role in this area as well.

References

1. Paolis, L.T., Ricciardi, F., Giuliani, F.: Development of a serious game for laparoscopic suture training. In: De Paolis, L.T., Mongelli, A. (eds.) AVR 2014. LNCS, vol. 8853, pp. 90–102. Springer, Cham (2014). doi:10.1007/978-3-319-13969-2_7
2. Laver, K.E., George, S., Thomas, S., Deutsch, J.E., Crotty, M.: Virtual reality for stroke rehabilitation. Cochrane Database Syst. Rev. (2), Art. No. CD008349 (2015). doi:10.1002/14651858.CD008349.pub3

3. Gobron, S.C., Zannini, N., Wenk, N., Schmitt, C., Charrotton, Y., Fauquex, A., Lauria, M., Degache, F., Frischknecht, R.: Serious games for rehabilitation using head-mounted display and haptic devices. In: Paolis, L.T., Mongelli, A. (eds.) AVR 2015. LNCS, vol. 9254, pp. 199–219. Springer, Cham (2015). doi:10.1007/978-3-319-22888-4_15
4. Seymour, N.E., Gallagher, A.G., Roman, S.A., OBrien, M.K., Bansal, V.K., Andersen, D.K., Satava, R.M.: Virtual reality training improves operating room performance: results of a randomized, double-blinded study. Ann. Surg. **236**(4), 458–464 (2002)
5. Henderson, A., Korner-Bitensky, N., Levin, M.: Virtual reality in stroke rehabilitation: a systematic review of its effectiveness for upper limb motor recovery. Top Stroke Rehabil. **14**(2), 52–61 (2007)
6. Dunn, J., Yeo, E., Moghaddampour, P., Chau, B., Humbert, S.: Virtual and augmented reality in the treatment of phantom limb pain: a literature review. NeuroRehabilitation **Preprint**, 1–7 (2016). doi:10.3233/NRE-171447. [Preprint]
7. Bourdin, P., Barberia, I., Oliva, R., Slater, M.: A virtual out-of-body experience reduces fear of death. PLOS ONE **12**(1), 1–19 (2017). doi:10.1371/journal.pone.0169343. e0169343
8. Foerster, R.M., Poth, C.H., Behler, C., Botsch, M., Schneider, W.X.: Using the virtual reality device Oculus Rift for neuropsychological assessment of visual processing capabilities. Sci. Rep. **6** (2016). doi:10.1038/srep37016. 37016
9. Abram, H.S., Buchanan, D.C.: The Gift of Life: a review of the psychological aspects of kidney transplantation. IJPM **7**(2), 153–164 (1976)
10. Baines, L.S., Joseph, J.T., Jindal, R.M.: Emotional issues after kidney transplantation: a prospective psychotherapeutic study. Clin. Transplant. **16**, 455–460 (2002)
11. Beck, A.T., Ward, C.H., Mendelson, M., et al.: An inventory for measuring depression. Arch. Gen. Psychiatry. **4**, 561–571 (1961)
12. Blanke, O., Metzinger, T.: Full-body illusions and minimal phenomenal selfhood. Trends Cogn. Sci. **13**, 7–13 (2009)
13. Blanke, O., Landis, T., Spinelli, L., Seeck, M.: Out-of-body experience and autoscopy of neurological origin. Brain **127**, 243–258 (2004)
14. Botvinick, M., Cohen, J.: Rubber hands touch that eyes see. Nature **391**, 756 (1998)
15. Brugger, P.: Reflective mirrors: perspective-taking in autoscopic phenomena. Cogn. Neuropsychiatry **7**, 179–194 (2002)
16. Burloux, G., Bachmann, D.: Psychology and hand transplantation: clinical experiences. In: Mac Lachlan, M., Gallagher, P. (eds.) Enabling Technologies: Body Image and Body Function, pp. 169–185. Churchill Livingston, Edingburgh (2004)
17. Corruble, E., Barry, C., Varescon, I., et al.: The transplanted organ questionnaire: a validation study. J. Psychosom. Res. **73**, 319–324 (2012)
18. Ehrsson, H.H., Spence, C., Passingham, R.E.: Thats my hand! activity in premotor cortex reflects feeling of ownership of a limb. Science **305**, 875–877 (2004)
19. Fogassi, L., et al.: Coding of peripersonal space in inferior premotor cortex (area F4). J. Neurophysiol. **76**, 141–157 (1996)
20. Fukunishi, I.: Psychosomatic problems surrounding kidney transplantation. Psychother. Psychosom. **57**, 42–49 (1992)
21. Graziano, M.S., Cooke, D.F., Taylor, C.S.: Coding the location of the arm by sight. Science **290**, 1782–1786 (2000)
22. Ionta, S., et al.: Multisensory mechanisms in temporo-parietal cortex support self-location and first-person perspective. Neuron **70**, 363–374 (2011)

23. Iriki, A., Tanaka, M., Iwamura, Y.: Coding of modified body schema during tool use by macaque postcentral neurones. Neuroreport **7**, 2325–2330 (1996)
24. Látos, M., Devecsery, Á., Lázár, G., Horváth, Z., Szederkényi, E., Szenohradszky, P., Csabai, M.: The role of body image integrity and posttraumatic growth in kidney transplantation: a 3-year longitudinal study. Health Psychol. Open **2**(1), 1–8 (2015). doi:10.1177/2055102915581214
25. Lenggenhager, B., Tadi, T., Metzinger, T., Blanke, O.: Video ergo sum: manipulating bodily self-consciousness. Science **317**, 1096–1099 (2007)
26. Makin, T.R., Holmes, N.P., Ehrsson, H.H.: On the other hand: dummy hands and peripersonal space. Behav. Brain Res. **191**, 1–10 (2008)
27. Maravita, A., Iriki, A.: Tools for the body (schema). Trends Cogn. Sci. **8**, 79–86 (2004)
28. Schlitt, H.J., Brunkhorst, R., Schmidt, II.II.J., et al.: Attitudes of patients before and after transplantation towards various allografts. Transplant. **68**, 510–514 (1999)
29. Slater, M., Perez-Marcos, D., Ehrsson, H.H., Sanchez-Vives, M.V.: Towards a digital body: the virtual arm illusion. Front. Hum. Neurosci. **2**, 6 (2008)
30. Tsakiris, M., Haggard, P.: The rubber hand illusion revisited: visuotactile integration and self-attribution. J. Exp. Psychol. Hum. Percept. Perform. **31**, 80–91 (2005)
31. Kammers, M.P., de Vignemont, F., Verhagen, L., Dijkerman, H.C.: The rubber hand illusion in action. Neuropsychologia **47**, 204–211 (2009)
32. Lo, W.T., So, R.H.: Cybersickness in the presence of scene rotational movements along different axes. Appl. Ergon. **32**(1), 1–14 (2001)
33. Blanke, O.: Multisensory brain mechanisms of bodily self-consciousness. Nat. Rev. Neurosci. **13**, 556–571 (2012). doi:10.1038/nrn3292
34. Beck, A.T., Ward, C.H., Mendelson, M., et al.: An inventory for measuring depression. Arch. Gen. Psychiatry **4**, 561–571 (1961)
35. Tedeschi, R., Calhoun, L.: The posttraumatic growth inventory: measuring the positive legacy of trauma. J. Trauma. Stress **9**, 455–471 (1996)

Patient Specific Virtual and Physical Simulation Platform for Surgical Robot Movability Evaluation in Single-Access Robot-Assisted Minimally-Invasive Cardiothoracic Surgery

Giuseppe Turini[1,2]([✉]), Sara Condino[2], Sara Sinceri[2], Izadyar Tamadon[3],
Simona Celi[4], Claudio Quaglia[3], Michele Murzi[4], Giorgio Soldani[5],
Arianna Menciassi[3], Vincenzo Ferrari[2,6], and Mauro Ferrari[2]

[1] Computer Science Department, Kettering University, Flint, MI, USA
gturini@kettering.edu
[2] Department of Translational Research on New Technologies in Medicine
and Surgery, EndoCAS Center, University of Pisa, Pisa, Italy
{sara.condino,sara.sinceri,vincenzo.ferrari,
mauro.ferrari}@endocas.unipi.it
[3] The Biorobotics Institute, Scuola Superiore Sant'Anna, Pisa, Italy
{izadyar.tamadon,claudio.quaglia,arianna.menciassi}@santannapisa.it
[4] Fondazione Toscana Gabriele Monasterio, Pisa, Italy
{simona.celi,michele.murzi}@ftgm.it
[5] Consiglio Nazionale delle Ricerche, Istituto di Fisiologia Clinica, Pisa, Italy
giorgio.soldani@ifc.cnr.it
[6] Information Engineering Department, University of Pisa, Pisa, Italy
vincenzo.ferrari@unipi.it

Abstract. Recently, minimally invasive cardiothoracic surgery (MICS) has grown in popularity thanks to its advantages over conventional surgery and advancements in surgical robotics.

This paper presents a patient-specific virtual surgical simulator for the movability evaluation of single-port MICS robots. This simulator can be used for both the pre-operative planning to rehearse the case before the surgery, and to test the robot in the early stage of development before physical prototypes are built.

A physical simulator is also proposed to test the robot prototype in a tangible environment. Synthetic replicas of the patient organs are able to replicate the mechanical behaviors of biological tissues, allowing the simulation of the physical interactions robot-anatomy.

The preliminary tests of the virtual simulator showed good performance for both the visual and physics processes.

After reviewing the physical simulator, a surgeon provided a positive evaluation of the organ replicas in terms of geometry and mechanical behaviors.

Keywords: Virtual reality · Unity game engine · Computer-assisted surgery · Minimally-invasive surgery · Cardiothoracic surgery · Robotic surgery · Surgical simulation

© Springer International Publishing AG 2017
L.T. De Paolis et al. (Eds.): AVR 2017, Part II, LNCS 10325, pp. 211–220, 2017.
DOI: 10.1007/978-3-319-60928-7_18

1 Introduction

Minimally invasive cardiothoracic surgery (MICS) has grown rapidly over the past decade, thanks to continuous innovations in surgical techniques, advances in surgical instruments, and the adoption of robotic technologies. According to literature evidence, major cardiac operations traditionally performed through a median sternotomy can be accomplished less invasively through small incisions, with equivalent safety and durability [12].

Robotic systems have been utilized successfully to perform complex surgical procedures such as mitral valve and tricuspid valve repairs [3,9], single and multiple vessel coronary artery bypass surgeries [9,11], atrial fibrillation ablations [20], intracardiac tumor resections, atrial septal defect closures, and left ventricular leads [2,18]. Moreover recent studies demonstrated the feasibility of performing aortic valve replacement in adults using surgical robots [10].

Single port access (SPA) surgery, which uses one skin incision for interventions, caught the attention of the surgical community in the past a few years because of its potential to further reduce the invasiveness of surgical procedures and post-operative complications. Looking at this potentiality, researchers have proposed various robotic systems to assist SPA surgery [21]. For example, an articulated robotic probe has been designed for cardiac surgery applications [8], and a flexible *"snakelike"* robotic systems have been developed to allow physicians to view, access, and perform complex procedures on the beating heart through a single-access port [14].

Despite the reduced invasiveness, SPA robotic surgery has its own limitations. One of the main issues is that the anatomical region reached from an incision site is restrained. So the access port placement has to be carefully chosen depending on: patient anatomy, steps of the surgical procedure, and robot workspace [19].

Patient-specific surgical simulators could overcome this limitation by allowing the surgeon to plan the intervention in order to evaluate the robot workspace and the optimal access port placement [13,19]. Moreover they can also be used by robot designers to evaluate the robot dimensioning and distal dexterity in a realistic scenario, thus improving the quality and shortening the design cycle.

In this paper we present a patient-specific virtual and physical simulation platform (Figs. 1 and 8b) for surgical robot evaluation in single-access robot-assisted minimally-invasive cardiothoracic surgery.

2 Modeling of the Patient Anatomy

A computed tomography dataset with contrast medium was used to generate the 3D model. The stack of medical images in DICOM format was processed using a specific segmentation pipeline, developed in VMTK, a software for the generation of 3D virtual models by integrating custom Python scripts. The segmentation algorithm is based on a hierarchical approach as previously described in [5]. Basically: once the most simple feature to be identified is reconstructed, the associated pixels are excluded from the subsequent segmentation phase. Finally,

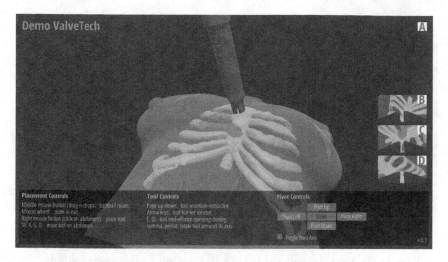

Fig. 1. Overview of the virtual simulator: the surgical robot initially positioned above the chest, 2 rib parts (in green) can be expanded to facilitate the robot insertion, the insertion point highlighted by a red dot on the skin, the 3 views from the robot end-effector cameras (right), and the GUI to control the virtual simulator (bottom). (Color figure online)

mesh reconstruction, artefacts removal, and holes filling stages were performed to generate the 3D models of the patient anatomy necessary for the surgical simulation, including: rib cage, aortic arch, ascending aorta, and aortic valve.

3 Development of the Virtual Simulator

The virtual simulator was designed to be a standalone desktop application for the Microsoft Windows platform (Fig. 1). We used Blender and Unity as the main tools for the 3D content creation and the software development respectively (Fig. 2). Both tools were chosen because they are cost-effective and technically suitable to implement virtual surgical simulators [7,15].

3.1 Modeling of the Virtual Surgical Robot

The virtual surgical robot was modeled accordingly to the current prototype as designed by the mechanical engineering team. This single-access surgical robot consists in: a mechanical flexible trunk with a user-controlled torsion, 3 distal blades allowing its insertion and anchoring into the aorta, and 3 distal cameras for the inspection of the aorta inner part once the robot is inserted (Fig. 4a).

In Unity, the entire behavior of the virtual robot was controlled by a C# script component, implementing the following mechanisms:

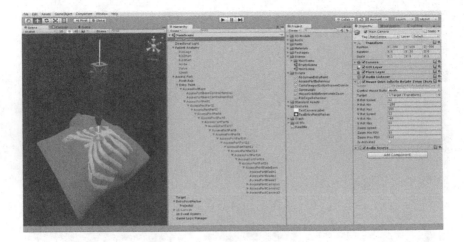

Fig. 2. The virtual simulator project in the Unity game engine editor.

- control the main body torsion using the keyboard arrow keys;
- robot insertion/extraction pressing *"page down"*/*"page up"* respectively;
- opening/closing of the robot end-effector blades with keys *"e"* and *"q"*;
- robot rotation around its axis using *"comma"* and *"period"* keys.

In order to enable the interactions between the virtual surgical robot and the virtual anatomy, we configured each robot part with a *Collider* component, and a *Rigidbody* component (Fig. 3). These Unity components enable collision-detection capabilities, and physics properties respectively.

All the robot Collider components have been configured using the proper type (i.e. shape) to approximate the 3D geometry of the respective part, and setting them to be *trigger* Colliders. In this way, Unity will be able to detect the collisions robot-anatomy, but these collisions will not affect the robot positioning.

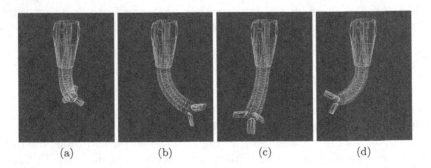

(a)   (b)   (c)   (d)

Fig. 3. The structure of the Collider components of the virtual robot in Unity: (a), (b), (c), and (d) show the torsion boundaries of the surgical robot.

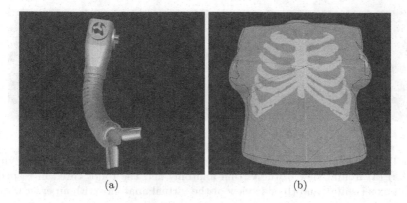

(a)   (b)

Fig. 4. Detailed view of: (a) the virtual robot end-effector (highlighted in orange), including 3 blades to open/close the tip and 3 cameras for endovascular inspection; and (b) the *navigation mesh* (in blue) baked on the chest of the patient, and used to implement the interactive navigation of the insertion point on the skin (Color figure online)

All the robot Rigidbody components have been configured to be *kinematic*. In this way, we can assign each part its own physics properties, but we disable any update of its position/orientation performed by the Unity physics engine.

This configuration provides the maximum control to the user, and preserves the capability to detect all the interactions between the robot and the anatomy.

3.2   Interactive Simulation of the Surgical Robot Movability

The virtual surgical simulator was designed to provide a user-friendly interface to enable the surgeon to rehearse the robot placement using only: the mouse, its 3 buttons, and a minimal set of keyboard keys (Fig. 1).

The complete interface includes some keyboard controls, a GUI panel (Fig. 1), and some interactions available directly on the 3D virtual anatomy:

- an invisible *trackball* allows the user to rotate, zoom in, and zoom out the main view (i.e. the point-of-view of the surgeon) using only mouse buttons and drag-and-drop (see Figs. 5a and 5b);
- the virtual chest is interactive, allowing the user to click on the skin to directly place the insertion point (see red dot in Fig. 1);
- the insertion point can also be precisely positioned by moving it on the skin using the *"WASD"* keys (Fig. 1);
- five buttons on the GUI panel (Fig. 1) allow the user to rotate the robot in respect to the access point pivot axis, orthogonal to the skin surface (Fig. 5a);
- an error message is shown on the GUI panel (and an audio signal is played) whenever a collision between the robot and the *rib cage* is detected (Fig. 5b).

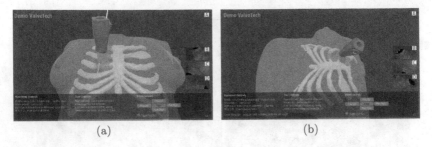

(a)   (b)

Fig. 5. Two different placements of the single-access surgical robot using the virtual simulator: (a) frontal view of the virtual anatomy and the robot tilted in respect to the pivot axis (white), and (b) side view of the virtual anatomy with an error message (red) signaling a collision between the robot and the rib cage.

The trackball was implemented in a C# script component attached to the main camera, and allows: the rotation of the main view around the virtual anatomy, with angular limits to avoid uncomfortable points of view; the zooming in and out implemented modifying the main camera *field-of-view* angle.

The interaction with the virtual chest was implemented through *ray-casting*, in a C# script component attached to it. Every time a mouse right click event was raised, the script converted it into a 3D ray using the *Camera* class *unprojection* capabilities. Then, the script used the Unity physics engine to cast the 3D ray, detecting its collision with the virtual chest thanks to a *Mesh Collider* component added to the skin.

The fine positioning of the insertion point is performed moving it on the skin using the keyboard. This implementation exploited a Unity *NavMesh*: a *navigation mesh* approximating the *"walkable"* surface and enabling artificial intelligence path-planning capabilities (Fig. 4b). In our project, a NavMesh has been baked on the chest, and it has been properly configured to allow movements only on the almost-flat part of the skin. A *NavMeshAgent* component attached to the insertion point enables the movement on the NavMesh. Finally, a C# script component attached to the chest controls the NavMeshAgent to perform the proper movement accordingly to the user inputs.

The GUI panel buttons allow the tilting of the virtual robot in respect to the access point pivot axis (Fig. 5a). This feature has been implemented simply exploiting the parenting between Unity *GameObjects*, in this case: the insertion point (the parent GameObject), and the virtual robot (the child GameObject).

Finally, collisions between the virtual robot and the rib cage are identified using Unity collision-detection capabilities. In fact, all the robot parts have their respective Colliders, and the rib cage has a MeshCollider.

4   Development of the Physical Simulator

The manufacturing of organ physical replicas involves rapid prototyping techniques as described in previous works [6,17]. More particularly a 3D printer

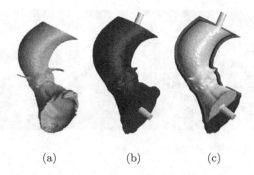

(a)   (b)   (c)

Fig. 6. Manufacturing of the ascending aorta distal part and aortic valve: (a) 3D virtual model of the portion to be reproduced, (b) CAD model of designed mold, and (c) CAD view of the mold inner core with pins for a correct positioning.

(Dimension Elite 3D Printer) is used to turn the 3D virtual model of the patient bones into tangible 3D synthetic replicas made of acrylonitrile butadiene styrene (ABS). This plastic is commonly used for the manufacturing of bone replica for orthopedic surgery simulations, since it sufficiently replicates the mechanical behavior of the natural tissue [1,16,17].

Soft synthetic replica of the whole or a part of an organ can be manufactured with casting technique, selecting plastic materials with properties tailored to the specific application [4]. Injection molds are designed using a computer-aided design (CAD) software starting from the organ 3D virtual models (Fig. 6).

Figure 7 shows the physical simulator developed for cardiac interventions involving the ascending aorta and the aortic valve, including a replica of:

- the rib cage with bones made of ABS, and a portion of costal cartilage made of a high hardness silicone rubber to reproduce the elastic behavior of the natural tissue (highlighted in red in Fig. 8b);
- the aortic arch (with brachiocephalic, left common carotid, and left subclavian arteries) made of ABS with a pin to anchor it to a base (Fig. 7b);
- the ascending aorta and the aortic valve, which are the anatomical targets of the intervention, made of soft silicone for a realistic interaction with surgical instruments (traditional and/or robotic devices);

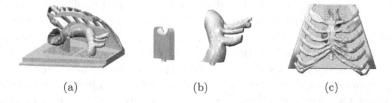

(a)   (b)   (c)

Fig. 7. Assembly of the physical simulator: (a) CAD assembly including a portion of the rib cage, the aortic arch, the ascending aorta, the aortic valve, an aortic valve support, and a base for a stable positioning of the anatomical parts; (b) the aortic arch and the aortic valve support with pins; and (c) the CAD assembly of whole simulator.

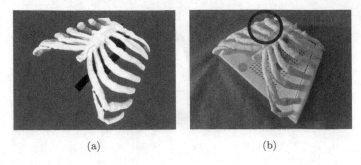

(a)   (b)

Fig. 8. Side-by-side views of the virtual and physical anatomies: (a) the virtual anatomy as imported in Unity for the virtual simulator; and (b) the physical anatomy built using 3D printing technology and silicones to have flexible and rigid parts. (Color figure online)

- an aortic valve support made of ABS with a pin for anchoring (Fig. 7b);
- a base with a grid of holes accommodates the pin of the aortic arch and the aortic valve support (labeled in green in Fig. 8b).

The assembly of the organ replicas can be customized using the grid of holes in the base of the physical simulator (see green label in Fig. 8b). This grid allows a *pin-hole coupling*, constraining 5 DOF, that can be used to simulate different anatomical configurations by repositioning the aortic arch and the aortic valve.

5 Preliminary Results and Future Work

The virtual surgical simulator was tested on a laptop running Microsoft Windows 7 (Intel Core i7 – 2.80 GHz, 16 GHz RAM, GPU nVidia GeForce GT 650 M), using a virtual 3D environment including: the patient anatomy composed of approximately 81k vertices and 150k triangles, and the surgical robot made with roughly 63k vertices and 64k triangles. The update frequency was ranging from 65 to 75 fps, with the physics engine running at 50 fps (default). The memory required to run the simulator was about 140 MB.

The physical simulator underwent a qualitative evaluation performed by a surgeon, and both the geometry and mechanical behavior of all the synthetic organ replicas were positively evaluated. A quantitative evaluation, considering all the factors affecting the generation of the 3D organ replicas, estimated an accuracy of less than 2 mm for the physical anatomy.

The virtual simulator described allows the pre-operative planning to rehearse the surgical case before the actual intervention, and the evaluation of the surgical robot during the design-development cycle. The physical simulator presented enables the evaluation of the surgical robot in a synthetic anatomy, testing the physical interactions between the robot prototype and the organ replicas. Thus, we can assess the robot *payload* and *compliance* performing a wide range of tasks (not included in the virtual simulation). Furthermore, the virtual and physical surgical simulators can also be efficiently integrated into the clinical context for teaching and training purposes.

In the future, we plan to combine the virtual and physical simulators into a single *mixed reality* system. Additionally, we will also perform validation studies to test the *face validity* of the simulator.

Acknowledgments. The research leading to these results has been supported by the scientific project ValveTech (*"Realizzazione di una Valvola Aortica Polimerica di Nuova Concezione ed Impiantabile Tramite Piattaforma Robotica con Tecniche di Chirurgia Mininvasiva"* 2016–2018) funded by the Tuscany Region (Italy) through the call FAS SALUTE 2014.

References

1. Baccarin, L.S., Casarin, R.C.V., Lopes-da Silva, J.V., Passeri, L.A.: Analysis of mandibular test specimens used to assess a bone fixation system. Craniomaxillofacial Trauma Reconstr. **8**(03), 171–178 (2015)
2. Bhatt, A.G., Steinberg, J.S.: Robotic-assisted left ventricular lead placement. Card. Electrophysiol. Clin. **7**(4), 649–659 (2015)
3. Bush, B., Nifong, L.W., Alwair, H., Chitwood Jr., W.R.: Video-atlas on robotically assisted mitral valve surgery. Ann. Cardiothorac. Surg. **2**(6), 846–848 (2013)
4. Carbone, M., Condino, S., Mattei, L., Forte, P., Ferrari, V., Mosca, F.: Anthropomorphic ultrasound elastography phantoms: Characterization of silicone materials to build breast elastography phantoms. In: 2012 Annual International Conference of the IEEE Engineering in Medicine and Biology Society (EMBC), pp. 492–494. IEEE (2012)
5. Celi, S., Berti, S.: In-vivo segmentation and quantification of coronary lesions by optical coherence tomography images for a lesion type definition and stenosis grading. Med. Image Anal. **18**(7), 1157–1168 (2014)
6. Condino, S., Carbone, M., Ferrari, V., Faggioni, L., Peri, A., Ferrari, M., Mosca, F.: How to build patient-specific synthetic abdominal anatomies. An innovative approach from physical toward hybrid surgical simulators. Int. J. Med. Robot. **7**(2), 202–213 (2011)
7. De Luca, V., Meo, A., Mongelli, A., Vecchio, P., De Paolis, L.T.: Development of a virtual simulator for microanastomosis: new opportunities and challenges. In: Paolis, L.T., Mongelli, A. (eds.) AVR 2016. LNCS, vol. 9769, pp. 65–81. Springer, Cham (2016). doi:10.1007/978-3-319-40651-0_6
8. Degani, A., Choset, H., Wolf, A., Zenati, M.A.: Highly articulated robotic probe for minimally invasive surgery. In: Proceedings of the 2006 IEEE International Conference on Robotics and Automation, ICRA 2006, pp. 4167–4172. IEEE (2006)
9. Folliguet, T.A., Dibie, A., Philippe, F., Larrazet, F., Slama, M.S., Laborde, F.: Robotically-assisted coronary artery bypass grafting. Cardiol. Res. Pract. **2010** (2010)
10. Folliguet, T.A., Laborde, F.: Robotic aortic valve replacement. In: Chitwood Jr., W.R. (ed.) Atlas of Robotic Cardiac Surgery, pp. 265–269. Springer, London (2014)
11. Gong, W., Cai, J., Wang, Z., Chen, A., Ye, X., Li, H., Zhao, Q.: Robot-assisted coronary artery bypass grafting improves short-term outcomes compared with minimally invasive direct coronary artery bypass grafting. J. Thorac. Dis. **8**(3), 459–468 (2016)

12. Iribarne, A., Easterwood, R., Chan, E.Y., Yang, J., Soni, L., Russo, M.J., Smith, C.R., Argenziano, M.: The golden age of minimally invasive cardiothoracic surgery: current and future perspectives. Future Cardiol. **7**(3), 333–346 (2011)
13. Moglia, A., Turini, G., Ferrari, V., Ferrari, M., Mosca, F.: Patient specific surgical simulator for the evaluation of the movability of bimanual robotic arms. Stud. Health Technol. Inf. **163**, 379–385 (2011)
14. Neuzil, P., Cerny, S., Kralovec, S., Svanidze, O., Bohuslavek, J., Plasil, P., Jehlicka, P., Holy, F., Petru, J., Kuenzler, R., et al.: Single-site access robot-assisted epicardial mapping with a snake robot: preparation and first clinical experience. J. Robot. Surg. **7**(2), 103–111 (2013)
15. Paci, A., Marcutti, S., Ricci, S., Casadio, M., Vercelli, G.V., Marchiolè, P., Cordone, M.: eBSim: development of a low-cost obstetric simulator. In: Paolis, L.T., Mongelli, A. (eds.) AVR 2016. LNCS, vol. 9769, pp. 101 110. Springer, Cham (2016). doi:10.1007/978-3-319-40651-0_9
16. Parchi, P., Condino, S., Carbone, M., Gesi, M., Ferrari, V., Ferrari, M., Lisanti, M.: Total hip replacement simulators with virtual planning and physical replica for surgical training and rehearsal. In: Proceedings of the 12th IASTED International Conference on Biomedical Engineering, BioMed 2016, pp. 97–101 (2016)
17. Parchi, P., Ferrari, V., Piolanti, N., Andreani, L., Condino, S., Evangelisti, G., Lisanti, M.: Computer tomography prototyping and virtual procedure simulation in difficult cases of hip replacement surgery. Surg. Technol. Int. **23**, 228–234 (2013)
18. Poffo, R., Toschi, A.P., Pope, R.B., Celullare, A.L., Benício, A., Fischer, C.H., Vieira, M.L.C., Teruya, A., Hatanaka, D.M., Rusca, G.F., et al.: Robotic surgery in cardiology: a safe and effective procedure. Einstein (Sao Paulo) **11**(3), 296–302 (2013)
19. Turini, G., Moglia, A., Ferrari, V., Ferrari, M., Mosca, F.: Patient-specific surgical simulator for the pre-operative planning of single-incision laparoscopic surgery with bimanual robots. Comput. Aided Surg. **17**(3), 103–112 (2012)
20. Wutzler, A., Wolber, T., Haverkamp, W., Boldt, L.H.: Robotic ablation of atrial-fibrillation. J. Vis. Exp. JoVE **99** (2015)
21. Xu, K., Zheng, X.: Configuration comparison for surgical robotic systems using a single access port and continuum mechanisms. In: 2012 IEEE International Conference on Robotics and Automation (ICRA), pp. 3367–3374. IEEE (2012)

Using of 3D Virtual Reality Electromagnetic Navigation for Challenging Cannulation in FEVAR Procedure

Roberta Piazza[1,2,3], Sara Condino[3(✉)], Aldo Alberti[4],
Davide Giannetti[2], Vincenzo Ferrari[2,3], Marco Gesi[4],
and Mauro Ferrari[1,3]

[1] Vascular Surgery Unit, Cisanello University Hospital, AOUP, Pisa, Italy
[2] Information Engineering Department, University of Pisa, Pisa, Italy
roberta.piazza@ing.unipi.it,
vincenzo.ferrari@unipi.it
[3] EndoCAS, Department of Translational Research and of New Surgical
and Medical Technologies, University of Pisa, Pisa, Italy
{sara.condino,vincenzo.ferrari,
roberta.piazza}@endocas.org,
mauro.ferrari@med.unipi.it
[4] Department of Translational Research and of New Surgical
and Medical Technologies, University of Pisa, Pisa, Italy
a.albertimd@gmail.com, marco.gesi@med.unipi.it

Abstract. Virtual Reality (VR) is promising not just for the game and entertainment industry, but also for the medical and surgical fields, to develop simulation systems and navigation tools for the intra-operative assistance. Electromagnetic (EM) tracking technology is today widely proposed in the context of computer-assisted medical interventions.

In this work we preliminary evaluate whether a three-Dimensional (3D) virtual reality EM navigator could simplify a challenging endovascular procedure, the fenestrated endovascular aneurysm repair (FEVAR), facilitating the collateral arteries cannulation. This paper describes the navigation system and presents results of in-vitro trials which provide preliminary evidence to prove the potentialities of the proposed technology for the specific surgical application.

Keywords: Computer assisted system · Electromagnetic navigation · Endovascular navigation · FEVAR · Cannulation · Catheterization

1 Introduction

New VR technologies will have a major impact on health care in the coming decades [1]. Clinically validated, powerful VR navigators and simulators are now available and in use across the world. VR navigation systems have emerged as a particularly useful tool for the guidance of minimally invasive surgical procedures to restore the 3D perception of the surgical field and augment the visual information available for the

© Springer International Publishing AG 2017
L.T. De Paolis et al. (Eds.): AVR 2017, Part II, LNCS 10325, pp. 221–229, 2017.
DOI: 10.1007/978-3-319-60928-7_19

surgical team. This work is focused on the application of VR navigation to endovascular surgery.

Endovascular surgery uses bi-dimensional (2D) fluoroscopic imaging (based on X-rays) to guide minimally invasive procedures employing guide-wires and catheters to access and treat various vascular diseases, including aneurysm pathology (permanent localized enlargement of an artery). In order to deal with the lack of depth perception, multimodal imaging strategies, involving the integration of live fluoroscopy with 3D images from rotational angiography (RA), magnetic resonance imaging (MRI) and computerized tomography (CT), have been developed [2]. For example available 3D road-mapping systems allow accurate superimposition between a live fluoroscopic image, containing the real-time information on interventional devices position, and its matching 2D projection of a 3DRA data set which provides useful and detailed 3D information regarding the vascular morphology. These systems can potentially reduce operative time, the fluoroscopy time and the amount of contrast media used in a procedure [3]. However the endovascular tool can only be localized in 2D.

In an attempt to further reduce the total amount of radiation dose, EM tracking technology has been proposed for monitoring the instruments position without an X-ray imaging system. The EM technology can allow the 3D localization of the endovascular tool, and registration/calibration methods can be used to integrate the EM data with the 3D VR model of the patient anatomy (extracted from intra-operative or pre-operative radiological data set) thus obtaining a 3D "radiation-free" VR navigation system [4–8].

In this work we present a novel guidance method for a challenging interventional procedure which could take advantage of 3D VR EM navigation: the fenestrated endovascular aneurysm repair. This latter is a catheter-based surgical technique allowing the minimally invasive repair of complex aortic aneurysms, thanks to patient-specific fenestrated endografts with customized holes for preserving blood flow to essential collateral arteries originating from the aorta (Fig. 1). FEVAR is technically challenging and time consuming since: (1) the endograft should be accurately positioned aligning fenestrations with the target collateral vessels; (2) the endograft fenestration and subsequent target vessel cannulation can be very difficult, even for an experienced surgeon, especially if the endograft is not optimally positioned (visceral ostial stenosis can further exacerbate any such difficulties in cannulation) [9, 10].

The aim of this work is to preliminarily evaluate whether the navigator could simplify this procedure, which requires a great deal of precision, by providing the surgeon with:

- a 3D EM navigation system able to accurately track, in real time, the guidewires and the catheters;
- a 3D visualization of the fenestrated stent graft inside the aorta;
- an additional "virtual endoscopic view" aligned with the catheter tip.

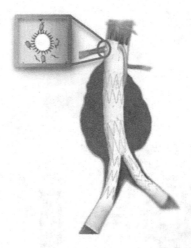

Fig. 1. Schematic illustration of a fenestrated endograft delivered within a juxtarenal infrarenal aneurysms

2 Materials and Methods

2.1 3D Electromagnetic Navigation System

The system (Fig. 2) has been developed starting from the EndoCAS general purpose navigation platform [11]. The software has been implemented in C++ language using the open source framework OpenSG to create 3D scenes, and the Qt platform to develop the GUI. The current version of the navigator prototype includes sensorized catheters and guidewires prototypes simultaneously tracked with the NDI Aurora (Northern Digital, Waterloo, Canada) EM localizer [12].

The 3D position and orientation of these instruments can be accurately showed in real-time within a 3D virtual model of the patient vasculature. Such model can be reconstructed from a 3DRA acquired after the endograft deployment with a previously calibrated rotational C-Arm, allowing the surgeon to visualize the collateral arteries and the endograft fenestrations labeled by radiopaque markers. A simple method to calculate the rigid static transformation between the 3DRA and the Aurora reference frames is described in [7].

2.2 In Vitro Experimental Set-up

The experimental setup comprises the B.E.S.T simulator, which consists of a transparent plastic model, with an engraved geometry representing the abdominal aorta with its principal bifurcations. More in particular, the model simulates an abdominal pararenal aneurysm [13].

A fenestrated endograft mock-up, with holes to match the simulator renal ostia, was manufactured (Fig. 3) for the simulation of the target surgical step.

The final experimental setup is showed in Fig. 4.

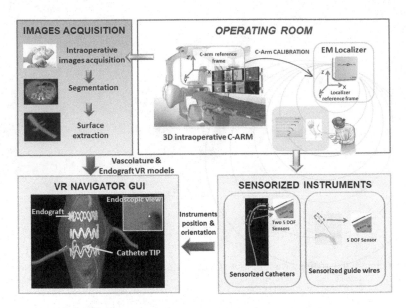

Fig. 2. Schematic representation of the proposed endovascular navigation system

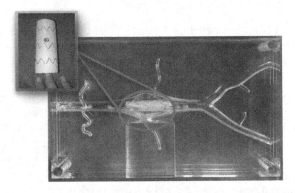

Fig. 3. In vitro set-up. A global view of the B.E.S.T. simulator is shown. The zoom detail shows the fenestrated endograft mock-up into the aorta mannequin to simulate the stent graft. Two metal rings are used to indicate the stent graft fenestration aligned with the renal ostia. Sensorized catheters and guidewire were manufactured according to [12].

2.3   Study Protocol

The fenestrated endograft mock-up was manually inserted into the B.E.S.T simulator by an experienced surgeon, aligning fenestrations with the renal ostia. Then, CT images of the simulator were acquired and processed with a semiautomatic tool, the EndoCAS Segmentation Pipeline integrated in the software ITK-SNAP (www.itksnap.org), to extract the 3D model of the vasculature and the endograft mock-up. Three fiducial markers were identified and used for a point-based registration.

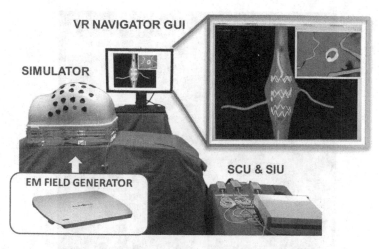

Fig. 4. Experimental setup of the electromagnetic (EM) trials. The picture shows the graphical user interface (GUI), the NDI Aurora system control unit (SCU), and sensor interface units (SIU), while the EM field generator is placed under the vascular model (this latter was covered with a simulated plastic abdomen during navigation trials).

To preliminarily assess whether the EM navigator can facilitate the cannulation of fenestration, four participants, including three vascular surgeons and one interventional radiologist, were recruited for this in vitro study. All participants were asked to cannulate the fenestration and the renal arteries using the EM navigator without fluoroscopic support (Fig. 5 shows an example of virtual scene showed by the navigator during a cannulation trial).

During the tests the simulator was covered with a simulated plastic abdomen and participants were not allowed to see the vascular model until the study was completed.

The trial was considered successful completed when the operator was able to cannulate both the renal arteries inserting the guide-wire or the catheter more than 2 cm into the vessel within 20 min.

Each trial was video-recorded and analyzed by a blinded and independent observer.

The following parameters were considered in the performance analysis: success in completing the task and total time (min).

As for the success in completing the task a score of: 4 was assigned if both fenestrations and both renal arteries were cannulated; 3 if both fenestrations but only one of the renal arteries were cannulated; 2 if both fenestrations but none of the renal arteries or alternatively a single fenestration and a renal artery were cannulated; 1 if only a single fenestration was cannulated; 0 if the operator was not able to cannulate any fenestrations.

Moreover, at the end of the experimental session, participants were asked to fill out a Likert questionnaire (see Table 2) to evaluate the navigator potentialities for the specific surgical task.

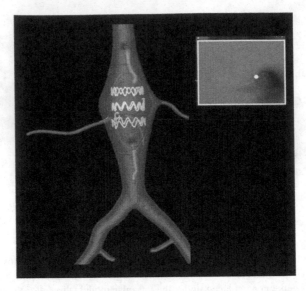

Fig. 5. Navigator scene showing the catheter distal part during the cannulation of the endograft fenestration (yellow circle). The endoscopic view is rendered from a virtual camera positioned at the catheter tip. (Color figure online)

3 Results

The SPSS Statistics Base 19 software was used for the statistical analysis.

Table 1 reports results obtained by each operator as well as median values with the interquartile range (IQR) of the measurements taken by the observer. Three operators obtained the maximum score and the median time to accomplish the cannulation task was 13:57 (min:sec). These results are very satisfactory given that the selected task is very difficult and time-consuming as highlighted in a recent multicenter clinical study on the use of fenestrated graft which reports a median time of 18 min and a maximum time of 92 min for renal cannulation [14].

Table 1. Operator performance analysis. Each operator performance and median values with interquartile range (IQR) (25th; 75th) are reported.

Performance analysis	Total time (min:sec)	Score on the task
Operator 1	14:10	4.0
Operator 2	15:00	3.0
Operator 3	13:44	4.0
Operator 4	11:10	4.0
Median	13:57	4.0
IQR	(13:05;14:22)	(3.8; 4.0)

Table 2 reports the central tendencies of responses to a single Likert item, summarized by using median with dispersion measured by IQR.

Table 2. Likert questionnaire results. The central tendency of responses is summarized by using median with dispersion measured by interquartile range (IQR) (25th; 75th).

Item	Median	IQR
1. The GUI is easy to use	4	3.8; 4.3
2. The GUI clearly shows the instruments position within the 3D model of the anatomy and the prosthesis	3.5	3.0; 4.0
3. The simulated endoscopic view is useful for the cannulation task	3	2.0; 4.0
4. It can be easier to cannulate the fenestrations with the navigator than with the fluoroscopic guidance	4	3.8; 4.3
5. It can be easier to cannulate the renal arteries with the navigator than with the fluoroscopic guidance	3.5	3.0; 4.3
6. The navigator can simplify and reduce the time of FEVAR	4	3.8; 4.3

Operators expressed a positive opinion (median score of 4) on the easiness of the GUI and they agreed with the following statements: it can be easier to cannulate the fenestrations with the navigator than with the fluoroscopic guidance; the navigator can simplify and reduce the time of FEVAR. However, a negative opinion (score of 2) was expressed by 50% of respondents on the usefulness of the simulated endoscopic view for the cannulation task.

4 Conclusion

This work provides a preliminarily proof-of-concept of the efficacy of the navigator to guide cannulation in FEVAR procedure. Obtained results should be confirmed in a larger study comparing the proposed EM navigation to standard fluoroscopic guidance and involving more operators (for statistically significant results).

For this in vitro study a static representation of the anatomy was used, however in a real surgical setting, the 3D virtual model of the anatomy showed by the navigator could be up-dated on the basis of predictive respiratory motion models [15], and and/or intraoperative data, such as 3D ultrasound [16, 17].

Acknowledgments. The research leading to these results has been partially supported by the scientific project LASER (electromagnetic guided in-situ laser fenestration of endovascular endoprosthesis, November 2014–November 2017) funded by the Italian Ministry of Health and Regione Toscana through the call "Ricerca Finalizzata 2011–2012".

References

1. McCloy, R., Stone, R.: Virtual reality in surgery. BMJ: Br. Med. J. **323**, 912–915 (2001)
2. Fagan, T.E., Truong, U.T., Jone, P.-N., Bracken, J., Quaife, R., Hazeem, A.A.A., Salcedo, E. E., Fonseca, B.M.: Multimodality 3-dimensional image integration for congenital cardiac catheterization. Methodist DeBakey Cardiovasc. J. **10**, 68–76 (2014)
3. Rossitti, S., Pfister, M.: 3D road-mapping in the endovascular treatment of cerebral aneurysms and arteriovenous malformations. Intervent. Neuroradiol. **15**, 283–290 (2009)
4. Pujol, S., Pecher, M., Magne, J.L., Cinquin, P.: A virtual reality based navigation system for endovascular surgery. Stud. Health Technol. Inform. **98**, 310–312 (2004)
5. Sidhu, R., Weir-McCall, J., Cochennec, F., Riga, C., DiMarco, A., Bicknell, C.D.: Evaluation of an electromagnetic 3D navigation system to facilitate endovascular tasks: a feasibility study. Eur. J. Vascul. Endovasc. Surg.: Official J. Eur. Soc. Vascul. Surg. **43**, 22–29 (2012)
6. Cochennec, F., Riga, C., Hamady, M., Cheshire, N., Bicknell, C.: Improved catheter navigation with 3D electromagnetic guidance. J. Endovasc. Therapy: Official J. Int. Soc. Endovasc. Spec. **20**, 39–47 (2013)
7. Condino, S., Ferrari, V., Freschi, C., Alberti, A., Berchiolli, R., Mosca, F., Ferrari, M.: Electromagnetic navigation platform for endovascular surgery: how to develop sensorized catheters and guidewires. Int. J. Med. Robot. **8**(3), 300–310 (2012)
8. Condino, S., et al.: Electromagnetic guided in-situ laser fenestration of endovascular stent-graft: endovascular tools sensorization strategy and preliminary laser testing. In: Zheng, G., Liao, H., Jannin, P., Cattin, P., Lee, S.-L. (eds.) MIAR 2016. LNCS, vol. 9805, pp. 72–83. Springer, Cham (2016). doi:10.1007/978-3-319-43775-0_7
9. Rodd, C.D., Desigan, S., Cheshire, N.J., Jenkins, M.P., Hamady, M.: The suitability of thoraco-abdominal aortic aneurysms for branched or fenestrated stent grafts – and the development of a new scoring method to aid case assessment. Eur. J. Vascul. Endovasc. **41**, 175–185 (2011)
10. Shahverdyan, R., Gray, D., Gawenda, M., Brunkwall, J.: Single centre results of total endovascular repair of complex aortic aneurysms with custom made anaconda fenestrated stent grafts. Eur. J. Vascul. Endovasc. **52**, 500–508 (2016)
11. Megali, G., Ferrari, V., Freschi, C., Morabito, B., Turini, G., Troia, E., Cappelli, C., Pietrabissa, A., Tonet, O., Cuschieri, A., Dario, P., Mosca, F.: EndoCAS navigator platform: a common platform for computer and robotic assistance in minimally invasive surgery. Int. J. Med. Robot. Comp. **4**, 242–251 (2008)
12. Condino, S., Calabro, E.M., Alberti, A., Parrini, S., Cioni, R., Berchiolli, R.N., Gesi, M., Ferrari, V., Ferrari, M.: Simultaneous tracking of catheters and guidewires: comparison to standard fluoroscopic guidance for arterial cannulation. Eur. J. Vascul. Endovasc. **47**, 53–60 (2014)
13. Sinceri, S., Carbone, M., Marconi, M., Moglia, A., Ferrari, M., Ferrari, V.: Basic endovascular skills trainer: a surgical simulator for the training of novice practitioners of endovascular procedures. In: Proceedings of the Annual International Conference of the IEEE Engineering in Medicine and Biology Society, EMBS, pp. 5102–5105 (2015)
14. Quiñones-Baldrich, W.J., Holden, A., Mertens, R., Thompson, M.M., Sawchuk, A.P., Becquemin, J.-P., Eagleton, M., Clair, D.G.: Prospective, multicenter experience with the ventana fenestrated system for juxtarenal and pararenal aortic aneurysm endovascular repair. J. Vascul. Surg. **58**, 1–9 (2013)

15. Turini, G., Condino, S., Postorino, M., Ferrari, V., Ferrari, M.: Improving endovascular intraoperative navigation with real-time skeleton-based deformation of virtual vascular structures. In: Paolis, L.T., Mongelli, A. (eds.) AVR 2016. LNCS, vol. 9769, pp. 82–91. Springer, Cham (2016). doi:10.1007/978-3-319-40651-0_7
16. Parrini, S., Zhang, L., Condino, S., Ferrari, V., Caramella, D., Ferrari, M.: Automatic carotid centerline extraction from three-dimensional ultrasound doppler images. In: 2014 36th Annual International Conference of the IEEE Engineering in Medicine and Biology Society, EMBC 2014, pp. 5089–5092 (2014)
17. Zhang, L., Parrini, S., Freschi, C., Ferrari, V., Condino, S., Ferrari, M., Caramella, D.: 3D ultrasound centerline tracking of abdominal vessels for endovascular navigation. Int. J. Comput. Assist. Radiol. Surg. 9(1), 127–135 (2014)

A Tailored Serious Game
for Preventing Falls of the Elderly

Estelle Courtial[1](✉), Giuseppe Palestra[2], and Mohamed Rebiai[2]

[1] Laboratory PRISME, University of Orléans, 8 rue Léonard de Vinci,
45072 Orléans, France
Estelle.Courtial@univ-orleans.fr
[2] Streamvision, 12 rue Pajol, 75018 Paris, France
{Giuseppe.Palestra,Mohamed.Rebiai}@streamvision.fr

Abstract. Serious games have shown to be particularly adapted to
address fall prevention and rehabilitation issues because they engage
the elderly in performing physical exercices in an entertaining way.
A tailored serious game was developed to take into account the ageing process, an adaptation to the physical status of the senior, and a
3D-visualization to better perform the exercices. The Health professional
creates the exergame-based program according to the needs and capabilities of the elderly. The proposed solution is easy to use, personalized
and based on low-cost and non-invasive technologies. An experimentation
was carried out in a day care center for the elderly. The pilot evaluation
illustrates the benefit of the system in terms of performance enhancement and points out the improvements that should be addressed in the
future.

Keywords: Fall prevention · Serious games · Rehabilitation

1 Introduction

Among priorities of Public Health the consequences of the population ageing
are at the heart of national policy in many developed countries. Indeed, the
world's population aged 60 years or over was 901 million people in 2015 and is
projected to grow to 1.4 billion in 2030 and to 2.1 billion by 2050 [11]. The
number of people at very advanced ages (80 years or over) will increase from 125
million in 2015 to 202 million in 2030 and to 434 million in 2050. The ageing
process induces a loss of physical and cognitive capabilities and a higher risk
of falls which are the main factors of the dependence for the elderly. Falls are
the second leading cause of accidental deaths worldwide and the first one among
people over 80 years old. One in three seniors falls at least one time during the
year. The direct and indirect costs related to a fall consumes the major part
of Health budget. For these reasons, the fall prevention is a real challenge for
Public Health both with social and economic issues.

L.T. De Paolis et al. (Eds.): AVR 2017, Part II, LNCS 10325, pp. 230–239, 2017.
DOI: 10.1007/978-3-319-60928-7_20

To cope to this challenge, games can be a solution both for preventive and curative actions. In this context, the name of "serious game" takes on full significance because what could be more serious than Health! Serious games are designed for a purpose other than entertainment. They are based on game thinking which provides the fun and joyful part of the game and game mechanics such as scores, rewards, trophies, leader boards. They are used to engage and motivate people in achieving goals.

Past studies have shown that physical exercice programs reduce the risk of falling and significantly improve the motor functions of the elderly [6]. Physical exercices are dedicated to enhance the balance, to strengthen muscles and to maintain the joint flexibility. Unfortunately, the low level of participation in the exercice programs, the lack of regularity and the scarce exercice intensity question the efficiency of such programs [10]. Recently numerous papers have explored solutions relating to the use of the exergames in rehabilitation and prevention contexts [2, 3, 7, 9]. The results of these different studies indicated that exergames are useful for improving the elderly's engagement in physical activity, and can significantly increase the physical capabilities of the elderly. Based on a review of more than 60 studies, Skjaeret et al. [8] analyzed affirmed that exergames have shown a promising future in rehabilitation programs and they provided recommendations for further research in order to successfully establish exergames as a prevention and rehabilitation tool for the elderly. A rehabilitation program has also been tested in home settings using a Kinect [5] and showed the feasibility of their system but further investigations are necessary for fall risk assessment. In most of the studies, the adaptation of the exergame to the elderly seems to be crucial: adaptation of the difficulty level, of the exercices, of the duration.

The aim of this work is to propose a rehabilitation system based on a tailored exergame program to enhance the physical status of the elderly. The Health Professional creates the exergame program according to the needs and capabilities of each senior. The set of exergames is equivalent to a rehabilitation session at the physiotherapist's premises. The proposed system is personalized with multilevel exergames, adapted to the senior's capabilities, based on low-cost and non-invasive technologies, and easy to use for the both end-users. An experimentation was carried out in a day care center for the elderly to evaluate the system efficiency.

This paper is organized as follows. Section 2 details the context and the requirements of serious games developed for fall prevention and rehabilitation purposes. The creation of exergames by the HP and the play of exergames by the elderly are described. Section 3 addresses the experimentation carried out in an elderly day care center. The results of the experimentation are analyzed in order to assess the usability and the efficiency of such system. Finally conclusions and perspectives are given in Sect. 4.

2 Fall Prevention and Rehabilitation Game

2.1 Context

Rehabilitation and prevention programs are usually long, costly and require an intensive training by performing repetitive exercices. Due to the repetitive exercices, patients find the program boring and rapidly loss their motivation. By against, a rehabilitation plan is effective if and only if the training program is fully performed. In this context, serious games can be an alternative and cost-efficient solution. Serious games take on the challenge of improving the engagement and the motivation of people involved in rehabilitation programs and of offering an enjoyable way to perform exercices. The Otago Exercice Program [6], set of easy exercices to improve strength and balance proved that falls can be reduced by an overall 35% and the Health cost expenses too. This fall prevention program is now used in several countries and is the backbone of several exergames for fall prevention.

Based on a users-requirement study conducted as part of a User Centered Design strategy, a rehabilitation system has to take care of several points for a successful serious game for the elderly:

- The elderly are a very heterogenous audience with different levels of physical and cognitive skills. Thus it requires that the game should be personalized according to the level of capabilities.
- The users are more engaged in games that can be adjusted to their skill levels and that can provide a gradual increase of the difficulty degree. They are discouraged if the game is too slow or too fast, if there are not sufficient game levels, if the progression on game levels is too slow. Physiotherapists should be involved in designing multilevel exercices which can be safety performed by the senior.
- The results and feedback information should be displayed in a gentle manner to avoid discouraging the seniors. A special attention should be given to the user interface: it should be attractive and easy to use. In any case, the senior should stop the activity because he/she does not understand what he/she has to do or how he/she can manage to do it. The elderly do not like young avatars in games.
- The social part of the game is crucial to maintain the social link and to avoid the loneliness of the elderly. It seems to be the keystone of the engagement in a long term perspective.

To address the aforementioned points, a fall prevention system has been developed as part of an European research project called KINOPTIM. This project aims at developing an innovative ICT-based system for fall prevention and rehabilitation for the elderly with a holistic management service [1]. Many functionalities were integrated. A tele-monitoring module based on image processing provides a fall risk index [4]. A rehabilitation module makes possible to create and to perform exergames. A medical business intelligence module offers several services through a web interface and contains a database and a data analysis functionality useful for the follow up of the rehabilitation.

2.2 Exergame Creation

First, a Health Professional (HP), generally a physiotherapist, evaluates the physical status of the senior and then defines a tailored exergame program for the senior. The exergame program represents in a way a session with the physiotherapist. An exergame session is thus constituted of exercices which are themselves decomposed into poses. The HP has two ways for creating exercices. He/she can perform the exercice very slowly while a camera records it. He/she can create the exercice by adding different poses from a set of basic poses available in a library (see Fig. 1). Different parameters can be adjusted: the duration of the pose, the angle for a joint motion, and also the weighting of the pose in the exercice score. The exergames are conceived to improve the balance, the gait, the muscle strength and the joint flexibility of the senior. The exergame programs have three kind of exercices respectively devoted to arms, legs and knees mobilization with multilevels of difficulty (easy, medium and hard). If a senior has serious difficulties in moving the left leg, the HP will give him/her a program that does not include left leg exergames. All the exercices are personalized and adapted to the senior's capabilities.

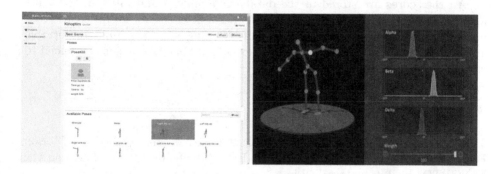

Fig. 1. Interfaces for exergame creation

2.3 Exergame Program

Through the KINOPTIM interface, the elderly is able to log in/out, to navigate in the menu and access to the tailored rehabilitation program. The rehabilitation game module relies on depth and optical sensors to estimate the body posture of the senior. When the elderly play an exergame they can visualize in real-time their posture, the desired one, and the score (see Fig. 2). The 3D-visualization (facial, left or right, and top views) makes possible to better perform the exercice. With commercial exergames focused on the gameplay (fun and entertaining part), one can reach high scores while badly performing the exercice because the matching of the posture is only in two-dimensions. For example, a person can raise the left leg while bending the body on the right side. It can be dangerous for the elderly because he/she could loss the balance.

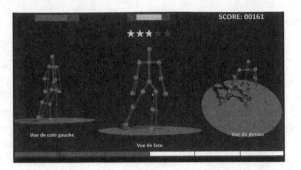

Fig. 2. 3D visualization of the pose (Color figure online)

The senior has to reach the desired posture in a given time defined according to the difficulty level of the exergame. The quality of the performance between the desired postures and the ones realized by the senior is scored and ranked in stars. Stars are a graphical evaluation of the matching quality of the postures. At the left top, a graphical timer (in blue) indicates the duration of the pose.

All the scores are stored in the database, analyzed and allow a "medical" follow-up of the senior. The HP takes into account the score evolution to gradually increase the level of difficulty while keeping the exergame comfortable and pleasant to play. The improvement, even low, between sessions is crucial to engage the elderly.

3   Experimentation

The experimentation took place at an elderly day care center called "La Maison Felippa" and located in Paris (France). Experiments were carried out on the KINOPTIM prototype installed in a special room of the pilot site.

3.1   Pilot Description and Setup

The experimental setup of the KINOPTIM prototype is composed of two cameras, an Asus Xtion PRO LIVE and a Full HD 1080p Logitech webcam which have been respectively selected as depth sensor and RGB camera to capture the posture of the senior, a 27" LCD monitor used to display exergames and to guarantee a sufficient quality of picture, and a workstation (Dell Precision Tower 7910). The distance between the display and the elderly person has been set at 2 m from the depth sensor placed 0.2 m in front of the monitor.

The participants were some of the seniors who attended the day care center. First of all, inclusion and exclusion criteria have been verified before the enrolment of the elderly. Inclusion criteria for participants were: age between 65 and 85 years, stable fall situation ($\geq$1 month from the last fall), independently mobile without a walking aid, adequate sight and sufficient cognitive capacity

Fig. 3. General overview of the experimental room

to understand instructions and to play exergames. Exclusion criteria for participants were: Parkinson disease and heavy medical treatment. According to the KINOPTIM ethical guidelines, the experiment procedure has been approved by the French National Commission on Informatics and Liberty (CNIL). All recordings have been anonymized by assigning a numerical identifier (ID) to each participant. Among the dozen of seniors who have tested the KINOPTIM system, only four healthy and voluntary seniors (3 women and 1 man) within the age range of 74–85 years (M = 81.25, SD = 5.19) regularly attended all the sessions of the experiment to this day. ID number, gender, age: (ID1,M,85); (ID2,F,74); (ID3,F,81); (ID4,F,85).

3.2 Evaluation

The experimentation started in the second half of January 2017 and is still ongoing. The four participants have been asked to perform five exergame sessions (S1 to S5) with the rehabilitation system. According to a preliminary assessment of the physical status of the senior, the physiotherapist has defined a tailored exergame program for each senior. The program comprised five exergames per session (one exercice for the arms extension, two exercices for the knees extension and two others for the legs) with the suited level. A session lasted 15 min and a frequency of two per week was required. The experiments were conducted by experts (physiotherapists and IT professionals) (Fig. 3).

Table 1. Percentages of the improvement between S1 and S5 for each participant.

	ID1	ID2	ID3	ID4
Arms	43.32	118.72	81.84	129.38
Knees	67.97	49.51	121.97	31.18
Legs	26.22	8.46	34.93	106.91
Average	45.83	58.90	79.58	89.15

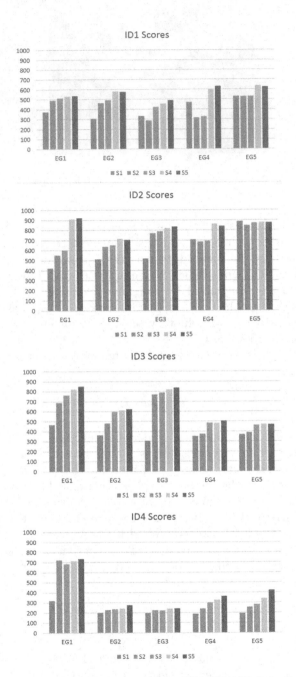

Fig. 4. Scores obtained by each participant (ID1, ID2, ID3, ID4) for 5 exergames (EG1, EG2, EG3, EG4, EG5) performing during 5 sessions (S1, S2, S3, S4, S5).

To assess the efficiency of the rehabilitation system, the focus has been put on the score reached to perform a correct posture in a right way. The score reached in each exergame indicates the level of similarity between the desired posture and the posture realized by the senior. The system considers 1000 points as the top score for each exergame which indicates that the exergame has been perfectly performed. It has been observed that all the participants have increased their scores after following the exergame program (see Fig. 4). They have improved the performance of their postural response of around 60%. In Table 1 are reported the percentages of improvement for each participant with respect to the different exercices gathered in arms, knees and legs.

At the end of the last session, a satisfaction questionnaire has been submitted to the elderly in order to evaluate the user-friendliness and the interaction quality of the system. Although the seniors are not familiar with new technologies they found very satisfactory the usability and the quality of the interaction with the system. They have appreciated to have a real-time feedback on what they were performing and a visualization of what they had to do (reference posture). However they suggested three points of improvements. First, a major color contrast in the graphical interface is necessary. During the experimentation, the HP gave explanations and orally guided the senior. The elderly well understood the 3D visualization of the exercice when it was explained. But while they were playing the game, they found it difficult and they didn't know where to look at. They missed time to react. The three views (facial, left and top) of the human skeleton should be more explicit and detailed. Finally, a vocal guide should be added to help the elderly in performing the exergames.

Concerning the gameplay, the elderly's requirements initially specified to integrate a musical background and a travel context. Following the first experimentation session, the music background was abandoned because the seniors were disturbed due to hearing disorders. The game context should be also investigated in order to not disturb the senior while performing the exercice.

4   Conclusions

In the context of fall prevention for the elderly, the rehabilitation system developed in this study proposed an efficient solution based on a tailored exergame program. The latter is defined by a physiotherapist according to the elderly's physical status. An experimentation was carried out at an elderly day care center. The participants have increased their scores after following the KINOPTIM exergame program whatever the kind of exercices (arms, knees or legs). The performance of the postural response, over one month training, has been improved of around 60%. Globally, the rehabilitation system encountered a great success in the elderly both for its efficiency in maintaining a physical activity and for its user-friendliness. The elderly really enjoyed to test the platform and were not afraid of new technologies. They found very satisfactory the usability and the quality of the interaction with the system. They have appreciated to have a real-time feedback on what they were performing. It created a real motivation to better perform the exercices. However, they have suggested several improvements of the KINOPTIM system: a vocal guide, a better color distinction, a more detailed and explicit 3D-visualization of the desired postures. We must pay attention to not over-use 3D graphic and animation because it seems to destabilize the elderly in performing exercices.

From the HP's point of view, the exergames creation is easy. They suggested to integrate exercices which could be performed sitting on a chair for people with balance impairments. At this stage, the image processing algorithms should be improved to deal with such exercices. Further investigations should be done in this domain.

Further experimentations will be carried out with a greater number of seniors in order to establish the efficiency of the rehabilitation system by comparing the obtained performance with a control group. The obtained results are very encouraging and allow to consider an experimentation at the elderly's home.

Acknowledgments. The authors would like to thank the pilot site "La Maison Felippa". This research was supported by a Marie Curie IAPP program within the FP7 under Grant 324491.

References

1. Barelle, C., Courtial, E., Vellidou, E., Tsirbas, H., Tagaris, T., Ibanez, F., Sanchez, E., Koutsouris, D.: Tele-monitoring and diagnostic for fall prevention: the KINOPTIM concept. In: IEEE-EMBS International Conference on Biomedical and Health Informatics (BHI), pp. 342–345 (2014)
2. Brox, E., Konstantinidis, S.T., Evertsen, G., Fernandez-Luque, L., Remartinez, A., Oesch, P., Civit, A.: GameUp: exergames for mobility-a project to keep elderly active. In: Kyriacou, E., Christofides, S., Pattichis, C. (eds.) XIV Mediterranean Conference on Medical and Biological Engineering and Computing 2016, vol. 57, pp. 1225–1230. Springer, Cham (2016)
3. Choi, S.D., Guo, L., Kang, D., Xiong, S.: Exergame technology and interactive interventions for elderly fall prevention: a systematic literature review. Appl. Ergon. (2016)
4. Courtial, E., Brulin, D.: A decision support system for preventing falls in elderly people. In: Proceedings of the 5th EAI International Conference on Wireless Mobile Communication and Healthcare, pp. 108–112. ICST (Institute for Computer Sciences, Social-Informatics and Telecommunications Engineering) (2015)
5. Ejupi, A., Gschwind, Y.J., Brodie, M., Zagler, W.L., Lord, S.R., Delbaere, K.: Kinect-based choice reaching and stepping reaction time tests for clinical and in-home assessment of fall risk in older people: a prospective study. Eur. Rev. Aging Phys. Act. **13**(1), 2 (2016)
6. Otago-Medical-School: Otago exercice programme to prevent falls in older adults, March 2003. http://www.acc.co.nz/PRD_EXT_CSMP/groups/external_providers/documents/publications_promotion/prd_ctrb118334.pdf
7. Paraskevopoulos, I., Tsekleves, E., Warland, A., Kilbride, C.: Virtual reality-based holistic framework: a tool for participatory development of customised playful therapy sessions for motor rehabilitation. In: 2016 8th International Conference on Games and Virtual Worlds for Serious Applications (VS-Games), pp. 1–8. IEEE (2016)

8. Skjaeret, N., Nawaz, A., Morat, T., Schoene, D., Helbostad, J.L., Vereijken, B.: Exercice and rehabilitation delivered through exergames in older adults: an integrative review of technologies, safety and efficacy. Int. J. Med. Inform. **85**(1), 1–16 (2016)
9. Smeddinck, J.D., Herrlich, M., Malaka, R.: Exergames for physiotherapy and rehabilitation: a medium-term situated study of motivational aspects and impact on functional reach. In: Proceedings of the 33rd Annual ACM Conference on Human Factors in Computing Systems, pp. 4143–4146. ACM (2015)
10. Tiedemann, A., O'Rourke, S., Sherington, C.: How is a yoga-based fall prevention program perceived by older people? J. Sci. Med. Sport **18**, e94 (2014)
11. World-Health-Organization: Fact sheet 344, September 2016. http://www.who.int/mediacentre/factsheets/fs344/en/

Application of VR/AR in Cultural Heritage

Finger Recognition as Interaction Media in Augmented Reality for Historical Buildings in Matsum and Kesawan Regions of Medan City

Mohammad Fadly Syahputra[✉], Ridho K. Siregar,
and Romi Fadillah Rahmat

Faculty of Computer Science and Information Technology,
Department of Information Technology,
University of Sumatera Utara, Medan, Indonesia
{nca.fadly,romi.fadillah}@usu.ac.id,
ridho_kurniawan@students.usu.ac.id

Abstract. Cultural heritage refers to the objects or symbolic attributes which resembles the identity of a society inherited from the previous generations, and will be preserved for the future generations. Despite of the importance of the cultural heritage, the interest of modern society for historic building has been decreased, as the cultural heritage is not considered as the main priority of development by the local government. This condition increases the necessity to restore the interest of modern society for historic building by implementing augmented reality. In this research, the finger recognition is utilized as the media of interaction between the 3-D objects and User. The system will identify the structure of human hand and calculate the number of fingers detected from the image obtained from web camera, by using convex hull and convexity defects. The research shows that the distance required to obtain the best performance is 30 to 50 cm with adequate light condition, while the distance required to perform marker detection in augmented reality is between 2.5 to 5 m, with the camera angle of 40°.

Keywords: Finger recognition · Augmented reality · Digital heritage preservation · Skin color detection

1 Introduction

Medan city is the third biggest city in Indonesia besides Jakarta and Surabaya city, it is also can be represented as the main gate of western Indonesia. Medan has been developed from the main export hub city in the colonial era into a metropolitan city in this era. The historical buildings built in the colonial era are the part of tourism objects in Medan. Some of the historical buildings in Medan are Grand Mosque of Al Mashun, Maimoon Palace, and Tirtanadi Water Monument in Matsum region; along with Tjong A Fie Mansion, Post Office, and Lonsum Office in Kesawan region. The majority of modern society in Medan do not have adequate knowledge about historical building in Medan. Therefore, the work to promote historical building in Medan is needed.

L.T. De Paolis et al. (Eds.): AVR 2017, Part II, LNCS 10325, pp. 243–250, 2017.
DOI: 10.1007/978-3-319-60928-7_21

One of the technology used to introduce historical buildings is augmented reality. Augmented reality is the technique of real world modification, enhanced with digital information, which will be displayed into the screen of a computer or a mobile phone [1]. Augmented reality is implemented as the education media and the information media. Augmented reality is the technology which implements computer vision in its process. Computer vision is one of the principles of image processing, which gives the compute the eyesight capability. By using computer vision, the computer can do decision making based on the image object.

In this research, an augmented reality application will be constructed to display the 3-D objects representing the historical buildings in Medan, along with the other 3-D objects. The finger recognition method is applied by to detect the input given by the user. In order to select the specific cultural heritage, we used the number of the finger that has been detected by the application.

The main obstacle of historical building preservation in Medan is the lack of interest from modern society, some of the problems is the lack of data [8]. Therefore, the approach to promote historical building by using image processing and 3-D animation is needed to attract interest of modern society and urban developers. An application with augmented reality is produced by developing 3-D models of historical buildings in Medan. In addition, the finger detection method by using OpenCV will be implemented to select the specific animation scene.

Various researches have been conducted about implementation of OpenCV and augmented reality. Brotos [2] build an interactive augmented reality panel for Android by using Microsoft Hololens. The finger detection process is started by color segmentation using HSV and processed by CAMSHIFT algorithm to determine the number of detected finger objects. The result shows that the performance of the detection process correlates to the color of the detected finger. Peng [3] researched about development of face detection and augmented reality in mobile platform by using various tools. Rios et al. [4] combines OpenCV with augmented reality to operate 6 instructions by detecting hand gesture. The detection process, which is done by implementing skin-color filtering, convex-hull, and convexity defects, shows that the accuracy of the detection process correlates to the lighting level of the skin. Liang et al. [5] performed palm pose tracking in augmented reality to control 3-D objects by using OpenGL. Lee et al. [6] performed skin color detection based on HSV value, with dilation and erosion method to process image morphology, before performing hand gesture recognition. The hand gesture recognition process is performed by using blob detection method. Other skin color detection has been described by Rahmat et al. [7], they performed skin color detection using multi-color space threshold.

2 Methodology

The steps performed in this research are image acquisition by using web camera, image resizing, RGB to HSV conversion, skin color detection by defining the desired HSV value, image optimization by median blur to minimize noise and dilation, feature extraction with contour and convex-hull detection from the detected contour, convexity defects calculation, and calculate the detected fingers. The number of detected fingers returned by the system will be used to determine the instruction given by the user to switch the scene, which is constructed in Unity3D. The general architecture of the system illustrated in this research is shown by Fig. 1.

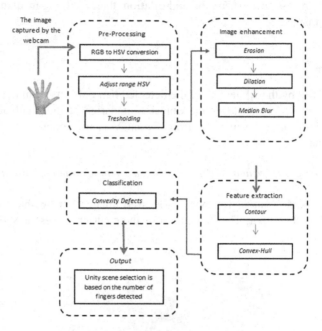

Fig. 1. General architecture of the system

2.1 Image Pre-processing

The image pre-processing steps is performed to identify hand object based on the skin colour. The result of this process correlates to the brightness level and the quality of the web camera. The HSV colour method is implemented to perform colour segmentation process. The image captured by the web camera will be converted into HSV colour space. The result of HSV conversion will be converted to binary image by using thresholding process. Skin colour detection is performed by defining the value of H, S, and V. The rule of color segmentation by HSV in this research is defined by Eq. 1 below.

$$w(x,y) = \begin{cases} 255, & if \ h_1 < h < h_2, \ s_1 < s < s_2 \\ 0 \end{cases} \tag{1}$$

where w(x,y) refers to the binary value of the color, h_1, h, and h_2 refers to H value of the color pixel, while s_1, s, and s_2 refers to S value of the color pixel.

2.2   Image Enhancement

The image produced by the pre-processing process will be inducted to the next phase in order to minimize noise and highlighting the object of the hand. The process starts with morphological process such as erosion and dilation, then applying median blur filter to the processed image.

2.3   Contour

Contour is defined by the white dots of the detected hand objects from the thresholding process result of the image, to define object boundaries of the hand object. In this research, the findContours() function from OpenCV is implemented to find the contours of the image.

$$findContours\,(src\,image, contours, hierarcy, mode, method, Point());\qquad(2)$$

In order to get single contour for every processed image, then we have to define the area for the biggest contour. The illustration of the contour process is shown in Fig. 2 below.

Fig. 2. Contour area

2.4   Convex Hull

The convex-hull process is the process to detect contour or objects in an image, which consists of set of dots connected with line, filling over the boundaries of the contour. The largest contour detected from the convex-hull process will be considered as the hand object. The result of the convex-hull process, which correlates with the brightness level of the image, will be utilized to calculate the number of fingers. To perform the convex hull we use convexHull() function. The result form this function is been used to count the fingers. In the reality, the illumination brightness will become main factors in hull detection.

2.5   Convexity Defects

The convexity defect, which is the last step of finger detection process, is the process where the system will search for the connection point between contour and convex-hull line. The start point of a convexity defect is an end of contour line which is synchronized with convex-hull line. The contour will be defined clockwise. The illustration of the start point is shown by Fig. 3(a). The red point is the point which is located in convex hull, and the next point is not located inside convex hull. The end point of the convexity defect will be defined as the point located in convex hull, where the preceding point is not located inside convex hull. As shown by Fig. 3(a), the violet point is the end point of convexity defects. The convexity defects area will be created by connecting the start point, the end point, and red point, as shown by Fig. 3(b). The result of the convexity defects process is shown by Fig. 4. As shown by Fig. 4, a hand with 4 fingers is detected, and we can get the tip of the finger from this process. This will lead us to control the application using finger movement recognition.

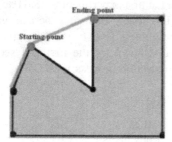 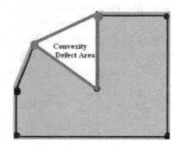

Fig. 3. (a) start and end points of convexity defects, (b) convexity defect area (Color figure online)

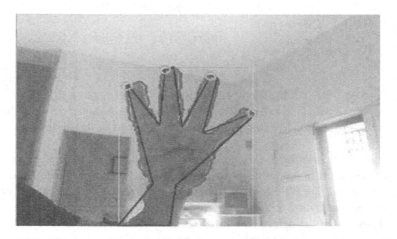

Fig. 4. Result of convexity defect

3 Experiment and Results

The experiment is conducted to know the accuracy level of the finger detection method. The command defined in the application will be used to determine user command in 3-D augmented reality application. The parameters implemented in the experiment is brightness level and the distance between hand and camera. Brightness and distance has the biggest impact in deciding the finger recognition in our system. In different level of brightness, it also gives different result. In different distance level, it will also give different results.

3.1 Brightness Level and Distance Level Experiments

In this section, the experiment is done by implementing different brightness level. The first experiment and the second experiment are done in the room with high brightness level. The accuracy level obtained from the first experiment is shown by Table 1. The result shows that the best accuracy level obtained in the first experiment is 98.61%. The second experiment is done in the room with low brightness level. The best accuracy level obtained by the method is 96.82%. The low brightness level cause the method to be unable to detect skin color. Based on the result shown by the first and second experiment, the mean accuracy level of the finger detection process is 97.71%.

Table 1. Brightness level

Experiment	Low brightness level		High brightness level	
Number of finger	1	2	1	2
Number of attempts	75	85	72	60
True positive	72	83	70	60
False positive	3	2	2	0
Accuracy	96.00	97.64	97.22	100
Error	4.00	2.36	2.78	0.00

The third and the fourth experiment is done by implementing different distance between hand and the camera. In the third experiment, the distance between the hand and the camera is 30 cm. The best accuracy level obtained in the third experiment is 99.33%.

In the fourth experiment, the distance between the hand and the camera is 60 cm. The result shows that in the fourth experiment, the hand could not be detected by the system, resulting in the 0% accuracy level. For the distance larger than 60 cm, the system could not recognize and count the fingers, and only obtaining the result for its contour. Thus, to get the defects, the calculation by the system will give bad results, because of the distance between fingers will be closer, it will also give impact to the depth point of contour area. The result of the third and fourth experiment is shown by Table 2. The average accuracy level of the third and the fourth experiment is 49.665%.

Table 2. Distance level

Experiment	Distance 30 cm		Distance 60 cm	
Number of finger	1	2	1	2
Number of attempts	75	65	50	65
True positive	74	65	0	0
False positive	1	0	50	65
Accuracy	98.66	100.00	0.00	0.00
Error	1.34	0.00	100.00	100.00

Fig. 5. The selection page (Color figure online)

3.2   Implementations

The application will display an animation video with the duration of 5 s, introducing the historical buildings constructed in this research. The scene selection page, which is shown by Fig. 5, will be shown after the playback of the short video has been finished. In this implementation, the background of the finger capturing process is in light green,

Fig. 6. (a) The main view of the application, (b) Matsum region, (c) Kesawan region

and using predefined HSV values. The user can select the scene by giving hand command with one or two fingers. The selected scene can be displayed for the maximum duration of 1 min. The appearance of the system is shown by Fig. 6.

4 Conclusion

The finger detection method is applied to the augmented reality application for displaying 3-D objects which represents some historical buildings in Medan. The result of this research shows that the best performance of finger detection method is produced while the image has adequate brightness level, and the hand is placed with the distance between 30–50 cm from camera, with the accuracy level of 98.61%. The minimum distance of the finger from the camera required for the best performance of 99.33% is 30 cm, while the maximum distance of the finger from the camera required to be detected by the method is 65 cm. The finger detection method in this research gives the best result when the background of the detection area should be in plain color and should not represent the skin color. The distance of the marker required to be detected by augmented reality system ranges between 2.5 to 5 m.

For the future research, the finger detection method should be modified to be able to detect finger with various background colors. The other methods should be implemented to prevent the other objects, such as arms and head. Also, the method should be modified to enable the method to be performed while there is the significant change of brightness level.

References

1. Hartanto, R., Nurtiantoro, M.A.: Perancangan Awal Antarmuka *Gesture* Tangan Berbasis visual. JNTETI **1**(1), 36–43 (2012)
2. Brotos, A.: Interactive augmented reality panel interface for android. Bachelor Thesis, Stanford University (2015)
3. Peng, H.: Application research on face detection technology based on OpenCV in mobile augmented reality (2015)
4. Rios, D., et al.: Hand-gesture recognition using computer-vision techniques. In: 21st International Conference on Computer Graphics, Visualization and Computer Vision (2013)
5. Liang, H., Thalmann, D., Magnenat, N.: AR in Hand: egocentric palm pose tracking and gesture recognition for augmented reality applications. Skripsi, Nanyang Technological University, Singapore (2015)
6. Lee, H., Tateyama, Y., Ogi, T.: Hand gesture recognition using blob detection for immersive projection display system. World Acad. Sci. Eng. Technol. Int. J. Comput. **2**, 116–119 (2012)
7. Rahmat, R.F., Chairunnisa, T., Gunawan, D., Sitompul, O.S.: Skin color segmentation using multi-color space threshold. In: 2016 3rd International Conference on Computer and Information Sciences (ICCOINS), Kuala Lumpur, pp. 391–396 (2016)
8. Syahputra, M.F., Permady, J.A., Muchtar, M.A.: Digital reconstruction of Darul Aman palace based on images and implementation into virtual reality environment. In: Paolis, L.T., Mongelli, A. (eds.) AVR 2016. LNCS, vol. 9769, pp. 269–279. Springer, Cham (2016). doi:10.1007/978-3-319-40651-0_22

An Innovative Real-Time Mobile Augmented Reality Application in Arts

Chutisant Kerdvibulvech[✉]

Graduate School of Communication Arts and Management Innovation,
National Institute of Development Administration,
118 SeriThai Rd., Klong-chan, Bangkapi, Bangkok 10240, Thailand
chutisant.ker@nida.ac.th

Abstract. Due to the popularity of music, motion tracking and augmented reality in recent years, the research topic in these fields is extremely popular. In contrast to every previous work, in this paper, we present an innovative real-time mobile application in arts for helping musicians by integrating motion tracking into augmented reality technology. A kinematic filtering algorithm is utilized for calculating the parameters. According to the computed parameters, each hand of musicians is then tracked by using the Microsoft Kinect. After that, an augmented reality application with an integrated multimedia feature is built based on the PixLive Maker synchronized with music being played. This hybrid application allows musicians to interact with the virtual piano in a new way that is similar to the way in which they are playing a real piano. By pressing any selected piano key on the air, the sound of each note is generated continuously into a song and incorporated with an interface in the smartphone. The new application achieves a suitable computed rate for real-time use. Representative experimental results have shown that the application is beneficial for piano players in arts by allowing them to practice and touch the virtual piano with lower cost and an interactive experience.

Keywords: Motion tracking · Augmented reality · Kinematic filtering · Microsoft Kinect · Multimedia · Musical instrument · Arts · Virtual piano · Real-time

1 Background

Nowadays, augmented reality (AR) technology is rapidly becoming a very popular field for assisting people in a new manner. This is done by combining between the computer system and the real world. At the same time, music also plays a very essential part of various cultures in many parts of the world, from western cultures to eastern cultures. Recently, there have been various interesting works related to augmented reality and computer vision visually for supporting musicians, especially guitarists (such as in the work of [1] presented previously many years ago for guitar chord recognition using stereo cameras) and pianists. We found many research works that are related for helping pianists. For example, Chow et al. [2] presented an augmented reality-based immersive experience system for improving the experience of people who are learning piano. Their system built the augmented reality interface and then used a

© Springer International Publishing AG 2017
L.T. De Paolis et al. (Eds.): AVR 2017, Part II, LNCS 10325, pp. 251–260, 2017.
DOI: 10.1007/978-3-319-60928-7_22

head-mounted display (HMD) to monitor their piano practice exercises visually. Moreover, Chouvatut and Jindaluang [3] created an augmented reality-based musical system, called Virtual Piano, for people with hearing disability who are not able to play a keyboard instrument. This system allowed people with hearing impairment to practice playing note by providing the sound of musical instrument. Nonetheless, both systems in [2, 3], they do not aim to deal with motion tracking for helping musicians to play the instrument. Next, Liang et al. [4] built a computer vision-based hand interaction application for supporting piano players. Their application visually segmented the hand from the plane painted white clearly. Then, the system created a kinematic chain for recovering the fingers' articulation parameters. However, this system did not challenge the background for plane, especially when it is challenging. Furthermore in [5], Oka and Hashimoto presented a computer vision-based prototype system to detect the differences in depth for keys by analyzing the movement of fingers in playing piano. They used sequential depth images to solve the problems. Nevertheless, it was not totally convenient to use the depth sensor in some certain situations. A similar work can be found in [6] by Goodwin and Green for focusing on piano. This work used a vision-based algorithm to identify a keyboard of piano from a low-cost camera (i.e., webcam) for helping piano teachers. A binary thresholding, Hough line transforms and Sobel operators were implemented in this work for determining a region of interest (ROI) resembling a keyboard. However, their aim was not to help pianists to create the music by pressing a piano key on the air. Also more recently, Deb and Rajwade [7] presented an image analysis methodology to generate the visual information for musical transcription played on musical instruments. Although their system can deal well with different lighting conditions, in their research work, they focused only on a keyboard-like instrument with several specific limitations. In addition, Randolph and Eugenio [8] created a Dactylize system for overlaying every key of a keyboard with foil tape as digital input from piano performances. Even though the system was economical and somehow practical to build, there still had some challenges about usability.

Moreover, rather than using augmented reality and computer vision, there have been several works using sensors to support pianists in recent years. For instance, Zhang et al. [9] proposed a piano biofeedback prototype system using a sensor-based digital glove. This system was virtually designed to help people with stroke which is a common condition in the elders. So their system attempted to determine proper methods for increasing some extra activities by taking some advantages from musical instruments. Moreover recently, an augmented reality-based interactive performance application was built by Dubnova and Wang [10] using IR markers and a depth sensing camera. However, their application did not aim to use for supporting musicians. To the best of our knowledge, in contrast to the existing works, we have a different research goal from each aforementioned system. In this paper, our research goal is to track hands and fingers of musicians for interacting with the hybrid virtual piano that include seven keys of piano, i.e. Do, Re, Mi, Fa, Sol, La and Ti.

This paper presents a novel hybrid system by integrating a kinematic filtering algorithm [11] with augmented reality for supporting musicians visually. Figure 1 demonstrates an example of our hybrid application between motion tracking and augmented reality-based multimedia and computer graphics. This system allows people to interact with the hybrid virtual piano in a way that is similar to the way in which they are playing a real piano. We track each hand and finger of musicians by using the Microsoft Kinect [12] technology for generating the kinematic parameter in real-time. After that, the parameter is implemented for creating the augmented reality application based on the PixLive Maker [13]. Therefore, people can get more interactive experience of playing the piano and keyboard in the virtual piano system because they do not have to touch the real piano using Pixlive Player via a smartphone. By pressing any selected piano key on the air, the sound of each note is generated continuously into a song and incorporated with an interface in the smartphone. Thus, it allows pianists to practice and touch the virtual piano or keyboard with lower cost, but at the same time it can create more uniquely interactive experience than the real one.

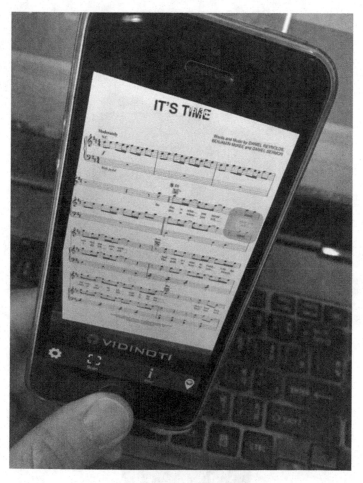

Fig. 1. An example of our hybrid system while the user is using the application via his/her smartphone

In the rest of the proposed paper, it is organized as following: Sect. 2 introduces the system overview of the presented hybrid application and demonstrates our representative experimental results; Sect. 3 concludes the paper and points out the directions of our possible future work.

2 Hybrid System Overview

In this section, we describe the overview of hybrid system and its implementation. In contrast to the previous works, this presented system is built for creating a new kind of playing music. Figure 2 shows the system overview. First, a user starts to scan QR

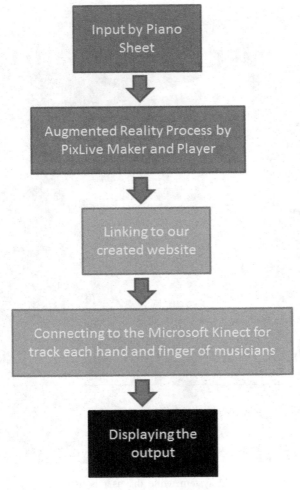

Fig. 2. System overview of the presented hybrid application using augmented reality and the Microsoft Kinect

code from the piano sheet for connecting with an augmented reality scenario we built. In this case, the input to our system is the piano sheet. Please note that we receive our piano sheets online from the websites of Choose-Piano-Lessons and Online-Pianist. Then, the PixLive Maker is used for displaying the scenario for interacting with people. After selecting the musical sheet in the website, the system is programmed to connect to the Microsoft Kinect for tracking the poses of hands and fingers based on the musical sheet they select. Then the system can estimate the kinematic parameter, and send this information to produce the sound of each note musically and interactively. Therefore, the output of our system is the sound of the selected music from the piano sheet based on the gestures of the musician. In addition, this application we built includes many functions such as video function, audio function, game function, practice piano note, instrument's shop and link to mobile website for supporting the musicians. For the video and audio functions, it allows people to choose other instruments as well such as piano, guitar, violin and flute. However, in this prototype system, we focus on the piano

Fig. 3. Examples of augmented reality-based application and its functions for practice each musical note

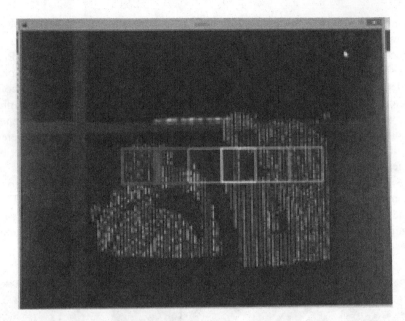

a.) Seven small boxes in different colors are connected to the Microsoft Kinect to represent each musical note.

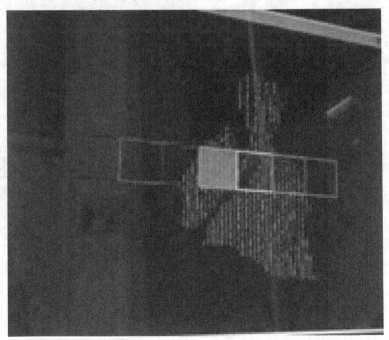

b.) When a player is moving his hand into the area (green region), the system can recognize it automatically.

Fig. 4. There are seven small boxes showing for seven musical notes. (Color figure online)

first. In this way, this application can practice in part of piano's and metronome's rhythm. Figure 3 shows some examples of the augmented reality-based application and its functions for practice each musical note.

Moreover, in this augmented reality application, we create a game for entertaining users and practicing knowledge about instruments. Each user can play the game we design to choose to answer each question which the system generates automatically. After the game finishes, the system will show scores which are achieved by each user. Also, this application is designed to allow people to access the mobile website for increasingly entertaining the users. Both the augmented reality-based application and the mobile website can connect with the Microsoft Kinect. The Microsoft Kinect is installed Processing 2.0, OpenNI, Microsoft Kinect SDK v.1.8, NiTE and SimpleOpenNI-1.96 library and is written with C programming. This programming is used in this work because it is supported with the Microsoft Kinect SDK for gesture. For implementation, to begin with, the Microsoft Kinect is utilized. Windows.h and Ole2.h are included for allowing the Microsoft Kinect work properly. We then obtain Red-Green-Blue data from this initialization. OpenGL is also used for drawing the texture. A camera viewpoint via an orthographic projection is set up for two dimensional images. Each box is drawn in each frame to the screen.

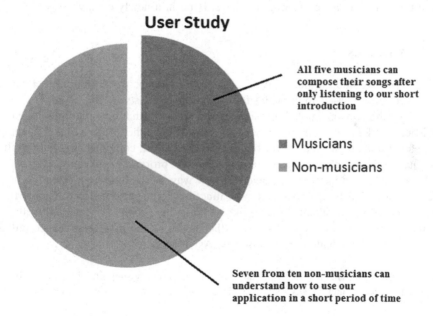

Fig. 5. A user study was conducted for assuring the effectiveness of the presented application.

For designing of the Microsoft Kinect, the program is designed by building seven boxes. These small seven boxes are represented as each musical note (C, D, E, F, G, A, and B). Figure 4 shows these seven boxes connected to the Microsoft Kinect via coding the programs. This figure also represents some representative experimental results. The sensor of the Microsoft Kinect detects hands and fingers of the musicians when they are in each small box, so that we gain rhythms and at the same time the color of the box will change over time. Therefore, by pressing any selected piano key on the air, the sound of each note from the augmented reality-based application is generated continuously into a musical song.

Finally, a user study was conducted for evaluating the application by randomly selecting fifteen people. Figure 5 shows this evaluation. Five of fifteen people were musician (i.e., pianist), while ten people were not musician. According to our experiments, all five pianists can use this presented application smoothly. They can compose their songs quickly after listening to our short introduction. However, three from ten non-musicians spent more than five minutes to understand how to use our application. Also, they cannot compose any song, even though they understand how to use the application. They suggested that it should be more explanation about the user interface in the application, so that it would help to those who have absolutely no experience of music before. Nevertheless, thirteen of fifteen people (i.e., 86.7%) liked our application. Two people wrote positively in the comment forms we gave that they would like to use this application for creating a musical band in a newly creative way.

3   Conclusions

In this paper, we built an innovative mobile application between motion tracking and augmented reality-based multimedia for supporting pianists in arts. A kinematic filtering algorithm was integrated into augmented reality with a new multimedia feature. The Microsoft Kinect technology was also utilized. Then the PixLive Maker is applied for creating this augmented reality-based multimedia and computer graphics application. Our experimental results have revealed that the proposed application is beneficial for those who would like to play piano in a new way. In the future, we intend to utilize several advanced techniques and add more functions to this application for supporting a wide variety of users. We also would like to refine the problem of the ease of the use interface. Moreover, we would like to further apply to use in several related-cultural heritage projects in Thailand and Southeast Asian (ASEAN).

Acknowledgments. This research presented herein was partially supported by a research grant from the Research Center, NIDA (National Institute of Development Administration).

References

1. Kerdvibulvech, C., Saito, H.: Real-time guitar chord recognition system using stereo cameras for supporting guitarists. Trans. Electr. Eng. Electron. Commun. (ECTI) **5**(2), 147–157 (2007)
2. Chow, J., Feng, H., Amor, R., Wunsche, B.C.: Music education using augmented reality with a head mounted display. In: Proceedings of the Fourteenth Australasian User Interface Conference, Melbourne, Australia, 29 January–01 February 2013, vol. 139, pp. 73–79 (2013)
3. Chouvatut, V., Jindaluang, W.: Virtual piano with real-time interaction using automatic marker detection. In: Proceedings of the International Computer Science and Engineering Conference (ICSEC), 4–6 September 2013, INSPEC Accession Number: 14022228. IEEE (2013)
4. Liang, H., Wang, J., Sun, Q., Liu, Y.-J., Yuan, J., Luo, J., He, Y.: Barehanded music: real-time hand interaction for virtual piano. In: Proceedings of the 20th ACM SIGGRAPH Symposium on Interactive 3D Graphics and Games (I3D), Redmond, Washington, 27–28 February 2016, pp. 87–94 (2016)
5. Oka, A., Hashimoto, M.: Markerless piano fingering recognition using sequential depth images. In: Proceedings of the 19th Korea-Japan Joint Workshop on Frontiers of Computer Vision, pp. 1–4, January 2013
6. Goodwin, A., Green, R.: Key detection for a virtual piano teacher. In: Proceedings of the 28th International Conference of Image and Vision Computing New Zealand (IVCNZ), 27–29 November 2013, INSPEC Accession Number: 14062333. IEEE (2013)
7. Deb, S.S., Rajwade, A.: An image analysis approach for transcription of music played on keyboard-like instruments. In: Proceedings of the Tenth Indian Conference on Computer Vision, Graphics and Image Processing (ICVGIP), Guwahati, Assam, India, 18–22 December 2016. Article No. 5
8. Randolph, D.A., Di Eugenio, B.: Dactylize: automatically collecting piano fingering data from performance. In: Proceedings of the Extended Abstracts for the Late-Breaking Demo Session of the 17th International Society for Music Information Retrieval Conference, August 2016
9. Zhang, T., Lu, J., Hu, F., F., Wu, F., Guo, M.: A sensor-based virtual piano biofeedback system for stroke rehabilitation. In: Proceedings of the Global Humanitarian Technology Conference (GHTC), 10–13 October 2014, INSPEC Accession Number: 14789792. IEEE (2014)
10. Dubnov, T., Wang, C.: Free-body gesture tracking and augmented reality improvisation for floor and aerial dance. arXiv:1509.04751v1, 15 September 2015
11. Wang, Q., Kurillo, G., Ofli, F., Bajcsy, R.: Evaluation of pose tracking accuracy in the first and second generations of microsoft kinect. In: Proceedings of the International Conference on Healthcare Informatics (ICHI), pp. 380–389 (2015)

12. Ofli, F., Kurillo, G., Obdrzalek, S., Bajcsy, R., Jimison, H.B., Pavel, M.: Design and evaluation of an interactive exercise coaching system for older adults: lessons learned. IEEE J. Biomed. Health Inform. (JBHI) **20**(1), 201–212 (2016). doi:10.1109/JBHI.2015. 2391671. INSPEC Accession Number: 15673370. IEEE

13. Kerdvibulvech, C., Wang, C.-C.: A new 3D augmented reality application for educational games to help children in communication interactively. In: Gervasi, O., et al. (eds.) ICCSA 2016. LNCS, vol. 9787, pp. 465–473. Springer, Cham (2016). doi:10.1007/978-3-319-42108-7_35

Augmented Reality and UAVs in Archaeology: Development of a Location-Based AR Application

Maria Concetta Botrugno[✉], Giovanni D'Errico,
and Lucio Tommaso De Paolis

Department of Engineering for Innovation, University of Salento, Lecce, Italy
{mariaconcetta.botrugno,giovanni.derrico,lucio.depaolis}@unisalento.it

Abstract. In addition to the current use of Unmanned Aerial Vehicles in archaeology, oriented to rebuild the historical evolution of an archaeological area by using aerial photogrammetry and relief of archaeological objects, is possible to consider the fruition through augmented reality. By using jointly UAVs and augmented reality, it is possible to explore sites which are not often directly accessible from the user and from different perspectives, by providing various types of contextual information (3d models, textual information, etc.) and directly on site. This work deals with a feasibility study for the development of a location-based AR Android application supporting the fruition of a given archaeological site from an aerial perspective, by exploiting UAVs and augmented reality. The main contribution of the work was the integration between the Wikitude SDK augmented reality framework and the DJI Mobile SDK and led to the development of DJIARcheoDrone, a first prototype of the application.

Keywords: Augmented reality · UAV · Mobile applications · Virtual cultural heritage · Archaeology

1 Introduction

The safeguard of the historical and artistic memory of the world cultural heritage has become in recent years the center of discussions, even on interdisciplinary intervention areas, because the perception of a progressive and irreversible depletion of this heritage is growing. The evolution of technology and the possibilities of interconnection in real time and anywhere offered by mobile technology provide an important bridge to the valorisation, the protection, and even the prevention of degradation.

In the last few years, technologies supporting cultural heritage include UAVs (Unmanned Aerial Vehicles), i.e. remotely piloted aircrafts without human pilot on board that provide an important contribution to the reconnaissance, interpretation and knowledge of the state of places.

© Springer International Publishing AG 2017
L.T. De Paolis et al. (Eds.): AVR 2017, Part II, LNCS 10325, pp. 261–270, 2017.
DOI: 10.1007/978-3-319-60928-7_23

In addition to the current use of UAVs in archaeology, oriented to rebuild the historical evolution of an archaeological area by using aerial photogrammetry and relief of archaeological objects, is possible to consider the fruition through augmented reality. This technology allows extending the observed reality without replacing it with a completely synthetic one, presenting a world in which real and virtual objects exist simultaneously.

UAVs and augmented reality are part of the large technological investments for the near future. A recent research conducted by Coleman Parkes Research reveals that both technologies will be an integral part of workstations by 2036 [1].

In addition, the emerged data from the report published by WinterGreen Research trace the business growth prospects of UAVs industry from a starting value of $600 million in 2014 up to $5 billion in 2021 [2]. These technologies have a strategic role in many application contexts, but a real bet for the future focuses on their synergy.

The aim of this work is to extend the current boundaries about the use of UAVs in archeology, with reference to improving the user fruition of the archaeological heritage, by combining both the advantages of aerial exploration and augmented reality.

2   Previous Works

The growing development of computer technologies and their involvement in the cultural heritage field not only helps to preserve sites of historical importance at disappearance risk, but it also allows artworks valorization and the improvement of the user experience. In particular, this improvement can be facilitated by technologies such as virtual and augmented reality, which enable to emotionally involve the visitor and increase his level of attention, thereby making easy the learning of useful and precious information regarding an artwork, a monument or an archaeological area.

Several projects are available in literature, where virtual reality appears to be an important tool for expanding and spreading the historical view of cultural heritage, traditionally limited to only a few professionals, scholars and researchers. De Paolis et al. [3–5] present the reconstruction of a town in the Middle Ages in order to develop a multi-channel and multi-sensory platform for the edutainment in cultural heritage. A digital didactic game oriented towards the knowledge of medieval history and society is proposed and it has permitted a didactic experimentation whereby simulation is considered as a precious teaching support tool. The educational game has prompted students to participate in and experience in a simulated and immersive environment of a town in the Middle Ages in order to connect the recreational actions, and to critically discover roles, functions and actions referring to Medieval life.

Vecchio et al. [6] propose the use of augmented reality and cloud computing technology in order to enrich the scenes of sites with a relevant cultural interest and improve the users cultural experience during the sightseeing of a city of art.

In archaeological field, augmented reality is used both as a tool for enhancing archaeological heritage and improving the visitor's fruition [7,8], as well as a tool useful for archaeologists in excavation and analysis works [9,10].

The joint use of augmented reality and UAVs currently responds to multiple needs, ranging from interactive videogames production [11] to improvement of the flight fruition experience, with the possibility to benefit of a first-person view (FPV) experience, as if UAV camera was a real extension of the user view. The most innovative solutions in this regard include the Epson MOVERIO BT-300 smartglasses, which allow the user piloting and keeping an eye on the aircraft, and enjoying at the same time of an augmented vision of the aerial images received from on board UAV camera [12].

Furthermore, this joint use involves the archaeological field, where until now the use of these devices was predominantly limited to the relief of archaeological objects [13] and aerofotogrammetry [14]. In this regard, the experiences investigated in literature still focuses on the videogames world as a useful educational tool to bring above all young people closer to art and cultural and archaeological heritage [15,16].

3 Work Hypothesis

Methodology. This work deals with a feasibility study for the development of an Android application for supporting the fruition of a given archaeological site from an aerial perspective, by exploiting UAVs and augmented reality.

A first and relevant choice involved the tracking methodology to be adopted for the scenario under consideration. The reference scenario is the outdoor one, where the complexity of a marker-based tracking shall be added to the objective difficulty of a markerless approach based on image recognition, because the environment is not prepared and dynamic, and requires a preliminary collection of a large set of scene photographs at different angles to allow a correct and continuous tracking.

Although some solutions available in literature are oriented towards a hybrid approach, there are several research lines exploiting a tracking based on GPS and inertial sensors [17,18], which represents the working solution adopted here, thanks to the current availability of position and movement sensors on board the most of UAVs on the market. The choice seems to be advantageous in terms of simplicity and ease of use, independently of changes in lighting, atmospheric conditions, and the environment.

Unmanned Aerial Vehicle. The choice of the UAV device that best fitting with project requirements was preceded by a survey phase oriented to choose, among all UAV devices currently available on the market, the product closest to some specific features, including the availability of a development software supporting both Android and iOS, the presence of a GPS receiver and a set of sensors on board, the remote video control, and the compatibility with augmented reality visors. Its important presence on the market and its consolidated use in the examined research projects oriented the choice on DJI devices and, specifically, on the Phantom 3 Professional model.

The remote controller allows an easy and stable aircraft piloting and the camera rotation only for pitch angle.

DJI Mobile SDK, compatible with both Android and iOS systems, is a software development kit provided by DJI in order to give developers the ability to manage all the aircraft potentiality, by developing customized mobile applications. Application development is simplified, because the software development kit takes care of the most of low-level functionality such as flight stabilization and communication between UAV and controller.

Augmented Reality Framework. In the choice of the augmented reality framework were taken into account some requirements in terms of compatibility with the Android operating system, specific support for a tracking based on GPS and inertial sensors, and 3D model registration in outdoor scenarios.

Trying to meet all these requirements by keeping a good generality level in the choice, the emphasis was given to the Wikitude SDK framework [19], that represents a multi-platform (Android, iOS, and Smartglasses) augmented reality mobile application library and currently supports location-based, marker-based and markerless tracking (Natural Feature Tracking and SLAM).

The Roman Pier of San Cataldo. As archaeological site to be used as scenario in the testbed phase, we focused on the ancient port of Lecce called "Adriano Pier", at San Cataldo. This site has been a great historical interest for the territory in the 2nd century A.D. and it is still possible to admire some original blocks, partly clearly detectable out of the water and partly submerged, and completely covered by marine vegetation.

4   DJIARcheoDrone Project

The software project is only made up of an Android mobile application, which runs on a mobile device connected to the UAV remote controller; the interacting systems are two, i.e. the Mobile Device and the DJI Product (consisting of UAV and remote controller in cascade systems). The mobile application uses first of all the DJI Mobile SDK and the Wikitude SDK, and finally the Android libraries. In addition, the connection between mobile device and remote controller is via USB.

4.1   Integration Between Wikitude SDK and DJI Mobile SDK

The integration work is based on four points: connection to the UAV, decoding of the video stream coming from the camera of the aircraft, telemetry data reception, and redirection of each of these components into the augmented reality experience.

In Fig. 1, a simplified version of the application class diagram is proposed. The main class is represented by the activity *MainActivity.java* which, on the

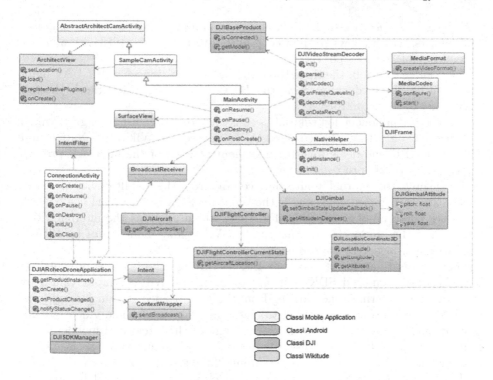

Fig. 1. Diagram class

one hand, interfaces with the logic of initializing, managing, and presenting AR experience and, on the other, with the classes allowing dialogue with the DJI Product, in order to receive and manage the external inputs. The connection to the DJI Product is performed by an application class, *DJIARcheoDroneApplication.java*, also responsible for monitoring any possible change in connectivity.

Starting with the sample code provided with the DJI Mobile SDK for Android [20], the entire logic for receiving raw video data, parsing, decoding, and rendering video images is inserted into the two classes *DJIVideoStreamDecoder.java* and *NativeHelper.java*. In particular, the first one represents a listener: when this class is instantiated, new raw data coming from the UAV camera can be received, analyzed, and transformed.

The ffmpeg library identifies syntax and semantics for the bitstream in accordance with the H.264 format, set as a contextual codec during the library initialization.

For hardware decoding, the Android *MediaCodec* class was used in order to access device low-level codecs and was configured through a surface parameter, on which decoded frames will be rendered.

In order to obtain updated values for telemetric parameters with reference to latitude, longitude, and altitude, a dialogue with the FlightController, the UAV on-board computer, must be established. This can be done by using

DJIFlightController, a DJI class containing a mapping to all on-board computer components, which allows reading both GPS and barometric altitude values at a frequency of 10 times per second.

Yaw, pitch and roll, the three rotation angles with respect to the UAV main axes, can be obtained by querying the *DJIGimbal* class, which allows the full UAV point of view control.

The core component for wikitude sdk is the computer vision engine, which is accessible only through dedicated APIs offered by Wikitude (Native and Javascript API) and deals with the management logic of the main AR process stages, from tracking to registration.

By default, the internal input values coming from the mobile device are used. One of the most important classes in the Wikitude SDK is *ArchitectView*, a views container made up of an OpenGL ES View, which contains the internal video stream and the augmented content, and a Web View, made up of an HTML page with a transparent background.

The goal is to access to Wikitude Engine through the features provided by both Wikitude Android SDK API and plugins, and redirect input values by injecting the "external" ones coming from the UAV (video stream coming from the UAV camera and telemetry data) into the framework. The video stream, in its default configuration, can come from any of the integrated mobile device cameras. In order to receive this stream from another source, a special plugin was used, developed starting from the Input Plugins API provided by Wikitude.

In the context under consideration, the plugin was exploited in order to exclude rendering of the internal video stream from the architectView, by switching off the relative view layer into the container. The video stream coming from the UAV is rendered by MediaCodec directly into a SurfaceView, which will be superimposed on architectView in the views composition (Fig. 2).

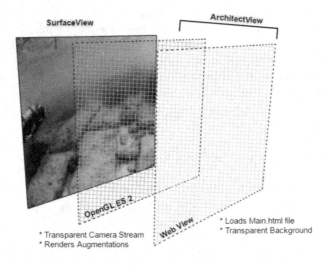

Fig. 2. View composition after integration

By using the ArchitectView setLocation() method, you can redirect geo-localization parameters by replacing the values provided by the embedded GPS in the mobile device with the values coming from the UAV.

Regarding sensor values redirection, Wikitude SDK does not offer any method to notify alternative values for the yaw, pitch, and roll angles provided by the sensors to the Wikitude Engine. This represents the greatest issue encountered in the integration work.

4.2 Augmented Reality Experience

Wikitude Javascript APIs allow writing cross-platform augmented reality experiences, called Architect Worlds, heavily based on web technologies (HTML, Javascript and CSS).

The augmented reality experience allows the user of an archaeological site visualizing a series of contextual information (superimposed on the aerial perspective of the real scenario) near a specific point of interest. The virtual contents will appear after the touch of a specific placemark, related to the desired point of interest and superimposed on the real scene. Once a placemark is selected, a panel containing textual information will appear on the right of the screen, in addition to a series of buttons enabling to choose the type of content to display (Fig. 3).

The visitor will be given the opportunity to visit the web site about the point of interest and enjoy other augmented reality contents, such as a picture

Fig. 3. DJARcheoDrone: screenshot of the augmented reality experience

slideshow, an audio guide and a video. In particular, the video content will offer a virtual tour within the 3D scenario showing the point of interest in the its ancient splendor.

The application is addressed primarily to the visitor user and the gradual improvement of his fruition experience of the historical-archaeological site. Let us imagine a scenario in which users are able to enjoy a truly flight experience in augmented reality, suitably assisted by an operator authorized to pilot the UAV in the overflight operations of a given site (Fig. 4).

Furthermore, in the archaeological field, this application would also be a valid support for the scientist, who could take advantage in the aerial reconnaissance surveys from a whole range of augmented information that helps him, for example, in the study of stratified evolution of the site in its various works of finding.

Huawei MediaPad M2-801L tablet with Android Lollipop 5.1.1 has been used for the tests of the application.

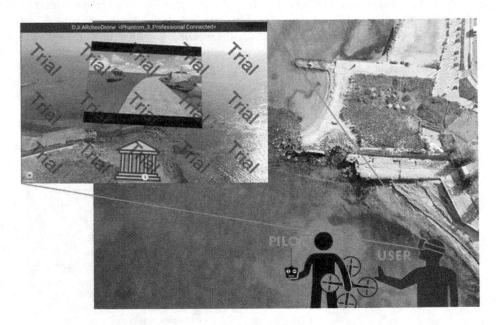

Fig. 4. DJARcheoDrone: user AR experience

5   Conclusions and Future Work

The carried out tests confirmed the effectiveness of the fruition experience of an archaeological site in augmented reality from an aerial view. Although the location-based approach suffers from the limits regarding GPS and sensor inaccuracies, it is simple and portable, allowing the use of the application for any kind of point of interest, independently from contextual conditions (lighting, atmospheric conditions, changes in environment).

Next steps of the research will be oriented to explore other tracking techniques such as hybrid ones that exploit pattern recognition in addition to the use of GPS and inertial sensors, in order to improve registration accuracy and enable even more complex augmented reality experiences, such as the superimposing of 3d models directly on the scene.

Another step will be to extend what is designed for Android systems even to iOS systems, allowing the use of DJIARcheoDrone even on iPhone and iPad devices.

Finally, along with the announced partnership between DJI and Epson, a further future development of the work will be to include the use of the Moverio smartglasses to improve the immersive flight experience in first person view by using augmented reality.

Acknowledgement. This work was carried out taking advantage of an educational partnership with DJI Enterprise, which provided the UAV for the entire research and testing period, and thanks to the collaboration with the LabTAF (Ancient Topography and Photogrammetry Laboratory) of the Department of Cultural Heritage of the University of Salento, and the CNR IBAM ItLab. In particular, the authors would like to thank Prof. Giuseppe Ceraudo, and Dr. Ivan Ferrari for their precious support.

References

1. Ricoh Europe. http://thoughtleadership.ricoh-europe.com
2. WinterGreen Research. http://www.wintergreenresearch.com
3. De Paolis, L.T., Aloisio, G., Celentano, M.G., Oliva, L., Vecchio, P.: A game-based 3D simulation of Otranto in the middle ages. In: Third International Conferences on Advances in Computer-Human Interactions, pp. 130–133. IEEE Press, St Maarten (2010)
4. De Paolis, L.T., Aloisio, G., Celentano, M.G., Oliva, L., Vecchio, P.: MediaEvo project: a serious game for the edutainment. In: Third International Conferences on Computer Research and Development, pp. 524–529. IEEE Press, Shanghai (2011)
5. De Paolis, L.T.: Walking in a virtual town to understand and learning about the life in the middle ages. In: Murgante, B., Misra, S., Carlini, M., Torre, C.M., Nguyen, H.-Q., Taniar, D., Apduhan, B.O., Gervasi, O. (eds.) ICCSA 2013. LNCS, vol. 7971, pp. 632–645. Springer, Heidelberg (2013). doi:10.1007/978-3-642-39637-3_50
6. Vecchio, P., Mele, F., De Paolis, L.T., Epicoco, I., Mancini, M., Aloisio, G.: Cloud computing and augmented reality for cultural heritage. In: De Paolis, L.T., Mongelli, A. (eds.) AVR 2015. LNCS, vol. 9254, pp. 51–60. Springer, Cham (2015). doi:10.1007/978-3-319-22888-4_5
7. Vlahakis, V., Karigiannis, J., Tsotros, M., Ioannidis, N.: Archeoguide: first results of an augmented reality, mobile computing system in cultural heritage sites. In: VAST, Proceedings of the Conference on Virtual Reality, Archeology, and Cultural Heritage, Glyfada, Greece, pp. 131–140. ACM (2001)
8. Pierdicca, R., Frontoni, E., Zingaretti, P., Malinverni, E.S., Colosi, F., Orazi, R.: Making visible the invisible. Augmented reality visualization for 3D reconstructions of archaeological sites. In: Paolis, L.T., Mongelli, A. (eds.) AVR 2015. LNCS, vol. 9254, pp. 25–37. Springer, Cham (2015). doi:10.1007/978-3-319-22888-4_3

9. Fernández-Palacios, B.J., Nex, F., Rizzi, A., Remondino, F.: ARCube the augmented reality cube for archaeology. Archaeometry **57**(Suppl.1), 250–262 (2015)

10. Eggert, D., Hücker, D., Paelke, V.: Augmented reality visualization of archeological data. In: Buchroithner, M., et al. (eds.) Cartography from Pole to Pole. Lecture Notes in Geoinformation and Cartography, pp. 203–216. Springer, Heidelberg (2013)

11. AR. Pursuit (Parrot SA). http://the-parrot-ardrone.com

12. Epson. http://www.epson.it

13. Ceraudo, G.: 100 anni di Archeologia aerea in Italia. Claudio Grenzi Editore, Foggia (2009)

14. Chen, L., Betschart, S., Blaylock, A.: Projeto Redentor: High-resolution 3D modelling of large, hard-to-reach objects. White Paper, Aeryon Labs Inc - Pix4D (2015)

15. Thon, S., Serena-Allier, D., Salvetat, C., Lacotte, F.: Flying a drone in a museum: an augmented-reality cultural serious game in Provence. In: Digital Heritage International Congress (DigitalHeritage), pp. 669–676. IEEE Press, Marseille (2013)

16. Bostanci, E., Unal, M.: Making visits to museums more fun with augmented reality using kinect, drones and games. In: The International Conference on Circuits, Systems, Signal Processing, Communications and Computers, pp. 7–10, Vienna (2016)

17. Behzadan, A.H.: Arviscope: Georeferenced Visualization of Dynamic Construction Processes in Three-Dimensional Outdoor Augmented Reality. University of Michigan (2008)

18. Stylianidis, E., Valaria, E., Smagasa, K., Pagani, A., et al.: LBS augmented reality assistive system for utilities infrastructure management through Galileo and Egnos. In: International Archives of the Photogrammetry, Remote Sensing and Spatial Information Sciences, XXIII ISPRS Congress, vol. XLI-B1, pp. 1179–1185, Prague (2016)

19. Wikitude SDK. http://www.wikitude.com

20. Android Video Stream Decoding Sample. http://developer.dji.com

Photogrammetric Approaches
for the Virtual Reconstruction
of Damaged Historical Remains

D. Costantino[1](✉), M.G. Angelini[1], and V. Baiocchi[2]

[1] DICATECh – Politecnico di Bari, V.le del Turismo, 8, 74121 Taranto, Italy
{domenica.costantino,
mariagiuseppa.angelini}@poliba.it
[2] DICEA – Sapienza Università di Roma,
Via Eudossiana, 18, 00184 Rome, Italy
valerio.baiocchi@uniromal.it

Abstract. The photogrammetrical techniques are, in this moment, experimenting new approaches based on innovative algorithms. The recent availability of high resolution cameras and sensors made possible the fast and accurate acquisition of complex geometries. On the other hand, manage such amount of data need for optimized procedure to automatize the geometric extraction of the geometric features. In this paper different photogrammetric techniques will be compared with direct measurement of the same site with laser scanner. The test site is the main door of the palace of the ex seminar archbishop's palace of Taranto town, whose construction goes up again to the XVII century, was surveyed. The survey has been realized, as we said, using two techniques: photogrammetrical survey and terrestrial digital laser scanner. In the portal the frieze is attributable to the Baroque style, while the molding has Rococo style features. The use of the photogrammetry has been finalized to the virtual reconstruction of the aforesaid portal, of which only lateral pillars and parts of the decoration are present in situ; the other elements found by the archaeologists have been summarily recomposed in laboratory. The photogrammetric survey has been performed on every element, moreover with the aid of the laser scanning survey, we have performed the resetting of the frieze, so that the whole portal has been semi-qualitatively reconstructed on the base of precise measurements.

The visualization of this element could be used for future interventions of portal restauration.

Keywords: Taranto · SfM · Laser scanning · Photogrammetry · Cloud points

1 Historical Notes

The former archdiocesan seminary of Taranto is one of the palaces of the old town of the city. He was one of the first seminary to be founded after the Council of TrentThe former seminary overlook the Great Sea, with the main entrance in the 'Vico Seminario' St. Peter and St. Paul islands.

© Springer International Publishing AG 2017
L.T. De Paolis et al. (Eds.): AVR 2017, Part II, LNCS 10325, pp. 271–281, 2017.
DOI: 10.1007/978-3-319-60928-7_24

The Seminaries draw origin from Tridentino Council, as said, in order to make the priesthood more accessible to the lower classes for obtain a cultural preparation more adherent to the necessities of the moment. Its institution was defined with a specific decree, which was signed also by the Archbishop of Taranto, Mons. M. Colonna that, between 1563 and 1568, officially founded the Seminary: it was opened on 1 June 1568 and had as its first rector the historian Giovanni Giovine (Fig. 1).

Fig. 1. Portal before frieze collapse

The original construction was approximately realized in three or four years. Soon it appeared insufficient to receive an increasing number of pupils and boarders, so appeared the necessity to widen and renew the plant.

Little is known regarding the original shape of the building, because of the continuous transformations it has undergone over the centuries. Traces of these modifications are found, among other things, by the presence of the coat of arms of the archbishops Sarria and Pignatelli that would have enlarged the building respectively in 1638 and in 1685. Another trace is the white marble portal wanted by Archbishop Mastrilli around 1770.

Afterward the French Revolution, when Napoleon arrived in Italy, and with the occupation of the Papal State, the property owner Orders and all the begging convents were suppressed.

So during the war between France, England and Turkey in 1801, the city of Taranto became a military centre, therefore the Seminary was employed to accommodate soldiers, so it lost its original use destination. While after the unification of Italy briefly housed the high school gymnasium "Archyta", The Seminary was solemnly reopened in 1885 from Mons. Jorio. Closed again during the first World war, it was finally abandoned in 1964, following the inauguration of the new seminary of Poggio Galeso.

Since May 6, 2011 is the seat of the Diocesan Museum.

The building has a quadrangular structure, and its rooms are arranged around the central cloister. The façade has a large portal, unusually oriented towards the sea, differently from surrounding constructions. The windows on the ground floor are unevenly distributed, probably inherited from the older structure, while the first and second floors are distributed on a regular basis.

2 Structure Condition

Restauration works of the entire building and, in particular, the architectonic restoration of the entrance portal of the Archbishopric, have been started. This architectonic element partially in situ was find; in fact, in the native place, the lateral moldings had remained (Fig. 2), while the upper frieze had collapsed.

Fig. 2. Portal before restoration

During the restoration work, several architectonic remains have been recovered inside the complex; they are dislocated in bulk, so it was necessary to recognize the remains that constitute the frieze. They were in a bad state of conservation (Fig. 3).

Fig. 3. Particular of one block of those composing the frieze

3   Survey Project for Restoration

In order to facilitate the restoration, it was essential to carry out an activity of integrated survey. This activity was aimed at the production of a simulation process of the interventions.

Firstly the execute the survey of moldings, a photogrammetric surveying has been realized using calibrated camera Nikon D5000. Natural Ground Control Points (GCP), necessary for the restitution, have been identified and surveyed. The coordinates of the 15 GCP, uniformly distributed, were determined for multiple intersection, of three station vertex (100, 200 and 300). The survey schema and the adjusted coordinates are shown in Fig. 4.

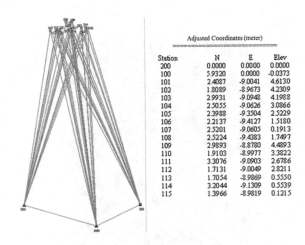

	Adjusted Coordinates (meter)		
Station	N	E	Elev
200	0.0000	0.0000	0.0000
100	5.9320	0.0000	-0.0373
101	2.4087	-9.0041	4.6130
102	1.8089	-8.9673	4.2309
103	2.9931	-9.0948	4.1988
104	2.5055	-9.0626	3.0866
105	2.3988	-9.3504	2.5229
106	2.2137	-9.4127	1.5180
107	2.5201	-9.0605	0.1913
108	2.5224	-9.4383	1.7497
109	2.9893	-8.8780	4.4893
110	1.9103	-8.9977	3.3822
111	3.3076	-9.0903	2.6786
112	1.7131	-9.0049	2.8211
113	1.7054	-8.9869	0.5550
114	3.2044	-9.1309	0.5539
115	1.3966	-8.9819	0.1215

Fig. 4. Ground control points coordinates

In the phase of recognition, 18 elements constituting the frieze have been identified. For these elements, an integrated survey has been executed in order to obtain a 3D model for each of this. In particular, have been carried out the TLS (Terrestrial Laser Scanner), topographic and photogrammetric survey [7, 8, 10, 11].

Due the complexity of the elements constituting the frieze, a laser scanning survey has been also executed using the TLS phase measurement which assures a higher resolution [5, 6].

The data collected have been processed with dedicated software. In particular, the acquisition of TLS data has been effectuated with *Cyclone* software; the exported point clouds have been with Geomagic and other software elaborated (Fig. 5).

The photogrammetric data has been pre elaborated with Agisoft Photoscan software (Figs. 6 and 7) and integrated at the laser scanner data in Geomagic. The registration in a local reference system of overall 3D model has been realized between the topographic survey.

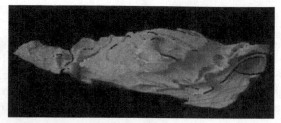

Fig. 5. TLS survey of elements

Fig. 6. Point cloud of moldings in PhotoScan

Fig. 7. Texture of frieze in PhotoScan

4   Reconstruction of 3d Models

The photograms of moldings and frieze have been processed with the Photoscan SW for the images registration. In Geomacic software have been imported the points cloud obtained with PhotoScan. The pre-elaboration and the production of wrap was made. Starting from 3D models thus obtained, the edges of elements were extracted [2–4, 12, 13]. The results of restitution in vectorial format are shown in Figs. 8 and 9.

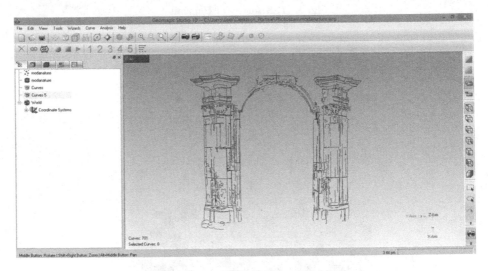

Fig. 8. Geometric definition of moldings

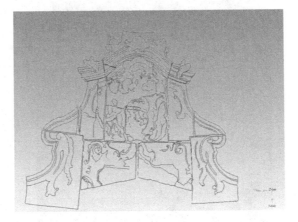

Fig. 9. Vectorial restitutions of the frieze

By means of the edges extracted of the individual frieze elements and with the use of historical photographic documentation, it was simulated a virtual assemblage used in the next fase of object reconstruction in site (Fig. 10).

Fig. 10. Historical photo (left) and photo mosaic (right) of the damaged frieze

In order to have the union of the two constituent architectonic elements, either of the whole portal, on the base of extracts edges, the support points were analyzed between frieze and moldings with the aide of historical image [9] (Fig. 11).

Fig. 11. Geometric elements used for whole portal reconstruction

The assemblage (Fig. 12) showed the results we expected from qualitative point of view as could be highlighted by the comparison between the historical photo and the vectorial restitution.

5   Result Comparison Post Restoration

The integrated survey have been executed also after restoration and processed through the same procedures above described. The results show intervention carried out on the basis of simulations performed (Figs. 13 and 14).

Fig. 12. Vectorial assemblage of whole portal

Fig. 13. Point cloud of TLS survey

In addition, the edges obtained by the two 3D model pre and post restoration (Fig. 15) were compared.

Fig. 14. 3D model of photogrammetric survey

Fig. 15. Comparison between 3D model pre and post restoration

In particular, comparing the graphic restitutions it can be said to have respected the valid basic criteria for any processing preservation and/or restoration artwork authenticity.

6 Conclusions

The restitution of the architectonic structure has been lead through two techniques: photogrammetric survey and terrestrial laser scanning.

The digital photogrammetric acquisition showed that, in the case of an archaeological structure, the digital image and digital processing could allow satisfactory results.

The photogrammetric restitution of complete mosaic of frieze should be very difficult to realize, so we have used laser scanning survey. Successively it was possible through a metric approach to create an assemblage of structural portions that allowed a reconstruction of the whole portal.

Elements of a damaged structure, that have been physically separated, have been virtually composed using two integrated methodologies that facilitates the steps of the conservative and integral restoration of the whole structure.

References

1. Putignani, A.: Il Seminario Arcivescovile di Taranto, pp. 1–32 (1964)
2. Armistead, C.C.: Applications of "Structure from Motion" Photogrammetry to River Channel Change Studies. Boston College University Libraries (2013). http://hdl.handle.net/2345/3086
3. Fonstad, M.A., Dietrich, J.T., Courville, B.C., Jensen, J.L., Carbonneau, P.E.: Topographic structure from motion: a new development in photogrammetric measurement. Earth Surf. Proc. Land. **38**(4), 421–430 (2013). doi:10.1002/esp.3366
4. Kersten, T.P., Lindstaedt, M.: Image-based low-cost systems for automatic 3D recording and modelling of archaeological finds and objects. In: Ioannides, M., Fritsch, D., Leissner, J., Davies, R., Remondino, F., Caffo, R. (eds.) EuroMed 2012. LNCS, vol. 7616, pp. 1–10. Springer, Heidelberg (2012). doi:10.1007/978-3-642-34234-9_1
5. Nex, F., Rinaudo, F.: LiDAR or photogrammetry? Integration is the answer. Ital. J. Remote Sens. **43**, 107–121 (2011). doi:10.5721/ItJRS20114328
6. Pirotti, F., Guarnieri, A., Vettore, A.: State of the art of ground and aerial laser scanning technologies for high-resolution topography of the earth surface. Eur. J. Remote Sens. **46**, 66–78 (2013). doi:10.5721/EuJRS20134605
7. Costantino, D., Angelini, M.G.: Three-dimensional integrated survey for building investigations. J. Forensic Sci. **60**(6), 1625–1632 (2015). doi:10.1111/1556-4029.12915
8. Costantino, D., Angelini, M.G.: Features and ground automatic extraction from airborne LIDAR data. In: International Archives of the Photogrammetry, Remote Sensing and Spatial Information Sciences - ISPRS Archives, vol. 38(5W12), pp. 19–24 (2011)
9. Costantino, D., Angelini, M.G.: Realization of a cartographic GIS for the filing and management of the archaelogical excavations in the Nelson's Island. In: Ioannides, M., Fellner, D., Georgopoulos, A., Hadjimitsis, D.G. (eds.) EuroMed 2010. LNCS, vol. 6436, pp. 513–527. Springer, Heidelberg (2010). doi:10.1007/978-3-642-16873-4_42
10. Costantino, D., Angelini, M.G., Caprino, G.: Laser scanner survey of an archaeological site - Scala di furno (Lecce, Italy). In: International Archives of the Photogrammetry, Remote Sensing and Spatial Information Sciences - ISPRS Archives, vol. 38(Part 5), pp. 178–183 (2010)

11. Pueschel, H., Sauerbier, M., Eisenbeiss, H.: A 3D model of Castle Landenberg (CH) from combined photogrammetric processing of terrestrial and UAV-based images. In: The International Archives of the Photogrammetry, Remote Sensing and Spatial Information Sciences, vol. XXXVII-B6b, pp. 93–98 (2008)
12. Ullman, S.: The interpretation of structure from motion. Roy. Soci. (1979). http://dx.doi.org/10.1098/rspb.1979.0006
13. Fabris, M., Achilli, V., Artese, G., Boatto, G., Bragagnolo, D., Cancheri, G., Meneghello, R., Menin, A., Trecroci, A.: High resolution data from laser scanning and digital photogrammetry terrestrial methodologies. In: Test Site: An Architectural Surface, International Archives of the Photogrammetry, Remote Sensing and Spatial Information Sciences, vol. XXXVIII, Part 3/W8, pp. 43–48 (2009)

Web Tool as a Virtual Museum of Ancient Archaeological Ruins in Peru

Eva Savina Malinverni[1]([✉]), Roberto Pierdicca[1], Francesca Colosi[2], and Roberto Orazi[2]

[1] Department of Civil Engineering, Building and Architecture, Universitá Politecnica delle Marche, Via Brecce Bianche 12, 60131 Ancona, Italy
{e.s.malinverni,r.pierdicca}@univpm.it
[2] CNR-ITABC, Via Salaria km. 29,300, Monterotondo Street, 00016 Rome, Italy
{francesca.colosi,roberto.orazi}@itabc.cnr.it

Abstract. A web-browser allows discovering and navigating between the bas-reliefs. This latter part of the exhibition represents the main novelty and it will be deepening during the dissertation.

The importance of the whole set of data gathered is twofold: first of all a complete metrical reconstruction of the site provides conservators with a fundamental starting point for restoration works; secondly, these data provide the possibility to create a virtual corner for their exposition, moving from the scheme of a classical exposition of findings towards a digital and interactive visualization.

Keywords: Archaeology · Digital photogrammetry · 3D model reconstruction · WebGL3D · Web-based 3D visualization · E-culture · Digital media · Web virtual museum · Web visitor

1 Introduction

The potential of using 3D models, at different details (buildings, bass-relieves, small findings, etc.) applied to archaeology, is growing at different levels: research and application. Nevertheless, the biggest challenge is nowadays to make this valuable source of information and documentation available to the whole mankind. The purpose of documenting a heritage site using 3D models as the main source of knowledge is twofold: on one hand, they represent a great resource in terms of preservation, since they can be used for further reconstructions in case of damage or loss. On the other, they are able to overcome the obstacles that prevent the fruition of archaeological findings, mainly when they are unreachable because of the site wideness or inaccessibility. A great benefit towards this direction is represented by the combination of geomatics techniques and the exploitation of web solutions.

In the archaeological domain, this trend has been undertaken so far and increased by well-established pipelines of data acquisition. Acquisition and digitization (i.e. virtual models, visualization, etc.), in fact, are a good practice

© Springer International Publishing AG 2017
L.T. De Paolis et al. (Eds.): AVR 2017, Part II, LNCS 10325, pp. 282–296, 2017.
DOI: 10.1007/978-3-319-60928-7_25

for every kind of ancient site, artefact or excavation [5]. The photogrammetric techniques from data acquisition to 3D reconstruction for the visualization in virtual way of rests are mandatory for both conservation/documentation and promotion of Cultural Heritage (CH), in particular archaeology. This geomatic approach provides free and low cost solutions, allowing: (i) unplanned data acquisition; (ii) fast and smart techniques to facilitate documentation during excavation work; (iii) high level of detail for the representation of complex 3D objects contextualizing the visualization of archaeological findings to share them on virtual web-based museums. At the same time, the development of new digital tools to enhance CH fruition is almost a well-established and widespread good practice [16]. It has been proved by several studies that CH can be largely exploited providing users with new media of knowledge. The ICT (Information and Communication Technologies) approach is carrying successful influence, for example increasing the interest of young people by means of new tools [2]. As well, the web represent the mainstream vehicle to exploit 3D virtual heritage in a more intuitive and appealing manner [12], also by increasing the accessibility of knowledge [6].

Given the above and in line with recent research trends, we present our work, that consists on the creation of a virtual museum, populated with the produced materials coming from a survey on site, processed like 3D textured models, virtual tour, images, details of one of the most wide and complex archaeological site in raw earth (adobe) in the work: Chan Chan, in Peru. Up to now, it is the first step that shows the information built on the site but in the future can be upgraded with other materials to complete in better way the knowledge of the archaeological site. This moreover share art, history and culture of these civilization even if only virtually. Specifically, the work consists on a web-based solution developed with the aim of showing a complex and wide archaeological site. The state-of-the-art of these technologies and their adoption is the demonstration of how cultural objects are protagonist only through a good information and interaction with the visitors/users.

After a 3D model reconstruction and virtual representation of some archeological goods located in the Chan Chan site, we chose a web-based approach for a complete dissemination and valorisation of them. The research moves between complexity and limitations of the offered tools that makes the use of new media an innovative choice. Two kinds of users can take advantage from this approach: the first ones are the insiders, such as archaeologists, experts and conservators. The second ones are the visitors, who can exploit the potentials of new ways of communication to improve their knowledge. In addition, this new browsing concept in an interactive web-site may not be easily accepted by the average of the users because they probably feel more comfortable with a standard web-site. New features could enhance the user-interaction experience and the improvement of the rendering stage. To share the knowledge of an archaeological settlement, built by direct survey in the last decades on the Chan Chan, we used 3DHOP software (3D Heritage Online Presenter) which is an open-source software package useful to create an interactive web presentations of high-resolution 3D models.

3DHOP is used by the museum curators with some ICT experience, web designers who want to embed 3D contents in their creations and from students in the CH field to small companies developing web applications for museum and CH institutions [11].

The paper, after an introduction on the aim of the web-based solution for CH, gives a general description of the investigated archaeological settlement of Chan Chan pointing the accent on the two huacas close to the site and belonging to Chimu pre-Incas civilization (Huaca Arco Iris and Huaca Esmeralda). We have collected spatial data by photogrammetry, creating 3D models and enhancing them to share their historical and geographical context by web. Following, we introduce briefly the Open Source software 3DHOP (3D Heritage Online Presenter) using this tool to customize and share a virtual visit. The contents are presented from the data acquisition to the processing from the surveying point of view. The provided 3D models of the two main temples underline not only the building structure of them but also show in detail all the decorative parts (bas-relieves) on the principal walls. The other important task was to give a readable object (assigning texture and other relevant aspects) to the program; the only readable format used by 3DHOP is NXS. The customization of the toolbar allows then to place the hotspot to link the 3D decorative part and any other information to the whole structure and to insert measuring functions. Before the final conclusions we give some details about several web pages of the whole project, linked together, which allow a panoramic view of the Chan Chan site and which will be upgraded in the future.

2   Operative Background

This section is devoted to describe the operative background in which the authors operated. Hence, in the first part will be reported the recent advances in the field of web visualization for CH, with a specific focus on the management of complex 3D models. Afterwards, we will provide a brief description of the case study.

2.1   Related Work

More than two decades ago, Falk and Dierkin [4] in their definition of the interactive museum experience described three key elements that influence the way visitors experience museums: the physical context, the personal context and the social context. Nowadays, the current web museum experience is dramatically changed, in contrast to the traditional museum visit; searching for information is not necessarily a solitary activity, since it can achieve different public and cultures at a worldwide scale. Semper's [14] survey of the use of museum educational material represents a good dissertation to be mentioned. Additionally, Twidale et al. [15], in their study of the use of library terminals, noted that in most cases the task of finding information was based on immediate collaboration of members of the same group or occasional collaboration with people outside the group, such as library staff and other researchers. Awareness of people's choices and engagement with the material, as well as direct exchange of opinions with co-users, are important aspects of the successful retrieval of information. Nevertheless, visiting a museum web site for big portion of web visitors is a leisure activity; it also seems to be an activity that is not rigidly tied to a potential visit to the physical site but can be enjoyed separately. In this respect, visiting a museum website may share similar intrinsic motivation with visiting the physical site of a museum. Whether it can satisfy the needs and the wants of remote visitors, to the extent the museum caters for on-site visitors appears to be a growing concern. The participant's experience itself is also based on the use of current museum web sites that mainly focus on delivery of information. However, the great potential of new tools of visualization is not exploited at all. The web is treated as an information medium (able to facilitate the educational and marketing activities of the museum), rather than a vehicle for complex objects that can be manipulated and experienced. Co-visiting between new remote audiences, who visit museums via the web, and more traditional visitors to the physical premises of a museum, has been supported by experimental technologies such as virtual environments, cameras, robots and remotely controlled interfaces. Muller, in a famous article appeared in the Museums Journal [8], argued for a change in the way museums treat their websites and he wonders how can museum curate virtual spaces that engage on-line museum visitors, encouraging them to do more than browse, but also to learn about and experience their artefacts. Museums nowadays make an effort to cater for the information needs of their diverse web audiences by increasing their educational resources and the information about their collections on-line. The question that arises, however, is whether information accessibility and diversity comprises an interactive museum experience.

It is not so tricky to transpose all the above within the context of an archaeological site. In fact, most of the findings are unreachable to the majority of the interested visitors. The web, in this latter case, could really represent a turning point in which the archaeology is experienced. On one side it can contribute to share with the world detailed information of remote site, boosting the curiosity of tourists to visit it. On the other, thanks to the growing potential of nowadays browsers and 3D technologies, we are able to convey complex shapes with a level of detail that is not reachable with the naked eye [1].

Several examples in the literature demonstrate that the exploitation of complex 3D models, arising from different data sources, has become paramount for their sharing [9]. The role of these new techniques of acquisition and their consequent visualization is to make remote places known by the mankind [7].

This opens a wider discussion about the nature of the museum experience and its audiences. Current museum practice emphasises respect to visitors' needs and wants, and the design of meaningful museum experiences that enhance people's lives. In this respect, virtual and real can cooperate, by introducing media that support shared interactions and meaning making between on-site and off-site visitors, beyond the place, the time and the media of a single visit. The more this happens, the more the virtual will be a real and useful part of modern museum practice. Different projects are an example of how the virtualization through the web is important, like the Zamani project of Capetown University, where authors capture the spatial domain of heritage with a current focus on Africa, by accurately recording its physical and architectural structures, dimensions and positions. Sites are seen in the context of their physical environment, and wherever possible, the topography of landscapes surrounding the documented sites is mapped based on satellite images and aerial photography [13]. The Virtual Amarna Museum presents a series of significant objects from the Egyptian site of Amarna, including stone steles, ceramics, pendants, moulds and selected architectural elements. Every research is based on acquisition and creation of digital representations of heritage must like a part of the knowledge of the whole site. The presented project is a showcase of how this trend should be stressed for the dissemination of high quality and complex models.

2.2   The Case Study: Chan Chan and the Huacas

Chimu is considered the second Andean civilization after the Incas for the vastness of its territory and for the political and social organization. The capital was the city's largest raw land in the world: Chan Chan. (which means Sun Sun), it was conquered by the Incas in 1470. It is located 4 Km north-east from the city of Trujillo in the Moche River valley (Fig. 1).

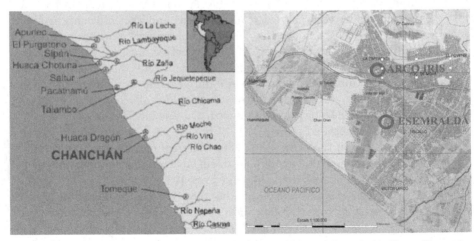

(a) Geographic location of the site   (b) Location of the whole Chan Chan site

Fig. 1. General overview of the geographic location of the Chan Chan archaeological site, pointing out the two huacas' position inside the archaeological area of Chan Chan.

For its size, architectural complex and its bas-relieves, it was the largest city in pre-Columbian age. Its remains reflect the organization of a policy and rigorous social strategy, underlined by the division into ten 'citadels' or 'palaces' forming independent units. The adopted material is adobe. It is subjected to

a decay for many human and physical events, and for this reason it is urgent
to take it under control, to preserve it or to restore as soon as possible. The
virtual solution is a good manner to preserve the existence and the knowledge.
There are intricate forms and drawings of two types of drawings: one realistic
character mostly zoomorphic and the other more stylized but always portraying
animals (fish, birds and small mammals). Religious practice was based on the
worship of the moon, and some particular temples were devoted places where
the population during the ceremonies offered large quantities of fruit, animal and
moreover human sacrifices. In some cases, however limited, there were sacrifices
of children in honour of more prestigious. The history of these ceremonies is decorated with friezes and relieves decorated on the wall of the temples (Huacas).
Huaca is a Quechua term used by the Incas defining places, objects or animate
beings considered sacred. It was estimated that the huaca retained within it
the power that created them and that they were able to influence the events of
human life. In particular, Huaca was not only a great religious and ceremonial
monument but also an administrative center built in adobe. There are two Huacas located surrounding the Chan chan site, included in the Trujillo city, which
varied in importance, each of these had a sacred object of worship associated
with a legend. In 1986 Chan Chan became part of the UNESCO World Heritage
List. Some important monuments, part of the archaeological complex of Chan
Chan, are the Huaca Arco Iris and the Huaca Esmeralda, now surrounded by
new buildings of the modern Trujillo. These buildings are the one used as a
demonstrator within the web-based solution of this paper. The first one, and in
particular its 3D reconstruction (realized adopting procedures of data fusion and
restitution from different geomatics techniques), is already published; interested
readers can refer to [10]. Huaca Esmeralda deserve a brief explanation, since its
reconstruction has not been published so far. Huaca Esmeralda (that covers an
area of 4.700 mq) has a shape of stepped pyramids and from time to time were
completely reconstructed by adjoining a new level of mud bricks to the existing
one (Fig. 2).

(a) Picture of the current state of Huaca   (b) General top view of Huaca Esmeralda

Fig. 2. Overview of Huaca Esmeralda.

The building has an important re-modeling: the oldest part was buried by a new construction that repeats the same scheme, even if with a variation of iconographic motifs and with the addition of two rooms and an atrium at the sides of the central ramp. The front and the sides of the monument are decorated with bas-reliefs with different patterns; the oldest is characterized from zoomorphic and geometric motifs very similar to those of Tschudi (a palace in Chan Chan settlement far from it few kilometres), the most recent is decorated with diamonds which enclose birds. Huaca Esmeralda was completely restored in 1964–1968. The site is not inside the Chan Chan complex but it is close to the Trujillo city and not always the tourist know it. The virtual tour in this case can help to discover another piece of the Chimu Empire, to improve the visit of the site, inform about its history and to have a preview of the fine bas-reliefs of the huaca.

3   Workflow

The bulk of information collected among the years over Chan Chan site is huge, operating within the framework of the Italian Mission in Peru (MIPE) since 2002 [3]. It is a wide collection of different multimedia sources like panoramic tours, historical information and 3D reconstruction that, up to now, are not collected within a unique container of knowledge. For this reason, we decided to implement the proposed web solution, which starts with the creation of the contents until their insertion within the browser. For the close purpose of this dissertation, we will report in the following the procedure of reconstruction of just one of the models present in the site, as an example for the other information that are already developed or in progress for the publication.

3.1   3D Models: Huaca Esmeralda 3D Reconstruction

For the acquisition of the digital images, we used a digital camera reflex Canon EOS 60D, time of exposure 1/160 s, sensibility ISO-80, focal distance 10 mm, with sensor CMOS from 18 Megapixels. The complete 3D model of the temple was carried out in a combination of different photogrammetric techniques, namely Structure from Motion and Multi View Stereo coupled with Multi Image Spherical Photogrammetry, following the rules and the procedures described in [10]. The final result of this process is visible in Fig. 3.

For the 3D model reconstruction of the bas-reliefs, three groups of frames have been acquired, concerning the wall of entrance, the second central ramp and the steps to this ramp. For the bass relieves of the wall of entrance, we performed 11 points of station, for the second ramp 13 and for the steps 24. The stations have been served as different anglings, so that to have different points of view and in such way to have the same points of the object recognizable on more photos (stereoscopy). This is essential for the phase of restitution in which, as we will see subsequently, to beat the homologous points is necessary above at least two photos. The realization of 3D surfaces, have been performed through

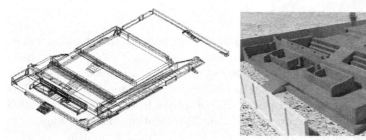

(a) Wireframe model of the temple.   (b) 3D virtual reconstruction.

Fig. 3. The virtual model of Huaca Esmeralda. Starting from the wireframe plotting of the structures, the 3D model with attached the bass-relieves was realized.

Agisoft Photoscan. Particularly, Dense Stereo Matching allows extracting three-dimensional information from images acquired also in low cost conditions. The principle on which these systems work is a photogrammetric approach: from a series of correspondences among images which go up again to the parameters of the camera and to the three-dimensional position of the points of correspondence. The Dense Stereo Matching, is able to find in automatic way the points of correspondence, useful to calibrate the camera and to produce a 3D dense point cloud using the homologous pixels among all the images. The 3D range are the input to create a 3D polygonal mesh bringing the geometric and chromatic information of the part of the visible surface from the direction of select images; in this case by mean Meshlab. PhotoScan supports different output and export formats. Orthoimages and digital models of elevation can be produced. It is also possible to specify the system of coordinates and to point out the applicable parameters of export to the type of selected file. For this job we exported the bas-relieves 3D file in OBJ, JPG, MTL. The same decisive procedure is applied for the development of the three-dimensional models both for the central ramp that for the attached steps to the second ramp (see Fig. 4 for more details).

(a) Significant mesh of a side wall of the Huaca   (b) Mesh of the side wall of the ramp

Fig. 4. The 3D computation of the bas-relieves pictures gave in output the 3D meshes

3.2   Optimisation for the Web

As stated in the introduction section, 3DHOP was chose for the visualization of
the 3D models. In order to convert a 3D models in the multi-resolution format,
one need to get also the NEXUS tools package. Nexus is a software package for
the creation and visualization of a batched multi-resolution mesh structure. The
main goal of such structure is to upgrade the primitive from 1 triangle to 10000
triangles, removing the CPU bottleneck in multi-resolution visualization. Main
features of this library are: out-of-core interactive visualization, multiple instanc-
ing of models, http streaming, compression, color per vertex, opensg Nexus node.
An NXS file is created starting from a standard single-resolution model, using a
conversion tool. NXS may be compressed for smaller server occupation and better network performances. Compression is slightly lossy, on smaller 3D models (1
million triangles or less) this can be visible and compression should be avoided;
on the other hand, for models above the 10 million triangles limit, compression
is strongly advised. For local, non-network use (e.g. local kiosks), uncompressed
NXS has better performances, for every size of 3D model.

At this point we can see the potential of the models. The use of 3DHOP allows
the user to navigate the model with simple and well established interactions.
Holding down the left mouse button you can rotate the object along the axis
x and along axis z, and view its particularities as desired, and with a double
click you can choose the axis of rotation center. The same can be done for the
bas-reliefs. In this case, however, we must add that, zooming in and displaying
the detail, the more we go close to the finest detail, the more the model increase
the detail. This property of the program will allow the user to browse on-line
by going to view and explore the parts that is interest to him/her, just by using
the mouse of the PC, or in the case of mobile simply use the touch screen.

It is necessary to underline an important aspect: all the meshes are loaded
with the spatial orientation and scale saved in their source file. This means,
obviously, that a model that is saved in its file with a non-straight orientation,
(e.g. upside down, tilted) will be rendered inside 3DHOP with its own non-
straight orientation. In these cases, to "compose" the scene by arranging the
models around, it is possible to apply transformations to each mesh and instance,
or we can modify the axis orientation, scale and positioning of the 3D models
(and save it in their source file) before opening them.

3.3   Features Development

To improve the 3DHOP usability experience together with the basic version
of the viewer, an ad-hoc tool bar and different method of interaction with the
models has been developed. In order to meet this need, 3DHOP provides a way
to create geometrical hotspots, and a series of events to detect user clicks on
3D models and hotspots. The idea is to provide basic building blocks, that can
be used to create a wide series of user interaction schemes, suitable for different
web pages layouts.

We will firstly describe how to add hosptots (*clickable* geometries) in the scene, by adding a new kind of element in the scene definition; then, we will detail how to detect user clicks on these geometries, by registering handler functions. Instead of having hotspots defined by a single point, as it happens in many 3D visualization tools, 3DHOP implements a more flexible system of *clickable* geometries. These geometries are rendered with a solid color using transparency, and can be turned visible/invisible at will during the visualization (like for the instance, it is possible to make visible/invisible single hotspots or groups of hotspots). An example of hot spots is reported in Fig. 5.

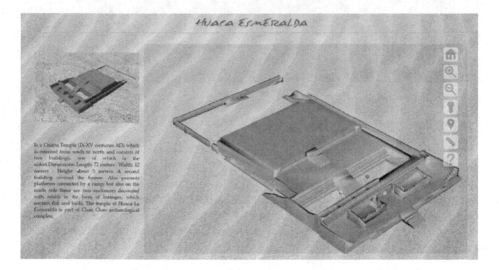

Fig. 5. Example of interaction with the model; in this case the hotspot reports significant information over the construction phases of the temple.

In this two cases, we have two meshes that will be used for instances (the *Huaca Emeralda* and the *Struttura* meshes) and three other that will be used for hotspots (the "Sphere", "Cube" and the "Wing" meshes). In this case, the three hotspots have a very simple geometry, so a single-resolution PLY file was used, but also multi-resolution NXS geometries, and even point clouds may be used as hotspots geometry. Once the hotspots were developed, we created the .htm for all 3D models relative to the bas-reliefs and saved them in the work folder by changing the .nxs file with the file .nxs alleging hotspot.

Completed the hotspot work, we developed the tool bar with some features like "measurement mode". 3D models coming from measuring devices such as 3D scanning are "metric", in the sense that their 3D coordinates corresponds to measurements taken in the real world, it makes sense, then, to offer a way to take measurements over the geometry. This especially useful for cultural heritage or scientific visualization. A virtual scene can be a faithful representation of the reality. However, as it often happens when the scene contains 3D models without

Fig. 6. With the rule mode, it is possible to query the 3D model over its real measures, since they have been scaled with the real measures.

specific landmarks or reference objects, it may be difficult to fully understand the scale and the size of the 3D entities; the measurement tools makes easier to understand the size of the depicted objects. 3DHOP uses the [X,Y,Z] coordinates exactly as they are stored in the 3D models: for this reason, any measurement taken on the 3D models displayed are in the measure unit of the 3D model (see Fig. 6).

4   Result and Discussion

The last part of the project was the creation of a website that could contain within it all the material of the Huaca Esmeralda and the Huaca Arco Iris who over the years had been produced. In particular, with reference to the Zamani Project, we have created a virtual museum that can enrich in the coming years with further work of other archaeological sites of Chan Chan. The web site was developed locally, using XAMPP, and working with Joomla.

It was decided to include these main sections:

1. HOME: in addition to the project description, in this section can be found, with the approximate geolocation, the map with various Points of Interests of Chan Chan (Fig. 7).
2. DATA TYPES: this section contains all the information and descriptions of the various contents present in every folder of the web site.
3. 3D VIEWER: all the work performed for the visualization of the 3D models has been included in this section.

Fig. 7. The home of the web site with the map representation of the point of interest.

4. GALLERY: an useful section is devoted to the visualization of informative material like pictures and information related to the main archaeological areas. This includes recording methods and metadata, discovery, access and citation of digital objects, analysis and study, reuse and re purposing of digital objects, and the critical role of a national/international digital archive.

5. VIRTUAL TUORS: the visual tour which has been constructed allows a previsit of the archaeological complex and of its different architectural structures. The system, through the definition of points of view situated in the most representative areas of the settlement, gives an accurate image of the actual state of conservation of the monument. The main architectural typologies which appeared in the panoramic views are identified by means of a short report and the whole system can be related to the dedicated GIS of the Archaeological Park that the MIPE is preparing as a managing instrument for the whole project (Fig. 8).

The web site is not available on the web so far. Even if we are planning to share with the community this work in the upcoming month, we also implemented a back end editor that can be useful for a simple upload of the models and contents that will be developed. For the archaeologists, as well as for the interested users that wish to deepen their knowledge about Chan Chan, the back end editor is noteworthy. In fact, the excavation and survey activities on the settlement are steady; this means that in the upcoming month we will collect several virtual reconstructions of findings that can be easily stored within the web service. Furthermore, it is important to underline the operational background in which these activities are carried out. In fact, providing a remote archaeological site with advanced digital tools means to bring it towards the digital era; this

Fig. 8. The integration of the virtual tours within the same container allows one to deepen the knowledge of Chan Chan.

is not trivial, since several heritage sites all over the world still suffer a lack of digital services that can share their knowledge over their borders. As stated, the archaeological site is huge and the models showed up to now represent a very small portion with respect to the huge material that we have at our disposal for further reconstructions. Anyhow, this works paves the way for further a implementation. The methodology described proved to be the best way in order to collect, within the same container, the information related to the site. The possibility to compute complex 3D models and share them through agile methods of visualization represent the first milestone of the project. We can thus declare that from now we can reach the extent of spreading Chan Chan site knowledge all over the world.

5   Conclusion and Outlook

In this paper, an integrated web-based solution for the visualization and sharing of several data source have been presented. As usual for archaeological complexes, and regretfully for the entire CH panorama, we faced with economic issues that obliged to use low cost techniques of acquisition (as well the computation of data arising from unplanned survey) together with the use of Open Source platforms for both data processing and data visualization tasks. Notwithstanding, the optimization of the model for their visualization is performing, lossless and performing for every web platform. Thanks to the merging of different digital technologies, it will be possible a cataloguing of scientifically validated contents, giving the possibility to monitor the state of conservation of the ancient findings. This is a great advantages for such scenario where the weather conditions and the quality of the materials make the damage and the possible loss very probable.

Back to the technological aspects, we can affirm that the back-end function, developed for future implementations, will give the possibility of expanding the information, as soon as new models and contents will be developed. We are actually working on the digitization of Palacio Tchudi with acquisition took with terrestrial and aerial platforms, that we seek to introduce inside the proposed web platform. Hence, the site is fundamental for both insiders and interested tourists. The visual tour will be published on Internet through a link with the site of the Ministerio de Cultura, thus assuming a promotional function of the north region of Peru that, although boast a rich archaeological heritage, is often excluded from international tourist circuits tend to prefer central and southern areas of the country as Machu Picchu e Nazca. It is our intention, in fact, to connect, in a single tour route, the complex of Chan Chan, the Esmeralda and Arco Iris even though these two last structures are now surrounded by modern buildings. This will allow to preserve the historical value of Chan Chan, its history and culture. Although only virtually, we can give new life to these invaluable goods, regardless of the care that the nature, or the menkind, will take care of them.

Acknowledgments. The authors would like to thanks, for their efforts, the students that helped on the development of this work. In particular a special thank goes to Riccardo Balletti for the implementation of the 3D models and for their optimization for the web tool. We also thanks Matteo Angelini who was in charge of the development of the whole web site. Finally, we thank Francesco Bergamotti for the work performed for the creation of the bas-relieves. Our students are our greatest resource.

References

1. Agosto, E., Bornaz, L.: 3D models in cultural heritage: approaches for their creation and use. Int. J. Comput. Methods Heritage Sci. (IJCMHS) **1**(1), 1–9 (2017)
2. Buhalis, D., Law, R.: Progress in information technology and tourism management: 20 years on and 10 years after the internet - the state of eTourism research. Tourism Manag. **29**(4), 609–623 (2008)
3. Colosi, F., Fangi, G., Gabrielli, R., Orazi, R., Angelini, A., Bozzi, C.A.: Planning the archaeological park of Chan Chan (Peru) by means of satellite images, GIS and photogrammetry. J. Cult. Heritage **10**, e27–e34 (2009)
4. Dierking, L.D., Falk, J.H.: Understanding free-choice learning: a review of the research and its application to museum web sites. In: Museums and the Web, vol. 98 (1998)
5. Lerma, J.L., Navarro, S., Cabrelles, M., Villaverde, V.: Terrestrial laser scanning and close range photogrammetry for 3D archaeological documentation: the upper palaeolithic cave of parpalló as a case study. J. Archaeol. Sci. **37**(3), 499–507 (2010)
6. Loran, M.: Use of websites to increase access and develop audiences in museums: experiences in British national museums. E-J. Humanit. Philology Stud. UOC **7**, 23–29 (2005)
7. Malinverni, E.S., Pierdicca, R.: Discovering and sharing of secret architectures: the hidden tomb of the pharaoh of El-khasneh, Jordan. In: Proceedings of 3D ARCH - 3D Virtual Reconstruction and Visualization of Complex Architectures (2017)

8. Müller, K.: Museums and virtuality. Curator: Mus. J. **45**(1), 21–33 (2002)
9. Petrovic, V., Vanoni, D.J., Richter, A.M., Levy, T.E., Kuester, F.: Visualizing high resolution three-dimensional and two-dimensional data of cultural heritage sites. Mediterr. Archaeol. Archaeometry **14**(4), 93–100 (2014)
10. Pierdicca, R., Frontoni, E., Malinverni, E.S., Colosi, F., Orazi, R.: Virtual reconstruction of archaeological heritage using a combination of photogrammetric techniques: Huaca Arco Iris, Chan Chan, Peru. Digit. Appl. Archaeol. Cult. Heritage **3**(3), 80–90 (2016)
11. Potenziani, M., Callieri, M., Dellepiane, M., Corsini, M., Ponchio, F., Scopigno, R.: 3DHOP: 3D heritage online presenter. Comput. Graph. **52**, 129–141 (2015)
12. Potenziani, M., Corsini, M., Callieri, M., Di Benedetto, M., Ponchio, F., Dellepiane, M., Scopigno, R.: An advanced solution for publishing 3D content on the web. In: Museums and the Web 2013 (2013)
13. Rüther, H., Held, C., Bhurtha, R., Schroeder, R., Wessels, S.: From point cloud to textured model, the Zamani laser scanning pipeline in heritage documentation. S. Afr. J. Geomatics **1**(1), 44–59 (2012)
14. Semper, R., Wanner, N., Jackson, R., Bazley, M.: Who's out there? a pilot user study of educational web resources by the science learning network (SLN). In: Museums and the Web, pp. 179–200 (2000)
15. Twidale, M.B., Nichols, D.M., Paice, C.D.: Browsing is a collaborative process. Inf. Process. Manage. **33**(6), 761–783 (1997)
16. Witcomb, A.: The materiality of virtual technologies: a new approach to thinking about the impact of multimedia in museums. Theorizing Digital Cultural Heritage Cambridge, pp. 35–48. MIT Press, Massachusetts (2007)

Virtual Reality Meets Intelligence in Large Scale Architecture

Ahmet Kose$^{(\boxtimes)}$, Eduard Petlenkov, Aleksei Tepljakov, and Kristina Vassiljeva

Tallinn University of Technology,
Ehitajate tee 5, 19086 Tallinn, Estonia
ahmet.kose@ttu.ee

Abstract. This paper presents the process for a case study concerning fully immersive application of physical environment. The paper considers intelligent systems integration to VR and self-learning activities with sociological aspects by significant experimental platform. Authors aim to detail the process of systematical design including modelling, computing, intelligence and an initial evolution of virtual environment. Also practical usage and futuristic aspects are included for the concept. As the project based on physical environment, target of the work is concentrated to give high presence feeling for end-users. To increasing presence feeling, authors aim to maximize immersion level. Self-learning activities based on the perception of supervised and unsupervised learning. The activities are engaged to immersive and entertaining structure. Heterogeneous intercontinental participants provide unique feedback source. The environment is research and development center of Tallinn University of Technology. The virtual environment of the center has been evaluated based on realistic conditions.

Keywords: Virtual Reality · Intelligent systems · Cyber-physical systems · Supervised learning · Architecture modelling · 3D modelling · Unreal Engine 4

1 Introduction

Virtual reality (VR) has become a significant field for computer-simulated environment recently. VR is a high-end human computer interface that strives to immerse the designers and users completely in a virtual interactive environment for a simulation of real world [1]. Although VR has been issued for more than half century, it has become more popular with rapid development of its technology in recent years [2]. Man et al. claims that VR is one of the three most promising computer technologies in the 21st century along with Internet technology and multimedia technology [3]. Interactive devices including head-mounted display, controllers are usually referred to VR technology. That development brought different experiences to world in virtual reality. Arguably, relevant implementations of virtual environment such as interactivity, presence, high degree of exposure etc. are applied successfully. Besides that, virtual environment (VE) may be

© Springer International Publishing AG 2017
L.T. De Paolis et al. (Eds.): AVR 2017, Part II, LNCS 10325, pp. 297–309, 2017.
DOI: 10.1007/978-3-319-60928-7_26

considered the crucial part of virtual reality. Additionaly VE gives access to users who are able to interact with objects and characters in virtual space. That advanced interaction may enhance the feeling of presence. Those approaches can be useful for improvements and teaching methods. Some researchers believe that virtual reality can bring new horizons in education and contemporary learning activities efficiently to students. They assume learning in 3D virtual reality environments can be stated as a desired reality among young students [4]. This paper presents an interactive walkthrough of immersive environment with unique self-learning activities by using virtual reality devices. The creation of immersive environment is based on large scale building located in Tallinn/Estonia. Artificial exterior architecture of the building is shown in Fig. 1. The building is contributed as a research and development center of Tallinn University of Technology. The center meets descent number of intercontinental visitors daily considering demonstration of current work including prototypes, futuristic applications, start-up ideas etc. The structure also contains intelligent systems in considerable fields such as telecommunication, logistics, healthcare, avionics. The center has welcomed around 200000 visitors in three years [5]. Those conditions also provide high effiency for self-learning based on physical activities. Hence, experimental evolution can be assumed to unique regarding universal participants where they can demonstrate their actual knowledge in immersive environment. In Cyber-Physical Systems (CPS), there are essential units such as systems, sensors and actuators, which follow different data models and interaction paradigms. The set-up of a CPS in an architecture that combines heterogeneous components and allows for the integrated processing of data is therefore challenging [6]. Designing an intelligent systems for architectures based on VR provides greater interaction and higher usability [7]. The application compiles human factors and CPS based on VR. That approach might help to improve the process for practical CPS integrated VR applications. Additionally, the terminology of joyful learning mainly originated from the concept of "Game Based Learning". It arranges the teaching content and concept with the game-design mode, applies fun, challenges, competition, cooperation, self satisfaction and a sense of achievement of games to provide the learners with motivation, promote continuous learning willingness, effectively retain and organize skills or knowledge, and further improve learning effectiveness. The inner process of learners' joyful learning can be divided into digital game learning mode [7] and experience game mode [8]. The basic concept of the two both corresponds with flow theory; they both think that with the guidance of game characteristics, the learners will be able to enter the learning cycle, repeat the same learning experience, and achieve the expected target in a joyful situation [9]. The centre organizes competitions, cooperations, challenges for their visitors constantly with particular aims. Therefore, the VE of the center has relevant conditions and possibilities to apply joyful learning approaches. Nevertheless, provided VR experience may take as replacements for real visitations by students and visitors. Hence the application is relevant and it has also high practical values.

Fig. 1. Virtual Environment of the physical building

2 System Design

Successful immersive applications based on realistic environment minimize difference between physical reality and virtual reality (VR). However large scale environments require longer period of time and intensive work for realistic representation [10]. The application integrates computer graphics and simulation, dynamic interaction in real-time, computational intelligence, motion capturing and interconnected computer networks etc. Regardless, teleportation feature of VR technology is implemented for the application. That feature allows users to move independently and effortless in computer simulated realistic architecture. Although the environment is unique and subsections are slightly relevant, the process for creating the virtual environment is familiar with related researches. The process is as follows: (A) Environmental Creation and System Design, (B) Modelling and Texturing, (C) Materials and Hardware Integration, (D) Web Camera Entegration, (E) Interactions (F) Optimization. Unreal Engine 4 is chosen to create the virtual environment as the engine is the one of most known and used physics engine. High efficiency for VR applications, compability and does not require high maintenance cost could be considered as some of prior advantages for the preferred physics engine. Furthermore, Unreal Engine meets beneficial expectations like other common game engines. The concept of object oriented programming, process of computer generated graphics, reusable code with libraries might be main benefits of using primary game engines [11]. Autodesk Maya 3D animation, modeling, simulation, and rendering software is used to model meshes and partly environment as a preference [12]. OpenCV is a opensource computer vision library and it is implemented to display a webcam in virtual environment. OpenCV allows to develop Mixed Reality (MR) environments. MR is usually represented in three forms. Those forms can be defined as Augmented Reality (AR), Augmented Virtuality (AV) and VR. In AR, the virtual and real content can be implemented through the physical world by mixing and registering. AV is slightly closer to VR, which refers to approaching physical objects in to a virtual world. Real objects can be integrated to the virtual world, hence it is possible to interact with them synchronously in MR [13]. Detailed process is shown in Fig. 2. Nevertheless, the hardware integration includes Oculus Rift Development Kit 2 (DK2) and HTC Vive. Integrating two VR devices allows us to compare usability and efficiency for the VE.

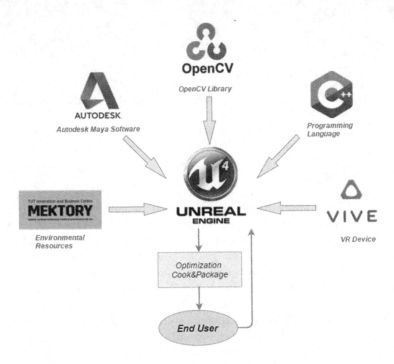

Fig. 2. Process of the application

2.1   Modelling and Texturing

In this phase, the 3D model and rendering of the building were progressed. Creating replicated components for virtual environment is another significant part of the process. The whole concept is accomplished to receive high efficiency for supervised and unsupervised human learning. Interior design is referred to the physical design. Hence, modelling and texturing for the center is based on physical assets which are located in the center. Those assets has been rendered and 3D modelled by using Autodesk Maya software [14]. The architecture components were developed using polygon shape and modified using functions such as extrudes, append etc. as shown in Fig. 3. The physics engine can respectfully identify the material components and map file (Textures) with FBX file format. Texture map is directly related to the quality of the model for the physics engine. In addition, Using Level of Detail (LOD) feature is utilized to simplify the 3D models. LOD is useful to reduce the number of polygons for rendering. It is important to receive better vision on VR devices with better performance. Overall, the design should ensure the virtual quality to achieve good results [15].

Fig. 3. Modelling and texturing interior part of architecture

2.2   Environmental Creation and Software Management

Visualization is applied in various fields related to such as education, product visualization, interactive multimedia and in architecture. Bresciani et al. [16] claims that visualization is useful to construct intellectual procedures. Successful immersive environments should include accurate design to give presence feeling for users. Additionally the virtual environment is used for multiple purposes such bridging CPS to VR interface, self-learning activities, physiological and psychological aspects of virtual reality. Floor plan of center is used for accurate virtual environment based on physical assets. Although creating an environment is the most time consuming of stage in process, significant accuracy would reduce harder rework. The chosen engine allows to create realistic environments and simulate realistic affects. Hence users can feel lifelike interaction during experiencing the application. Flexible massive terrain is done by the Landscape tool in Unreal Engine 4. The landscape system can be applied for different devices [17]. Terrain is an essential part of environment where the artificial building lie on. Otherwise the user would be in fully infinitive virtual environment where the presence feeling may not be applied. Fundamental parts such as walls, columns etc. are inserted in physics engine according to suggested scale compability of physics engine (1 unreal unit is equal to 1 cm) [18]. Repeating some fundamental parts are applicable regarding the floor plan. Once modelling and texturing are processed, all the content is created in the physics engine. In other words, we assembly all the artificial models based on physical world in the immersive environment. The world includes more than 4400 actors including navigation meshes collision, lights, blocking volumes, light mass importance volumes, ambient sounds, brushes, trigger boxes, materials and meshes. The principle logic of the application is referred to predefined VR class of the engine: Motion Controller Pawn, HUD, VR GameMode, Player Controller. The operation in physics engine is shown in Fig. 4.

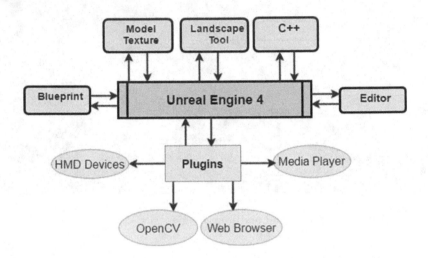

Fig. 4. Working process of the physics engine

2.3   Materials and Hardware Integration

Materials are significant for 3D models. Reactions of those models to the lighting depend on information from the materials. We also use roughness to identify how rough the material is, metallic to reflect model surface, emissive color and normal 3D model. Head tracking devices are in charge of dynamic alterning for the vision of users. The application with the main VR devices provides physical mobility in real room scale, real-time positioning and tracking with advanced display resolution. Oculus Rift DK2 is used in the first stage of application [19]. Although the development started with Oculus Rift DK2 in the early stage of project, authors accomplished the application with HTC Vive VR headset. Independent navigational benefits, convenient hand-held controllers, high resolution display are some facts to prefer HTC Vive. The HMD provides 1080×1200 resolution per eye, and the 9-DOF with 2 lighthouse base stations for tracking. Also the HMD set has two sets of controller. The controller features 24 sensors, dual-stage trigger and multifunction trackpad [20]. The application was implemented using the Unreal Engine 4.14 game engine. Developing with the engine and running the serious game require specific hardware and software requirements. The application run on a PC equipped with a 4.00 GHz Intel i7-6700 processor, 32 GB RAM, and an NVidia GTX 980 graphic card. HTC Vive HMD used for running the project.

2.4   Web Camera Integration

HMD devices can still be considered very new hardware devices for VR. Those devices also have somehow limited ergonomics. During testing period, some difficulties for users such as insecure emotions were observed. Some participants were not satisfied to experience HMD devices. Furthermore they did not want to be isolated from the physical world in some points. The engine provides the features and interfaces needed for camera integration. In order to display actual web-camera in the room where the application is presented for participants, an OpenCV plugin is utilized [21]. The plugin enables to display user physical environment in virtual world. Additionaly this setup of the camera provides more than single camera application for scenarios. Web camera implementation is shown by Fig. 5. That feature will be used for future work. Although the plug-in further takes care of all the HMD-specific tasks such as rendering the viewport separately for each eye, and dealing with the pre-warping of the image [22].

Fig. 5. Real time camera implementation

2.5   Interactions

Human - Machine Interaction (HMI) has always been significant research approaches. Merging interactions in virtual reality, brings different perspective to HMI. In other words, HMI can be obtained to maximize in artificial reality conditions [23]. A sample of HMI in Blueprint design is shown in Fig. 6. The figure presents display structure for CPS [24]. Nevertheless, one of the main attitude of VR development is allow user to interact as much as they desire. It gives them independent movement, thinking and improving themselves with support of VE. Moving in the scene of VR can be operated through HMD controller using teleporting, physicalmovement etc. Users can direct any locations where navigation maps are implemented. The application allows users to manipulate by handles are provided with VR device. Manipulations such as: open and close doors, switch lights, turn on and offf display screens are implemented in two different approaches. Those approaches can be described as self-controlled systems and an automated systems. We aim to allow users to have meaningful CPS experience in VE. We believe that users might have better understanding for CPS. Additionaly it is possible to grab some objects in architecture to interact independently by physics handle component. Furthermore, those interactions grant us to sense self-learning activities in VE. As soon as we complete the process, the application has been tested. The test period was purposed to recognize usability scale of the application and to concrete heuristic evolution for valuable feedback. Received feedbacks are considered to improve the project. Also those feedbacks are used to analyse human behaviours in immersive environment.

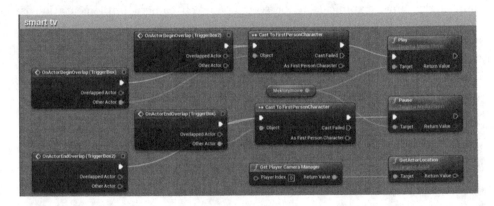

Fig. 6. Blueprint implementation of display located at lobby

2.6   Optimization

Optimization is processed in the last stage synchronously with the testing period. We insert advance details in the architecture like sounds, lights and CPS and artificial intelligence (AI). The editor of the engine allows us to implement three kind of lights: Stationary, Movable and Static. Besides atmospheric light source, particular point lights and spot lights are set up stationary in immersive environment to understand evolution of user experience. Stationary lights are also engaged to the virtual environment where the interactions are not actively applicable. The Blueprints Visual Scripting system in Unreal Engine is a complete gameplay scripting system based on the concept of using a node-based interface to create gameplay elements from within Unreal Editor [25]. The Blueprint system allowed us to create CPS and AI prototypes.

3 Evolution

3.1 Preparation

The VR application is referred to the research and development center of Tallinn University of Technology. The center welcomes numerous international visitors continuously. In addition, those visitors often concern to experience VR applications. Hence, we had relevant conditions to demonstrate different cases to evaluate different approaches. Although we collaborate with heterogeneous participants, we preferred to divide participants randomly into two groups. To establish a baseline, first group of participants had excursions inside of the large scale building. The guide directed those participants to accomplish the practice. Subsequently, members of the first group experienced in a virtual replica of the physical environment. Second group of participants repeated the same process backwards. In other words, second group of people had an excursion individually in VE. We navigated participants to complete their virtual excursion then in real world. This allowed us to evaluate differences between VE and the physical architecture. The part of experimental platform is shown by Fig. 7. Furthermore we received relevant outcomes from both groups. We ask seven questions to participants and we expected to receive ranking between 0 to 10 (0 = not agree at all, 10 = completely agree). Questions are shown in Table 1. Finally, we asked them to inform us concerning their preferences in four different segments including AI, CPS, hardware and interactions.

Fig. 7. Evolutionary platform of the architecture

3.2 Results

According to participants, we experienced that there is no major differences between real building and virtual replica. However functionalities of virtual environment is limited considering some participants would like to demonstrate practical life activities such as using coffee machine, ordering a food in cafeteria etc.

Table 1. Questionnaire result. Proportion is referred to average of responses

Questions for participants	First group	Second group
How was your recognition between VE and real world?	6	7
What was difference between VE and real world?	4	3
Do you prefer to experience VE again?	8	9
Do you think physical world can be replicated?	3	5
Could VR be alternated to physical environments?	6	7
Did you enjoy VR experience?	8	9
Are HMD devices are suitable?	6	6

Besides that, major participants claim that experiencing immersive environment is definitely worth it and presence feeling is considerably high. Also they would prefer to run the application in their residences whether the application could integrate another players in real time. They desire to arrange meeting in the application and using functions what can be placed in real life such as voice communication, document presentation, social interaction. Participants have experienced CPS in different cases. We deployed two different cases for CPS. CPS prototypes are self-controlled for first case. In other words, users can control functionalities of components. In second case, CPS components are set due to activities in VE. Major part of participants preferred self-controlled CPS. They claim that self-dependency is crucial point to optimize systems. Analysis of the results for CPS and interactions is shown in Table 2. VE is cost-free environment to recognize whether standard practical solutions are suitable. Density, brightness, lighting color might be changed in order to preferences in VE. Also they would optimize sensibility distance for CPS by deployments in VE. Moreover, users are able to experience optimization segments such as sensors activities, contrast and size for realistic visualization devices. Large amount of participants experienced VE and majority of those people claimed that HTC Vive would be their primarily VR headset. Independent movement in room scale, motion controllers and high degree resolution are some facts for their selection. Besides that some participants mentioned that Oculus Rift DK2 with default controller caused motion sickness. Some researchers also determined statements of motion sickness recently [26,27]. Additionally, the controller for Oculus Rift DK2 is some how limited. Therefore, presence feeling was not applicable for participants. Analysis results for hardware preferences and AI perspective is shown in Table 3. As we thought in the first stage of project, huge portion of participants like to interact actively with objects in their VE. They claim that it definitely would be joyful to learn with VR technology. Moreover, independent and unlimited actions make them feel self-confident. Some of them also claims that interacting with meshes could be helpful for designing creative environment.

Table 2. Hardware and artificial intelligence analysis

	Oculus DK2	HTC Vive		The guide in VE	Real guide
Participants	80	200	Participants	80	200
Preferences	22	155	Preferences	34	186

Table 3. CPS and interactions analysis

	Self control CPS	Automated CPS
Participants	120	200
Preferences	69	117
	Active interactions	Passive interactions
Participants	200	120
Preferences	174	58

4 Conclusion

This paper introduced the fully immersive environment based on the physical architecture. The architecture is named Mektory House is used as a research and development center of Tallinn University of Technology. Then we proposed the process for creating virtual environment. We investigated approaches for maximize immersion level. We also presented integration of several relevant software programs to the physics engine. We created a virtual environment to demonstrate CPS, AI and self learning activities. Nevertheless, entire process of the application was effort more than 800 working hours including evolution stage. Finally, we allow users to experience our approaches. It brought us valuable feedback to recognize expectations. We received relevant outcomes by participants during demonstration. We also compared two VR devices and evoluated them according to participants.

4.1 Future Work

People suffering from severe physical disabilities (paraplegia, amyotrophic lateral sclerosis, etc.) have very limited movement options [28]. We believe that VR might be relevant solution and the application might help those people to experience immersive environment based on physical center of Tallinn University of Technology. Hence, we aim to set up convenient physical platform for those people to experience the VE. We also believe that platform will provide us unique feedback source. Nevertheless, we aim to create relevant integration tools with physical objects locate in the center related to intelligent systems such as logistics, healthcare, avionics etc. Nevertheless, the VE would give possibilities to implement joyful learning approaches adequately.

Acknowledgements. The research was supported by TUT Innovation and Entrepreneurship Center Mektory and the Information Technology Foundation for Education. We thank the division of Department of Computer and Systems Engineering at Tallinn University of Technology for the ordinary working environment and extremely friendly atmosphere.

References

1. Zhu, L., Wang, J., Chen, E., Yang, J., Wang, W.: Applications of virtual reality in turn-milling centre. In: 2008 IEEE International Conference on Automation and Logistics, pp. 2302–2305. Institute of Electrical and Electronics Engineers (IEEE), September 2008
2. Jiang, L., Gao, B., Zhao, J.: Kinematic and static analysis of a cable-driven parallel robot with a flexible link spine. In: 2015 IEEE International Conference on Robotics and Biomimetics (ROBIO), pp. 31–36. Institute of Electrical and Electronics Engineers (IEEE), December 2015
3. Man, W., Qun, Z.: The deconstruction and reshaping of space: the application of virtual reality in living space. In: 2017 9th International Conference on Measuring Technology and Mechatronics Automation (ICMTMA), pp. 410–413. Institute of Electrical and Electronics Engineers (IEEE), January 2017
4. Grivokostopoulou, F., Perikos, I., Hatzilygeroudis, I.: An innovative educational environment based on virtual reality and gamification for learning search algorithms. In: 2016 IEEE Eighth International Conference on Technology for Education (T4E), pp. 110–115. Institute of Electrical and Electronics Engineers (IEEE), December 2016
5. Mektory: Mektory - a way of thinking! (2017). https://www.ttu.ee/mektory-eng
6. Kafer, T., Harth, A., Mamessier, S.: Towards declarative programming and querying in a distributed cyber-physical system: the i-VISION case. In: 2016 2nd International Workshop on Modelling, Analysis, and Control of Complex CPS (CPS Data), pp. 1–6. Institute of Electrical and Electronics Engineers (IEEE), April 2016
7. Garris, R., Ahlers, R., Driskell, J.E.: Games, motivation, and learning: a research and practice model. Simul. Gaming **33**(4), 441–467 (2002)
8. Kiili, K.: Digital game-based learning: towards an experiential gaming model. Internet High. Educ. **8**(1), 13–24 (2005)
9. Yin, T.-L., Sun, K.-T., Chan, H.-T.: A case study on building Web3D virtual reality and its applications to joyful learning. In: 2011 7th International Conference on Digital Content, Multimedia Technology and its Applications (IDCTA), pp. 49–54, September 2011
10. Poullis, C., You, S.: Photorealistic large-scale urban city model reconstruction. IEEE Trans. Vis. Comput. Graph. **15**(4), 654–669 (2009)
11. Torres-Ferreyros, C.M., Festini-Wendorff, M.A., Shiguihara-Juarez, P.N.: Developing a videogame using unreal engine based on a four stages methodology. In: 2016 IEEE ANDESCON, pp. 1–4. Institute of Electrical and Electronics Engineers (IEEE), October 2016
12. Autodesk Maya Software: Features (2017). http://www.autodesk.com/products/maya/features/all
13. Jayawardena, A.N., Perera, I.: A framework for mixed reality application development: a case study on Yapahuwa archaeological site. In: 2016 Sixteenth International Conference on Advances in ICT for Emerging Regions (ICTer), pp. 186–192. Institute of Electrical and Electronics Engineers (IEEE), September 2016

14. Rosmani, A.F., Mazlan, U.H., Ahmad, S.Z., Apendi, A.A.M.K.: Developing an architectural visualization using 3D for photo tourism. In: 2014 International Conference on Computer, Communications, and Control Technology (I4CT), pp. 429–433. Institute of Electrical and Electronics Engineers (IEEE), September 2014

15. Jing, X.: Design and implementation of 3D virtual digital campus - based on unity3d. In: 2016 Eighth International Conference on Measuring Technology and Mechatronics Automation (ICMTMA), pp. 187–190. Institute of Electrical and Electronics Engineers (IEEE), March 2016

16. Bresciani, S.: The design process: a visual model. In: 2015 19th International Conference on Information Visualisation, pp. 354–359. Institute of Electrical and Electronics Engineers (IEEE), July 2015

17. Unreal Engine: Creating landscapes (2017). https://docs.unrealengine.com/latest/INT/Engine/Landscape/Creation/

18. Ue4/maya lt: Set up grid in maya lt/maya to match Unreal Engine 4, 2008–2016. http://www.worldofleveldesign.com/categories/ue4/ue4-set-up-maya-grid-to-match-unreal-engine4.php

19. LaValle, S.M., Yershova, A., Katsev, M., Antonov, M.: Head tracking for the oculus rift. In: 2014 IEEE International Conference on Robotics and Automation (ICRA), pp. 187–194. Institute of Electrical and Electronics Engineers (IEEE), May 2014

20. Dempsey, P.: The teardown: HTC vive virtual reality headset. Eng. Technol. **11**(7), 80–81 (2016)

21. Ginku: Integrating OpenCV into Unreal Engine 4 (2015). https://wiki.unreal engine.com/Integrating_OpenCV_Into_Unreal_Engine_4

22. Schneider, A., Cernea, D., Ebert, A.: HMD-enabled virtual screens as alternatives to large physical displays. In: 2016 20th International Conference Information Visualisation (IV), pp. 390–394. Institute of Electrical and Electronics Engineers (IEEE), July 2016

23. Combefis, S., Giannakopoulou, D., Pecheur, C., Feary, M.: A formal framework for design and analysis of human-machine interaction. In: 2011 IEEE International Conference on Systems, Man, and Cybernetics, pp. 1801–1808. Institute of Electrical and Electronics Engineers (IEEE), October 2011

24. Ben Ormstad: Unreal Engine 4 tutorial - simple in-game movie screen (2015). https://www.youtube.com/watch?v=VeQtyrVJkMU&t=471s

25. Blueprints visual scripting, 2004–2017. https://docs.unrealengine.com/latest/INT/Engine/Blueprints/

26. Kawamura, S., Kijima, R.: Effect of head mounted display latency on human stability during quiescent standing on one foot. In: 2016 IEEE Virtual Reality (VR), pp. 199–200. Institute of Electrical and Electronics Engineers (IEEE), March 2016

27. White, P.J., Byagowi, A., Moussavi, Z.: Effect of viewing mode on pathfinding in immersive virtual reality. In: 2015 37th Annual International Conference of the IEEE Engineering in Medicine and Biology Society (EMBC), pp. 4619–4622. Institute of Electrical and Electronics Engineers (IEEE), August 2015

28. Naves, E.L.M., Bastos, T.F., Bourhis, G., Silva, Y.M.L.R., Silva, V.J., Lucena, V.F.: Virtual and augmented reality environment for remote training of wheelchairs users: social, mobile, and wearable technologies applied to rehabilitation. In: 2016 IEEE 18th International Conference on e-Health Networking, Applications and Services (Healthcom), pp. 1–4. Institute of Electrical and Electronics Engineers (IEEE), September 2016

A Virtual Travel in Leonardo's Codex of Flight

Marcello Carrozzino[1]([✉]), Chiara Evangelista[1], Claudia Faita[1],
Mihai Duguleana[2], and Massimo Bergamasco[1]

[1] Perceptual Robotics Laboratory, Institute of Communication,
Information and Perception Technologies, Scuola Superiore Sant'Anna,
Pisa, Italy
{m.carrozzino,c.evangelista,c.faita,
m.bergamasco}@santannapisa.it
[2] Department of Automotive and Transport Engineering,
Transylvania University of Brasov, Brasov, Romania
mihai.duguleana@unitbv.ro

Abstract. This paper presents a museum exhibition based on Immersive Multimedia (IM) and Virtual Reality (VR). Several researches showed that the use of IM and VR in exhibition increase the involvement of the visitor and improve communication with the public. The goal of our project is relive the ancient Leonardo's manuscript "Codex of Flight" using immersive multimedia, video projection systems and VR technology. In a museum tour, the visitors contemplate projections and 3D installation and become aware of the historical research process which led to the birth of the Leonardo's manuscript and the subsequent achievements.

Keywords: Virtual Reality · Immersive technologies · Cultural heritage · Museum exhibition · Virtual Environment

1 Introduction

Museums are institutions created to collect, preserve and make available to the public artworks and, in general, cultural assets. In recent years there was a growing interest in the use of information and communication technologies (ICT) for museum exhibitions, with the aim of a better and more engaging communication [1]. In particular, evaluation studies show that the use of ICT in exhibitions can improve learning and communication with the public [2,3]. Moreover, new ICT technologies such as Virtual Reality (VR) and Immersive Multimedia (IM) are nowadays starting to be effectively used in traditional museums in order to improve the involvement of visitors [4]. These technologies can also provide richer and more engaging web-based pre-visit information on museums [1], and sites [5] in what becomes an experience in itself. The advantage of both VR and IM technologies is mainly given by the immersive conditions provided by these medium. Virtual Environments (VE) have been proved to recreate in users the feeling to be completely immersed and present in the scene. The sense of immersion and

© Springer International Publishing AG 2017
L.T. De Paolis et al. (Eds.): AVR 2017, Part II, LNCS 10325, pp. 310–318, 2017.
DOI: 10.1007/978-3-319-60928-7_27

presence provided by such technological tools improves visitors' engagement and emphasizes the learning process of the exhibition content [6]. For this reason, VR has been used in the field of cultural heritage not only in museums but also in libraries, for instance to restore and disseminate the content of ancient books [7]. Previous studies showed that 3D technologies play a role in improving the understanding of book content [8].

In this work we present the design and development of a museum exhibition in which IM and VR technologies were used to relive the Leonardo Da Vinci's manuscript "Codex of Flight". The general aims of our project was to use video projection and 3D technologies in order to highlight the historical and research process which led to the birth of the text and the subsequent achievements in this topic.

2   Related Work

An interesting new way that VR is being used in museums is the experience of entering artworks. Recently released, the VR exhibit titled "Dreams of Dali" get visitors to explore the world of the artist through an Oculus Rift headset, which enable them to walk through and explore the elements of the painting enriched by elements coming from other Dali paintings[1]. The "Van Gogh Alive" exhibition[2] is instead based on the immersive and emotional effect generated by multiple projected screen which surround visitors with more than 3000 images of the artist at big scale, synchronized with a music soundtrack. Woofbert VR (now Boulevard VR)[3] is an app for Oculus Rift which, initially, enabled panoramic tours in art galleries and was subsequently improved to enable exploring artworks themselves with a paradigm similar to the Dali one. Another immersive multimedia experience has been hosted at the Muse des Beaux des Arts de Montral, dealing with a multisensory experience of a Pompeii's roman aqueduct coming to life followed by a volcanic eruption[4]. When dealing with books and manuscripts, rather than with paintings, it is often necessary to elaborate on the book content as it might not present sufficient visual material to be represented in immersive environments. In [9] a methodology to deal with children's narrative in order to produce interactive VEs is proposed, although immersion was limited to a desktop experience. Cauchard et al. [10] propose virtual learning environments offering visitors the opportunity of engaging with virtual manuscripts and of accessing the heritage and other cultural information contained in them. These "Living Manuscripts" can be experienced either in a web-based approach or using onsite immersive systems. An interesting opportunity is provided by Information Landscapes (ILs), abstract VEs composed of text, images and 3D content, which can provide highly immersive experiences like in the case of the Lilienskiold's Travel Log [11] which originated an IL that can be experienced in a CAVE-like environment.

---

[1] http://thedali.org/dreams-of-dali/.
[2] http://grandeexhibitions.com/traveling-exhibitions/van-gogh-alive/.
[3] http://blvrd.com/artculture/.
[4] http://www.graphicsemotion.com/gem/portfolio/pompeii-mbam/.

3   The Project

The project presented is a museum exhibition, opened in Rome in January at Musei Capitolini. The exhibition is conceived as a cultural journey aimed at communicating the heritage of the ancient Leonardo's manuscript "Codex of Flight", using immersive multimedia, video projection systems and VR technology in a museum tour in which visitors, at the end of the itinerary, are finally able to contemplate the original copy of the manuscript. When designing the multimedia exhibition tour we were motivated by:

- recalling the preeminence of Leonardo's ideas and studies about flight
- showing the real-life consequences of Leonardo's concepts
- creating a historically faithful reconstruction of the manuscript

3.1   Leonardo and the Book

The "Codex on the flight of the birds" is an ancient manuscript written by Leonardo da Vinci around 1505. The book can be considered as a sum of the thoughts of Leonardo about flying. The author in fact harbored the ambitious project to build the most advanced flying machine. The machine design starts with the observation of the behavior of birds with special attention to the flight of kites, which is dedicated to the name of the *"fly machine"*. The manuscript is composed of eighteen paper sheets each measuring 21×15 cm and begins with an investigation of the behavior of flying birds, proposing subsequently possible mechanisms for achieving flight by means of mechanical machines. In addition to the representations of the flight of birds, in almost all of the eighteen pages a set of geometric figures, mechanical and architectural drawings enrich the text, written, as usual in Leonardo, using mirror writing. In order to preserve the

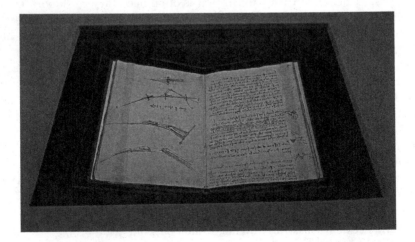

Fig. 1. The original manuscript of Leonardo's Codex of the flight

precious manuscript, the codex is commonly not accessible to the public except during special exhibitions where, in any case, it is protected by a special case able to keep the right environmental conditions. It is preserved by the 1893 at the Royal Library in Turin, Italy. In Fig. 1 the book located in the exhibition case is showed.

3.2 The Museum

The exhibition took place at the Capitoline Museums, a group of art and archeological museums located in Piazza del Campidoglio (Capitoline Hill), one of the most important historical locations in Rome, Italy. The museums' collection has grown to include a large number of ancient Roman statues, inscriptions and other artifacts; a collection of medieval and Renaissance art; other collections of jewels, coins, and other items. The Capitoline Museums are composed of four main buildings:

- Palazzo Senatorio, built during the 13th and 14th centuries and modified according to Michelangelo's designs;
- Palazzo dei Conservatori, built in the mid-16th century and redesigned by Michelangelo with the first use of the giant order column design;
- Palazzo Nuovo, constructed between 1603–1654. Its facade duplicates to that of Palazzo dei Conservatori
- Palazzo Caffarelli-Clementino, built between 1538 and 1680 by Gregory Canonico for Gian Pietro Caffarelli II; it was added to the complex of Capitoline Museums in 2000.

The Leonardo exhibition takes place at Palazzo Caffarelli-Clementino. Figure 2 shows the map of the exhibition room. The exhibition entrance is in

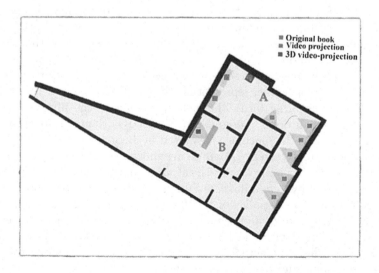

Fig. 2. Map of the exhibition (Color figure online)

room A, where a sequence of video projections leads to the room where the original manuscript are located. The exhibition continues in the hall B, where the VR stereoscopic system is presented.

4   Multimedia Content

The exhibition itinerary is divided in two parts. The first part presents six large video projections in which the history of Leonardo's inspiration and the manuscript content is presented. This part introduces the room where the original manuscript and a theca with several ancient copies are shown. In the second part visitors attend to a 3D video installation recalling the realization of the dream of flying.

4.1   The Video Projections

The exhibition begins with an evocative-explanatory path characterized by six large video projections placed consecutively in the entrance hallway. The path of video projections is illustrated in details in Fig. 2, where they are identified with a green square and capital letters representing a certain projection station. Each projection shows a particular phase of Leonardo's research on flight presented through animations realized starting from Leonardo drawings. In order to faithfully reconstruct the historical path of the studies conducted by Da Vinci, we have used original pictures of drawings presented in Leonardo's notes related to the fly, not only the Code of the Flight, but also the Codex Atlanticus. Moreover, each animation is correlated to explanatory texts in English and Italian, as shown in Fig. 3. The choice of written text against vocal narration was necessary because of the simultaneous presence of several co-located projections which would have compromised the understandability of the narration. For this reason, audio was limited to a few sound effects (like birds tweeting, tide sounds, etc.) carefully synchronized in order to create an atmosphere without making the environment too noisy.

The video-projections have a sequential structure (Table 1): starting from the images of the flight of Icarus, representing the ill-fated dream of flying, and of kites (Leonardo's inspiring bird), the itinerary leads to the illustration of the first prototype of helicopter, designed by Enroico Forlanin in 1877, which is structurally similar to the machine speculated by Leonardo (F). In B two flying machine prototypes designed by Leonardo are shown: the Aerial Screw and a sort of parachute. In C four pictures show the studies concerning the structure of the wing as investigated by Leonardo. The D and E video-projections are dedicated to the illustration of the studies of the flight of birds as natural phenomena, including spiral trajectories and the exploitation of thermals close to seashores in order to soar. The journey in Leonardo's concepts eventually flows into the exhibition space where the actual book is presented, together with other paper material historically connected to the manuscript.

Fig. 3. Examples of video projections in the exhibition

Table 1. List of projection content in the sequential structure presented in the museum

Projection	Frame picture	Content
A	2 small on the left 1 on the right	The Flight of Icarus Kite Flight Inspiration
B	1 on the left 2 small on the center 1on the right	Machine with a rotating and helitical wing Parachute
C	4 same size	Wing structure
D	2 same size	Birds flight trajectories
E	1 large	Thermal soaring of birds
F	6 same size	Original video and photo of helicopter prototypes and first airplanes

4.2 Immersive VR System

Finally, visitors entering in room B are able to experience a non-interactive immersive VR system aiming at suggesting the realization of Leonardo's dream (Fig. 4). The objective of this installation is to emphasize the importance of Leonardo's intuition, imagination and determination in chasing is dream. The room features a Powerwall using passive stereoscopy, in order to provide visitors with disposable paper glasses with polarized lenses both for health and economical reasons. The projection station is composed of a PC driving two Optoma W505 projectors, chosen because of the offered lens-shift features allowing a fast and precise calibration of the two images. A wooden counter hides the projectors from the audience and offers support for visitors standing up in front of the Powerwall. The expected consistent flow of groups of visitors has favored the choice on a non-interactive experience against the initially foreseen interactive

Fig. 4. Top: a screenshot of the VR installation content. Bottom: audience experiencing the VR content.

one. The experience starts with an excerpt of David Attenborough's "Conquest of the sky" 3D documentary, featuring very suggestive images related to flight kindly offered by SKY3D channel of SKY Italia broadcasting. Subsequently, the immersive experience continues with a VR animation (realized with Autodesk 3DSMax and rendered in real-time with XVR) starting with images of a fast browsing of the pages of Leonardo's manuscripts on flight, eventually focusing on the Ornithopter Flying Machine which, suddenly, becomes "real" and start flying in the Tuscan Countryside side to side with a kite. After a while, the visual passes from third to first person and the viewer "becomes" the man powering

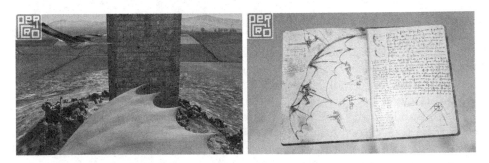

Fig. 5. Screenshots of the VR installation content. Left: first person view of the experience. Right: virtually browsing the manuscript pages

the flying machine. The animation fades out with the flying machine pointing to the sun, to suggest the realization of the dream of flying as opposed to the fall of Icarus (Fig. 5).

5 Conclusion

The exhibition aims at producing a sophisticated storytelling through a series of suggestions and sensory extensions. Immersive Multimedia and VR technologies have been used as a means acting as a digital guide in an experience where content is generated by different forms of knowledge and not as the result of aesthetical choices of a curator. The fundamental objective was to create an open cultural itinerary where visitors, after their visit, are pushed to investigate, ask questions and refine their experience. We are currently conducting a user study, attempting at understanding if the set objectives have been actually reached. In particular we will try to determine if the exhibition has been able to narrate a story, to raise awareness on the topic and the desire to delve into it, to set up a cultural journey which visitors have felt to be part of. For this purpose we are evaluating the user experience by collecting an after-exhibition questionnaire and by observing the visitor's behavior.

Ackwnowledgment. The realization of the exhibition was realized together with Associazione Culturale Metaforfosi and Zetema Progetto Cultura. The cultural itinerary was curated by Giovanni Saccani (Biblioteca Reale di Torino) and Claudio Giorgione (Museo Scienza e Tecnologia Leonardo Da Vinci di Milano). The theoretical framework underlying the use of Immersive Multimedia and VR for cultural communication and the user study has been carried out in the context of the EU 2020-TWINN-2015 eHERITAGE project (grant number 692103).

References

1. Wojciechowski, R., Walczak, K., White, M., Cellary, W.: Building virtual and augmented reality museum exhibitions. In: Proceedings of the Ninth International Conference on 3D Web Technology, pp. 135–144. ACM (2004)
2. Tost, L.P., Economou, M.: Evaluating the social context of ICT applications in museum exhibitions. In: Proceedings of the 7th International Conference on Virtual Reality, Archaeology and Intelligent Cultural Heritage, pp. 219–228. Eurographics Association (2006)
3. Kirkup, G., Kirkwood, A.: Information and communications technologies (ICT) in higher education teaching a tale of gradualism rather than revolution. Learn. Media Technol. **30**(2), 185–199 (2005)
4. Brondi, R., Carrozzino, M., Lorenzini, C., Tecchia, F.: Using mixed reality and natural interaction in cultural heritage applications. Informatica **40**(3) (2016)
5. Carrozzino, M., Brogi, A., Tecchia, F., Bergamasco, M.: The 3D interactive visit to Piazza dei miracoli, Italy. In: Proceedings of the 2005 ACM SIGCHI International Conference on Advances in Computer Entertainment Technology, pp. 192–195. ACM (2005)

6. Roussou, M.: The components of engagement in virtual heritage environments. In: Proceedings of New Heritage: New Media and Cultural Heritage, pp. 225–241 (2008)
7. Carrozzino, M., Angeletaki, A., Evangelista, C., Lorenzini, C., Tecchia, F., Bergamasco, M.: Virtual technologies to enable novel methods of access to library archives. SCIRES IT Sci. Res. Inf. Technol. **3**(1), 25–34 (2013)
8. Martín-Gutiérrez, J., Saorín, J.L., Contero, M., Alcañiz, M., Pérez-López, D.C., Ortega, M.: Design and validation of an augmented book for spatial abilities development in engineering students. Comput. Graph. **34**(1), 77–91 (2010)
9. Baroni, A., Evangelista, C., Carrozzino, M., Bergamasco, M.: Building 3D interactive environments for the children's narrative: a didactic project. In: Proceedings of the 2005 ACM SIGCHI International Conference on Advances in Computer Entertainment Technology, pp. 350–353. ACM (2005)
10. Costantino, D., Angelini, M.G.: Realization of a cartographic GIS for the filing and management of the archaelogical excavations in the Nelson's Island. In: Ioannides, M., Fellner, D., Georgopoulos, A., Hadjimitsis, D.G. (eds.) EuroMed 2010. LNCS, vol. 6436, pp. 513–527. Springer, Heidelberg (2010). doi:10.1007/978-3-642-16873-4_42
11. Carrozzino, M., Evangelista, C., Bergamasco, M., Belli, M., Angeletaki, A.: Information landscapes for the communication of ancient manuscripts heritage. In: Digital Heritage International Congress (DigitalHeritage), vol. 2, pp. 257–262. IEEE (2013)

Visualising a Software System as a City Through Virtual Reality

Nicola Capece, Ugo Erra$^{(\boxtimes)}$, Simone Romano, and Giuseppe Scanniello

Dipartimento di Matematica, Informatica ed Economia,
Università degli Studi della Basilicata, Potenza, Italy
{nicola.capece,ugo.erra,simone.romano,giuseppe.scanniello}@unibas.it

Abstract. We describe a technique developed using C++ language and
Unreal Engine 4 that allows users to visualise software systems written in
object-oriented Java through virtual reality and using the city metaphor.
Our aim is to use virtual reality to visualise the metrics of classes and
packages of a software system. In this paper, we present a prototype.
The ultimate goal will be to demonstrate that it is possible to use virtual
reality to better understand software.

Keywords: Software visualisation · Virtual Reality · CodeCity

1 Introduction

Among the new display systems, virtual reality (VR) is an emerging field with
enormous potential. Most research focuses on immersive VR technologies that
have replaced sensorial information from the real world with synthetic stimuli such as 3D images and sounds. The goal of immersive virtual environments
(VEs) is to allow the user to experiment in a world generated by computers as
if it were real [5]. The industry showing the greatest demand for VR is certainly
the videogames industry. For a long time, small and large companies have been
developing hardware and software technology to bring VR to a higher level,
gradually improving its features in terms of performance and level of immersion. However, in recent years, VR's context of use has also expanded to other
application contexts such as military, educational, and engineering fields.

Software visualisation has in particular been extensively explored and used in
software maintenance to comprehend the features of the software itself. However,
as software engineering evolves, software systems developed today are becoming
more complex and difficult to understand. The goal of software visualisation is
to help software comprehension.

More and more approaches and metaphors based on 2D and 3D techniques
[6,7,16] are being proposed. In this paper, we propose a VR system to visualise
a software system by using the city metaphor [14] to represent software using
3D objects that compose the scene. In the city metaphor, software systems are
represented as real cities, in which classes are visualised as buildings and packages
as districts. Because cities are familiar to most users, they are easy to move

© Springer International Publishing AG 2017
L.T. De Paolis et al. (Eds.): AVR 2017, Part II, LNCS 10325, pp. 319–327, 2017.
DOI: 10.1007/978-3-319-60928-7_28

around and explore, especially through an immersive technology such as VR. We developed a 3D graphics application through a game engine called Unreal Engine 4, which, given an XML file generated in a previous step and containing information about the analysed software system, creates a building for each class; each building is represented by a parallelepiped, whose dimensions and colour are determined by the properties of the class. Because we are visualising object-oriented applications written using Java, even packages are represented, whose width and depth are optimised using a bin-packing algorithm to visualise all the buildings belonging to the same package in as less space as possible; the height has a constant value.

The remainder of this paper is structured as follows: Sect. 2 provides an overview of related works. Section 3 provides background information about the technologies used. Section 4 describes our VR system and preliminary results. Section 5 ends with final remarks and future directions for our research.

2   Related Works

As mentioned above, VR is used in several fields of application. Maletic et al. [10] describe a system called Imsovision for visualisation of object-oriented software through VR. Their aim is to develop a language that uses few metaphors and constructs, but is capable of representing a variety of elements without ambiguity or loss of meaning. The elements distinguishing the software are represented in the visualisation, the specific information on classes, the dependencies among classes, and so on. Their system allows recognition of the software system using a VE, taking advantage of all the possibilities offered by this type of visualisation, such as 3D browsing. The dimension of objects in the VE represents the source code's metrics and attributes. Visualisation in VR is performed using a system where the display is a 10 square feet room in which are projected stereoscopic images, creating the illusion of coexistence between objects in the room and the user. The user wears liquid crystal glasses for visualising stereoscopic images and uses a controller to interact with the VE.

Kapec et al. [9] presented a visualisation system that allows visual analysis through graphs representing the software system using a VR interface based on a standard desktop environment (icons, menus, etc.) and augmented reality. The software systems analysed were written using the Lua programming language [8]. Information was extracted from these systems and used to encode visual attributes of the graphs and to perform visual analysis. Visualisation through augmented reality uses a "spatial optical see-through display" a Kinect v1, and a Leap motion sensor for interaction. Souza et al. [12] proposed visualising software systems through augmented reality by using the city metaphor to represent the software's evolution. Augmented reality allows the user to interact with the city using a marker, a computer, and a camera. Their system, called SkyscrapAR, represents packages as districts, sub-packages as stacked districts, and classes as buildings positioned in their respective packages, in the same way as CodeCity. The visualisation of the city is projected in the environment of the user using the camera and the marker. The user interacts with the visualised object manipulating the marker using his or her hands to obtain the representation of the city from the desired point of view. Our goal is to use VR technology currently available on the market, such as Oculus Rift and HTC Vive. Through these two hardware systems, we experimented with the sensation of full immersion in the software system visualised using the city metaphor. The sensation of immersion arises because these technologies allow interaction with the VE without the need for external instruments. Both Oculus Rift and HTC Vive are equipped with controllers that allow easy interaction with the VE.

3   Background

Our system was developed using several technologies. The analysed software systems are written in Java and are composed of two main entities: packages and classes. In particular, the analysis of the software was performed using an Eclipse [2] plugin called CodePro AnalytiX [1]. This plugin aims to enhance the quality and security of the source code and helps developers to reduce the number of errors and security vulnerabilities. CodePro allows the desired metrics to be selected from the analysed software, generating an XML file containing the information. 3D city construction and rendering are performed using the well-known videogames engine Unreal Engine 4 [4]. This engine allows 3D applications to be developed using two different styles of programming: (i) Blueprints visual scripting, based on the concept of using a node-based interface to create gameplay elements, and (ii) the C++ programming language. These programming styles are interchangeable. In our work, we used both. 3D elements were positioned based on the bin-packing algorithm [11]. This algorithm represents a possible solution to an intractable NP-complete problem. The proposed algorithm allows 3D objects to be positioned within the 3D environment in a way that optimises the occupied space, computing sub-package dimensions based on the package's classes dimensions. As mentioned above, the visualisation in VR is performed using HTC Vive [3] and Oculus Rift [3]. HTC Vive uses a technology called room-scale that allows the user to move in a 3D space in the real world. Each of these technologies allows the user to be fully immersed in the VE and to interact in a realistic way with it.

4   The VR System

We propose an approach comprising two steps: (i) analysis of the source code to visualise the software system and (ii) construction and rendering of the 3D scene. In the first step, we analysed different software systems using the Eclipse plugin CodePro AnalytiX. This plugin takes as its input the directory containing the Java source code of the software system, analysing it and extracting the desired metrics. Initially, we decided to extract for each class: the structure of its package through the fully qualified name of the class itself, the number of methods, and the number of attributes. When the metrics have been obtained, the results can be exported in several ways, for example as plain text or HTML. We chose to use the XML format because it represents a generic standard that may also be used in other application contexts. The generated XML file is then analysed by the game engine, which performs the parse. Because this file is structured as a list of classes, and in XML sub-tags represent the classes' parameters, analysis of the file and reconstruction of the software system schema through a tree-type data structure was needed.

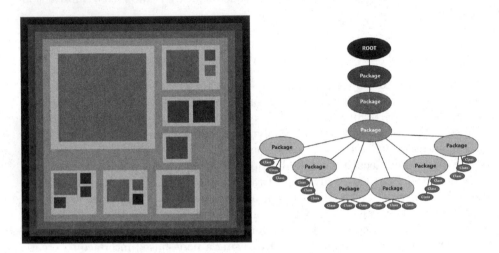

Fig. 1. Left: the positioning algorithm. Right: the software system schema under analysis.

As shown in Fig. 1, the tree is composed of intermediate nodes, which represent the packages, and leaf nodes, which represent the classes. After constructing the tree, we computed the dimension of the packages using the bin-packing algorithm. This algorithm computes the dimension of a block based on the objects that are inside it, optimising the layout to minimise the space occupied.

The algorithm is executed recursively, starting from the leaves, to compute the dimension and positions in the 3D scene for all packages. This can be seen in Fig. 2, which shows only the packages from two different software systems on Unreal Engine 4 and all classes belonging to the analysed software system.

The second step consists of building the 3D scene based on the position and the dimension of each package and class in the tree. Packages are shown as colourful blocks in grey scale in a range from dark grey to light grey according to the nesting level [15] of the package in the software system. The height of the package is a constant value. Classes are represented as blocks in blue scale, represented on a scale from 0 to 1, where 0 means dark blue and 1 means light blue. The colour value is given by the number of lines of code, which is composed of a certain class that has been normalised between 0 and 1, to display a class

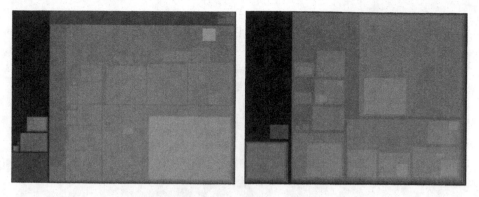

Fig. 2. Showing only the packages in Unreal Engine 4 from two different software systems, viewed from the top.

composed of a few lines of code with a darker colour and a class composed of many lines of code with a lighter colour. The dimension of the buildings is given the number of attributes that belong to the class. This number is multiplied by a scaling factor to represent the city in proportion to the user. The final displayed parameter represents the height of each building, which is given the number of methods belonging to the class. This number is also multiplied by a scaling factor equal to the previously mentioned scaling factor. To facilitate user orientation within the city and to better understand the structure of the source code being analysed, we included signs in each district/package that contain its name. The same feature was implemented for classes, where in addition to the name are also shown the analysed metrics. Our system also allows some interactions with the user. We exploited the potential of Unreal Engine 4 by using ray casting [13] to locate and select objects in the 3D scene. In ray casting, a ray is shot orthogonally to the controller position. This ray is represented by a vector of the constant module and allows the user to point the controller towards the desired object. When the ray hits a building, it changes the building's colour, giving the illusion of selection of the building. After the building has been selected, the user can view detailed information on metrics belonging to the represented class. Integration with the head-mounted display is also realised using its native controllers. Using the right controller it is possible to move into the VE. The user uses the track-pad to move in the scene. Using the left controller it is possible to interact with the objects in the scene. As explained above, we use ray casting to identify the object pointed to by the user. The user selects the buildings by pointing the controller, and the application changes the material and colour of the selected object, as shown in Fig. 3.

The user can visualise detailed information about the metrics belonging to the class represented by the object in the scene. We also implemented a teleport system through the scene. If the user points the right controller to a space occupied by a district, the user can "teleport" to that point, speeding the movement through the scene. We also improved the photo-realism of the scene by adding

Fig. 3. HTC Vive interaction. (Color figure online)

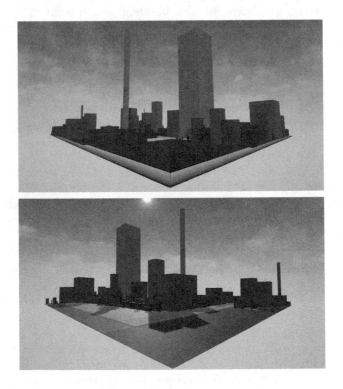

Fig. 4. Visualisation software system jEdit.

Fig. 5. Visualisation software system JFreeChart.

two lights: ambient light and directional light. The first is useful for viewing well even in shadow zones, and the second is useful for displaying the shadows of buildings.

4.1   Preliminary Results

To test our visualisation system, we used the source code of three software systems. Figure 4 shows the city that represents the jEdit[1] version 7.0.6 software system, which consist of 251 packages, 188267 lines of code, 7153 methods, and 4192 fields. Figure 5 shows the city that represents the JFreeChart[2] version 1.0.19 software system, which consists of 43 packages, 233369 lines of code, 8183 methods, and 2961 fields. The third software system, shown in Fig. 6, is JHotDraw[3] version 7.0.6, which consists of 36 packages, 57020 lines of code, 3377 methods, and 900 fields (Fig. 7).

---

[1] www.jedit.org.

[2] www.jfree.org/jfreechart/.

[3] www.jhotdraw.org.

Fig. 6. Visualisation software system JHotDraw.

Fig. 7. Virtual reality visualisation.

5   Conclusions and Future Work

We have presented a technique to visualise object-oriented software systems written in Java through VR. This system is an extension of the city metaphor proposed by Wettel et al. [16] and enables the user to visualise the characteristics of each class comprising the software system being analysed, by the user's full immersion in VR. The idea is to increase and further improve user interaction with the 3D scene, visualising other metrics such as the class dependencies. In fact, it would be possible to obtain a better perception of the structure of the analysed software system by selecting a class and determining the classes on which it depends. This work is a first step towards quantifying the use of VR for software analysis. This is a work in progress at a preliminary stage. The post-implementation step consists of user experimentation. This will allow a group of computer science students to test the system to verify both the usability and the primary goal, which is simplification of the comprehension of the source code. Future works will include real empirical studies to investigate how this proposed work contributes to research and development communities that use VR.

References

1. CodePro AnalytiX. www.marketplace.eclipse.org/content/codepro-analytix
2. Eclipse Mars. www.eclipse.org
3. HTC Vive. www.vive.com/eu/
4. Unreal Engine 4. www.unrealengine.com
5. Bowman, D.A., McMahan, R.P.: Virtual reality: how much immersion is enough? Computer **40**(7), 36–43 (2007)
6. Ducasse, S., Lanza, M.: The class blueprint: visually supporting the understanding of glasses. IEEE Trans. Softw. Eng. **31**(1), 75–90 (2005)
7. Hattori, L., D'Ambros, M., Lanza, M., Lungu, M.: Software evolution comprehension: replay to the rescue. In: 2011 IEEE 19th International Conference on Program Comprehension, pp. 161–170, June 2011
8. Ierusalimschy, R., de Figueiredo, L.H., Filho, W.C.: Lua - an extensible extension language. Softw. Pract. Exper. **26**(6), 635–652 (1996)
9. Kapec, P., Brndiarov, G., Gloger, M., Mark, J.: Visual analysis of software systems in virtual and augmented reality. In: 2015 IEEE 19th International Conference on Intelligent Engineering Systems (INES), pp. 307–312 (2015)
10. Maletic, J.I., Leigh, J., Marcus, A., Dunlap, G.: Visualizing object-oriented software in virtual reality. In: Proceedings 9th International Workshop on Program Comprehension, IWPC 2001, pp. 26–35 (2001)
11. Skiena, S.S.: The Algorithm Design Manual, 2nd edn. Springer Publishing Company Inc., Heidelberg (2008)
12. Souza, R., Silva, B., Mendes, T., Mendonça, M.: Skyscrapar: an augmented reality visualization for software evolution. In: Proceedings of 2nd Brazilian Workshop on Software Visualization (WBVS 2012) (2012)
13. Stoakley, R., Conway, M.J., Pausch, R.: Virtual reality on a WIM: interactive worlds in miniature. In: Proceedings of the SIGCHI Conference on Human Factors in Computing Systems, CHI 1995, pp. 265–272. ACM Press/Addison-Wesley Publishing Co., New York (1995)
14. Wettel, R., Lanza, M.: Program comprehension through software habitability. In: 15th IEEE International Conference on Program Comprehension (ICPC 2007), pp. 231–240, June 2007
15. Wettel, R., Lanza, M.: Visualizing software systems as cities. In: 2007 4th IEEE International Workshop on Visualizing Software for Understanding and Analysis, pp. 92–99, June 2007
16. Wettel, R., Lanza, M.: CodeCity: 3D visualization of large-scale software. In: Companion of the 30th International Conference on Software Engineering, ICSE Companion 2008, New York, NY, USA, pp. 921–922. ACM, New York (2008)

Implementation of Player Position Monitoring for Tanjung Pura Palace Virtual Environment

Mohammad Fadly Syahputra[✉], Muhammad Iqbal Rizki,
Siti Fatimah, and Romi Fadillah Rahmat

Department of Information Technology, Faculty of Computer Science
and Information Technology, University of Sumatera Utara, Medan, Indonesia
{nca.fadly, romi.fadillah}@usu.ac.id,
{m.iqbalrizki, chitifatimah}@students.usu.ac.id

Abstract. Previously we had developed 3d model in virtual environment for palace in Tanjug Pura Region. For enchachment and enrichment of this application in order to introduce historical place in Tanjung Pura region, such as Darul Aman Palace, Darussalam Palace and the other historical buildings, we developed player positioning monitoring feature and implement it on its virtual environment. In this research, the player position mapping is performed inside a mini-map in Tanjung Pura Palace virtual reality application. The result of this research shows that the implemented method can be used to track the location of the user Tanjung Pura Palace virtual reality application.

Keywords: Minimap · Virtual reality · Tanjung pura palace · Player positioning monitoring

1 Introduction

In 1946, Darul Aman Palace in Tanjung Pura region was destroyed as the result of social revolution [1]. At the present, there are no signs of the former palace construction on the palace site. The palace acts as the important historical building of Malay culture in North Sumatera. For the preservation effort of Malay culture in North Sumatera, the reconstruction work is required.

Various researches about the implementation of virtual reality have been conducted for historic learning and industrial sector. Angeloni et al. constructed a virtual reality application to display Flemish artworks, and the background of each artwork to the user, in an environment inspired by museum in the real world [2]. Li and Hu conducted the research about history leaving method for tour guide candidates by using virtual reality. With this application, candidates can learn about historical objects and soft skills as a tour guide [3]. The research conducted for mapping the motion of the player inside the virtual environment, as done by Charles [4]. The research utilized Kinect to track motion and location of player body part inside the virtual environment.

Bruno et al. [5] presented the guidelines in the VR system development for digital archaeological exhibition. The work illustrates a complete methodology to create a virtual exhibition system based on realistic high-quality 3D model. Calabria that built between 18th and 9th BC was the subject of his study. The research is done by using a

L.T. De Paolis et al. (Eds.): AVR 2017, Part II, LNCS 10325, pp. 328–334, 2017.
DOI: 10.1007/978-3-319-60928-7_29

low-cost multimedia stereoscopic system called MNEME (from the Ancient Greek 'memory'), which allows user to interact easily.

Previously, Darussalam Palace and Darul Aman Palace has been reconstructed using Image-Based Modeling and Game Engine as the Virtual Environment [4]. In this research, we use Virtual Reality (VR) environment, which is integrated with Head-Mounted Display device in order to improve its immersive graphic. This research aims on implementation of Player Position Monitoring in Darul Aman Palace Virtual Reality to obtain player position in virtual environment.

2 Methodology

The methodology of this study consists of several phases, i.e. virtual reality environment, player position monitoring and colliding, which is shown by Fig. 1.

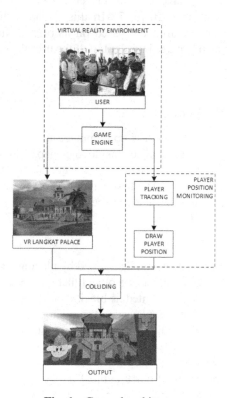

Fig. 1. General architecture

2.1 Virtual Reality Environment

Virtual Reality environment is constructed as the main container of 3D objects that will be shown to the user. In this research, virtual reality environment contains the 3D objects required to constructed the real-world condition of the Darul Aman Palace [8].

Game Engine is a software to build a game application, however the purpose of game engine has been expanded in to building educational applications, industrial applications, and animation for entertainment sectors. In this research, we use Unity 3D as our game engine, this is particularly because we need the ability of its functions and libraries that will connect user to their virtual environment.

2.2   VR Langkat Palace

Virtual Reality for Langkat Palace is an application that displays the area, environment, and history of Langkat Palace to the user. Therefore, the experience excitement will be their benefit rather than showing the 3D without using virtual reality. This particular Langkat Palace is divided by two main Palaces, the first palaces is Istana Darul Aman (Darul Aman Palace), the second palace is Istana Darussalam (Darussalam Palace). These two historical palaces have been resurrected and rebuild in Virtual Reality environment by Fadly et al. in 2016 [6, 7]. In this research, those two places were placed in one virtual reality environment based on its original historical place in real world, and we add mini-map features in order to tell the user their position in the virtual reality environment.

2.3   Player Position Monitoring

Player position monitoring is the process implemented to track user location in virtual environment and place the player object inside the map, where the object position depends on user location. In this research, two camera objects will be utilized to support player position monitoring. The first camera object represents of main view of the player inside virtual environment, while second camera is placed on virtual environment to display map and user location.

2.3.1   Player Tracking

User location in virtual environment can be tracked by placing a game object inside the player object. In our particular case, a game object that has been induced in other game object (such as player) will be represented as black cubical object. If this black cubical object is attached to group that has player as the main object then the black cubical object will continuously be depending on user movement.

2.3.2   Draw Player Position

Because of the x and y positions of black cubical object and player is equal, then we can assume that the position of black cubical object is the position of the player too. The difference between these two entities is the height or z-axis. Black cubical object is build taller than the player's height, therefore it will decrease user distraction when they use the application. The location continuation will be obtained from the game object will be draw inside the map at second camera (Fig. 2a and b).

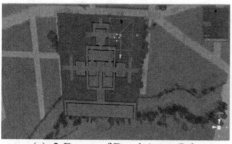

(a). 2-D map of Darul Aman Palace	(b) User Marker

Fig. 2. Player position monitoring

2.4 Colliding

A function provided by unity named as Collider, it works as the outline if a game object for implementing certain effects on actions on selected game object. Colliding is the technique performed to switch between two or more maps. Colliding process performed by creating a collider as the boundaries between every area which are present in each map. A function is implements to switch over each map in virtual environment when the user passes through the collider, which in turn will return information about current position of user in virtual environment by viewing the mini-map. Without using collider, several processes have to be performed, such as defining all points included in every game objects to produce the same result as shown by using collider (Figs. 3 and 4a, b, c and d).

Fig. 3. Collider option in unity

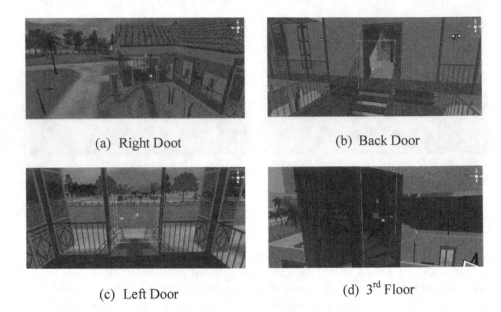

(a) Right Doot

(b) Back Door

(c) Left Door

(d) 3rd Floor

Fig. 4. Collider in darul aman palace

3   Result

Generally, the mapping process of Darul Aman Palace in virtual environment does not have difference with the real world. Also, the placement of player in virtual environment does not have significant difference with the placement of the second camera (Fig. 5a and b).

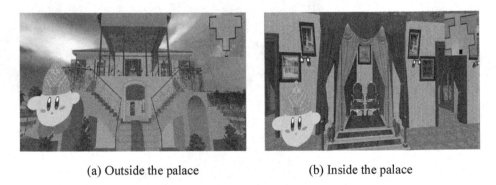

(a) Outside the palace

(b) Inside the palace

Fig. 5. 3D model and minimap result

We have performed several experiments to know percentage of tracking accuracy. As shown by Table 1, average tracking accuracy obtained in this research is 66%.

Table 1. Tracking accuracy by 10 times of experiment

Location	True positive	False positive		Percentage		
		Reversed	Untracked	Tracked	Reversed	Untracked
Front door	10	0	0	100%	0%	0%
Right door	10	0	0	100%	0%	0%
Left door	10	0	0	100%	0%	0%
Back door	10	0	0	100%	0%	0%
3rd door	5	5	0	50%	50%	0%
Average	9	1	0	90%	10%	0%

4 Conclusion

The main aim of this research is to implements real-time position mapping of the user in virtual reality of Darul Aman Palace. The mapping process is done by embedding a game object inside the player object. The game object, acting as player tracker, will be placed inside the camera object in order to monitor the location of user in the virtual environment from the map inside the second camera. For the future research, mapping process can be done by placing the second camera beneath the virtual environment without placing the map in front of the camera. Also, the objects placed in the virtual environment should utilize collider with finite boundaries.

References

1. Ramadhan, F.: Revolusi Sosial di Kesultanan Langkat Pada Tahun 1946. http://eprints.uny.ac.id/17777/1/Skripsi%20Full%2010407141001%20Fitra%20Ramadhan.swf. Accessed 10 Oct 2015
2. Angeloni, I., Bisio, F., De Gloria, A., Mori, D., Capurro, C., and Magnani, L.: A Virtual Museum for Flemish artworks. A digital reconstruction of Genoese collections. In: 18th International Conference on Virtual Systems and Multimedia (VSMM) 2012, pp. 607–610 (2012)
3. Li, N., Hu, W.: Virtual reality applications in simulated course for tour guides. In: 2012 7th International Conference on Computer Science & Education (ICCSE, pp. 1672–1674 (2012)
4. Charles, S.: Real-time human movement mapping to a virtual environment. In: 2016 IEEE Region 10 Symposium (TENSYMP), Bali, Indonesia (2016)
5. Bruno, F., Bruno, S., Sensi, G.D., Luchi, M.L., Mancuso, S., Muzzupappa, M.: From 3D reconstruction to virtual reality: a complete methodology for digital archaeological exhibition. J. Cult. Heritage 11(1), 42–49 (2009)
6. Syahputra, M.F., Permady, J.A., Muchtar, M.A.: Digital reconstruction of darul aman palace based on images and implementation into virtual reality environment. In: Paolis, L.T., Mongelli, A. (eds.) AVR 2016. LNCS, vol. 9769, pp. 269–279. Springer, Cham (2016). doi:10.1007/978-3-319-40651-0_22

7. Syahputra, M.F., Siregar, B., Purnamawati, S.: Aplikasi virtual Tour Istana Darussalam menggunakan teknologi virtual reality. In: Proceedings of SENARAI USU, Medan, pp. 249–253 (2014)
8. Syahputra, M.F., Annisa, T., Rahmat, R.F., Muchtar, M.A.: Virtual application of Darul Arif Palace from Serdang Sultanate using virtual reality. J. Phys. Conf. Ser. **801**(1), 012009 (2017)

Computer Graphics

Differential G-Buffer Rendering for Mediated Reality Applications

Tobias Schwandt$^{(\boxtimes)}$ and Wolfgang Broll

Ilmenau University of Technology, Ilmenau, Germany
{tobias.schwandt,wolfgang.broll}@tu-ilmenau.de

Abstract. Physically-based approaches are increasingly used in a wide field of computer graphics. By that, modern graphic engines can provide a realistic output using physical correct values instead of an analytical approximation. Such applications apply the final lighting on a geometry buffer to reduce the complexity. Using this approach for Mediated Reality applications, some changes have to be made in order to fuse the real with the virtual world. In this paper, we present an approach with a focusing on the extraction of real world environment information and saving them directly to the geometry buffer. Therefore, we introduce a solution using spatial geometry to integrate the real world into the virtual environment. Hereby, the approach is usable in real-time and allows for visual interaction between virtual and real world objects. Moreover, a manipulation of the real world is easily possible.

Keywords: Mediated reality · Mixed reality · Augmented reality · Differential rendering · Physically based rendering

1 Introduction

Mediated Reality [24,25], especially the subset Mixed Reality (MR) and Augmented Reality (AR), are fast growing technologies that have already started to enhance our daily life. As previous work in research as well as in industry has shown, they have the potential to be used in a huge range of different application areas, including, but not limited to medicine, education, and entertainment. Applications in these areas share three key challenges: 1. the objects should be tracked properly, 2. the objects' geometry has to be seamlessly integrated into the world, and 3. the illumination of the objects has to be as real as possible. Therefore, modern graphic pipelines take use of Physically Based Rendering (PBR) [1,15]. Thus, virtual objects are rendered by using real world metrics like smoothness, and reflectance for a material, or photometric values for light sources rather than analytical approximation.

In order to achieve a realistic illumination inside a Mediated Reality application, a correct photometric registration is required. This can be achieved by using Differential Rendering (DR) [3]. Hereby, the lighting has to be calculated twice, one time for the virtual content including the world approximation and a

© Springer International Publishing AG 2017
L.T. De Paolis et al. (Eds.): AVR 2017, Part II, LNCS 10325, pp. 337–349, 2017.
DOI: 10.1007/978-3-319-60928-7_30

second time for the approximation only. Finally, the result is combined with the current image stream. However, using PBR, such approach so far could not be applied in real-time because of the high complexity of lighting equations.

In this paper, we present an approach for extracting data from the real world and save this data as a virtual object inside the geometry buffer. By this, our approach achieves a plausible and realistic lighting of the virtual as well as the real world without additional lighting calculations. Moreover, by using the geometry, we can enroll some effects inside the real environment that wouldn't be possible in a traditional AR or MR approach. Our approach does not need any extra draw calls for lighting, shadowing, indirect lighting, tone mapping, and post effects. Therefore, our approach allows for applying physically-based manipulation of light and geometry to Mediated Reality applications in real-time.

In Sect. 2 we will investigate into previous work in the areas of DR and PBR, whereas Sect. 3 we will introduce our approach regarding the structure and the generation of the G-Buffer. We will present our lighting mechanism in Sect. 4, before showing results from different scenarios in Sect. 5. Results and limitations of our approach are discussed in Sect. 6 before we finally conclude and take a look into future work in Sect. 7.

2   Related Work

In this section, we will review previous work in the area of Differential Rendering with a focus on lighting and Physically Based Rendering. DR originally was developed by Fournier et al. for augmenting photographs by virtual content applying the correct lighting [4].

Paul Debevec presented a first AR application showing a real world scene with a plausible light interaction between real and virtual objects [3]. The illumination of the real scene was made by capturing reflections from a mirroring sphere. A corresponding shadow cast from a virtual object onto the real surface was calculated by using DR. Two global lighting results are generated: 1. the illumination of the real and virtual world, and 2. the illumination of the real world depending on the virtual light sources. Depending on the number of light sources calculations may become quite complex, especially when using PBR. Finally, the result is a combination of both preliminary results. The result of the real world lighting is subtracted from the real and virtual world output. In combination with current image stream, the result is a real world setup with virtual objects including the lighting.

Gibson and Murta presented an approach using DR for a far-field illumination [8]. The implementation was completely done on the GPU. Hereby, real-time capability could be achieved, making the approach widely usable. Later, the approach was further developed by Gibson et al. for a constant near-field illumination [7]. Therefore, a combination of point light sources and an irradiance volume is needed.

So far, this approach was used for DR in many cases. Especially as basis for several global illumination approaches such as instant radiosity [16–18], progressive path tracing [14], and light propagation volumes [5,6].

Knecht et al. showed a method for a "single-pass" DR [16–18]. This approach also needs two buffers that are generated at runtime. Both buffers are subtracted from each other and finally combined with the camera image. The lighting has to be done for every buffer which makes the performance very low especially in the case of many lights.

Gruber, Richter-Trummer and Schmalstieg presented an approach for DR based on a voxel structure [9,10]. Reciprocating shadows between real and virtual world can be achieved just by a transformation of the real world into a voxel-based structure. Due to the rather coarse structure of the voxels, the approach does not allow for high-quality output. By using pre-defined geometry this limitation can be overcome.

Other approaches for the presentation of Mediated Reality scenes make use of one of the previously mentioned methods. They are used for realizing indirect lighting [20–22], photo-realistic illumination on mobile devices [29,30], and reflections on mirror-like surfaces on virtual objects [32].

3 Creation of the G-Buffer

To deal with many virtual objects at once, a simplification of the lighting calculation is required. In this section, we take a closer look on the G-Buffer – especially its structure in order to save material and geometry information.

The G-Buffer is used to store all the information of the geometry including the material that is visible from the current camera. Traditionally the G-Buffer provides information of the: 1. albedo color, 2. normal and 3. depth of the object. Depending on the graphics engine some extra information may be stored. However, in when using PBR further information for storing the objects in the buffer is required [1,15,19]. In our case, we use a G-Buffer structure similar to the Frostbite engine [19]. The G-Buffer is divided into three RGBA8 buffers with information of: 1. albedo color, 2. normal, 3. roughness, 4. reflectance color $f0$, 5. Ambient Occlusion (AO) of the object, and 6. an ID that can be used to distinguish between reconstructed and virtual objects. Figure 1 provides some details regarding the structure of the information in the G-Buffer.

The reflectance albedo is the final result depending on the metalness of the object. As provided in [19], the reflectance color and albedo color can be computed by considering the base color and the metalness of the objects. Equation (1) shows the calculation of the albedo value and Eq. (2) shows the calculation of the reflectance term. With R as reflectance value, M as metalness and C as base color of the material.

$$A = C * (1 - M) \tag{1}$$

$$f0 = 0.16 * R^2 * (1 - M) + C * M \tag{2}$$

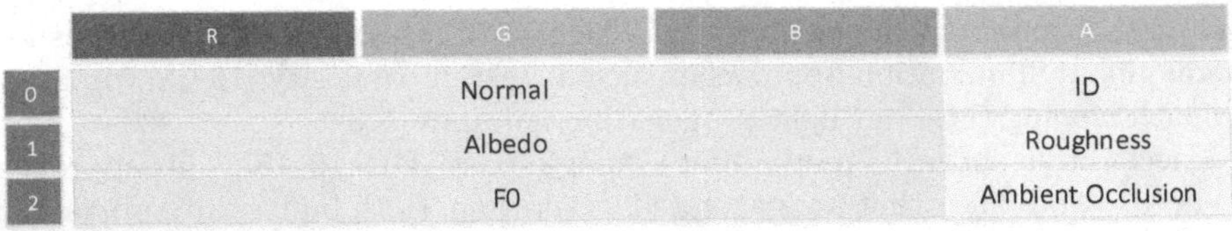

	R	G	B	A
0		Normal		ID
1		Albedo		Roughness
2		F0		Ambient Occlusion

Fig. 1. The structure of the G-Buffer is based on a two-color deferred base material layout as used by Frostbite [19]. $f0$ can be computed while filling the G-Buffer based on the material information metalness and reflectance. The roughness/smoothness is saved for further calculations.

The extraction of the information of the real world is the next step during the G-Buffer pass. Based on the approach by Gruber, Richter-Trummer and Schmalstieg [9,10], this approach takes each pixel in screen-space and interprets it as a voxel inside the scene. This high-quality voxel structure is defined by manually arranged geometry. Therefore, it is possible to fill in correct and well-defined data inside the G-Buffer. The data that will be stored in the buffer has no information about the color but is defined by an assigned material. In general, this material information is a combination of metalness, reflectance, roughness/smoothness, and a base color. Finally, the material information, the geometry, and the current image stream are combined and stored in the G-Buffer.

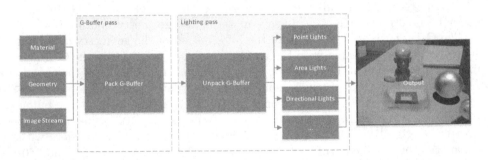

Fig. 2. This figure represents the pipeline. In general, material and geometry information are provided to the G-Buffer. In the case of a reconstruction of the real world, the image stream of the application is additionally uploaded. The screen-space color of the image stream is used as the albedo color of the material and is then multiplied with the color of the material.

Figure 2 shows the structure of the pipeline. It is possible to define multiple geometry entities with individual material information. The defined geometry is used as input data to fill the G-Buffer. Normal and depth are given by the geometry of the object. Metalness and reflectance are given by the material information. The albedo color is a multiplication of the material color and the image stream. The image stream is linearly sampled in screen-space. The calculation of

$f0$ depends on the albedo color, metalness, and reflectance. No special adoption of the equation is necessary.

The construction phase of the "Differential G-Buffer" is done by using the default G-Buffer pass of the pipeline. In addition to the material and geometry, the current image stream from a webcam is uploaded to the graphics card. Based on this information, for each pixel in screen-space, the G-Buffer is filled with the required data. In Listing 1.1 an excerpt of the shader code to pack and store the data is shown.

Listing 1.1. Creation of the G-Buffer to represent the real geometry in the virtual world.

```
void PackGBuffer(vec3 C, vec3 N, float S, vec3 R, float M,
         out SGBuffer Out)
{
    vec3 A  = C * (1 - M);
    vec3 F0 = C * M + 0.16 * R * R * (1 - M);

    Out.m_C0 = vec4(N , ID);
    Out.m_C1 = vec4(A , S);
    Out.m_C2 = vec4(F0, AO);
}

void main(void)
{
    vec3 C = FETCH_STREAM(fs_BackgroundColor, TexCoord);

    SGBuffer GBuffer;

    PackGBuffer (...);
}
```

Any non-transparent object inside the scene can be saved in the G-Buffer. Depending on the material and geometry information, the G-Buffer is filled with the given parameter. After every geometry is stored in the buffer, the lighting pass can use this data to calculate the illumination. Transparent objects are calculated by using a forward rendering pass after the lighting pass.

4 Lighting

Applying the G-Buffer, the virtual scene may be illuminated in a single lighting pass (see Fig. 2). The result of the lighting pass is stored into one RGBA16F render target. Since the entire light calculation uses floating-point numbers, this enables us to use High Dynamic Range (HDR) within the final virtual scene. High Dynamic Range is needed in order to be able to properly represent extreme physical values with respect to the defined light sources. High dynamic range values can be handled by building a histogram. An exposure value is computed. Finally, a tone mapping step converts the HDR values to the color space of the screen by using the exposure value.

4.1 Light Sources

Various types of light sources are supported which may be placed inside the virtual scene conventionally. Since the real geometry is transferred to the virtual world, illumination can be done without special attention to the real world. Therefore, point light sources, directional lights, spot lights, light probes, and area lights can be included in the light pass without extra draw calls, extra lighting calculations, or an extra lighting buffer. In Fig. 3 a basic lighting with a directional light from the top of the scene is shown. On the left side of the image, a graph shows the dependency of the resulting Bidirectional Reflection Distribution Function (BRDF) from the view angle. The right side of the image is the final result of a virtual non-metal sphere inside a MR application.

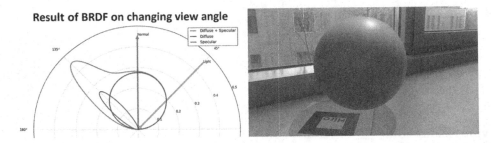

Fig. 3. This scene shows a default lighting when using a directional light. On the left side, a graph shows the result of the BRDF with changing view angle over the hemisphere. In this example the light vector is 45° and the normal is perpendicular to the surface. Material values are: roughness 0.4, reflectance, 0.6, metalness: 0.0. On the right side, the final result of a sphere with a shadow on the surface is shown.

To achieve a good lighting quality, the virtual light sources have to be good approximations of the real world light sources. Under such condition a realistic illumination of the scene and the objects involved can be achieved. The light sources illuminate the geometry of the G-Buffer and accumulate the result in the light buffer. After this, a histogram is generated according to the light values inside the light buffer. The values are converted into the color-space of the screen by considering a global exposure value in the final tone mapping. In order to achieve an even more realistic output, a local histogram and tone mapping should be considered. However, a global tone mapping seems to be sufficient in most cases.

4.2 Shadowing

Shadow calculation for the integrated light sources is possible without any extra calculations. The approximated real geometry is inserted into the shadow pass as an additional object. By rendering the geometry from the point of view of the virtual light source the real world information can be considered. Because of the view of the light source, the color information from the image stream can't be used. As a fallback solution, the color value defined in the material can be applied. That is important in the case of indirect lighting with a Reflective Shadow Map (RSM) [2]. However, the generated shadow map contains the geometry information of the real world and can be used within the lighting pass. By that, a correct shading of the virtual objects on the real geometry can be achieved automatically. Moreover, the real world geometry may also cast a shadow on virtual objects. As already stated, in addition to the shadow map, the pass can be used for indirect lighting by rendering a RSM. Shadows, indirect light, caustics, and striking light features were created in a correct way without extra or multiple draw calls. Hereby, a photometric registration of the virtual objects in the real scene is done automatically by using the pre-defined geometry and material definition.

5   Results

The following figures show various scenarios applying individual light sources and geometry information inside the G-Buffer. The general illumination of the scene is based on Schwandt and Broll [32]. They used a reconstructed global light probe sampled from the current camera image.

5.1   Scenarios

Point Lights. A point light source is a basic light source, which has a major influence on the final scene. In the first scenario, the surface of the desk is approximated by a plane provided with material properties corresponding to the real world material. Moreover, a tablet computer is placed inside the scene with virtual geometry and related material information. The point light illuminates the virtual and real scene in the same way, whereby the specular information of the point light is different depending on the material information. In Fig. 4, the scenario is depicted and shows the desired effect.

Directional Light. A directional light can be used for a more sophisticated lighting of the scene. In Fig. 5 a plane is used to represent the wooden table and desk. Moreover, a direction light is facing the scene and illuminates the virtual objects. On the left side of the image, it is clearly visible that the shadow of the book is casting on the blue plastic "Chinese Dragon". On the right side, the ball is properly illuminated within the scene, casting a correct shadow on the surface.

Area Lights. In Fig. 6 the reflections of the area light are displayed correctly on a smooth, reflective surface. The reflection of the area light on the surface of the tablet computer is based on using different planes with a smooth, non-metallic, and reflective material. Similar to the point light, the area light shows different reflection types on the surface. Even where some information is shown on top of the display, the results are still plausible.

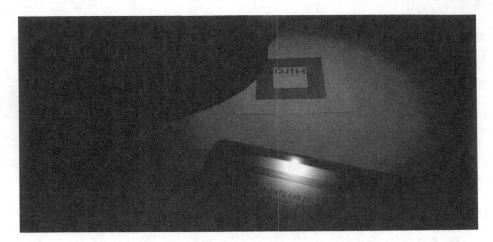

Fig. 4. This picture was made inside a closed room without any daylight. The only light is a point light source in the middle of the room. A virtual point light source is placed in the scene and shows different specular reflections on the surface of the tablet computer depending on the individual material properties.

Fig. 5. Based on the directional light, a correct shadow is shown inside the scene. On the left side, a book casts a shadow onto the Stanford dragon. On the right side, the directional light represents the sun and the shadow is casted onto the wooden surface. (Color figure online)

Fig. 6. The left side shows the results with the area light turned off, while the right side shows the same scene with an active area light. Area lights are implemented according to Heitz, Dupuy, Hill and Neubelt [12].

Manipulation. As previously explained, real world surfaces are approximated by virtual geometry and material information. Hereby, it is possible to add virtual objects inside the scene which has a different geometry from the real surface. Doing so, a manipulation of the real world may be applied, allowing for a variety of effects. Indentations, elevations, and even abstract geometry may be used for the manipulation of the real world. Figure 7 shows the effect of non-realistic geometry. Inside the scene, a rock-like object is used as real world approximation. The figure depicts that the look of the desk has changed depending on the surface information. Moreover, the result is correctly shaded and consists of the physical behavior of the object. By that, a manipulation of the Mediated Reality output can be achieved easily.

Fig. 7. A manipulation of the surface can be achieved by using non-realistic geometry information instead of plausible data. This can replace the real world inside the Mediated Reality application. Thus, as shown in this figure, elevations can be generated in the table which should not actually be there.

5.2   Rendering

The hardware configuration used for testing was a desktop PC with an Intel Core i7 3770, Nvidia GeForce 670GTX, and 8GB DDR3 RAM. A self-developed in-house graphics engine "Saltwater" has been used to render the scenarios. The engine is based on C++ with OpenGL 4.5 and uses PBR to display virtual environments. As post effect Screen Space Reflections (SSR), Screen-Space Ambient Occlusion (SSAO), and Subpixel Morphological Antialiasing (SMAA) are activated. Tracking is done via ARToolKit using a Logitech c920 webcam. The frame rate of all recordings is above 60 FPS @ 1280 × 720 pixel. All shown results are rendered for a monoscopic display. Using this approach within a stereoscopic system should not affect the final performance. In the case of a 3D projection, the pre-defined geometry has to be rendered as often as other objects (once per eye). Afterwards, the lighting can be done in a traditional way.

6   Discussion and Limitations

Using our "Differential G-Buffer" provides a great potential for enhancing the visual output in Mediated Reality scenarios and in particular for MR and AR applications. By a minimal adjustment of the rendering pipeline, an integration of virtual content into the real environment is possible and allows for the utilization of physically-based virtual light sources. Hence, calculations of indirect light, shadows, caustics, and other light properties is significantly simplified and can be mutually computed for the real and the virtual environment. Our approach avoids the drawbacks of a traditional DR approach where multiple draw calls in the lighting pass are required. At the same time, our approach may be used to manipulate certain aspects of the real environment. By that, it is possible to assign physical properties to real world objects and surfaces not existing in the actual real environment.

While our approach allows for some quite convincing results, some limitations were encountered. The effort for manual post-processing and scene setup is still pretty high and should be reduced or entirely replaced by automatic approaches. Applying our "Differential G-Buffer" allows for a correct representation of virtual light sources, geometry and material according to the real environment. However, the virtual environment must be adequately prepared to leave the impression of a seamless integration into the virtual environment. This problem might be reduced by more sophisticated approaches for the extraction of material properties or detection of real light sources from a camera image. A geometric extraction of objects could be done by using Simultaneous Localization and Mapping (SLAM) based techniques [11,27,31]. The problem of manual adjustment of light sources might be reduced by using an image-based light source detection from the current camera image [9,13,23,26,28]. Some of these approaches allow simultaneously the extraction of material properties. Another problem is the double shadowing of real world objects because they cast a shadow onto an already existing shadow. The final shadow is darker than it should be. Therefore, real world shadows have to be considered during the lighting pass. This can be done by the – until now – unused ID inside the G-Buffer. Besides, the problem seems to be negligible because it does not affect the final output.

7   Conclusion and Future Work

In this paper, we presented our approach for realizing Differential Rendering not only for AR and MR, but even for Mediated Reality application. This approach uses the G-Buffer for saving real and virtual world data in order to achieve plausible mutual lighting and reflections between the real and the virtual environment. To save the real world data into the G-Buffer, a proper geometry and material information is needed. Therefore, we manually place elements inside the scene and use them for generation of the buffer. This "Differential G-Buffer" represents the data of both worlds with information about normal, reflectance, albedo color, roughness/smoothness, and ambient occlusion. Inside the lighting pass, this information is used to visualize several physically-based lighting effects such as specular and diffuse reflections. Moreover, the approach allows us to support shadowing. It supports casting shadows from real world geometry onto virtual objects and vise-versa. Saved geometry inside the geometry buffer can be different from the real world and provide a manipulation of the look-and-feel of the environment.

In our future work, we will investigate into a more sophisticated reconstruction of the real world environment by using SLAM based techniques and material estimation to overcome any additional manual adjustment. Moreover, we would like to integrate the information into a voxel-based structure and reuse already detected information. In addition, a light estimation shall be implemented to automatically extract important global lighting information and light sources.

References

1. Burley, B.: Practical physically based shading in film and game production. In: Physically-based shading at disney, part of ACM SIGGRAPH 2012 Course (2012)
2. Dachsbacher, C., Stamminger, M.: Reflective shadow maps. In: Proceedings of the 2005 Symposium on Interactive 3D Graphics and Games, pp. 203–231 (2005)
3. Debevec, P.: Rendering synthetic objects into real scenes. In: Proceedings of the 25th Annual Conference on Computer Graphics and Interactive Techniques - SIGGRAPH 1998, pp. 189–198. Association for Computing Machinery (ACM) (1998). http://dx.doi.org/10.1145/280814.280864
4. Fournier, A., Gunawan, A.S., Romanzin, C.: Common illumination between real and computer generated scenes. Technical report Vancouver, BC, Canada (1992)
5. Franke, T.A.: Delta light propagation volumes for mixed reality. In: 2013 IEEE International Symposium on Mixed and Augmented Reality (ISMAR), pp. 125–132. Institute of Electrical and Electronics Engineers (IEEE), October 2013. http://dx.doi.org/10.1109/ISMAR.2013.6671772
6. Franke, T.A.: Delta voxel cone tracing. In: 2014 IEEE International Symposium on Mixed and Augmented Reality (ISMAR), pp. 39–44. Institute of Electrical and Electronics Engineers (IEEE), September 2014. http://dx.doi.org/10.1109/ISMAR.2014.6948407
7. Gibson, S., Cook, J., Howard, T., Hubbold, R.: Rapid Shadow Generation in Real-World Lighting Environments. In: Dutre, P., Suykens, F., Christensen, P.H., Cohen-Or, D. (eds.) Eurographics Workshop on Rendering. The Eurographics Association (2003)
8. Gibson, S., Murta, A.: Interactive rendering with real-world Illumination. In: Pèroche, B., Rushmeier, H. (eds.) Rendering Techniques. Eurographics Workshop on Rendering, pp. 365–376. Springer, Vienna (2000). https://doi.org/10.1007%2F978-3-7091-6303-0_33
9. Gruber, L., Richter-Trummer, T., Schmalstieg, D.: Real-time photometric registration from arbitrary geometry. In: 2012 IEEE International Symposium on Mixed and Augmented Reality (ISMAR), pp. 119–128. Institute of Electrical and Electronics Engineers (IEEE), November 2012. http://dx.doi.org/10.1109/ISMAR.2012.6402548

10. Gruber, L., Ventura, J., Schmalstieg, D.: Image-space illumination for augmented reality in dynamic environments. In: 2015 IEEE Virtual Reality (VR), pp. 127–134. Institute of Electrical and Electronics Engineers (IEEE), March 2015. http://dx. doi.org/10.1109/VR.2015.7223334

11. Han, Y., Lee, J.Y., Kweon, I.S.: High quality shape from a single RGB-D image under uncalibrated natural illumination. In: 2013 IEEE International Conference on Computer Vision, pp. 1617–1624. Institute of Electrical and Electronics Engineers (IEEE), December 2013. http://dx.doi.org/10.1109/ICCV.2013.204

12. Heitz, E., Dupuy, J., Hill, S., Neubelt, D.: Real-time polygonal-light shading with linearly transformed cosines. ACM Trans. Graph. **35**(4), 41:1–41:8 (2016). http://doi.acm.org/10.1145/2897824.2925895

13. Jachnik, J., Newcombe, R.A., Davison, A.J.: Real-time surface light-field capture for augmentation of planar specular surfaces. In: 2012 IEEE International Symposium on Mixed and Augmented Reality (ISMAR), pp. 91–97. Institute of Electrical and Electronics Engineers (IEEE), November 2012. http://dx.doi.org/10.1109/ISMAR.2012.6402544

14. Kán, P., Kaufmann, H.: Differential progressive path tracing for high-quality previsualization and relighting in augmented reality. In: Bebis, G., Boyle, R., Parvin, B., Koracin, D., Li, B., Porikli, F., Zordan, V., Klosowski, J., Coquillart, S., Luo, X., Chen, M., Gotz, D. (eds.) ISVC 2013. LNCS, vol. 8034, pp. 328–338. Springer, Heidelberg (2013). doi:10.1007/978-3-642-41939-3_32

15. Karis, B.: Real shading in unreal engine 4. In: ACM SIGGRAPH 2013 Course: Physically Based Shading in Theory and Practice (2013)

16. Knecht, M., Traxler, C., Mattausch, O., Purgathofer, W., Wimmer, M.: Differential instant radiosity for mixed reality. In: 2010 IEEE International Symposium on Mixed and Augmented Reality. Institute of Electrical and Electronics Engineers (IEEE), October 2010. https://doi.org/10.1109/ISMAR.2010.5643556

17. Knecht, M., Traxler, C., Mattausch, O., Wimmer, M.: Reciprocal shading for mixed reality. Comput. Graph. **36**(7), 846–856 (2012). http://dx.doi.org/10.1016/j.cag.2012.04.013

18. Knecht, M., Traxler, C., Winklhofer, C., Wimmer, M.: Reflective and refractive objects for mixed reality. IEEE Trans. Visual. Comput. Graph. **19**(4), 576–582 (2013). http://doi.acm.org/10.1145/2897824.2925895

19. Lagarde, S., Rousiers, C.D.: Moving frostbite to physically based rendering. In: ACM SIGGRAPH 2014 Course: Physically Based Shading in Theory and Practice (2014)

20. Lensing, P., Broll, W.: Fusing the real and the virtual: a depth-camera based approach to mixed reality. In: 2011 IEEE International Symposium on Mixed and Augmented Reality (ISMAR), pp. 261–262. Institute of Electrical and Electronics Engineers (IEEE), October 2011. http://dx.doi.org/10.1109/ISMAR.2011.6143892

21. Lensing, P., Broll, W.: Instant indirect illumination for dynamic mixed reality scenes. In: 2012 IEEE International Symposium on Mixed and Augmented Reality (ISMAR), pp. 109–118. Institute of Electrical and Electronics Engineers (IEEE), November 2012. http://dx.doi.org/10.1109/ISMAR.2012.6402547

22. Lensing, P., Broll, W.: LightSkin: Real-time global illumination for virtual and mixed reality. In: Proceedings of Joint Virtual Reality Conference of EGVE - EuroVR, pp. 17–24. The Eurographics Association (2013). http://dx.doi.org/10.2312/EGVE.JVRC13.017-024

23. Lombardi, S., Nishino, K.: Reflectance and natural illumination from a single image. In: Fitzgibbon, A., Lazebnik, S., Perona, P., Sato, Y., Schmid, C. (eds.) ECCV 2012. LNCS, vol. 7577, pp. 582–595. Springer, Heidelberg (2012). doi:10. 1007/978-3-642-33783-3_42

24. Mann, S.: Mediated Reality. Technical report 260, M.I.T. Media Lab Perceptual Computing Section, Cambridge, Massachusetts (1994)

25. Mann, S.: Mediated reality. Linux J. **1999**(59es), 5 (1999). http://dl.acm.org/citation.cfm?id=327697.327702

26. Morgand, A., Tamaazousti, M., Bartoli, A.: An empirical model for specularity prediction with application to dynamic retexturing. In: 2016 IEEE International Symposium on Mixed and Augmented Reality (ISMAR), pp. 44–53. Institute of Electrical and Electronics Engineers (IEEE), September 2016. http://doi.org/10. 1109/ISMAR.2016.13

27. Newcombe, R.A., Fox, D., Seitz, S.M.: DynamicFusion: reconstruction and tracking of non-rigid scenes in real-time. In: 2015 IEEE Conference on Computer Vision and Pattern Recognition (CVPR), pp. 343–352. Institute of Electrical and Electronics Engineers (IEEE), June 2015. http://dx.doi.org/10.1109/CVPR.2015.7298631

28. Richter-Trummer, T., Kalkofen, D., Park, J., Schmalstieg, D.: Instant mixed reality lighting from casual scanning. In: 2016 IEEE International Symposium on Mixed and Augmented Reality (ISMAR), pp. 27–36. Institute of Electrical and Electronics Engineers (IEEE), September 2016. http://doi.org/10.1109/ISMAR.2016.18

29. Rohmer, K., Buschel, W., Dachselt, R., Grosch, T.: Interactive near-field illumination for photorealistic augmented reality on mobile devices. In: 2014 IEEE International Symposium on Mixed and Augmented Reality (ISMAR), pp. 29–38. Institute of Electrical and Electronics Engineers (IEEE), September 2014. http:// dx.doi.org/10.1109/ISMAR.2014.6948406

30. Rohmer, K., Grosch, T.: Tiled frustum culling for differential rendering on mobile devices. In: 2015 IEEE International Symposium on Mixed and Augmented Reality (ISMAR), pp. 37–42. Institute of Electrical and Electronics Engineers (IEEE), September 2015. http://dx.doi.org/10.1109/ISMAR.2015.13

31. Salas-Moreno, R.F., Glocken, B., Kelly, P.H.J., Davison, A.J.: Dense planar SLAM. In: 2014 IEEE International Symposium on Mixed and Augmented Reality (ISMAR), pp. 157–164. Institute of Electrical and Electronics Engineers (IEEE), September 2014. http://dx.doi.org/10.1109/ISMAR.2014.6948422

32. Schwandt, T., Broll, W.: A single camera image based approach for glossy reflections in mixed reality applications. In: 2016 IEEE International Symposium on Mixed and Augmented Reality (ISMAR), pp. 37–43. Institute of Electrical and Electronics Engineers (IEEE), September 2016. http://doi.org/10.1109/ISMAR. 2016.12

Solid Angle Based Ambient Obscurance in Image Space

Dario Scarpa[1] and Ugo Erra[2](✉)

[1] SpinVector, Benevento, Italy
darioscarpa@gmail.com
[2] Dipartimento di Matematica, Informatica ed Economia,
Università degli Studi della Basilicata, Potenza, Italy
ugo.erra@unibas.it

Abstract. We derive a new approximation of ambient obscurance to improve the quality of state-of-the-art techniques used in real-time rendering. We attempt to stay close to the original definition of ambient obscurance and, while building on the deferred rendering approach, bring into image-space information that is suitable for accurate estimations of visibility that take account of the position and orientation of near occluding geometry. The approach is based on the approximation of a covered solid angle, considering the area of surfaces, and hemisphere partitioning that gives directional information about coverage, both done in image space. The immediate advantage of our technique is that we avoid over-occlusion caused by multiple occluders covering each other but covering from the same direction. In some cases our implementation achieves lower performance with respect to some currently popular and widely adopted screen-space ambient obscurance approximations, but still obtains real-time frame rates on the current generation of hardware.

Keywords: Ambient Obscurance · Screen-space · Hemisphere partitioning

1 Introduction

Shadowing of ambient light is called ambient occlusion. It has been shown in [8] that ambient occlusion offers a better perception of the 3D shape of displayed objects, and its effectiveness is evident in its popularity in videogame engines [11]. The mathematical definition of ambient occlusion is related to the concept of the solid angle. In fact, the occlusion $A_\mathbf{p}$ at a point $\mathbf{p}$ on a surface with normal $\mathbf{n}$ can be computed by integrating the visibility function over the hemisphere Ω with respect to the projected solid angle:

$$A_\mathbf{p} = \frac{1}{\pi} \int_\Omega V_{\mathbf{p},\omega}(\mathbf{n} \cdot \omega) \, d\omega \tag{1}$$

where $V_{\mathbf{p},\omega}$ is the visibility function at $\mathbf{p}$ along a direction ω. A simple method to approximate this integral in practice, in off-line rendering, is based on ray-tracing. Rays are shot in a uniform pattern across the hemisphere over point

© Springer International Publishing AG 2017
L.T. De Paolis et al. (Eds.): AVR 2017, Part II, LNCS 10325, pp. 350–368, 2017.
DOI: 10.1007/978-3-319-60928-7_31

p, and an occlusion value can be calculated as the number of rays that hit the geometry divided by the total number of rays shot. Rays can be restricted to a certain length, avoiding distant geometry to be taken into account while calculating the occlusion value. This is fundamental in closed environments, which would otherwise result in total occlusion at every point and subsequently the complete removal of ambient light.

Ambient Obscurance (AO) is an extension of ambient occlusion defined in [20]. A falloff function that reduces the influence of occlusion with distance is introduced in the formula:

$$AO_{\mathbf{p}} = \frac{1}{\pi} \int_{\Omega} \rho(D_{\mathbf{p},\omega})(\mathbf{n} \cdot \omega) \, d\omega \qquad (2)$$

Comparing this expression with the formula of ambient occlusion, in place of the binary visibility function $V_{\mathbf{p},\omega}$ we have the function $\rho(D_{\mathbf{p},\omega})$, where $D_{\mathbf{p},\omega}$ is the distance between **p** and the first intersection point along ω. If there are no intersections along ω, its value is $+\infty$. Here, ρ is the decreasing falloff function, with $\rho(0) = 1$ and $\rho(x) = 0$ if $x > r$, where r is the maximum distance at which any intersecting geometry is considered as producing occlusion.

In this paper, we derive a new approximation of ambient obscurance focused on improving the quality of state-of-the-art techniques used in real-time rendering. Our approach is called Solid-angle Screen Space Ambient Obscurance (SaSSAO). We attempt to remain close to the original definition of ambient obscurance and, while building on the deferred rendering approach, bring into image-space information that is suitable to an accurate estimate of visibility that takes account of the position and orientation of near occluding geometry. The main idea is to track the amount of occlusion from the set of directions. This approach handles the over-occlusion that results from the same directions where thin objects are stacked. To the best of our knowledge, the approximation of a covered solid angle (used in our occlusion estimate) considering the area of surfaces, and the hemisphere partitioning that gives directional information about coverage, both done in image space, are original contributions to the field.

To evaluate the quality of results, we compare screen-shots from our implementation with images rendered off-line in Blender, a popular open-source 3D graphics software that features a configurable ray-traced calculation of ambient occlusion. For the comparison, we use the Structural Similarity Index [19], a metric that attempts to measure similarity between images in a way that is consistent with human eye perception. In some cases our implementation achieves lower performances with respect to some currently popular and widely adopted screen-space ambient obscurance (SSAO) approximations, but still obtains real-time frame rates on the current hardware generation. Moreover, it offers many parameters that can be adjusted to trade quality for efficiency.

2   Related Works

Real-time global illumination is a "hot topic" in computer graphics research, and an impressive number of related works have been published. The 2012 survey [14] provides a general overview of the field, and works about ambient occlusion offer further insights. Here, we restrict the scope to techniques most closely related to our own: ambient occlusion/obscurance approximations suitable to real-time rendering that operate in image space (also called screen space).

Even considering only this category of algorithms, a variety of approaches exist. Some sources attempt to correlate, compare and evaluate such techniques, and the interested reader may like to consult [1,6], two recent theses that both agree that the Alchemy algorithm is the current state of the art. In the following sections, we briefly cover the more influential works.

In his seminal work [3], Micheal Bunnell of NVIDIA corporation describes a technique that approximates polygon meshes as a set of surface elements (discs) that can emit, transmit, or reflect light and that can shadow each other. He defines an approximation of ambient occlusion on the basis of the calculated coverage between discs, and an approximation of indirect lighting by estimating the disc-to-disc radiance transfer. Major drawbacks of this algorithm are the dependence on scene complexity and the need to preprocess geometry, which must be well tessellated to give good results. This also implies that the technique is not suitable for deformable objects. Note that this is not an image-space technique, but a geometry approximation one. Nevertheless, we mention it because it has to some extent inspired subsequent works, including our own.

In [16] Shanmugam and Arikan approximate ambient occlusion through spherical proxies. Their interesting idea is to reconstruct approximately the surface represented by a pixel using a sphere in world-space that roughly projects to that pixel on the screen. By using deferred rendering, a ND -buffer storing normals and depths is created. From this information, each pixel can be mapped to a sample of some surface in world-space, which can be considered as an occluder to other pixels. The algorithm also uses a separate calculation (non-screen space) for low-frequency occlusion due to distant occluders, and then combines the results. Despite its original and interesting ideas, this technique is perhaps over-complicated and had little success and was subsequently surpassed in both quality and speed by simpler techniques.

In [11] the denomination "screen-space ambient occlusion" appears for the first time. In its CryEngine, Crytek implements this technique, which works by sampling the surroundings of a pixel and, on the basis of the z-buffer, performs depth comparisons. Sample positions are distributed in a sphere around the pixel, and some randomness is introduced by reflecting position vectors on a random plane passing through the sphere origin. The occlusion factor depends only on the depth difference between sampled points and the current point. This, combined with the simple distribution of samples (around a sphere and not a hemisphere) causes some over-darkening: even flat, non-occluded areas result in some samples considered as occluders.

Some improvements over the CryEngine approach are shown in [5]. Samples are offset in 3D space from the current point being computed, and then projected back to screen space to sample the depth of the sample location. Normals (this algorithm is also based on deferred rendering) are used to flip the vectors that fall in the hemisphere below the current point, avoiding the self-occlusion exhibited by the Crytek algorithm. An occlusion function maps the relationship between the depth delta and the amount of occlusion. A number of details are taken care of (sample randomization, filtering, down-sampled calculation) to improve performance and to obtain a production-ready solution.

The method in [2] interprets the depth buffer as a height field and works by performing a type of ray marching in screen space. It considers the tallest occluder along each azimuthal direction to determine the visible horizon on the hemisphere around the current point. This assumes a continuous depth buffer, so the occlusion does not take into account the unoccluded portion of hemisphere in case of floating occluders. Subsequent refinements of the method have been published, but the method remains expensive in relation to the quality it produces.

The Alchemy SSAO algorithm, presented in [10], has been developed with the goal of artistic expressiveness rather than physically grounded realism. The strength of Alchemy is in the way it derives its estimator: the chosen falloff function cancels some expensive operations while staying meaningful. The obtained highly efficient estimator is then applied to points sampled in the hemisphere, as in some previous methods. Alchemy features a number of artist-tweakable parameters and generally gives good quality results with high performance. Some improvements and modifications of the algorithm are discussed in [9].

3   Hemisphere Partitioning

To derive an approximation close to ambient obscurance into image space, we adopt a scheme to discretize the sphere into solid angles as proposed in [7]. Let us consider a unit sphere centred on the origin of Euclidean space. The origin divides each of the axes into two halves: a positive and a negative semi-axis. Let us refer to the slice of sphere delimited by the three positive semi-axes as the positive octant of the sphere (see Fig. 1).

Let us consider the $x + y + z = 1$ plane and the equilateral triangle that lies on it with vertices $\mathbf{v_0} = (1, 0, 0)$, $\mathbf{v_1} = (0, 1, 0)$, and $\mathbf{v_0} = (0, 0, 1)$.

We split each of the $\overline{\mathbf{v_0 v_1}}$, $\overline{\mathbf{v_0 v_2}}$, and $\overline{\mathbf{v_1 v_2}}$ edges into n equal units. For edge $\overline{\mathbf{v_0 v_1}}$, we connect subdivisions between the other two edges with line segments parallel to $\overline{\mathbf{v_0 v_1}}$. Then, we repeat the same process for the remaining two edges, obtaining a tessellation of the original triangle into n^2 triangles. The process is illustrated in Fig. 2.

If we project onto the surface of the sphere the vertices of this tessellation, by normalization we obtain a partition of the octant into spherical triangles. Each of these spherical triangles represents a solid angle ω, associated with the direction Θ_ω passing through the triangle centroid. Individual triangles are assigned unique identifiers, as shown in Fig. 2.

Given an arbitrary direction ϑ starting from the sphere's centre, we can identify the associated triangle in constant time by using the procedure illustrated

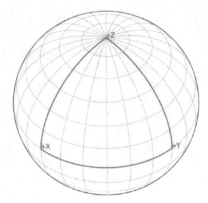

Fig. 1. The surface above the positive octant of a sphere.

in [7]. Then, from the unit vector along ϑ, the procedure takes as input its intersection point p_ϑ with the $x + y + z = 1$. We report the procedure for simplicity below.

Algorithm 1. getTriangle

---

procedure GETTRIANGLE(p_ϑ)

    $x = np_\vartheta$; $z = np_\vartheta$

    $x_i = \lfloor x \rfloor$; $z_i = \lfloor z \rfloor$

    $\xi_\vartheta = z_i(2n - z_i) + 2x_i$

    $diag = (x - x_i) + (z - z_i)$

    return $\xi'_\vartheta = \xi_\vartheta + \lfloor diag \rfloor$

For the ambient obscurance calculation, we are interested only in directions associated with the hemisphere "surrounding" the normal of the point, so we repeat the process for four octants, building a pyramid. We have shown how for n subdivisions we obtain n^2 triangles, so for four octants we obtain $4n^2$ total triangles. The triangle identifiers follow the pattern shown in Fig. 2, but with an additional offset added, depending on the slice of hemisphere to which they are related: for example, the third slice will have triangle identifiers ranging between $2n$ and $3n - 1$.

The solid angle covering the full hemisphere is 2π, so the solid angle associated with every "bucket" is

$$\omega = \frac{2\pi}{4n^2} \tag{3}$$

The algorithm to find the bucket associated with any direction vector is easily adapted: the signs of the vector coordinates indicate in which of the four octants of the hemisphere we have to look.

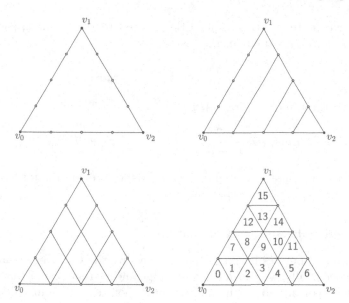

Fig. 2. Steps of triangle subdivision for $n = 4$. The last triangle has numeric identifiers for each individual triangles.

4   Solid-Angle-based Ambient Obscurance

On a higher level, our approach proceeds in three passes. In the first pass, the geometry shader computes an area value relative to each triangle processed, then forwards it to the fragment shader, which saves it in the G-buffer together with normals and depths. In the second pass, for each pixel, a fragment shader samples the G-buffer to calculate the ambient obscurance (AO). In the third pass, the AO-buffer is filtered to lower the noise caused by the sampling and used to modulate the ambient factor in the final compositing of the rendered image. In the following sections, we provide details of each pass.

4.1   Area Calculation

Whereas the vertex shader operates on a per-vertex level, the geometry shader can access whole primitives (in our implementation, we use only triangles). So, for each triangle, the camera space position of its vertices is used as a basis to compute an area that will later be used in the AO calculation. The main idea is to approximate triangle meshes as a set of circumscribed circles or of inscribed circles that will be used as occluders for calculating the AO for a given point.

Given a triangle in the camera space position, we calculate the lengths of its sides, a, b, and c. Then, by using the Heron formula, in which s is the semi-perimeter of the triangle, we can calculate the triangle area A_t:

$$A_t = \sqrt{s(s - a)(s - b)(s - c)} \tag{4}$$

We can calculate additional quantities related to the triangle, such as the area of the circumscribed circle A_{cct} as

$$radius_{cct} = \frac{abc}{4A_t} \Rightarrow A_{cct} = \pi \cdot radius_{cct}^2 \tag{5}$$

or the area of the inscribed circle A_{ict} as

$$radius_{ict} = \frac{2A_t}{(a+b+c)} \Rightarrow A_{ict} = \pi \cdot radius_{ict}^2 \tag{6}$$

Further area calculations are possible, and as we show in the following, these can be taken as a configurable parameter.

4.2 Ambient Obscurance Calculation

The second pass operates in image space, accessing the G-buffer created in the first pass. Specifically, we can retrieve some geometry-related information from the G-buffer according to a sampling pattern, then use it in our calculation of the ambient obscurance.

For a pixel p, at screen coordinates x_p and y_p, from the G-buffer we have the following data:

- d_p: the depth of the pixel p, from the z-buffer, normalized to $[0..1]$
- $\mathbf{n}_p$: the normal of the geometry surface at p
- $\mathbf{c}_p$: the camera space position of p
- a_p: the area related to the triangle to which p belongs, calculated as described in Sect. 4.1.

Selection of the screen-space positions to take samples for calculating the AO for point p is important. Basically, two categories of approaches are possible, both involving a radius around p, named $samplingRadius$, often scaled by d_p, which limits the distance samples can be taken. The flat sampling locates points around p, in a circle of radius $samplingRadius$, considering the 2D screen-space coordinates x_p and y_p. While the 3D sampling considers the hemisphere around $\mathbf{n}_p$ having radius $samplingRadius$ and takes points in the screen-space area delimited by this hemisphere.

Perspective projection introduces same complications when returning to camera space. Pixels selected with both approaches may result in useless samples, related to points outside the area considered in the AO calculation. Randomization is a crucial aspect of every sampling technique adopted. If we adhere to a static, regular pattern, some banding artefacts will appear in the calculated AO. By applying some form of randomization, we avoid such artefacts, at the price of some high-frequency noise that can be handled with filtering, as will be shown in Sect. 4.3. A simple way to introduce randomization is to use some form of rotation dependent on a random value derived from the pixel coordinates. In flat sampling, a kernel of points randomly placed around the centre p is rotated around p. While in 3D sampling, a kernel of vectors reaching random points in

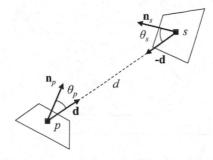

Fig. 3. The angles and vectors related to the solid-angle approximation between two pixels p and s.

the hemisphere is rotated by using the normal of point p as the rotation axis. In our experiment, we tested both approaches (including some variants) to evaluate the best option.

Solid-angle estimator. In [3], scene geometry is approximated with oriented discs considered as occluders to calculate per-vertex occlusion on the GPU. Our approach takes inspiration from this technique but brings it to the image-space domain.

Let us consider two pixels, p and s, which belong to two different triangles. We want to estimate the solid angle at pixel p that is covered by the surface to which the point s belongs. Figure 3 visualizes the involved entities.

Let $\mathbf{d} = \mathbf{c}_s - \mathbf{c}_p$ be the normalized vector from the camera space position of p to the camera space position of s, and let d the distance between $\mathbf{c}_s$ and $\mathbf{c}_p$. We also define θ_p as the angle formed by $\mathbf{d}$ and $\mathbf{n}_p$ and θ_s as the angle formed by $-\mathbf{d}$ and $\mathbf{n}_s$. A possible solid-angle approximation is

$$s_p = \frac{a_s \max(0, \mathbf{d} \cdot \mathbf{n}_p)}{d^2} \tag{7}$$

The key idea is that $\max(0, \mathbf{d} \cdot \mathbf{n}_p)$ decreases the impact of occluders that block only incident light at shallow angles (which is radiometrically correct). Conversely, multiplying by the area related to the occlusor surface modulates the contribution according to the dimensions of the surface.

If we want to also consider the orientation of the occlusor, we must introduce θ_s into the equation. Ideally, if we consider a disc of area a_s and oriented according to $\mathbf{n}_s$, its projected solid angle would be

$$\omega_s = \frac{a_s \cos \theta_s}{d^2} \tag{8}$$

This is based on the differential area being related to the differential solid angle (as viewed from point p) by

$$d\omega = \frac{dA \cos \theta}{r^2} \tag{9}$$

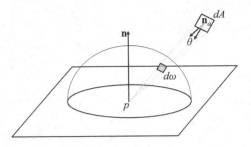

Fig. 4. Differential solid angle and differential area (image taken from [13]).

where θ is the angle between the surface normal of dA and the vector to p, and r is the distance from p to dA, as shown in Fig. 4.

This equation can be understood intuitively as follows. If dA is at distance 1 from p and it is aligned so that it is exactly perpendicular to $d\omega$, then $d\omega = dA$ and $\cos\theta = 1$, and the equation holds. As dA moves farther away from p, the r^2 term increases, and so dividing by it reduces $d\omega$ accordingly. Conversely, as dA rotates so that it is not aligned with the direction of $d\omega$, the $\cos\theta$ term decreases, reducing $d\omega$ accordingly.

Unfortunately, applying this equation with screen-space estimators results in bad artefacts, because often the portion of an object visible to the camera is not the same one that is oriented towards the surface for which we are calculating the occlusion, as shown in Fig. 5.

A possible approximate solution can be obtained by flipping the normal in such cases: after all, regarding solid-angle coverage, we are interested in whether or not there is some geometry occluding light, not whether or not it is oriented towards the occluded surface.

In terms of calculations, instead of holding the cosine value to 0, we can take its absolute value: so, if the θ_s angle falls in the $[90...180]$ degrees range, the negative cosine value relative to $\mathbf{n}_s$ becomes a positive value for $-\mathbf{n}_s$.

$$\omega'_s = a_s \cdot \mathrm{abs}(\mathbf{d} \cdot \mathbf{n}_s) \tag{10}$$

Modifying our approximation according to this factor, we obtain:

$$s_{p,s} = \frac{a_s \cdot \mathrm{abs}(\mathbf{d} \cdot \mathbf{n}_s) \cdot \max(0, \mathbf{d} \cdot \mathbf{n}_p)}{d^2} \tag{11}$$

Our approximation of ambient obscurance allows the solid-angle approximation formula to be changed to evaluate different approaches easily. As for instance, in [12] the authors derive an analytical expression for the solid angle subtended by a plane triangle at some arbitrary point in the space. This expression should be used to obtain ambient obscurance in our approach in place of 11. However, this expression is more expensive because its computation involves 32 multiplications, 20 additions, 3 square roots, and 1 ATAN2.

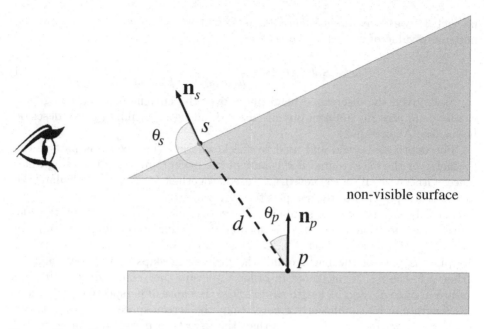

Fig. 5. No occlusion would be calculated if applying the basic solid-angle formula calculation.

Algorithm 2. SaSSAO.

---

procedure AMBIENTOBSCURANCE(p)
    if $foreground(d_p)$ **then**
        for $i \leftarrow 0, k - 1$ **do**
            $S_i \leftarrow sample\_pixel(p)$
            if $foreground(d_{S_i})$ **then**
                $sampleDir \leftarrow c_{S_i} - c_p$
                if $length(sampleDir) \leq maxDist$ **then**
                    $t_{id} \leftarrow getTriangle(S_i)$
                    $b \leftarrow bucket(t_{id})$
                    if $b \leq bucketSolidAngle$ **then**
                        $s_{p,s} \leftarrow getSolidAngle(p, S_i)$
                        $b \leftarrow min(bucketSolidAngle, b + s_{p,s})$
        for $i \leftarrow 1, hemisphereBuckets$ **do**
            $em \leftarrow em + b_i$
        $AO = em/2\pi$

A falloff function relative to the occluding geometry distance allows the obscurance contribution to be smoothed with distance. We adopt the falloff function proposed by the Alchemy SSAO algorithm in [10].

SaSSAO algorithm. Let *triangleDivs* be the triangle subdivision factor, which defines how the hemisphere is discretized. From this factor (as explained in Sect. 3), we derive $hemisphereBuckets$, which is $4 \cdot triangleDivs^2$ and the maximum value of the solid angle of each bucket as:

$$bucketSolidAngle = \frac{2\pi}{hemisphereBuckets} \qquad (12)$$

Now, given the discretized hemisphere over the current pixel p, a fragment shader computes the ambient obscurance estimating its visibility as we describe below (see Algorithm 2).

The depth d_p is read and used to check whether the pixel p is part of the geometry or the background. If it is part of the background, no processing takes place. Otherwise, $\mathbf{n}_p$ is retrieved and used, together with d_p, to calculate the screen-space position of the samples to be taken.

Let k be the number of samples to take, and $S_i, i \in [0...k-1]$, be the i-th sample pixel position in screen space, located depending on the adopted sampling pattern, as discussed in Sect. 4.2. Then, for each S_i, the depth d_{S_i} is read. If the pixel is part of the background, the processing skips to the next sample. Otherwise, the c_{S_i} is calculated in order to obtain the vector $sampleDir$ that goes from c_p to c_{S_i} and its length $sampleDist$. Because of perspective projection, this length can be significantly greater than the screen-space distance between p and S_i. If $sampleDist$ is greater than the $maxDist$ parameter, the sampled point is too distant to be taken into account for the AO calculation, and so processing skips to the next sample.

Otherwise, by the process described in Sect. 3 and adapted to work for the four octants of the hemisphere, the triangle id in which $sampleDir$ falls is found. So, let t_i be the triangle id found for S_i. We check whether the bucket t_i is already fully covered (meaning that we know that the direction to which the sample belongs is already occluded). If it is, we skip to the next sample. Otherwise, we compute an estimate of the covered solid angle as described in the approximation formula 11, and we add it to the current coverage value for the bucket. The last check is to determine whether in the current bucket an over-occlusion from the same directions occurs. If this is the case, the value of the current bucket is set to the maximum value $bucketSolidAngle$.

After processing all the samples, we have an estimate of the visibility around the current processing point in the form of the coverage values for all the buckets of our discretization. We know that the solid angle for the full hemisphere is 2π, so we sum the coverage values of all the buckets and divide this sum by 2π to obtain a global occlusion value. Of course, random sampling is no guarantee that samples will be obtained on every near-field occluder, but this is true for every SSAO technique. The immediate advantage of our technique is that we avoid over-occlusion caused by multiple occluders covering each other but covering from the same direction.

4.3 AO Filtering

Random sampling avoids banding issues, but introduces high-frequency noise. This could be removed with a basic Gaussian blur but the main problem with using this filter with AO is that it would also cause some shadow bleeding between surfaces at different depths or orientations. Because we have normals and depths at our disposal, so a more intelligent filtering can be done.

We decided to use a filtering function defined in [6], that is, a filter with bilateral weights based on normal and depth differences, and not Gaussian weights:

$$I^{\text{filtered}}(x) = \frac{\sum_{x_i \in \Omega} color(x_i) w(x, x_i)}{\sum_{x_i \in \Omega} w(x, x_i)} \tag{13}$$

where

$$w(x, x_i) = w_{normal}(x, x_i) w_{depth}(x, x_i) \tag{14}$$

$$w_{normal}(x, x_i) = \left(\frac{n_x \cdot n_{x_i} + 1}{2} \right)^{k_n} \tag{15}$$

$$w_{depth}(x, x_i) = \left(\frac{1}{1 + |d_x - d_{x_i}|} \right)^{k_d} \tag{16}$$

Here, k_n and k_d are two constants that can be tuned to alter the contribution of the normal/depth discriminators in the weight calculation.

5   Results

In this section, we present our methodology for evaluating the validity of our rendering technique. In terms of quality, we use Blender to off-line render ray-traced ambient occlusion as the reference image. The Blender renderings were conducted setting the number of samples to 64, a high number that gives excellent quality images. The resolution of all the images is 1280×720 pixels. To define the similarity between two images, we adopted the Structural Similarity Index (SSIM) [19] as a metric to measure similarity between images in a way that is consistent with human eye perception. In terms of efficiency, we implemented the Alchemy algorithm to allow us to evaluate SaSSAO against an already established technique. We implemented Alchemy while performing the minimal changes needed to our already active pipeline, so that we could share many parameters between the two techniques and make meaningful comparisons. However, evaluating the validity and efficiency of the technique against other techniques is complicated. Many parameters are involved, and even if the source code of some other technique is available, comparisons are not straightforward: different algorithms in many cases do not use the same parameters, and even minor adjustments may dramatically change the quality of results and performance. Moreover, there may be some scene dependency, causing one technique to perform better than others in only some scenes, and then the results are merely indicative.

5.1   Test Results

Our testing system was equipped with an Intel Core i7-3820 CPU 3.60 GHz, 16 GB of RAM, and a GeForce GTX TITAN GPU. The model used in our experiments was Sponza by Crytek [4]. For SaSSAO, we used the area of circumscribed circle as area approximation, and hemisphere sampling. These parameters showed the best results during our tests. We also used an angle bias parameter. This parameter often appears in SSAO techniques and is used to limit the self-occlusion and the artefacts caused when the geometry is almost co-planar with the geometry of the current point. If the cosine of the angle between the current point normal and the direction to the occluder was less than the angle bias, the sample was ignored. Tables 1 and 2 list the test scenes and associated parameters used. For Alchemy, we used flat sampling because it clearly shows good results. Other parameters were adjusted manually in an attempt to improve results or to show some particular behaviour. However, because of the difficulty of performing a comparison, we attempted to obtain for each selected scene the best result by tuning the parameters manually. Figures 6, 7, 8, 9, 10 and 11 show some results from the Atrium Sponza 3D model [4].

Table 1. Test scenes used with maximum distance, angle bias, and radius sampling chosen as shared parameters.

Scenes	Max distance	Angle bias	Radius
Lion head close up	0.5	0.3	0.4
Lion head close up	1.0	0.3	1
Lion head and drapes	0.25	0.6	0.2
Lion head and drapes	1.5	0.4	1.5
Atrium (from top)	0.8	0.3	0.8
Atrium	0.8	0.3	0.5

Table 2. Test scenes used with values associated with the SaSSAO and Alchemy approaches. Note that we tuned these values independently to obtain the best results for each one in terms of Structural Similarity Index (SSIM) and FPS.

Scenes	SaSSAO				Alchemy		
	SSIM	FPS	Samples	tDivs	SSIM	FPS	Samples
Lion head close up	92.80%	35.90	16	4	92.71%	22.26	64
Lion head close up	91.87%	22.86	32	4	92.95%	22.96	64
Lion head and drapes	92.64%	14.32	64	3	91.07%	55.41	16
Lion head and drapes	90.46%	11.53	64	4	84.81%	83.19	16
Atrium (from top)	85.51%	35.59	64	4	81.16%	84.10	16
Atrium	87.77%	13.28	64	4	86.91%	84.52	16

Fig. 6. Lion head close up - max distance 0.5, angle bias 0.3. Up: SaSSAO, SSIM 92.80%, 35.90 fps - Down left: Blender - Down right: Alchemy, SSIM 92.71%, 22.26 fps.

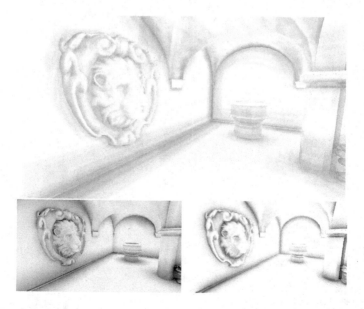

Fig. 7. Lion head close up - max distance 1.0, angle bias 0.3. Up: SaSSAO, SSIM 91.87%, 22.86 fps - Down left: Blender - Down right: Alchemy, SSIM 92.95%, 22.26 fps.

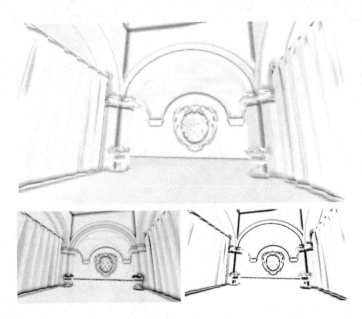

Fig. 8. Lion head and drapes - max distance 0.25, angle bias 0.6. Up: SaSSAO, SSIM 92.64%, 14.32 fps - Down left: Blender - Down right: Alchemy, SSIM 91.07%, 55.41 fps.

Fig. 9. Lion head and drapes - max distance 1.5, angle bias 0.4. Up: SaSSAO, SSIM 90.46%, 11.53 fps - Down left: Blender - Down right: Alchemy, SSIM 84.81%, 83.19 fps.

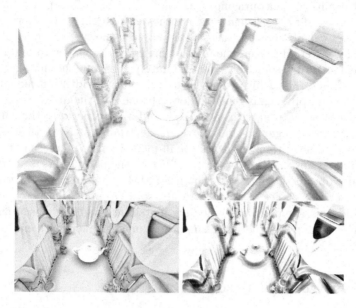

Fig. 10. Atrium (from top) - max distance 0.8, angle bias 0.3. Up: SaSSAO, SSIM 85.51%, 35.59 fps - Down left: Blender - Down right: Alchemy, SSIM 81.16%, 84.10 fps.

Fig. 11. Atrium - max distance 0.8, angle bias 0.3. Up: SaSSAO, SSIM 87.77%, 13.28 fps - Down left: Blender - Down right: Alchemy, SSIM 86.91%, 84.52 fps.

Overall results are encouraging, with our algorithm often producing results of comparable quality to Alchemy (sometimes even slightly superior). Alchemy performs fewer calculations for each sample, so with the same number of samples it is generally faster. However, the interesting aspect is that with fewer samples and more calculations, sometimes approximately the same quality was obtained at a similar frame rate, which could be useful in bandwidth-limited situations. FPS count in our approach is generally lower because of the many access into the triangle buckets associated with each pixel, and also to perform the comparison to check whether a region is fully covered by triangles. Nevertheless, we are confident that some optimizations can be implemented to increase performance.

Ultimately, it appears that properly adjusting the parameters is a large factor in the results obtained. Moreover, a higher-SSIM image may not always match a human observer's choice of the best result, so we are not completely confident that this index is a particularly effective metric for ambient obscurance comparisons. For example, sometimes, smoother images taken with more samples receive a lower SSIM.

6   Conclusions and Future Work

We have developed a new technique for ambient obscurance exploiting screen space. The approach common in the literature is based on deferred rendering and G-buffer sampling and is shared by a number of algorithms in the field. Our novel contributions are the use of a geometry shader to approximate the area of occluders and the adoption of a hemisphere discretization technique to classify the occluders according to their positions. To estimate coverage, we used a solid-angle approximation derived from our experiments with other algorithms and from some observations related to the lack of data inherent to image-based algorithms.

This type of approach, in which we evaluated the level of occlusion considering the direction from which coverage originated, storing the result in our "triangle buckets", allowed us to avoid over-occlusion and generally produced better quality results because of the implicit weighting of sample contributions. Quality is our primary concern, and we evaluated our results by comparing the structural similarity with off-line rendered images calculated through ray-tracing in Blender.

Ambient obscurance and, generically, global illumination approximations (for real-time rendering) are constantly improving, following the evolution of hardware, APIs, and the literature. Here, we share some ideas that we wish to explore in the near future. Our pyramid of "triangle buckets" does not only tell us how much a point is covered, but also from where (with a customizable level of precision). This may be exploited to achieve other types of results such as "directional occlusion" [15] and may be used to calculate direct lighting by using "bent normals", which are normals adjusted to consider the direction from which more incoming light will potentially reach the surface (i.e., where there are no occluders).

The compute shaders, introduced in OpenGL 4.3, add another level of freedom in utilization of the GPU (in the direction of other general-purpose APIs that exploit GPUs and other parallel hardware, such as OpenCL and CUDA). Compute shaders operate differently from other shader stages: for example, they have no well-defined set of input values and no frequency of execution specified by the nature of the stage (once per vertex, once per fragment...). More efficient sampling may be key : our technique performs a number of texture fetch operations (particularly relevant to the efficiency of the technique) for each fragment, and a possible way of optimizing fetch operations is to use the GPU shared memory. Recent results in the SSAO field, based on CUDA implementations, recently appeared in [17,18] with interesting implications for SaSSAO.

References

1. Aalund, F.P.: A comparative study of screen-space ambient occlusion methods. Technical University of Denmark, Technical report (2013)
2. Bavoil, L., Sainz, M., Dimitrov, R.: Image-space horizon-based ambient occlusion. In: ACM SIGGRAPH 2008 Talks, p. 22. ACM (2008)
3. Bunnell, M.: Dynamic ambient occlusion and indirect lighting. In: GPU Gems, vol. 2, no. 2, pp. 223–233 (2005)
4. Crytek: Atrium Sponza Palace. www.crytek.com/cryengine/cryengine3/downloads
5. Filion, D., McNaughton, R.: Effects & techniques. In: ACM SIGGRAPH 2008 Games, pp. 133–164. ACM (2008)
6. Gravås, L.O.: Image-space ambient obscurance in WebGL. Technical report, Institutt for datateknikk og informasjonsvitenskap (2013)
7. Khanna, P., Slater, M., Mortensen, J., Yu, I.: A non-parametric guide for radiance sampling in global illumination. In: Computer Graphics, Imaging and Visualisation, CGIV 2007, pp. 41–48 (2007)
8. Langer, M.S., Bülthoff, H.H.: Depth discrimination from shading under diffuse lighting. Perception 29(6), 649–660 (2000)
9. McGuire, M., Mara, M., Luebke, D.: Scalable ambient obscurance. In: Proceedings of the Fourth ACM SIGGRAPH/Eurographics Conference on High-Performance Graphics, pp. 97–103. Eurographics Association (2012)
10. McGuire, M., Osman, B., Bukowski, M., Hennessy, P.: The alchemy screen-space ambient obscurance algorithm. In: Proceedings of the ACM SIGGRAPH Symposium on High Performance Graphics, pp. 25–32. ACM (2011)
11. Mittring, M.: Finding next gen: CryEngine 2. In: ACM SIGGRAPH 2007 Courses, pp. 97–121. ACM (2007)
12. Oosterom, A.V., Strackee, J.: The solid angle of a plane triangle. IEEE Trans. Biomed. Eng. BME 30(2), 125–126 (1983)
13. Pharr, M., Humphreys, G.: Physically Based Rendering: From Theory to Implementation. Morgan Kaufmann Publishers Inc., San Francisco (2010)
14. Ritschel, T., Dachsbacher, C., Grosch, T., Kautz, J.: The state of the art in interactive global illumination. Comput. Graph. Forum 31(1), 160–188 (2012)
15. Ritschel, T., Grosch, T., Seidel, H.P.: Approximating dynamic global illumination in image space. In: Proceedings of the 2009 Symposium on Interactive 3D Graphics and Games, pp. 75–82. ACM (2009)

16. Shanmugam, P., Arikan, O.: Hardware accelerated ambient occlusion techniques on GPUs. In: Proceedings of the 2007 Symposium on Interactive 3D Graphics and Games, pp. 73–80. ACM (2007)
17. Timonen, V.: Line-sweep ambient obscurance. In: Computer Graphics Forum (Proceedings of EGSR 2013), vol. 32, no. 4, pp. 97–105 (2013)
18. Timonen, V.: Screen-space far-field ambient obscurance. In: Proceedings of the 5th High-Performance Graphics Conference, HPG 2013, pp. 33–43. ACM, New York (2013)
19. Wang, Z., Bovik, A.C., Sheikh, H.R., Simoncelli, E.P.: Image quality assessment: from error visibility to structural similarity. IEEE Trans. Image Process. **13**(4), 600–612 (2004)
20. Zhukov, S., Iones, A., Kronin, G.: An ambient light illumination model. In: Drettakis, G., Max, N. (eds.) Rendering Techniques 1998. Eurographics, pp. 45 55. Springer, Vienna (1998)

"Shape-Curvature-Graph": Towards a New Model of Representation for the Description of 3D Meshes

Arnaud Polette[1(✉)], Jean Meunier[2], and Jean-Luc Mari[3]

[1] Arts et Métiers ParisTech, CNRS, LSIS UMR 7296, Aix-en-provence, France
arnaud.polette@ensam.eu
[2] DIRO, University of Montreal, Montreal, Canada
[3] Aix-Marseille Université, CNRS, LSIS UMR 7296, Marseille, France

Abstract. This paper presents a new shape descriptor for 3D meshes, that aims at representing an arbitrary triangular polyhedron using a graph, called SCG for "Shape-Curvature-Graph". This entity can be used to perform self-similarity detection, or more generally to extract patterns within a shape. Our method uses discrete curvature maps and divides the meshes into eight categories of patches (peak, ridge, saddle ridge, minimal, saddle valley, valley, pit and flat). Then an adjacency graph is constructed with a node for each patch. All categories of patches cannot be neighbors in a continuous context, thus additional intermediary patches are added as boundaries to ensure a continuous consistency at the transitions between areas. To validate the relevance of this modular structure, an approach based of these shape descriptor graphs is developed in order to extract similar patterns within a surface mesh. It illustrates that these "augmented" graphs obtained using differential properties on meshes can be used to analyze shape and extract features.

1 Introduction

Triangular meshes are currently a standard structure for 3D representation in many domains related to computer graphics. These meshes are becoming increasingly large with the rapid development of 3D scanners. Therefore, geometric analysis is of crucial interest. Shape feature extraction and comparison on meshes is an important step in several graphical 3D applications, such as shape recognition, shape modeling, and shape registration.

A non-trivial problem in 3D shape analysis is the definition of a method to characterize features independent of scaling or rigid transformations.

In this study, we propose a curvature-based analysis technique to build a representative graph of the shape features of a surface mesh (based on our previous work [13]). The object is divided into eight categories of patches, depending on the local curvature: *peak, ridge, saddle ridge, minimal, saddle valley, valley, pit* and *flat*. This process characterizes the local shape in a low-level semantic manner, regardless of the scaling. We propose to enrich the graph with transition

© Springer International Publishing AG 2017
L.T. De Paolis et al. (Eds.): AVR 2017, Part II, LNCS 10325, pp. 369–384, 2017.
DOI: 10.1007/978-3-319-60928-7_32

boundaries between patches to ensure continuous consistency at the transitions between areas. These additional transitions lead to a more consistent and robust descriptor graph.

The goal is to build a descriptor graph from a discrete object that closely approximates the graph based on the original continuous objects that have been sampled to create this discrete object.

There are many studies regarding shape or feature extraction on meshes using discrete curvatures, e.g., via a skeleton using mean curvature [8], via crest lines [5,22], via a mesh split into patches using a region growing method driven by curvature variation [9], or mean-shifted curvature [23], using Gaussian curvature to extract salient features in a multi scale frame [21] (the concept of *saliency feature* has been previously described by [10]), by extracting a list of minimal and maximal specific curvature positions on a mesh [6].

In addition, some recent studies point to shape analysis, such as feature extraction or local self-similarity extraction, e.g., via a *regularity graphs* [18] and via linear programming [7], or mesh segmentation and labeling, e.g., via *consensus of deformable shapes* [14], via *multi-objective approach* [16], via *hierarchical planar symmetry* [15], and via machine learning [19].

Our objective is to propose a modular structure with which to extract specific features via semantic description based on a graph using a specific pattern.

Graph and sub-graph processing for the analysis of shapes is a known methodology [1] used to detect shape symmetries, [4] extract feature on points clouds using sub-graphs selection; [23] also used graphs to perform mesh segmentation, and [17] used skeleton graphs to achieve global matching of shapes.

Following [3], our main objective is to locally match the surface parts using discrete curvature as an invariant descriptor, using a graph-based approach to be able to use surface propagation schemes, common sub-graphs matching and region growing algorithms. The main challenge with this approach is related to the natural discontinuity of meshes; by its nature, discrete curvatures of meshes are dependent on the sampling of the mesh.

The key idea of the proposed approach is to build a surface graph from a mesh. This graph, called SCG for "Shape-Curvature-Graph", is made of nodes (patches) represent different types of parts of the shape, with a node adjacency that respects specific rules (related to continuous properties) to build similar types of features of a shape with a similar surface-graph.

2   Basic Notions on Curvatures

Geometrically, the curvature at a regular point on a curve (belonging to a plane) is defined as the inverse of the radius of the *osculating circle* passing through this point (the osculating circle is the circle that fits the curve on a region infinitesimally small around this point).

With a radius of the osculating circle r (the *radius of curvature*), the curvature k is defined as:

$$k = 1/r$$

This definition is not directly applicable to surfaces. An additional definition is needed to allow the curvature estimation on surfaces.

The value of the curvature being calculated on a curve, a cutting plane is used to obtain an intersection curve to compute the curvature value on a surface. As illustrated in Fig. 1, the cutting plane is the *normal plane* and is defined with the *normal vector* N to the surface and the *tangential vector* v, passing through the point P. This plane intersects the surface in a curve (the *intersection curve*). This curve gives the *normal curvature* using the osculating circle in the intersection plan. As it exists an infinity of *tangential vectors*, an infinity of *intersection curves* can be built at the same point. This *normal curvature* reaches two maximal and minimal values $k1$ and $k2$ (with $k1 \geq k2$) called *principal curvatures* in the direction of the two respective vectors $t1$ and $t2$ called *principal directions*. Moreover, these two vectors are orthogonal.

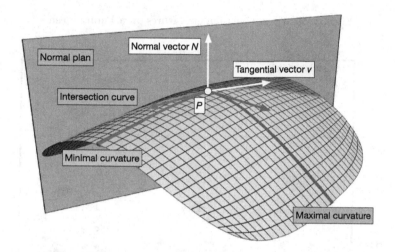

Fig. 1. The cutting plane is defined with the *normal vector* N to the surface and the *tangential vector* v, passing through the point P. This plane intersects the surface in a curve (the *intersection curve*).

Two other quantities are widely used to describe the local differential properties on surfaces - the mean curvature H and the Gaussian curvature K, defined as follows:

$$H = (k1 + k2)/2$$

$$K = k1 \cdot k2$$

Figure 2 shows two bunny meshes colored by the values of H and K.

The sign of these values gives eight categories of local shapes (categorization described by [2]): *peak, ridge, saddle ridge, minimal, saddle valley, valley, pit* and *flat* (see Fig. 3).

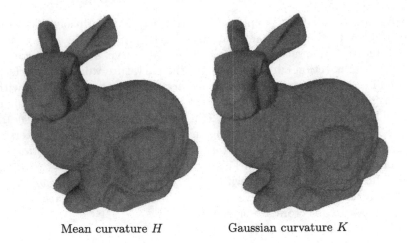

Mean curvature H Gaussian curvature K

Fig. 2. Mean and Gaussian curvatures on a bunny mesh

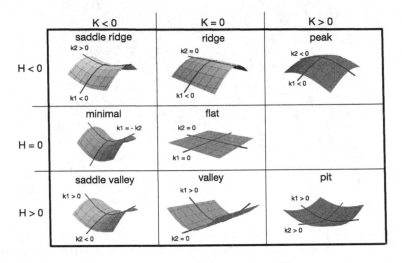

Fig. 3. Shape categories using mean and Gaussian curvatures.

Figure 4 shows a category map on a bunny mesh. This map is independent of the scale of the mesh; two identical meshes with a different scaling will give two different mean and Gaussian curvature maps but will have the same category map because the classification is only based on the sign of the curvature.

3 Shape Curvature Graph (SCG) Construction Method

In our work, we use the discrete curvature estimator of Meyer *et al.* [11] to obtain the mean curvature H and the Gaussian curvature K. This robust curvature

Fig. 4. Category map on a bunny mesh.

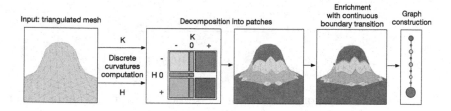

Fig. 5. Overview of the graph construction.

estimation is based on Voronoï cells and a finite-element/finite-volume method and ensure a fast and robust curvature estimation (Fig. 5).

3.1 Decomposition into Patches

Depending on the size of the features to be detected, before the decomposition procedure, an additional step can be used to extract the mean local curvature at different scales. A small scale extracts the texture and small features (Fig. 4 and first column of Fig. 6), and a large scale produces targeted macro-global features (Fig. 6 last column). We use a mean filter (a smoothing mathematical morphology filter applied on the surface) to locally compute the local mean curvature (the mean value of *Gaussian* and *mean curvature*) of a vertex group, with an adaptive structuring element based on a maximal Euclidian distance threshold.

The filter is defined as follows, where v is the current vertex, t is the distance threshold, S the total amount of selected vertices, and $SelectedVerts_i H$ and $SelectedVerts_i K$ are the mean and the Gaussian curvatures, respectively, corresponding to the selected vertex $SelectedVerts_i$. The selection function $SelectVerts(startingVertex, threshold)$ uses a propagation scheme to recursively select vertices, starting from a given vertex and bounded by an Euclidian distance threshold.

Fig. 6. Three examples of the influence of the distance parameter on the *bunny* mesh, the radius distance is shown as a grey disk.

$$SelectedVerts = SelectVerts(startingVertex, threshold)$$

$$meanH = \frac{\sum_{i=1}^{S} SelectedVerts_i H}{S}$$

$$meanK = \frac{\sum_{i=1}^{S} SelectedVerts_i K}{S}$$

This method allows for the selection of vertices with a maximum distance threshold, constrained to only accessible vertices by a local propagation and avoiding the selection of unwanted vertices, as illustrated in Fig. 7.

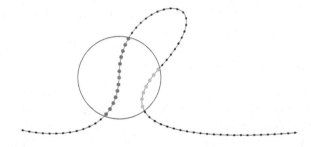

Fig. 7. The selection starts from the red vertex, with a threshold represented by a circle; the selected vertices are in blue, and orange vertices are below the threshold value but are not selected using the propagation scheme. (Color figure online)

Figure 8 shows the vertices used with the same distance on three similar shapes represented by different meshes. Due to this distance, it is possible to compute a local mean estimation of the curvature, regardless of the sampling of the mesh, in a multi-scale way.

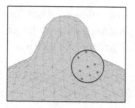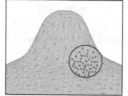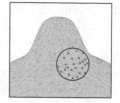

Fig. 8. Vertices used for the local curvature estimation of a vertex group with the same distance for three different meshes of the same object.

3.2   Continuous Boundary Between Areas

By its nature, discrete curvatures are dependent on the sampling of the mesh. Our goal is to build a graph using the previously presented curvature patches as robust as possible. The approach to achieve this goal is to build a graph that closely approximates the graph that would be built if a continuous object was used to obtain this graph. In a continuous context, all patches cannot be adjacent. Continuity rules are defined to ensure a continuous consistency in transitions between patches. Figure 9 shows the adjacency rules between them (corresponding categories are presented in Fig. 3).

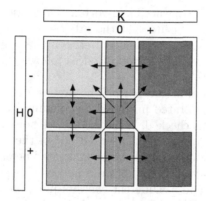

Fig. 9. Adjacency rules between patches. (Color figure online)

These rules involve an implicit interpolation of the curvatures between areas to establish the permitted adjacency for each category. These complementary areas on the mesh aim to achieve the same differential transitions between each category. For example, on a C^2-surface, it is not possible to have a peak area and a pit region without passing a flat or a ridge area. Thus, a graph can be built from a discrete object as close as possible to the original continuous objects that have been sampled to create the discrete object.

Using these rules, only one shortest path exists between two patches. Being a type of interpolation, nothing can ensure that the real continuous path between two nodes is built, but we can choose the most probable one that obeys the continuous adjacency rules. As a result, two non-planar adjacent patches that need an intermediate junction to be consistent will produce a path without a planar node (purple area).

Figure 10 shows an "augmented" mesh with continuous transition boundaries. Each area between two red areas is found to form a ring. The yellow parts are now linked and considered to be a unique area.

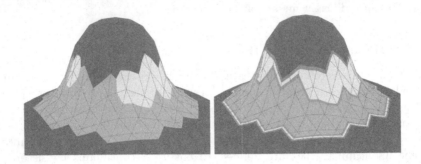

Fig. 10. Continuous boundary enrichment on a simple bumped mesh

To enrich the mesh with these sub-vertex boundaries, each face (triangle) of the mesh is checked to ensure that the adjacency rules are respected for all edges. If not, then new areas are added between them and properly linked to their neighbors. The procedure is described as follows (different configurations are presented in Fig. 11).

This process is divided in two parts. The first one is the addition of missing nodes; this process is illustrated in Fig. 11 in columns 1 and 2. Before adding a new node, its existence is checked. If the node does not exist, then a new one is built. Otherwise, the existing one is used (if one of the edges has be processed before, some additional nodes may have been created before). The second part is the creation of links between the additional nodes. This procedure is illustrated in Fig. 11 in columns 2 and 3. Different cases of junction addition are described in Fig. 11 (a, b and c). The addition of nodes on each edge is performed using the adjacency rules presented Fig. 9.

3.3   Construction of the SCG

After the continuous boundary enrichment, a SCG is built using the patch neighborhood, and then a propagation algorithm is used to select all contiguous vertices and build a list of patches by category. A node is defined for each patch; each node contains the category, the patch area, and a link to each neighboring patch (Fig. 12).

To show how the boundary enrichment affects graph consistency, three meshes from the same shape with different sampling are presented (Fig. 13).

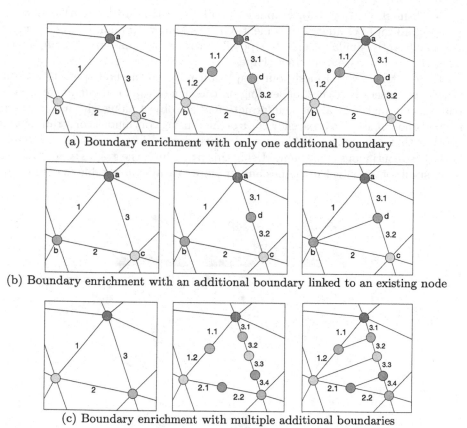

(a) Boundary enrichment with only one additional boundary

(b) Boundary enrichment with an additional boundary linked to an existing node

(c) Boundary enrichment with multiple additional boundaries

Fig. 11. Continuous boundary enrichment.

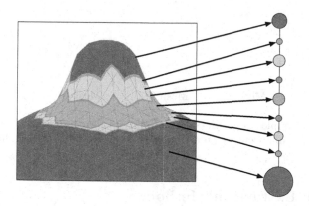

Fig. 12. Graph construction procedure

For each mesh (1, 2 and 3), graphs are built with (Fig. 13 bottom) and without (Fig. 13 top) boundary enrichment. Graphs built with boundary enrichment are significantly similar; thus, it is possible to use a simple graph comparison algorithm to compare or extract shapes.

From a triangulated mesh, our graph construction method splits the whole object into a set of patches, depending on the sign of the local curvature. These patches contain the local shape information of the object along with a structured neighborhood based on adjacency rules defined using continuous constraints: two patches that cannot be neighbors on a continuous object cannot be neighbors with these continuous constraints. Using this procedure, the graphs we obtain are more similar for equivalent shapes and are more easily comparable (see Fig. 13).

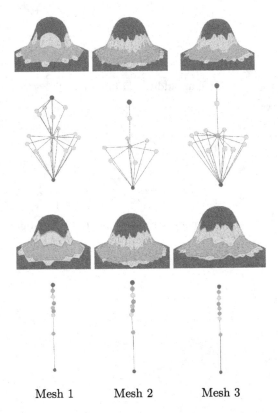

Mesh 1   Mesh 2   Mesh 3

Fig. 13. Three examples of graph construction with (bottom) and without (top) continuous boundary enhancement on a similar shape with different sampling.

4   Pattern Extraction Method

The pattern extraction procedure can be formulated as a partial sub-graph matching problem. This is a well-known problem for standard graphs. However,

SCG are categorized and sized for each node, and with specific adjacency rules, a dedicated matching method is proposed for these specific graphs. Thanks to the neighborhood consistency given by the adjacency rules, a weighted pairing node-to-node algorithm can be used to solve this problem with SCG.

The methodology consists of three steps:

- construction of the *similarity matrix S*
- starting node pairs selection
- recursive node pairing from starting pairs.

Construction of the Similarity Matrix. Consider two graphs G_1 and G_2 as inputs defined as $G_1 = (V_1, E_2)$ and $G_2 = (V_2, E_2)$, where V is a set of nodes and E is a set of edges, $|V_1|$ and $|V_2|$ represent the number of nodes in each graph, and the *similarity matrix S* is a $|V_1| \cdot |V_2|$ matrix, with S_{ij} the similarity between the nodes V_{1i} and V_{2i}, $S_{ij} \in \mathbb{R}$ and $0 \leq S_{ij} \leq 1$. Two strictly identical nodes give a similarity value of 1, and two strictly different nodes give a value of 0.

The similarity matrix is built using the method described by [12], using the assumption "two nodes $i \in VA$ and $j \in VB$ are considered to be similar if neighbor nodes of i can be matched to similar neighbor nodes of j".

The matrix S is initialized first by a node-to-node similarity function using the category C_V and the area size A_V; this value is set to zero if the nodes do not belong to the same category:

$$simil(V_i, V_j) \begin{cases} min(A_{V_i}, A_{V_j})/max(A_{V_i}, A_{V_j}), & \text{if } C_{V_i} = C_{V_j} \\ 0, & \text{otherwise} \end{cases}$$

Next, the similarity matrix S is iteratively built by neighbor matching; for each existing pair V_i and V_j, the similarity value S_{ij}^k for the kth iteration is updated using the following function, where $d(V)$ is the degree of the node V:

$$S_{ij}^{k+1} = \frac{1}{max(d(V_i), d(V_j))} \sum_{x=1}^{min(d(V_i), d(V_j))} f_{ij}^k(x)$$

With $f_{ij}^k(x)$, the enumeration function of the optimal matching ij gives the xth highest similarity value between the neighborhood of V_i and V_j at the kth iteration.

The original method defined by [12] is designed to compute the similarity between two entire graphs and iterates until the similarity matrix is stable. Our goal is to locally compute the similarity between two nodes. The number of iterations required depends on the number of nodes to take in consideration in the similarity computation: starting from a node, for k iterations, nodes to a depth of k are taken into account.

Starting Nodes Selection and Node Pairing. Using the computed similarity matrix, common sub-graphs can be extracted by recursive node pairing. Starting pairs are first found by testing the similarity value using a threshold t; a ij pair is a starting pair if $S_{ij} > t$. Starting from each selected pair, each node of their neighborhoods is recursively paired by the maximal similarity value. This pairing function is recursively called on each new pair ij if $S_{ij} > t$. The maximal size of each ij pair of paired sub-graphs is saved in a new $|V_1| * |V_2|$ matrix M.

Finally, the matrix M is used to extract maximal similar patterns, beginning with the maximal values of M_{ij}. Similar sub-graphs are reconstructed using the same previous recursive method. Corresponding pairs are indexed as a new extracted pattern. Multiple similarities can be found by a propagation of this index to all the same maximal values through the rows and columns of each indexed node.

5   Examples and Validation

In this section, examples are presented to illustrate our methods for each proposed scheme.

5.1   Semantic Description of a Feature

A desired feature can be explicitly described with a pattern via a semantic description. Figure 14 shows a feature extraction on the wing of the *gargoyle* mesh. The sub-graph used (Fig. 14(d)) describes "a pit bounded by a saddle ridge that can contain one or more peaks, the whole area being bounded by a saddle valley". 81% (9 out of 11) of the features are extracted. Undetected ones being linked to bigger patches.

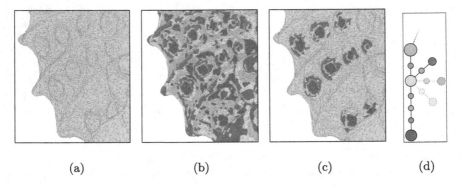

(a)   (b)   (c)   (d)

Fig. 14. Feature extraction by terminal sub-graph recognition: (a) source mesh, (b) mesh split into patches defining a graph, (c) extracted features and (d) terminal sub-graph used as a feature descriptor, 81% (9 out of 11) of the features are extracted. Undetected ones being linked to bigger patches.

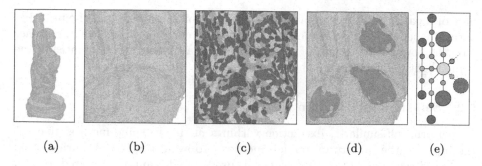

(a)   (b)   (c)   (d)   (e)

Fig. 15. Extraction of flowers on the Buddha mesh (b), categories (c), extracted parts (d) and the extraction pattern used (e), 75% (3 out of 4) of the features are extracted. The missing one being slightly different from the others. (Color figure online)

To achieve this extraction the pattern includes some conditional nodes. During the extraction process, the conditional nodes are taken into account only if they can be paired and if the value of the degree is adapted to fit to the paired nodes.

The next example (Fig. 15) uses the same approach to extract lotus flowers from the Buddha mesh (this extraction is also performed in [3]). In this example, an additional constraint is used during the graph building process: patches are limited to a maximal size; this allows for the extraction of a feature made of a

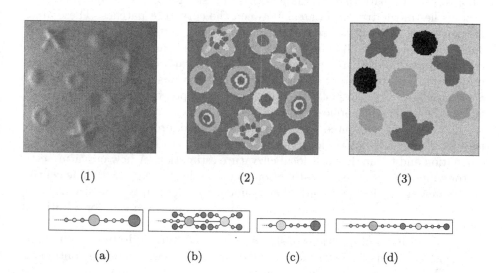

(1)   (2)   (3)

(a)   (b)   (c)   (d)

Fig. 16. Self-similarity extraction on a mesh: (1), (2) and (3) show the input mesh, the computed list of patches and the output classification of sub-graphs. Extracted sub-graphs produced by the method are presented in (a), (b), (c) and (d). This example was built using 3D brushes on Blender. Each feature is correctly extracted, the detection rate is 100%.

part of a patch. In this example, the yellow part of the flowers and the branches naturally belong to the same node. By limiting the size of patches, we can extract only the flowers. 75% (3 out of 4) of the features are extracted. The missing one being slightly different from the others.

5.2 Self-similarity Within a Mesh

To perform self-similarity extraction within a mesh, the same mesh is given as the input to the pattern extraction method. To avoid the trivial pairing of all nodes to itself, an additional constraint is used: a node cannot be paired to itself in the final pairing procedure.

Figure 16 shows an example of self-similarity extraction on a mesh. Four maximal sub-graphs are found multiple times; as an additional output, the method computes the sub-graphs. Figure 16 shows the following patterns: a peak (a), a cross (b), a pit (c), and a crater (d). This example was built using 3D brushes on Blender. Each feature is correctly extracted, the detection rate is 100%.

6 Conclusion and Future Work

In this paper, we presented a new feature extraction approach based on a SCG (Shape Curvature Graph). In the proposed approach, the mesh decomposition is performed using curvature maps defined by the signs of mean and Gaussian curvatures. The patterns are characterized by sub-graphs. One of our contributions lies in the transition areas between the curvature patches. These areas are constructed by analogy to the continuous world, and they define new predefined nodes on the graph. The extraction of features is more robust because the transition possibilities are very restricted. A sub-graph extraction method was proposed to perform pattern extraction and similarity or self-similarity detection. Some examples were presented to illustrate the proposed schemes of extraction and to show different applications of SCG.

The approach presented in this paper can be improved upon. The curvature estimator method could support multi-scaling to combine the curvature estimation and the multi-scale local curvature estimation. A new curvature estimator supporting multi-scale estimation could be chosen (e.g., [20]). The continuous boundary enrichment method adds nodes with an empty area size. Adding an interpolation step could help to determine a proper area size for additional boundaries.

Some specific configurations of shapes could lead to the addition of junctions that can be chosen in a better way to be closer to the corresponding continuous object. For example, additional junctions between a peak node and a saddle valley node could have more than one path. By default, the most probable path is chosen: ridge, saddle ridge or minimal. However, a shape with a potential plane between to nodes could exist. Some additional adjacency rules could be added to find theses specific cases.

With shapes being represented by SCG, the extraction of features is based on the neighborhood between nodes. A localization of patches could be added to the properties of the nodes to find a specific spatial configuration of the nodes.

Moreover, these graphs can be extended in the future to semantic feature extraction within 3D databases, because they can be used to describe any kind of 3D shapes in a more simplified way, without carrying the geometry of the shape (in the literal sense).

Acknowledgments. This work was supported by the Natural Sciences and Engineering Research Council of Canada (NSERC). The Bunny and the Happy Buddha data sets were provided courtesy of the Stanford University Computer Graphics Laboratory. The Gargoyle and the Chinese dragon data sets were provided courtesy of the AIM@SHAPE consortium.

References

1. Berner, A., Bokeloh, M., Wand, M., Schilling, A., Seidel, H.-P.: A graph-based approach to symmetry detection. In: Proceedings of the Fifth Eurographics/IEEE VGTC Conference on Point-Based Graphics, SPBG 2008, pp. 1–8. Eurographics Association, Aire-la-Ville, Switzerland, Switzerland (2008)
2. Besl, P.J., Jain, R.C.: Segmentation through variable-order surface fitting. IEEE Trans. Pattern Anal. Mach. Intell. **10**(2), 167–192 (1988)
3. Gal, R., Cohen-Or, D.: Salient geometric features for partial shape matching and similarity. ACM Trans. Graph. **25**(1), 130–150 (2006)
4. Gumhold, S., Wang, X., Macleod, R.: Feature extraction from point clouds. In: Proceedings of the 10th International Meshing Roundtable, pp. 293–305 (2001)
5. Hildebrandt, K., Polthier, K., Wardetzky, M.: Smooth feature lines on surface meshes. In: Proceedings of the Third Eurographics Symposium on Geometry Processing, SGP 2005, pp. 085–090. Eurographics Association, Aire-la-Ville, Switzerland, Switzerland (2005)
6. Ho, H.T., Gibbins, D.: Curvature-based approach for multi-scale feature extraction from 3D meshes and unstructured point clouds. IET Comput. Vis. **3**(4), 201–212 (2009)
7. Huang, Q., Guibas, L.J., Mitra, N.J.: Near-regular structure discovery using linear programming. ACM Trans. Graph. **33**(3), 23:1–23:17 (2014)
8. Kudelski, D., Viseur, S., Mari, J.-L.: Skeleton extraction of vertex sets lying on arbitrary triangulated 3D meshes. In: Gonzalez-Diaz, R., Jimenez, M.-J., Medrano, B. (eds.) DGCI 2013. LNCS, vol. 7749, pp. 203–214. Springer, Heidelberg (2013). doi:10.1007/978-3-642-37067-0_18
9. Lavoué, G., Dupont, F., Baskurt, A.: A new CAD mesh segmentation method, based on curvature tensor analysis. Comput.-Aided Des. **37**(10), 975–987 (2005)
10. Lee, C.H., Varshney, A., Jacobs, D.W.: Mesh saliency. ACM Trans. Graph. **24**(3), 659–666 (2005)
11. Meyer, M., Desbrun, M., Schröder, P., Barr, A.H.: Discrete differential-geometry operators for triangulated 2-manifolds. In: Hege, H.-C., Polthier, K. (eds.) Visualization and Mathematics III. Mathematics and Visualization, pp. 35–57. Springer, Berlin (2003)
12. Nikolić, M.: Measuring similarity of graph nodes by neighbor matching. Intell. Data Anal. **16**(6), 865–878 (2012)

13. Polette, A., Meunier, J., Mari, J.-L.: Feature extraction using a shape descriptor graph based on discrete curvature patches. In: Computer Graphics International (CGI 2015), Strasbourg, France (2015)
14. Rodola, E., Rota Bulo, S., Cremers, D.: Robust region detection via consensus segmentation of deformable shapes. Comput. Graph. Forum **33**(5), 97–106 (2014)
15. Simari, P., Kalogerakis, E., Singh, K.: Folding meshes: hierarchical mesh segmentation based on planar symmetry. In: Proceedings of the Fourth Eurographics Symposium on Geometry Processing, SGP 2006, pp. 111–119. Eurographics Association, Aire-la-Ville, Switzerland, Switzerland (2006)
16. Simari, P., Nowrouzezahrai, D., Kalogerakis, E., Singh, K.: Multi-objective shape segmentation and labeling. In: Computer Graphics Forum: Eurographics Symposium on Geometry Processing. Eurographics Association, Switzerland, Aire-la-Ville, Switzerland, March 2009
17. Sundar, H., Silver, D., Gagvani, N., Dickinson, S.: Skeleton based shape matching and retrieval. In: Proceedings of the Shape Modeling International 2003, SMI 2003. IEEE Computer Society, Washington, DC, USA (2003)
18. Tevs, A., Huang, Q., Wand, M., Seidel, H.-P., Guibas, L.: Relating shapes via geometric symmetries and regularities. ACM Trans. Graph. **33**(4), 119:1–119:12 (2014)
19. Xie, Z., Kai, X., Liu, L., Xiong, Y.: 3D shape segmentation and labeling via extreme learning machine. Comput. Graph. Forum **33**(5), 85–95 (2014)
20. Yang, Y.-L., Lai, Y.-K., Hu, S.-M., Pottmann, H.: Robust principal curvatures on multiple scales. In: Polthier, K., Sheffer, A. (eds.) SGP 2006: 4th Eurographics Symposium on Geometry processing, pp. 223–226. Eurographics Association (2006)
21. Yang, Y.-L., Shen, C.-H.: Multi-scale salient features for analyzing 3D shapes. J. Comput. Sci. Technol. **27**(6), 1092–1099 (2012)
22. Yoshizawa, S., Belyaev, A., Seidel, H.-P.: Fast and robust detection of crest lines on meshes. In: Proceedings of the 2005 ACM Symposium on Solid and Physical Modeling, SPM 2005, pp. 227–232. ACM, New York (2005)
23. Zhang, X., Li, G., Xiong, Y., He, F.: 3D mesh segmentation using mean-shifted curvature. In: Chen, F., Jüttler, B. (eds.) GMP 2008. LNCS, vol. 4975, pp. 465–474. Springer, Heidelberg (2008). doi:10.1007/978-3-540-79246-8_35

Semantics-Supported Collaborative Creation of Interactive 3D Content

Krzysztof Walczak[✉]

Poznań University of Economics and Business,
Niepodległości 10, 61-875 Poznań, Poland
walczak@kti.ue.poznan.pl
http://www.kti.ue.poznan.pl/

Abstract. Interactive 3D techniques offer a new quality in the design of user interfaces of computer applications, in particular when 3D applications are accessible remotely over the internet. A critical element for building practical 3D applications is adequate 3D synthetic content. However, designing high-quality interactive 3D content is a complex and challenging task. This difficulty is one of the major obstacles preventing widespread use of 3D techniques on the web in many promising application domains. In this paper, a new approach to 3D content creation is presented. The approach employs a range of techniques for simplification of the content creation process, but its main novelty lies in the fact that properly structured content can be created by communities of designers, regardless of whether they explicitly collaborate or not. Appropriate organization and consistency of the user-contributed content is enforced by the use of semantic web techniques with external domain ontologies. The presented approach is consistent both with the existing content creation pipelines and business models, aiming at enhancing and not replacing the current practices in digital content creation. A prototype of a tool for 3D content design implemented as an extension to the Unity IDE is also presented.

Keywords: 3D content · 3D web · Semantic web · Content creation · Unity IDE

1 Introduction

Increasing use of interactive three-dimensional techniques, such as virtual reality (VR) and augmented reality (AR), for building rich multimedia human-computer interfaces has been made possible by significant advances in the performance of computing equipment (including mobile devices), steadily increasing throughput and availability of computer networks and increasingly sophisticated forms of content presentation and interaction with the content on end-users' equipment.

The development of graphics hardware and applications based on three-dimensional interactive user interfaces is largely driven by the rich and rapidly growing market of computer games. However, these techniques can be – and

© Springer International Publishing AG 2017
L.T. De Paolis et al. (Eds.): AVR 2017, Part II, LNCS 10325, pp. 385–401, 2017.
DOI: 10.1007/978-3-319-60928-7_33

in fact are – successfully used also in other areas, such as rapid prototyping of products, architectural design and visualization, as well as simulation and training.

An entirely new level of applicability of the three-dimensional techniques is achievable by the development of standards that enable describing interactive synthetic multimedia content in a way which is independent of hardware and software, and publishing such content on the web. Therefore, extensive research and standardization effort has been recently conducted aiming at the development of universal data formats for describing interactive three-dimensional VR/AR content available on the web. These works led to the development of standards, such as VRML/X3D [45,46], MPEG-4 [18], COLLADA [19], and U3D [10]. With these standards it is possible to encode, transmit over the network, and present on the end-user's equipment three-dimensional high-quality interactive multimedia content. A number of imperative programming libraries employing web standards, such as HTML5, JavaScript, jQuery, SVG and CSS have been also designed. Prominent examples include WebGL [20], Three.js [31], Sprite3D.js [29], Phoria.js [26], Voxel [37] and Photon [15]. Also, X3DOM [14] is a notable example of the use of such imperative programming libraries to enable presentation of declarative content (X3D) in web browsers.

Users can use virtual environments available over the network in the same way as they can use their local counterparts. The importance of this technology is difficult to overestimate. Remote access to three-dimensional interactive multimedia content and services enables creation of a wide range of services and applications, such as access to geographically dispersed cultural content, travel guides, e-learning systems, e-commerce applications, social and entertainment services, and tele-work environments. The use of VR/AR techniques not only can lead to the implementation of better versions of already available services, but can also enable the implementation of entirely new services, which are not possible without this kind of technology. It has been proven that in many cases viable business models accompany such developments.

Availability of universal standards enabling content description has much further reaching implications than just the ability to access pre-designed content over the network. In conjunction with the availability of easy to use and inexpensive tools for content creation, it may open the possibility of social 3D content co-creation by users that are both producers and consumers (prosumers), as it is possible today in the classical "two dimensional" web, leading to the development of Social 3D Web or "3D Web 2.0". Content creation is understood here as the design and programming of basic content elements as well as combining elements of previously created content – including those created by other users. The possibility of involving large groups of prosumers in content creation is critical for the development of content, which is interesting for users, up-to-date and of adequate quality.

However, creation, searching and combining distributed three-dimensional interactive content is much more complex and challenging than in the case of standard web pages. The relationships between components of an interactive three-dimensional virtual scene may include, in addition to its basic meaning and presentation form, also spatial, temporal, structural, logical, and behavioral aspects. This problem can be – at least to some extent – tackled by the use of semantic web techniques.

Research on the Semantic Web has been initiated by T. Berners-Lee and the W3C (World-Wide Web Consortium) in 2001 and led to the development of standards such as RDF/RDF(S), OWL and SPARQL. The goal is to transform the current web into a distributed semantic database, linking structured content and documents (Linked Data). Semantic descriptions enable achieving a new quality in building web applications that can "understand" the meaning of particular components of content and services as well as their relationships, leading to better methods of creating, recombining and presenting content.

Even for content with relatively low structural complexity, such as HTML pages, the use of semantic techniques provides a significant increase in the ability to automatically process and integrate the content. In the case of content with a high degree of structural complexity, such as interactive 3D components and virtual scenes (e.g., encoded in X3D), where the variety of types of relationships between different content components is much higher, the use of semantic techniques can help to develop an entirely new class of distributed multimedia applications, which can be described as *3D Semantic Web*.

In this paper, a new approach to 3D content creation, called *SemFlex*, is presented. The approach employs a range of techniques for simplification of the content creation process, but its main novelty lies in the fact that highly structured 3D content can be created by communities of developers, regardless of whether they explicitly collaborate or not. Appropriate organization and consistency of the user-contributed content is enforced by the use of semantic web techniques with external domain ontologies. The presented approach is consistent with the existing content creation pipelines and business models, aiming at enhancing and not replacing the current practices in digital content creation. The overall architecture of the *Semantic Content Design Environment* based on SemFlex is also presented, together with a prototype of a tool for semantic 3D content design implemented as an extension to the Unity IDE [34].

The rest of this paper is organized as follows. In Sect. 2, a review of the state of the art in the field of 3D content creation is presented. In Sect. 3, the concept, the requirements and the overall architecture of a distributed environment for semantic 3D content creation are discussed. Section 4 describes implementation of the *Semantic Content Design Environment* and provides a step-by-step content design example. Finally, Sect. 5 concludes the paper.

2   State of the Art

Different approaches to the simplification of the 3D content creation process have been elaborated. All these methods aim at reducing the amount and the complexity of information that designers need to provide to create 3D content. This can be achieved in several ways, as presented below.

2.1 3D Scanning

Automatic or semi-automatic 3D scanners can be used to capture the geometry, the appearance and the movement of objects [2]. Specialized active scanners based on laser ToF, triangulation, photogrammetry and structured light analysis are available [4]. More affordable – but less precise – techniques enable 3D reconstruction from series of images – often performed in the cloud, e.g., Autodesk 123D and 3DSOM. Scanners largely simplify content creation and produce high-quality naturally-looking 3D models. Scanning is useful for creating digital representations of real objects and places. However, scanning cannot be used for modeling objects and places that do not exist, e.g., because they were destroyed or are simply a product of designer's imagination. Also, scanning does not help in modeling interactivity and behavior of objects. As a result, 3D scanning is often used in combination with other methods of content creation, which allow designers to have more influence on the process and the created content.

2.2 Visual Content Modeling

A number of visual environments have been developed for 3D content modeling. Examples of software designated for traditional modeling or sculpting of 3D objects include: 3ds Max, Blender, Maya, Modo, 3D-Coat and Zbrush.

Advanced environments – intended for professional users – offer rich capabilities of designing various content elements, but their complexity requires expertise in 3D modeling. 3D content creation may be facilitated by narrowing the domain of application and the set of available operations. Environments of this kind (e.g., Sweet Home 3D, AutoCAD Civil 3D and Ghost Productions), designed for domain experts, provide tools enabling relatively fast and efficient modeling, without requiring users' extensive experience in 3D content creation. This, however, significantly reduces the generality of the content creation process.

2.3 Parameterized and Procedural Modeling

Creation of 3D content can be simplified by using content templates that enable automatic generation of content on demand [41,44]. Templates can be parameterized, so that content designers can influence the content creation process. The use of templates reduces flexibility of content design, but it enables creating high quality content, while keeping the amount of information required at the content creation stage relatively low. There is an obvious trade-off between the flexibility and the simplicity of content creation with templates. Templates are also useful for visualization of various types of data in 3D. Templates often employ elements created with the use of 3D scanners and visual modeling environments, and are often used in combination with other content creation methods.

Sophisticated general-purpose procedural modeling software packages enable employing parametrization in the creation of various types of objects, e.g., Houdini [27], City Engine [11] and Vue [9]. Specialized procedural software enables employing parametrization in the creation of selected types of objects, e.g., SpeedTree [17], Plant Factory [8], Terragen [24], Acropora [38], Meta-Elements [22].

2.4 Content Models and Patterns

Increasing number and structural complexity of content generation parameters require the development of content models – well defined structures, which describe how content is organized [40]. Based on such models, content generation software can automatically create final form of the content. The main benefits of using content models are better organized and easier to understand and maintain content structures, automatically verifiable data consistency, and elimination of redundancy in content representation. Content models can be stored in different types of repositories, depending on particular system requirements. Content patterns add another conceptual layer on top of the content models, providing well-defined roles for specific elements of a content model [23, 25].

2.5 Content Componentization

Instead of using fixed content models, rules of combining different types of content elements can be defined, allowing designers to flexibly set up content from predefined building blocks – components [5,36,39,40]. Components may include geometrical objects, sounds, scenarios, interaction elements and others. Although creation of content based on configuration of components constrains possible final forms of the created content, the process is simpler and more efficient than creating content from scratch, while usually still providing more flexibility than content templates and content models.

2.6 Separation of Concerns

Further simplification of content modeling requires separation of concerns between users with different expertise, who are equipped with different modeling tools. For example, limitations of component-based content creation can be mitigated by providing means of extending the library of the available components. This can be achieved by assigning different roles to different content designers. A non-expert content creator may build virtual scenes by assembling ready-to-use components. It is relatively easy to compose a scene, but the process is constrained. New content creation capabilities can be provided by introducing new types of components. This task can be performed by programmers or 3D designers.

The presented solutions significantly facilitate modeling of 3D content, but they still have important limitations, which result from their orientation on the modeling of content instead of the modeling of concepts. As a consequence, 3D content modeling experts do not use methods specific to the particular application domain, but methods specific to 3D graphics. It is also necessary – at some stage – to describe all components of the created 3D content.

2.7   Semantic Modeling

Further progress in modeling of 3D content is possible through the use of semantic web techniques [1, 28, 35, 47]. Semantic web techniques enable modeling 3D content using high-level concepts from a particular application domain, instead of low-level concepts specific to 3D graphics. Inference can be used to enhance and simplify the content creation process. Also, semantic modeling enables designing content in a platform independent way. A number of approaches have been proposed to enable modeling of synthetic 3D content with the use semantic web techniques [3, 7, 12, 21, 42, 43]. A comprehensive study of the use of semantic web techniques for 3D content representation and modeling has been presented in [13].

2.8   Social Content Creation

Availability of easy to use methods of content creation, in particular methods based on the semantic web, opens the possibility of social 3D content co-creation by users that are both producers and consumers (prosumers), as it is currently possible in the "two-dimensional" Web 2.0. There are number of on-line 3D content sharing sites with large and active communities of users. Examples include Turbosquid [32], Unity Asset Store [33], 3D ContentCentral [6], Highend3D [16] and many others (e.g., Creative Crash, CG People Network, Falling Pixel, 3d Export, The 3D Studio, Evermotion, Renderosity, 3D Ocean, Daz 3D).

In some cases, 3D object library websites enable obtaining the required 3D models in a quick and easy way. However, this is typically only true, if the user's requirements are modest and flexible. Even if the number of models on such websites is typically high, the models greatly differ in style, quality, format and functionality, which makes it difficult to find objects of strictly defined features. Moreover, the process of searching through such on-line databases is time-consuming because of the large number of objects and only roughly structured organization of the libraries. Often it is also impossible to verify the models' quality before downloading (or purchasing) them.

2.9   Summary

Great structural and conceptual complexity of 3D content and multitude of aspects that must be taken into account in the content design process make the 3D content creation an inherently complex task. Several methods suitable in different contexts have been proposed to simplify this process. Practical applications must combine different methods to provide the necessary trade-off between the conflicting requirements of generality and simplicity of content creation and high quality of the created content.

3   Semantic Social Content Creation

3.1   Requirements

In Sect. 2, a number of approaches aiming at the simplification of the content creation process have been discussed. To provide further progress in this field, these approaches need to be combined into a user-friendly and efficient design ecosystem in such a way that the complementary benefits offered by particular approaches are preserved and employed in a synergistic manner. The main functional requirements for such a content creation method are discussed below.

1. The method should enable the use of content created with scanning systems and modeling packages as well as the use of existing libraries of content. It is important that the content elements can be imported in various formats, including formats which are currently popular (e.g., FBX, OBJ, 3DS), but not limiting further extensibility of the supported set of file formats.
2. The method should enable parameterization of content. The use of parameters with well-defined meaning and range of values greatly decreases the amount (entropy) of information that designers need to pass to the system when designing content.
3. The method should enable the use of components. Components enable creation of higher-level building blocks, which are easier and quicker to use. Although by themselves constraining, used in connection with parameterization, components provide a very powerful tool.
4. The method should enable the use of high-level content models, which can greatly simplify understanding and management of complex content structures.
5. The method should enable separation of concerns, thus enabling specialization of designers and development of more efficient tools providing particular functions.
6. The method should enable the use of semantics as a formal way of describing the role and the structure of virtual scene components, thus defining their possible usage and simplifying search and parameterization.
7. Finally, the method should enable creation of content by groups of users either explicitly or implicitly collaborating in the content design process.

Requirements 1 and 3 are met by currently available VR/AR authoring environments, such as the *Unity Game Engine IDE* [34]. Requirement 2 – the use of parameters – is commonly used for built-in elements of editing tools, but rarely available for elements created by designers. Requirement 4 – the use of high-level models – is also available, through the use of scene models, scene graphs and predefined complex elements, such as *Prefabs* in Unity. Requirement 5 is achieved by good practices in the current content creation pipelines, but not explicitly supported by content design tools. Requirement 6 is currently not supported, while requirement 7 only partially – by the use of content sharing websites.

3.2   The SemFlex Approach

To enable the use of parameterized user-contributed content elements, the use of semantics in content design, social creation of content by multiple distributed users, as well as separation of concerns in the design process, a new approach to collaborative semantic content creation, called *SemFlex*, is proposed in this paper.

In the SemFlex approach, the 3D content creation process is performed in an open distributed architecture, which enables sharing semantically described content. Content creation is understood here as both designing basic content elements and combining elements of previously created content – including those created by other users – thus enabling designers to contribute content in a truly social manner. The possibility of involving large groups of prosumers in the 3D content creation process is a necessity for the development of content, which is interesting for users, up-to-date and of adequate quality.

The basic unit of content in the SemFlex approach is a semantically described parameterized content element, called *Flex Object* (*FO*). Semantic editing tools (IDEs – Integrated Design Environments) are used by content designers both to create 3D virtual scenes based on FOs retrieved from shared content repositories and to create new FOs and upload them to a shared repository. Different types of FOs can be created, depending on their primary content (e.g., scene objects, materials, animations). FOs may represent simple independent generic components intended for publication in a library (e.g., furniture, plants, cars, people, equipment) or complex ready-to-use environments that can form a basis for building games, animations and videos. FOs may be offered in the shared repositories using various licensing and pricing models.

Each of the FOs may be *parameterized* – regardless of whether it is simple or complex. Parameterization enables producing more generic components with wider possibilities of reuse, and enable users of these components to adjust them to their particular requirements. Default values of parameters permit designers to use FOs without setting all parameters.

Parameters are not intended to replace basic functionality of the used IDEs, but to enhance them with additional functionality. For example, characteristics such as position, orientation and scale of objects are well handled by exiting IDEs, so they do not need to be represented as parameters (although they could). However composition of objects from sub-objects (e.g., objects to put onto a shelf), identification of materials (e.g., material to be used for a table), physical properties or objects, animations and behavior are typically much more difficult to handle. For example, a query in the Unity Asset Store "table material" returns 1540 results (as of Feb 28th, 2017), but no materials for the use in table design are really found. Instead, there is a variety of different tables and furniture sets in different prices (Fig. 1). A designer has to use a specific texture library (e.g., [30]) to find an appropriate image and build a material from scratch. More than one texture is typically needed to create a realistic material, which makes the process even more complex and time consuming.

Fig. 1. Searching for a table material in the Unity Asset Store.

Parameterization in SemFlex encompasses different types of features of the Flex Objects (Fig. 2). The list is extensible – new types of parameters may be added in particular implementations. Basic types of FO parameters include:

- *Sub-Object* – this type of parameters is used for composition of objects. An object may consist of several geometrical elements (e.g., a building may consist of a facade, a number of identical windows positioned in specific places and a door – these would be three different *Sub-Object* parameters). It is important that a *Sub-Object* may be left empty, and that the same *Sub-Object* may be used multiple times in an FO (e.g., windows, people in a crowd, cars in streets).
- *Visual Material* – this type of parameters is used for defining visual appearance of geometrical objects. Each of the materials used in an FO may be declared as a parameter. Visual material encompasses such elements as color, texture, smoothness, normal map, height map, occlusion, emission, etc. The same *Visual Material* parameter can be assigned to several components of an FO (e.g., parameter *Furnishing Textile* could set a material for several objects: a sofa, an armchair, and a number of chairs).
- *Physical Material* – this type of parameters is used for defining physical properties of objects in a virtual scene. This includes such elements as static friction, dynamic friction and bounciness. Again, the same *Physical Material* can be assigned to several components of an FO to ease and speed up the virtual scene design process.
- *Animation* – this type of parameters is used for establishing animation properties of objects. This includes the animator (i.e., a state machine used for animation) and a number of animation clips associated with the state machine.

– *Animation Clip* – this type of parameters is used when an animator is fixed in the object or selected by the *Animation* parameter, and there are still independent animation clips to be assigned to the object.

– *Behavior* – this type of parameters is used for assigning scripts describing behavior of objects in the scene. This can include both individual behavior of objects (e.g., a window handle rotates when pushed) or interaction between components (e.g., window opens when the handle is rotated). When the behavior scripts describe internal behavior of an FO, they can be automatically assigned to sub-objects through a name or a tag. When behavior scripts are to govern interaction between elements created within different FO parameterization sessions, the corresponding objects may have to be set later by the designer.

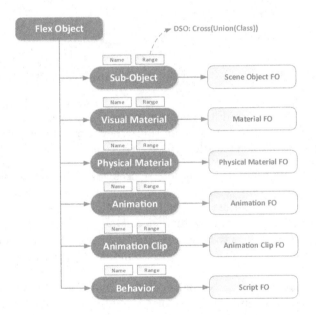

Fig. 2. Types of Flex Object parameters.

4   The Semantic Content Design Environment

4.1   Implementation

The SemFlex approach has been implemented within the *Semantic Content Design Environment* – an open distributed architecture consisting of three kinds of communicating nodes: *Semantic IDEs*, *Shared Content Repositories* (SCRs) and *Domain Ontology Services* (DOSs), as presented in Fig. 3.

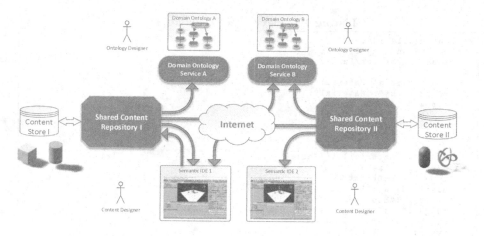

Fig. 3. Architecture of the semantic content design environment.

The Semantic IDEs, implemented as an extension to the Unity IDE (Fig. 4), communicate with SCRs and DOSs implemented as REST services running on web servers. The Unity IDE has been selected because it is a popular cross-platform and feature-rich game engine and IDE [34]. Unity can be extended with custom menus, editor windows, custom component editors and property drawers using JavaScript and C#. The SemFlex Unity extension enables both creating virtual scenes using remote semantically described resources (FOs) and creating and uploading such resources in the form of parameterized FOs to remote SCRs.

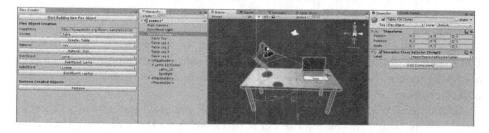

Fig. 4. Semantic IDE implemented as an extension to Unity IDE

To achieve maximum uniformity in the use of SemFlex content, the Unity package file format is used for all kinds of SemFlex resources. To keep the format of resources intact, the parameterization information, which is necessary for SemFlex, is added as external metadata files. These files are encoded in JSON and contain information about the name and the type of the Flex Object (Scene Object, Material, Animation, etc.), the name of the asset folder where the resource should be stored (to maintain compatibility with non-SemFlex content creation pipelines) and SemFlex parameters. An example of a SemFlex metadata file is provided in Listing 1.1 below.

Listing 1.1. Flex Object metadata file.

```
{"name":"Table FO",
 "type":"Scene Object",
 "folder":"Interior/Furniture",
 "parameters":[
  {"type":"Visual Material",
   "displayName":"Material",
   "target":["Table Top",
             "Table Leg 1",
             "Table Leg 2",
             "Table Leg 3",
             "Table Leg 4"]
   "range":"(Material) & (Table)",
   "empty":"false"}
  {"type":"Sub-Object",
   "displayName":"Left Object",
   "target":"Sub-Object 1",
   "range":"(Office equipment, Computers) & (Desk)",
   "empty":"true"}
  {"type":"Sub-Object",
   "displayName":"Right Object",
   "target":"Sub-Object 2",
   "range":"(Office equipment, Computers) & (Desk)",
   "empty":"true"}
 ]}
```

4.2   Content Design Example

Instantiation of a Flex Object starts with opening the *Flex Creator* window available in the Semantic IDE menu (Fig. 5). Top-left part of the figure is the scene hierarchy panel – initially containing only a light source, a camera and a single object – Floor. Bottom-left part is the Flex Creator tool. The right part contains a preview of the created 3D scene. The Flex Creator editor provides a field for entering the URI of an SCR and the button "Start Building New Flex Object". When the button is pressed, a list of available categories and objects is displayed as a pop-up menu. The list of categories is taken from a DSO used by the repository (cf. Fig. 7). After selection of the object to create, a corresponding "Create:" button appears. When a user confirms, the actual object creation process starts.

The object creation process consists of several phases. First, the object package (.unitypackage) containing the FO is retrieved from the server together with the SemFlex metadata file (.meta). After the package has been imported and stored in a temporary directory, the SemFlex editor installs the content of the package in the original location retrieved from the metadata file. Preserving the original package location is important to guarantee the reuse of already downloaded packages and compatibility with non-SemFlex content used by the designer. Regardless of whether a particular element has been downloaded as a SemFlex FO or as an independent asset – it can be used in the IDE in the same way. After installing the package content, the Flex Object is created in the scene and attached to the current parameterization context. Next, based on the parameters described in the metadata file, further parameterization elements are created in the Flex Creator window, enabling continuation of the instantiation and parameterization process.

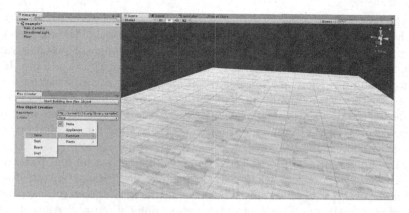

Fig. 5. Flex Creator – selection of a Flex Object

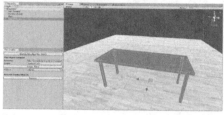

(a) FO created without the Material parameter set.

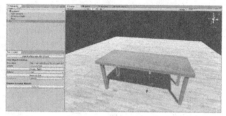

(b) FO with assigned material "Oak".

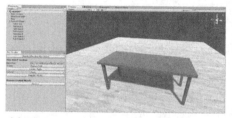

(c) FO with assigned material "Plastic".

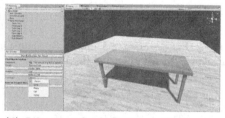

(d) Selection of a Sub-Object FO by a semantic category.

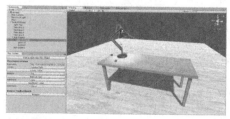

(e) Sub-Object "Lamp" instantiated in a placeholder associated with a sub-object parameter.

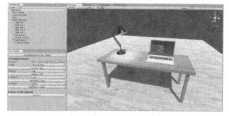

(f) Second sub-object parameter "Laptop" assigned.

Fig. 6. Flex Creator – instantiating a Flex Object.

In the presented example (Fig. 6), the *Table FO* is associated with an *Material FO*, whose selection is indicated as the *Material* parameter. The parameter has clearly indicated domain (table top and legs) and a range of possible values. The range identification is performed through the use of DSO concepts. In the presented example, the texture needs to be an instance of two classes (or their subclasses) from the domain ontology: *Material* and *Table*. A generalization could be achieved, when instead the *Table* class, the *Furniture* class were used. This would provide more results, but not necessarily all of them would be usable in the given context.

Such a fine-grained approach to content componentization and parameterization has two important advantages: (1) it simplifies the content creation by enabling the designer to select only suitable elements in the given context, and (2) it contributes to the establishment of large collections of reusable content (FOs). Subsequent steps of instantiating the Table FO are presented in Fig. 6(a)–(f).

Fig. 7. Fragment of a Domain Specific Ontology used for categorization of interior furniture objects specified in OWL.

5   Conclusions

In this paper, a new approach to collaborative content creation in a distributed environment has been presented. The approach, called *SemFlex*, is based on the concept of the *Flex Object* – a semantically-described shared parameterized object, which is a unit of content reuse and extension. The method is flexible in that it enables both transition from non-parameterized to parametrized content and vice versa, i.e., providing the ability to use existing content libraries to create new parameterized content and use parameterized content to create final virtual scenes. Therefore a mechanism is provided to reuse user-generated content to create new user-generated content in a structured way, which forms a foundation for *social content creation in 3D*.

The content creation process is performed in a distributed architecture with multiple collaborating designers. Collaborating designers can work with a single repository (SCR), but multiple SCRs can be set up for different teams or subject domains. Content design is simplified by the use semantics. A taxonomy is used to describe classes of objects. These classes are used to define ranges of FO parameter values, therefore reducing the target object sets when parameterizing a particular feature of an object.

Currently, the Semantic IDE – implemented as an editor extension to the Unity IDE – provides a wizard-like instantiation of semantic FOs, import of content from SCRs and creation of parameterized FO packages from existing content elements (Fig. 4). Parameterization of the created FOs is performed manually, by editing the generated metadata file. In future work, we plan to extend the semantic FO exporter to support selection of parameterized components and indication of their semantic ranges based on DSOs. This will further simplify the FO design process.

The presented method of building semantic parameterized content elements and their instantiation has been tested with limited number of relatively simple design scenarios. In future work, we plan to perform larger design trials, which will involve higher number of designers building more complex 3D environments.

Acknowledgments. This work was supported by the Polish National Science Centre (NCN) under Grant No. DEC-2012/07/B/ST6/01523.

References

1. Alpcan, T., Bauckhage, C., Kotsovinos, E.: Towards 3D internet: why, what, and how? In: International Conference on Cyberworlds, CW 2007, pp. 95–99. IEEE (2007)
2. Berger, M., Tagliasacchi, A., Seversky, L., Alliez, P., Levine, J., Sharf, A., Silva, C.: State of the art in surface reconstruction from point clouds. In: Eurographics 2014 - State of the Art Reports. EUROGRAPHICS star report, Strasbourg, France, vol. 1, pp. 161–185, April 2014. https://hal.inria.fr/hal-01017700
3. Chaudhuri, S., Kalogerakis, E., Giguere, S., Funkhouser, T.: Attribit: content creation with semantic attributes. In: Proceedings of the 26th Annual ACM Symposium on User Interface Software and Technology, pp. 193–202. ACM (2013)
4. Creaform: Metrology Products (2017). https://www.creaform3d.com/en/metrology-solutions/creaform-product-overview
5. Dachselt, R., Hinz, M., Meissner, K.: Contigra: An XML-based architecture for component-oriented 3D applications. In: Proceedings of the Seventh International Conference on 3D Web Technology, Web3D 2002, NY, USA, pp. 155–163. ACM, New York (2002)
6. Dassault Systèmes: 3D ContentCentral (2017). https://www.3dcontentcentral.com/
7. De Troyer, O., Bille, W., Romero, R., Stuer, P.: On generating virtual worlds from domain ontologies. In: Proceedings of the 9th International Conference on Multi-Media Modeling, Taipei, Taiwan, pp. 279–294 (2003)
8. E-on software Inc.: PlantFactory (2017). http://www.plantfactory-tech.com/
9. E-on software Inc.: VUE - Solutions for Digital Nature (2017). http://www.e-onsoftware.com/

10. ECMA International: Universal 3D File Format (2007). http://www. ecma-international.org/
11. Esri: Esri CityEngine (2017). http://www.esri.com/software/cityengine
12. Flotyński, J., Walczak, K.: Ontology-based creation of 3D content in a service-oriented environment. In: Abramowicz, W. (ed.) BIS 2015. LNBIP, vol. 208, pp. 77–89. Springer, Cham (2015). doi:10.1007/978-3-319-19027-3_7
13. Flotyński, J., Walczak, K.: Ontology-based representation and modelling of synthetic 3D content: a state-of-the-art review. In: Computer Graphics Forum (2017). http://dx.doi.org/10.1111/cgf.13083
14. Fraunhofer I.G.D: X3DOM (2017). http://www.x3dom.org/
15. Giannattasio, T.: PHOTON - CSS 3D Lighting Engine (2017). http://photon. attasi.com/
16. Highend3D: High Quality 3D Models, Scripts, Plugins and More! (2017). https:// www.highend3d.com/
17. Interactive Data Visualization Inc.: Speedtree (2017). http://www.speedtree.com/
18. ISO/IEC: MPEG-4 Information technology - Coding of audio-visual objects (2017). http://mpeg.chiariglione.org/standards/mpeg-4
19. Khronos Group: COLLADA - 3D Asset Exchange Schema (2017). https://www. khronos.org/collada/
20. Khronos Group: WebGL - OpenGL ES for the Web (2017). https://www.khronos. org/webgl/
21. Latoschik, M.E., Blach, R., Iao, F.: Semantic modelling for virtual worlds a novel paradigm for realtime interactive systems? In: VRST, pp. 17–20 (2008)
22. META-Elements: META-Elements (2017). https://www.meta-elements.com/
23. Pellens, B., De Troyer, O., Kleinermann, F.: CoDePA: a conceptual design pattern approach to model behavior for X3D worlds. In: Proceedings of the 13th International Symposium on 3D Web Technology, Web3D 2008, NY, USA, pp. 91–99 ACM, New York (2008). http://doi.acm.org/10.1145/1394209.1394229
24. Planetside Software LLC: Terragen 4 (2017). http://planetside.co.uk/
25. Polys, N., Visamsetty, S., Battarechee, P., Tilevich, E.: Design patterns in componentized scenegraphs. In: Proceedings of SEARIS. Shaker Verlag (2009)
26. Roast, K.: Phoria (2014). http://www.kevs3d.co.uk/dev/phoria/
27. SideFX: Houdini VFX and Animation Tools (2017). https://www.sidefx.com/
28. Spagnuolo, M., Falcidieno, B.: 3D media and the semantic web. IEEE Intell. Syst. **24**(2), 90–96 (2009)
29. Sprite3D.js: A small library for generating and manipulating CSS 3D transforms (2017). http://minimal.be/lab/Sprite3D/
30. Textures.com: Textures for 3D, graphic design and Photoshop (2017). http://www. textures.com/
31. Three.js: Javascript 3D library (2017). https://threejs.org/
32. TurboSquid Inc.: 3D Models for Professionals (2017). https://www.turbosquid. com/
33. Unity Technologies: Asset Store (2017). https://www.assetstore.unity3d.com/en/
34. Unity Technologies: Unity Game Engine v. 5.5.2 (2017). https://unity3d.com/ unity
35. Van Gool, L., Leibe, B., Müller, P., Vergauwen, M., Weise, T.: 3D challenges and a non-in-depth overview of recent progress. In: 3DIM, pp. 118–132 (2007)
36. Visamsetty, S.S.S., Bhattacharjee, P., Polys, N.: Design patterns in X3D toolkits. In: Proceedings of the 13th International Symposium on 3D Web Technology, Web3D 2008, NY, USA, pp. 101–104. ACM, New York (2008). http://doi.acm. org/10.1145/1394209.1394230

37. Voxel.js: An open source voxel game building toolkit for modern web browsers (2014). http://voxeljs.com/
38. Voxelogic: Acropora (2017). http://www.voxelogic.com/
39. Walczak, K.: Flex-VR: configurable 3D web applications. In: Proceedings of the Conference on Human System Interactions, pp. 135–140. IEEE (2008)
40. Walczak, K.: Structured design of interactive vr applications. In: Proceedings of the 13th International Symposium on 3D Web Technology, Web3D 2008, NY, USA, pp. 105–113. ACM, New York (2008). http://doi.acm.org/10.1145/1394209.1394231
41. Walczak, K., Cellary, W.: X-VRML for advanced virtual reality applications. Comput. **36**(3), 89–92 (2003)
42. Walczak, K., Flotyński, J.: On-demand generation of 3D content based on semantic meta-scenes. In: De Paolis, L.T., Mongelli, A. (eds.) AVR 2014. LNCS, vol. 8853, pp. 313–332. Springer, Cham (2014). doi:10.1007/978-3-319-13969-2_24
43. Walczak, K., Flotyński, J.: Semantic query-based generation of customized 3D scenes. In: Proceedings of the 20th International Conference on 3D Web Technology, Web3D 2015, NY, USA, pp. 123–131. ACM, New york (2015). http://doi.acm.org/10.1145/2775292.2775311
44. Walczak, K., Wojciechowski, R., Wójtowicz, A.: Interactive production of dynamic 3D sceneries for virtual television studio. In: The 7th Virtual Reality IC VRIC - Laval Virtual 2005, pp. 167–177, April 2005. http://www.laval-virtual.org/en/pres-colloque.php
45. Web3D: The Virtual Reality Modeling Language - ISO/IEC 14772-1 (2006). http://www.web3d.org/standards/all
46. Web 3D: X3D Specifications - ISO/IEC-19775-1 (2013). http://web3d.org/x3d/specifications/
47. Zahariadis, T., Daras, P., Laso-Ballesteros, I.: Towards future 3D media internet. In: NEM Summit, pp. 13–15 (2008)

Feature Fusion of HOG and GSP
for Smile Recognition

Hemant Kumar Meena[1][(✉)], Kamlesh Kumar Sharma[1], and S.D. Joshi[2]

[1] Department of Electronics and Communication Engineering,
Malaviya National Institute of Technology, Jaipur, Rajasthan, India
hmeena.ee@mnit.ac.in
[2] Department of Electrical Engineering,
Indian Institute of Technology Delhi, New Delhi, India

Abstract. Recognizing smile conveys the information about the happy mood and the acceptability of the message. The Histogram of Oriented Gradient (HOG) has been used to find out the face detection and the facial expression recognition. However, due to the large feature length of facial expression, there is a challenge to decrease the size of the feature vector. This paper demonstrates the proposed method for smile recognition on JAFFE dataset and Cohn-Kanade dataset by combining the HOG with Graph Signal Processing (GSP). Not only, the feature length is significantly reduced but also, the accuracy has been increased in the smile recognition using the proposed method.

1 Introduction

The innate ability of human being that helps to effectively communicate each other is through the understanding of non verbal expressions [1]. Facial expression are the important component of the non verbal gestures. Due to the wide application of smile detection in interactive systems, video conferences, digital video cameras and patient monitoring [2], the smile recognition is a hot research topic. The facial expression recognition can be divided into the three stages as shown in Fig. 1:

During the preprocessing, the noise removal/enhancement is done. After the face detection, the facial features including the eyes, nose, mouth, eyebrows etc. are extracted. The different techniques for feature extraction include Gabor filter [3], Principal Component Analysis(PCA) [4], Independent Component Analysis (ICA), Linear Discriminant Analysis (LDA), LBP (Local Binary patterns). In the last step, the classifier using the methods Support Vector Machine (SVM), k-Nearest Neighbor (kNN), Neural Network and now, Deep Learning are used to categorize the expression into different labels.

To extract the information of the facial expression lying in the edges, HOG has been used for smile recognition [5,6,13]. Thereafter, the reduction in feature dimension is focused. Because the information in facial expression contains the joint relationship of the edges at local level (e.g. mouth and eye pair here), the Graph signal processing (GSP) preserves the relationship of the edges at local

© Springer International Publishing AG 2017
L.T. De Paolis et al. (Eds.): AVR 2017, Part II, LNCS 10325, pp. 402–409, 2017.
DOI: 10.1007/978-3-319-60928-7_34

Fig. 1. Facial expression recognition system.

neighborhood level. It can be used to reduce the dimension of the feature vector significantly as well. Our objective is to improve the accuracy as well as to reduce the size of feature vector simultaneously.

For smile recognition mouth plays an important role in comparison with the other regions on a face [7]. HOG operator is introduced for extracting the mouth region shape. In addition, the eye pair further distinguishes the smile in the subtle face expressions. After concatenating these features from the face, the length of the feature vector becomes very large. In this paper, the focus is upon addressing the length of the concatenated feature vector of a smile expression. The graph signal approach has been applied to reduce the length of the concatenated feature. Then the nearest neighbor classifier is applied to distinguish the expression into either the smile or non smile.

The remainder of the paper is organized as follows: Sect. 2 introduces proposed approach, GSP and HOG in brief. Section 3 explains upon the experimental performance using the combination of the GSP and HOG. Finally, the derived conclusions based upon the experimental performance are given in the Sect. 4.

2 Feature Selection Approach

2.1 Proposed Method of HOG and GSP for Smile Recognition

As the information of the facial expression lies in the form of edges esp. across the specific regions of face, the gradients across the edges is used to extract that information. HOG has been found to be effective for computing such gradients. The size of the feature vector resulted from HOG is further reduced by taking the projection of the signal on the significant Laplacian basis using the GSP approach. Moreover, the specific facial expression are differentiated from each other by their joint relationship of the edges at local level of the mouth and the eye pair. By capturing that co-relationship of the edges structure, GSP approach has been found to improve the accuracy of the smile recognition. Finally, the accuracy has been increased along with the reduction in the size of the feature vector. The brief description about the functional block of the proposed method framework is given in the following sections.

Figure 2 illustrates the flowchart of the proposed smile recognition method.

2.2 Feature Extraction with HOG

The Histogram of Orientation Gradients (HOGs), proposed by Dalal and Triggs [8], is well suited to robustly extract features for visual object recognition. In

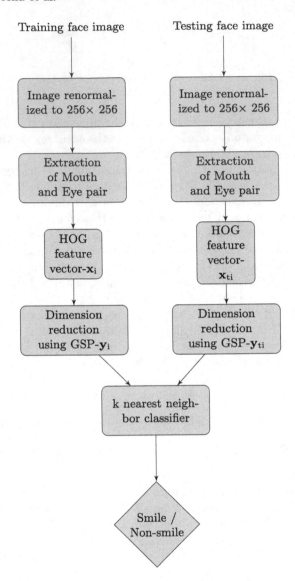

Fig. 2. The block diagram of the proposed method

HOG descriptor computation, the gradient of the image is computed and the phase is quantized according to a predefined number of orientation intervals, which will represent the bins in the histogram. Thereafter the image is divided in small regions called cells from which the orientation histogram is built by votes of the quantized orientation of each pixel. These votes are weighted by the magnitude of the gradient for each pixel. Subsequently cells are grouped in blocks which are the normalization units of the algorithm. This normalization

Fig. 3. The HOG feature of the smiley mouth.

Fig. 4. The HOG feature of the smiley eyes.

constitutes an important part of the algorithm, because it represents a smoothing factor and limits the effect of the variations of the gradient in local areas due to illumination and object/background contrast. Finally the descriptor $\mathbf{x}_i$ is created by the concatenation of the block-normalized histograms of all the cells. The HOG features for the smiley mouth and the eyes is shown in Fig. 3 and Fig. 4 respectively.

2.3   Feature Extraction with Graph Signal Processing

In order to reduce the dimension of the above computed feature vector $\mathbf{x}_i$ using the HOG, the GSP is applied. The GSP requires the signal to be represented as the graph, shown in Fig. 5.

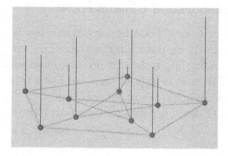

Fig. 5. A random positive graph signal on the vertices of the Petersen graph.

For building a graph, let each facial image be considered as the vertex (denoted as red in Fig. 5) and X be the graph signal with N nodes on the vertices $V=\{v_1, v_2, ... v_N\}$ connected by the edges $E=\{e_{ij}:v_i,v_j \epsilon$ V$\}$. Here, the computed feature vector $\mathbf{x}_i$ is taken as the i-th component of the graph signal X lying on vertex v_i, shown in blue in Fig. 5. The edges of the graph are undirected here. The level of connectivity for an edge joining vertices v_i and v_j is specified by the associated weight W_{ij} and it is defined as [12]

$$W_{ij} = \begin{cases} exp\frac{(-\|\mathbf{x_i}-\mathbf{x_j}\|)^2}{t}, & \text{if } \|\mathbf{x_i} - \mathbf{x_j}\|)^2 < \varepsilon \\ 0, & \text{elsewhere} \end{cases} \tag{1}$$

where the symbol ($\|\mathbf{x}\|$) stands for L_2 norm of a vector.

A graph is compactly represented by its adjacency matrix W where each entry is given by W_{ij}. Along with the degree matrix (defined as $D = \text{diag}\{d_1, d_2, \ldots d_N\}$, where each d_i is the sum of the weights of all edges connected to v_i), the matrix L gives the graph Laplacian: $\boldsymbol{L} = \boldsymbol{D} - \boldsymbol{W}$. The Laplacian is a difference operator when applied to a graph signal X [9]:

$$L\mathbf{x_i} = \sum_{v_j : e_{ij} \epsilon E} W_{ij}[\mathbf{x_i} - \mathbf{x_j}] \tag{2}$$

where, $\mathbf{x}_i$ indicates the value of X at vertex v_i. Then, the eigenvectors and eigenvalues for the generalized eigenvector problem are computed as follows [12]:

$$XLX^\mathsf{T}\mathbf{a} = \lambda XDX^\mathsf{T}\mathbf{a} \tag{3}$$

Let the column vectors $\mathbf{a}_0,\ldots,\mathbf{a}_{l-1}$ be the solution of (3) corresponding to the eigenvalues, $\lambda_0 < \ldots\ldots < \lambda_{l-1}$. The reduced vector $\mathbf{y}_i$ is given as follows:

$$\mathbf{y_i} = A^\mathsf{T}\mathbf{x_i}, A = (\mathbf{a}_0, \ldots, \mathbf{a}_{l-1}) \tag{4}$$

where $\mathbf{y_i}$ is a l-dimensional vector ($l << n$), and A is a $n \times l$ matrix. Finally, the k-Nearest Neighborhood classifier (kNN) is trained and used to classify each testing facial image.

2.4 k-Nearest Neighborhood Classifier(kNN)

kNN is a non parametric lazy learning algorithm i.e. it does not make any assumptions on the underlying data distribution. The term 'lazy' implies that it does not use the training data points to do any generalization. Thus, it keeps all the training data. The cost is high in terms of both time and memory. Yet it is preferred due to its simplicity in implementation.

Suppose there are 'C' known pattern classes and the number of samples in each class are n_i (i=1,2,.....C). For a given new sample 'Y', the nearest neighbor can be found out as follows:

$$d_i(Y) = \| Y - Y_{ir} \|^2 \tag{5}$$

where Y_{ir} is the training sample of class i as well as the nearest neighbor to the sample Y. $d_i(Y)$ is the distance based upon the similarity (generally,the Euclidean distance is selected) in (5). 'Y' is considered as belonging to the class 'q' in case the distance between 'Y' and the class 'q' is minimal, shown as follows:

$$d_q(Y) = min_i d_i(Y) \tag{6}$$

3 Experiment and Results

Two standard facial databases have been used to study the performance of our method. The two databases are as follows: JAFFE database [10] and Cohn-Kanade AU Coded Facial Expression (CKAUCFE) database [5]. In JAFFE database, there are 213 images of 10 subjects with 7 expressions viz. "anger", "disgust", "fear", "happy", "neutral", "sad" and "surprise". CKAUCFE database includes around 2000 image sequences of around 200 subjects, and consists of 100 university students ranging in age from 18 to 30 years.

3.1 Experimental Data

(a) JAFFE database: Every subject has 3–4 samples for each of the expression. The happy expression is considered as the smile, shown in Fig. 6 and the other expressions are considered as the non smile. For our experiments, training images (90) are taken from the separate female subjects and testing images (36) are different from those female images in the training set. (b) CKAUCFE database: The 267 frames have been selected from it. For each expression of a subject, the last five frames from each set were selected as peak expression images. Then the frames were divided into two classes: smile (shown in Fig. 7) and non-smile facial expressions. Finally, the total number of positive samples (smile) and negative samples (non-smile) were 90 and 177 respectively. For the training, total samples include 65 positive sample and 127 negative sample. The remaining samples were used for testing. The images of the training and testing were selected from the different subjects i.e. the subject selected for the training sample is not selected in the testing for either of the positive or the negative sample.

3.2 Experimental Performance

The images are resized into the size of 256×256. The face from the given image has been detected by the Viola-Jones Face Detection algorithm [11]. Further, the active face patches including the mouth and eye pair are extracted from the face using the Viola-Jones algorithm again. On extracting the features from HOG algorithm, the feature vector $\mathbf{x}_i$ is computed. Using the GSP, the final feature vector $\mathbf{y}_i$ is computed. The number of nearest neighbor is taken as 8. As the appropriate size of the HOG cell for the mouth and the eye pair is selected, the feature length and the recognition rate for the JAFFE and CKAUCFE databases are calculated and shown in Table 1. Thereafter, on using the GSP along with

Fig. 6. Sample of JAFFE database-Smile.

Fig. 7. Sample of Cohn-Kanade database-Smile.

the HOG, the feature vector length has been significantly decreased (due to more redundancy) but also leads to the improvement in the recognition rate for both the databases, as shown in Table 1.

Table 1. The overall comparison of HOG and HOG+GSP on the JAFFE and CKAUCFE database

Method	Database	Feature dimension	Overall recognition rate (in %)
HOG	JAFFE	2484	88.88
HOG+GSP	JAFFE	29	91.66
HOG	CKAUCFE	6084	89.93
HOG+GSP	CKAUCFE	86	93.33

On comparing the proposed method with the existing methods in [5,6] for smile recognition, Table 2 shows that the proposed method is equally comparable to the existing methods on the basis of the recognition rate and significantly outperforms the existing methods in the feature dimension.

3.3   Discussion of Result

The application of GSP brings closer the similar neighboring points of the smiley face nearer in the whole image space while the dissimilar points in the neighborhood of the smiley face are placed farther in the whole space. As a result of the reorganization of the neighboring points, the influence of significant related

Table 2. Comparison of the proposed method with the existing methods for smile recognition

Method	Features used	Database	Feature dimension	Overall recognition rate (in %)
[5]	HOG+LBP	JAFFE	Not given	90.47
Proposed method	HOG+GSP	JAFFE	29	91.66
[6]	PHOG+Gabor	Cohn-Kanade	840	**93.48**
Proposed method	HOG+GSP	Cohn-Kanade	86	93.33

regions is increased while the influence of unrelated regions are minimized on each other. Henceforth, the recognition of the correct smile has been increased by the fused method of HOG and the GSP.

4 Conclusion

This paper proposes an improved method for the smile recognition based on the Histogram of oriented gradients and Graph signal processing. Henceforth, the feature size is decreased along with the improved recognition rate of the smile recognition from this new fused method of HOG and the GSP.

References

1. Mehrabian, A.: Communication without words. Psychol. Today **2**, 53–55 (1968)
2. Mandal, M.K., Pandey, R., Prasad, A.B.: Facial expressions of emotions and schizophrenia: a review. Schizophr. Bull. **24**(3), 399–412 (1998)
3. Lyons, M.J., Budynek, J., Akamatsu, S.: Automatic classification of single facial images. IEEE Trans. Pattern Anal. Mach. Intell. **21**(12), 1357–1362 (1999)
4. Turk, M.A., Pentland, A.P.: Face recognition using eigenfaces. In: IEEE Computer Society Conference on Computer Vision and Pattern Recognition (CVPR 1991), pp. 586–591 (1991)
5. Li, Y.: Smile recognition based on face texture and mouth shape features. In: IEEE Workshop on Electronics, Computer and Applications, pp. 606–609 (2014)
6. Bai, Y., Guo, L., Jin, L., Huang, Q.: A novel feature extraction method using pyramid histogram of orientation gradients for smile recognition. In: 16th IEEE International Conference on Image Processing (ICIP), pp. 3305–3308 (2009)
7. Fridlund, A.I.: Human facial expression: An evolutionary view. Academic Press, San Diego (1994)
8. Dalal, N., Triggs, B.: Histograms of oriented gradients for human Detection. In: IEEE Computer Society Conference on Computer Vision and Pattern Recognition (CVPR 2005), vol. I, pp. 886–893 (2005)
9. Shuman, D.I., Narang, S.K., Frossard, P., Ortega, A., Vandergheynst, P.: The emerging field of signal processing on graphs: extending high-dimensional data analysis to networks and other irregular domains. IEEE Signal Process. Mag. **30**(3), 83–98 (2013)
10. Lyons, M.J., Akemastu, S., Kamachi, M., Gyoba,J.: Coding facial expressions with gabor wavelets. In: 3rd IEEE International Conference on Automatic Face and Gesture Recognition, pp. 200–205 (1998)
11. Viola, P., Jones, M.: Rapid object detection using a boosted cascade of simple features. In: Proceedings of the IEEE Computer Society Conference on Computer Vision and Pattern Recognition (CVPR), vol. 1, pp. I-511–I-518 (2001)
12. He, X., Niyogi, P.: Locality preserving projections. In: NIPS, vol. 16 (2003)
13. Hong, L., Gao, Y., Wu, P.: Smile detection in unconstrained scenarios using self-similarity of gradients features. In: 2014 IEEE International Conference on Image Processing (ICIP), pp. 1455–1459 (2014)
14. Kanade, T., Cohn, J.F., Tian, Y.: Comprehensive database for facial expression analysis. In: Fourth IEEE International Conference on Automatic Face and Gesture Recognition, pp. 46–53 (2000)

Real-Time 3D Modeling with a RGB-D Camera and On-Board Processing

Wilbert G. Aguilar[1,3,4]($\boxtimes$), Guillermo A. Rodríguez[2,3],
Leandro Álvarez[2,3], Sebastián Sandoval[2,3], Fernando Quisaguano[2,3],
and Alex Limaico[2,3]

[1] Dep. Seguridad y Defensa, Universidad de las Fuerzas Armadas ESPE,
Sangolquí, Ecuador
wgaguilar@espe.edu.ec
[2] Dep. Eléctrica y Electrónica, Universidad de las Fuerzas Armadas ESPE,
Sangolquí, Ecuador
[3] CICTE Research Center, Universidad de las Fuerzas Armadas ESPE,
Sangolquí, Ecuador
[4] GREC Research Group, Universitat Politècnica de Catalunya,
Barcelona, Spain

Abstract. In this article we present a three dimensional modeling system that generates precise real-time mapping using a RGB-D camera. With the use of the light weight sensors Microsoft Kinect and small and powerful computers like the Intel Stick Core M3 Processor, our system can run all the computation and sensing required to smoothly run SLAM (Simultaneous Localization and Mapping) on-board and in real-time, removing the dependence on unreliable wireless communication. We use visual odometry, loop closure and graph optimization. Our approach is capable of generating accurate maps of several objects analyzing the data yielded by several tests of the system.

Keywords: SLAM · RGB-D · Loop closure detection · Graph optimization · Visual odometry · RANSAC · UAVs

1 Introduction

The 3D modeling of objects or environments has become a popular task, with applications in the field of medicine, games, movie industry, or architecture community. Many approaches have been developed over the last two decades, including laser range scans [1, 2], a set of different photos [3], monocular cameras [4] and stereo cameras [5], each technology with its advantages and limitations. Most of these approaches rely on the use of expensive specialized hardware, usually not affordable for many people interested in three dimensional modeling. Our proposed solution is the use of the SLAM (Simultaneous Localization and Mapping). This method provides a approximation of the solution, but the process for obtaining relevant reference points gives up important information that compromises the accuracy of the system.

Interest in RGB-D cameras like Microsoft Kinect or ASUS Xtion Pro has experienced an exponential grow because of their ability to provide real-time color images

© Springer International Publishing AG 2017
L.T. De Paolis et al. (Eds.): AVR 2017, Part II, LNCS 10325, pp. 410–419, 2017.
DOI: 10.1007/978-3-319-60928-7_35

and depth maps. SLAM solution, based on scale information of 3D depth sensing with the visual information of the cameras, is a new low-cost approach to create real time 3D environment maps. Some methods use dense visual odometry [6, 7], showing accurate results on the main problematic, but using desktop or laptop computers to process the visual data. This represents a considerable complication when modeling large objects or environments, because of the mobility needed to map them. This inconvenience can be solved by on-board processing using portable and powerful mini computers.

Our approach consists in an implementation of the SLAM solution by the rtabmap libray from ROS, using dense color and depth images obtained from RGB-D cameras, and is based on contributions made in loop closure detection [8] and graph-based SLAM [9]. We show that our system is able to perform SLAM for three dimensional modeling using an Intel Stick M3 computer, allowing for the optimization of communication resources while doing real-time processing of the algorithms.

2 Related Works

The Simultaneous Localization and Mapping (SLAM) problem has been a widely known topic of the history of robotic mapping [10–13], computer graphics [14, 15] and computer vision [16–19]. The desire to create a truly autonomous robot [20–23] has led to the creation of Visual SLAM systems [24, 25], which are commonly used to extract interest points from the camera images [26–28], simplifying data association. For online loop closure detection, the bag-of-words [29] approach is commonly used [30, 31]. The bag-of-words approach consists in representing each image by visual words taken from a vocabulary. Graph pose optimization approaches [32, 33] can then be used to reduce odometry errors using poses and link transformations inside each map and also between the maps.

Different sensor procedures have been used in SLAM, including 2D scanners [34, 35], monocular cameras [36, 37], and recently RGB-D sensors such as the Microsft Kinect [38] or the Asus Xtion Pro Live. Several SLAM approaches for modeling systems have been made in the last few years, including autonomous mapping and localization in outdoor environments [39], but performing all the hard processing work off-board in a ground station, taking away the real time capabilities from the system.

3 Our Approach

In our work, the basic structure of the map is a graph with nodes and links. These nodes store information like the odometry poses for every location taken in the map, the visual information of the RGB and depth images of the Kinect, and the visual words used for loop closure detection. As for the links, they save the rigid geometrical transformations within nodes. Close links are added among the current and the previous nodes with their corresponding odometry transformation. Loop closure links are added when a loop closure is detected within the current node and one from the same or previous map. We combined visual odometry, loop closure detection [6] and resource optimization to provide a method smooth enough to run real time SLAM in an Intel Stick M3 for three dimensional modeling.

3.1   Visual Odometry

We use visual odometry to estimate the trajectory of the RGB-D sensor from a specific region within the image. This method is useful for the pose estimation problem which will be linked directly to the measurements given by the RGB-D sensor via a non-linear model. This model is responsible for the 3D geometric configuration of the current environment. The Fig. 2 shows the visual odometry performed by the system.

For a robust visual odometry model, the approach used on [40] is used. This method defines a RGB-D sensor with a color brightness function $I(p,t)$ and a depth function $D(p,t)$, where $p = (u,v)$ are pixel locations within the image acquired at time t. After defining a series of motion models and mathematical transformations, a non-linear least square cost function

$$C(x) = \sum_{P^* \in \mathcal{R}^*} \left(\mathcal{J}\left(w\left(P^*; T(x)\hat{T}\right)\right) - \mathcal{J}^*(P^*)\right)^2 \qquad (1)$$

is obtained, where $P^* = \{p, D\} \in \mathbb{R}^{nx3}$ and are the 3D points associated with the depth image and the image points p, the current image $\mathcal{J} = \{I, D\}$ which is the set containing both brightness and depth, w the motion model that defines the 3D geometric deformation of a structured light RGB-D camera, $T(x)$ the incremental pose to be estimated, $\hat{T}$ the estimated pose of the current image and $\mathcal{I}^*$ the reference image. By minimizing the cost function (1), the pose and trajectory of the camera can be estimated. We use the minimization approach in [40] to estimate these parameters (Fig. 1).

Fig. 1. Visual odometry performed by the system

3.2   Loop Closure Detection

Our approach uses a Bayesian filter to evaluate loop closure hypotheses over all previous images, based on the method described in [8]. The loop closure detector uses a bag-of-words (visual words, which are SURF features quantized to an incremental visual dictionary) approach to determinate the likelihood that a new image comes from a previous or new location. When a loop closure hypothesis is accepted, a new

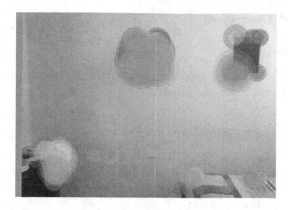

Fig. 2. Loop Closure detection performed by the system

constraint is added to the map graph, following by a graph optimizer that minimizes the errors in the map, which will be explained in the following section. A loop closure is detected when a pre-defined threshold H is reached by the loop closure hypothesis. We use the map memory management approach of [9] to limit the number of locations used for loop closure detection and graph optimization algorithms, thus respecting the real-time limitations on large-scale environments.

The visual words are extracted from the RGB image. This image is registered with the depth image, knowing that a 3D position can be computed using the calibration matrix and the depth information provided by the depth image for each point in the RGB image, giving us the 3D positions of the visual words. The RANSAC algorithm [41] uses the 3D visual word matches to compute the rigid transformation between the corresponding images when a loop closure is detected. The loop closure is accepted and a link with this transformation between the loop closure hypothesis node and the current node is added to the graph, only in the case of a minimum of I inliers are found.

3.3   Graph Optimization

We use the tree based parametrization [11] to describe an efficient configuration of the nodes in the graph. To acquire such a tree, one can construct a graph with the given trajectory of the UAV. In this procedure, the pose and link transformations are used as the limitations. Errors produced by the visual odometry estimation can be propagated to all the links when a loop closure is found, and correcting the map at the same time. In order to not overload the system and decrease the computation work of the algorithms, we are not going to use the approach proposed in [8]. Instead, we will use a more straightforward method, using the tree based parametrization algorithm [11] to create a tree from the map graph with only one map. By this procedure the tree of the algorithm will only have one root, removing the necessity of a robust memory management for the system.

4   Results and Discussion

4.1   Metric Evaluation

The metric of evaluation for our approach is based on root-mean-square error (RMSE) of measurements taken, defined as follows:

$$RMSE = \sqrt{E\left((EV - OV)^2\right)} \tag{2}$$

Where EV is the estimated value measured by our device and OV is the observed value of the real dimension of the object mapped. We will also test the response of the system to different light intensity variations.

4.2   Modeling of a Small Object

The first object to be mapped is a small box, as shown in Fig. 3. We used this object to test the precision of the system at a close range. We used the pose estimated from the corners of the box to calculate its dimensions.

Fig. 3. Test box (left) and 3D model of the box (right)

To obtain the values of the estimated dimensions of the box, we took the average value of five measurements acquired by our system. The results these measurements and the error calculated are shown in Table 1.

In Table 1, we can appreciate the small error between the real and the estimated dimensions of the object. Our system shows positive results with small objects.

4.3   Modeling of a Medium Sized Object

The next object to be mapped is a hybrid quadrotor, as can be seen in Fig. 4. Similar to the previous procedure, we used this object to test the precision of the system at a medium range. This time we used the pose estimated from the tip of the wings and the motors of the quadrotor to calculate its dimensions.

Table 1. Root mean squared error of the measurements

Measurement	Real dimensions (cm)	Estimated dimensions (cm)	RMSE
Width	30,3	30,9	0,6
Length	39,5	40,4	0,9
Height	29,3	30,1	0,8

Fig. 4. Hybrid quadrotor (left) and its 3D model (right)

Values of the estimated dimensions of the quadrotor were obtained in the same manner, taking the average value of five measurements. The results these measurements and the error calculated are shown in Table 2.

Table 2. Root mean squared error of the measurements

Measurement	Real dimensions (cm)	Estimated dimensions (cm)	RMSE
Height	15,4	14,7	0,70
Wing Length	119,35	120,7	1,35
Distance between motors	74,1	74,0	0,10

In Table 2, we can see that the estimated measurements have a small percentage of error, meaning that our system is capable of generating precise 3D maps with medium sized objects.

4.4   Modeling of a Large Object

The last object to be mapped is a large arrangement of tables, as can be seen in Fig. 5. We took a similar to the previous procedures, but we used the pose estimated from the all the corners of the tables to calculate its dimensions.

Values of the estimated dimensions of the quadrotor were obtained in the same manner, taking the average value of five measurements. Thirteen different measurements were necessary to calculate the dimensions of the object. The results these measurements and the error calculated are shown in Table 3.

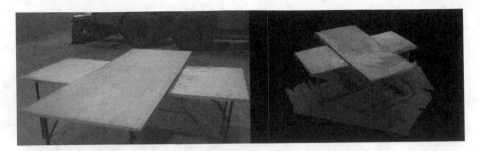

Fig. 5. Table arrangements (left) and its 3D model (right)

Table 3. Root mean squared error of the measurements

Measurement	Real dimensions (cm)	Estimated dimensions (cm)	RMSE
Side 1	65,0	67,2	2,2
Side 2	65,0	63,5	1,5
Side 3	89,5	91,2	1,7
Side 4	65,0	63,7	1,3
Side 5	65,0	64,2	0,8
Side 6	89,5	90,3	0,8
Side 7	65,0	63,8	1,2
Side 8	65,0	62,9	2,1
Side 9	89,5	91,7	2,2
Side 10	65,0	65,9	0,9
Side 11	65,0	64,2	0,8
Side 12	89,5	87,8	1,6
Height	80,3	80,9	0,6

In Table 3, we can see that the estimated measurements have a small percentage of error, but higher than previous tests. We hypothesize that because of the short range of the RGB-D camera, the error increases as the test object gets bigger. Nonetheless, the modeling is precise enough to generate a useful map of the object.

5 Conclusions and Future Work

Our proposal for on-board SLAM can perform three dimensional modeling and run smoothly on an Intel Stick core M3 computer in real time, removing the dependence on unreliable wireless communication. As shown in Table 1, our system can perform mapping in real time with a small error in measurements.

The system does not behave in the same way while doing the mapping with a weaker light source. In order to obtain the best results from the system, the mapping needs to be performed during the day. Our approach makes use of the loop closure detection algorithm to relate reference points in different instances in time. At the current state, the system is not capable of updating its map in order to adapt to the environment. We are currently developing a solution to this inconvenience.

In the future, there is necessary a wider distance of mapping. We will use a LIDAR to improve the range of action of our system, and test several algorithms in order to optimize the processing of the information.

Acknowledgement. This work is part of the projects VisualNavDrone 2016-PIC-024 and MultiNavCar 2016-PIC-025, from the Universidad de las Fuerzas Armadas ESPE, directed by Dr. Wilbert G. Aguilar.

References

1. May, S., Droschel, D., Holz, D., Fuchs, E., Malis, S., Nuchter, A., Hertzberg, J.: Three-dimensional mapping with time-of-flight cameras. J. Field Robot. **26**(1), 11–12 (2009)
2. Thrun, S., Burgard, W., Fox, D.: A real-time algorithm for mobile robot mapping with applications to multi-robot and 3D mapping. In: Proceedings of the IEEE International Conference on Robotics & Automation (2000)
3. Furukawa, Y., Curless, B., Seitz, S., Szeliski, R.: Reconstructing building interiors from images. In: Proceedings of the International Conference on Computer Vision (2009)
4. Clemente, L., Davison, A., Reid, I., Neira, J., Tardos, J.: Mapping large loops with a single hand-held camera. In: Proceedings of Robotics: Science and Systems (2007)
5. Konolige, K., Agrawal, M.: FrameSLAM: from bundle adjustment to real-time visual mapping. IEEE Trans. Rob. **25**, 5 (2008)
6. Whelan, T., Kaess, M., Leonard, J., McDonald, J.: Deformation based loop closure for large scale dense RGB-D SLAM. In: IEEE/RSJ International Conference on Intelligent Robots and Systems (2013)
7. Kerl, C., Sturm, J., Cremers, D.: Dense visual slam for RGB-D cameras. In: Proceedings of the International Conference on Intelligent Robot Systems (IROS) (2013)
8. Michaud, M., Labbe, F.: Appearance-based loop closure detection for online large-scale and long-term operation. IEEE Trans. Rob. **29**(3), 734–745 (2013)
9. Michaud, M., Labbe, F.: Online global loop closure detection for large-scale multi-session graph-based SLAM. In: Proceedings IEEE/RSJ International Conference Intelligent Robotic Systems, pp. 2661–2666 (2014)
10. Thrun, S.: Robotic mapping: A survey. Exploring Artificial Intelligence in the New Millennium (2003)
11. Grisetti, G., Grzonka, S., Stachniss, C., Pfaff, P., Burgard, W.: Efficient estimation of accurate maximum likelihood maps in 3d. In: Proceedings of the International Conference on Intelligent Robots and Systems (IROS), 2007
12. Dellaert, F.: Square root SAM. In: Proceedings of Robotics: Science and Systems (RSS), pp. 177–184 (2005)
13. Kaess, M., Ranganathan, A., Dellaert, F.: iSAM: Incremental smoothing and mapping. IEEE Trans. Robot. **24**(6), 1365–1378 (2008)
14. Jin, H., Favaro, P., Soatto, S.: Real-time 3-D motion and structure of point features: front-end system for vision-based control and interaction. In: IEEE Conference on Computer Vision and Pattern Recognition (CVPR) (2000)
15. Stuhmer, J., Gumhold, S., Cremers, D.: Real-time dense geometry from a handheld camera. In: DAGM Symposium on Pattern Recognition (DAGM) (2010)

16. Aguilar, W.G., Angulo, C.: Estabilización de vídeo en micro vehículos aéreos y su aplicación en la detección de caras. In: IX Congreso de Ciencia y Tecnología ESPE, Sangolquí, Ecuador (2014)
17. Aguilar, W.G., Angulo, C.: Estabilización robusta de vídeo basada en diferencia de nivel de gris. In: VIII Congreso de Ciencia y Tecnología ESPE, Sangolquí, Ecuador (2013)
18. Aguilar, W.G., Angulo, C.: Compensación y aprendizaje de efectos generados en la imagen durante el desplazamiento de un robot. In: X Simposio CEA de Ingeniería de Control, Barcelona, Spain (2012)
19. Aguilar, W.G., Angulo, C.: Compensación de los efectos generados en la imagen por el control de navegación del robot Aibo ERS 7. In: VII Congreso de Ciencia y Tecnología ESPE, Sangolquí, Ecuador (2012)
20. Aguilar, W.G., Verónica, C., José, P.: Obstacle avoidance based-visual navigation for micro aerial vehicles. Electronics 6(1), 10 (2017)
21. Aguilar, W.G., Morales, S.: 3D Environment Mapping Using the Kinect V2 and Path Planning Based on RRT Algorithms. Electronics 5(4), 70 (2016)
22. Cabras, P., Rosell, J., Pérez, A., Aguilar, W.G., Rosell, A.: Haptic-based navigation for the virtual bronchoscopy. In: 18th IFAC World Congress, Milano, Italy (2011)
23. Aguilar, W.G., Angulo, C., Costa, R., Molina, L.: Control autónomo de cuadricópteros para seguimiento de trayectorias. In: IX Congreso de Ciencia y Tecnología ESPE, Sangolquí, Ecuador (2014)
24. Murray, G., Klein, D.: Parallel tracking and mapping for small AR workspaces. In: Proceedings IEEE and ACM International Symposium on Mixed and Augmented Reality (ISMAR) (2007)
25. Strasdat, H., Montiel, J.M., Davison, A.: Scale drift-aware large scale monocular slam. In: Proceedings of Robotics: Science and Systems (2010)
26. Aguilar, W.G., Angulo, C.: Real-time model-based video stabilization for microaerial vehicles. Neural Process. Lett. 43(2), 459–477 (2016)
27. Aguilar, W.G., Angulo, C.: Real-time video stabilization without phantom movements for micro aerial vehicles. EURASIP J. Image Video Process. 1, 1–13 (2014)
28. Aguilar, W.G., Angulo, C.: Robust video stabilization based on motion intention for low-cost micro aerial vehicles. In: 11th International Multi-Conference on Systems
29. Zisserman, J., Sivic, A.: Video Google: a text retrieval approach to object matching in videos. In: Proceedings 9th International Conference on Computer Vision, pp. 1470–1478 (2003)
30. Botterill, T., Mills, S., Green, R.: Bag-of-words-driven, single-camera simultaneous localization and mapping. J. Field Rob. 28(2), 204–226 (2011)
31. Konolige, K., Bowman, J., Chen, J., Mihelich, P., Calonder, M., Lepetit, V., Fua, P.: View-based maps. Int. J. Rob. Res. 29(8), 941–957 (2010)
32. Christensen, H.I., Folkesson, J.: Closing the loop with graphical SLAM. IEEE Trans. Rob. 23(4), 731–741 (2007)
33. Johannsson, H., Kaess, M., Fallon, M., Leonard, J.J.: Temporally scalable visual SLAM using a reduced pose graph. In: RSS Workshop on Long-term Operation of Autonomous Robotic Systems in Changing Environments (2012)
34. Montemerlo, M., Thrun, S., Koller, D., Wegbreit, B.: FastSLAM: a factored solution to the simultaneous localization and mapping problem. In: Proceedings of the National Conference on Artificial Intelligence (AAAI) (2012)
35. Grisetti, G., Stachniss, C., Burgard, W.: Improved techniques for grid mapping with rao-blackwellized particle filters. IEEE Trans. Robot. (T-RO) 23, 34–46 (2007)

36. Weiss, S., Scaramuzza, D., Siegwart, R.: Monocular-SLAM-based navigation for autonomous micro helicopters in GPS-denied environments. J. Field Robot **28**(6), 854–874 (2011)
37. Mur-Artal, R., Montiel, J., Tardo, J.: ORB-SLAM: a versatile and accurate monocular SLAM system. IEEE Trans. Robot. **31**(5), 1147–1163 (2015)
38. Engelhard, N., Endres, F., Hess, J., Sturm, J., Burgard, W.: Realtime 3D visual SLAM with a hand-held RGB-D camera. In: RGB-D Workshop on 3D Perception in Robotics at the European Robotics Forum (2011)
39. Fraundorfer, F., Heng, L., Honegger, D., Lee, G., Meier, L., Tanskanen, P., Pollefeys, M.: Vision-based autonomous mapping and exploration using a quadrotor MAV. In: Intelligent Robots and Systems (IROS) (2012)
40. Audras, C., Comport, A., Meilland, M., Rives, P.: Real-time dense appearance-based SLAM for RGB-D sensors. In: Australasian Conference on Robotics and Automation (2011)
41. Bolles, M.A., Fischler, R.C.: Random sample consensus: a paradigm for model fitting with apphcatlons to image analysis and automated cartography. Commun. ACM **24**, 381–395 (1981)

Real-Time Detection and Simulation of Abnormal Crowd Behavior

Wilbert G. Aguilar[1,4,5(✉)], Marco A. Luna[2], Julio F. Moya[2],
Marco P. Luna[3,7], Vanessa Abad[6], Hugo Ruiz[1,8],
and Humberto Parra[1,7]

[1] Dep. Seguridad y Defensa,
Universidad de las Fuerzas Armadas ESPE, Sangolquí, Ecuador
wgaguilar@espe.edu.ec
[2] Dep. Eléctrica y Electrónica,
Universidad de las Fuerzas Armadas ESPE, Sangolquí, Ecuador
[3] Dep. Tierra y Construcción,
Universidad de las Fuerzas Armadas ESPE, Sangolquí, Ecuador
[4] CICTE Research Center,
Universidad de las Fuerzas Armadas ESPE, Sangolquí, Ecuador
[5] GREC Research Group, Universitat Politècnica de Catalunya,
Barcelona, Spain
[6] Universitat de Barcelona, Barcelona, Spain
[7] PLM Research Center, Purdue University, West Lafayette, IN, USA
[8] Universidad Politécnica de Madrid, Madrid, Spain

Abstract. In this paper, we propose an algorithm for abnormal crowd behavior detection and simulation for real time surveillance applications. Our method is a low computational cost approach based on moved pixel density modelling. Using statistical methods, we obtain the model of pixel densities in normal behaviors based on datasets available in the literature. During abnormal anomalous event detection we run a simulation of people motion and save the data for future analysis. We test the execution time of our algorithm for motion detection to validate its usage in fast applications. Finally we validate our method comparing it with other approaches in the literature in two datasets.

Keywords: HAAR · HOG · LBP · Saliency maps · People detection · Cascade classifiers · UAVs

1 Introduction

According to [1] abnormal or unusual behavior are somehow the interesting things that catch the attention of human observers, and often quite easy to identify. Anomalous event detection is a critical task; it requires a lot of work and attention of human employees without stop. This is an exhausting process because the abnormal events occur with a low probability, making that the major part of the effort be wasted watching regular videos [2]. The technological advance has allowed that improved and intelligent monitoring and surveillance systems based on human behavior could be developed [3, 4, 5]. In the field of computer vision, real-time applications [6, 7],

© Springer International Publishing AG 2017
L.T. De Paolis et al. (Eds.): AVR 2017, Part II, LNCS 10325, pp. 420–428, 2017.
DOI: 10.1007/978-3-319-60928-7_36

and crowd behavior analysis has become a topic of interest and it has captured the attention of several research groups [8]. Many of these algorithms works with computer simulations [9, 10]. In [11], the behavior of people in crowds could be different depending on situation, it makes more difficult to represent the dynamic models of a crowd.

Our approach is focused on fast abnormal events detection based on analysis of inter-frame pixel motion. We obtain a model of pixel density behavior in human crowds using statistical concepts, and replicate the abnormal crowd behavior in computer simulations.

This paper is organized as follows: Sect. 2 describes the related work on abnormal crowd behavior detection. Next the statistical modelling and our algorithm are presented in the Sect. 3. In Sect. 4 we present the experimental results, followed by the summary. Finally conclusions and future works are presented in Sect. 5.

2   Related Works

In the literature, there are several techniques focused on abnormal crowd behavior detection. Multiple authors have divided all these methods in two main approaches: model based detection and particle advection based detection. The choose of the model will depend of the density of the crowd to be analyzed [12].

Model based methods use detection and segmentation of individuals to analyze their behavior, for example, in [13, 14] they analyze the motion patterns using people tracking and in [15, 16] the extracted trajectories were used to represent normal patterns, atypical values were considered abnormal.

Particle advection based models [17, 18, 4] represents a holistic vision of a crowd. According to [15], common approaches in this field include: optical flow [4, 18, 19], gradients [20], spatio-temporal features [21], and others.

Unlike other approaches in the state of art, our method for anomaly detection uses a particle advection based algorithm; we analyze pixel densities with statistical modelling to identify abrupt movements in the image and detect abnormal behavior.

3   Our Approach

Our method for abnormal crowd behavior and simulation include three main tasks: Motion detection and analysis, statistical modelling of normal behavior, and finally abnormal crowd behavior detection and simulation.

3.1   Motion Detection and Analysis

For motion detection and background subtraction, we use an algorithm based on image differences in consecutive frames. First, we read three consecutive frames: previous frame, current frame and next frame. Then, we applicate RGB to Gray transformation to each frame for color channels simplification. We operate between images as color matrices obtaining the absolute difference between consecutive frames using the Eq. 1:

$$absdiff = |Current\,Frame - Previous\,Frame| \tag{1}$$

With the results of the operations we apply the logical operation AND to these differences, finding pixels that have moved in current frame. This algorithm is graphically presented in Fig. 1.

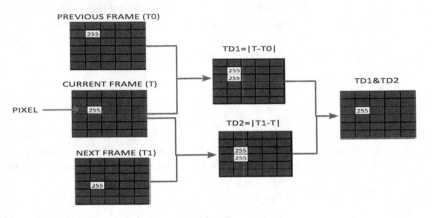

Fig. 1. Motion detection algorithm

Once we obtain moved pixel obtained, adjacent pixels are grouped to get little contours of moved pixels. Background subtraction approaches like [22] proposes that with the increase of the speed in the motion, increases the density of these grouped pixels. We group this moved pixels inside bounding boxes as show the Fig. 2.

Fig. 2. Motion pixel detection

The Fig. 2 shows that the algorithm generates bounding boxes around moved pixels; the computational advantage of this approach is to reduce the image analysis to simple matrix operations.

3.2   Statistical Modelling

Normal Behavior. In the literature, several datasets for abnormal behavior detection have been created. For pixel density modelling, we get the average area of the bounding boxes by frame during normal crowd behaviors. We use 3 video datasets focused on abnormal crowd behavior detection:

- UMN dataset [4]: Abnormal behavior are panic situations resulting in evacuation or scape.
- UCSD ped1 dataset [15]: Abnormal behavior represent different objects like bikes or cars with different speed in comparison with common pedestrians.
- Avenue Dataset [2]: Abnormal behavior are individuals running or moving with abnormal speeds respect to other pedestrians.

In order to have small variation in data, we set all videos to the same size (320 × 240 pixels). We tabulate the data for each frame. In total, 12154 frames were analyzed. The results of histograms are presented in Fig. 3.

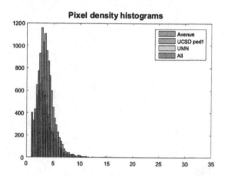

Fig. 3. Histograms of pixel density

As we can see in Fig. 3, all datasets present similar trends. Data of mean, standard deviation and coefficient of variability are tabulated in Table 1.

Table 1. Statistical values of pixel density

Dataset	Mean	Standard deviation	Coefficient of variation
Avenue [2]	3.025	**2.087**	**0.6899**
UCSD ped1 [15]	3.6130	1.1341	0.3139
UMN [4]	**4.474**	1.9378	0.4331
All	3.401	1.888	0.5554

According to standard deviation and coefficient of variation, Avenue dataset [2] is the most unstable for the application of this method.

Abnormal Crowd. For abnormal crowd behavior we compute the atypical values in pixel densities, i.e. when the algorithm detects an atypical value in pixel density we will assume that is an abnormal behavior. For this, we calculate the upper limit for atypical values given by the equation:

$$Ul = Q_3 + 3\,IQR \qquad (2)$$

Where Q_3 represent the third quartile and IQR is the interquartile range. We only take values over the upper limit because there are not atypical values under lower limit. The interquartile range is defined as:

$$IQR = Q_3 - Q_1 \qquad (3)$$

Where Q_1 is the first quartile. The box plot for tabulated data is presented in the Fig. 4.

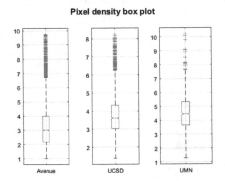

Fig. 4. Box plots for different datasets

The value for upper limit for extreme atypical values in each dataset is presented in Table 2.

Table 2. Upper limits for different datasets

Dataset	Upper limit
Avenue [2]	9.76
UCSD ped1 [15]	8.26
UMN [4]	**9.93**

3.3 Detection and Simulation Algorithm

Giving the results of atypical values, we determinate that abnormal crowd behaviors occurs when the pixel density exceed upper atypical values. During abnormal behaviors, we display "Abnormal Crowd", as seen in the Fig. 5.

(a)   (b)

Fig. 5. Abnormal crowd behavior detection algorithm. (a) Normal behavior. (b) Abnormal behavior

Simulation. For simulation algorithm we obtain the center points of bounding boxes during abnormal crowd in function of time that they appear. In video screens the position $y = 0$ begins at up-left corner, to match it with Cartesian coordinates, we must subtract 240 minus "y" positions. Graphical results are present in Fig. 6. Video results are presented in https://www.youtube.com/watch?v=6fPFR1beaRk.

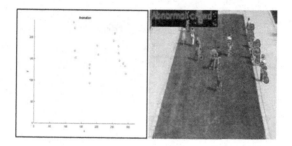

Fig. 6. Simulation of abnormal crowd

4 Results and Discussion

4.1 Execution Time

The results of execution time in 2.4 GHz, 2 GB RAM PC are presented in Table 3.

Table 3. Execution time of the algorithm in datasets

Dataset	Execution time (fps)
Avenue [2]	**72.6**
UCSD ped1 [15]	71.02
UMN [4]	71.39

Table 3 shows that computers with low features the algorithm works fast, thus the algorithm can be used in real time applications.

4.2   Algorithm Performance

To evaluate the algorithm performance, we count the number of bounding boxes that present atypical values, defining a threshold to determinate an abnormal behavior. In each threshold we tabulate the true positive and false positive rates. We compare our algorithm based on statistical pixel density model (SPDM) in two datasets: UMN [4] and UCSD ped1 [15] according to their respective ground – truth annotations. In the first dataset we evaluate our approach and social-force model [4]. In the second dataset we compare our method with: MPPCA+SF [15], Adam [23], y subspace [24]. Results are presented in Fig. 7.

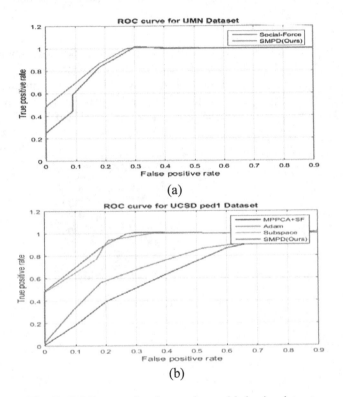

Fig. 7. ROC curves for abnormal crowd behavior dataset

In Fig. 7, our algorithm presents better performance that methods presented in the state of art for frame level analysis. In UCSD ped1 [15], many approaches determinate the performance at pixel level, this paper not deal with this task.

5   Conclusions and Future Work

Despite the videos for statistical modeling are different, they present similar features during density pixel estimation; it allows generating a global model that works in different applications.

Due to the low computational cost of image processing, the proposed method for motion detection works for real time applications as show the Table 3.

In our method, we use abrupt changes in pixel density to detect anomalies. This proposal for abnormal crowd behavior detection is robust compared with approaches in the literature.

In the future, we will improve the detection including pixel level analysis; however it is necessary to include more variables in the process. It will allow improving the simulation too.

Acknowledgement. This work is part of the projects VisualNavDrone 2016-PIC-024 and MultiNavCar 2016-PIC-025, from the Universidad de las Fuerzas Armadas ESPE, directed by Dr. Wilbert G. Aguilar.

References

1. Popoola, O.P., Wang, K.: Video-based abnormal human behavior recognition—a review. IEEE Trans. Syst. Man Cybern. Part C Appl. Rev. **42**(6), 865–878 (2012)
2. Lu, C., Shi, J., Jia, J.: Abnormal event detection at 150 fps in matlab. In: Proceeding IEEE International Conference on Computer Vision, pp. 2720–2727 (2013)
3. Aguilar, W.G., Luna, M.A., Moya, J.F., Abad, V., Parra, H., Ruiz, H.: Pedestrian detection for UAVs using cascade classifiers with meanshift. In: IEEE 11th International Conference on Semantic Computing (ICSC), pp. 509–514 (2017)
4. Mehran, R., Oyama, A., Shah, M.: Abnormal crowd behavior detection using social force model. Comput. Vis. Pattern (2009)
5. Aguilar, W.G., Alulema, D., Limaico, A., Sandoval, D.: Development and verification of a verbal corpus based on natural language for Ecuadorian Dialect. In: IEEE 11th International Conference on Semantic Computing (ICSC), pp. 515–519 (2017)
6. Aguilar, W.G., Angulo, C.: Real-time model-based video stabilization for microaerial vehicles. Neural Process. Lett. **43**(2), 459–477 (2016)
7. Aguilar, W.G., Angulo, C.: Real-time video stabilization without phantom movements for micro aerial vehicles. EURASIP J. Image Video Process. **2014**(1), 46 (2014)
8. Jacques Jr., J.S., Musse, S., Jung, C.: Crowd analysis using computer vision techniques. IEEE Signal Process. Mag. **27**(5), 66–77 (2010)
9. Cabras, P., Rosell, J., Pérez, A., Aguilar, W.G., Rosell, A.: Haptic-based navigation for the virtual bronchoscopy. IFAC Proc. **18**(1), 9638–9643 (2011)
10. Aguilar, W., Morales, S.: 3D environment mapping using the kinect V2 and path planning based on RRT algorithms. Electronics **5**(4), 70 (2016)
11. Lemercier, S., Jelic, A., Kulpa, R., Hua, J., Fehrenbach, J., Degond, P., Appert-Rolland, C., Donikian, S., Pettré, J.: Realistic following behaviors for crowd simulation. EURO-GRAPHICS **31**(2) (2012)

12. Raghavendra, R., Cristani, M., Bue, A., Sangineto, E., Murino, V.: Anomaly detection in crowded scenes: a novel framework based on swarm optimization and social force modeling. In: Ali, S., Nishino, K., Manocha, D., Shah, M. (eds.) Modeling, Simulation and Visual Analysis of Crowds. TISVC, vol. 11, pp. 383–411. Springer, New York (2013). doi:10. 1007/978-1-4614-8483-7_15
13. Basharat, A., Gritai, A., Shah, M.: Learning object motion patterns for anomaly detection and improved object detection. In: IEEE Conference on Computer Vision and Pattern Recognition, pp. 1–8 (2008)
14. Stauffer, C., Grimson, W.E.L.: Learning patterns of activity using real-time tracking. IEEE Trans. Pattern Anal. Mach. Intell. $22(8)$, 747–757 (2000)
15. Mahadevan, V., Li, W., Bhalodia, V., Vasconcelos, N.: Anomaly detection in crowded scenes. In: IEEE Computer Society Conference on Computer Vision and Pattern Recognition, pp. 1975–1981 (2010)
16. Wu, S., Moore, B.E., Shah, M.: Chaotic invariants of lagrangian particle trajectories for anomaly detection in crowded scenes. In: Computer Vision and Pattern Recognition, pp. 2054–2060 (2010)
17. Mehran, R., Moore, Brian E., Shah, M.: A streakline representation of flow in crowded scenes. In: Daniilidis, K., Maragos, P., Paragios, N. (eds.) ECCV 2010. LNCS, vol. 6313, pp. 439–452. Springer, Heidelberg (2010). doi:10.1007/978-3-642-15558-1_32
18. Ali, S., Shah, M.: A lagrangian particle dynamics approach for crowd flow segmentation and stability analysis. In: Computer Vision and Pattern Recognition 2007 (2007)
19. Andrade, E.L., Blunsden, S., Fisher, R.B.: Modelling crowd scenes for event detection. In: 18th International Conference Pattern Recognition, ICPR 2006, vol. 1, pp. 175–178 (2006)
20. Ke, Y., Sukthankar, R., Hebert, M.: Event detection in crowded videos. In: IEEE 11th International Conference Computer Vision, ICCV 2007, pp. 1–8 (2007)
21. Kratz, L., Nishino, K.: Anomaly detection in extremely crowded scenes using spatio-temporal motion pattern models. In: IEEE Conference Computer Vision Pattern Recognition, pp. 1446–1453 (2009)
22. Zivkovic, Z., Van Der Heijden, F.: Efficient adaptive density estimation per image pixel for the task of background subtraction. Pattern Recogn. Lett. $27(7)$, 773–780 (2006)
23. Adam, A., Rivlin, E., Shimshoni, I., Reinitz, D.: Robust real-time unusual event detection using multiple fixed-location monitors. IEEE Trans. Pattern Anal. Mach. Intell. $30(3)$, 555–560 (2008)
24. Elhamifar, E., Vidal, R.: Sparse subspace clustering. In: IEEE Conference on Computer Vision and Pattern Recognition, pp. 2790–2797 (2009)

Human Computer Interaction

Steering Versus Teleport Locomotion for Head Mounted Displays

Chris G. Christou$^{(\boxtimes)}$ and Poppy Aristidou

University of Nicosia, Nicosia, Cyprus
christou.ch@unic.ac.cy

Abstract. We compared the ability to navigate from one point to another in a virtual environment using Gaze-Directed, Pointing and Teleport locomotion. Participant's start position and destination were shown to them on a map at the beginning of each trial. Participants also had to deviate from their route to collect 'Pokémon' tokens: testing their spatial updating ability. Results showed that the two steering methods resulted in increased levels of cybersickness compared to teleporting. In terms of performance, teleporting resulted in faster traversal times but surprisingly was just as effective in allowing users to complete their journey, indicating that user disorientation was not a major issue. The main failing of the teleport method was that it increased the likelihood of missing collectable tokens en route. These results suggest that restricted variants of the teleport method should be explored for use in commercialized VR applications in which real walking is not necessary.

Keywords: Virtual reality · Navigation · Spatial updating · Locomotion · Immersive gaming · Motion control · Steering

1 Introduction

The hardware requirements for Virtual Reality (VR) systems include sensors for tracking a user's body, a display for sensory feedback, and a means of user interaction for grabbing objects and for controlling locomotion through a scene. VR systems come in many varieties depending on how they implement these requirements. For example, the VR CAVE situates the user in a 'room' consisting of back-projected screens and tracking of the user's head position is used to update their view of the virtual world as projected on the screens [1]. With head-mounted display (HMD) systems the user wears the visual display on their head and their position and orientation in physical space are tracked by sensors coupled to a virtual camera located in the scene. In general, this coupling between movements of the user's body and concomitant sensory feedback contributes to the impression of immersion within the depicted virtual environment and immediately the user forgets their physical surroundings and feels situated in the virtual world instead [2].

A key component of VR interaction is that of locomotion, or the control of movement through the depicted virtual world. Although body tracking enables real walking, virtual worlds may be vast and require the traversal of large distances to be experienced. Body tracking however is limited by the extent of the physical space in

© Springer International Publishing AG 2017
L.T. De Paolis et al. (Eds.): AVR 2017, Part II, LNCS 10325, pp. 431–446, 2017.
DOI: 10.1007/978-3-319-60928-7_37

which the simulation occurs. In the CAVE, for example, this limitation is the distance between the back-projected walls. For HMDs, the restriction is the extent of the tracking area and the size of the physical space in which the user is situated. The challenges for methods of locomotion therefore are that they should allow the traversal of distances larger than the physical space of the system while being comfortable, relatively effortless and without interfering with the objectives of the task. This latter requirement relates in part to the locomotion method being able to support the same spatial awareness that we would expect in the real world.

In order to preserve and exploit the naturalness of real walking researchers have devised numerous imaginative devices and techniques that allow free walking while maintaining the user's position within the enclosing space. Such methods include treadmills, which allow walking on a moveable surface [3, 25, 26], and walking in place [23, 39] in which walking is 'mimed' and interpreted by a computer to determine pace and direction. This emphasis on real walking is based on evidence from several studies which suggest that only through real walking can a user maintain spatial updating and therefore spatial awareness [18, 27], ensuring a comfortable experience and that users do not get 'lost' in the virtual world. However, real walking can also cause fatigue, especially when large distances must be traversed during a simulation. Furthermore, recent advances in VR displays has in turn resulted in a flurry of development activity aimed at the commercialization of VR for home and educational use. The commercialization of VR necessitates that hardware requirements be kept to a minimum. Real walking devices are costly but, moreover, few users may be prepared to play immersive games for extended periods if this involves excessive physical activity. We therefore also need to explore other methods of locomotion that are cheap, expedient, do not induce fatigue, are enjoyable to use and which still maintain reasonable spatial awareness.

The locomotion metaphor most often used in traditional computer games is that of Gaze-Directed locomotion. This belongs to a class of locomotion techniques known as steering methods, in which simulated walking is achieved using a hand-held controller. The user orients their 'gaze' (heading) with the controller and makes translations only in this direction. It is expedient and easy to use and therefore was adopted by non-immersive desktop VR systems [5, 8]. In such systems, the field of view is relatively small and it makes sense to only allow movement in the direction of gaze: movements in directions other than the gaze direction may cause collisions with objects in the scene. The Gaze-Directed method has also been used in immersive systems. However, immersive systems use sensors to track the orientation of the users' head. Users can therefore make head and body rotations to change gaze direction directly instead of using a controller. The controller is only required for initiating translation. The ability to make independent head movements while walking provides an alternative to Gaze-Directed locomotion. This is facilitated by the *Pointing method*, another steering method, in which the user indicates their direction of travel by pointing with a tracked controller while being free to look wherever they like [5, 8]. Pointing is more akin to real world locomotion. In previous experiments comparing Gaze-Directed and Pointing in a CAVE display we found that the Pointing method resulted in better performance in a wayfinding task requiring participants to navigate to fixed destinations in a realistic virtual setting [32].

The utility of a given locomotion method may depend on the type of display used. For example, Gaze-Directed locomotion is more appropriate for desktop VR systems whereas Pointing is more beneficial in a CAVE display. From our own observations, both of these steering methods, when used in a HMD, have a propensity to induce nausea and motion sickness, a condition known as cybersickness. This apparently is a common view among VR developers who have recently been experimenting with an alternative method known as Teleporting. Teleporting dispenses with smooth motion and instead the user points to some location in the environment using a tracked controller and is instantly transported there. Teleporting may reduce cybersickness by eliminating the cue conflict involved in perceived visual motion and the vestibular system [33]. However, initial studies of teleporting have found it to result in disorientation [21].

In this paper, we compare these two steering methods and teleporting with respect to navigation and spatial awareness in VR. Our comparisons are made based on objective performance variables but we also place strong emphasis on the degree to which each method induces cybersickness.

2 Background

2.1 Navigation in VR

Virtual worlds are built to be navigated and navigation is a combination of two components, wayfinding and locomotion [6, 7]. Wayfinding employs the cognitive skills that allow people to orient themselves in 3D space to get from one place to another. [9] identified different types of knowledge that people may gain and use from such behavior, the most useful of which is survey-type knowledge. Survey knowledge is geocentric in nature and develops over a prolonged period of familiarization with an environment. However, survey-type knowledge may also be acquired directly from a map [10, 11]. This process is beneficial in that it reduces the time required to familiarize oneself with an environment. However, distance estimation and orientation judgements have been found to be inferior in individuals who have gained their spatial knowledge in this manner [10, 12]. Also, survey type knowledge derived only from maps is still somewhat egocentric in nature, being dependent on the orientation of the user in relation to the map used to learn the environment [14]. This orientation-dependency was studied by [13] in terms of map design. They found that in order to facilitate efficient map use, the map must be congruent with the environment it represents. This is illustrated in the forward-up equivalence principle, which states that the upward direction of a map must correspond with what is in front of the viewer for them to make efficient use of it and proceed from where they are to where they wish to go. If the user's position, as specified on a map, is not congruent with the environment in front of them then cognitive effort (in the form of imagined rotations) is required to navigate to their destination. This is something that people find difficult to do [12, 42] and we make use of this in our experiment.

Locomotion methods should not impede normal cognitive function. Initial experiments that studied navigation in VR found that it was more difficult than in equivalent real world scenarios, e.g. [14, 15]. It was found that subjects became disorientated and lost their way. This was initially attributed to impoverished visual cues in VR compared to the real-world [16]. Other research suggests that visual fidelity is not entirely the problem. Instead, it has been argued that the lack of proprioceptive and vestibular feedback during locomotion makes navigation in virtual environments more difficult [17–19]. Proprioceptive feedback informs us of the position and orientation of our limbs and head. Vestibular feedback gives us a sense of linear acceleration (translation) and rotation in space. It has been shown that observers are capable of reconstructing complex displacements of the body using just proprioceptive and vestibular inputs alone, e.g. [43, 44]. It may therefore be that such non-visual cues contribute to successful navigation and when they are lacking, as in some VR systems, this leads to diminished spatial cognition. According to [20] the main ability that is lacking in VR systems is spatial updating. Spatial updating is the dynamic process of adjustment of a cognitive map based on one's movements within an environment. For example, if we started from a given point in space and walk directly ahead, make a turn and walk directly head for some distance, we would be able to pin-point our original start position. Performing this as an experiment with objective measurement of errors in pin-pointing one's original start point [20] found that only with real walking did subjects perform the test relatively accurately. When this procedure is performed in a HMD with simulated walking and rotation, there are systematic errors suggesting lack of path integration, or spatial updating. These results suggest that spatial updating is sub-served by non-visual proprioceptive and vestibular cues. This in turn has important connotations for the design of VR motion control.

2.2 Cybersickness in VR

One of issues that has plagued VR from the beginning and that stands as an obstacle to its commercialization is cybersickness. Similar to motion sickness, cybersickness involves a number symptoms including nausea and headaches. Unlike motion sickness, cybersickness occurs when the optic field of the observer implies movement of the body, but their body is stationary. Because this implied movement is determined by the method of locomotion the ultimate success of a given mode of locomotion must also be determined with respect to propensity to induce cybersickness.

There is still debate as to the causes of cybersickness and also how to combat it [33, 35]. Quantifying the degree if cybersickness is usually done by a questionnaire that probes associated symptoms. The most commonly used questionnaire was devised by [34] who used a series of factor analyses to identify sixteen symptoms of cybersickness. The sixteen symptoms were found to cluster into three categories, oculomotor, disorientation and nausea. The oculomotor cluster includes eyestrain, difficulty in focusing, blurred vision and headache. The disorientation cluster includes dizziness and vertigo. The nausea cluster includes stomach awareness, increased salivation and burping. A weighted average of these three factors comprises a 'Total Score', which reflects the severity of the symptoms for an individual and can be used to assess the likelihood that a VR system will cause cybersickness [4].

2.3   Locomotion in VR

The ability of VR systems to track the position and orientation of the user's head, hands and body has inspired many novel techniques that go beyond the abstract steering methods used in computer games (see [37] for review). Locomotion techniques may be classified as follows:

- Physical Walking or Miming. These methods involve actual walking, walking in place with the aid of a treadmill [3, 25, 26] or redirected walking [38, 40]. In some cases, the user 'mimes' the actions necessary to control their movements through space [23, 24, 39].
- Steering. The continuous movement and rotation in space using a movement metaphor. Can be either gaze-directed or pointing [5, 28].
- Target-Based locomotion. For example, the destination can be chosen using a pointer and the camera position is set to that position instantaneously.

All physical walking methods share a common problem: performing walking movements for extended periods of time causes fatigue. An alternative to real walking is provided by steering methods which allow smooth motion through a virtual space. Gaze-Directed locomotion allows the user to rotate their head and/or body and move in the direction in which they are facing. Pointing methods are similar but the direction of translation is independent of the direction of gaze: the user is free to look around and the direction of locomotion is chosen by pointing in a particular direction using a tracked controller.

A serious problem with steering methods is that the implied smooth movement of the body while it is actually at rest (also known as vection) may cause cybersickness. This limits the amount of time people are prepared to use VR applications. This problem may be eliminated by target-based locomotion such as teleporting. Teleporting allows the user to select their destination and be instantly transported there. The destination is usually chosen as the intersection between the ground and a projected beam emanating from a tracked controller. This method may be as deficient as steering in terms of not providing proprioceptive and vestibular inputs. Moreover, there are no smooth visual flow cues either which may cause disorientation in VR [21, 22]. On the other hand, because there is no vection experienced with teleporting and this may eliminate the possibility of cybersickness. We explicitly test this in our experiment.

3   Experiment

We compared Gaze-Directed, Pointing and Teleport methods in a primed-search navigation task requiring spatial awareness and spatial updating for successful completion. In particular, we wanted to address the following:

- Whether there are advantages in using the Pointing method compared to Gaze-Directed method with a HMD, as was previously found in the CAVE [32].
- Whether the two steering methods increase the likelihood of cybersickness as compared with teleporting.

- Whether the Teleport method increases the likelihood of users becoming disorientated in comparison to steering methods.

We devised a task that required the user to navigate from a given start position to a destination shown to them on a map at the beginning of each trial. This use of maps was an expedient way to allow participants to form knowledge of the spatial layout of the environment without extensive learning in advance. A similar map-based method has been used in [32]. Because participants vary greatly in navigation abilities a repeated measures experimental design was used. Repeated measures, often referred to as within-subject designs, require the same subject to perform all conditions of the experiment: in our case, they would use all three locomotion methods. The main problem with this type design is the possibility of an effect of learning and therefore appropriate randomization of conditions had to be performed. The advantage however is that there is less variability in the data and fewer participants could be employed.

To reduce the effects of random variables within each trial, multiple trials were used and performance variables averaged. In order to generate multiple trials a 3D model of a desert city consisting of self-similar buildings was used as a starting point. This allowed us to create 3 different cities with different configurations of buildings for repeated trials. The destinations were always exactly in the middle of each city (see Fig. 1). In order to vary the difficulty of the task the start position, as shown on the map, was either directly below, to the left, on top and to the right of the final destination. Thus, if the customary way of viewing a map with the 'you-are-here' at the bottom is 0° then the other positions where located at 90°, 180° and 270°. In ego-centric terms the final destination was always directly ahead of the start direction, and the 'beeline' distance was identical. However, different buildings impeded direct walking to the target and participants had to navigate around them. Therefore, the total distance was different for each route (Fig. 2).

As a further test for spatial-updating we also required participants to collect 'tokens' that they encountered along each route. These tokens were 'Pokémon' type characters (Fig. 3), approximately 1 m high, and positioned away from, but within viewing distance of, the route to each target. Spatial updating would be required to collect each token and continue their route to the target. There were 5 tokens visible for each route. These became visible only when the participant was close enough (10 m). Similarly, the final target destination was only made visible when the user came within 20 m, thus testing participant's memory for the target's position rather than allowing its presence to guide their movements.

Because the Teleport method allows long leaps from one location to another the fact that participants had to collect tokens *en route* served to restrict extra-long leaps. Long leaps were also restricted by the presence of buildings: Movements through buildings were not permitted. Nevertheless, it was expected that the Teleport method would produce faster route navigations than the steering methods, which were restricted to a speed of 3 m/s. The latter was chosen based on our own subjective impressions of comfort and the fact that maximum walk speed for 20–30 year-olds is around 2.5 m/s [36].

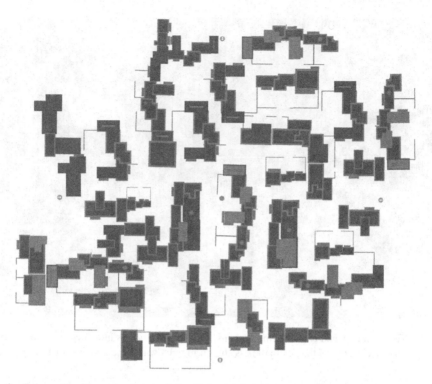

Fig. 1. Schematic diagram of one of the three 'cities' showing 4 start locations (green) and destination (red, centered). This is *not* the map seen at the beginning of each trial. The maps used in the experiment (see Fig. 3) showed only the region of the city that included the start and end locations and were generated from a 'live' orthographic projection camera situated above the city. (Color figure online)

Fig. 2. View of one 'city' from above and behind the start position showing the map and direction to target. These disappeared as soon as the participant moved out of the circle. (Color figure online)

Fig. 3. View of a map and two Pokémon tokens. The start location is indicated by a green circle on the right of the map, and the destination is shown in red towards the left. (Color figure online)

3.1   Design

The objective performance measures used were the number of successful trials and the average number of tokens collected for each condition. Although less informative, we also recorded the time taken to reach the destination. Because the routes consisted of navigations around different buildings, the optimal route times were different for each route. We therefore used average recorded time for each condition in the analysis.

We used a between-subject repeated-measures design in order to limit the effects of inter-subject differences in performance and response biases in the questionnaires. The three locomotion methods formed the three conditions of the experiment. In order to make fair comparisons between conditions we used random presentation of the same three cities for each condition. However, the cities were rotated 90 degree clockwise about their center for each new condition: thus, the final condition performed by participants used the same cities as the first but rotated by 180°. Order effects were eliminated by altering the order of the conditions for each participant according to a Latin square design.

To summarize, the experiment consisted of three conditions (Pointing, Gaze-Directed and Teleport) and each condition was tested by three different scenes (cities) whose presentation order was randomized between subjects. Each scene consisted of four trials with four different start positions around the same target, presented in random order.

3.2   Participants

Eighteen participants were recruited by advertisement. The mean age was 24 years, median age was 22 years. 11 participants were male and 7 were female. The majority (>90%) were students and had regular interaction with computers, but the minority (<10%) had prior experience with VR technology.

Participants gave informed consent to the data collection and agreed to visit the lab for testing on three separate occasions. Tests for each condition were performed on different days with no more than a two-day intervening gap between tests. All tests were completed over a three-week period.

3.3   Setup

The VR display used was a HTC Vive HMD with a resolution of 1080 × 1200 pixels per eye and 110° field of view. Each of the two screens of the HMD had a refresh rate of 90 Hz. User input was achieved with a single hand-held controller, a virtual depiction of which was also visible in the virtual environment. The position and orientation of the display and the controller were tracked within a space of 3 square meters, although the participants were not required to make physical translations. The head and controller tracking was based on a lighthouse system with lighthouses placed at opposite ends of the tracking area and approx. 4 meters apart. A positional tracking accuracy of 2 mm has been reported for this system[1].

The virtual environment was rendered by a Windows 7 workstation with Intel Core i5-4690 K 3.5 GHz CPU & 8 GB RAM with NVidia GeForce GTX 970 GPU with 8 GB on-board memory.

The Unity3D game engine was used to create the game level design with lighting, buildings, terrain, trees etc. In total 11 scenes were created: 9 scenes for the different trials (3 conditions × 3 cities), 1 practice scene and 1 experiment scene in which each session started. Custom C# scripts controlled the flow of the experiment. We used an *Experiment* class to control the onset of the practice and test scenes, and a *TrialManager* class to control each scene including loading of appropriate locomotion controls, randomization and presentation of trials and data collection. The SteamVR SDK[2] was used to handle scene display and implementation of the locomotion techniques.

The Pokémon characters and the buildings of the 3D environment were derived from a public domain source. The buildings were adjusted for our purposes using the graphical editor 3DS Studio Max. These models were chosen because they had simplistic self-similar detail and could be positioned 'Lego-style' to restrict user movements. For each start-stop pair, there was only one viable route that would lead users to the target location.

---

[1] http://www.roadtovr.com/analysis-of-valves-lighthouse-tracking-system-reveals-accuracy/.

[2] http://www.steamvr.com/.

3.4   Procedure

Each test began with participants reading written instructions explaining the task and how to perform locomotion using the current locomotion method. The HMD was then fitted and adjustments made for inter-pupillary distance, and clear focus by adjustment of the eye-screen distance. The participant then had the opportunity to practice using the locomotion technique in a demo scene. This consisted of 5 token Pokémon characters randomly positioned within a 20 m virtual space. Participants navigated to each character and 'collected' them by passing over them.

Each trial consisted of the following: One of the four routes was chosen at random without replacement and the subject's virtual position was changed to the start of the route and their orientation was changed so that they were facing towards the direction of the target. To the participants' right they could see a map of their route. The map was dynamically generated by a virtual camera situated above and in front of the participant. The orthographic image of this camera was just large enough to show the location of the start platform (shown in green with an arrow indicating the correct direction) and the location of the target (shown as a red disk). Participants were instructed to memorize the route from the start location to the target location and collect any tokens that were visible en route. As soon as they moved out of the start region it disappeared, together with the map. They then had to proceed as quickly as possible to the target destination. If after 120 s they had not reached the target location, they were informed by text display that they had failed and to wait for the next trial which proceeded automatically. Immediately following each test a cybersickness questionnaire was administered. The questionnaire was derived from [34].

3.5   Results

Three participants (all female) dropped out of the experiment after the first or second condition complaining of nausea and their data was discarded from the analysis. Averaged cybersickness scores are shown in Table 1. According to [34] scores for the nausea scale range from 0 to 200, scores on the oculomotor scale range from 0 to 159, scores on the disorientation scale range from 0 to 292, and total simulator sickness scores range from 0 to 235. The higher the score, the greater the cybersickness. A total score of less than 10 indicates minimal symptoms, whereas a total score over 20 indicates a problem simulator [41]. Table 1 indicates that Pointing resulted in the highest level of cybersickness and Teleport the least. The average score for the Pointing method is indicative of motion sickness which carries a high likelihood that a user would terminate their use of a VR simulation [29]. We performed a repeated-measure ANOVA with mode of locomotion as repeated-measures factor with three levels. The result showed that the mode of locomotion was significant [$F(2,28) = 3.68$, $p < 0.05$]. Post hoc comparisons using the Fisher LSD test indicated that the Teleport method produced significantly lower cybersickness scores than the Pointing method. There was no statistical difference between Gaze-Directed locomotion and either Pointing or Teleport.

Table 1. Cybersickness mean scores and standard deviations (in brackets, n = 15).

	Pointing	Gaze-directed	Teleport
Nausea	36.0 (37.2)	21.0 (21.1)	10.8 (14.4)
Oculomotor	23.8 (25.9)	18.7 (20.6)	13.6 (17.5)
Disorientation	39.0 (46.8)	29.7 (33.2)	24.1 (31.3)
Total	36.4 (37.8)	25.4 (25.4)	17.5 (19.7)

In terms of performance, Fig. 4 shows the mean number of successful trials averaged across all subjects for each of the three conditions. Each participant performed 12 trials using each of the three locomotion methods. The Pointing method resulted in fewer successful trials than either of the other two methods. A general linear models repeated-measures ANOVA showed that locomotion had a significant effect on success rate [$F(2, 28) = 5.65$, $p < 0.01$]. A Fisher LSD post-hoc comparison of means showed that the Pointing produced significantly lower success rates than both Gaze-Directed or Teleport (mean diff -1.33 and -1.47 respectively), and that the Gaze-Directed and Teleport means were not significantly different (mean difference= -0.13) from each other.

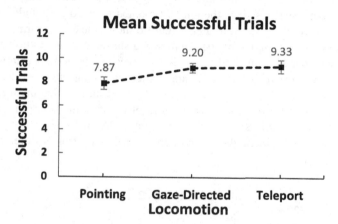

Fig. 4. The mean number of successful trials for each method of locomotion. Participants completed 12 trials in total for each condition.

A similar analysis was performed on the total number of tokens collected (regardless of eventual outcome). The reader should remember that each locomotion test involved exactly the same environments (displayed differently on the maps) and token positions. Figure 5 shows that the two steering methods resulted in similar performance and better than the Teleport method. A repeated measures ANOVA compared the effect of mode of locomotion on tokens collected. There was a significant effect of locomotion on tokens collected at the $p < .05$ level for the three conditions [$F(2,28) = 3.74$, $p = 0.036$]. Post hoc comparisons using the Fisher LSD test indicated that the mean tokens collected for Teleport ($M = 40$, $SE = 1.99$) was significantly lower than those

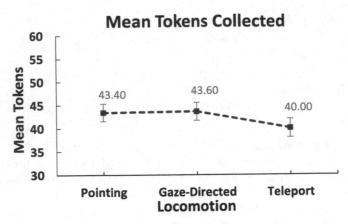

Fig. 5. There were 5 tokens available per trial therefore the maximum number of tokens that could be collected was 60.

collected using Pointing (M = 43.4, SE = 1.89) and the Gaze-Directed (M = 43.6, SE1.94) methods. The latter were not significantly different from each other.

Finally, we consider the time taken to complete the routes, which is the least informative of our measures since the teleport method allowed unbounded leaps to be made whereas steering was speed limited. Figure 6 shows the average traversal time for successful trials for each mode of locomotion and shows that teleporting was indeed faster than the other two methods. A within-subjects repeated measures ANOVA indicated that locomotion mode significantly affected average time to destination [F (2,28) = 40.56, p < .005]. A post hoc analysis of means showed that the mean time for Teleport (M = 34.8, SE = 2.74) was significantly different from the means for Gaze-Directed (M = 54.59, SE = 1.85) and Pointing (M = 58.63, SE2.5). The latter two modes were not significantly different from each other (mean difference = 4.04, SE = 2.83, p = 0.16).

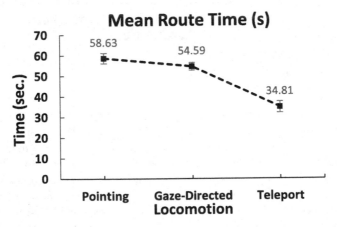

Fig. 6. Average time taken to complete each trial. The maximum time allowed was 120 s. Data shown only for successful trials.

4 Summary and Discussion

There are many ways in which a user may interact with a virtual environment but perhaps the most important is the ability to navigate through it. Navigation is a combination of wayfinding and locomotion and since our wayfinding abilities are developed in the real world from an early age locomotion for VR should enable and exploit the cognitive machinery that we have at our disposal. Although real walking is therefore the best way to do this it may not always be feasible and it may not even be necessary. Effective spatial updating may still be possible as long as bodily rotations are enabled [19, 20, 44]. In a head and body tracked VR system there are many ways to do this. In this paper, we have compared three such methods. Our results, in terms of performance in finding a target position specified on a map, shows that even with the worst performing method participants could find the target on 66% of trials. This was the case even though we deliberately violated the forward up equivalence principle of map use by depicting the user start position at 90°, 180° and 270° offsets around the target as depicted on the maps. In these offset cases participants had to employ more cognitive effort to form their route knowledge, thereby making the task more difficult.

In terms of our comparison of the three methods of locomotion, our initial prediction was that Pointing would be most successful in the wayfinding task. This is because it is more natural (after all, we commonly walk in one direction while looking in another), and because recent tests have shown it to be more effective than Gaze-Directed loco-motion [32]. This experiment was similar to the one reported here, however the display used was a CAVE. The CAVE does provide a larger field of view than the HMD used in the current tests and this could be a contributing factor. A restricted field of view may have caused participants to employ a different strategy to that used in the CAVE [30, 31]. We believe, however, that the difference is more likely related to the relative level of cybersickness experienced. Although the cybersickness scores for the Pointing and Gaze-Directed conditions were not statistically different, those of the Pointing method were consistently higher in all sub-categories and the final score. A participant who is experiencing high levels of nausea and disorientation is not going to perform very well in wayfinding and this may be the principle contributing factor to this result.

The Teleport method, as expected, allowed participants to navigate faster to their destination than either of the steering methods but surprisingly it produced comparable results in terms of successful navigations. This is not to say that users did not get lost using teleporting. Our observation of the participants performing the trials was that they did, on occasion, become disorientated, particularly after disengaging from their route to collect a token. However, in some cases they still had enough time to backtrack to the point where they made a wrong turn.

There was also less evidence of cybersickness using the Teleport method compared to the steering methods. Nausea scores for the Teleport method were one third those for the Pointing method. Again, some care must be taken in interpreting this result as the Teleport method required less time and therefore less opportunity for our participants to feel discomfort. Nevertheless, these results suggest that steering using a HMD elevates cybersickness and furthermore that the primary reason for this is the vection produced by smooth motion with a display that allows only restricted field of view.

Our results suggest that Teleport locomotion does not result in substantial disorientation. The mean sub-score for disorientation in the cybersickness survey was lowest for Teleport locomotion. Disorientation is often maintained as the main problem with teleport methods. However, our results show that participants were able to successfully navigate to destinations with teleporting equally well as with Gaze-Directed locomotion and better than Pointing. The main problem with teleporting that we observed was that users had a propensity to miss detail: in our case the tokens that had to be collected en route. In application, this can be handled by restricting the size of teleport leaps. Indeed, we observed that a few participants adapted to the method by making rapid yet small teleport leaps. However, developments in this field are ongoing. In order to maintain awareness of the environment during a teleport leaps the game developer id Software LLC have developed a variant of teleporting known as Dash Teleport in which, instead of moving instantaneously to a new location, the user selects the leap destination and is propelled there with accelerated speed. This 'warp-speed' movement may reduce any element of disorientation and allow the user to see detail in between. However, its propensity for inducing cybersickness is yet to be assessed.

References

1. Cruz-Neira, C., Sandin, D.J., DeFanti, T.A.: Surround-screen projection-based virtual reality: the design and implementation of the CAVE. In: Proceedings of the 20th Annual Conference on Computer Graphics and Interactive Techniques, pp. 135–142 (1993)
2. Bowman, D., McMahan, R.P.: Virtual reality: how much immersion is enough? Computer **40**, 36–43 (2007)
3. Darken, R.P., Cockayne, W.R, Carmein, D.: The omni-directional treadmill: a locomotion device for virtual worlds. In: Proceedings of the 10th Annual ACM Symposium on User Interface Software and Technology. ACM (1997)
4. Davis, S., Nesbitt, K., Nalivaiko, E.: A systematic review of cybersickness. In: Proceedings of the 2014 Conference on Interactive Entertainment, pp. 1–9. ACM (2014)
5. Bowman, D.A., Kruijff, E., LaViola Jr., J.J., Poupyrev, I.: An introduction to 3-D user interface design. Presence: Teleoperators Virtual Environ. **10**, 96–108 (2001)
6. Montello, D.R.: Navigation. In: Miyake, P.S.A. (ed.) The Cambridge Handbook of Visuospatial Thinking, pp. 257–294. Cambridge University Press, Cambridge (2005)
7. Wiener, J.M., Büchner, S.J., Hölscher, C.: Taxonomy of human wayfinding tasks: a knowledge-based approach. Spatial Cogn. Comput. **9**, 152–165 (2009)
8. Bowman, D.A., Kruijff, E., LaViola Jr., J.J., Poupyrev, I.: 3D User Interfaces: Theory and Practice. Addison-Wesley, Redwood City (2004)
9. Thorndyke, P.W., Goldin, S.E.: Spatial Learning and Reasoning Skill. Springer, New York (1983)
10. Thorndyke, P.W., Hayes-Roth, B.: Differences in spatial knowledge acquired from maps and navigation. Cogn. Psychol. **14**, 560–589 (1982)
11. Ruddle, R.A., Payne, S.J., Jones, D.M.: Navigating buildings in 'desk-top' virtual environments: experimental investigations using extended navigational experience. J. Exp. Psychol. Appl. **3**, 143–159 (1997)
12. Presson, C.C., Hazelrigg, M.D.: Building spatial representations through primary and secondary learning. J. Exp. Psychol. Learn. Mem. Cogn. **10**(4), 716 (1984)

13. Levinew, M., Marchon, I., Hanley, G.: The placement and misplacement of you-are-here maps. Environ. Behav. **16**(2), 139–157 (1984)
14. Richardson, A.E., Montello, D.R., Hegarty, M.: Spatial knowledge acquisition from maps and from navigation in real and virtual environments. Mem. Cogn. **27**, 741–750 (1999)
15. Lessels, S., Ruddle, R.A.: Movement around real and virtual cluttered environments. Presence Teleoperators Virtual Environ. **14**, 580–596 (2005)
16. Darken, R.P., Sibert, J.L.: A toolset for navigation in virtual environments. In: Proceedings of the 6th Annual ACM Symposium on User Interface Software and Technology, pp. 157–165. ACM (1993)
17. Chance, S.S., Gaunet, F., Beall, A.C., Loomis, J.M.: Locomotion mode affects the updating of objects encountered during travel: the contribution of vestibular and proprioceptive inputs to path integration. Presence **7**, 168–178 (1998)
18. Ruddle, R.A., Lessels, S.: For efficient navigational search, humans require full physical movement, but not a rich visual scene. Psychol. Sci. **17**, 460–465 (2006)
19. Riecke, B.E., Bodenheimer, B., McNamara, Timothy P., Williams, B., Peng, P., Feuereissen, D.: Do we need to walk for effective virtual reality navigation? Physical rotations alone may suffice. In: Hölscher, C., Shipley, T.F., Olivetti Belardinelli, M., Bateman, J.A., Newcombe, Nora S. (eds.) Spatial Cognition 2010. LNCS, vol. 6222, pp. 234–247. Springer, Heidelberg (2010). doi:10.1007/978-3-642-14749-4_21
20. Klatzky, R.L., Loomis, J.M., Beall, A.C., Chance, S.S., Golledge, R.G.: Spatial updating of self-position and orientation during real, imagined, and virtual locomotion. Psychol. Sci. **9**, 293–298 (1998)
21. Bowman, D., Koller, D., Hodges, L.F.: Travel in immersive virtual environments: an evaluation of viewpoint motion control techniques. In: Virtual Reality Annual International Symposium, pp. 45–52, 215. IEEE (1997)
22. Bowman, D.A., Koller, D., Hodges, L.F.: A methodology for the evaluation of travel techniques for immersive virtual environments. Virtual Reality **3**, 120–131 (1998)
23. Slater, M., Usoh, M., Steed, A.: Taking steps: the influence of a walking technique on presence in virtual reality. ACM Trans. Comput.-Hum. Interact. (TOCHI) **2**, 201–219 (1995)
24. Adamo-Villani, N., Jones, D.: Travel in immersive virtual learning environments: a user study with children. IADIS Int. J. Comput. Sci. Info. Syst. **2**, 151–161 (2007)
25. Souman, J.L., Giordano, P.R., Schwaiger, M., Frissen, I., Thümmel, T., Ulbrich, H., Luca, A.D., Bülthoff, H.H., Ernst, M.O.: CyberWalk: enabling unconstrained omnidirectional walking through virtual environments. ACM Trans. Appl. Percept. (TAP) **8**, 25 (2011)
26. Giordano, P.R., Souman, J., Mattone, R., De Luca, A., Ernst, M., Bulthoff, H.: The CyberWalk platform: humna-machine interaction enabling unconstrained walking through VR. In: First Workshop for Young Researchers on Human-Friendly Robotics (2008)
27. Ruddle, R.A., Lessels, S.: The benefits of using a walking interface to navigate virtual environments. ACM Trans. Comput.-Hum. Interact. **16**, 1–18 (2009)
28. Mine, M.: Virtual environment interaction techniques. UNC Chapel Hill computer science technical report TR95-018 507248-507242 (1995)
29. Balk, S.A., Bertola, M.A., Inman, V.W.: Simulator sickness questionnaire: twenty years later. In: Proceedings of the Seventh International Driving Symposium on Human Factors in Driver Assessment, Training, and Vehicle Design, pp. 257–263 (2013)
30. Alfano, P.L., Michel, G.F.: Restricting the field of view: perceptual and performance effects. Percept. Mot. Skills **70**, 35–45 (1990)
31. Arthur, K.: Effects of field of view on task performance with head-mounted displays. In: Conference Companion on Human Factors in Computing Systems, pp. 29–30. ACM (1996)

32. Christou, C., Tzanavari, A., Herakleous, K., Poullis, C.: Navigation in virtual reality: comparison of gaze-directed and pointing motion control. In: Proceedings of 18th Mediterranean Electrotechnical Conference (MELECON), pp. 1–6 (2016). doi:10.1109/MELCON.2016.7495413

33. LaViola, Jr., J.J.: A discussion of cybersickness in virtual environments. ACM SIGCHI Bull. **32**, 47–56 (2000)

34. Kennedy, R.S., Lane, N.E., Berbaum, K.S., Lilienthal, M.G.: Simulator sickness questionnaire: an enhanced method for quantifying simulator sickness. Int. J. Aviat. Psychol. **3**, 203–220 (1993)

35. Stanney, K.M., Kennedy, R.S., Drexler, J.M.: Cybersickness is not simulator sickness. In: Proceedings of the Human Factors and Ergonomics Society annual meeting, pp. 1138–1142. SAGE Publications Sage CA, Los Angeles (1997)

36. Bohannon, R.W.: Comfortable and maximum walking speed of adults aged 20–79 years: reference values and determinants. Age Ageing **26**, 15–19 (1997)

37. Hollerbach, J.M.: Locomotion interfaces. In: Handbook of Virtual Environments: Design, Implementation, and Applications, pp. 239–254 (2002)

38. Interrante, V., Ries, B., Anderson, L.: Seven league boots: a new metaphor for augmented locomotion through moderately large scale immersive virtual environments. In: IEEE Symposium on 3D User Interfaces. IEEE (2007)

39. Usoh, M., Arthur, K., Whitton, M.C., Bastos, R., Steed, A., Slater, M., Brooks, Jr., F.P.: Walking > walking-in-place > flying, in virtual environments. In: Proceedings of the 26th Annual Conference on Computer Graphics and Interactive Techniques, pp. 359–364. ACM Press/Addison-Wesley Publishing Co. (1999)

40. Steinicke, F., Bruder, G., Ropinski, T., Hinrichs, K.: Moving towards generally applicable redirected walking. In: Proceedings of the Virtual Reality International Conference (VRIC), pp. 15–24 (2008)

41. Kennedy, R.S., Drexler, J.M., Compton, D.E., Stanney, K.M., Lanham, D.S., Harm, D.L.: Configural scoring of simulator sickness, cybersickness and space adaptation syndrome: similarities and differences. In: Virtual and Adaptive Environments: Applications, Implications, and Human Performance Issues, p. 247 (2003)

42. Levine, M., Jankovic, I.N., Palij, M.: Principles of spatial problem solving. J. Exp. Psychol. Gen. **111**, 157 (1982)

43. Berthoz, A., Israël, I., Georges-François, P., Grasso, R., Tsuzuku, T.: Spatial memory of body linear displacement: what is being stored? Science **269**, 95 (1995)

44. Klatzky, R.L., Beall, A.C., Loomis, J.M., Golledge, R.G., Philbeck, J.W.: Human navigation ability: tests of the encoding-error model of path integration. Spatial Cogn. Comput. **1**, 31–65 (1999)

Mixed Reality-Based User Interaction Feedback for a Hand-Controlled Interface Targeted to Robot Teleoperation

Laura Cancedda, Alberto Cannavò, Giuseppe Garofalo, Fabrizio Lamberti, Paolo Montuschi, and Gianluca Paravati[✉]

Dipartimento di Automatica e Informatica, Politecnico di Torino,
Corso Duca degli Abruzzi, 24, 10129 Torino, Italy
{laura.cancedda,alberto.cannavo,s239732}@studenti.polito.it,
{fabrizio.lamberti,paolo.montuschi,gianluca.paravati}@polito.it
http://grains.polito.it

Abstract. The continuous progress in the field of robotics and the diffusion of its related application scenarios in today's modern world makes human interaction and communication with robots an aspect of fundamental importance. The development of interfaces based on natural interaction paradigms is getting an increasingly captivating topic in Human-Robot Interaction (HRI), due to their intrinsic capabilities in providing ever more intuitive and effective control modalities. Teleoperation systems require to handle a non-negligible amount of information coming from on-board sensors as well as input devices, thus increasing the workload of remote users. This paper presents the design of a 3D User Interface (3DUI) for the control of teleoperated robotic platforms aimed at increasing the interaction efficiency. A hand gesture driven controller is used as input modality to naturally map the position and gestures of the user's hand to suitable commands for controlling the platform components. The designed interface leverages on mixed reality to provide a visual feedback to the control commands issued by the user. The visualization of the 3DUI is superimposed to the video stream provided by an on-board camera. A user study confirmed that the proposed solution is able to improve the interaction efficiency by significantly reducing the completion time for tasks assigned in a remote *reach-and-pick* scenario.

Keywords: Human-robot interaction · Robot teleoperation · 3D user interface · Mixed reality · Visual feedback · Hand-based control

1 Introduction

Due to the recent advances in robotics, performing remote tasks with the support of robotic systems, possibly involving several interfaces to different robot functionalities, is becoming ordinary practice for a growing number of activities in several application fields, ranging from search and rescue in dangerous

© Springer International Publishing AG 2017
L.T. De Paolis et al. (Eds.): AVR 2017, Part II, LNCS 10325, pp. 447–463, 2017.
DOI: 10.1007/978-3-319-60928-7_38

environments, to inspection of industrial plants and assistance for home-care, to name a few [1].

Human-robot interaction (HRI) plays a key role in teleoperation scenarios, since most of the developed system are still based on supervisory control by the human operator. In this scenario, it is of paramount importance to develop ever more effective and intuitive interaction modalities to let the operator focus on the relevant aspects of the task to be carried out, rather than getting distracted from the complexity of the interaction. Several factors influences the performance and the efficiency in carrying out teleoperation tasks. Along these lines, a careful design of the overall system is needed by considering, aside from technical aspects, interaction modalities, user interfaces as well as human factors.

The first factor influencing human-robot interaction is the input method. Several possibilities may be considered, ranging from the use of the most common user interfaces (i.e. keyboard, mouse, gamepad, etc.) to the adoption of the most recent technologies capable to elaborate and interpret human's voice and gestures. The latter category allows the operator to interact with the robot more naturally, by following the principles of Natural User Interaction (NUI) to increase the level of empathy and confidence [2].

Another important factor influencing the efficiency in robot teleoperation is the design of the Graphical User Interface (GUI), considered that the operator is remotely located and cannot directly check the maneuvering of a robot in response to issued commands. Furthermore, as argued in the remainder of the manuscript, despite their intuitiveness NUIs may introduce the need for additional information to be conveyed to the operator. Indeed, HRI relying on vision-based techniques lacks direct feedback concerning the working volume of the input device. In this scenario, mixed reality assumes a key role for enhancing the spatial awareness concerning the control of remote mobile robots by providing both virtual and physical information [3]. As a consequence, an essential and fundamental design principle is to provide the user with various forms of feedbacks. Indeed, feedback can be visual, tactile, auditory and, in general, may involve all senses together, but it is also tightly related to the selected input device.

Moved by the above considerations, this paper presents the design and development of a 3D user interface to control a multi-functional teleoperated system composed by a rover equipped with a robotic arm. The interface allows the user to interact with the system through the use of hand gestures captured by a Leap Motion controller, which has been.selected due to its high accuracy [4]. A mixed reality interface is built by combining teleoperation information (e.g. concerning the surrounding environment, available functionalities, etc.) and visual feedback concerning user interaction in a single interface. Test results confirmed the ability of the designed interaction modality to reduce task completion times for telemanipulating a robotic arm with respect to common teleoperation approaches. Moreover, a subjective user study conducted on 12 participants revealed a preference for the proposed interface.

The remainder of this paper is organized as follows. Section 2 reviews related works concerning teleoperation systems by focusing on aspects related to interaction modalities as well as the design of the graphical user interface and motivates the design choices given in Sect. 3, which presents both architectural details and the design of the interaction modality. Section 4 reports both on the objective and subjective results obtained by testing the interface in a *reach-and-pick* scenario. Finally, conclusion are drawn in Sect. 5.

2   Background

In past years, many approaches have been proposed in the development of user interfaces for teleoperation systems [5,6]. Several interaction modalities have been investigated based on the specific task should be carried out by the robot itself. For instance, force-reflecting manual controllers are suitable for manipulating grippers and robotic arms, though they introduce time delays and suffer stability problems [7]. Datagloves have been widely used coupled with force feedback devices to give the remote user the perception of the situation faced by the controlled robot in the real environment as, for instance, in [8].

Despite the diversity of adopted interaction forms, control sticks and game controllers are definitely the most common interfaces used in human-robot interaction. The reasons behind their widespread diffusion in mass-market rest on their cost effectiveness, their accurate control capabilities and their general-purpose orientation. Complex teleoperation tasks involving robotic platforms with multiple degrees of freedom (DOF), like a robot manipulator, could be addressed by leveraging on the combination of multiple input devices. For instance, in [9] a couple of control sticks and a gamepad have been used to control a robotic arm by acting on different DOFs simultaneously, or by separately controlling each joint, respectively.

As widely known, the presence of a physical device for robot control permits to establish a feedback channel to be exploited for different purposes. A bidirectional system for teleoperation has been developed in [10], where a control stick has been used as input device to send commands to a mobile platform and information concerning the environment is sent back to the operator in the form of feedback forces through the control stick itself. Vibro-tactile feedback is also investigated in [11], where the interface shows a virtual space representing the robot and its adjacent objects in the real environment, superimposed to images coming from an on-board camera. The vibro-tactile feedback is used as complementary hint to visualization to improve spatial awareness by providing information about the distance from objects in the environment.

The functionalities of a teleoperation system may be difficult to be properly activated by means of control sticks and gamepads, in particular for inexperienced users. This is the situation when a large number of DOFs should be remotely controlled [12], e.g., for manipulating a robotic arm. Indeed, button- or stick-based input devices may require to operate simultaneously on numerous levers or buttons thus having a huge impact on the intuitiveness of the interface.

This shortcoming may be overcome by leveraging on intuitive gestures performed by the operator, which can be implemented in several ways from a technological standpoint, e.g., ranging from the use of wearable intertial sensors, to body tracking using vision based techniques, and so forth. Techniques able to capture user's poses and gestures are often referred to as Natural User Interfaces (NUIs). They have been proven to improve several aspects of human-robot interaction in teleoperation systems, e.g. by reducing the operator training time, cognitive load and enhancing situation awareness [13]. As a matter of example, in [13] gestures are defined to pick objects in a virtual environment by mapping the movement of users with a virtual representation of their hand. Virtual reality is exploited as well in [14] to let the user control a real robot through its virtual counterpart in a virtual setting. It is worth to outline that, although it is possible to virtually reconstruct the real environment, e.g., through simultaneous localization and mapping techniques, virtual reality decreases the user's sense of awareness with respect to a real image flow streamed by a camera [6].

As widely known, augmented reality techniques permit to retain real world vision by enlarging its level of knowledge. In [15], a robotic arm is controlled through an augmented reality interface exploiting an exocentric vision of the robot (i.e., slightly behind and above) built by means of a Kinect sensor and a head-mounted display. Hand tracking and gestures recognition relying on vision-based techniques are exploited to generate control commands. Similarly, a mixed reality user interface for teleoperation robots has been developed in [16] to visualize predicted scenarios. In this case, images coming from the onboard camera of a rover are augmented with a virtual representation of the wheeled platform itself, thus realizing an augmented reality exocentric view. The user directly operates by giving commands to drive the virtual robot, which is followed by the real one.

Despite the intuitiveness provided by NUIs through vision-based techniques, the main drawback with respect to handheld controllers is constituted by the impossibility to rely on vibro-tactile feedback to convey information to the operator. Indeed, NUI devices improve the situation awareness and naturalness of the interface, as noted by [17], but they need to provide an adequate visual feedback through additional information which could overload the screen. As a matter of example, in [18], the feedback has been provided in the form of visual information to develop an immersive interface to control a snake-like robot. The interaction is provided by a Leap Motion controller. The visual feedback is provided to the user by means of two separate devices: information concerning the environment is represented in the main screen of a workstation whereas control information relating to the field of view of the input device are provided through a tablet device. It is worth noticing that the decoupling of visualization information may increase the mental workload required to users due to repeated gaze switches among several devices.

Different sources of information may be provided in different viewports of the same interface, eventually by adapting contents and layout to the need of the user [19]. In [20], an application for remotely controlling an arm and grasp objects has been presented. In this case, the interface shows different views side by side: the real environment, the virtual corresponding scene, and the webcam stream from a ceiling camera above the robot; eventually in the virtual scene a hand skeleton mirrors the state of the tracked real hand. The dissociation among the hand representation, the arm virtual mapping and the image of the real arm could bring to a sense of unawareness [21] and does not improve the learnability of the interface. Similarly, in [22], the video coming from the onboard camera and the feedback concerning the field of view of the hand gesture driven controller are shown in distinct viewports. Furthermore, the field of view of the hand gesture driven controller is represented through two distinct two-dimensional views (front view and top view), which increases the complexity of the user interface.

By moving from the above considerations, we designed a system for interacting with remotely located robots which leverages on a Natural User Interface for effectively carrying out teleoperation tasks. The presented solution is able to overcome the above mentioned limitations of hands-free interaction modalities by means of a mixed reality-based feedback with the aim of integrating the robot egocentric vision with three dimensional information concerning the working volume of the hand gesture driven controller.

3   Teleoperation System

This section describes the main architectural components of the teleoperation system which has been used to test the mixed reality-based user interaction method. A multi-robotic platform composed by a rover (Lynxmotion A4WDI) and a robotic arm (Lynxmotion AL5D) can be remotely controlled.

Both of them are connected through a Wi-Fi network shield to communicate with a distributed controller software by receiving commands and sending information about sensors status. The rover moves reacting to directional and speed commands, while the arm is a 5-DoF manipulator as shown in Fig. 1a. The latter is controlled through an inverse kinematics solver by mapping the spatial coordinates of the user's wrist to the end effector of the robotic arm. Roll and pitch of the gripper are controlled through forward kinematics. A Web Cam Logitech C525 is mounted over the end effector of the robotic arm and connected to a Raspberry Pi to provide real-time visualization capabilities to the remote user, which can inspect the surrounding environment. The video is streamed through a Wi-Fi network.

The high-level architecture of the interaction system is illustrated in Fig. 1b. The user interacts with the system through a hand gesture based controller (in particular, a Leap Motion device has been used in this work), which is in charge to locate and track in real-time the user's hand within its working volume. Its interaction field is approximately shaped as an inverted pyramid centered at the device's center and extending upwards. The range of the tracking volume depends from the device's field of view, which is approximately 150 degree. Outside this region the tracking is lost.

An application is responsible for recognizing input commands for the rover and the arm and providing visual feedback, presented by its interface. Once recognized, numeric values associated to the gesture (i.e. spatial coordinates)are translated into actionable commands and then they are sent to the robot to properly activate its servomotors.

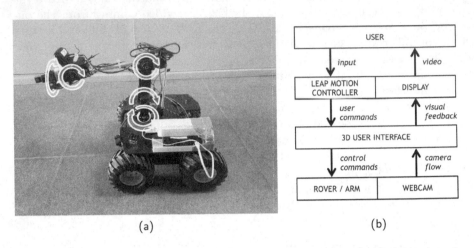

(a)   (b)

Fig. 1. The teleoperation system developed for testing the mixed reality user interface: (a) the multi-robotic platform is composed by a rover and a 5-DOF robotic arm, (b) high-level architecture of the designed interaction system.

Interfaces for teleoperation systems like the one developed for testing the presented user interface should permit a simple and direct interaction with the environment and objects. An interface is defined as effective when the user can reach his or her goals, when the important tasks can be done better, easier, or faster than by using another system, and when users are not frustrated or uncomfortable [20]. The user should be always in control of what is happening as a consequence of his/her commands; the less effort the user has to make to understand how the system is operating, the more attention he/she can pay to the task to be performed [21].

Any system based on gesture recognition requires an adequate feedback able to don't distract the user from the main task is being carried out. For this purpose we designed a mixed reality interface to overlap hints concerning the hand-gesture based controller (which intrinsically lacks feedback information otherwise available with other interfaces, e.g. handheld-based) to information aimed at providing situational awareness in a teleoperated system (in this case, the streaming flow provided by the front-facing camera mounted on board). Data related to the input controller are displayed by leveraging on a 3D visualization to enhance the user's perception of the controller's working limits. Dynamically adjusted 3D volumes represent the workable area where the user can effectively move his/her hands. A set of discrete commands are activated by the user by leveraging on some symbolic gestures previously defined (e.g., open hand to the left/right, roll the hand facing the palm upwards/downwards, close hand, etc.). It is worth to recall that interfaces for teleoperation benefit in naturalness and learnability by maintaining a coherence between the mapped gesture and the movement the user would do in real circumstances to reach a target, since real-world physical metaphors constitute a valid help for the user to remember associated actions [20, 21].

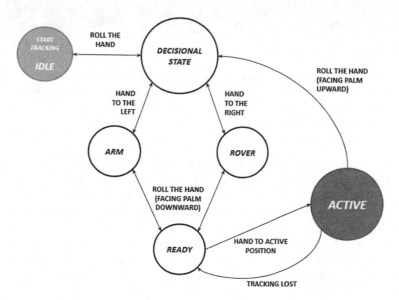

Fig. 2. State diagram of the devised interaction schema. Starting from the *Decisional State* it is possible to choose a control mode (*Arm/Rover*) to be selected (*Ready*); the interaction starts (*Active*) when a setup position is reached.

The interaction schema is based on the state diagram shown in Fig. 2. In the idle state, the hand tracker calculates the position and orientation of the user's hand. When the hand's palm is facing upwards, the application enters into a decisional state, in which the graphical user interface is divided into three main areas: two on the sides, which are labelled with the relative control mode that can be enabled (namely, "Arm" and "Rover" areas), and one centrally located, not associated to any control mode (i.e., a "Transition" area). Figure 3a shows a screenshot of the interface in the decisional state.

Once the user reaches one of the two sides, the specific operational states (i.e. arm- and rover-control modes) are activated through the rotation of the palm downwards. The reverse operation (i.e. rolling the hand's palm upwards) can be used to come back to the decisional state in any moment. For this reason, the latter represents a safe gesture always available. For safety reasons, the interaction does not start directly after the selection of the operational state. Indeed, although the hand position may be correct during the decisional state, abrupt or

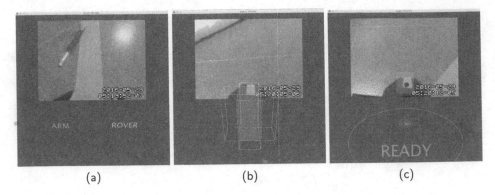

(a)　　　　　　　　　　　(b)　　　　　　　　　　　(c)

Fig. 3. Screenshots of the user interface for the selection of the robotic functionality to be controlled. (a) Decisional state with three areas, Arm area, Transition area and Rover area. (b) Setup position to be reached in rover driving mode. (c) Setup position to be reached in arm-control mode.

unwanted commands (e.g., sudden movements of the rover or the arm) may be produced when an operational state is activated. The user's hand – represented by a sphere in the interface – should reach a safe setup position within the 3D workspace of the hand gesture driven controller before the interaction with the selected robotic component begins. This way the user is driven to assume an initial pose which maximizes the available interaction volume. Figure 3 shows the setup position (highlighted in green) to be reached in the 3D user interface for each control mode. As soon as the user achieves the indicated volume, the interaction with the selected component begins.

When the arm functionality is selected, a grid – representative of the rover's base where the arm is mounted on – is overimposed to the streaming flow of the on-board camera. The relationship between the physical position of the hand and the underlying hand gesture driven controller is graphically represented together with the current tracking limits. In fact, a graphical indicator of the working area related to the hand tracking module is displayed on the screen in the form of an ellipsoid, which represents the projection of the tracking boundary on the surface grid. The border of this safe area should not be overrun by the sphere representing the hand of the user to avoid tracking failures. The tracking area is dependent from the height of the tracked hand with respect to the tracking hardware. For this reason, the size of the tracking area has been designed to be adaptive. In fact, the size of the projection reflects the width available for the movements on the horizontal plane at a certain height. As a result, the ellipsoid resizes as the hand moves in the vertical axis. To correctly track, the sphere's shadow should remain inside the indicated boundary. Otherwise, a tracking failure may occur, since the hand is located near the borders (or beyond) the working volume. In this case, the system detects the tracking failure and jumps to the idle state to avoid the triggering of unwanted commands.

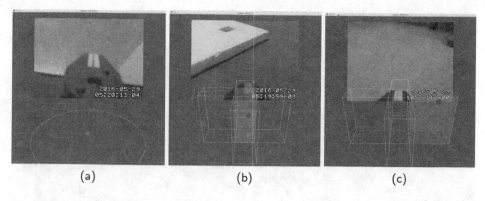

Fig. 4. Workspace limits of the hand gesture driven controller. Their size is determined by the physical height of the tracked hand with respect to the input controller. (a) Interface for controlling the robotic arm and the tongs: the ellipsoid represents the boundary of the tracking volume. (b) Interface for driving the robot: a steady zone is used as a rest pose for the rover. (c) Interface for driving the robot: each (dynamically resized) volume represents a command.

Furthermore, to increase the spatial awareness, two concentric ellipses supplementing the sphere indicate the hand's roll (Fig. 4a). The user's hand position allows to configure in real-time all the robotic arm's joints through an inverse kinematics solver: it enables the movement of the robotic arm in all directions as well as the use of a tongs located in the arm's edge, which can rotate and further grab objects by opening and closing movements.

When the user selects the Rover area, the wheeled platform can be directly controlled. In this case, a custom shape represented by two perpendicular parallelepipeds in a cross configuration is overimposed to the camera stream flow (Fig. 4). The volume currently containing a sphere, representing the hand position, is highlighted by using different colours to give the user a prompt and immediate feedback about the state of the interaction tool: light blue for the central one corresponding to the steady position (Fig. 4b), green for forward, backward, left and right ones (Fig. 4c); when the sphere exits from one interaction shape, it returns to be transparent. As in the case of the arm control, graphical borders represents the physical boundaries of the tracking area. In fact, the size of the shape is dynamically changed according to the height reached by the hand with respect to the input controller in order to give to the user the perception that the tracked area becomes wider by increasing the distance between his/her hand and the controller itself. The right and the left sections are used to send rotational commands to the robot, while by moving forward or backward the hand, a user will trigger the movement of the wheels in the same direction of the moving hand.

Transitions between states (e.g. from Ready to Active state) as well as wrong movements (i.e. tracking losses) are associated to a visual feedback. For instance, tracking loss is particularly relevant in the interface due to the disorientation

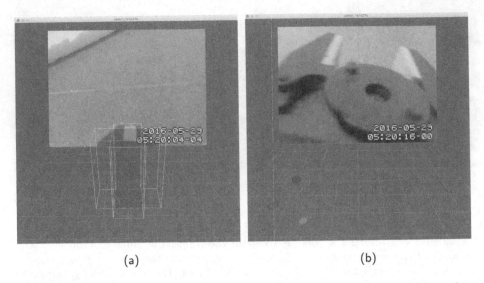

(a)   (b)

Fig. 5. Visual feedback for (a) tracking loss occurring in driving mode and (b) tracking loss occurring in arm-control mode.

generated to the user, thus slowing down the completion of the tasks. For this reason, as illustrated in Fig. 5, the tracking loss is clearly highlighted in both control modes by highlighting in red the interface elements. A video showing the interaction modalities with the robotic platform is available for download[1].

4   Results

To evaluate the usability and possibly identify the elements of the teleoperated system which can take more advantage from the designed 3D user interface, a user study has been conducted by involving the participation of 12 students at the University. The test consisted in carrying out a *reach-and-pick* task with three different user interfaces, with the aim of comparing the proposed one with a user interface based on a gamepad and another implementation based on a hand gesture driven controller [22] (in the following referred to as 3DUI, gamepad and 2DUI, respectively). The gamepad interaction method is related to the use of a long-established input device, where the teleoperation interface simply consisted in the real-time streaming flow of the on-board camera. The latter concerns the use of a Leap Motion controller to track user's hand position, orientation and status (open/closed), as in the current work, presented to the user by means of a 2D interface [22].

Participants were allowed to get accustomed with each interface by freely operating with the two components of the tele-manipulated platform, i.e., the

---

[1] Video: https://www.dropbox.com/sh/uxje5n18t41iyhu/AABBhfwCc1I1xfIIu6IYJo M4a?dl=0.

rover and the robotic arm, both by using the hand gesture driven controller and the gamepad. During this training session, participants were instructed about the interpretation of the information provided by the different user interfaces and they were invited to try to tele-control the rover and the arm by leveraging on the video stream received from the on-board camera.

The *reach-and-pick* scenario consisted in two consecutive sub-tasks, i.e., navigation and picking. The first one consisted in driving the rover along a predefined path drawn on the ground (Fig. 6). The first sub-task was considered as completed as soon as the rover reached a target point (i.e., on the top of a ramp). The latter consisted in grasping a small target object placed on the ground at the end of the path by using the robotic arm. In this case, the task was considered as concluded once the target object was grabbed. The two sub-tasks will be referred to as *Rover* and *Arm*. The overall scenario was designed to test the driving of the rover and the arm-control mode separately; each participant repeated three times the experiment, one for each interface. In order to reduce possible learning effects, the sequence of user interfaces to be used by each participant was randomly generated.

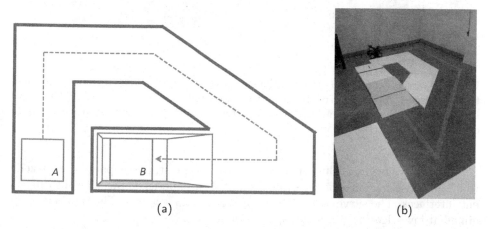

(a)   (b)

Fig. 6. *Reach-and-pick* scenario designed for the user study: A. start position of the rover for the navigation sub-task, B. target destination of the navigation sub-task and position of the picking sub-task.

Objective and subjective results were carried out to assess the designed user interface. The performance indicator selected for the objective evaluation was the task completion time, which has been measured for carrying out both sub-tasks. Subjective evaluations were collected to supplement the performance analysis with the users' opinions through a questionnaire filled in at the end of the experimental test.

Results obtained with the objective evaluation in terms of completion time for the two sub-tasks are reported in Fig. 7. On average, the completion time with the proposed 3DUI was lower both for the navigation (i.e., Rover) and picking (i.e., Arm) tasks. The statistical significance of the objective results was analyzed by running independent samples t-tests on collected data with significance level $\alpha = 0.05$. According to the statistical analysis, the proposed interface outperformed both the 2DUI and Gamepad ones in the picking scenario ($p = 0.0148$ and $p = 0.0460$, respectively). Concerning the navigation scenario, the average completion time was significantly lower by using the proposed interface with respect to the 2DUI ($p = 0.0189$).

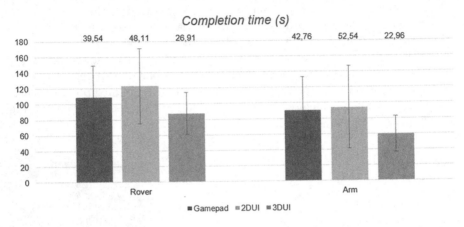

Fig. 7. Average completion time for the sub-tasks (carried out by tele-manipulating the rover and the robotic arm) by using the Gamepad, the 2DUI and the 3DUI. Bars height indicate the average value (lower is better) whereas labels indicate the standard deviation.

As said, after the conclusion of the experimental test, participants were asked to fill in a questionnaire for the evaluation of their experience by using the different interfaces. The survey was divided in three main sections. The first one was aimed at investigating usability aspects defined by Nielsen [23]. To this aim, five questions were included to determine whether a participant was satisfied in terms of learnability, memorability, efficiency of the user interface controls, pleasantness during the interaction, and number of errors made. The second section was created by considering the SASSI methodology [24], which was originally targeted to speech interfaces. In this work, the questionnaire was integrated with questions derived from the SASSI methodology to possibly evaluating usability factors not covered by Nielsen. In particular, participants were asked to evaluate the following five usability factors: System Response Accuracy (SRA), Cognitive Demand (CD), Annoyance (AN), Habitability (HAB) and Speed (SPE). Lastly, the preference for a particular interface was asked in the last section of the questionnaire. Overall, the survey had 10 statements to be evaluated on a five-point Likert scale from 0 (strong disagreement) to 4 (strong agreement) for each interface and for each task separately.

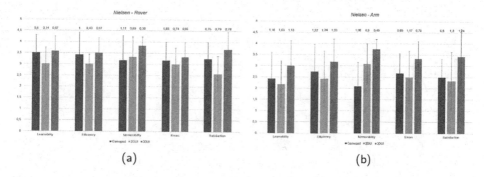

Fig. 8. Overview of the subjective results for the two sub-tasks using the three interfaces based on the Nielsen methodology and concerning Learnability, Efficiency, Memorability, Errors and Satisfaction. Bars height indicate the average value (higher is better), labels indicate standard deviation.

Figure 8 reports an overview of the average subjective results gathered with the Nielsen methodology. Results are plotted using a worse-to-better scale. Again, the statistical significance was checked by adopting the same procedure used for the objective evaluation. According to the outcomes of the statistical analysis for the Nielsen methodology, the proposed user interface always scored better than or equal to the other user interfaces. In particular, memorability reached the highest score for the 3DUI, demonstrating the easiness in gaining expertise and remembering commands in the use of the interface. Analyzing the picking sub-task more in the detail (Fig. 8b), the proposed interface proved to be robust from the point of view of the errors (i.e., perception of committed errors, easiness of recovery, and how severe they are) beside memorability. In fact, both the usability factors scored significantly better than Gamepad ($p = 0.0020$ for memorability, $p = 0.0389$ for errors) and 2DUI ($p = 0.0046$ for memorability, $p = 0.0437$ for errors). A significant preference over the 2DUI was observed for learnability ($p = 0.0021$), efficiency ($p = 0.0054$) and satisfaction ($p = 0.0053$). Results concerning the perception of efficiency are not statistically significant by comparing the 3DUI and the Gamepad, but the above objective results give evidence of how quickly users can perform tasks.

Figure 9 show the results for the second section of the questionnaire based on the SASSI methodology. Average results indicate that the proposed interface always scored better than or equal to the other ones. The Habitability usability factor was significantly higher than the Gamepad and 2DUI in both sub-tasks ($p = 0.0388$ and $p = 0.0015$, respectively, for the Rover; $p = 0.0116$ and $p = 0.0019$, respectively, for the Arm). The 3DUI outperformed the 2DUI also in terms of System Response Accuracy. In fact, statistical significance is achieved both for the navigation ($p = 0.0069$) and picking ($p = 0.0209$) interaction scenarios. Objective results are confirmed by the Speed usability factor. In this case, only results concerning the manipulation of the robotic arm are statistically significant (the 3DUI is perceived to provide a faster way to execute

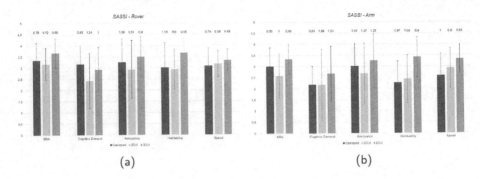

(a)   (b)

Fig. 9. Overview of the subjective results for the two sub-tasks using the three interfaces obtained based on the SASSI methodology and concerning System Response Accuracy (SRA), Cognitive Demand (CD), Annoyance (AN), Habitability (HAB) and Speed (SPE). Bars height indicate the average value (higher is better), whereas labels indicate standard deviation.

tasks than the Gamepad, $p = 0.0209$), totally in accordance with the previous measurements of the task completion time.

In the last part of the questionnaire, participants were asked to express their preference for a particular user interface among those analyzed. According to the scores summarized in Fig. 10, the overall preference for the whole experiment was 46% in favor of the proposed interface, 31% of participants indicated the Gamepad, and 24% preferred the 2DUI. To get more insights about the usability of the 3DUI for different tasks and to possibly identify the elements of the teleoperated system which can take more advantage from the proposed interaction modality, users were asked to express their preference for each of the different phases of the *reach-and-pick* scenario. For the first sub-task, i.e. navigation, neither of 3DUI and Gamepad emerged clearly as preferred interface (they were judged as first choice by 39% and 38% of participants, respectively). For the

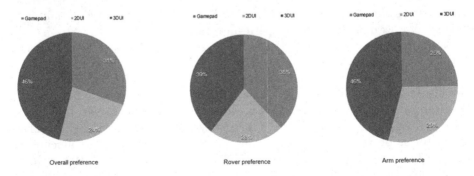

Fig. 10. Overall preference, Rover preference, Arm preference expressed in the questionnaires.

last phase, i.e. grabbing, 46% of participants preferred the proposed interface, 25% the gamepad, and 29% the 2DUI.

Based on the above results, the designed interface proved to be effective in particular when the teleoperation task involved the control of complex robotic components. Indeed, the "reaching" mode actually required to drive the rover by acting on a few commands. Conversely, "picking" mode required to concurrently act on several degrees of freedom.

5 Conclusion and Future Works

In this work, a mixed reality-based user interface aimed at improving the interaction efficiency for controlling multi-task mobile robots during teleoperation tasks is presented. The interaction is based on a hand gesture driven approach, which requires to provide users with additional status advices to effectively interact with the remote platform (e.g., concerning the physical workspace limits of the input controller), in addition to information related to situational awareness (i.e., data coming from on-board sensors, e.g., a camera). The proposed interface blends the ego-centric vision of the remote platform with a 3D representation of the interaction space for hand gesture based input controllers as well as the real-time position of the user's tracked hand. The combination of these elements into the same visualization area constitutes the strength of the proposed approach, as it allows to increase the usability of the interface as demonstrated by the experimental tests carried out in a *reach-and-pick* scenario, which involved the comparison with two different interfaces (based on a gamepad and on hand tracking with a 2D visualization of the same input data, respectively). The mobile platform was composed by a rover and a robotic arm, both controlled by the same user interface. Objective and subjective results confirm the ability of the proposed solution to make easier and efficient the interaction with the teleoperation platform, as well as pleasant to use. In particular, the designed mixed-reality based interface allowed participants to reduce execution times in the task involving the control of the robotic arm. Moreover, subjective evaluations pointed out that the presented solution outperforms the gamepad implementation in terms of memorability and habitability, thus suggesting that the determination of appropriate gestures and actions for reaching the task goal was easier than common approaches.

Given the encouraging results obtained, future works will be addressed to improve several features of the considered teleoperation interface. Several cameras and sensors (e.g. proximity) showing different points of view may be used to improve the spatial awareness and reduce the so-called "key-hole" effect [25]. In this case, additional information to be visualized on the interface should be taken into account. Other interaction possibilities will be considered as well, e.g., by adding additional gestures to move or change the current point of view.

References

1. Boboc, R.G., Moga, H., Talaba, D.: A review of current applications in teleoperation of mobile robots. Bull. Transilvania Univ. Brasov Ser. I Eng. Sci. **5**(54), 9–16 (2012)
2. Sriram, S., Wijnand, I.: Survey and classification of spatial object manipulation techniques. IPO, Center for User-System Interaction, Eindhoven University of Technology, pp. 1–2 (2000)
3. Ricks, B., Nielsen, C.W., Goodrich, M.A.: Ecological displays for robot interaction: a new perspective. In: Proceedings of the IROS, p. 2 (2004)
4. Coelho, J.C., Verbeek, F.J.: Pointing task evaluation of Leap Motion Controller in 3D virtual environment. In: Proceedings of the Chi Sparks 2014 Conference on Creating the Difference, pp. 78–85 (2014)
5. Nielsen, C.W., Goodrich, M.A., Ricks, R.W.: Ecological interfaces for improving mobile robot teleoperation. Trans. Robot. **23**(5), 927–941 (2007)
6. Chen, J.Y., Haas, E.C., Barnes, M.J.: Human performance issues and user interface design for teleoperated robots. IEEE Trans. Syst. Man Cybern. Part C: Appl. Rev. **37**(6), 1231–1245 (2007)
7. Cui, J., Tosunoglu, S., Roberts, R., Moore, C., Repperger, D.W.: A review of teleoperation system control. In: Proceedings of the Florida Conference on Recent Advances in Robotics (FCRAR), pp. 1–12 (2003)
8. Hu, H., Li, J., Xie, Z., Wang, B., Liu, H., Hirzinger, G.: A robot arm/hand teleoperation system with telepresence and shared control. In: Proceedings, 2005 IEEE/ASME International Conference on Advanced Intelligent Mechatronics, Monterey, CA, pp. 1312–1317 (2005)
9. Crainic, M.F., Preitl, S.: Ergonomic operating mode for a robot arm using a gamepad with two joysticks. In: IEEE 10th Jubilee International Symposium on Applied Computational Intelligence and Informatics, Timisoara, pp. 167–170 (2015)
10. Cho, S.K., Jin, H.Z., Lee, J.M., Yao, B.: Teleoperation of a mobile robot using a force-reflection joystick with sensing mechanism of rotating magnetic field. IEEE/ASME Trans. Mechatron. **15**(1), 17–26 (2010)
11. De Barros, P.G., Lindeman, R.W., Ward, M.O.: Enhancing robot teleoperator situation awareness and performance using vibro-tactile and graphical feedback. In: Proceedings of IEEE 2011 Symposium on 3D User Interfaces. 3DUI 2011, pp. 47–54 (2011)
12. Hashimoto, S., Ishida, A., Inami, M., Igarashi, T.: TouchMe: an augmented reality interface for remote robot control. J. Robot. Mechatron. **25**, 529–537 (2013)
13. Levine, S.J., Schaffert, S., Checka, N.: Natural User Interface for Robot Task Assignment, pp. 1–5 (2010)
14. Cheng-jun, D., Ping, D., Ming-lu, Z., Yan-fang, Z.: Design of mobile robot teleoperation system based on virtual reality. In: IEEE International Conference on Automation and Logistics, Shenyang, pp. 2024–2029 (2009)
15. Peppoloni, L., Brizzi, F., Avizzano, C.A., Ruffaldi, E.: Immersive ROS-integrated framework for robot teleoperation. In: IEEE Symposium on 3D User Interfaces 2015, pp. 23–24, March 2015
16. Sauer, M., Zeiger, F., Schilling, K.: Mixed-reality user interface for mobile robot teleoperation in ad-hoc networks. IFAC Proc. Volumes **43**(23), 77–82 (2010). ISSN 1474-6670
17. Hu, C., Meng, M.Q., Liu, P.X., Wang, X.: Visual gesture recognition for human-machine interface of robot teleoperation. In: Proceedings of the 2003 IEEE/RSJ International Conference on Intelligent Robotics System, pp. 1560–1565 (2003)

18. Krupke, D., Lubos, P., Bruder, G., and Steinicke, F., Zhang, J.: Natural 3D inter-action techniques for locomotion with modular robots. In: Mensch und Computer 2015: Gemeinsam Arbeit Erleben (2015)

19. Kawamura, K., Nilas, P., Muguruma, K., Adams, J.A., Zhou, C.: An agent-based architecture for an adaptive human- robot interface. In: Hawaii International Con-ference on System Sciences (HICSS 2003) (2003)

20. Krupke, D., Einig, L., Langbehn, E., Zhang, J., Steinicke, F.: Immersive remote grasping: realtime gripper control by a heterogenous robot control system. In: VRST 2016 Proceedings of the 22nd ACM Conference on Virtual Reality Software and Technology, pp. 337–338 (2016)

21. Bowman, D., Koller, D., Hodges, L.: A methodology for the evaluation of travel techniques for immersive virtual environments. Virtual Reality Res. Develop. Applicat. **3**(2), 120–131 (1998)

22. Bonaiuto, S., Cannavò, A., Bazzano, F., Paravati, G., Lamberti, F.: Tele-operation of Robot Teams: A Comparison of Gamepad-, Mobile Device and Hand Tracking-based User Interfaces. Unpublished

23. Nielsen, J., Molich, R.: Heuristic evaluation of user interfaces. In: Proceedings of the ACM CHI 1990 Conference (Seattle, WA, 1–5 April), pp. 249–256 (1990)

24. Hone, K.S., Graham, R.: Towards a tool for the subjective assessment of speech system interfaces (SASSI). Nat. Lang. Eng. **6**, 287–303 (2000)

25. Plemmons, D., Mandel, P.: Designing intuitive interfaces. In: Introduc-tion to Motion Control. https://developer-archive.leapmotion.com/articles/designing-intuitive-applications

Development and Heuristic Evaluation of Semi-immersive Hand-Gestural Virtual Reality Interface for Luxury Brands Online Stores

Samar Altarteer[1(✉)], Vassilis Charissis[2], David Harrison[2], and Warren Chan[2]

[1] Dar Al-Hekma University, Jeddah, Kingdom of Saudi Arabia
Samaraltarteer@gmail.com
[2] Glasgow Caledonian University, Glasgow, Scotland, UK
{Vassilis.Charissis, D.K.Harrison,
Warren.Chan}@gcu.ac.uk

Abstract. This paper introduces HCI design approach for an online shopping gestural-based interface. The proposed semi-immersive Virtual Reality (VR) interface aims to elevate the user experience in such indirect environment, where effective delivering of functional yet distinguishable experience effectively is crucial. The system comprises product customisation and personalization service, in which the product is visualized in a three-dimensional highly interactive manner.

The level of flexibility and realism of the aforementioned system and its impact on the experience presents new prospects for e-commerce systems, particularly for luxury markets. A preliminary heuristic evaluation was conducted by HCI experts prior to user trials to uncover potential usability issues. The heuristic session's outcome emphasised valuable components and design aspects within the system with regards to the system functionality, visualisation and interaction quality. Some factors and design issues for optimising and further enhancing the system were also highlighted.

Keywords: HCI · Virtual Reality · Luxury brands · Hand gesture · Semi-immersive · Product visualization

1 Introduction

Immersing customers into the shopping experience and providing exceptional services are some of the luxury brands key success strategies. Despite the fact that purchasing luxury products online is still in its infancy, due to the delay in e-store establishment, there are particular important factors making the digital presence of these brands even more influential and consistent with the other market channels. In luxury online stores, customers have essential considerations of the perceived value of the experience that in turn has a significant impact on customer satisfaction (Maklan and Klaus 2011; Bagdare and Jain 2013; Klaus and Maklan 2013). Customer attitude towards these

© Springer International Publishing AG 2017
L.T. De Paolis et al. (Eds.): AVR 2017, Part II, LNCS 10325, pp. 464–477, 2017.
DOI: 10.1007/978-3-319-60928-7_39

e-stores is determined by different aspects, which could be task-related such as product information, convenience, and time and effort exerted, as well as aesthetic and experiential-related such as web design (Kim et al. 2015). The role that the online stores play in delivering efficient information about products not only affecting positively customers' attitude but also influences about 45% of the actual offline luxury goods sales (Dauriz et al. 2014). Correspondingly, Google Think Insights (2013) found that 78% of customers rely mainly on online searches before purchasing luxury items. Although 69% purchase luxury products online because they find it convenient, the same percentage of customers still prefer to do offline shopping in order to investigate the products comprehensively (Google Think Insights 2013; Dauriz et al. 2014). In addition, about 19% of the customers attributed their offline preference to the lack of luxury customer experience in online stores (Google Think Insights 2013). Luxury brands like Herme's, Louis Vuitton, Chanel, Gucci, Dior and Ferragamo, approach different procedures in expressing the brand heritage and offer Know-How experience in online stores in order to convey a luxury experience (Maman Larraufie and Kourdoughli 2014). However, other signs and indications of luxury like rarity, accessibility and visual emotion are not expressed in these stations (Maman Larraufie and Kourdoughli 2014).

Hence, there is a challenge for the experience design and the interface design to compensate for the lack of direct interaction and explicit luxury experience. This dictates the need for a multisensory experience that involves high-task and low-task related factors to satisfy customers' demands (Kapferer 2012). This could be achieved by utilising appropriate technological solutions in order to satisfy the target customers' requirements and achieve the ideal online experience.

2 Proposed Interface Rational

In order to deliver a typical service for luxury brands, a 3D VR HCI interface was developed to facilitate the online store journey. The main objective of this research is to utilize Virtual Reality technology in order to deliver immersive experience to luxury brand customers. In addition, the proposed system encompasses product customisation capacity to enable the user to participate in the design process and allow for even higher levels of interactivity and engagement (Altarteer et al. 2016).

Advance 3D visualisation and real time interaction methods are integrated to mimic the real-life experience and provide customers with more accurate and comprehensive information about the products. A large 3D display is utilised to maximize the stereoscopic data delivery and to allow 1–1 scale product visualisation. Kober et al. (2012) and Clemente et al. (2014) empirical studies found that 3D large screen enhances motion stimuli and the perceived presence more than the desktop screen. The interaction with this large 3D display could possibly be delivered in a natural experience, where no device is required to accomplish the shopping task. The use of traditional wireless mouse in similar scenario was deemed non-immersive and blunts (Altarteer et al. 2013). A freehand Gestural Interaction system can best fit the task environment and the 3D large display (Ni 2011) and functions as an attractive solution for the expected limitations. These limitations can be met when using a mouse to navigate over giant or multiple displays, where the far ends, or one particular display out of many, can be reached or located smoothly and quickly with gestures (Wilson and Oliver 2003). It is also likely to elevate the perceived presence and engagement (McMahan et al. 2012). Therefore, in order to provide immersive experience the interaction with the interface is accomplished through hand gesture in a typical living-room environment, presented through large 3D-capable TV set equipped with 3D glasses.

2.1   Tasks and Predefined Configuration

Within the proposed system, the experience is divided into five tasks; the main task is to choose a specific product style, a travelling bag in this case. Sub-task 1 is to visualize the product features including opening the bag from inside and open the exterior compartments. Sub-task 2 is to manipulate the bag directly and freely (scale-rotate) to obtain all possible visual information. Sub-task 3 is to choose the desired product features and examine the changes in a real-time manner. Sub-task 4 is to obtain information and written description about the product features.

Options provided included three different product materials (Fig. 1) and two configurations of the exterior compartment style (long or short compared to the length of the bag) in addition to a choice between having flat pockets or zipped pockets, or both. Some of the choices were designed to be mutually exclusive (e.g., a short exterior compartment with both flat and zipped pockets). These options allow the user to evaluate the product, taking into account all product permutations, which should be adequate for testing purpose.

Fig. 1. The 3D model of the bag shows the three provided materials

2.2   Hand Gesture HCI Design Requirements

Designing the hand gesture interaction initiated by identifying the taxonomy of the gestures (discriminate categorization of the hand gestures' inputs and their interpretation by the recognition device). Task primitives have to be identified in relation to the hand actions as well as the gesture recognition device capabilities (Billinghurst and

Fig. 2. Handgrip dynamic gesture to perform interaction input

Buxton 2011). A vital challenge in gesture control is the gesture delimiters, which is the system performance in distinguishing the natural movements from the intended gestures that are meant as signs to execute commands and also define a gesture start and end correctly (Benko and Wilson 2010). For this reason, the gesture vocabulary has to be designed in a way that minimizes the accidental activation of the system command performance (Benko and Wilson 2010). Other important factors that have to be considered in gestures design are fatigue, accuracy, naturalness, duration (Barclay et al. 2011) and ease of recall and performance (Kortum 2008). Further, it should consider the application domain; the motions capture technology, the distance of the display monitor, and the context in which the interaction is accomplished.

Since this system is designed for online shopping, ubiquitous "off-the-shelf", easy-to-set-up devices was selected. Commonly owned devices for personal use are the console games motion capture devices. Kinect is one of those devices that do not require handheld trackers or controller, which was used for this study. Kinect (by Microsoft) technology can track motions by analyzing the input video stream of both hand and body movement, which provides input information about the height, depth and direction of the movements. The information received from hand gestures and movement can navigate, manipulate, select and accomplish commands throughout the interface.

A previous study investigating interface development for Gesture Interaction (GI) in VR environments identified four components of gesture interface: selection, navigation, manipulation and control of the VR environment (Pentiuc et al. 2012). The present system design requires the same gesture set although the implementation should be accomplished differently due to the nature of the task. Since the target users' age group is large, minimal effort in executing commands should be appropriate. Therefore, only the palms of both hands were required to interact with the system.

An option to perform the hand gesture was to use finger joint movement recognition that gives wider gestures possibilities and requires less physical activity like pinching gestures. However, Benko and Wilson (2010) in a study for Microsoft Research as a base interaction gesture for the purpose of identifying the start and end point of the interaction, while combining other hand movements to perform panning, zooming, rotation and navigation in different visualisation environments. The user's feedback from this study stated that the pinch gesture was not easy to learn nor self-evident. Hand gripping is another procedure of identifying the gesture's start and end times. The current study utilized hand gripping (Fig. 3) as an indicator of start and end times of command to avoid "False Positives", where the natural hand movement is

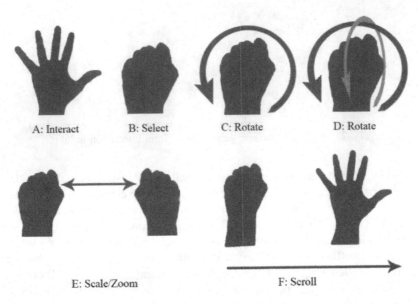

A: Interact   B: Select   C: Rotate   D: Rotate

E: Scale/Zoom   F: Scroll

Fig. 3. Hand gestures used in the system

mistakenly registered by the system as an intentional gesture to perform commands (Microsoft 2013b).

2.3   Hand Gesture Set Design

The gesture set developed intended to be harmonious, convergent and coincided to be memorable. Four primaries and one secondary gesture were developed. The *Interact* gesture initiates the interaction with the system (Fig. 4-A).

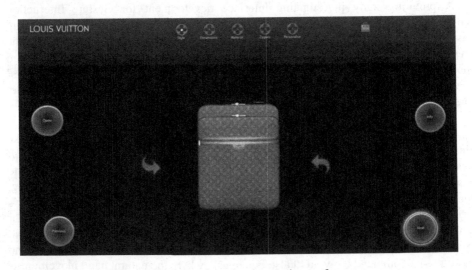

Fig. 4. Guiding arrows for the rotation performance

Select command is performed by gripping, then opening the hand over a navigational button or a choice on the screen (Fig. 4-B). Kinect embedded gestures for selecting are either hovering or pressing/pushing and release or both of them together (pushing and holding then release). However, Microsoft (2013a) prefers a *press* action as the user performance could improve on it by practicing, rather than the hover, which causes frustration. Using an appropriate gesture for the particular task is essential (Billinghurst and Buxton 2011). *Press* actions are less suitable for the present system since the interaction is not required only with the 2D interface; 3D object manipulation action is also required, and the use of one method for both actions is more efficient. Moreover, the chance of misinterpreting the press gesture with the slide gesture by the system is high, since both of them use an open hand form. Further, handgrip shares similar features with finger pinch in the way of providing an identifiable start and end of the gesture. Performing hand gripping does not require arm movement or body movement, thus it is expected to be comfortable to perform in a repetitive manner.

Rotation action is performed only for the 3D object interaction. The ***Rotate*** gesture is an extension of the ***Select*** action and was chosen because it mimics the real world and harmoniously matches the set of gestures used. The user selects the 3D object by gripping the hand, then moving the hand to the X-axis and Y-axis (Fig. 4-C, D).

To ***Zoom*** in, the distance between both separating and gathering gripped hands in any XY direction scales the 3D object up and down (Fig. 4-E). In the Kinect for Xbox One Instruction manual, this gesture was suggested for opening notifications but in the Kinect Xbox 360, this gesture performs page scaling.

Finally, to ***slide*** pages, the same gripping gesture performed dynamically, starting by hand grip over any empty place on the screen and moving the hand to pull the pages to the right or left navigates between stages (Fig. 4-F). This method of scrolling enables longer distance precision without fatigue or frustration compared to hovering and is adopted by Microsoft for the same purpose (Microsoft 2013a).

All of the gestures except the scale are one-handed gestures, in which users can use either hand up to their preferences or switch between both hands (Figure 3).

In order to facilitate the user mission in finding the right method to interact with the VR system, and particularly for novice users, a video tutorial explaining the gestures performance procedure is presented to the user. Microsoft promotes playing such videos of the gestures at the beginning of the experience, so that the user can draw from it in the subsequent experience (Microsoft 2013a). For the manipulation of the bag, a further visual assistant on how to perform the gestures is presented during the interaction with the products.

2.4   Interface Development

The VR simulation was developed in the *Unity 3D* cross platform game engine. The 3D models of the bags were designed including all the fine details and material characteristics of the bag in order to be as realistic and informative as possible. The modeling of the bags' three-dimensional meshes was developed in *Autodesk 3Ds max* software. For optimal system performance, several issues were taken into consideration in the procedure of designing the bag, such as low polygon count and minimum number of materials. This is crucial for real-time system to enable loading the models for the end user instantly. Adobe Photoshop was also used to create the maps and materials as well as the other interface elements. All the required assets were imported to *Unity 3D,* including 3D meshes in *FBX* format, defuse materials and normal maps, and interface elements including background and icons. After the editing of the shaders and after the scene preparation, the real-time interface functions and objects behavior were developed using C# language.

2.5   Menu Design and Layout

Although the sequential or linear menu design has some limitation in long scenarios, which is not the case with the current system, the great contextual advantage of it is that it enables utilization of the screen space to provide the user with large icons and a final rendering of the available choices for easier comparison. Moreover, a linear menu was used for its advantage in guiding the user through the customisation journey, as Shneiderman and Plaisant (2005) suggests that the use of such menu design is "effective for the novice user performing a simple task". Five different customization menus were included: *Style*, *Dimensions*, *Material*, *Hardware* and finally the *Personalization* of the bag using initials, strips and colors.

To this end, the system starts with the bag in the first menu -*Style*- and after choosing one of the options and gap the next icon, the next menu -*Material*- get initiated and so on.

For the reason of providing direct investigation of the product, selecting any choice from the sub-menu will isolate the choice and allow the user to manipulate the product, see inside the product and read the product features description (Fig. 5).

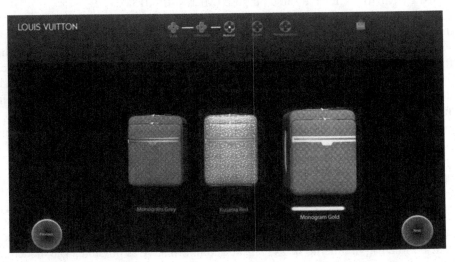

Fig. 5. The interface design, sub-menu options (Material)

The core element of the system interface in the online shopping journey is the product itself. Nielsen (2011) emphasised the effectiveness of utilizing the screen space and providing as large representation of elements on the monitor as possible for a better user experience. The product occupies two-thirds of the screen space taking into consideration optimal interaction setting using both hands. The navigational icons on the other hand occupy the remaining third in a way that is accessible for both hands matching natural arm movements. This alignment with the display size allows real-life scale item representation on the screen, which expected to enhance the user engagement.

For the alignment of the sub-menu choices, instead of having GUI for the choices to select from, the choices were designed to show real-time updates and all of the choices appear as large as possible for the user to select from. In other words, the sub-menu represents the choices on the 3D model directly and responsively by providing actual 3D models to visualize the choices (Fig. 6).

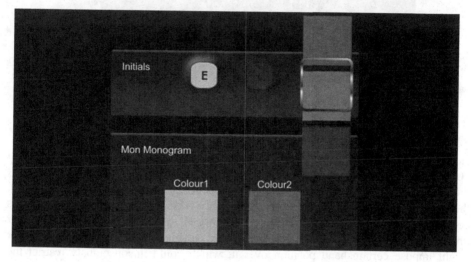

Fig. 6. Wheel scroll menu for product personalisation

To investigate the bag from inside, the **Open** icon enclose three different options to unfold different parts of the bag. Additional information about the product like the material characteristics, the metal type and other related features can be obtained from the **Info** icon by the right side of the screen.

The design of the Personalization menu was challenging. The users need to select a letter from a list with 26 options in addition to the color menu. A wheel scroll menu is thought to be one solution for this. Although horizontal scrolling is ergonomically easier than vertical scrolling (Microsoft 2013a), caroling the letters vertically in the present system can easily conflict with scrolling pages. The same menu style was also used in the color choices for the personalization strips and initials (Fig. 7).

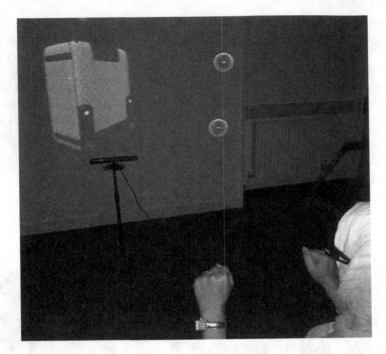

Fig. 7. The researcher interacting with the system using hand gestures

Turning to the icons design, icons have to be an effective target for easy selection, clearly recognizable and enhancing the aesthetic appeals of the interface (Bedford 2014). For gesture interaction, the icon shape can take a form that matches the shape of the hand performing different gestures. For the opened hand and gripped hand gestures, the hand profile or outline mimics the circular shape. A circular shape expresses continuity, which could give the button a sense of flexibility and forgiveness for unrestricted natural hand alignment (Fig. 3). A rectangular or square icon however might impose certain hand position over it, which could unconsciously restrict the alignment of the user's hand over the icon. Finally, progress indicator icons were added to the top of the screen to keep the user informed about the achieved, current and remained tasks.

3   Heuristic Evaluation

In order to appraise the interface validity and attain reflection of the interface design usability prior to user trials, the study conducted a heuristic evaluation. The heuristic utilised in this study is a refined version of the general heuristics of Nielsen and Molich (1990) and field-related heuristics of Sutcliffe and Gault (2004) that investigates the perceived sense of presence, natural engagement and compatibility with the task domain.

Four experts in User Centered Interfaces design from GCU have participated in the study. Inspectors were supplied with a document presenting the study aim and objectives as well as the list of heuristics and the feedback form. Without specifying any task, the experts were required to evaluate the system by finding usability issues, and score it out of five; zero means no problem found and 4 means usability catastrophe that has to be fixed. Testing was accomplished in the VRS Lab in GCU. Each expert conducted the evaluation study independently for the duration of about 60 min.

As anticipated, several usability issues were identified from the heuristic study. In general, the issues that scored three and four based on the provided scale were considered in the fixing process. The other issues scored between 2 and 0 and were taken into consideration in the analysis of the final evaluation study results.

4 Results and Discussion

Visibility of system status:
The system status was entirely clear for 50% of the experts although the rest of them had a complete understanding of the system half way through usage of the system. It was suggested that the strength of the feedback of the progress indicator icons required exaggeration, particularly with regards to the display size and distance. This issue was reported to be a minor usability problem by half of the experts and 25% believed that fixing it was necessary.

Match between system and the real world:
In terms of the consistency between the system and the real world, the experts complimented the level of detail in the 3D models and the way in which the dimensions were explained pictorially alongside human figures and elements that closely replicated the real world experience. Additionally, the progress of the system was considered to be "logical", "nice" and "natural".

User control and freedom:
Most of the experts (75%) stated that they would prefer to have "undo/reset" button for the bag orientation and for the personalisation menu and gave this issue a rating of 3–4. Although the perspective of the bag is readjusted automatically from stage to stage, the undo function within each stage was thought to be essential. This feature was originally provided in the prototype tested in the pilot study, but as none of the users utilised it, it was eliminated from the later version.

Consistency and standards:
Consistency and standards were discussed in a twofold approach: the hand gesture design and the compatibility of the gesture to the assigned task. Half of the evaluators believed that the gestures could come naturally with the users, whereas the other group suggested that they might be more familiar to gamers. One of the experts detected a problem in performing the "gripping" gesture, which is registering a vertical or horizontal movement for the hand that causes the target to be missed (rated 3 on the usability scale). Since changing the gripping gesture would have required amending the whole set of gestures, and due to time restrictions, a temporary solution was

determined. Instructing the users to aim slightly higher from the target before gripping the hand can prevent this problem from occurring. Further, this issue occurs clearly in certain circumstances, where the size of the icons are small or during the rotation of the 3D element around the restricted axis. Therefore, the icons were also enlarged in size, particularly the personalisation menu icons, which were rated 4 on the usability scale.

Error prevention:
Experts found the system efficient in preventing errors in most cases. The issue with the icon size in the personalisation menu (rating 4) was a notable exception. They suggested that the main consequence of this is that with the small icon size, the interaction feedback was unclear, and may require several tries from the user to achieve the desirable interaction, in a way that could results in fatiguing or confusing (rate 2).

Recognition rather than recall:
The user would not have to recall information, as everything is visible and consistent, which is considered, from the experts' perspective, to be one of the main benefits of the system. Moreover, an expert stated that the sliding command was easier to perform than picking buttons; however, a continuous visual reminder for the user is required as the "Next" and "Back" buttons are always visible, which could lead the user to using them spontaneously even if they preferred the page sliding method.

Flexibility and efficiency of use:
It was agreed by 75% of the experts that by the end of the session, even with only a session's practice, the system had become far easier and they were able to determine the right distance from the display screen and the required speed and accuracy. In terms of flexibility, the provided alternatives for task performance such as swiping the page for next and back were considered to be useful, particularly if they could also be implemented in the rotation function (3). On the other hand, the experts expressed a strong preference for the swiping command over the buttons "Next and Back".

Aesthetic and minimalist design:
The information on the screen was "carefully considered", which aids clarity and helps users to focus on the task. As previously mentioned, the need for the interaction hints was expected.

Help users recognize, diagnose, and recover from errors:
There was a common suggestion for undo/reset for the bag perspective/angle and the personalisation menu, as stated previously. It was considered to be a minor issue (2) more relevant to the enjoyment of the experience than to system functionality.

Sense of presence:
The experts admired the high level of detail in the model: "even down to the stitching it was very clear", Further, "the detail of the object 360 is excellent" provides a very high level of presence, which is accomplished by the contribution of the physical interaction with the system. In addition, the minimalist design with clear figures enhances the presence as the experts stated.

Compatibility with the user task and domain:
Compatibility was discussed in a two-fold approach: the interface and the 3D model. The evaluators stated that the interface design was compatible to what they would expect from an online shopping application, "conventional" and "in appropriate order". With regards to the interaction with the 3D model, all of the evaluators agreed that the hand gesture design reflected the real world. However, in relation to the rotation, conflicted feedback was received. 50% of the evaluators thought that the rotation gesture could be improved to better mimic real world, and the other 50% found it very compatible and that it corresponded "well to real life". The use of the gripping gesture for the interaction with the 3D model was perceived to be easier and more natural than performing it in the interaction with the menu icons (usability rated between 2 to 4).

Natural engagement:
Exaggerating the interaction feedback in certain cases would increase the engagement. Further, although the rotation gesture did not receive any complaints from half of the experts, the other group thought that improving it would have a great impact on the engagement.

To this end, the experts appreciate the amount of details such system is able to provide customers knowing that a considerable investment is involved. 3D highly interactive models with highly detailed textures helps in understanding the product details and characteristics. While the authenticity of models is crucial in being emerged in such environment, the interaction method with the system and the minimalist interface design plays a strong role in generating immersive experience. However, the usability of a relatively new interaction method in facilitating fast response interaction and effective feedback is crucial.

5   Conclusion and Future Work

This paper illustrates general consideration and design challenges in the development of semi-immersive VR hand gestural interface for luxury online shopping. HCI experts were involved into preliminary heuristic evaluation for system optimization. The required system improvements were outlined; further functionality and advance control possibility were highlighted.

Heuristic evaluation of the proposed system proved to be an efficient method to learn about the system usability and shed light on its pros and strength, involving a small number of participants in a relatively short time. It would be difficult to obtain the same level of information and solutions from user trials.

For future work, further enhancements of the system functionality and visual aspects based on this study are considered. Usability and acceptability of the system using psychometric tools and observation will be conducted involving representative users in user trials session in order to get comprehensive understanding of the impact of such technology in this specific context. A comparative evaluation of the hand gesture against a traditional interaction method can also help in underlining the functional as well as the experiential factors that gesture interactions can convey.

References

Altarteer, S., Charissis, V., Harrison, D., Chan, W.: Product customisation: virtual reality and new opportunities for luxury brands online trading. In: International Conference on 3D Web Technology/ACM SIGGRAPH, pp. 22–24. ACM, Anaheim (2016)

Altarteer, S., Charissis, V., Harrison, D., Chan, W.: Interactive virtual reality shopping and the impact in luxury brands. In: Shumaker, R. (ed.) VAMR 2013. LNCS, vol. 8022, pp. 221–230. Springer, Heidelberg (2013). doi:10.1007/978-3-642-39420-1_24

Bagdare, S., Jain, R.: Measuring retail customer experience. Int. J. Retail Distrib. Manage. **41**, 790–804 (2013)

Barclay, K., Wei, D., Lutteroth, C., Sheehan, R.: A quantitative quality model for gesture based user interfaces. In: Proceedings of the 23rd Australian Computer-Human Interaction Conference. ACM, Canberra (2011)

Bedford, A.: Icon Usability. Nielsen Norman Group (2014). http://www.nngroup.com/articles/icon-usability/. Accessed 7 Aug 2015

Benko, H., Wilson, A.D.: Multi-point interactions with immersive omnidirectional visualizations in a dome. In: ACM International Conference on Interactive Tabletops and Surfaces. ACM, Saarbrücken (2010)

Clemente, M., Rey, B., Rodríguez-Pujadas, A., Barros-Loscertales, A., Baños, R.M., Botella, C., Alcañiz, M., Ávila, C.: An FMRI study to analyze neural correlates of presence during virtual reality experiences. Interact. Comput. **26**, 269–284 (2014)

Billinghurst, M., Buxton, B. (2011): Gesture based interaction. Haptic Input (2011). 24

Dauriz, L., Michetti, A., Sandri, N., Zocchi, A.: Digital luxury experience 2013: keeping up with changing customers. McKinsey & Company, Italy (2014)

Google Think Insights: Fashion Online: How Affluent Shoppers Buy Luxury Goods: Think with google (2013). http://www.google.co.uk/think/research-studies/fashion-online-affluent-shoppers-luxury.html. Accessed 4 Aug 2015

Kapferer, J.N.: The Luxury Strategy: Break the Rules of Marketing to Build Luxury Brands. Kogan Page Publishers, London (2012)

Kapri, A., Wong, K., Hunter, S., Gillian, N., Pattie, M.: InReach: manipulating 3D objects remotely using your body. In: International Conference on Human Factors in Computing (CHI 2013). Association for computing machinery, Paris (2013)

Kim, H., Choi, Y.J., Lee, Y., Hayes, S., Taylor, G.: Web atmospheric qualities in luxury fashion brand websites. J. Fashion Mark. Manag. Int. J. **19**, 384–401 (2015)

Klaus, P.P., Maklan, S.: Towards a better measure of customer experience. Int. J. Mark. Res. **55**, 227 (2013)

Kober, S.E., Kurzmann, J.,Neuper, C.: Cortical correlate of spatial presence in 2D and 3D interactive virtual reality: an EEG study. Int. J. Psychophysiol. **83**, 365–374 (2012)

Kortum, P.: HCI Beyond the GUI: Design for Haptic, Speech, Olfactory, and Other Nontraditional Interfaces. Morgan Kaufmann, Amsterdam (2008)

Maklan, S., Klaus, P.: Customer experience: Are we measuring the right things? Int. J. Mark. Res. **53**, 771 (2011)

Maman Larraufie, A.F., Kourdoughli, A.: The e-semiotics of luxury. J. Global Fashion Mark. **5**, 197–208 (2014)

McMahan, R.P., Bowman, D.A., Zielinski, D.J., Brady, R.B.: Evaluating display fidelity and interaction fidelity in a virtual reality game. IEEE Trans. Vis. Comput. Graph **18**, 626–633 (2012)

Microsoft: Kinect Gestures, Wave to Kinect and Kinect Xbox Dashboard (2013a). Microsoft web site: xbox.com, http://support.xbox.com/en-US/xbox-360/kinect/body-controller#b0621460e 98a42198e6b455ed1e674a3. Accessed 13 Sept 2014

Microsoft: Kinect for Windows Human Interface Guidelines v1.8.0 (2013b). Msdn.microsoft. com, https://msdn.microsoft.com/en-us/library/jj663791.aspx. Accessed 1 Nov 2014

Ni, T.: A framework of freehand gesture interaction: techniques, guidelines, and applications. Virginia Polytechnic Institute and State University (2011)

Nielsen, J.: Utilize Available Screen Space (2011). Nielsen Norman Group. http://www.nngroup. com/articles/utilize-available-screen-space/

Nielsen, J., Molich, R.: Heuristic evaluation of user interfaces. In: Proceedings of the SIGCHI Conference on Human Factors in Computing Systems, pp. 249–256. ACM (1990)

Pentiuc, S.G., Craciun, E., Grisoni, L.: Interface for gestural interaction in virtual reality environments. Elektronika ir Elektrotechnika **121**, 97–100 (2012)

Shneiderman, B., Plaisant, C.: Designing the User Interface: Strategies for Effective Human-Computer Interaction. Addison-Wesley, Reading (2005)

Sutcliffe, A., Gault, B.: Heuristic evaluation of virtual reality applications. Inter. Comput. **16**, 831–849 (2004)

Wilson, A., Oliver, N.: Gwindows: towards robust perception-based UI. In: Conference on Computer Vision and Pattern Recognition Workshop. CVPRW 2003, 16–22 June 2003, pp. 46–46 (2003)

Remote Touch Interaction with High Quality Models Using an Autostereoscopic 3D Display

Adriano Mancini[1(✉)], Paolo Clini[2], Carlo Alberto Bozzi[2],
Eva Savina Malinverni[2], Roberto Pierdicca[2], and Romina Nespeca[2]

[1] Department of Information Engineering, Universitá Politecnica delle Marche,
Via Brecce Bianche 12, 60131 Ancona, Italy
m.mancini@univpm.it
[2] Department of Civil Engineering, Building and Architecture,
Universitá Politecnica delle Marche, Via Brecce Bianche 12, 60131 Ancona, Italy
{p.clini,e.s.malinverni,r.pierdicca,r.nespeca}@univpm.it,
carloalbertobozzi@gmail.com

Abstract. The use of 3D models to document archaeological findings witnessed to boost in the latest years, mainly thanks to the large adoption of digital photogrammetry for the virtual reconstruction of ancient artifatcs. For this reason, the widespread availability of digital 3D objects obliges the research community to face with a hard challenge: which is the best way for allowing visitors being in contact with the real estate of cultural goods? The work described in these pages answers to these questions by describing a novel solution for the enhanced interaction and visualization of a complex 3D model. The installation consists in an autostereoscopic display paired with a remotely connected (with a wired connection) touch-pad for the interaction with the contents displayed in it. The main advantage of using such technology is represented by the fact that one is not obliged to wear cumbersome devices but at the same time one can have a 3D view of the object without any additional aid. The system allows, through a touch-pad, to manage the 3D views and interact with a very small object that in its virtual dimension is magnified with respect to a classical museum arrangement. The research results, applied to the real case exhibition presented, have proved the innovation and usability of the multimedia solutions, which required the use of complex hardware components and a tricky implementation of the whole software architecture. The digital disruption in the CH domain should be also entrusted in the use of advanced interfaces that at the same time are intuitive and usable interaction methods.

Keywords: Human-computer interaction · Autostereoscopic · Cultural Heritage · 3D reconstruction · 3D visualization

1 Introduction

Digital technologies are becoming more and more the mainstream for the communication of Cultural Heritage (CH) goods. Indeed, the virtualization of real

L.T. De Paolis et al. (Eds.): AVR 2017, Part II, LNCS 10325, pp. 478–489, 2017.
DOI: 10.1007/978-3-319-60928-7_40

objects proved to enhance the cognition of the users, and it is also, probably, the only viable solution to put in contact the user with objects that, otherwise, might remain unknown to the majority of the mankind [3]. The use of 3D models to document archaeological findings witnessed to boost in the latest years, mainly thanks to the large adoption of digital photogrammetry for the virtual reconstruction of ancient artifatcs. Close range photogrammetry in fact, allows achieving faithful results in terms of both the 3D model accuracy and the quality of the outcomes visualization. The use of minimal hardware, (essentially, just a digital camera is enough to collect an useful dataset for documentation aims), and the ease of use in almost every environmental condition, make 3D sampling solutions based on Multiple View Stereo (MVS) matching and Structure from Motion techniques ideal for the documentation of archaeological findings [10, 16].

For these reasons, it has become a common practice within the international panorama. Notwithstanding, the widespread availability of digital 3D objects obliges the research community to face with a hard challenge: which is the best way for allowing visitors being in contact with the real estate of cultural goods? The variables to achieve such a difficult task are many. The quality of the reproductions, the devices (or platforms) in which these contents should be displayed, the type of interaction that better fits with the expectations of the users.

The work described in these pages answers to these questions by describing a novel solution for the enhanced interaction and visualization of a complex 3D model; specifically, the Venus model (mesh and texture) showed in Fig. 1a has been chosen as a case study for a new exhibition in the Museum of Genga, Marche Region, Italy. The Venus is a little statue belonging to the Paleolitic period, realized with stalactite stones with a high of only 8.7 cm. Due to its small dimensions, for the acquisition of the images it was used the so called focus stacking, a close range techniques adopted to solve the problems related to the depth of field and to obtain a 3D model with high quality resolution. The survey was done capturing more than 900 pictures, obtaining a point cloud of more than 42 million points and a mesh of more than 9 millions faces and texture resolution of 8192×8192. The installation basically consists in an autostereoscopic display paired with a remotely connected (with a wired connection) touch-pad for the interaction with the contents displayed in it. Autostereoscopic screen is not novel itself, but represents a strong enhancement for museums installations, since its use for museums exhibitions is not widespread so far. With respect to a classical 2D view approach, this technology allows, among the others: *stereo parallax, movement parallax, accommodation* and *convergence*. All 3D display technologies (stereoscopic displays) provide at least stereo parallax, whilst autostereoscopic displays provide the 3D image without the viewer needing to wear any special viewing gear. We refer the reader to [7] for a more exhaustive discussion over this technology. The main advantage of using such technology is hence represented by the fact that one is not obliged to wear cumbersome devices but at the same time one can have a 3D view of the object without any additional aid. The system allows, through a touch-pad, to manage the 3D views and interact with a very small object that in its virtual dimension is magnified with respect to a classical museum arrangement.

Besides the representation of the high quality of the model (75K faces, 7 MB weight of 3D model in obj format with 1,83 MB jpeg texture), which allows a large variability of outputs (e.g. 3d printing, stereoscopic view and 3D visualization), 3D stereo technologies can be applied to the world of CH as a vessel for preservation, reconstruction, documentation, research and promotion (see Fig. 1b for the details of the acquisition). In fact, 3D stereo technology is able to support artifact exploration activities, bringing new excitement for the museums and, more important, for the end-user. As a demonstration of that, the recent study conducted by Sooai et al. [19] is a clear demonstration of how novel interaction techniques can help the user to interact and understand the 3D object. Thus, the main objective of this work is to enable new scenarios in the human-machine interaction applied to the Cultural Heritage, through an User-Centered approach where it is necessary to involve actively all the stakeholders modelling user(s) deriving a set of functional and not-functional requirements that is the base for the system design.

The research results, applied to the real case exhibition presented, have proved the innovation and usability of the multimedia solutions, which required the use of complex hardware components and a tricky implementation of the whole software architecture. The digital disruption in the CH domain should be also entrusted in the use of advanced interfaces that at the same time are intuitive and usable interaction methods.

The reminder of the paper is organized as follows: following this introduction which consists on the showcase of this work, Sect. 2 is devoted to a critical state

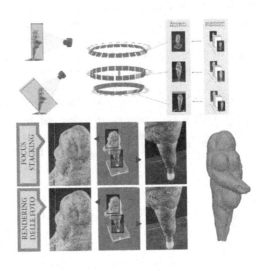

(a) The original Venus standing on a plexiglass pedestal.

(b) A brief description of the steps performed to achieve the 3D virtual reconstruction.

Fig. 1. The photogrammetric survey of the Venus of Frasassi.

of art analysis of the related works in the field of advanced interactive solutions used in the CH scenario. The full description of the architecture is reported in Sect. 3, with a specific focus on the implementation details. Concluding remarks, together with a prospective outlook of our future works is reported in Sect. 4.

2   Related Work

Creating an interactive installation which combines a 3D view of the artifact and the manipulation of it with a remote controller requires combining state-of-the-art results in several technological areas, besides a requiring a multi-disciplinary design team. In this section we thus outline different kinds of technologies and interactions that, in the last years, have been adopted in the CH panorama, discussing those methods that most relate to the solution described in this paper.

Since we deal with the interaction with complex 3D models, it is necessary to remind the strong enhancement we witnessed in the last years with respect to the exploitation of virtual reconstruction, especially in the archaeological field. Even if the web put at the disposal of the research community many possibilities to remotely navigate virtual museums [20], nowadays the approach of making museums more interactive and attractive is growing. The use of autostereoscopic display, as stated in the introduction section is not a common practice; however, in some cases is used exploiting motion parallax to allow visitors of a science museum to interact with virtual contents [12].

Dealing with 3D models, several pipelines of work have been set up, which range from the data collection, acquisition and processing to the visualization in complex exhibition. The work by Bruno et al. is a good example to be noted [2]. Thanks to the introduction of fast and agile tools for the visualization of 3D models (just think to the development of Web GL, Open GL and other real time rendering engine available) and to the growing availability of tools which enable one to simplify the models without loosing their quality, we can consider the issue of a high quality visualization solved. What is become paramount in the CH panorama is how to make these models, reconstructions or virtual scenario interactive for the users. Several projects and researches attempt to solve this issue. It is the case of *Keys to Rome* project [14]. This project has the purpose of creating an interactive journey to discover the Roman culture in different venues and making a massive use of different technological installations. In the literature, other examples are worth to be mentioned. In [4] for instance, the proposed solution allows new interactions based on gestures. An important feature is the one to one navigational input based on Kinect skeleton tracking. The framework was used to configure a virtual museum art installation using a real museum room where the user can move freely and interact with virtual contents by adding and manipulating 3D models.

In [11], a natural exploration of extremely detailed surface models with indirect touch control in a room-sized workspace, suitable for museums and exhibitions is showed. Interested readers would find of interest several requirements to be respected, besides an accurate review of the different kinds of interactions and gestures. According to these requirements, several experiences have been set up in the CH panorama [18] to enjoy an immersive and attractive experience, allowing the users to observe 3D archaeological finds, in their original context.

Notwithstanding, several technical and technological issues are commonly related to the design of virtual museum exhibits [1]. One of the main issue when developing solutions for the interaction with CH goods is the design of gestures. In fact, whilst the interaction with touch displays has become a de-facto standard at a worldwide scale (thanks to the diffusion of smartphones), body gestures are related to the user's cultural and provenance background. Hence the user have to be trained to allow him to experience the installation. A good dissertation about this topic can be found in [15]. Another example of complex architectures developed for the engagement of the users is reported in [9]. In this occasion, the Vitruvian man's model was used to engage the user with a gamification approach. The latter case study is of interest also because it included an holographic view of the Vitruvian man reconstruction. Holograms show virtual objects floating within a box, and there are also examples where the user can interact with the model with touch-less model [6]. Even if the feedback from the users was surprisingly good, one of the most crucial point to consider when designing such types of installation in museums is the simplicity of the system and easiness of maintenance of the multimedia product. This could represent a drawback for every kind of installation, regardless the type of interaction chosen.

Both Virtual and Augmented Reality have become important technologies, more and more used in the CH panorama. In fact they allow to see ancient artifact reconstructions as if they are existing with the same point of view of the users. With respect to the kind of installation that should be set up inside museum environment, one important kind of VR experience is represented by the Cave Automatic Virtual Environment (CAVE). It is a polyhedral projection display technology that allows multiple users to experience fully-immersive 3D scenes. A good example is reported in [8]. Also in the case of VR experience, the gesture interaction is an important aspect to be taken into account, as shown in [5] where the user is enabled to virtually interact with virtual contents.

Finally, the world of mobile technologies is the one that is probably taking ground in the field of museums navigations, since they can reach the majority of the users thanks to the publications of apps. Some real case exhibitions make use of this kind of CH diffusion. Relevant examples can be found in [13, 17].

3   System Architecture

The installation is composed of two main hardware components: the autostereoscopic display DIMENCO 50 in. (127 cm) professional QFHD 3D display DM504MAS for the visualization of the contents (both 2D and 3D) and the Microsoft Surface 3 tablet for the touch interaction. An explanatory description of the components, in their physical installation inside the museum, is showed in Fig. 2a, while a schematic view of the installation can be found in Fig. 2b.

In order to enable the visitor for an in-depth analysis of the Venus, a specific application was designed; the latter presents a simple interface with 8 buttons

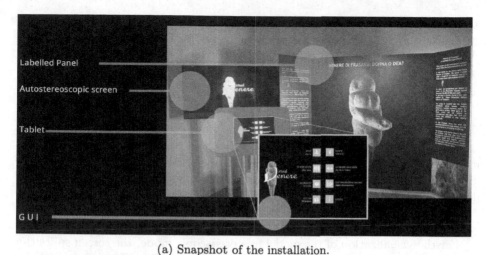

(a) Snapshot of the installation.

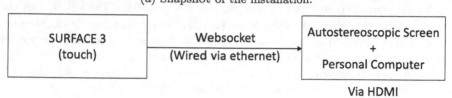

(b) Schematic representation of the core components of the system.

Fig. 2. The whole installation is composed of a touchpad used as a remote controller for the interaction with the contents displayed on the screen of the autostereoscopic display. The picture also reports the GUI, designed to switch among 2D/3D contents.

which bring the user to different sheets and multimedia contents related to the artifacts, the history of similar statues in the worlds and information about the museum. The main multimedia contents that are displayed in the autostereoscopic monitor can be summarized as follows:

- **HD images**: To permit the use of huge imagery for users visualization purposes, we used a virtual texturing technique, a combination of classical MIP-mapping and loading only the tiles needed to perform the texture at user request. For each level of zoom, the set of tiles corresponding to the observed texture appears (2D+LoDs/scale coordinates). In this case were used leaflet libraries[1];
- **3D model**: it can be visualized in different modes. Classical 3D visualization, anaglyph visualization and Stereoscopic view thanks to the autostereoscopic screen;
- **Gallery**: direct interaction with photographic documentation of the museums and in particular of the Venus.

For the storage of the contents we built up a webserver (Apache) that was installed in both tablet and the personal computer used to control the monitor.

---

[1] http://leafletjs.com/ - last access March 2017.

The communication between the two hardware was performed using websockets[2], a computer communications protocol, providing full-duplex communication channels over a single TCP connection. This was done for three main reasons, explained below:

- Communicate the content's changes from the GUI;
- Management of the switching between 2D/3D mode;
- Data exchange of gesture interactions.

The whole architecture was designed with the twofold aim of browsing all the information related to the Venus model and of displaying the model in its third dimension without the use of any wearable device. Its development is tricky and deserves a deep explanation. The general schema can be found in Fig. 3.

The software has been developed to be modular, efficient optimizing the use of resources as the CPU and GPU.

For the visualization of the model in stereoscopic mode, the screen splits the visualization into two separate areas thank to the parallax. The left half of the screen contains the textured model, while the right parts contains the depth map. Of course, the above mentioned contents have to be synchronizes for the proper visualization. Hence, on the same canvas, the PC have to generate the render of the model and the depth map within the same canvas. Moreover, a header file should be communicated to match both values. There is no existing autostereoscopic monitor that is able to manage the information as described above.

The Dimenco autostereoscopic display requires the 2D-plus-Depth format. The format contains the following data:

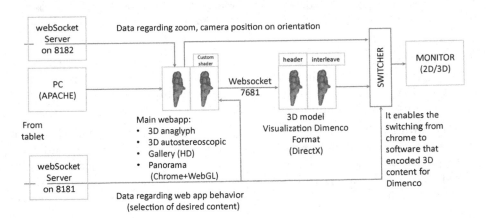

Fig. 3. Overall software architecture. Thank to the use of websocket protocol it was possible to convey the contents according to the following schema: 8181 - to manage the switch of the pages towards the browser and the switch into autostereoscopic mode; 8182 - to manage touch gesture as pan, zoom and rotate towards the browser; 7861 - to manage the rasterization of the web page thanks to the 3D visualiser.

---

[2] https://tools.ietf.org/html/rfc6455 Last - RFC 6455 The WebSocket Protocol - last access March 2017.

- Header
- 2D sub-image with a resolution 960×540
- Depth sub-image with a resolution 960×540

A Depth map in grey scale picture. This depth map belongs to the 2D sub-image. Figure 4(c) shows an example of the 3D frame layout for the 2D-plus-Depth format.

Basically the idea is to use the webGL as a render engine that will broadcast the 2D sub-image + Depth image to a dedicated software by using a websocket. This software exploits the Dimenco PlayerAPI based on the Microsoft DirectX9. The processing pipeline is the following one:

- configure the monitor;
- instantiate a server websocket;
- when the socket client connects to the server the incoming base64 image is decoded;
- image is encoded into the Dimenco frame format;
- encoded image is presented by a full-screen window.

From the client side the 2D+depth image is generated by using a webGL page rendered in Chrome by using the threejs to create a dual scene view. Left scene is dedicated to the 2D image while the right one for the depth. Depth image is created by our custom vertex shared as it follows.

```
<script id="vertexShader" type="x-shader/x-vertex">
// switch on high precision floats
#ifdef GL_ES
precision highp float;
#endif
varying vec4 vpos;
void main()
{
gl_Position = projectionMatrix * modelViewMatrix * vec4(position,1.0);
vpos = projectionMatrix * modelViewMatrix * vec4(position,1.0);
}
</script>
<script id="fragmentShader" type="x-shader/x-vertex">
#ifdef GL_ES
precision highp float;
#endif
varying vec4 vpos;
float zmin = 0.97;
float zmax = 1.0;
void main()
{
vec4 v = vec4(vpos);
v /= (v.w);
float gray = 1.0 - (v.z - zmin) / (zmax - zmin);
gl_FragColor = vec4(gray);
}
```

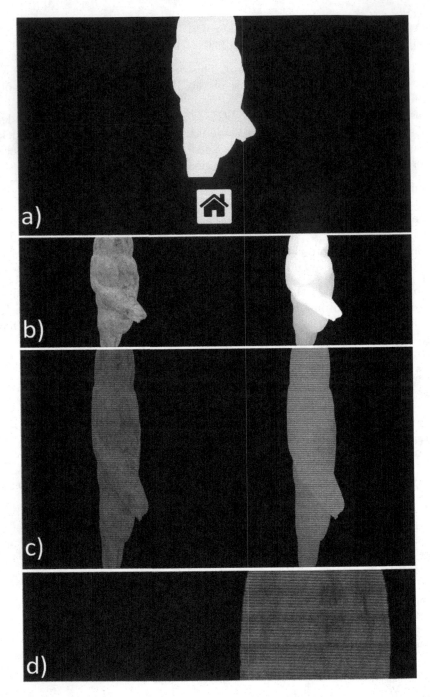

Fig. 4. Different renders of Venus by tablet and 2D + depth image processors. (Color figure online)

The left and right cameras are synchronized and share the same coordinates (x,y,z) and orientation (roll, pitch, yaw). When the renderering of the frame is completed than a base64 image resulting from the scene is generated. This image is sent by using the websocket to the software that is responsible for the conversion to the Dimenco format. Zooming is limited to guarantee a proper level of usability.

The position and orientation of synced cameras is transmitted by the Surface tablet over the websocket. This aspect is fundamental to reflect the user's desired point of view on the final render.

Figure 4 shows an example of rendering on tablet and server side. In particular Fig. 4 (a) shows the desired view (tablet side) while (b) represents the rendered 2D + depth images with cameras synced to the tablet one. Figure 4 (c) shows the Dimenco encoded image and (d) depicts a detailed area where it is possible to see the header (top-left blue pixels) and the row-interleaved content.

The measured delay during the transmission of position from table and rendering to the Dimenco screen is 60 ms on average. User has also the capability to select the anaglyph view of the 3D model. Anaglyph image is generated through the `AnaglyphEffect.js` library of ThreeJS.

High definition images of the Venus could also be explored by using a tiled pyramidal representation. Tiles are generated by using GDAL[3] and are visualized by using the Leaflet js library. Each high-resolution image could be considered as a tiled map service (TMS) layer. User is able to pan and zoom image to focus on a particular region of interest.

Panoramic images could be also viewed. In this case the tablet sends the coordinates to the server that will properly change the camera parameters to match with the user's preference.

4   Conclusion and Outlook

In this paper we presented a novel interactive installation to enhance the visitor's perception of the complex 3D model of a small size artifact. The use of a touch pad for the remote interaction with high quality contents into a stereoscopic display proved to be a valuable solution to increase the attractiveness of the museum. The advantage is mainly represented by the fact that the interaction is simple and the user do not need to be trained before to start the experience. It is well known that, generally, it is difficult to understand the gestures in more complex installation, where the intuitiveness of the gestures needs more investigations. Moreover, the visualization of the 3D model into an autostereoscopic display can represent a turning point with respect to similar visualization where the user is required to wear cumbersome and uncomfortable headsets.

The software solution developed for this case study is a step forward with respect to the autostereoscopic display, since with this solution the contents to be shown can be personalized end incorporated within a wider GUI. Platform is object independent. In this way other 3D objects could be easily integrated.

---

[3] http://www.gdal.org/ - Last access March 2017.

As a future work, we plan to extend the already developed gesture towards a touchless interaction. To achieve this result, we plan to use leap motion[4] sensor, making the experience of interaction more faithful and attractive.

Acknowledgments. Thanks to the Archaeological Museum of Marche and its director Nicoletta Frapiccini, the Polo Museale Marche and its director Peter Aufreiter. The digital acquisition and the implementation of the three-dimensional model have been carried out by the research team DiStoRi Heritage of the Department of Civil Engineering, Construction and Architecture of the Polytechnic University of Marche. The technological and interactive exhibition is provided by EVE-Enjoy Visual Experiences, a spin-off of the Polytechnic University of Marche. Scientific manager: prof. Paolo Clini. Digital documentation: Ludovico Ruggeri, Romina Nespeca, Gianni Plescia. Technological equipment: Adriano Mancini, Carlo Alberto Bozzi. Texts and archaeological consulting: Dr. Gaia Pignocchi.

References

1. Barbieri, L., Bruno, F., Mollo, F., Muzzupappa, M.: User-centered design of a virtual museum system: a case study. In: Eynard, B., Nigrelli, V., Oliveri, S.M., Peris-Fajarnes, G., Rizzuti, S. (eds.) Advances on Mechanics, Design Engineering and Manufacturing. LNME, pp. 155–165. Springer International Publishing, Cham (2017). doi:10.1007/978-3-319-45781-9_17
2. Bruno, F., Bruno, S., De Sensi, G., Luchi, M.L., Mancuso, S., Muzzupappa, M.: From 3D reconstruction to virtual reality: a complete methodology for digital archaeological exhibition. J. Cult. Heritage **11**(1), 42–49 (2010)
3. Clini, P., Frontoni, E., Quattrini, R., Pierdicca, R.: Augmented reality experience: from high-resolution acquisition to real time augmented contents. Adv. Multimedia **2014**, 18 (2014)
4. Dias, P., Pinto, J., Eliseu, S., Santos, B.S.: Gesture interactions for virtual immersive environments: navigation, selection and manipulation. In: Lackey, S., Shumaker, R. (eds.) VAMR 2016. LNCS, vol. 9740, pp. 211–221. Springer, Cham (2016). doi:10.1007/978-3-319-39907-2_20. https://www.scopus.com/inward/record.uri?eid=2-s2.0-84978891255&doi=10.1007%2f978-3-319-39907-2_20&partnerID=40&md5=8677cbf2dd0aecb82474d1d75442e83a, cited By 0
5. Dias, P., Pinto, J., Eliseu, S., Santos, B.S.: Gesture interactions for virtual immersive environments: navigation, selection and manipulation. In: Lackey, S., Shumaker, R. (eds.) VAMR 2016. LNCS, vol. 9740, pp. 211–221. Springer, Cham (2016). doi:10.1007/978-3-319-39907-2_20
6. Dingli, A., Mifsud, N.: Using holograms to increase interaction in museums. In: Chung, W., Shin, C. (eds.) Advances in Affective and Pleasurable Design. AISC, vol. 483, pp. 117–127. Springer, Cham (2017). doi:10.1007/978-3-319-41661-8_12. https://www.scopus.com/inward/record.uri?eid=2-s2.0-84986265771&doi=10.1007%2f978-3-319-41661-8_12&partnerID=40&md5=5793f0ad27aeb9243331e4dbff422c54, cited By 0
7. Dodgson, N.A.: Autostereoscopic 3D displays. Computer **38**(8), 31–36 (2005)

---

[4] https://www.leapmotion.com/ - last access March 2017.

8. He, Y., Zhang, Z., Nan, X., Zhang, N., Guo, F., Rosales, E., Guan, L.: vConnect: perceive and interact with real world from cave. Multimedia Tools Appl. **76**(1), 1479–1508 (2017). https://www.scopus.com/inward/record.uri?eid=2-s2.0-8494 9777242&doi=10.1007%2fs11042-015-3121-4&partnerID=40&md5=d0aa965578f8 9a8bc556ee6075a5ce89, cited By 0

9. Maliverni, E.S., d'Annibale, E., Frontoni, E., Mancini, A., Bozzi, C.A.: Multimedia discovery of the leonardos vitruvian man. SCIRES IT Sci. Res. Inf. Technol. **5**(1), 69–76 (2015)

10. Manferdini, A.M., Gasperoni, S., Guidi, F., Marchesi, M.: Unveiling damnatio memoriae. the use of 3D digital technologies for the virtual reconstruction of archaeological finds and artefacts. Virtual Archaeol. Rev. **7**(15), 9–17 (2016)

11. Marton, F., Rodriguez, M., Bettio, F., Agus, M., Villanueva, A., Gobbetti, E.: Isocam: interactive visual exploration of massive cultural heritage models on large projection setups. J. Comput. Cult. **7**(2) (2014). https://www.scopus. com/inward/record.uri?eid=2-s2.0-84979824803&doi=10.1145%2f2611519& partnerID=40&md5=8a3e89038916901d10557d308cf31ba2, cited By 2

12. Mizuno, S., Tsukada, M., Uehara, Y.: Developing a stereoscopic CG system with motion parallax and interactive digital contents on the system for science museums. Multimedia Tools Appl. **76**(2), 2515–2533 (2017)

13. Ozden, K.E., Unay, D., Inan, H., Kaba, B., Ergun, O.O.: Intelligent interactive applications for museum visits. In: Ioannides, M., Magnenat-Thalmann, N., Fink, E., Žarnić, R., Yen, A.-Y., Quak, E. (eds.) EuroMed 2014. LNCS, vol. 8740, pp. 555–563. Springer, Cham (2014). doi:10.1007/978-3-319-13695-0_55. https://www. scopus.com/inward/record.uri?eid=2-s2.0-84911873985&doi=10.1007%2f978-3-31 9-13695-0&partnerID=40&md5=b1329a6b8a3fac60a89eb1d336f833f2, cited By 0

14. Pescarin, S.: Museums and virtual museums in Europe: reaching expectations. SCIRES IT Sci. Res. Inf. Technol. **4**(1), 131–140 (2014)

15. Pescarin, S., Pietroni, E., Rescic, L., Omar, K., Wallergard, M., Rufa, C.: Nich: a preliminary theoretical study on natural interaction applied to cultural heritage contexts. In: Digital Heritage International Congress (Digital Heritage) 2013, vol. 1, pp. 355–362. IEEE (2013)

16. Pierdicca, R., Frontoni, E., Malinverni, E.S., Colosi, F., Orazi, R.: Virtual reconstruction of archaeological heritage using a combination of photogrammetric techniques: Huaca Arco Iris, Chan Chan, Peru. Digital Appl. Archaeol. Cult. Heritage **3**(3), 80–90 (2016)

17. Pierdicca, R., Frontoni, E., Zingaretti, P., Sturari, M., Clini, P., Quattrini, R.: Advanced interaction with paintings by augmented reality and high resolution visualization: a real case exhibition. In: Paolis, L.T., Mongelli, A. (eds.) AVR 2015. LNCS, vol. 9254, pp. 38–50. Springer, Cham (2015). doi:10.1007/ 978-3-319-22888-4_4

18. Pietroni, E., Pagano, A., Rufa, C.: The etruscanning project: gesture-based interaction and user experience in the virtual reconstruction of the regolini-galassi tomb. In: Digital Heritage International Congress (Digital Heritage) 2013, vol. 2, pp. 653–660. IEEE (2013)

19. Sooai, A.G., Sumpeno, S., Purnomo, M.H.: User perception on 3D stereoscopic cultural heritage ancient collection. In: Proceedings of the 2nd International Conference in HCI and UX on Indonesia 2016, pp. 112–119. ACM (2016)

20. Sundar, S., Go, E., Kim, H.S., Zhang, B.: Communicating art, virtually! psychological effects of technological affordances in a virtual museum. Int. J. Hum. Comput. Interact. **31**(6), 385–401 (2015). https://www.scopus.com/inward/ record.uri?eid=2-s2.0-84930032158&doi=10.1080%2f10447318.2015.1033912&part nerID=40&md5=d458ce86d7ce5720030d86301b3bbc15, cited By 0

Versatile Augmented Reality Scenes
for Tangible Interaction
in Real-World Environments

Rafał Wojciechowski[✉]

Poznań University of Economics and Business, Poznań, Poland
rawojc@kti.ue.poznan.pl

Abstract. An increasing interest of large IT companies in the area of augmented reality (AR) technology has been observed recently. This opens up new possibilities for a wide adoption of the AR technology in the daily lives of users. However, a major problem is the lack of useful AR content, which could be presented in different real-world environments of multiple users. In this paper, a new approach to AR content creation is presented. The approach, called VARS (Versatile Augmented Reality Scenes), enables to create versatile AR scenes that can be presented in a variety of real-world environments containing different physical objects. This approach is based on semantic loose coupling of physical objects present in the user's environment with abstract objects defined in the AR scenes. Also, an example application of the proposed approach in an education domain is presented.

Keywords: Augmented reality · Tangible user interfaces · Semantics

1 Introduction

In the recent years, an increasing interest in the VR technology has been observed. Introducing a number of new head mounted displays on the market, such devices as Oculus Rift [1], HTC Vive [2], aroused hopes of both game developers and investors. In the past, yet never so many major IT companies invested such huge resources in the development of new VR devices and the content. The most evident examples of such companies are: Facebook, HTC, Sony and Microsoft.

An extension of VR technology is augmented reality, which allows users to present synthetic content in the context of real environments [3]. In comparison to virtual reality, which is aimed at immersing a user in a synthetic environment, augmented reality supplements the user's perception of the real world by the addition of computer–generated content registered to real-world locations. The AR technology enables merging virtual objects with the views of real objects, resulting in augmented reality environments. In augmented reality environments, both virtual and real objects can coexist and interact in real time [4].

An increasing interest of large IT companies in the area of AR glasses has been observed recently. For example, Microsoft has introduced HoloLens [5], which is the first self-contained, cordless computer, enabling users to engage with digital content

© Springer International Publishing AG 2017
L.T. De Paolis et al. (Eds.): AVR 2017, Part II, LNCS 10325, pp. 490–500, 2017.
DOI: 10.1007/978-3-319-60928-7_41

and interact with AR holograms in the real world. Another notable project in the domain of AR visualization is Magic Leap [6], supported by Google, whose the main idea is supposed to be projection of digital images directly onto users' eyes [7]. However, the existing AR glasses are still not perfect and suffer from childhood diseases, such as a narrow viewing angles, low image resolution, latency. However, still new improved AR devices are introduced to the market, such as Meta [8] and ODG [9], which become lighter and offer better visualization quality [10].

Despite the growing number of AR devices on the market, the proliferation of useful interactive AR applications is very limited. The vast majority of existing AR applications are focused mainly on the presentation of synthetic content in the context of real-world environments, but they offer very limited user interaction with the content [11]. The existing AR applications enabling tangible user interaction are mostly prototypes and usually are used by a narrow group of users. A major limitation of these systems is tight coupling of presented synthetic content with components of real-world environments. Most often, it is assumed that specific markers and/or physical objects must exist in a target real-world environment [12]. These markers and objects are tracked in the environment and used for content positioning. Such solutions significantly restrict the reuse of AR content by multiple users in different real-world environments.

In this paper, a new approach to AR content creation is presented. The approach, called VARS (Versatile Augmented Reality Scenes), enables to build AR scenes that can be presented in a variety of real-world environments containing different physical objects. This approach is based on semantic loose coupling of physical objects present in the user's environment with abstract objects defined in the AR scenes.

The proposed approach moves away from defining specific markers and objects in an AR scene, which must exist in a target real-world environment. Instead, the scene contains high-level semantic definitions of the real-world environment components, based on their characteristics. Also, the target real-world environment and its components are described using semantic descriptions. The specification of both the AR scene and the real-world environment are defined based on a common ontology.

In computer science, an ontology is defined as a formal, structured representation of a set of concepts within a particular domain [13, 14]. A concept represents a group of individuals, that share common characteristics. Concepts are typically represented as classes and their characteristics are represented as properties. Class properties are used for modeling general facts about individuals, i.e., attributes and relationships with other individuals. The individuals are usually referred to as class instances and may represent both concrete and abstract objects [15].

In the VARS approach, AR environments are created based on versatile AR scenes. To this end, physical objects existing in real-world environments are automatically assigned to abstract objects defined in the scene, based on their semantic similarity. As a result, one versatile AR scene can be presented in a number of different real-world environments. To present an AR scene in a real-world environment, it is required to create semantic description of the configuration of its components in advance. However, once semantically described the real-world environment can be used for presenting a number of different versatile AR scenes.

The rest of this paper is organized as follows. In Sect. 2, an overview of the state of the art in the field of interactive AR applications is presented. In Sect. 3, the concept of Versatile Augmented Reality Scenes (VARS) is introduced. Also, the Sect. 3 contains an overview of a prototype system implementing the proposed approach. In Sect. 4, an example application of the prototype system in an education domain is presented. Finally, conclusions are presented in Sect. 5.

2   State of the Art

In contrast to virtual reality, which is aimed at immersing a user in a completely synthetic environment, augmented reality superimposes computer-generated content onto the view of the real world perceived by a user. Therefore, AR supplements reality, rather than completely replacing it [3]. Azuma points to the following three characteristics that define AR:

- combines real and virtual content,
- is interactive in real time,
- is registered in three-dimensional space.

This definition of augmented reality excludes 2D virtual overlays (even interactive but not merged with a real environment in 3D), and non-interactive contents (e.g., movies featuring photorealistic virtual objects seamlessly blended with a real environment in 3D). The definition does not limit augmented reality to the use of standard closed-view head-mounted displays (HMDs), which do not allow any direct view of the real world, but also it allows the use of monitors, projectors, and see through HMDs.

There are two approaches to generation of the AR views on head-mounted displays: optical see-through and video see-through [3]. Most of currently available AR glasses are based on the optical combining synthetic content with views of the real world [5, 8, 9]. However, for many recent years, a number of prototype systems have been developed, based on overlaying the synthetic content on the video image captured with a camera. They were built based on VR head-mounted displays with one or two cameras attached to the front. However, these solutions were mostly prototypes or expensive bulky devices, targeted to a narrow group of professionals. Furthermore, these devices were connected by a cable to a computer and were mainly intended for indoor use.

These problems have been alleviated with the advent of AR systems based on mobile devices, such as smartphones and tablets. In these systems, a user can observe on a device's screen the synthetic content superimposed on video image captured with a built-in camera. This type of AR visualization is currently the most widespread, since virtually everyone, who has a smartphone or a tablet, can enjoy the benefits of AR without buying sophisticated equipment. To this end, a user has to install an AR-enabled application on his/her mobile device. Recently, the most recognized application of this type is Pokemon GO [16], which achieved enormous popularity. However, the main disadvantage of AR systems based on mobile devices is the need to hold the device with one or two hands, which significantly reduces the possibility of user interaction with the presented content.

A solution to this problem is the use of mobile VR headsets (e.g., Samsung Gear VR), which enable mounting a smartphone into it [17]. The mobile VR headsets are primarily dedicated to VR visualization. However, they can be also used for AR visualization based on combining the synthetic content with video images captured with a device camera. These solutions enable users hands-free interaction with both presented synthetic content and real-world environments, also through a tangible user interface (TUI) [18, 19].

The mobile VR headsets are particularly promising in the context of interactive applications, since they do not require significant financial investments. In the simplest version, they can even be made of cardboard, such as Google Cardboard [20].

In the existing approaches to creating AR environments, AR content is tailored to a specific real-world environment, which contains a specific and predefined set of physical objects. In most of existing AR systems, these objects have a form of physical markers that do not represent any semantic meaning in the context of presented AR content [12]. Any change to the configuration of the environment entails the need to update the content. Also, any attempt to present an AR scene in an environment containing a different configuration of markers or physical objects requires appropriate adjustment of the scene to this configuration. The need for modifying the AR scene usually requires the participation of qualified personnel, which entails time and additional costs. Moreover, such content modifications would cause creation of a large number of different but redundant AR scene versions tailored to the needs of multiple individual users.

In the ideal case, an AR presentation should be made available over the Internet for multiple users. Each user should be able to run the presentation in his/her own real-world environment. The main problem is the diversity of real-world environments in which AR content could be presented. In most of existing AR systems, it is assumed that all users have exactly the same set of markers or physical objects, which can be tracked within an environment. In practice, however, it is difficult to guarantee identicalness of different real-world environments of multiple users, who may be geographically dispersed, due to organizational reasons.

A possible solution to this problem is to provide an AR presentation in a bundle with markers to be printed by users. Another option is to distribute digital AR content as a supplement to printed paper materials. In recent years, a number of books and product catalogues containing printed AR tags on their pages have been published [21, 22]. Readers are able to scan these pages using mobile devices with a special application installed. The application enables them to view additional AR content that is a synthetic addition to the content presented in the printed materials. In this embodiment, however, the interaction with the presented content is very limited or impossible.

In most existing AR systems, the process of creation of advanced interactive AR environments requires involvement of highly qualified skilled IT professionals, who are experts in design and implementation of interactive 3D content. Also, any changes in the content often cannot be made without assistance of the programmers. On the one hand, programmers do not have sufficient domain knowledge required to build a complete AR environment. On the other hand, domain experts do not have appropriate technical knowledge to create and modify the AR content on their own.

All these problems related to the adaptation of AR content to different real-world environments make it difficult to reuse the content by multiple users. As a consequence, the prevalence of interactive AR content which may coexist with physical objects in users' environments is still in its infancy.

3 VARS Approach

3.1 Overview

The VARS approach, which stands for Versatile Augmented Reality Scenes, allows to design interactive AR scenes, which can be presented in the context of multiple real-world environments surrounding different users. Users are able to intuitively manipulate the synthetic content using physical objects existing in their environments. The main advantage of the VARS approach is the ability of adaptation of AR scenes to various configurations of users' environments based on their semantic descriptions. Consequently, once created a versatile AR scene can be repeatedly used by a number of users in their real-world environments containing different sets of physical objects. The general concept of the VARS approach is presented in Fig. 1.

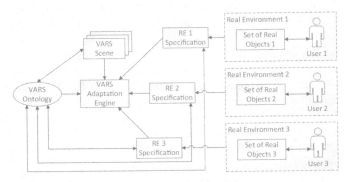

Fig. 1. The concept of the VARS approach

On the right side of the figure, three different *Real Environments* (RE) are presented. Each of them contains a different set of real objects. Each real environment is semantically described in a form of *RE Specification* using classes defined in *VARS Ontology*, presented on the left. AR environments are defined in the form of Versatile AR Scenes (*VARS Scenes*), which specify presentation content, behavior, and possible user interaction. The content objects defined in VARS scenes are also described with semantic annotations based on the classes defined in the *VARS Ontology*.

The central component of the proposed approach is *VARS Adaptation Engine*, which is responsible for adjusting VARS scenes to different configurations of real-world environments. The *VARS Adaptation Engine* performs automatic adaptation of a VARS scene to the sets of real objects found in different real-world environments.

For this purpose, the module matches the real objects to the semantic specifications of abstract objects specified in the scene definition based on their semantic similarity.

3.2 Versatile AR Scenes

Each VARS scene is composed of *content objects* and a *scenario* of an AR presentation created in a real-world environment. The content objects are divided into the following categories:

- *virtual objects* – represented as three-dimensional models, such objects are always presented as synthetic objects,
- *real objects* – represented by physical objects, which must exist in a real-world environment in which the scene is presented,
- *abstract objects* – represented either by physical or synthetic objects.

The scenarios specified in VARS scenes describe:

- *content* – objects presented in AR environments,
- *behavior* – spatial, temporal, and logical relationships between the presented objects,
- *interaction* – possible user actions in relation to the presented content.

Virtual objects can coexist with the real objects in a real-world environment. Real objects can affect the virtual objects, which means that they can be used for user interaction with the virtual objects. Also, the virtual objects may interact with each other. Depending on physical objects available in an environment, possible user interaction may vary.

Abstract objects are used both for presentation of virtual objects, as well as for user interaction with the presented objects. Abstract objects are components crucial for the versatility of VARS scenes. They are specified by semantic descriptions of the characteristics of real and virtual objects, which can be assigned to them. One VARS scene can be presented in the context of different real environments containing different physical objects. Users can interact with virtual objects using physical objects within their environment. If there are abstract objects defined in a VARS scene, which cannot be successfully matched with appropriate physical objects, then they can be instantiated with appropriate virtual objects defined in the scene. Additionally, such a virtual object can be assigned to a physical object, which features some characteristics (e.g., shape, behavior, functionality) similar to the object that could not be found in the scene.

The adaptation of VARS scenes to real-world environments is performed on the basis of a common VARS ontology containing semantic representation of the characteristics of abstract, real, and virtual objects defined in the scene, as well as physical objects existing in a target real-world environment. In particular, these semantic descriptions specify: geometry, appearance, behavior, functionality, and possible interaction with other objects and a user. These features are semantically expressed based on the concepts defined in the VARS ontology.

In AR environments created according to the proposed approach, users are able to use physical objects for tangible interaction with the presented synthetic content.

For example, in a chemistry laboratory these objects can be: chemistry vessels, beakers, pipettes, plates, etc. In this case, VARS scenes can contain generalized semantic descriptions of these objects, so the scenes can be adapted to different real chemistry laboratories featured with different equipment.

3.3 VARS System

The proposed approach has been implemented in a prototype system, called VARS. The system is based on video see-through visualization of AR environments. For presentation of AR environments based on VARS scenes, a dedicated mobile application, called *VARS Application*, has been developed. The VARS scenes are presented via Samsung Gear VR glasses equipped with a smartphone [17]. The environment of a user is captured with a phone camera. A user can see through the glasses the video image from the camera with 3D stereoscopic virtual content superimposed on it. A user interacting through a tangible user interface with an example AR environment created based on a VARS scene is presented in Fig. 2.

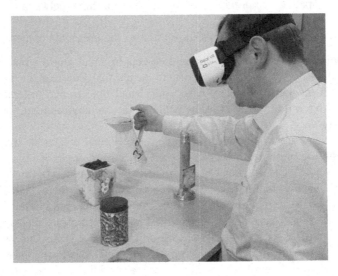

Fig. 2. VARS system – tangible user interaction in an AR environment

A user can see through the glasses the real-world environment augmented with additional virtual objects. The virtual objects are presented relatively to the physical objects, as depicted in Fig. 3(a). A user can interact with the virtual objects by manipulating the physical objects and observe behavior of the presented content.

The VARS Application has been implemented using the Unity game development platform [23]. Tracking of physical objects in real-world environments has been implemented using the Vuforia library [24]. The library enables tracking of physical objects based on their visual features, such as distinctive images on their surface. Some of the objects contain such features themselves, whereas some of them must be

(a)

(b)

Fig. 3. Examples of AR environments created based on a VARS scene within two different real-world environments

supplemented with additional visual markers. The Vuforia tracking library supports recognition of four categories of visual targets: 2D images, cuboids, cylinders, and user-defined 3D objects. In the presented example, there are the following visual targets defined: a 2D image for a plant pot, a 2D image for a visual marker attached to a flash light, and two cylinder targets for a jug and a tin. The physical objects present in the environment are semantically described to enable their matching to abstract objects defined in presented VARS scene.

4   Example Application

4.1   Education Domain

One of the most promising application domains for the AR technology is education. The main advantages of AR applications in the education domain are: activity of learners, cost and safety. AR environments can be used for visualization of three-dimensional objects, which learners can manipulate and observe from desired viewpoints. The AR technology has the potential to increase learners' motivation and engagement, facilitate learning, increase learners' spatial skills, etc. Augmented reality learning environments bring students exceptional freedom of experimentation, because the students can play an active role in a wide range of learning scenarios [25]. Augmented reality environments may be particularly useful for presenting phenomena, which are potentially dangerous (e.g., chemical experiments), very fast or very slow (e.g., explosive reactions and bio-chemical reactions), abstract concepts (e.g., magnetic fields).

Usually, learning systems offer the same learning materials to all learners. However, different learners may be characterized with different learning styles. According to the VARK theory, four basic learning styles can be distinguished: *visual, aural, read/write, kinesthetic* [26]. The AR technology may offer a great help for both the visual and the kinesthetic learning styles.

Providing learning materials appropriate for the visual learning style can be achieved in a variety of ways by preparing learning multimedia content. Conversely, to ensure kinesthetic learning is a much more challenging task, because it requires preparing hands-on experiments. However, there are serious limitations associated with the experiments performed in teaching labs, since they may require much space, expensive equipment, appropriate safety measures, and trained staff. In this context, the AR technology can be successfully used for kinesthetic learning, by providing learners with an opportunity to performing hands-on experiments in real-world environments with the use of physical objects.

4.2   Experiment

The VARS system has been successfully used to create an example AR Scene for kinesthetic learning on factors influencing the growth of plants. Experiments on the growth of plants usually require a lot of time, from several days to several weeks. Therefore, conducting such experiments in a class environment during one lesson is impossible. Such an experiment can be successfully performed in an AR environment in a short time, since a faster flow of time can be simulated.

During the experiment, learners can use physical objects existing in their real-world environment. The objects can be used for both positioning the synthetic content within the environment and user interaction through a tangible user interface. To this end, the position and orientation of the physical objects is tracked during the whole experiment.

In Fig. 3, two examples of AR environments created based on one VARS scene are presented. These environments have been constructed within real-world environments containing different sets of physical objects for tangible user interaction.

In the experiment, users should sow a virtual plant, next they should water it and provide light. They can see a flow of time on a virtual clock. During the whole experiment, the users can observe the process of plant growth and influence of different factors on this process. During the experiment, users can use a number of physical objects, which are represented in the form of the following abstract objects:

- a plant pot,
- package of seeds for planting plants,
- a watering can,
- a flash light for providing light.

The presented real-world environments contain different sets of physical objects, which are used for positioning virtual objects and for user interaction. The physical objects from the both environments are assigned accordingly to the abstract objects defined in the scene based on their semantic similarity. The physical objects existing in the two environments have different geometry and appearance, but their semantics is consistent with the semantics of the corresponding abstract objects defined in the scene.

In the environment depicted in Fig. 3(a), there is a real light torch, which can be tracked using a visual marker attached to it, so it can be used for tangible user interaction with the scene content. However, in the environment depicted in Fig. 3(b), there is no physical object corresponding to a flash light. Therefore, an appropriate virtual object representing a flash light has been assigned to the corresponding abstract object. In this case, another physical object of cylindrical shape has been selected for tangible user interaction with the virtual flash light.

5   Conclusions

The VARS approach to modeling augmented reality environments allows content creators to design versatile scenes that can be dynamically adapted to different real-world environments containing different physical objects. In VARS scenes, abstract objects are represented by their semantic properties based on a shared ontology. Also, the configuration and physical objects existing in target real-world environments are semantically specified using the concepts defined in the ontology. In the runtime, the abstract objects defined in the scene are matched to the physical objects existing in a given real-world environment based on their semantic similarity.

The proposed approach fosters reuse once developed AR content in different contexts by a number of users. The approach can contribute to a greater spread of AR technology due to the improvement of the process of creating the content for multiple real-world environments. The application of the VARS approach in practice should help to reduce the cost of developing AR content required to disseminate AR environments on a massive scale. Potential application areas of the developed approach include: education, training, medicine, maintenance and repair procedures.

Acknowledgements. This research work has been supported by the Polish National Science Centre (NCN) Grant No. DEC-2012/07/B/ST6/01523.

References

1. Oculus Rift. https://www.oculus.com/rift/
2. HTC Vive. https://www.vive.com/eu/
3. Azuma, R.: A survey of augmented reality. Presence Teleoperators Virtual Environ. **6**(4), 355–385 (1997)
4. Milgram, P., Kishino, F.: A taxonomy of mixed reality virtual displays. IEICE Trans. Inf. Syst. **77**(12), 1321–1329 (1994)
5. Microsoft HoloLens. https://www.microsoft.com/microsoft-hololens/en-us
6. Magic Leap. https://www.magicleap.com/
7. Wired: The Untold Story of Magic Leap, the World's Most Secretive Startup. https://www.wired.com/2016/04/magic-leap-vr/
8. Meta International. https://www.metavision.com/
9. ODG. http://osterhoutgroup.com/products
10. Tech Crunch: ODG unveils its first consumer AR/VR glasses, built on Qualcomm's Snapdragon 835 chip. https://techcrunch.com/2017/01/03/odg-unveils-its-first-consumer-ar-glasses-built-on-qualcomms-snapdragon-835-chip/
11. Billinghurst, M., Kato, H., Myojin, S.: Advanced interaction techniques for augmented reality applications. In: Shumaker, R. (ed.) VMR 2009. LNCS, vol. 5622, pp. 13–22. Springer, Heidelberg (2009). doi:10.1007/978-3-642-02771-0_2
12. Wojciechowski, R., Walczak, K., White, M., Cellary, W.: Building virtual and augmented reality museum exhibitions. In: Proceedings of 9th International Conference on 3D Web Technology, Web3D 2004, pp. 135–144. ACM (2004)
13. Gruber, T.R.: Toward principles for the design of ontologies used for knowledge sharing? Int. J. Hum Comput Stud. **43**(5–6), 907–928 (1995)
14. Gruber, T.R.: Ontology. In: Liu, L., Özsu, M.T. (eds.) Encyclopedia of Database Systems. Springer, Heidelberg (2009). http://tomgruber.org/writing/ontology-definition-2007.htm
15. Lord, P.: Components of an Ontology. Ontogenesis (2010). http://ontogenesis.knowledgeblog.org/514
16. Pokemon GO, http://www.pokemongo.com/
17. Samsung Gear VR. http://www.samsung.com/global/galaxy/gear-vr/
18. Billinghurst, M., Kato, H., Poupyrev, I.: Collaboration with tangible augmented reality interfaces. In: Proceedings of HCI International, pp. 234–241 (2001)
19. Billinghurst, M., Kato, H., Poupyrev, I.: Tangible augmented reality. In: Proceedings of ACM SIGGRAPH ASIA 2008, pp. 1–10 (2008)
20. Google Cardboard. https://vr.google.com/cardboard/
21. Tomi, A.B., Rambli, D.R.A.: An interactive mobile augmented reality magical playbook: learning number with the thirsty crow. In: International Conference on Virtual and Augmented Reality in Education. Procedia Computer Science, vol. 25, pp. 123–130. Elsevier (2013)
22. Grasset, R., Dünser, A., Billinghurst, M.: Edutainment with a mixed reality book: a visually augmented illustrative children's book. In: Proceedings of International Conference on Advances in Computer Entertainment Technology, ACE 2008, pp. 292–295. ACM (2008)
23. Unity. https://unity3d.com/
24. Vuforia. https://www.vuforia.com/
25. Wojciechowski, R., Cellary, W.: Evaluation of learners' attitude toward learning in ARIES augmented reality environments. Comput. Educ. **68**, 570–585 (2013)
26. Fleming, N.D.: VARK: A Guide to Learning Styles. http://www.vark-learn.com/

Cascade Classifiers and Saliency Maps Based People Detection

Wilbert G. Aguilar[1,3,4(✉)], Marco A. Luna[2], Julio F. Moya[2],
Vanessa Abad[5], Hugo Ruiz[1,6], Humberto Parra[1,7],
and William Lopez[3]

[1] Dep. Seguridad y Defensa,
Universidad de las Fuerzas Armadas ESPE, Sangolquí, Ecuador
wgaguilar@espe.edu.ec
[2] Dep. Eléctrica y Electrónica,
Universidad de las Fuerzas Armadas ESPE, Sangolquí, Ecuador
[3] CICTE Research Center,
Universidad de las Fuerzas Armadas ESPE, Sangolquí, Ecuador
[4] GREC Research Group, Universitat Politècnica de Catalunya,
Barcelona, Spain
[5] Universitat de Barcelona, Barcelona, Spain
[6] PLM Research Center, Purdue University, IN West Lafayette, USA
[7] Universidad Politécnica de Madrid, Madrid, Spain

Abstract. In this paper, we propose algorithm and dataset for pedestrian detection focused on HCI and Augmented Reality applications. We combine cascade classifiers with saliency maps for improving the performance of the detectors. We train a HAAR-LBP and HOG cascade classifier and introduce CICTE_PeopleDetection dataset with images from surveillance cameras at different angles and altitudes. Our algorithm performance is compared with other approaches from the state of art. In the results, we can see that cascade classifiers with saliency maps improve the performance of pedestrian detection due to the rejection of false positives in the image.

Keywords: HAAR · HOG · LBP · Saliency maps · People detection · Cascade classifiers · HCI

1 Introduction

In the field of HCI (Human Computer Interaction) and Augmented Reality, there are multiple applications in pedestrian detection for mobile cameras like surveillance [1, 2], robotics [3–5], navigation [6–8], driver assistance systems [9, 10], and others.

Developments in HCI have been introduced for UAVs (Unmanned Aerial Vehicles) [11–13]. Pedestrian detection can be used with UAVs taking into consideration that they have a complex dynamic and altitude variation [14, 15], that adding extra challenges to the detection [16, 17]. Conventional classifiers fail when altitude increases generating more false positives.

© Springer International Publishing AG 2017
L.T. De Paolis et al. (Eds.): AVR 2017, Part II, LNCS 10325, pp. 501–510, 2017.
DOI: 10.1007/978-3-319-60928-7_42

Our proposal for pedestrian detection in mobile HCI test cascade classifier algorithms of the state of art in combination with saliency maps [18] to provide detection robustness. Considering the altitude variations and lighting changes, we introduce CICTE-PeopleDetection dataset with images captured from surveillance cameras. We use two trained algorithms: The first one based on a combination of the feature extraction methods HAAR-LBP, and the second one based on HOG. Both algorithms use cascade classifiers with Adaboost training.

This paper is organized as follows: Sect. 2 describes the related work on pedestrian detection. Next, our proposal for pedestrian detection and dataset creation is described in Sect. 3. In Sect. 4 we present the experimental results, followed by the summary. Finally conclusions and future works are presented in Sect. 5.

2 Related Works

In the literature, two important algorithms have been developed for pedestrian detection and object detection in general: Haar-like features [19] by Viola and Jones, and Dalal and Triggs algorithm called HOG [20]. Both algorithms have generated over 40 new approaches [21]. Several methods for pedestrian detection includes feature extraction algorithms: HAAR [19], HOG [20, 22], HOG-HAAR [23] and HOG-LBP [24]; working with machine learning approaches based on SVMs [20, 25] or Adaboost [10, 26].

Several research groups have created different datasets and methods for pedestrian detection. According to [21, 27] there are two types of datasets: photo datasets and video datasets. Photo datasets like INRIA [20], MIT [28], CVC [10], NICTA [29] aboard the classification problem: train binary classification algorithms. Video datasets as ETH [30], TUD-Brussels [31] or Dalmier (DB) [26] are focused on detection problem: design and test full image detection systems and human locomotion modeling.

The applications of computer vision in HCI are manifold: people assistance systems [11, 32, 33], navigation control [12, 13, 34], etc. The use of saliency maps in UAVs is widely used for object and motion detection in aerial images [35, 36]. Works like [37] use saliency maps to detect people reducing the search space, they fuse the results using mean-shift procedure applied in flights from 10 to 40 m of altitude.

3 Our Approach

3.1 Training Process

Our approach consists in the combination of two algorithms for extraction of the feature set: Local Binary Patterns (LBP) and Haar-like features. We use Adaptive Boosting (AdaBoost) as training algorithm and a combination of Haar-LBP features due to them are algorithms of low computation time. To create our Haar-LBP algorithm we divided the all images in 70% for training and the other 30% for testing, after that we use the algorithm with a UAV images in different scenarios. Additionally, we train a HOG cascade classifier and compare it with Opencv HOG to validate our Dataset. The training processes are shown Fig. 1.

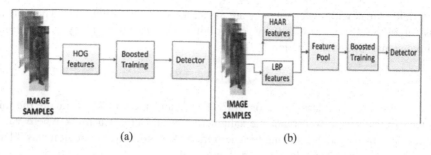

(a)   (b)

Fig. 1. Pedestrian detection training. (a) HOG features with Adaboost. (b) Haar-LBP features with Adaboost

The methods used for training the cascade classifiers are described as follows:

Local Binary Patterns (LBP)
This feature extractor was presented in [38] as a texture descriptor for object detection, and compares a central pixel with the neighbours.

Haar-like Features
Viola and Jones uses a statistical approach describing the ratio between light and dark areas within a defined kernel [19, 39].

Histogram of Oriented Gradients (HOG)
In this algorithm introduced in [20], the image window is separated into smaller parts called cells. For each cell, we accumulate a local 1-D histogram of gradient orientations of the pixels in the cell.

Adaboost
Adaboost is a machine learning algorithm [40] that initially keeps uniform distribution of weights in each training sample. In the first iteration the algorithm trains a weak classifier using a feature extraction methods or mix of them achieving a higher recognition performance for the training samples. In next iterations, the training samples, misclassified by the first weak classifier, receive higher weights.

For training we use positive and negative images. Positive images are the images that contain pedestrians. Negative images are frames without pedestrians. The main difference of CICTE-PeopleDetection with other photo datasets is the location and perspective of the cameras that emulate the onboard camera perspective UAVs. We use surveillance cameras because UAVs videos are stable and comparable with fixed cameras. Our dataset has 3900 positive images and 1212 negative images. Positives images were captured during the day and the night in different scenarios.

3.2   People Detection Algorithm

We implement a combination of cascade classifier with saliency maps presented in [18]. The purpose of saliency maps is to locate prominent areas at every location in the visual field. Areas with lower saliency are associated to background [41]. The saliency maps algorithms are deduced by convolving the function f by an isotropic bi-dimensional Gaussian function [42]:

$$S(X) = f(X)G_\sigma(X) \tag{1}$$

Where σ is the standard deviation of the Gaussian function. To eliminate the false positives in the image we obtain the salient region and create a mask where values greater than a threshold will belong to salient map. Additionally, this region was dilated to give it robustness. This algorithm is shown in Fig. 2.

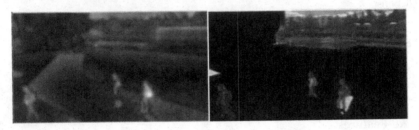

Fig. 2. Saliency maps algorithm. (a) Saliency map (b) Saliency regions.

Once it has been obtained the salient region, we take as true positives only the cascade classifier detections inside this region. To determinate if a detection bounding box is inside the salient region, we compute the center point of the bounding box.

We take the center point as reference to avoid false positives that could have small parts of their bounding box in salient regions. Our proposal is presented graphically in Fig. 3.

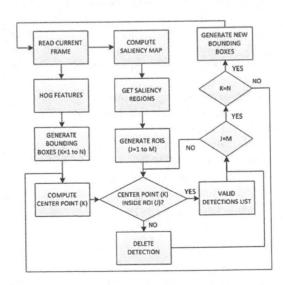

Fig. 3. Algorithm for people detection using HOG Cascade classifier and Saliency Maps

The results of the application of this algorithm are presented in the Sect. 4.

4   Results and Discussion

4.1   Training Evaluation

The metrics of evaluation for our approach are based on the miss rate (False negative rate-FNR). Defined as follows:

$$FNR = \frac{FN}{TP + FN} * 100\% \tag{2}$$

We evaluate our dataset training a cascade classifier based on HOG features and compared this classifier with the OpenCV HOG cascade classifier in UAV videos. Experimental results are presented in Table 1.

Table 1. Dataset training performance

Algorithm	Miss rate (%)
HOG-CICTE	**48.32%**
HOG [43]	65.22%

The Table 1 shows that HOG-CICTE PeopleDetection has a lower miss-rate than HOG from the OpenCV library. Result shows our approach has better performance; the miss rate of our proposal is 17% approximately lower than the other classifier.

4.2   Algorithm Evaluation

We compare HAAR-LBP features and HOG features (trained with CICTE-PeopleDetection) respect to other cascade classifiers at different scenarios. The average results are presented in Table 2.

Table 2. Cascade Classifiers Performance

Algorithm	Altitude (m)	Miss rate (%)
HAAR-LBP	2–5	92.24
HAAR [19]	2–5	97.5
LBP [44]	2–5	67.25
HOG CICTE	2–5	**36.1**

In Table 2, the combination of HAAR-LBP features has high miss rate compared with the other methods; however the proposal is better than HAAR features. With altitude increasing, sensitivity decrease in all cascade classifiers. Performance curves are presented in the Fig. 4.

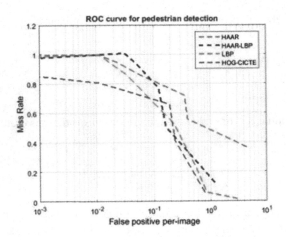

Fig. 4. Comparison of ROC curves for different approaches.

In the Fig. 4, the performance of the HAAR-LBP features algorithm is better than HAAR individually applied. HAAR-LBP features generate a lower rate of false positives. True positive rate of HAAR-LBP features is higher than HAAR features but lower than LBP. Nevertheless, the HOG-CICTE cascade classifier still has the best performance due to its higher true positives rate and lower false positives rate.

4.3 Cascade Classifier- Saliency Maps Combination

Based on the results of the Table 2 we choose HOG CICTE cascade classifier to implement our algorithm. Graphical results are shown in the Fig. 5.

As we can see in the Fig. 5, the use of saliency region helps to reject the false positives in the images. For the evaluation we take an additional metric of evaluation that is precision or positive predictive value (PPV), given by:

$$PPV = \frac{TP}{TP + FP} * 100\%$$ (3)

Where TP are the true positive values and FP are the false positives. The results of precision of the detector with the application of the saliency region algorithm (SR) are shown in the Table 3.

In Table 3, the application of saliency region algorithm improves the precision of detection in 20% approximately, this denote an improvement in the performance too.

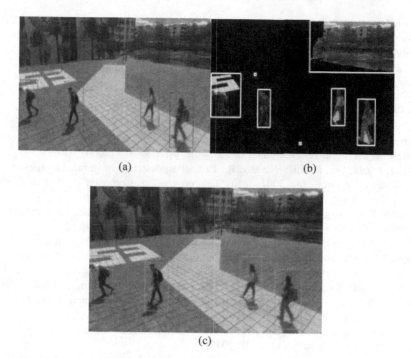

Fig. 5. Combination of Saliency Maps and Cascade classifier. (a) Cascade classifier result (b) Saliency regions (c) Final Result

Table 3. Comparison of precision between algorithms

Algorithm	Precision (%)
HOG-CICTE	69.23%
HOG-CICTE +SR	**88.1%**

5 Conclusions and Future Work

Our proposal based on HOG features has higher performance that OpenCV HOG respect to the miss rate (with an improvement of 16%), as shown in the Table 1, because the images used for training emulate UAVs perspective.

In order to improve the HAAR algorithm performance we combine two algorithms (HAAR and LBP). The miss rate decreased as shows Table 2; however the performance is lower in comparison with HOG-CICTE and LBP algorithm.

The use of saliency maps improves the performance detectors, saliency map helps to eliminate background regions even in mobile cameras like UAVs, and these regions may contain objects that confuse the classifier that is important to decrease the number of false positives.

In the future is necessary to develop HCI applications based on robust pedestrian detection in mobile cameras, as people assistance systems or driver assistance systems.

Acknowledgement. This work is part of the projects VisualNavDrone 2016-PIC-024 and MultiNavCar 2016-PIC-025, from the Universidad de las Fuerzas Armadas ESPE, directed by Dr. Wilbert G. Aguilar.

References

1. Torresan, H.: Advanced surveillance systems: combining video and thermal imagery for pedestrian detection. In: Proceeding of the SPIE, pp. 506–515 (2004)
2. Zhang, L.Z.L., Wu, B.W.B., Nevatia, R.: Pedestrian detection in infrared images based on local shape features. In: 2007 IEEE Conference on Computer Vision and Pattern Recognition, pp. 0–7 (2007)
3. Aguilar, W.G., Angulo, C.: Real-time video stabilization without phantom movements for micro aerial vehicles. EURASIP J. Image Video Process. **2014**(1), 46 (2014)
4. Jafari, O.H., Mitzel, D., Leibe, B.: Real-time RGB-D based people detection and Tracking for mobile robots and head-worn cameras. In: Proceedings of IEEE International Conference on Robotics and Automation, April 2016, pp. 5636–5643 (2014)
5. Kobilarov, M., Sukhatme, G., Hyams, J., Batavia, P.: People tracking and following with mobile robot using an omnidirectional camera and a laser. In: IEEE International Conference on Robotics and Automation. ICRA 2006, pp. 557–562 (2006)
6. Aguilar, W., Casaliglla, V., Pólit, J.: Obstacle Avoidance Based-Visual Navigation for Micro Aerial Vehicles. Electronics **6**(1), 10 (2017)
7. Aguilar, W.G., Angulo, C., Costa, R., Molina, L.: Control autónomo de cuadricopteros para seguimiento de trayectorias. In: Memorias del IX Congreso de Ciencia y Tecnología ESPE 2014 (2014)
8. Aguilar, W.G., Morales, S.: 3D environment mapping using the Kinect V2 and path planning based on RRT algorithms. Electronics **5**(4), 70 (2016)
9. Gavrila, D.M.: Pedestrian detection from a moving vehicle. In: Vernon, D. (ed.) ECCV 2000. LNCS, vol. 1843, pp. 37–49. Springer, Heidelberg (2000). doi:10.1007/3-540-45053-X_3
10. Gerónimo, D., López, A.M., Sappa, A.D., Graf, T.: Survey of pedestrian detection for advanced driver assistance systems. IEEE Trans. Pattern Anal. Mach. Intell. **32**(7), 1239–1258 (2010)
11. Avila, M., Funk, M., Henze, N.: DroneNavigator. In: Proceedings of the 17th International ACM SIGACCESS Conference on Computers & Accessibility - ASSETS 2015, pp. 327–328 (2015)
12. Kosmyna, N., Tarpin-Bernard, F., Rivet, B.: Brains, computers, and drones: think and control. Interactions **22**(4), 44–47 (2015)
13. Hansen, J.P., Alapetite, A., MacKenzie, I.S., Møllenbach, E.: The use of gaze to control drones. In: Proceedings of the Symposium on Eye Tracking Research and Applications - ETRA 2014, pp. 27–34 (2014)
14. Aguilar, W.G., Angulo, C.: Robust video stabilization based on motion intention for low-cost micro aerial vehicles. In: 2014 11th International Multi-Conference on Systems, Signals Devices (SSD), pp. 1–6 (2014)
15. Aguilar, W.G., Angulo, C.: Real-time model-based video stabilization for microaerial vehicles. Neural Process. Lett. **43**(2), 459–477 (2016)
16. Rudol, P., Doherty, P.: Human body detection and geolocalization for UAV search and rescue missions using color and thermal imagery

17. Aguilar, W.G., Luna, M.A., Moya, J.F., Abad, V., Parra, H., Ruiz, H.: Pedestrian detection for UAVs using cascade classifiers with meanshift. In: 2017 IEEE 11th International Conference on Semantic Computing (ICSC), pp. 509–514 (2017)
18. Itti, L., Koch, C., Niebur, E.: A model of saliency-based visual attention for rapid scene analysis. IEEE Trans. Pattern Anal. **20**, 1254–1259 (1998)
19. Viola, P., Jones, M.: Rapid object detection using a boosted cascade of simple features. In: Conference on Computer Vision and Pattern Recognition, pp. 1–9 (2001)
20. Dalal, N., Triggs, W.: Histograms of oriented gradients for human detection. In: 2005 IEEE Computer Society Conference on Computer Vision and Pattern Recognition. CVPR 2005, vol. 1, no. 3, pp. 886–893 (2004)
21. Benenson, R., Omran, M., Hosang, J., Schiele, B.: Ten years of pedestrian detection, what have we learned? In: Proceedings of Computer Vision-ECCV 2014 Work, pp. 613–627 (2014)
22. Zhu, Q., Avidan, S., Yeh, M.C., Cheng, K.T.: Fast human detection using a cascade of histograms of oriented gradients. In: IEEE Conference on Computer Vision and Pattern Recognition, vol. 2, pp. 1491–1498 (2006)
23. Wojek, C., Schiele, B.: A performance evaluation of single and multi-feature people detection. In: Jt. Pattern Recognition Symposium, pp. 82–91 (2008)
24. Wang, X., Han, T.X., Yan, S.: An HOG-LBP human detector with partial occlusion handling. In: IEEE 12th International Conference on Computer Vision (ICCV 2009), pp. 32–39 (2009)
25. Imamura, Y., Okamoto, S., Lee, J.H.: Human tracking by a multi-rotor drone using HOG features and linear SVM on images captured by a monocular camera, vol. I, pp. 8–13 (2016)
26. Enzweiler, M., Gavrila, D.M.: Monocular pedestrian detection: survey and experiments. IEEE Trans. Pattern Anal. Mach. Intell. **31**(12), 2179–2195 (2009)
27. Dollár, P., Wojek, C., Schiele, B., Perona, P.: Pedestrian detection: an evaluation of the state of the art. IEEE Trans. Pattern Anal. Mach. Intell. **34**(4), 743–761 (2012)
28. Papageorgiou, C., Poggio, T.: Trainable system for object detection. Int. J. Comput. Vis. **38**(1), 15–33 (2000)
29. Overett, G., Petersson, L., Brewer, N., Andersson, L., Pettersson, N.: A new pedestrian dataset for supervised learning. In: Proceedings of the IEEE Intelligent Vehicles Symposium, pp. 373–378 (2008)
30. Ess, A., Leibe, B., Schindler, K., van Gool, L.: Robust multiperson tracking from a mobile platform. IEEE Trans. Pattern Anal. Mach. Intell. **31**(10), 1831–1846 (2009)
31. Wojek, C., Walk, S., Schiele, B.: Multi-Cue onboard pedestrian detection. In: 2009 IEEE Computer Society Conference on Computer Vision and Pattern Recognition Workshops. CVPR Work 2009, pp. 794–801 (2009)
32. Aguilar, W.G., Alulema, D., Limaico, A., Sandoval, D.: Development and verification of a verbal corpus based on natural language for Ecuadorian dialect. In: 2017 IEEE 11th International Conference on Semantic Computing (ICSC), pp. 515–519 (2017)
33. Cabras, P., Rosell, J., Pérez, A., Aguilar, W.G., Rosell, A.: Haptic-based navigation for the virtual bronchoscopy. IFAC Proc. Vol. **18**(PART 1), 9638–9643 (2011)
34. Cavett, D., Coker, M., Jimenez, R., Yaacoubi, B.: Human-computer interface for control of unmanned aerial vehicles. In: 2007 IEEE Systems and Information Engineering Design Symposium, pp. 1–6 (2007)
35. Andriluka, M., Schnitzspan, P., Meyer, J., Kohlbrecher, S., Petersen, K., Von Stryk, O., Roth, S., Schiele, B.: Vision based victim detection from unmanned aerial vehicles. In: 2010 IEEE/RSJ International Conference on Intelligent Robots and Systems (IROS), pp. 1740–1747 (2010)

510   W.G. Aguilar et al.

36. Siam, M., Elhelw, M.: Robust autonomous visual detection and tracking of moving targets in UAV imagery. In: Proceedings of the International Conference on Signal Processing (ICSP), vol. 2, pp. 1060–1066 (2012)
37. Blondel, P., Potelle, A., Pegard, C., Lozano, R.: Human detection in uncluttered environments: from ground to UAV view. In: 2014 13th International Conference on Control Automation Robotics & Vision ICARCV 2014, pp. 76–81 (1997)
38. Wang, L., He, D.: Texture classification using texture spectrum. Pattern Recognit 23, 905–910 (1990)
39. Papageorgiou, C.P., Oren, M.: A general framework for object detection. In: IEEE International Conference on Computer Vision, pp. 555–562 (1998)
40. Schapire, R.E., Singer, Y.: Improved boosting algorithms using confidence-rated predictions. Mach. Learn. 37(3), 297–336 (1999)
41. Moosmann, F., Larlus, D., Jurie, F.: Learning saliency maps for object categorization. In: International Workshop on The Representation and Use of Prior Knowledge in Vision (2006)
42. Le Meur, O., Baccino, T.: Methods for comparing scanpaths and saliency maps: strengths and weaknesses. Behav. Res. Methods 45, 251–266 (2013)
43. Dalal, N., Triggs, B.: Histograms of oriented gradients for human detection. In: 2005 IEEE Computer Society Conference on Computer Vision and Pattern Recognition, vol. 1, pp. 886–893 (2005)
44. Ojala, T., Pietikäinen, M., Mäenpää, T.: A generalized local binary pattern operator for multiresolution gray scale and rotation invariant texture classification. Adv. Pattern Recognit. 2013, 399–408 (2001)

Author Index

Printed in the United States
By Bookmasters